HIGHLIGHTS

Law of Electronic Banking

by Melanie L. Fein

Law of Electronic Banking is a timely and authoritative guide for analyzing the legal issues raised by the emergence of new electronic technologies, focusing on actions by federal and state banking regulators and other government agencies that define the scope of permissible electronic banking activities.

This comprehensive treatise discusses current issues concerning: the role of the government; regulatory framework; the payment system; electronic fund transfers; home banking and Internet services; electronic money; joint ventures and strategic alliances; antitrust issues; new regulatory compliance issues; industry self-regulatory initiatives; and much more.

2001 Supplement

The 2001 Supplement to *Law of Electronic Banking* expands the scope of the main volume to provide essential new information, including:

- Overview of the **Uniform Money Services Act** which provides a framework for safety and soundness regulation of non-bank entities that engage in money transmission;
- Discussion of the **Uniform Computer Information Transactions Act** which covers the licensing of information, including software, and the sale of mass marketed software;
- Discussion of **electronic payment mechanisms** that play a significant role in facilitating electronic commerce, including credit cards, person-to-person payments, electronic checks, and business-to-business payments;

7700000262

- New chapter analyzing the Electronic Signatures in Global and National Commerce Act, or **"E-Sign Act"** which eliminates various legal impediments to the use of electronic signatures and records;
- Discussion of the special requirements imposed on newly chartered **Internet Banks** by the federal banking agencies;
- Overview of **"finder activities"** and **"account aggregation services"** permitted by banking organizations, including financial holding companies;
- Summary of joint guidelines issued by the federal banking agencies, the FTC, and the SEC pursuant to the Gramm-Leach-Bliley Act to establish standards for financial institutions relating to the **safekeeping of customer records** and information;
- Discussion of the risks associated with the **outsourcing of technology functions** by financial institutions and regulatory guidance in managing these risks, including analysis of due diligence, contracting with and oversight of service providers, and examination procedures;
- Overview of the latest laws enacted by Congress and a listing of recent studies, bulletins, reports, and pronouncements of the OCC and other federal banking agencies.

This supplement revises the Index to incorporate all the additions and changes to the text.

7/01

For questions concerning this shipment, billing, missing pages, or other customer service matters, call our Customer Service Department at 1-800-234-1660.

For toll-free ordering, please call 1-800-638-8437.

ASPEN LAW & BUSINESS

LAW OF ELECTRONIC BANKING
2001 Supplement

FILING INSTRUCTIONS

Before filing your 2001 Supplement, please make sure that your copy of the book is up to date. If the Filing Instructions for the 2000 Supplement are filed immediately inside the cover of your book, your volume is up to date and you may proceed to file the 2001 Supplement. If the Filing Instructions for the 2000 Supplement are missing from your copy, please contact our Customer Service Department at 1-800-234-1660 for assistance

Check as done	Remove and discard old page(s):	Insert new page(s):
☐	Title Page to xxviii	Title Page to xxx
☐	1-9 to 1-17	1-9 to 1-19
☐	2-1 to 2-16.3	2-1 to 2-16.4
☐	4-1 to 4-16	4-1 to 4-18
☐	5-1 to 5-12	5-1 to 5-13
☐	6-1 to 6-10	6-1 to 6-10.2
☐	6-19 to 6-23	6-19 to 6-28
☐	8-1 to 8-10	8-1 to 8-10.5
☐	9-1 to 9-6	9-1 to 9-6.1
☐	9-21 to 9-26	9-21 to 9-31
☐	10-5 to 10-8	10-5 to 10-9
☐	11-1 to 11-4	11-1 to 11-4.1
☐	11-13 to 11-24	11-13 to 11-27
☐	12-1 to 12-2	12-1 to 12-2
☐	12-11 to 12-17	12-11 to 12-18
☐	13-3 to 13-14.5	13-3 to 13-14.9
☐	13-21 to 13-25	13-21 to 13-26
☐	15-1 to 15-49	15-1 to 15-51
☐	—	16-1 to 16-13
☐	TC-1 to TC-4	TC-1 to TC-4
☐	IND-1 to IND-26	IND-1 to IND-31

When you have finished your 2001 Supplement, please place these instructions immediately inside the cover of your binder.

7/01

LAW OF ELECTRONIC BANKING

Melanie L. Fein

Aspen Law & Business
A Division of Aspen Publishers, Inc.
New York Gaithersburg

2001 SUPPLEMENT

A Division of Aspen Publishers, Inc.
A Wolters Kluwer Company
www.aspenpublishers.com

Printed in the United States of America

1 2 3 4 5 6 7 8 9 0

Library of Congress Cataloging-in-Publication Data

Fein, Melanie L.
Law of electronic banking / Melanie L. Fein.
p. cm.
Includes bibliographical references and index.
ISBN 0-7355-0372-9
1. Electronic funds transfers—Law and legislation—United States.
2. Point-of-sale systems—Law and legislation—United States.
3. Banks and banking—United States—Automation. I. Title.
KF1030.E4F447 1999
346.73′0821′0285—dc21 99-41882
CIP

2001 SUPPLEMENT

About Aspen Law & Business

Aspen Law & Business is a leading publisher of authoritative treatises, practice manuals, services, and journals for attorneys, corporate and bank directors, accountants, auditors, environmental compliance professionals, financial and tax advisors, and other business professionals. Our mission is to provide practical solution-based how-to information keyed to the latest original pronouncements, as well as the latest legislative, judicial, and regulatory developments.

We offer publications in the areas of accounting and auditing; antitrust; banking and finance; bankruptcy; business and commercial law; construction law; corporate law; criminal law; environmental compliance; government and administrative law; health law; insurance law; intellectual property; international law; legal practice and litigation; matrimonial and family law; pensions, benefits, and labor; real estate law; securities; and taxation.

Other Aspen Law & Business products treating banking law issues include:

Mutual Fund Activities of Banks
Securities Activities of Banks
Banking Law and Regulation
Bank Directors', Officers', and Lawyers' Civil Liabilities
Banking Policy Report: A Journal on Trends in Regulation and Supervision
Federal Deposit Insurance Corporation Enforcement Decisions and Orders
Fair Housing-Fair Lending, A Service
Insurance Activities of Banks
Law of Payment Systems and EFT
Standby and Commercial Letters of Credit

ASPEN LAW & BUSINESS
A Division of Aspen Publishers, Inc.
A Wolters Kluwer Company
www.aspenpublishers.com

SUBSCRIPTION NOTICE

This Aspen Law & Business product is updated on a periodic basis with supplements to reflect important changes in the subject matter. If you purchased this product directly from Aspen Law & Business, we have already recorded your subscription for the update service.

If, however, you purchased this product from a bookstore and wish to receive future updates and revised or related volumes billed separately with a 30-day examination review, please contact our Customer Service Department at 1-800-234-1660, or send your name, company name (if applicable), address, and the title of the product to:

ASPEN LAW & BUSINESS
A Division of Aspen Publishers, Inc.
7201 McKinney Circle
Frederick, MD 21704

ABOUT THE AUTHOR

MELANIE L. FEIN is a private practitioner specializing in the law of banking and financial services. Until 1999, Ms. Fein was a partner in the law firm of Arnold & Porter where she advised the firm's clients on a variety of financial services regulatory issues, including those involving electronic banking and financial services.

Prior to joining Arnold & Porter in 1986, Ms. Fein was a senior counsel at the Board of Governors of the Federal Reserve System where her responsibilities included a wide range of bank and bank holding company regulatory and legislative matters. While at the Federal Reserve, Ms. Fein served on the interagency legislative drafting committee for the Vice President's Task Group on Regulation of Financial Services.

Before joining the Federal Reserve Board in 1979, Ms. Fein worked as a law clerk in the Office of the Comptroller of the Currency and the Securities and Exchange Commission, and was a legislative secretary to Congressman John F. Seiberling.

Ms. Fein is the author of *Securities Activities of Banks, Third Edition* (Aspen Law & Business, 2001), *Mutual Fund Activities of Banks* (Aspen Law & Business, 1993 & Supps. 1992-2000), and *Federal Bank Holding Company Law, Second Edition* (Law Journals Seminars-Press, 1998), and has written numerous articles on banking law.

Ms. Fein is vice-chair of the Executive Council of the Federal Bar Association's Banking Law Committee and has served in other leadership roles in the American Bar Association.

Ms. Fein has taught Banking and Financial Institutions Law at Yale Law School (1992, 1993, 1997, 1999) and at the Catholic University Columbus School of Law (1985-1990), from which she received her law degree and was comment editor of the law review. Ms. Fein is a member of the bars of the U.S. Supreme Court and the U.S. Courts of Appeal for the District of Columbia Circuit and the Fourth Circuit.

To
JPV and DLR

SUMMARY OF CONTENTS

CONTENTS

Chapter 8
INTERNET SERVICES 8-1

Chapter 9
ELECTRONIC COMMERCE AND RELATED APPLICATIONS 9-1

Chapter 12
YEAR 2000 ISSUES 12-1

Chapter 13
CONSUMER PROTECTION AND PRIVACY 13-1

PREFACE

This volume is a book in search of the law where little is to be found at present. Unlike the law of banking or securities regulation, which abounds in the statute books and court reports, the law of electronic banking and financial services is scarce, making it a difficult subject for a book intended to be a useful guide for practicing attorneys and an unusual challenge for an author accustomed to having huge amounts of material to work with. Readers expecting to find a discernable body of law in this book will be disappointed. For this, the author is unapologetic and suggests that readers instead blame the federal government—and in particular the Clinton Administration—which has taken an uncharacteristically non-regulatory stance.

Rather than purporting to be a treatise on the law, this book aspires to become one, if and when the law acquires sufficient bulk and form to be considered a body of law. It is poised to capture legal developments as they occur and to report on the governing framework as it evolves from its current infant state.

Readers familiar with the banking laws will find many familiar points of reference in the book. Those becoming newly acquainted with the banking laws may wonder at the oddity of it all. As the former can attest, however, the banking laws are far more rational than they were five years ago and are becoming more so as the regulators and Congress strive daily to adapt the regulatory structure to what is surely one of the most dynamic periods in banking history.

In many ways, this book is a journey into the unknown, both for the author and readers. Where the journey will take us depends on technological and economic forces of unprecedented domestic and global magnitude that are redefining the financial services industry in ways unthinkable just yesterday. This book will attempt to chronicle the journey as it unfolds with the hope of illuminating the path of the law as it ventures into a new universe in the 21st Century.

Melanie L. Fein
August 1999

ACKNOWLEDGMENTS

I would like to thank the Honorable Eugene A. Ludwig for so generously sharing his thoughts on the electronic banking revolution in his Introduction to this book. As one of the nation's great Comptrollers of the Currency, Mr. Ludwig presided over the national banking system when many of the developments described in this book occurred. His vision and leadership during a time of unprecedented change in banking and finance is reflected in many of the regulatory decisions and interpretations issued by his Office that will continue to shape the course of electronic banking and financial services for years to come. As a former regulator, renowned banking lawyer, vice chairman of a major bank, and chairman of the Treasury Department's Working Group on Electronic Money and Banking, Mr. Ludwig has an exceptionally learned and authoritative perspective on the book's subject matter, and his Introduction is a valuable feature for readers.

I also am indebted to David Balto who authored the chapter on antitrust implications of electronic banking and financial services. Mr. Balto's chapter reflects his antitrust expertise and experience at the Federal Trade Commission and adds an important dimension to the book that undoubtedly will become even more significant as banks and other financial service providers seek new competitive parameters in the dynamically changing marketplace for electronic banking products and services.

Finally, this book would never have seen the light of day had it not been for the efforts of my long-term editor and friend, Ellen Fischer, who had the foresight to recognize the need for such a book and the energy to work with me in bringing it to fruition. I am grateful to Ellen for her persistence in helping me trek through the uncharted territory of this exciting new frontier in the law.

INTRODUCTION

by Hon. Eugene A. Ludwig*

We are in the midst of one of the greatest revolutions in banking and finance in all of history. Virtually all of the chess pieces on the worldwide financial chessboard are moving simultaneously and even the pieces themselves are changing.

Three forces are propelling this worldwide revolution: changes in information technology, changes in communications technology, and globalization.

The phrase "changes in information technology" is too tame. Indeed, using the word "revolution" is too tepid. Every 12 to 18 months the speed with which we are able to manipulate and store information is doubling. This phenomenon has been going on for more than a decade, and is likely to continue for at least the next decade. Moreover, the equipment that manipulates and stores information is becoming cheaper, smaller, and more ubiquitous. This trend too is almost certain to continue for the next decade.

Many sectors of the economy are being changed by the rapid advances in information technology, but none more so than finance. Finance is at its core an information business. So technological changes that increase the availability of information, the ability to manipulate information, and the speed of information retrieval can profoundly change the financial sector.

The revolution in communications technology is no less extraordinary. The advent and rapid improvements in modems, satellite communications, fiber optics, and compression technologies have allowed us to obtain information from around the globe virtually anywhere, anytime, and at great speed. Here too the pace of change should continue well into the next century.

For finance, a discipline so rooted in information, the ability to communicate information quickly, in various forms, and over large areas, is obviously of immense importance. As with the revolution in information technology, the

---

* Mr. Ludwig is currently Vice-Chairman of Deutsche Bank. From 1993-1998, he was United States Comptroller of the Currency. From 1995 until 1998, Mr. Ludwig was Chairman of the Treasury Department's Working Group on Electronic Money and Banking, which coordinated issues in this area for the Administration. Mr. Ludwig also has been a member of the Board of the Federal Deposit Insurance Corporation, a member of the President's Working Groups on Financial Institutions, and the Basle Committee on Bank Supervision.

revolution in communications technology has fundamentally changed the business of finance.

Globalizations (or, as some might say, internationalization) is in large part derivative of the changes in information and communications technologies. It is also a force unto itself with political and social antecedents. Irrespective of the causes, we are living through a profound globalization of culture and commerce. Everything from movie stars to fast food are becoming *lingua franca* from Oshkosh to Azerberzan. The same is increasingly true for finance. Trading in a wide variety of financial instruments is now global. Even sophisticated forms of finance, such as exotic derivatives, are increasingly available globally. Again, this trend will continue into the next century.

It is not possible to prognosticate all of the ways in which these revolutionary changes will affect finance. The crystal ball is clear with regard to some changes, however many of which are now obvious both on the product side and on the delivery side.

I divide products into four categories: credit (including both equity and debt), savings (including safe keeping and money management), money transfer, and insurance (including risk management services). In all of these areas we are witnessing, and can expect, great change.

For instance, we have already seen significant changes in insurance products with the advent of derivatives. Although derivatives are the result to a considerable degree of the Black/Scholes option pricing model, derivatives are also a product of the information technology revolution, which has allowed for a dramatic expansion of modeling capabilities. We are by no means at the end of product development in this area. On the contrary, enhancements in information and communications technologies will produce even more exotic derivative forms as well as broader and deeper international markets for these products.

In the area of money transfer, we are only in the early stages of the electronic money revolution. For a variety of reasons, including infrastructure costs and the success of competitive technologies, using smart card technology to replace coins and bills on a worldwide basis has been slower than some had predicted. However, there is no doubt in this writer's mind that at some point in the next century specie will all but disappear and electronic money will be the primary means of exchange.

I am also of the view that money will be exchanged and our banking and brokerage needs satisfied through handheld devices that communicate in a wireless fashion. These devices will both communicate with each other, with the markets, and, if needed, with a bank or brokerage house.

Money management is also an area where some frames of the future tableaux are easily seen. What has been an art will for many become more and more a science. There will be even more mathematical modeling of individual and collective portfolios, and the modeling will be more complex and more effective. Products, including mutual funds, will be more personally tailored on the one hand and more collective options will be available on the other.

Not only the product development, but also the product delivery area will be greatly changed by the forces I have described above. At some point in the next century, electronic banking and brokerage will be the norm. Most human contact at the retail level will be through the use of interactive screens. Branch banks will finally diminish markedly in number. Moreover, competition for banking and brokerage services will be global. Both retail and wholesale needs will be handled electronically by entities headquartered all over the world.

Of even greater consequence, both wholesale and retail customers will bypass financial intermediaries and transact business directly with the markets and directly among themselves. We can already see this happening.

Beyond changes in the product development and delivery areas, the new world of finance will fundamentally change banking and finance itself. Once an icon of tradition and stability, banking will be about innovation and change. The economics that drive this phenomenon are both powerful and unrelenting. More international competition means slimmer margins in traditional products and a rush for new products with fatter margins at least for a time.

Only fairly recently an industry under local or at most national control, banking and finance in the future will be an international phenomenon under international or at least multilateral control. Innovations in communications, including the Internet, will decrease the effectiveness of local supervision. Markets will be ever more linked and volatility will increase. National control will not be adequate to achieve a stable financial environment, and a less stable environment will be unacceptable politically. Hence, the inevitability of more powerful international financial stability mechanisms.

Until fairly recently an industry of relatively small companies, often geographically focused, banking and finance will eventually be dominated by a relatively few enormous enterprises with worldwide reach. At the same time, there will be a variety of successful innovators that will, at least for a time, be able to dominate certain market sectors.

This brave new world of finance is inevitable given the technological forces at work. Its advent, however, can be slowed or distorted by government intervention.

During my era in government, our policy was to alter existing rules to facilitate change and innovation and avoid new governmentally imposed regulation that would inhibit development. Our view was that, by allowing innovation in the financial sector, we would help create a stronger economy through increased price competition, new products, and through stronger and more profitable firms.

At the same time, we were mindful that some standards are essential to avoid abuse and excessive financial instability that can bring unacceptable levels of disruption and loss. Particularly in the emerging areas of electronic money and banking, we encouraged the industry itself to develop standards. Where we felt a greater degree of government involvement was in order, we favored guidance instead of legislation or regulation. In addition, we strove for internationalization and harmonization of standards to achieve an effective, level playing field wherever possible.

Whether governmental intervention is restrained or excessive, the new world of finance will be faced with an amalgam of existing and new governmental and self-regulatory efforts. Threading one's way through this regulatory environment will, alas, be as essential to the successful financial institution of the future as it has been in the past.

Unfortunately, precious few books and other reference sources are available to assist either the legal practitioner or financial institution with the laws and regulations applicable to modern banking and finance. Thus, a fine work of the type Melanie Fein has created in this book is both welcome and needed. The book is rooted both in a tradition of careful scholarship on the one hand and farsighted vision on the other. It will be, I am sure, an important adjunct to the library of scholars, practitioners, and businesspeople alike.

Eugene A. Ludwig
August 1999

CHAPTER 1

ELECTRONIC BANKING—NEW OPPORTUNITIES AND CHALLENGES

§ 1.01 NEW OPPORTUNITIES AND CHALLENGES

The technology revolution has dramatically altered the business of banking and presented banks with new business opportunities and competitive challenges. The development of electronic banking, smart cards, and new data processing techniques has made it possible for banking organizations to deliver traditional banking services in new formats as well as to provide new financial products and services with greatly enhanced efficiency and customer convenience.

Banks may participate in electronic banking in any number of capacities, including as system developers, issuers or distributors of stored value cards, transaction processors, transaction recordkeepers, trusted third parties providing authentification and certification services, as owners or investors through equity investments or joint ventures, and various combinations of the above. Under recent regulatory interpretations, banks may even participate in electronic commerce. Each of these activities presents new sources of diversified revenues for banks that will enhance shareholder value and make banks stronger competitors in the financial marketplace of the future.

§ 1.02 NEW CUSTOMER SERVICE OPPORTUNITIES

Electronic banking technology has increased the convenience and efficiency with which banks can deliver banking services to their customers and broadened the range of financial products available from banks. Advanced information processing and communication capabilities have made it possible for banks to tailor their services to more closely fit individual customer needs and to offer services on an integrated basis while maintaining a high degree of privacy and security of confidential customer information.

Banking customers have become increasingly comfortable with the concept of electronic banking through the widespread use of ATM machines and credit cards and the growing popularity of the Internet as a communications and purchasing device. As consumers gain experience with the convenience and security of electronic banking, banks will have increasing opportunities to offer their services electronically. The reduction in overhead and transaction costs that can be achieved with the new technology gives banks a strong incentive to encourage customer acceptance and usage of the new electronic banking systems.[1]

Internet customers are reported to be "significantly more profitable and loyal" than the average bank customer, giving their bank a 40 percent wallet share compared to the average 25 percent.[2] The wallet share increases to 50 to 60 percent for online customers who use electronic bill payment.

§ 1.03 NEW COMPETITIVE CHALLENGES

The technology revolution has brought new service providers to the financial marketplace and exposed banks to competition from unexpected sources.[3] Nonbank information technology companies, such as Microsoft and various Internet providers, have substantial capabilities in the business of transmitting secure financial information. Telecommunications companies, such as AT&T and regional telephone companies, also are direct participants in the communication link between banks and their customers. These and other companies have the capability to offer secure transaction processing services, including electronic bill payment services, credit cards, smart cards, and digital "money."[4] While nonbank technology companies have not yet embarked on large-scale efforts to compete with banks for banking business, they have the capability to come between banks and their customers in ways that could divert the customer relationship away from banks.

The widespread use of PCs and the Internet by bank customers has created additional competitive pressures by giving bank customers access

---

[1] Allowing customers to access monthly statements online rather than mailing them, for example, is a major cost saving that can be shared with customers. *See* "NextCard Splits the Savings from Not Mailing Statements," Am. Banker (Sept. 21, 1999) (reporting that NextCard Visa pays its credit card customers 50 cents per month to forego paper statements).

[2] Jeffrey Kutler, "From American Banker's Online '99 Conference: Internet Customers Really Are Profitable," Am. Banker (Oct. 4, 1999). A "wallet share" is a percentage of a customer's total financial services portfolio. *But see* "Dropout Rate Is Nearly 33% for Web Banking Customers," Am. Banker (Aug. 25, 1999).

[3] *See* "Viewpoints: Technology Companies Could Take the Lead in Financial Services," Am. Banker (Dec. 3, 1999).

[4] *See* "Banks Urged to Defend Turf in E-Payments," Am. Banker (Sept. 21, 1999) (reporting that Yahoo Inc. announced a new electronic bill payment service) ("As Internet commerce expands, bankers may have to turn to new technologies if they hope to keep their payment services businesses from slipping away to nonbanking competitors, industry observers say.").

to alternative sources of financial services and thereby reducing the traditional role of banks as intermediaries. Banking customers can shop for home mortgages, credit cards, insurance,[5] and other financial services directly on the Internet.[6] Through a variety of online calculators, search engines, and other aids, customers can make their own amortization, interest rate and other financial calculations, obtain financial advice, buy and sell securities, and purchase insurance. Customers with computer capability have less need for traditional banking services and can switch from one financial service provider to another with relative ease, thus reducing customer loyalty to any single bank. In order to capture and retain customers in the electronic marketplace of the future, banks will need to offer a full array of user-friendly electronic financial services.

While the technology revolution has increased competition in the financial services marketplace, it also has contributed to increased concentration in the structure of banking. The high start-up costs of new computer hardware and software systems[7] have forced banks to seek economies of scale by joining with other banks, financial firms, and technology companies in partnerships, joint ventures, and networks in order to share the costs of providing electronic banking services. For some banks, the price of acquiring the new technology has been too high and these banks have merged with or been acquired by larger banking organizations. The costs of Year 2000 preparedness undoubtedly contributed to increased consolidation in the industry. Much of the merger and acquisition activity in the banking industry over the past decade has been spurred by the need to achieve economies of scale in offering new banking technology. The continuing need for computer hardware and software upgrades is likely to pose continuing pressures toward consolidation.

§ 1.04 NEW REGULATORY CHALLENGES

Electronic banking presents new challenges to federal and state banking regulators. The regulators have been faced with novel proposals by banks to offer financial services in ways never contemplated before.

---

[5] "Insurance: Internet, Direct Marketing Expected to Fuel Life Sales," Am. Banker (July 27, 1999).

[6] *See* "Study Sees Steady Growth for Internet-Only Lenders," Am. Banker (Oct. 15, 1999).

[7] *See* "Financial Tech Spending Up 31%; Few Gauge Benefits," Am. Banker (Sept. 29, 1999).

For the most part, the banking agencies have viewed electronic banking as a positive development and have interpreted the regulatory framework as flexibly as possible to accommodate new computer and information technologies to the business of banking. The regulators have even gone so far as to charter "virtual banks" that operate solely in cyberspace.

The existing bank regulatory framework was not designed with electronic banking in mind, however, and many traditional bank regulatory concepts apply awkwardly to the new forms of electronic financial services. It remains to be seen whether the old regulatory tools can be adapted to fit the new technology without impeding the growth of emerging electronic banking products, or whether altogether new regulatory concepts need to be devised. The challenge for the regulators is to find ways of applying regulatory and supervisory norms to an emerging industry without retarding or otherwise inappropriately influencing its development.

The challenge of regulating electronic banking in large measure is how not to regulate it. The Clinton Administration's policy has been to let the private sector take the lead in developing self-regulatory measures.[8] The challenge of regulation thus is one that banks and other financial service firms share with the regulators.

§ 1.05 NEW POLICY ISSUES

Electronic banking and commerce raise a host of policy issues with broad ramifications for the financial services industry as a whole and for banks in particular. Some of these issues call into question the very nature of banking and have forced banks and their regulators to reconsider fundamental regulatory policies governing the industry.

Not only has the new technology provided new ways of conducting the very old business of banking, it has fundamentally transformed the nature of banking. The proliferation of stored value cards, digital cash, home banking systems, and cyberbanks has added new complexity to the age old questions of what is a "bank," what is a "deposit," what is "money," and how they should be regulated.

Many of the policy issues go beyond banking and encompass broad spheres of electronic commerce. Other policy issues implicate sociological considerations, such as which sectors of the population have Internet access

[8] *See* The White House, *A Framework for Global Electronic Commerce* (July 1, 1997).

and which do not.[9] Issues involving copyright, privacy, cryptography, and cyber-fraud, for example, affect not only banks but all entities involved in electronic commerce. Some of these issues are addressed in this book, but many of them are beyond the scope of the author's expertise and are left for others to address.

§ 1.06 CHRONOLOGY OF ELECTRONIC BANKING DEVELOPMENTS

The following chronology shows the evolution of electronic banking in the United States through regulatory actions and related developments:

1971 Federal Reserve Board issues policy statement on the payments system in anticipation of the substitution of electronic payments for checks. 57 Fed. Res. Bull. 546.

Federal Reserve Board amends Regulation Y to authorize bank holding companies to offer data processing services to the public. 57 Fed. Res. Bull. 512.

1973 Federal Reserve approves BankAmerica application to engage in issuance of travelers checks. 59 Fed. Res. Bull. 544.

1975 Federal Reserve Board issues interpretation clarifying and limiting the scope of data processing activities permissible under Regulation Y. 61 Fed. Res. Bull. 245.

1977 National Commission on Electronic Funds Transfers issues final report: "EFT in the United States: Policy Recommendations and the Public Interest."

1978 Congress enacts Electronic Funds Transfer Act. 15 U.S.C. §§ 1693 *et seq.*

[*Next page is 1-7.*]

[9] *See* U.S. Department of Commerce, *Falling Through the Net: A Report on the Telecommunications and Information Technology Gap in America* (July 1999).

1979 Federal Reserve Board authorizes bank holding companies to sell money orders, traveler's checks, and U.S. savings bonds. 65 Fed. Res. Bull. 249, 265.

Federal Reserve Board authorizes bank holding companies to provide check verification services. 65 Fed. Res. Bull. 263.

1980 Federal Reserve Board authorizes Citicorp to engage in expanded data processing activities. 66 Fed. Res. Bull. 85.

Federal Reserve Board denies bank holding company application to offer key entry services. 66 Fed. Res. Bull. 666.

1981 Federal Reserve Board authorizes Citicorp to engage in retail check authorization. 67 Fed. Res. Bull. 740.

Federal Reserve Board approves application by The Conifer Group to provide payroll processing, accounts receivable processing, accounts payable processing, automated lock box services, item processing, and automated accounting services. 67 Fed. Res. Bull. 449.

1982 Federal Reserve Board approves home banking services by Citicorp. 68 Fed. Res. Bull. 505.

Federal Reserve Board expands scope of data processing activities permissible under Regulation Y and is sued by the Association of Data Processing Service Organizations. 47 Fed. Reg. 37,368.

1984 Regulation Y data processing activities upheld. *Association of Data Processing Serv. Orgs., Inc. v. Board of Governors,* 745 F.2d 677 (D.C. Cir. 1984).

Federal Reserve Board authorizes group of banking organizations to operate EFT system for interchange of financial transactions of banks among different EFT networks (a network of networks). 70 Fed. Res. Bull. 113.

Federal Reserve Board approves pilot bank holding company program offering home shopping and travel planning services. F.R.R.S. 4-472.

1985 Office of the Comptroller of the Currency (OCC) permits national bank to provide electronic gateway and communications services. OCC Interpretive Letter No. 346.

1986 Federal Reserve Board approves Citicorp application to acquire Quotron Systems, Inc. 72 Fed. Res. Bull. 497.

Federal Reserve Board approves Citicorp application to acquire Northeast Exchange and thereby operate an ATM network. 72 Fed. Res. Bull. 583.

Federal Reserve Board authorizes bank holding company to operate nondiscriminatory ATM network in Giant grocery stores. 72 Fed. Res. Bull. 347.

1987 Federal Reserve Board authorizes bank holding company to provide computer output to microfilm services. 52 Fed. Reg. 45, 160.

1992 OCC authorizes national bank to sell computerized "smart phone" telephones. OCC Interpretive Letter No. 611.

1993 Smart Card Forum is founded.

Financial Services Technology Consortium is founded.

Federal Reserve Board authorizes bank holding companies to operate electronic data interchange services that furnish retail merchants with data collected from sales in format useful for inventory control and targeted marketing. 79 Fed. Res. Bull. 1158.

1994 Federal Reserve Board authorizes Banc One *et al.* to provide electronic benefit services. 79 Fed. Res. Bull. 1158.

Federal Reserve Board authorizes Banc One to operate network for processing medical payment data between physicians and hospitals and health insurance companies. 80 Fed. Res. Bull. 139.

Federal Reserve Board authorizes 15 bank holding companies to operate a worldwide retail "Infinet" ATM network for stored value cards and to dispense travelers' checks and postage stamps from ATMs. 80 Fed. Res. Bull. 1107.

Department of Justice issues consent decree in antitrust case against network rules that required small banks to have ATMs driven by network switch and exclusively routed through the network. 59 Fed. Reg. 44,757.

1995 Congress holds hearings on "The Future of Money." House Subcommittee on Domestic and International Monetary Policy (Oct. 11).

OCC authorizes national banks to acquire interest in MECA and its "Managing Your Money" software. OCC Interpretive Letter No. 677 (June 28).

Federal Reserve Board approves merger and expansion of MAC Network. 81 Fed. Res. Bull. 492.

Federal Reserve Board authorizes BNCCORP to process certain limited nonfinancial data. 81 Fed. Res. Bull. 295.

Federal Reserve Board authorizes State Street Boston Corporation and Bank of Boston joint venture to provide shareholder, bankruptcy, and class action electronic processing services. 81 Fed. Res. Bull. 1049.

Federal Reserve Board authorizes Norwest Corporation to offer money transmittal services. 81 Fed. Res. Bull. 1130.

OTS approves first banking institution to operate on the Internet.

European Union adopts "Directive on the Protection of Personal Data."

1996 OCC adopts revised interpretive ruling allowing national banks broadened powers to engage in electronic banking activities. 12 C.F.R. § 7.1019.

OCC permits national bank to provide ATM dispersal of tickets, phone cards, and gift certificates. OCC Interpretive Letter No. 718.

OCC permits national bank to build and operate electronic toll collection system. OCC Interpretive Letter No. 731.

OCC permits national bank to provide electronic data interchange services that provide for payments by EFT. OCC Interpretive Letter No. 732.

OCC permits national bank to operate closed stored value system and to provide computer hardware for ancillary functions; permits national bank to develop and deliver stored value systems for universities, hospitals, theme parks, military installations, and business centers. OCC Interpretive Letter No. 737.

OCC permits national bank to operate system that allows automobile dealers to track information on customers and generate market statistics such as buying trends and cycles. OCC Interpretive Letter No. 741.

OCC permits national bank to operate on Internet and sell excess Internet access service to the public. OCC Interpretive Letter No. 742 (Apollo).

OCC permits national bank to provide computer networking packages for other banks and to assist in installation and maintenance of networks. OCC Interpretive Letter No. 754.

OCC issues bulletin on stored value risks. OCC Bulletin 96-48.

OCC permits national banks to own interest in Mondex. OCC Conditional Approval No. 220.

OCC permits national bank consortium to operate electronic gateway for other banks to provide home banking services. OCC Conditional Approval No. 221.

American Bankers Association Payments System Task Force issues report on "The Role of Banks in the Payments System of the Future."

Court orders Federal Reserve Board to hold hearing on MAC network expansion but later vacates ruling. *Money Station, Inc. v. Federal Reserve Board,* 81 F.3d 1128, *vacated,* 94 F.3d 658.

Congress orders all federal benefit payments to be made electronically by 1999. 31 U.S.C. § 3332.

Court rules that Treasury cannot exclude nonbank financial firms from bidding for electronic benefit transfer contracts. *Transactive Corp. v. United States,* 91 F.3d 232 (D.C. Cir. 1996).

Congress clarifies that banks can share confidential customer information with their affiliates subject to right of customer to opt out. Pub. L. No. 104-208.

Interagency Consumer Electronic Payments Task Force is created to provide a forum for consideration of electronic banking policy issues.

FDIC issues General Counsel Opinion No. 8 concluding that most stored value cards are not FDIC-insured deposits.

The Bankers Roundtable forms Banking Industry Technology Secretariat ("BITS").

United Nations Commission on International Trade law adopts model law on electronic commerce.

Federal Reserve Board authorizes bank holding company to offer computer network consulting services to banks, including design, selection, acquisition, installation, and operation of computer networks. 82 Fed. Res. Bull. 82.

Federal Reserve Board authorizes Compagnie Financiere de Paribas to provide electronic billing services for digital mobile telephone network. 82 Fed. Res. Bull. 348.

Federal Reserve Board authorizes Royal Bank of Canada to acquire interest in MECA Software. 82 Fed. Res. Bull. 363.

Federal Reserve Board authorizes Cardinal Bancshares to acquire Five Paces, Inc. and assist other banks in offering Internet banking services. 82 Fed. Res. Bull. 674.

Federal Reserve Board proposes regulation to subject certain stored value cards to Regulation E. 61 Fed. Reg. 37,229.

Congress orders Federal Reserve Board not to adopt regulation but to report to Congress. Pub. L. No. 104-208.

Federal Reserve Board forms Committee on the Federal Reserve in the Payments Mechanism chaired by Alice Rivlin.

1997 White House issues "A Framework for Global Electronic Commerce."

Federal Reserve Board adopts Regulation Y provision expanding data processing authority by allowing 30 percent of a bank holding company's data processing revenues to come from nonfinancial data processing activities. 12 C.F.R. § 225.28(b)(14).

Federal Reserve Board issues "Sound Practices Guidance for Information Security for Networks." SR 97-32 (SUP).

Federal Reserve Board authorizes bank holding companies to form inter-bank clearinghouse for multilateral netting of foreign exchange transactions. 83 Fed. Res. Bull. 127.

Federal Reserve Board approves merger of Southeast Switch with other EFT networks. 83 Fed. Res. Bull. 131.

Federal Reserve Board authorizes 15 major banking organizations to enter Integrion joint venture with IBM to design, develop, and operate a data processing and transmission system parallel to the Internet. 83 Fed. Res. Bull. 135.

Federal Reserve Board authorizes Toronto-Dominion Bank to develop and sell software to allow brokerage customers to buy and sell securities over the Internet from personal computers. 83 Fed. Res. Bull. 335.

Federal Reserve Board authorizes Banc One Corporation to engage in merchant card processing including merchant contract acquisition, front-end network processing and back-end merchant accounting. 83 Fed. Res. Bull. 602.

Interagency Consumer Electronic Payments Task Force holds hearings on consumer disclosure and protections, access to electronic money, the financial condition of issuers, and privacy. 62 Fed. Reg. 19,173 and 29,392.

ABA Task Force on Stored-Value Cards issues analysis of commercial law issues involving stored-value cards. 52 Bus. Law. 653.

Federal Reserve Board issues report to Congress on application of EFT Act to stored value cards.

OTS permits savings bank to offer Internet banking services. OTS 97-2.

FDIC issues guidance on "Security Risks Associated with the Internet." FIL-131-97.

General Accounting Office issues report on "Payments, Clearance, and Settlement: A Guide to the Systems, Risks, and Issues," GAO/GGD-97-73.

General Accounting Office issues report on "Automated Teller Machines." GAO/GGD-97-90 (May).

Congress amends Fair Credit Reporting Act to facilitate information sharing among banks and their affiliates.

Federal Reserve Committee on the Federal Reserve in the Payments Mechanism issues report concluding that Federal Reserve has important role to play in payments system of the future.

Congress holds hearings on the payments system.

Federal banking regulators issue guidance on reporting of computer-related crimes by banks.

FinCen proposes regulations to subject electronic banking transactions to Bank Secrecy Act. 62 Fed. Reg. 27,890.

OCC issues Advisory Letter 97-6 establishing scheduling requirement for Year 2000 ("Y2K") readiness by national banks.

FFIEC issues guidance on Y2K risks and readiness.

Basle Committee on Banking Supervision issues paper on Y2K readiness.

FDIC and Federal Reserve Board take cease and desist action against Georgia banks for lack of Y2K readiness plans. FDIC Press Release 83-97.

Congress holds hearings on Y2K problem.

Treasury Department proposes regulations to implement electronic benefit transfer program. 62 Fed. Reg. 48,714.

Germany and Italy adopt digital signature laws.

European Commission issues paper on electronic commerce.

Organization for Economic Cooperation and Development issues voluntary guidelines for use of cryptography in electronic commerce.

International Chamber of Commerce issues nonbinding general usage guidelines for digital transactions over the Internet.

North American Securities Administrators Association adopts model rule to govern activities of broker-dealers on the Internet (April 27).

OTS issues "Statement on Retail On-Line Personal Computer Banking" for savings associations. OTS Press Release 97-39 (June 23).

National Telecommunications and Information Administration issues report on "Privacy and Self-Regulation in the Information Age." (June).

OCC charters Compubank, a national bank that will conduct business solely on the Internet. OCC Interpretive Letter No. 253 (Aug. 20).

Consumer Electronic Payments Task Force holds hearings. *See* 62 Fed. Reg. 19,173 and 29,392 (1997).

Banking agencies issue guidance on reporting of computer-related crimes by banks.

NASDR issues guidance as to when a broker-dealer will be deemed responsible for the content and filing of material on hyperlinked Web sites (Nov. 11).

SEC issues concept release inviting public comment on ways to update federal regulatory framework to address changes in U.S. securities markets resulting frcm Internet usage.

OCC authorizes Barnett Bank to operate Web site providing consumers and dealers with information on used cars, i.e., a virtual used car lot. Corporate Decision 97-60.

1998 Congress holds further hearings on Y2K problem.

OCC establishes Privacy Working Group to develop guidance for national banks on consumer privacy issues.

GAO issues report on "Electronic Banking: Experiences Reported by Banks in Implementing On-Line Banking." GAO/GGD-98-34 (Jan.).

OCC authorizes Zions National Bank to act as certification authority for verifying digital signatures. Conditional Approval No. 267 (Jan. 12).

Basle Committee on Banking Supervision issues report on "Risk Management for Electronic Banking and Electronic Money Activities." (Mar. 20).

European Commission issues proposal for a "Directive on a Common Framework for Electronic Signatures." (May 13).

President Clinton signs directive on Critical Infrastructure Protection establishing government policy of protecting against intentional acts that can disrupt essential computer systems. Presidential Decision Directive (PDD) 63 (May 22).

Federal Trade Commission issues "Privacy Online: A Report to Congress." (June).

European Commission issues "A Framework for Action on Combating Fraud and Counterfeiting of Non-Cash Means of Payment." (July).

Congress enacts Year 2000 Information and Readiness Disclosure Act. Pub. L. No. 105-271.

Congress enacts Examination Parity and Year 2000 Readiness for Financial Institutions Act. Pub. L. No. 105-164.

OCC issues bulletin on rights and responsibilities of national banks under Fair Credit Reporting Act when sharing customer information with affiliates. OCC Bulletin No. 98-33 (Aug. 3).

FDIC issues guidance on "Online Privacy of Consumer Personal Information." FIL 86-98 (Aug. 17).

Federal banking agencies and FBI alert banks to practice of "pretext phone calling" by account information brokers. OCC Advisory Letter No. 98-11 (Aug. 20).

OCC issues guidance on technology risk management for PC banking. OCC Bulletin 98-38 (Aug. 24).

European Central Bank issues proposed framework for regulation of electronic money in a "Report on Electronic Money." (Aug.).

OTS authorizes savings associations to use electronic means to perform any functions or service permissible under federal charter. 63 Fed. Reg. 65,673.

Federal banking agencies issue advisories on Y2K compliance, including guidance on management responsibilities, customer awareness, vendor compliance, and safety and soundness.

SEC issues Year 2000 reporting requirements for broker-dealers, investment advisers, and transfer agents.

OECD issues "Ministerial Declaration on Protection of Privacy on Global Networks." (Oct.).

Treasury adopts final regulation to implement requirement for electronic payment of all federal payments. 63 Fed. Reg. 51,490.

Department of Commerce proposes "safe harbor" for U.S. bank compliance with European Privacy Directive and commences negotiations with European Union.

SEC issues statement on how investment advisers, broker-dealers, mutual funds, and issuers of securities can use Web sites to solicit offshore securities transactions without triggering registration requirements. 63 Fed. Reg. 14,806.

1999 OCC authorizes bank-owned EFT network to operate scrip terminals that dispense vouchers redeemable for merchandise. OCC Interpretive Letter No. 854 (Feb. 25).

OCC authorizes national bank to offer electronic bill payment and presentment services via Internet. Conditional Approval No. 304 (March 5).

OCC authorizes national bank to host Internet Web sites for business customers. OCC Interpretive Letter No. 856 (Mar. 5).

OCC issues bulletin on "Infrastructure Threats from Cyber-Terrorists." (Mar. 5).

OCC issues guidance on compliance with customer opt-out provision in Fair Credit Reporting Act. OCC Advisory Letter 99-3 (Mar. 29).

Clinton Administration releases "Clinton-Gore Plan for Financial Privacy and Consumer Protection in the 21st Century." (May 4).

SEC brings enforcement antifraud actions in connection with fraudulent Internet securities sales practices.

OCC issues guidance on certification authority systems to national banks. OCC Bulletin 99-20 (May 4).

OCC issues guidance to national banks on Web Site Privacy Statements. OCC Advisory Letter 99-6 (May 4).

OCC charters NextBank as subsidiary of NextCard, Inc., which becomes second national bank chartered as Internet bank. Conditional Approval No. 312 (May 8).

Banking agencies issue further guidance on Year 2000 readiness.

FTC holds workshop on how to protect consumers in global electronic commerce (June 8-9).

U.S. Department of Commerce issues report "Falling Through the Net: A Report on the Telecommunications and Information Technology Gap in America" (July).

FTC issues report to Congress on "Self-Regulation and Privacy Online" (July).

GAO issues report on federal regulatory oversight of Internet banking. GAO/GGD-99-91 (July 6).

Year 2000 Readiness and Responsibility Act enacted (July 20).

Federal Reserve Board creates Payments System Development Committee to advise on public policy issues raised by developments in the retail payments system (July 20).

OCC issues Examination Handbook on Internet Banking (Oct. 14).

OCC authorizes banks to engage in "Spectrum" electronic bill presentment joint venture. OCC Conditional Approval No. 332 (Oct. 18).

OCC authorizes national bank to provide Web design services to merchant customers. Interpretive Letter No. 875 (Oct. 31)

Federal banking agencies release Interagency Financial Institution Web Site Privacy Survey Report (Nov.).

Gramm-Leach-Bliley Act enacted authorizing cross-industry affiliations, expanded powers for financial holding companies, and new consumer protections for financial information privacy, among other provisions (Nov. 12).

OCC authorizes consortium of banks to operate a global, interoperable network to serve as certification authority for digital signatures. OCC Conditional Approval No. 339 (Nov. 16).

Anti-Cybersquatting Consumer Protection Act enacted (Nov. 29).

OCC authorizes national bank to refer merchant customers to a third party that would provide Web site development and hosting services. Corporate Decision No. 99-50 (Dec. 23).

Uniform Electronic Transactions Act is finalized and adopted in California.

FDIC issues guidance on tools and practices designed to facilitate online banking risk assessment process. FIL-68-99.

Council for Electronic Billing & Payment releases "Electronic Bill Payment/Presentment Business Practices."

Federal Reserve Board proposes to allow financial institutions to deliver consumer disclosures electronically under Truth in Lending Act, Equal Credit Opportunity Act, and other consumer laws. 64 Fed. Reg. 49,688.

FFIEC adopts Uniform Rating System for Information Technology. 64 Fed. Reg. 3109 (1999).

2000 OCC reports that 541 national banks have transactional Web sites. 65 Fed. Reg. 4895.

OCC authorizes national banks to provide hyperlinks from bank Web sites to third-party service providers. OCC Interpretive Letter No. 347 (Jan. 29).

OCC authorizes EFS National Bank to acquire company that owns software enabling users to change their Web sites. Corporate Decision No. 99-50 (Jan. 29).

OCC charters AeroBank.com as first Internet-only national bank to focus on small business market. Conditional Approval No. 347 (Jan. 29).

OCC issues bulletin warning national banks of the threat of distributed denial of service "DdoS" attacks involving flooding of targeted Web sites and interruption of customer service. OCC Alert 2000-1 (Feb. 11).

OCC authorizes national bank to provide information on current events and weather in conjunction with hosting virtual mall. Conditional Approval No. 369 (Feb. 25).

FRB issues guidance on Information Technology Examination Frequency. SR 00-3 (SUP) (Feb. 29).

OCC authorizes Anexsys national bank, under finder authority, to develop and host a Web site for a government agency allowing the public to access or purchase services, information, forms, and products from the agency. Conditional Approval No. 361 (March 3).

FFIEC issues report on "Lessons Learned from the Year 2000 Project" (Mar. 21).

FDIC hosts Interagency Public Forum on Consumer Privacy in the Financial Services Industry. (Mar. 23); 65 Fed. Reg. 11,062.

OCC charters Pointpathbank as a full-service Internet-only bank with no banking offices open to the public. Conditional Approval No. 368 (Apr. 3).

OCC charters Hutton National Bank as Internet-only bank with a small business equipment leasing focus. Conditional Approval No. 383 (Apr. 13).

OCC authorizes national bank to make minority investment in registered broker-dealer that will use Internet to provide retail brokerage services. Interpretive Letter No. 889 (Apr. 24).

OCC issues bulletin advising national banks on how to prevent, detect and respond to intrusions into bank computer systems. OCC Bulletin 2000-14 (May 15).

OCC issues guidance on protecting Internet address of national banks. OCC Alert 2000-9 (July 19).

OCC issues working paper 2000-9 on "Internet Banking: Developments and Prospects" (Sept.).

OCC issues study on "Internet Banking: Developments and Prospects" (Sept.).

OCC charters eComm National Bank as a "bricks-and-clicks" national bank. Conditional Approval No. 430 (Nov. 13).

OCC charters Bridge Bank of Silicon Valley as "bricks-and-clicks" national bank to deliver products and services through both brick-and-mortar office and a transactional Internet site. Conditional Approval No. 427 (Nov. 17).

Congress enacts Electronic Signatures in Global and National Commerce Act ("E-Sign Act"). Pub. L. No. 106-229, *codified at* 15 U.S.C. § 7001.

FFIEC issues Statement on Risk Management of Technology Outsourcing. (Nov. 29, 2000).

FRB authorizes financial holding companies to act as "finders" and operate electronic marketplaces and host Internet Web sites. 65 Fed. Reg. 80,735 (2000).

2001 Federal banking agencies adopt Interagency Guidelines Establishing Standards for Safeguarding Customer Information. 66 Fed. Reg. 8616 (Feb. 1).

OCC issues bulletin on risks of account aggregation services. OCC Bulletin 2001-12 (Feb. 28, 2001).

CHAPTER 2

THE ROLE OF GOVERNMENT

§ 2.01 IN GENERAL

The development of electronic banking and commerce technologies has strained traditional regulatory concepts and raised questions as to whether, when, and how the government should regulate the new products and services that are emerging. Federal regulators generally have resisted the urge to adopt a comprehensive regulatory framework for electronic banking for fear of retarding the development of an infant industry or channeling it in inappropriate ways. State regulators, on the other hand, have appeared more eager to adopt regulations, but designed to facilitate rather than restrict, the development of electronic commerce within their states.

The Clinton Administration established a philosophy of relying on private industry to take the lead in self-regulation and to avoid undue governmental restrictions on electronic commerce. In announcing White House policy in *A Framework for Global Electronic Commerce*, President Clinton stated that "[f]or electronic commerce to flourish, the private sector must lead" and directed the federal executive agencies to refrain from imposing unnecessary regulations where effective industry self-regulation measures are in place.[1]

The policy of regulatory restraint was articulated by the Federal Trade Commission:

> What is the appropriate role of government in the development and deployment of new electronic payment systems? On the one hand, it can be argued that without effective government regulation, there will not be sufficient public confidence in the security, effectiveness and fairness of these new electronic payment systems to permit their development. On the other hand, premature government regulation could chill or prevent the market from developing optimal solutions. Particularly at the early stages of new technologies—where new issues will take shape gradually over time—there is a good case for government restraint. The regulatory decisions that are made in the near future will have an enormous impact not just on electronic payment systems but on the whole marketing revolution that is occurring in the new high technology, global marketplace. For now, government should continue to monitor the development of the marketplace for electronic payment systems to ensure that consumers

[1] The White House, *A Framework for Global Electronic Commerce* (July 1, 1997).

> are getting the information they need to make informed choices about protecting the privacy of their financial transactions.[2]

The Federal Reserve Board also endorsed a policy of non-intervention in the development of electronic banking. In a 1997 report to Congress, the Board presented an analytical framework for examining the effects of government regulation on technological innovation based on an analysis of the relationship between technological progress and social welfare and the rationales and effects of government regulation on emerging technologies.[3] An underlying premise of the Board's framework was:

> Given the close link between technical progress and improvements in social welfare, policymakers have an obligation to consider the effects of their actions on incentives to invest in research and development (R&D) activities that can lead to product and process innovations. Research and development are risky activities with highly uncertain outcomes. Investors require high expected rates of return in exchange for bearing the risk associated with funding such ventures. Government policies, which may alter the riskiness of or the return to R&D investments, have the potential to foster or to hinder technological progress and product development and may influence firms' choices among alternative technologies.[4]

The Board's report noted that regulation "does not always achieve the desired outcome," "provides an imperfect substitute for competition," and that "regulatory mistakes . . . may be costly to correct." Therefore, the Board concluded, "[o]n balance, it seems prudent for government to proceed cautiously and to engage in early regulation only when the benefit-cost tradeoff is particularly compelling."[5] Federal Reserve Chairman Greenspan has reiterated this view:

---

[2] Statement of the Federal Trade Commission before the House Subcommittee on Financial Institutions and Consumer Credit (Sept. 18, 1997), 1997 WL 14151407. *See also* Federal Communications Commission, Office of Plans and Policy, *The FCC and the Unregulation of the Internet* (July 19, 1999).

[3] Board of Governors of the Federal Reserve System, *Report to Congress on the Application of the Electronic Fund Transfer Act to Electronic Stored-Value Products,* (Mar. 1997); § II. of the Report, "Analytical Framework: The Economics of Innovation, Technology, and Regulation."

[4] *Id.* at 8.

[5] *Id.* at 13–14.

> The Federal Reserve also clearly recognizes the need to foster innovation in the private sector and to help remove barriers to the development and adoption of new payment services for electronic and traditional commerce. As I have often said, to continue to be effective, government's regulatory role must increasingly be focused on assuring that adequate risk management systems are in place in the private sector. As financial systems have become more complex, detailed rules and standards have become both more burdensome and less effective. If we wish to foster financial innovation, we must first be careful not to impose rules that inhibit it, and we must be especially watchful that we not unduly impede our increasingly broad electronic payments system.
>
> Thus, the private sector needs to play the pivotal role in determining what payment services consumers and businesses actually demand and in supplying those services. In a period of change and uncertainty there may be a temptation, and a desire by some market participants, to have the government step in and resolve the uncertainty, whether through standards, regulation, or other policies. In the case of electronic payment innovations, only consumers and merchants will ultimately determine what new products are successful in the marketplace. Government action can retard progress, but almost certainly cannot ensure it.
>
> One important role government can play, however, is to help identify and, where appropriate, help remove barriers to innovation.[5.1]

Industry groups have been loathe to disagree that the marketplace is the best regulator and generally have supported only a limited role for government.[6] On the other hand, industry members recognize that government regulation can be an important tool for gaining customer confidence in new electronic banking applications. For example, the benefits of regulation are recognized as a means of facilitating electronic banking and commerce through uniform standards in areas such as digital signatures where a plethora of conflicting state law requirements would stifle the use of this new technology.[7] A uniform regulatory framework

---

[5.1] Remarks by Chairman Alan Greenspan before the National Automated Clearinghouse Association Annual Meeting, April 10, 2000.

[6] *See, e.g.,* Testimony of Marcia Z. Sullivan, Vice President and Director of Government Relations, Consumer Bankers Association, before the House Subcommittee on Financial Institutions and Consumer Credit (Sept. 18, 1997); ABA Task Force Report at 25.

[7] *See generally* "Electronic Authentication—State and Federal Jurisdictional Questions," Electronic Banking Law and Commerce Report (June 1997) (different viewpoints on state vs. federal regulation).

for authentication and nonrepudiation also is viewed as desirable, if not essential, to promote the development of compatible systems across international boundaries. In order to assure United States industry participants a competitive position in the global electronic marketplace, some industry members have urged the U.S. government to take the lead in developing international standards.[8]

Internationally, the Basle Committee on Banking Supervision also has urged banking supervisors to avoid unnecessary regulation of electronic banking: "Given the degree of uncertainty about future technological and market developments, it is important that supervisory authorities avoid policies that hamper useful innovation and experimentation."[9]

In a major departure from the general policy of government nonintervention, however, the European Central Bank ("ECB") in 1998 proposed a regulatory framework for electronic money, stating:

> The ECB is convinced that appropriate regulation at an early stage has a positive impact on innovation by reducing the likelihood of the failure of a scheme, which would damage the confidence of customers and merchants in the payment instrument. Moreover, if such a regulatory framework were only to be designed after a variety of products had already developed, it might entail substantial changes to the products or restrictions on the parties involved and the related costs might endanger the business case for such products. In addition, the more electronic money schemes progress, the higher the risk that the absence of regulation may create "droits acquis," which would soon become impossible to challenge.[10]

The proposed European framework for electronic money is discussed in Chapter 6, **Electronic Money**.

---

[8] *See* Robert O. Ball, III, "Answering the Call for a Uniform Legal and Regulatory Framework for Electronic Banking and Commerce," Electronic Banking Law and Commerce Report (Jan. 1998) ("For the U.S. to compete in the world market and remain a dominant player, it needs a proper infrastructure and it needs it now. If a U.S. financial institution cannot facilitate my conducting Internet commerce, an EU bank can and will.").

[9] Basle Committee on Banking Supervision, Risk Management for Electronic Banking and Electronic Money Activities, Press Statement (Mar. 20, 1998).

[10] European Central Bank, *Report on Electronic Money* (Aug. 1998), at 20.

§ 2.02 FEDERAL GOVERNMENT ACTIVITIES

Various initiatives at all levels of government are being taken to monitor the impact of electronic banking on the financial system and to assess whether, when, and how government regulation may be appropriate. Although few regulatory initiatives have been proposed and adopted, much general guidance has been given.

[A] The Administration

[1] The White House

In 1997, President Clinton released *A Framework for Global Electronic Commerce* setting forth the Administration's policy on electronic commerce and establishing a set of principles to guide the U.S. government's actions in the electronic age.[11] The following key principles formed the basis of the framework:

- The private sector should lead.
- Governments should avoid undue restrictions on electronic commerce.
- Where governmental involvement is needed, its aim should be to support and enforce a predictable, minimalist, consistent and simple legal environment for commerce.
- Governments should recognize the decentralized qualities of the Internet and its tradition of "bottom-up governance" and revise existing laws to accommodate Internet commerce.
- Electronic commerce over the Internet should be facilitated on a global basis through rules that are consistent across geopolitical boundaries.

President Clinton directed executive department and agency heads to be guided by these principles in any future federal actions relating to electronic commerce.

The President's report addressed a number of policy issues, including customs and taxation, electronic payments systems, a "Uniform Commer-

[11] The White House, *A Framework for Global Electronic Commerce,* posted at ⟨⟨*http://www.iitf.nist.gov/eleccomm/ecomm.htm*⟩⟩.

cial Code" for electronic commerce, intellectual property protection, privacy, security, telecommunications infrastructure and information technology, regulation of content, technical standards, and the need for a coordinated electronic commerce strategy.

With respect to electronic commerce, the Administration recommended that the following rules should govern:

- Parties should be free to order the contractual relationship between themselves as they see fit.
- Rules should be technology-neutral (*i.e.,* not assume or require a particular technology) and forward looking (*i.e.,* not hinder the use or development of technologies in the future).
- Existing rules should be modified and new rules should be adopted only as necessary or substantially desirable to support the use of electronic technologies.
- The process should involve the high-tech commercial sector as well as businesses that have not yet moved online.

The Administration's non-regulatory approach to electronic commerce was reiterated by the U.S. Government Working Group on Electronic Commerce in 1998.[12]

[2] Treasury Department

The Treasury Department acquired a major role in the development of electronic banking when Congress ordered it to disburse all federal payments electronically rather than by check as of January 1, 1999.[13] The new law generally requires all payment recipients to have a bank account and thus is expected to extend electronic banking to a large number of individuals who currently do not use the banking system.

[3] FinCEN

Electronic banking has created new opportunities for criminals to access and manipulate financial information for unlawful purposes, posing

---

[12] *See* U.S. Government Working Group on Electronic Commerce, First Annual Report (Nov. 1998).

[13] 31 U.S.C. § 3332. *See* Chapter 10, **Electronic Transfer of Federal Payments.**

new challenges for law enforcement agencies. Among other measures aimed at electronic banking, the Treasury Department's Financial Crimes Enforcement Network ("FinCEN") in 1997 proposed regulations to subject electronic banking and commerce to the anti-money laundering provisions of the Bank Secrecy Act.[14]

[4] Department of Commerce

The Department of Commerce has played an active role in the Administration's policy on electronic commerce. The Secretary of Commerce chairs the President's Information Infrastructure Task Force. In April 1998, the Department of Commerce issued a report entitled *The Emerging Digital Economy* describing the impact of electronic commerce and the Internet on the nation's economy.

In June 1998, in connection with the preparation of a report to the President on privacy, the Department requested public comment on industry efforts to establish self-regulatory regimes to ensure online privacy and to develop technological means of protecting information privacy.[15]

[5] National Infrastructure Protection Center

The National Infrastructure Protection Center ("NIPC") was established in 1998 by the Department of Justice and the Federal Bureau of Investigation ("FBI") to serve as a national focal point for attacks on the Nation's critical infrastructures, including telecommunications, banking and finance, water supply systems, transportation, emergency services, government operations, electrical power, and gas and oil storage and delivery. NIPC was founded as a joint government and private sector partnership that includes representatives from agencies of federal, state and local governments. Its mission is to increase the sharing of information between government and private industry on vulnerability and threats to the critical infrastructures.

A key focus of NIPC's initiatives have been on technology-based threats and "cyber-terrorism." Among other things, NIPC issues advisory bulletins on "E-Commerce Vulnerabilities" warning of computer viruses

---

[14] 62 Fed. Reg. 27,890 (1997). *See* Chapter 11, **System Security and Risk**.

[15] 63 Fed. Reg. 30,729 (1998).

and hacker activity targeted at financial institutions and the availability of system "patches" to safeguard computer systems.[15.1]

[B] Federal Banking Agencies

[1] Comptroller of the Currency

The Office of the Comptroller of the Currency ("OCC") charters and supervises national banks. The OCC has played an important role in helping banks meet the opportunities and challenges posed by electronic banking and commerce.

In 1996, the OCC revised its interpretive rule governing data processing activities to broaden the scope of electronic banking services that national banks can offer[16] and has approved numerous proposals by national banks to offer electronic banking and services. In 1996, the OCC approved a charter proposal by a national bank to offer its customers Internet access services[17] and in 1997 chartered a national bank that proposed to operate solely on the Internet without any retail banking facilities.[18] In 1999, the OCC authorized a national bank to host Internet Web sites for its business customers and thereby facilitate commerce on the Internet.[19]

The OCC established an internal Bank Technology Committee—which subsequently was established as a division of the OCC—to identify and assess supervisory issues and risks arising from bank-related electronic technology. The Division includes representatives from the Chief National Bank Examiner's Office, each of the OCC's six district offices, the Multinational Banking Division, Law Department, Economics Department, Consumer and Fiduciary Compliance Department, and the Information Resources Management Department. Among other things, the Division issues guidance to national banks on supervisory concerns regarding account aggregation services offered by banks.[19.1]

The OCC is the coordinator for the Treasury Department's policy on electronic money issues and has taken the lead in a wide range of

---

[15.1] *See, e.g.,* NIPC Advisory 00-060, "E-Commerce Vulnerabilities" (Dec. 1, 2000) and update Advisory 01-003 (Mar. 8, 2001).

[16] 12 C.F.R. § 7.

[17] OCC Interpretive Letter No. 742 (1996) (Apollo Trust Company).

[18] OCC Conditional Approval No. 253 (Aug. 20, 1997) (Compubank).

[19] OCC Interpretive Letter No. 856 (Mar. 5, 1999).

[19.1] *See* OCC Bulletin 2001-12 (Feb. 28, 2001).

supervisory issues relating to electronic banking. Among other guidance, the OCC issued a bulletin addressing the risks inherent in developing and operating stored value cards[20] and provided guidance on technology risk management.[21] In 1998, the OCC established a Privacy Working Group to develop guidance for national banks on consumer privacy issues.[22]

In 2000, the OCC issued an advanced notice of proposed rulemaking soliciting public comment on a wide range of issues arising from national bank involvement in electronic banking activities to determine whether the OCC needs to revise its regulations to facilitate the use of new technologies by national banks.[22.1] Among the issues on which the OCC invited public comment are the following:

- How should the OCC adapt its regulations or supervisory policies to facilitate national banks' use of electronic technology consistent with safety and soundness?
- What statutes administered by the OCC could be interpreted more flexibly to accommodate new technologies, particularly those that reference a bank's "location"?
- How can the OCC enhance the operational flexibility of banks engaging in electronic banking consistent with safety and soundness?

[2] Federal Reserve Board

The Federal Reserve Board ("Federal Reserve" or "Board") supervises state member banks of the Federal Reserve System and bank holding companies. The Board has taken several actions to facilitate the use of electronic banking technology by these institutions.

In 1997, the Board revised its Regulation Y to authorize broader electronic banking activities by bank holding companies.[23] Of particular note was a new provision allowing bank holding companies to engage in data processing activities of any kind subject to a 30 percent revenue

[20] OCC Bulletin 96-48 (Sept. 10, 1996).

[21] OCC Bulletin 98-38, "Technology Risk Management: PC Banking" (Aug. 24, 1998).

[22] *See* OCC Press Release 98-59 (June 12, 1998).

[22.1] 65 Fed Reg. 4895 (2000).

[23] 12 C.F.R. § 225.28(b)(14).

limitation. The total annual revenue derived by a bank holding company from those activities may not exceed 30 percent of the company's total annual data processing revenues.

As indicated in subsequent chapters, the Board has approved numerous applications by bank holding companies under Regulation Y to engage in a wide range of electronic banking activities.

[3] FDIC

The Federal Deposit Insurance Corporation ("FDIC") provides deposit insurance to the banking industry and supervises state nonmember banks.

In 1996, the FDIC's general counsel issued a legal opinion addressing when stored value cards will be deemed to be FDIC insured.[24] The opinion concluded that, in most cases, such cards would not be covered by federal deposit insurance.

Among other measures, the FDIC has adopted Safety and Soundness Examination Procedures for Electronic Banking and issued other supervisory guidance to banks.

[4] Office of Thrift Supervision

The Office of Thrift Supervision ("OTS") is a bureau of the U.S. Treasury that regulates and supervises the thrift industry. Among other initiatives, the OTS has proposed regulations to streamline and update its electronic operations regulations for savings associations to give them electronic banking powers similar to those of national banks.[25]

The OTS in 1997 requested comment on all aspects of banking affected by electronic operations "to enhance OTS's understanding of new electronic banking technologies and the impact of these technologies on the regulation of Federal savings associations."[26] Based on the comments received, the OTS in 1998 adopted a proposal to require savings associations to provide advance notice to the OTS when they establish transactional Web sites in order to enable the OTS to address potential safety and soundness issues raised by such sites.[27]

---

[24] 61 Fed. Reg. 40,490 (1996). *See* discussion of the general counsel's opinion in Chapter 6, **Electronic Money**.

[25] 62 Fed. Reg. 51,817 (1997).

[26] 62 Fed. Reg. 15,626 (1997).

[27] 63 Fed. Reg. 65,673 (1998).

In 1995, the OTS approved the first depository institution to operate solely on the Internet[28] and has approved several additional Internet banks since then.[29] The OTS issued a "Statement on Retail On-Line Personal Computer Banking" in 1997 providing guidelines for online electronic banking activities of savings associations.[30]

[5] Interagency Actions

The federal banking agencies have issued numerous joint bulletins and advisories to guide the industry on supervisory and regulatory issues raised by electronic banking. The agencies frequently act through the Federal Financial Examination Council ("FFIEC"), established by Congress in 1978 for the purpose of prescribing uniform principles and standards for the federal examination of financial institutions and making recommendations to promote uniformity in the supervision of such institutions.[31]

Among other interagency actions, the FFIEC in 1998 proposed and in 1999 adopted a new Uniform Rating System for Information Technology that will enable regulators to uniformly assess the risks posed by information technology and identify institutions and service providers requiring special supervisory attention.[32] The FFIEC was particularly active in providing guidance on the Year 2000 problem.[33]

Another interagency initiative is the Consumer Electronic Payments Task Force, established in 1996 by the Secretary of the Treasury. Its mission is to identify consumer issues raised by electronic money and electronic payment systems, to evaluate the extent to which these issues are addressed under existing law and to develop innovative, nonregulatory responses where needed to meet consumer protection needs.[34] The Task Force is chaired by the Comptroller of the Currency and includes the FDIC, Federal Reserve Board, Office of Thrift Supervision, Federal Trade Commission, Financial Management Service of the Department of the Treasury, and the

---

[28] Security First Network Bank.

[29] *See, e.g.,* Atlanta Internet Bank and Principal Bank (owned by the Principal Mutual Life Insurance Company).

[30] OTS Press Release 97-39 (June 23, 1997).

[31] 12 U.S.C. §§ 3301 *et seq.*

[32] 63 Fed. Reg. 31,468 (1998); 64 Fed. Reg. 3109 (1999). The proposal would revise the existing Uniform Interagency Rating System for Data Processing Operations to reflect changes in information technology since the rating system was first adopted in 1978.

[33] *See* Chapter 12, **Year 2000 Issues**.

[34] 62 Fed. Reg. 19,173, 29,392 (1997).

Federal Reserve Bank of Atlanta. The Task Force held a series of hearings in 1997 on Consumer Disclosure and Protections, Access to Electronic Money, the Financial Condition of Issuers, and Privacy.[35]

In 2000, the FFIEC issued guidance on managing risks associated with outsourcing technology services.[35.1] In 2001, the federal banking agencies jointly issued interagency guidelines establishing standards for safeguarding customer information.[35.2]

[C] Federal Trade Commission

The Federal Trade Commission ("FTC") has broad consumer protection jurisdiction under the Federal Trade Act,[36] including jurisdiction over the Internet. The FTC has described its regulatory role as follows:

> The mission of the FTC is to promote the efficient functioning of the marketplace by protecting consumers from unfair or deceptive acts or practices and increasing consumer choice by promoting vigorous competition. The Commission undertakes this mission by enforcing the Federal Trade Commission Act, which prohibits unfair methods of competition and unfair or deceptive acts or practices in or affecting commerce. The Commission's responsibilities are far-reaching. With the exception of certain industries, this statute provides the Commission with broad law enforcement authority over virtually every sector in our economy. Commerce on the Internet falls within the scope of this statutory mandate.[37]

Although banking institutions generally are exempt from the FTC's jurisdiction,[38] the FTC's actions influence general standards of consumer protection that affect the banking industry.

---

[35] *See* Consumer Electronic Payments Task Force, Notice of Public Meeting and Request for Comments, 62 Fed. Reg. 19,173 (1997); 62 Fed. Reg. 29,392 (1997). *See* Task Force hearings of July 17, 1997, hosted by the Federal Trade Commission.

[35.1] Federal Financial Institutions Examination Council, *Statement on Risk Management of Technology Outsourcing* (Nov. 29, 2000).

[35.2] 66 Fed. Reg. 8616 (2001).

[36] 15 U.S.C. § 45(a).

[37] Testimony of David Medine, Associate Director for Credit Practices, Bureau of Consumer Protection, Federal Trade Commission, before the House Judiciary Committee (Mar. 26, 1998).

[38] 15 U.S.C. § 45(a)(2).

[D] Securities and Exchange Commission

The Securities and Exchange Commission ("SEC") regulates securities broker-dealers, mutual funds, and other intermediaries that offer electronic investment services. Among other actions, the SEC has issued advisories on the Year 2000 readiness obligations of securities firms and issuers of securities, including bank holding companies,[39] and has taken enforcement action against firms that have failed to make timely Year 2000 disclosures.[40]

In 1998, the SEC created an Office of Internet Enforcement to coordinate and oversee its regulatory efforts relating to the Internet. This office supervises a 125-person "cyberforce" devoted to "surfing the Internet looking for questionable securities-related activities."[41] The SEC reported in 1999 that it had brought 66 Internet-related cases since 1995.[42]

[E] Commodity Futures Trading Commission

The Commodity Futures Trading Commission ("CFTC") regulates the commodities markets in the United States and has taken similar actions to address the impact of technology on participants in those markets.

§ 2.03 CONGRESSIONAL ACTIVITIES

A flurry of legislative activity has emanated from Congress on electronic banking and commerce issues. Numerous Congressional committees and subcommittees have held hearings on various aspects of electronic banking and commerce, including the House and Senate Banking Committees, the House Commerce Committee, the House Judiciary Subcommittees on Crime and Courts and Intellectual Property, the House

---

[39] 63 Fed. Reg. 37,668 (1998); 63 Fed. Reg. 41,394 (1998); 63 Fed. Reg. 54,308 (1998); 63 Fed. Reg. 58630 (1998); 64 Fed. Reg. 12,127 (1999).

[40] *See* Chapter 12, **Year 2000 Issues**, § 12.05[C], *infra.*

[41] *See* U.S. Securities and Exchange Commission, Statement Concerning the Effect of Technology on the Capital Markets, by Laura S. Unger, Commissioner, before the House Subcommittee on Capital Markets, Securities, and Government Sponsored Enterprises (Mar. 25, 1999).

[42] *Id.*

International Relations Committee, and the Senate Special Committee on the Year 2000 Technology Problem.[43]

A multitude of legislative proposals was introduced in the 105th Congress, including the following:

- Consumer Internet Privacy Protection Act (H.R. 98)
- Internet Protection Act of 1997 (H.R. 2372)
- Electronic Financial Services Efficiency Act of 1997 (H.R. 2937)
- Electronic Commerce Enhancement Act of 1997 (H.R. 2991)

---

[43] *See, e.g.*, Hearings on "The Future of Electronic Payments: Roadblocks and Emerging Practices," before the House Subcomm. on Domestic and International Monetary Policy (Sept. 19, 2000); Hearings on the Year 2000 Problem, before the Subcommittee on Financial Services and Technology of the Senate Committee on Banking, Housing, and Urban Affairs (July 30, 1997); Hearings on the Implications of Emerging Electronic Payment Systems on Individual Privacy, before the House Subcommittee on Financial Institutions and Consumer Credit (Sept. 18, 1997); Testimony of Alan Blinder, Vice Chairman, Federal Reserve Board, at Hearings on "The Future of Money," before the House Subcommittee on Domestic and International Monetary Policy (Oct. 11, 1995), 1995 WL 10732104; Hearing before the House Subcommittee on Domestic and International Policy on "Internet Banking" (Aug. 2, 1999); Hearing before the Joint Economic Committee, "Cyber-Threats and the US Economy" (Feb. 23, 2000); Hearing before the Senate Judiciary Subcommittee on the Constitution, Federalism, and Property Rights on "Privacy in the Digital Age: Encryption and Mandatory Access" (Mar. 17, 1998); Hearing before the Senate Subcommittee on Financial Services and Technology on "The Digital Signature and Electronic Authentication Law of 1998" (Mar. 11, 1998); Hearing before the Commerce Committee on "Electronic Commerce: The Global Electronic Marketplace" (July 29, 1998); Hearings before the House Subcommittee on Telecommunications, Trade and Consumer Protection on "Consumer Protection in Cyberspace" (June 25, 1998), and on "Doing Business Online" (May 21, 1998); Hearings before the House Subcommittee on Finance and Hazardous Materials on "Investing On-Line" (July 18, 1998), and on "New Methods for Making Electronic Purchases"; Hearings before the House Judiciary Committee on the "Internet Freedom Act" and the "Internet Growth and Development Act of 1999" (June 30, 1999); House Judiciary Joint Oversight Hearing with the Senate Subcommittee on Criminal Justice Oversight, "Internet Denial of Service Attacks and the Federal Response" (Feb. 29, 2000), and Oversight Hearing on "Internet Domain Names and Intellectual Property Rights" (July 28, 1999); Hearing before the Domestic and International Monetary Policy Subcommittee on "Biometrics and the Future of Money" (May 20, 1998).

- Safety and Freedom Through Encryption Act of 1997 (H.R. 695)
- Encrypted Communications Privacy Act of 1997 (S. 376)
- Promotion of Commerce On-Line in the Digital Era (S. 377)
- Secure Public Networks Act (S. 909)
- Computer Security Enhancement Act of 1997 (H.R. 1903)
- Tax-Free Internet Act of 1997 (H.R. 995)
- Internet Tax Freedom Act (S. 442, H.R. 1054).

While most of these bills died, Congress enacted two bills dealing with the Year 2000 problem: the Examination Parity and Year 2000 Readiness for Financial Institutions Act[44] and the Year 2000 Information and Readiness Disclosure Act.[45] These laws are discussed in Chapter 12, **Year 2000 Issues**.

Numerous bills addressing various electronic banking and commerce matters were introduced and considered in the 106th Congress, including the following:

- Internet Tax Elimination Act (H.R. 3252) (to prohibit state and local governments from collecting sales and use taxes on Internet transactions); S. 1611 (similar bill);
- Electronic Signatures in Global and National Commerce Act (H.R. 1714) and Third Millennium Electronic Commerce Act (S. 761) (to make electronic signatures legally binding) (passed by both House and Senate, respectively, in 1999);
- Electronic Disclosures Delivery Act (H.R. 2626) (to allow financial institutions to provide legally required notices and disclosures over the Internet rather than through the mail);
- Collections of Information Antipiracy Act (H.R. 354) (to prohibit misappropriations of collections of information);
- Consumer and Investor Access to Information Act (H.R. 1858) (similar to H.R. 354);

[44] Pub. L. No. 105-164, 105th Cong., 2d Sess. (1998).

[45] Pub. L. No. 105-271, 105th Cong., 2d Sess. (1998).

- H.R. 850 (to relax export controls over encryption products);
- H.R. 1291 (to prevent the Federal Communications Commission from imposing interstate access charges on Internet service providers);
- Health Information Privacy Act (H.R. 1941);
- Electronic Securities Transaction Act (S. 921) (to establish a framework for broker-dealers, transfer agents, and investment advisers conducting business over the Internet by clarifying the legal status of electronic signatures in securities transactions);
- Internet Growth and Development Act (H.R. 1685) and Internet Freedom Act (H.R. 1686) (to open high-speed cable networks to Internet competition);
- Internet Regulatory Freedom Act (S. 1043) (to provide local phone companies regulatory parity with cable companies in supplying high-speed Internet services to local customers);
- Online Investor Protection Act (S. 1015) (to give SEC enhanced authority to monitor online brokers, increase fines for online fraud, give investors information on the speed of a broker's execution, and require online brokers and investment advisers to provide Internet hyperlinks to investor education Web sites).

Congress enacted the following laws:

- Year 2000 Readiness and Responsibility Act, Pub. L. No. 106-37, known as the "Y2K Act" (enacted July 20, 1999) (to curb the possibility of a flood of frivolous litigation arising from Y2K failures by adopting procedural and substantive law changes, including provisions to curb joint and several liability, more rigorous pleading standards, limitation of types of damages and damage amounts, and barriers to class action lawsuits);
- Title V of the Gramm-Leach-Bliley Act, Pub. L. No. 106-102 (enacted Nov. 12, 1999) (establishing new consumer protections for financial information privacy);

- Anti-Cybersquatting Consumer Protection Act, Pub. L. No. 106-113 (enacted Nov. 29, 1999) (to create a new cause of action for trademark owners against misappropriation of trademarks as Internet domain names);
- Electronic Signatures in Global and National Commerce Act ("E-Sign Act"), Pub. L. No. 106-229, *codified at* 15 U.S.C. § 7001 (enacted in 2000).

§ 2.04 STATE GOVERNMENT ACTIVITIES

The states have been active in enacting legislation addressing electronic banking and commerce issues.

Most states have consumer protection and privacy laws that encompass electronic banking. Massachusetts law, for example, contains 239 separate sections dealing with various aspects of privacy or confidentiality of information.[46] A majority of states already have adopted or are considering electronic signature legislation and are at work on electronic authentication laws.[47]

In general, state lawmakers appear to be motivated by a desire not to impose restrictions but to create a favorable legal environment in order to attract and retain business for their states. The various state approaches to regulating electronic commerce, however, create the prospect of inconsistent and confusing laws governing an area that by its nature is multijurisdictional and defies piecemeal regulation.[48] Electronic banking and commerce transcends state boundaries and, in many cases, it may be difficult to determine which state law applies. Moreover, the substantive state law requirements at times are unclear or conflicting. There appears to be little consensus on digital signature laws, for example, with states differing on what qualifies as an electronic signature and when electronic signatures are acceptable.

---

[46] *See* Testimony of Daniel J. Greenwood, Deputy General Counsel, Information Technology Division, Commonwealth of Massachusetts, before the House Subcommittee on Financial Institutions and Consumer Credit (Sept. 18, 1997).

[47] *See* Thomas J. Smedinghoff, "Analyzing State Digital Signature Legislation," Electronic Banking Law and Commerce Report (June 1997) ("A wave of digital signature and electronic signature legislation is sweeping across the country.").

[48] *See* Robert O. Ball, III, "Answering the Call for a Uniform Legal and Regulatory Framework for Electronic Banking and Commerce," Electronic Banking Law and Commerce Report (Jan. 1998) ("A patchwork quilt of inconsistent laws and regulations will also undoubtedly lead to incompatible and non-interoperatible systems, as well as less secure and less trustworthy authentification systems, all of which could ultimately undermine the safety and soundness of electronic banking and commerce.").

Although defenders of state law initiatives argue that the law of electronic banking is nothing more than contract law traditionally within the realm of state law,[49] major banks are working for national uniformity and preemption of inconsistent state laws, particularly in the area of digital signature and certification laws.[50]

It is likely that Congress will take over the field of electronic commerce regulation to establish uniformity if the inconsistencies among state laws are not minimized, particularly in view of the growing need for national uniformity to promote the participation of U.S. business in global electronic commerce.[51]

The National Conference of Commissioners on Uniform State Laws ("NCCUSL") in 1996 commenced the drafting of a Uniform Electronic Transactions Act in recognition that "many of the individual states have embarked on a rapid course of developing separate legislative approaches to these issues, and that serious inconsistencies and commercial confusion would inevitably result."

[*Next page is 2-17.*]

[49] *See, e.g.,* Daniel J. Greenwood, "The Role of the States: Sovereign Laboratories of Innovation or Irrelevant Sub-National Road Blocks?," Electronic Banking Law and Commerce Report (June 1997) ("State courts have, for over 200 years proven to be quite capable of adjudicating commercial disputes between parties from multiple jurisdictions and dealing with technological advances. Paternalistic concerns over state government competence are not called for. In fact, states are often better suited to producing innovative, responsive, and accountable policy models than the federal government.").

[50] *See* P. Michael Nugent, "Bank Arguments for National Uniformity in Legislation," Electronic Banking Law and Commerce Report (June 1997) ("Fifty state regimes governing digital signatures and certificates will . . . diminish the likelihood of seamless and uniform electronic banking and commerce . . . reduce the incentive for new market entrants . . . confuse customers . . . and result in a patchwork quilt of differing legal protections, commercial standards and levels of security.").

[51] *See* John Lopez, "The Need for a Federal Role in Electronic Authentication Legislation," Electronic Banking Law and Commerce Report (June 1997) ("United States investment in the current and future businesses dependent on the concept [of electronic authentication] will inevitably lag behind Europe and Asia if we wait for the states to reach consensus. . . . Business abhors uncertainty. Serial state action and the UCC process prolong the period of uncertainty. Besides, any sub-jurisdictions such as states are an increasingly irrelevant concept in cyberspace. Attempts to assert jurisdiction over informational or commercial activities initiated and carried out far from their borders has an air of the ridiculous, much like King Canute asserting his dominion over the tides.").

§ 2.05 INTERNATIONAL ACTIVITIES

Electronic banking and commerce is a global phenomenon and other nations apart from the United States are considering whether and how to regulate it. Varying regulatory approaches have been taken or are under consideration, particularly in the areas of digital signature and encryption, which are viewed as critical to the establishment of secure electronic commerce systems across international boundaries.[52]

The proliferation of different approaches among countries has the potential to cripple international electronic commerce by giving rise to a patchwork of conflicting laws.[53] Various international bodies are working in cooperative efforts to achieve greater global uniformity, as described below.

[A] European Commission

The European Commission ("Commission") in 1997 issued a paper entitled "A European Initiative in Electronic Commerce" with four parts: The Electronic Commerce Revolution; Ensuring Access to the Global Marketplace; Creating a Favorable Regulatory Framework; and Promoting a Favorable Business Environment.

Among other recommendations, the Commission has urged the creation of a European framework for digital signatures and cryptography to stimulate a European industry for these products as well as to ensure appropriate regulation.

In 1995, the European Union ("EU") adopted a Directive on the Protection of Personal Data ("Privacy Directive").[54] The Directive requires EU countries to adopt laws governing the processing of personal data and prohibits a company operating in the EU from transferring data outside EU borders unless adequate protections are in place. The EU member

---

[52] *See* Theodore S. Barassi, "International Developments in Digital Signature Legislation," Electronic Banking Law and Commerce Report (June 1997).

[53] *Id.* ("Not only do these various efforts suggest a legal landscape comprised of widely varied treatment of digital authentication issues, but they indicate that a seeming preference for vigorous state intervention in the emerging infrastructure appears to be, if not ascendant, at least widely contemplated. This could very well create not just disharmony, but outright conflict between the increasing number of national jurisdictions that are intent upon dealing with digital authentication legislatively.").

[54] Directive 95/46 of the European Parliament and of the Council (Nov. 23, 1995), Official Journal of the European Communities, No L. 281, posted at ⟨⟨*http://www.privacy.org/pi/intl_orgs/ec/dp-directive_final.txt*⟩⟩.

states were required to have enacted implementing legislation by October 24, 1998. The Directive has raised concerns among U.S. companies doing business in Europe because of the lack of a national privacy protection law in the United States, as discussed in Chapter 13, **Consumer Protection and Privacy**.

In 1998, the European Commission proposed a regulatory framework for the marketing of financial services via the Internet.[55]

[B] European Central Bank

In a departure from the non-regulatory approach of the United States, the European Central Bank in 1998 proposed a regulatory framework for electronic money.[56] The framework is intended to address the need for prudential supervision, reserve requirements, legal transparency, technical security, protection against crime, and other issues. *See* Chapter 6, **Electronic Money**, for a discussion of the European Central Bank's regulatory proposal.

[C] European Committee for Banking Standards

The European Committee for Banking Standards ("ECBS") was established in 1993 to produce European banking standards, technical reports, and other documents on standards related issues to support the European single market and a Europe-wide technical banking infrastructure. Among its projects, ECBS develops technical standards for automated cross-border transfers, direct debits, prepaid cards, and banking related security issues. ECBS is developing a standard for an interoperable European Electronic Purse.

[D] Basle Committee on Banking Supervision

The Basle Committee on Banking Supervision has been active in addressing supervisory and regulatory issues raised by electronic banking. In 1998, for example, the Basle Committee issued a paper on the risk management implications of electronic banking.[57]

---

[55] Posted at ⟨⟨*http:/europa.eu.int/comm/dg15/en/finances/consumer/891.htm*⟩⟩.

[56] European Central Bank, *Report on Electronic Money* (Aug. 1998).

[57] Basle Committee on Banking Supervision, *Risk Management for Electronic Banking and Electronic Money Activities* (Mar. 20, 1998).

[E] UNCITRAL

The United Nations Commission on International Trade Law ("UNCITRAL") was established by the General Assembly of the United Nations in 1966 to "further the progressive harmonization and unification of the law of international trade." UNCITRAL has taken a number of actions affecting electronic banking and commerce.

In 1996, UNCITRAL adopted a model law on electronic commerce.[58] The model law establishes rules that validate and recognize contracts formed through electronic means, sets default rules for contract formation and governance of electronic contract performance, defines the characteristics of a valid electronic writing and an original document, provides for the acceptability of electronic signatures for legal and commercial purposes, and supports the admission of computer evidence in courts and arbitration proceedings.

In 1997, UNCITRAL sponsored an inter-governmental meeting on digital signatures, resulting in draft uniform rules on digital signatures and certification authorities.

[F] OECD

The Organization for Economic Cooperation and Development ("OECD")[59] provides a forum for the exchange of information and harmonization of policy with a view towards maximizing economic growth within OECD member countries and assisting non-member countries to develop more rapidly. In 1997, the OECD issued voluntary guidelines for the use of cryptography in electronic commerce.

The OECD has long been concerned with the protection of personal privacy in electronic commerce and in 1980 issued "Guidelines Governing the Protection of Privacy and Transborder Data Flow of Personal Data." These Guidelines have been the basis for recent approaches to privacy in the context of electronic banking and commerce in the United States

[58] For the text of the model law, *see* ⟨⟨*http://www.un.or.at/uncitral/texts/electcom/ml-ec.htm#TOP*⟩⟩.

[59] The OECD refers to itself as "the international organization of the industrialized, market-economy countries." The OECD was originally created as the Organization for European Economic Cooperation in 1948 to administer Marshall Plan funding on the European side. In 1960, the organization was named the Organization for Economic Cooperation and Development ("OECD").

and other countries and the OECD has determined that it is unnecessary to update them.[60]

[G] International Chamber of Commerce

The International Chamber of Commerce ("ICC") in 1997 issued nonbinding general usage guidelines for digital transactions over the Internet and in 1998 issued draft guidelines for consumer protection in electronic commerce.

[H] Year 2000 Council

The Year 2000 Council was created in 1998 to ensure a high level of global attention to the Y2K problem, to share information on regulatory and supervisory strategies and approaches to the problem, to discuss possible contingency measures, and to serve as a point of contact with national and international private-sector initiatives.[61] The Council is sponsored jointly by the Basle Committee on Banking Supervision, the G-10 central bank governors' Committee on Payment and Settlement Systems, the International Association of Insurance Supervisors, and the International Organization of Securities Commissions.

[I] Individual Countries

In addition to global cooperative actions, individual countries have adopted laws addressing electronic banking and commerce issues. In 1997, for example, Germany adopted the first digital signature law creating a framework for the secure use of digital signatures for business transactions in an open network, involving government licensing and certification authorities. Italy adopted a similar law in 1997. Other countries are expected to follow suit.

Just as coordination of individual state actions in the United States is needed to ensure that electronic banking and commerce is not stifled by fragmented, duplicative, or inconsistent regulation, cooperation at the international level is also needed.

---

[60] *See* discussion of OECD Privacy Guidelines in Chapter 13, **Consumer Protection and Privacy**.

[61] *See* Statement by Ernest T. Patrikis, First Vice President, Federal Reserve Bank of New York and chairman of the Joint Year 2000 Council, before the House Committee on Banking and Financial Services (June 23, 1998).

CHAPTER 3

INDUSTRY SELF-REGULATION

The policy of the federal government that "the private sector should lead" in the regulation of electronic banking and commerce has placed a major self-regulatory burden, as well as opportunity, on the private sector. The banking industry and other private sector groups have responded to this challenge by undertaking major efforts to address the policy and operational issues raised by electronic banking through existing and new self-regulatory organizations. Some of these are described below.

§3.01 BITS

The Bankers Roundtable in 1996 formed the Banking Industry Technology Secretariat ("BITS") to "foster the growth and development of electronic banking in an open environment that will encourage greater choices in banking software, access devices, and development of more efficient processing capabilities, for the benefit of bank customers."[1] The board of directors of BITS includes the chairmen and CEOs of the 10 largest bank holding companies in the United States as well as representatives from the American Bankers Association ("ABA") and the Independent Bankers Association of America ("IBAA"). A major concern of BITS is to "promote safety and soundness in payment systems and the electronic delivery of banking products through secure, efficient and low-cost services, with appropriate privacy safeguards."[2]

A major initiative of BITS is the creation of a Financial Services Security Laboratory to test commercial software products against a rigid set of security criteria. The Laboratory will issue a "BITS Tested Mark" certifying that a product or service has met the security criteria.[2.1]

§3.02 INTERNET COUNCIL

The Internet Council was created by the National Automated Clearing House Association ("NACHA")[3] to "facilitate the development of

---

[1] *See* Statement of Catherine A. Allen, CEO, The Bankers Roundtable Banking Industry Technology Secretariat, before the Consumer Electronic Payments Task Force (July 17, 1997); Statement of Catherine A. Allen on Internet Banking before the House Subcommittee on Domestic and International Monetary Policy of the Committee on Banking and Financial Services (Aug. 3, 1999).

[2] *Id.*, July 17, 1999 Statement.

[2.1] *See* Peter Bowne and Cheryl Charles, "Financial Services and Electronic Commerce Security," Electronic Banking Law and Commerce Report (Oct. 1999), at 9.

[3] NACHA develops operating rules for the Automated Clearing House Network and represents more than 13,000 financial institutions.

global electronic commerce by enabling businesses, governments and consumers to utilize present and future payments over open networks in a secure and cost-effective manner."

The Internet Council has developed an interoperability framework for banks serving as verifiers of digital certificates used in electronic commerce. In 1998, the Internet Council issued draft guidelines intended to help state governments and other organizations develop interoperable public key infrastructures ("PKI") for digital signatures.[4]

The Payment Systems Interface Work Group of the Internet Council is developing business models for electronic commerce that leverage the existing payments infrastructure to support Internet commerce.

The Certification Authority Rating and Trust Task Force ("CARAT") is a coalition of state government organizations, state and federal government agencies, and private sector companies working together under the auspices of the Internet Council to develop certificate policies for multiple digital certificates. In 1998, CARAT issued preliminary *Guidelines for Constructing Policies Governing the Use of Identify-Based Public Key Certificates* to help organizations create closed but interoperable public Key infrastructures that can facilitate pilot projects employing public key technology.

§3.03 FINANCIAL SERVICES TECHNOLOGY CONSORTIUM

The Financial Services Technology Consortium ("FSTC") was founded in 1993 as a not-for-profit research organization of banks, financial service firms, industry partners, national laboratories, universities, and government agencies. FSTC sponsors collaborative research and development projects affecting the financial services industry with emphasis on new technologies that help banks enhance customer relationships, improve operational efficiency and expand market presence.

Among its projects, FSTC has published a Bank Internet Payment System ("BIPS") specification designed to promote electronic commerce through banks by providing a protocol for the sending of payment instructions to banks safely over the Internet and a payment server architecture for processing those instructions.[5]

---

[4] National Automated Clearing House Association, *Guidelines for Constructing Policies Governing the Use of Identity-Based Public Key Certificates* (Oct. 1998).

[5] *See* FSTC Press Release (Aug. 24, 1998).

FSTC also has developed an electronic check or "e-check" to work like a paper check in electronic form.

FSTC also has initiated Paperless Automated Check Exchange and Settlement ("PACES") to enable a nationwide interoperable check image exchange system providing image-based check truncation and an image-based return process as an alternative to the current exchange of paper documents.

§3.04 SMART CARD FORUM

The Smart Card Forum was formed in 1993 to promote the widespread acceptance of smart cards in North America. The Forum is comprised of smart card issuers and users, including banks, telecommunication companies, software companies, equipment providers, and card manufacturers, and 27 state and federal government agencies. Among its missions is to "lead the smart card industry forward by establishing a vision for interoperability and to develop cross-industry positions on issues relevant to technology, business, and legal and public policy."[6]

The Smart Card Forum encourages its members to adopt consumer protections and has established a Privacy Task Force to address privacy concerns relating to smart card usage.

§3.05 ELECTRONIC PAYMENTS FORUM

The Electronic Payments Forum ("EPF") is an alliance of standard-setting organizations, commercial entities, non-profit organizations, universities, and government agencies committed to furthering the development of interoperable electronic payment systems in support of global electronic commerce. The EPF provides a forum for discussion and resolution of issues relating to electronic payments problems.

§3.06 BILL PAYMENT COUNCIL

The Bill Payment Council was established by NACHA to further the development of electronic bill presentation and payment. Among its projects, the Bill Payment Council is working with BITS to develop business practice standards for open electronic bill presentment and pay-

[6] Statement of the Smart Card Forum's representative before the Consumer Electronic Payments Task Force (July 17, 1997).

ment.[7] The Bill Payment Council was renamed the Council for Electronic Billing & Payment. The Council released Electronic Bill Payment/Presentment Business Practices in 1999 to create a framework for security, privacy, timeliness, swift error resolution, and effective communication in the electronic bill payment process.

§3.07 INTERNET FRAUD ADVISORY PROTECTION COUNCIL

The Internet Fraud Advisory Protection Council is a consortium of online merchants and credit card issuers and processors. Its mission is to reduce the risk and costs of Internet credit card fraud through research, industry data analysis, and education.[7.1]

§3.08 ELECTRONIC BENEFITS TRANSFER COUNCIL

The Electronic Benefits Transfer Council was established by NACHA to facilitate electronic benefits transfer. In 1996, the Council created the Quest Operating Rules to provide interoperability among state EBT programs.

§3.09 OTHER BANKING INDUSTRY ACTIVITIES

The bank trade associations have established a variety of task forces and working groups to address issues raised by electronic banking. As noted above, The Bankers Roundtable has established the Banking Information Technology Secretariat ("BITS"). The ABA has established a subsidiary, ABAecom, dedicated to facilitating electronic banking and commerce over the Internet by providing high-level encryption services for financial institutions. America's Community Bankers has established an Electronic Banking and Community Banks task force. Both the American Bankers Association and The Bankers Roundtable have established groups to address payments system issues.[8]

As noted above, NACHA has undertaken efforts to develop emerging electronic payment solutions in the areas of Internet commerce, bill pay-

---

[7] *See* NACHA Press Release (Aug. 12, 1998).

[7.1] *See* Joe Barrett, "Internet Fraud Prevention Council Formed to Fight Growing Online Problem," Electronic Banking Law and Commerce Report (Oct. 1999), at 12.

[8] *See* ABA Task Force on the Payments System and The Bankers Roundtable's Committee on Payments and Technology.

ment and presentment, financial electronic data interchange, cross-border transactions, electronic checks, and electronic benefits transfer.

The banking industry also has been active in developing privacy guidelines for information exchanged on the Internet in response to the Clinton Administration's call for private industry to take the lead in privacy protection. In 1997, the Consumer Bankers Association, long interested in issues of consumer privacy, issued uniform industry guidelines in conjunction with the American Bankers Association and The Bankers Roundtable. The Smart Card Forum adopted similar consumer privacy guidelines for smart cards issuers.[9]

Other private sector initiatives are underway also. MasterCard and Visa, for example, have developed a protocol, called the "SET Protocol" to permit the secure use of credit cards over the Internet using digital signatures.

§3.10 BAR ASSOCIATION ACTIVITIES

Various bar associations have taken initiatives to assist in the revision of existing laws and the development of new ones to address the legal issues raised by electronic banking and commerce.

The American Bar Association has created a variety of subcommittees addressing electronic banking and commerce. The Information Security Committee, a part of the ABA's Section on Science and Technology, issued Digital Signature Guidelines to establish a legal framework for the development and use of secure computer-based signatures to enable reliable authentication of electronic documents and facilitate electronic commerce.[10] While nonbinding, the guidelines are available for use by various states considering digital signature legislation.

The ABA's Business Law Section has formed a Committee on Law of Commerce in Cyberspace, a Subcommittee on Domestic and International Payments and EFT Transactions, and a Task Force on Stored-Value Cards. The Task Force on Stored-Value Cards in 1997 issued a paper analyzing commercial law issues raised by stored value payment systems.[11]

---

[9] *See* Chapter 13, **Consumer Protection and Privacy**.

[10] ABA Information Security Committee, *Digital Signature Guidelines: Legal Infrastructure for Certification Authorities and Secure Electronic Commerce* (1996).

[11] *See* "A Commercial Lawyer's Take on the Electronic Purse: An Analysis of Commercial Law Issues Associated with Stored-Value Cards and Electronic Money," 52 Bus. Law. 653 (1997).

CHAPTER 4

THE REGULATORY FRAMEWORK

§ 4.01 IN GENERAL

No comprehensive regulatory framework exists for electronic banking. Various provisions of the existing banking laws are applicable to the electronic banking activities of banks and their affiliates, as described below. Because many of these laws were not adopted with electronic banking in mind, however, it is not always clear to what extent they apply.

In general, the federal banking regulators have not imposed major restrictions on banks in the offering of electronic banking services. The absence of a constituency of politically powerful competitors in the electronic banking arena has enabled banks to expand their activities largely without opposition.[1] Banking regulators thus have not felt compelled to impose restrictions of the type they imposed in response to objections by securities and insurance competitors of banks in the 1980s that were designed to limit bank participation in the marketplace. Moreover, electronic banking is not generally viewed by banking regulators as involving the types of risks that would require the imposition of "firewalls" or similar regulatory restrictions.

The following is an overview of the statutory and regulatory framework applicable to electronic banking activities of banks and their affiliates.

§ 4.02 NATIONAL BANK ACT

The National Bank Act[2] authorizes national banks to engage in the "business of banking" and activities incidental thereto.[3] The Office of the Comptroller of the Currency ("OCC") and the courts have interpreted this language in light of changes in the financial marketplace "so as to permit the use of new ways of conducting the very old business of banking."[4]

With respect to electronic banking, the OCC in 1996 revised its interpretive rules to provide broad powers for national banks to offer banking services through electronic means:

---

[1] Data processing companies failed in their attempt to limit the scope of data processing activities permissible for bank holding companies in the 1980s. *See Association of Data Processing Service Orgs., Inc. v. Board of Governors,* 745 F.2d 677 (D.C. Cir. 1984).

[2] 12 U.S.C. §§ 1 *et seq.*

[3] 12 U.S.C. § 24(Seventh).

[4] *M & M Leasing Corp. v. Seattle First Nat'l Bank,* 563 F.2d 1377 (9th Cir. 1977), *cert. denied,* 436 U.S. 956 (1978).

> A national bank may perform, provide, or deliver through electronic means and facilities any activity, function, product, or service that it is otherwise authorized to perform, provide, or deliver. A national bank may also, in order to optimize the use of the bank's resources, market and sell to third parties electronic capacities acquired or developed by the bank in good faith for banking purposes.[5]

On the basis of this authority, the OCC has authorized national banks to engage in a broad range of electronic banking activities as described in later chapters. In 1997, for example, the OCC chartered a national bank that proposed to conduct business solely in cyberspace without any retail banking offices.[6]

The OCC has interpreted the National Bank Act to authorize national banks to act as "finders" in "bringing parties together for transactions that the parties themselves negotiate and consummate."[7] The OCC has stated that "the means that national banks use to act as finders for their customers have evolved due to technological advancements" and has interpreted finder activities broadly to include, for example, hosting Internet Web sites for banking customers.[8] The OCC's interpretation authorizing finder activities has been upheld by at least one court.[9]

As a finder activity, the OCC has allowed national banks to provide hyperlinks from bank Web sites to third-party service providers both as a value-added service and to generate fee income through finders fees.[10] The OCC requires a bank offering such hyperlinks to take reasonable steps to clearly distinguish between the bank's products and services and those of the third party: "Bank customers should be able to identify when they are dealing with the Bank and when they are not, and the Bank should indicate that it does not provide, endorse, or guarantee any of the products or services available through the third party Web sites."[11] The OCC has stated that a national bank may negotiate arrangements with

---

[5] 12 C.F.R. § 7.1019.

[6] OCC Interpretive Letter No. 742 (1996) (Apollo Trust Co.).

[7] 12 C.F.R. § 7.1002(b).

[8] *See* OCC Interpretive Letter No. 856 (Mar. 5, 1999), discussed in Chapter 9, **Electronic Commerce and Related Applications**, *infra*.

[9] *Norwest Bank v. Sween Corp.*, 118 F.3d 1255 (8th Cir. 1997).

[10] OCC Conditional Approval No. 347 (Jan. 29, 2000), n.6.

[11] *Id.*

linked merchants to provide reduced rates to the bank's customers consistent with its role as a finder."[12]

§ 4.03 FEDERAL DEPOSIT INSURANCE ACT

The Federal Deposit Insurance Act ("FDI Act")[13] does not specifically regulate electronic banking activities of banks. It provides for the federal insurance of deposits and thus is relevant to stored value and other electronic money products that function like deposits. As noted elsewhere, the Federal Deposit Insurance Corporation's ("FDIC's") general counsel has interpreted the FDI Act as not providing insurance coverage for most stored value cards.[14]

The FDI Act assigns to the FDIC the primary federal regulatory responsibility for state banks that are not members of the Federal Reserve System—so-called state nonmember banks. The FDIC generally does not restrict the activities of state banks unless such activities pose safety and soundness risks.

Under Section 24 of the FDI Act, state banks may not engage as principal—as opposed to as agent—in any activity that is not permissible for a national bank to engage in, unless the FDIC determines that the activity would pose no significant risk to the federal deposit insurance funds.[15]

§ 4.04 FEDERAL RESERVE ACT

The Federal Reserve Act[16] imposes reserve requirements on banks, subjects state member banks to regulation by the Federal Reserve Board ("Federal Reserve" or "Board"), and restricts transactions between banks and their affiliates, among other provisions.

[A] Reserve Requirements

The Federal Reserve Act imposes reserve requirements on deposits maintained by depository institutions.[17] Issuers of stored value products

---

[12] OCC Conditional Approval No. 347 (Jan. 29, 2000), n.7.

[13] 12 U.S.C. §§ 1813 *et seq.*

[14] *See* FDIC General Counsel's Opinion No. 8, published at 61 Fed. Reg. 40,490 (1996), discussed in Chapter 6, **Electronic Money**.

[15] 12 U.S.C. § 1831a.

[16] 12 U.S.C. §§ 221 *et seq.*

[17] 12 U.S.C. § 461.

need to consider whether such products give rise to a "deposit" subject to reserve requirements under the Federal Reserve Act. The Board has testified to Congress that stored value products issued by a bank in at least some circumstances would be deemed to be transaction accounts subject to reserve requirements.[18]

[B] Regulation H

State banks that become members of the Federal Reserve System—so-called state member banks—are subject to regulation by the Federal Reserve Board under the Federal Reserve Act and the Board's Regulation H, which implements the Act.[19] As a general rule, if an activity is permissible for bank holding companies to engage in, the Board does not object to performance of the activity by a state member bank.

[C] Sections 23A and 23B

Sections 23A and 23B of the Federal Reserve Act restrict transactions between banks and their affiliates. Section 23A limits "covered transactions" with any one affiliate to no more than 10 percent of the bank's capital and surplus and with all affiliates in the aggregate to no more than 20 percent.[20] A "covered transaction" includes an extension of credit to an affiliate, a purchase of or investment in securities issued by an affiliate, a purchase of assets from an affiliate, the acceptance of an affiliate's securities as collateral for a loan to another person, or the issuance of a guarantee, acceptance, or letter of credit on behalf of an affiliate. All covered transactions must be on terms and conditions consistent with safe and sound banking practices. All extensions of credit to an affiliate must be secured by collateral according to a formula specified in the statute.

Section 23B[21] requires that covered transactions between a bank and its affiliates are offered only on terms and conditions that are substantially the same, or at least as favorable to the bank, as those prevailing at the time for comparable transactions involving nonaffiliated companies. In the absence of comparable transactions, such transactions must be on terms that in good faith

---

[18] *See* Testimony of Alan Blinder, Vice Chairman, Federal Reserve Board, at Hearings on "The Future of Money," before the House Subcommittee on Domestic and International Monetary Policy (Oct. 11, 1995), 1995 WL 10732104.

[19] 12 C.F.R. § 208.

[20] 12 U.S.C. § 371c.

[21] 12 U.S.C. § 371c-1.

would be offered to nonaffiliated companies. Section 23B applies to the purchase of assets by a bank from an affiliate as well as other covered transactions.

§ 4.05 BANK HOLDING COMPANY ACT

Under the Bank Holding Company Act ("BHC Act"), the activities of bank holding companies are limited to those that were found by the Federal Reserve Board, prior to November 12, 1999, to be "so closely related to banking . . . as to be a proper incident thereto."[22] The Federal Reserve Board found that electronic banking and related data processing activities met this standard.[23] The Board's initial finding in this regard was challenged in 1984 by the Association of Data Processing Service Organizations but was upheld by the reviewing court.[24]

The Gramm-Leach-Bliley Act amended the BHC Act in 1999 to authorize bank holding companies to become "financial holding companies" and thereby engage in a broad array of expanded activities deemed to be "financial in nature."[25]

[A] Regulation Y

Prior to 1997, Regulation Y authorized bank holding companies to engage in data processing activities only if the data was financial, banking, or economic. Regulation Y was substantially broadened by the Board in 1997, and bank holding companies now may engage in the following activities:

> (i) Providing data processing and data transmission services, facilities (including data processing and data transmission hardware, software, documentation or operating personnel), data bases, advice, and access to such services, facilities, or data bases by any technological means, if:
>
> (A) the data to be processed or furnished must be financial, banking, or economic; and
>
> (B) the hardware provided in connection therewith must be offered only in conjunction with software designed and marketed for the processing and transmission of financial,

[22] 12 U.S.C. § 1843(c)(8).

[23] *See generally* 12 C.F.R. § 225.28(b)(14).

[24] *Association of Data Processing Serv. Orgs., Inc. v. Board of Governors*, 745 F.2d 677 (D.C. Cir. 1984).

[25] 12 U.S.C. § 1843(k).

> banking, or economic data, and where the general purpose hardware does not constitute more than 30 percent of the cost of any packaged offering.
>
> (ii) A company conducting data processing and data transmission activities may conduct data processing and data transmission activities not described [above] if the total annual revenue derived from those activities does not exceed 30 percent of the company's total annual revenues derived from data processing and data transmission activities.[26]

This language allows a bank holding company to render advice to anyone regarding the processing and transmitting of banking, financial, and economic data and eliminates the former requirement that data processing facilities must be designed, marketed, and operated for processing and transmitting of financial, banking or economic data.

Prior to the adoption of the revised regulation, Regulation Y required all data processing services to be provided pursuant to a written contract with a third party that described and limited the services. This provision was eliminated in 1997.

The new 30 percent leeway authority in Regulation Y provides additional flexibility for bank holding companies that was not included in the prior regulation. It is unclear whether the 30 percent is measured against the parent company's consolidated data processing revenues or only against those of each separate subsidiary. The former method would allow greater flexibility.

Bank holding companies also have broad authority to perform data processing services for their affiliates under the BHC Act and Regulation Y.[27]

In 2000, the Board amended Regulation Y to significantly broaden the ability of financial holding companies to engage in electronic banking and commerce activities by authorizing them to engage in "finder" activities.[28] Pursuant to this authority, for example, a financial holding company may host an electronic marketplace on its Web site and operate an Internet Web site allowing multiple buyers and sellers to exchange information concerning products and services they are willing to purchase or sell, much like E-Bay. *See* Chapter 9, **Electronic Commerce and Related Applications,** § 9.17, for a discussion of "finder" activities.

---

[26] 12 C.F.R. § 225.28(b)(14).

[27] 12 U.S.C. § 1843(c)(1)(C).

[28] 65 Fed. Reg. 80,740 (2000).

[B] Anti-Tying Provisions

Section 106 of the BHC Act Amendments of 1970[29] prohibits certain tying arrangements between a bank and its affiliates. Section 106 provides that a bank shall not "in any manner extend credit, lease or sell property of any kind, or furnish any service, or fix or vary the consideration for any of the foregoing" on the condition or requirement that the customer obtain some additional credit, property, or service from the bank (other than a loan, discount, deposit, or trust service) or from an affiliate of the bank. Banks also are prohibited from conditioning their services on the customer not obtaining services from competitors of the bank or its affiliates.

The Federal Reserve Board is authorized by regulation or order to permit such exceptions as it considers will not be contrary to the purposes of the anti-tying prohibitions. In 1994 and 1995, the Board adopted an exemptive rule permitting banks and their affiliates to offer discounts on packaged products.[30]

Prior to 1997, the Board by regulation applied the anti-tying provisions to bank holding companies as well as to their subsidiary banks.

§ 4.06 BANK SERVICE COMPANY ACT

The Bank Service Company Act ("BSCA")[31] authorizes national and state banks to acquire shares of entities called "service companies." A bank service company may perform services for the bank itself, other depository institutions, and third parties generally. Such services include any service (other than deposit taking) that the parent bank is authorized to perform at locations in the state where the parent bank is located. In addition, a bank service company may perform at any geographic location, with the Federal Reserve Board's approval, any service that the Board has determined by regulation to be permissible for bank holding companies under the BHC Act.

In determining whether to approve or deny an application by a bank to acquire an interest in a bank service company, the appropriate bank regulatory agency is required to consider factors similar to those required under the BHC Act, although, unlike the BHC Act, the BSCA does not impose a public benefits test.

---

[29] 12 U.S.C. §§ 1971 *et seq.*

[30] 12 C.F.R. § 225.7(b).

[31] 12 U.S.C. § 1861 *et seq.*

A bank service corporation is subject to examination and regulation by the primary supervisor of its parent bank or, if the company is owned by more than one bank, by the regulator of the bank that is its principal investor.

The BSCA also includes a provision relevant to nonbank data processing and other technology companies to which banks outsource their operations. Section 7(c) of the Act subjects such companies to examination and regulation by the federal banking agencies. Specifically, the Act provides:

> Whenever a bank . . . or any subsidiary or affiliate of such a bank . . . causes to be performed for itself, by contract or otherwise, any services authorized under this chapter, whether on or off its premises—
>
> (1) such performance shall be subject to regulation and examination by such agency to the same extent as if such services were being performed by the bank itself on its own premises, and
> (2) the bank shall notify such agency of the existence of the service relationship within thirty days after the making of such service contract or the performance of the service, whichever occurs first.[32]

The federal banking agencies have utilized this authority to examine data processing and other companies that perform services for banks.

The OCC generally expects a national bank to notify potential vendors in writing of the OCC's examination and regulatory jurisdiction should they contract with the bank and to recognize the OCC's jurisdiction in all vendor contracts. The OCC has stated that, to the extent that a third-party vendor performs services for a bank, the vendor is subject to federal banking regulation and examination to the same extent as if such services were being performed by the bank itself.[33]

§ 4.07 HOME OWNERS' LOAN ACT

The Home Owners' Loan Act ("HOLA")[34] provides for the chartering and regulation of federal savings associations. Although these institutions are intended primarily to provide credit for housing, they also have broad powers to engage in commercial banking activities and frequently are indistinguishable from commercial banks.

---

[32] 12 U.S.C. § 1867(c).

[33] *See* OCC Conditional Approval No. 347 (Jan. 29, 2000) (AeroBank.com).

[34] 12 U.S.C. §§ 1461 *et seq.*

The Office of Thrift Supervision ("OTS") charters and regulates federal savings associations. The OTS in 1998 amended its rules to authorize savings associations to engage in "prudent innovation through the use of emerging technology" and to use electronic means to perform any function, or provide any product or service, permissible under its charter.[35] The first banking institution to operate mainly on the Internet was a savings association chartered by the OTS under HOLA.

§ 4.08 ELECTRONIC FUNDS TRANSFER ACT

The Electronic Funds Transfer Act ("EFT Act")[36] is the primary federal statute governing EFT transactions. The EFT Act establishes the basic rights, liabilities, and responsibilities of financial institutions that offer EFT services and of consumers who use them. Its primary objective is the protection of individual consumer rights.[37]

The EFT Act was enacted in 1978 following the report of the National Commission on Electronic Fund Transfers established by Congress to study EFT and make legislative recommendations.[38] The Act reflected the following Congressional findings:

> The Congress finds that the use of electronic systems to transfer funds provides the potential for substantial benefits to consumers. However, due to the unique characteristics of such systems, the application of existing consumer protection legislation is unclear, leaving the rights and liabilities of consumers, financial institutions, and intermediaries in electronic fund transfers undefined.[39]

[A] Scope of EFT Act

The EFT Act applies to any financial institution that offers a consumer a card, code, or other means of access to the consumer's account for the purpose of initiating an electronic fund transfer.[40] An "electronic fund transfer" is defined to mean:

---

[35] 12 C.F.R. Part 555, Electronic Operations; 63 Fed. Reg. 65,673 (1998).

[36] 15 U.S.C. §§ 1693 *et seq.*

[37] 15 U.S.C. § 1693.

[38] *See* EFT in the United States: Policy Recommendations and the Public Interest, Final Report of the National Commission on Electronic Fund Transfers (1977).

[39] 15 U.S.C. § 1693.

[40] *See also* § 13.02[B] for a further discussion of the EFT Act.

> any transfer of funds, other than a transaction originated by check, draft, or similar paper instrument, which is initiated through an electronic terminal, telephonic instrument, or computer or magnetic tape so as to order, instruct, or authorize a financial institution to debit or credit an account. Such term includes, but is not limited to, point-of-sale transfers, automated teller machine transactions, direct deposits or withdrawals of funds, and transfers initiated by telephone.[41]

The term "financial institution" for purposes of the EFT Act encompasses not only depository institutions but "any other person who, directly or indirectly, holds an account belonging to a consumer."[42] Thus, nonbank entities, as well as banks, are subject to the Act.

Rulemaking authority is assigned to the Federal Reserve Board under the EFT Act. Each of the federal banking agencies is empowered to enforce the Act against the banks for which they are the primary federal regulator. The Securities and Exchange Commission ("SEC") enforces the Act with respect to broker-dealers and the Federal Trade Commission ("FTC") with respect to any other entity subject to the Act.[43]

State law is preempted by the EFT Act to the extent it is inconsistent with the Act.[44] A state law is not deemed to be inconsistent with the Act if it affords greater consumer protections than the Act.

[B] Regulation E

Regulation E of the Federal Reserve Board implements the EFT Act.[45] Regulation E imposes disclosure requirements, limitations on consumer liability, written receipt and periodic statement requirements, and error resolution procedures.

Under Regulation E, a financial institution may issue an access device (*i.e.*, a card, code, or other means of access to a customer's account) only in response to an oral or written request or as a renewal of or substitute for any already issued access device.[46] A financial institution may distribute an unsolicited access device only if the device is not validated, accompanied by a clear explanation that it is not validated, and

---

[41] 15 U.S.C. § 1693a(6).

[42] 15 U.S.C. § 1693a(8).

[43] 15 U.S.C. § 1693o.

[44] 15 U.S.C. § 1693q.

[45] 12 C.F.R. Part 205. *See also* § 13.02[B] for a further discussion of Regulation E.

[46] 12 C.F.R. § 205.5(a).

other disclosures, and can be validated only in response to the consumer's oral or written request.[47]

The EFT Act and Regulation E limit the liability of a consumer for a lost or stolen credit card or other access device to $50 if the consumer notifies the financial institution within two business days after learning of the loss or theft.[48] If the consumer fails to provide notice, the liability is limited to no more than $500. With respect to unauthorized transfers, a consumer's liability is limited to those that occur after 60 days following the transmittal of a periodic statement on which the first unauthorized transfer appeared if the consumer fails to notify the financial institution.

Regulation E also requires a financial institution to make a written receipt available to a consumer at the time the consumer initiates an electronic fund transfer at an electronic terminal.[49] This requirement is problematic for stored value card systems that operate independently of any online hookup to a central computer system.

As noted in Chapter 10, **Electronic Transfer of Federal Payments,** the Federal Reserve Board in 1996 issued a proposed amendment to Regulation E pertaining to stored value cards, but was ordered by Congress not to adopt it and instead to conduct a study, which the Board released in 1997.

§ 4.09 FEDERAL TRADE COMMISSION ACT

The Federal Trade Commission Act[50] prohibits unfair or deceptive acts or practices in or affecting commerce.[51] The Act requires each of the federal banking agencies to establish a separate division of consumer affairs to handle consumer complaints regarding unfair or deceptive acts or practices, including violations of an institution's privacy policies and procedures.[52] Banking institutions are exempt from FTC jurisdiction under the Federal Trade Commission Act[53] but the FTC's

[47] 12 C.F.R. § 205.5(b).

[48] 15 U.S.C. § 1693g; 12 C.F.R. § 205.6(b).

[49] 12 C.F.R. § 205.9.

[50] 15 U.S.C. §§ 41 *et seq., enforced under* 12 U.S.C. § 1818.

[51] 15 U.S.C. § 45(a)(1).

[52] *See, e.g.*, Regulation AA, Unfair or Deceptive Acts or Practices, of the Federal Reserve Board, 12 C.F.R. Part 227.

[53] 15 U.S.C. § 45(a)(2).

decisions on unfair and deceptive acts and practices often are relevant to bank activities.[54]

§ 4.10 UNIFORM COMMERCIAL CODE ("UCC")

Most commercial transactions involving negotiable instruments or bank deposits are governed by the Uniform Commercial Code ("UCC"). The UCC establishes principles for commercial transactions such as finality and non-repudiation that are essential to the flow of commerce. The U.S. Court of Appeals for the Fifth Circuit has described the UCC as follows:

> At first glance the UCC may appear to be a compendium of confusing and seemingly contradictory rules enacted to govern myriad business transactions. Upon closer scrutiny the UCC is found to be a finely tuned statutory mechanism containing interlocking provisions designed to provide certainty in commercial transactions. Once the pieces of this puzzle are correctly aligned, the UCC furnishes the answer to almost any question involving the rights and liabilities of the parties to a covered transaction.[55]

The UCC was drafted by academic and practicing attorneys under the auspices of the National Conference of Commissioners on Uniform State Law. The UCC has been periodically updated over the past 40 years to reflect changes in commercial practice. Although the UCC is not binding on the states, each state has enacted some version of the UCC. Not all state laws conform to the uniform code, however, and court decisions interpreting one state's version of the UCC are not binding on courts in other states.[56]

The UCC Articles most relevant to banking are Articles 3, 4, and 4A, none of which is currently deemed to be applicable to electronic payments.[57]

---

[54] *See also* § 13.03[D], *infra* for a discussion of FTC actions to protect consumer privacy on the Internet under the Federal Trade Commission Act.

[55] *Union Bank of Benton, Ark. v. First Nat'l Bank in Mount Pleasant, Tex.*, 29 UCC Rep. Serv. 598, 621 F.2d 788, 790 (5th Cir. 1981).

[56] *See* Richard L. Field, "Survey of the Year's Developments in Electronic Cash Law and the Laws Affecting Electronic Banking in the United States," 46 Am. U. L. Rev. 967 (1997) ("Ultimately, U.C.C. provisions that look alike may come to have different or even contradictory interpretations in the various states.").

[57] Article 5 of the UCC deals with letters of credit, Article 7 with warehouse receipts, and Article 8 with investment securities.

[A] Article 3

Article 3 is entitled "Commercial Paper" and applies to drafts, checks, certificates of deposit, and notes to the extent not governed by Article 4, which deals with bank deposits and collections. Under Article 3, no person is liable on an instrument unless his signature appears on the instrument or he subsequently ratifies it. The risk of forgery falls on the recipient of the instrument. Article 3 requires all negotiable instruments to be in writing.

[B] Article 4

Article 4 of the UCC is entitled "Bank Deposits and Collections" and is primarily concerned with the transfer and collection of payment "items" to and from bank accounts. Article 4 was recently redrafted to address check truncation and electronic presentment.[58]

[C] Article 4A

Article 4A of the UCC pertains to commercial wire transfers and contains provisions recognizing that a transaction need not be in writing to be valid. Article 4A is not applicable to most transactions by consumers.

[D] Article 2B

Article 2B was drafted to become part of the UCC covering licenses of information, including software and sales of mass-marketed software. It was subsequently approved as the Uniform Computer Information Transaction Act rather than as Article 2B. *See* § 4.15 *infra.*

§ 4.11 UNIFORM ELECTRONIC TRANSACTIONS ACT

The National Conference of Commissioners on Uniform State Laws ("NCCUSL") for several years has been drafting a model law on electronic commerce. The model law will not be a part of the Uniform Commercial

---

[58] *See* UCC § 4-406(a) (amended 1990), 2B U.L.A. 65-66 (1991 & Supp 1996) (facilitating truncation by streamlining the duties of banks to their customers); UCC § 4-110 (amended 1990), 2B U.L.A. 25 (1991 & Supp. 1996) (providing that transmission of an image may constitute presentment without delivery of an item under agreement for electronic presentment).

Code and will not address electronic payments systems but will apply to electronic commercial transactions.

A final draft of the Uniform Electronic Transactions Act ("UETA") was approved by the UCCUSL for adoption by the states in the summer of 1999. The final draft limits the UETA to electronic records and signatures in commercial transactions, including transactions with consumers.[59] California has adopted the UETA effective January 1, 2000, and at least 27 state legislatures are expected to consider the UETA in 2000.[60] The UETA provides, *inter alia*, that a record or signature may not be denied legal effect or enforceability under state law solely because it is in electronic form and, if a state law requires a signature, an electronic signature satisfies the law. The UETA applies only when the parties agree to conduct a transaction electronically.

§ 4.12 UNCITRAL MODEL LAW ON ELECTRONIC COMMERCE

The United Nations Commission on International Trade Law ("UNCITRAL") in 1996 adopted a model law on electronic commerce.[61] The model law establishes rules that validate and recognize contracts formed through electronic means, sets default rules for contract formation and governance of electronic contract performance, defines the characteristics of a valid electronic writing and an original document, provides for the acceptability of electronic signatures for legal and commercial purposes, and supports the admission of computer evidence in courts and arbitration proceedings.

§ 4.13 UNIFORM MONEY SERVICES ACT

The National Conference of Commissioners of Uniform State Laws in 2000 approved for adoption by the states the Uniform Money Services Act. The Act provides a framework for safety and soundness regulation

---

[59] The draft is available at ⟨⟨*www.law.upenn.edu/library/ulc/uecicta/etaam99.htm*⟩⟩.

[60] *See generally* Robert Ballen and Thomas Fox, "The New Uniform Electronic Transactions Act: A Framework for Electronic Commerce," Electronic Banking Law and Commerce Report (Sept. 1999), at 8.

[61] For the text of the model law *see* ⟨⟨*http://www.un.or.at/uncitral/texts/electcom/ml-ec.htm#TOP*⟩⟩.

of entities other than banks that engage in money transmission. The term "money transmission" is defined in the Act to mean:

> To engage in the business of selling or issuing payment instruments, selling or issuing stored value, or receiving money or monetary value for transmission to a location within or outside the United States. The term does not include the provision of package delivery services, online services, network access, and telecommunications services, unless the provider receives compensation for the transmission of money, payment instruments, or stored value that is different from the compensation received for other transmissions.

The term "payment instrument" means a "check, draft, money order, traveler's check, or other instrument for the transmission or payment of money or monetary value, whether or not negotiable" but does not include a credit card voucher, letter of credit, or instrument that is redeemable by the issuer in goods or services. "Stored value" means "monetary value that is evidenced by an electronic record."

The Act prohibits a person from engaging in money transmission without obtaining a license from the relevant state. A state must consider financial and managerial criteria in considering whether to license a money transmitter and must determine that "it is in the interest of the public" to permit the applicant to engage in money transmission. A surety bond of up to $250,000 may be required and may be increased up to $1 million if the licensee's financial condition is impaired at any time. The Act gives the licensing state authority to examine and require reports of licensees and to issue cease and desist orders and impose civil and criminal penalties for violations. The Act also imposes restrictions on investments by licensees under which investments in equity securities generally may not exceed 50 percent of the total permissible investments of a licensee.

The Act does not apply to banks, bank holding companies and similar banking organizations, futures commission merchants, broker-dealers, or clearinghouses.

§ 4.14 E-SIGN ACT

The Electronic Signatures in Global and National Commerce Act, or "E-Sign Act"[62] establishes the validity of electronic signatures. The Act will

[62] Pub. L. No. 106-229, *codified at* 15 U.S.C. § 7001.

facilitate electronic banking and commerce and greatly reduce the paperwork burden associated with traditional paper-based transactions by allowing commercial contracts to be formed, documented and stored electronically.[63] The E-Sign Act generally preempts state law unless the state law constitutes an enactment of the Uniform Electronic Transactions Act as approved and recommended for enactment in all of the states by the National Conference of Commissioners on Uniform State Laws in 1999.

§ 4.15 UNIFORM COMPUTER INFORMATION TRANSACTIONS ACT

The Uniform Computer Information Transactions Act ("UCITA") was approved by the Conference of Commissioners on Uniform State Laws for adoption by the states in 2000. Originally drafted as Article 2B of the UCC, the Act covers licenses of information, including software and sales of mass-marketed software. The Act validates so-called "shrink-wrap" and "click-on" licenses.

The Act does not apply to "financial services transactions" or "insurance services transactions." The official comments to the Act state:

> Financial services transactions are similar in many ways to computer information transactions in that they entail trade in symbols, albeit symbols of very different use and effect, and share some common legal issues: e.g., authenticity, data integrity, and authority . . . . However, they will often be governed by very different rules in that, in many cases, the digital subject matter of a financial transaction *is* the value it represents. An appropriate book entry, for example, *is* a securities entitlement.

The Act excludes "core banking, payment and financial services activities" because they are "mature subjects of other bodies of law" including various UCC Articles. Nevertheless, banks as entities are not excluded and banks may be subject to the Act when they license or use licensed software. For example, where a bank provides software to a customer to be used in an on-line banking program, UCITA would govern the software license except with respect to any questions specifically excluded or dealt with in an article of the UCC or any preemptive federal law.

---

[63] *See* Chapter 16 for a more detailed discussion of the E-Sign Act.

CHAPTER 5

THE PAYMENTS SYSTEM

§ 5.01 IN GENERAL

The term "payments system" refers to the mechanism by which financial transactions between purchasers and sellers of goods and services are effectuated and settled in the United States. It is the vehicle for the transfer of the monetary value and related information necessary for the flow of commerce and has been referred to as the "life-blood of our economy."[1]

Access to the payments system is carefully guarded by the Federal Reserve Board, which views the integrity of the payments system as critical to economic stability, and by the banking industry, which views its role in the payments system critical to its competitive position in the financial services industry.

Both the American Bankers Association and The Bankers Roundtable have established groups to address payments system issues and ensure a predominant role for banks in the payments systems of the future.[2] The Internet Council similarly has established a Payment Systems Work Group to identify and pursue business models for electronic commerce that leverage the existing payments system infrastructure to support current and future Internet commerce.

§ 5.02 STRUCTURE OF THE PAYMENTS SYSTEM

Although often referred to as a single "system," the payments system is not a single mechanism but rather a series of mechanisms that serve different payment transfer needs. While the Federal Reserve System plays a major role in the operation and regulation of the payments system, key components of the system are privately operated and regulated. What the role of the Federal Reserve should be in the payments system is a subject of ongoing discussion and debate.[3]

The principal payments systems are Fedwire, the Clearing House Interbank Payment System ("CHIPS"), and a number of small-dollar check

---

[1] American Bankers Association, Payments System Task Force, *The Role of Banks in the Payments System of the Future* (Oct. 1996) (hereinafter "ABA Payments System Report"), Mission Statement.

[2] ABA Task Force on the Payments System and The Bankers Roundtable's Committee on Payments and Technology.

[3] *See* Hearings before the House Subcommittee on Domestic and International Monetary Policy, 1997 WL 14150817. *See* Chapter 6, **Electronic Money**, § 6.03[B], *infra*.

clearing house associations, including automated clearing house ("ACH") networks. Most large-dollar payments are processed through the system electronically whereas check payments generally are processed manually, although electronic check presentment is increasingly common.[4]

[A] ACH Networks

ACH networks process batches of payments such as employer payroll payments, consumer bill payments such as mortgage and insurance premium payments, corporate tax payments, and government benefit payments. Four such networks exist in the United States. They are operated by the Federal Reserve System (which processes approximately 80 percent of all ACH payments), the American Clearing House Association, New York Automated Clearing House, and VISANet under rules established by the National Automated Clearing House Association ("NACHA"). In 1996, the number of ACH payments totaled 4 billion worth $12.1 trillion with an average transaction value of approximately $4,000.[5]

The ACH networks are used by over 20,000 financial institutions, 500,000 businesses, and 60 percent of all households. Direct deposit is an example of an ACH processed payment. Over 55 percent of all full-time employees in the private sector receive their pay by this method.[6] Notwithstanding the widespread use of ACH payments, however, over 15 times more checks are processed each year than ACH payments.[7]

The OCC in 2000 issued supervisory guidance to national banks concerning the potential liability of banks for losses that result from the failure of their customers to meet ACH operating standards as a result of credit and debit entries initiated through the Internet.[8] The OCC emphasized the increased need for banks to implement ACH risk management measures, citing an amendment in NACHA's operating rules under which, as of March 16, 2001, banks are required to warranty compliance with

---

[4] General Accounting Office, *Payments, Clearance, and Settlement: A Guide to the Systems, Risks, and Issues*, GAO/GGD-97-73 (June 1997) (hereinafter "GAO Report"), at 102.

[5] *Id.* at 117–119.

[6] *See* The Role of the Federal Reserve and the Automated Clearing House Network, Statement of Elliott C. McEntee, President and CEO, National Automated Clearing House Association, before the House Subcommittee on Domestic and International Monetary Policy.

[7] *Id.*

[8] OCC Advisory Letter 2001-3 (Jan. 29, 2001).

NACHA's rules by their merchant and other customers that initiate debits through the Internet. Originators of WEB entries (i.e., debit entries initiated pursuant to an authorization obtained through the Internet to effect a transfer of funds from a customer account) are required to:

- Employ commercially reasonable fraudulent-transaction detection systems to screen the entries in order to minimize the risk of fraud related to Internet-initiated payments.
- Use commercially reasonable procedures to verify that routing numbers are valid.
- Establish a secure Internet session with each receiver prior to the key entry by the receiver of any banking information.
- Conduct an annual audit to ensure that the financial information obtained from receivers is protected by prescribed security practices and procedures. The first audit must be completed by December 31, 2001.

Under the NACHA rule, banks must ensure that their customers that originate WEB entries are in compliance with the above requirements on an ongoing basis and are deemed to warrant that originators have conformed to the new requirements. Banks also are required to establish the identity of the originator, monitor the originator's creditworthiness, establish and review exposure limits for originators, and monitor entries by each originator relative to its exposure limit across multiple settlement dates.

[B] Fedwire and CHIPS

"Fedwire" and "CHIPS" are primarily wholesale payment systems that process large-value payments made by banks and large corporations.

Operated by the Federal Reserve System, Fedwire allows any depository institution with a Federal Reserve account to transfer funds from its account to the Federal Reserve account of any other depository institution. Fedwire handled daily transactions totaling $989 billion in 1996, with an average amount per transaction of $3 million.[9] Under Regulation J, which governs Fedwire transfers, each transfer is final and irrevocable upon

[9] GAO Report at 15.

notice of it, thus avoiding credit exposure to the parties. The Federal Reserve Banks provide the intraday credit needed for this purpose and are exposed to the risk that a depository institution may not have sufficient funds in its Reserve account at the end of the day to meet its obligations. Accordingly, daylight overdrafts through Fedwire are carefully monitored and limited by the Federal Reserve.

The Clearing House Interbank Payments System, known as CHIPS, is owned and operated by an association of large New York banks. CHIPS handled daily transactions totaling $1.3 trillion in 1996, with an average value per transaction of $6.2 million.[10] The exposure to daylight overdrafts in CHIPS is born by the participating banks rather than the Federal Reserve.

Payments processed through Fedwire generally are related to domestic transactions whereas CHIPS payments generally involve foreign transactions and the settlement of foreign exchange transactions.

[C] SWIFT

The Society for Worldwide Interbank Financial Telecommunications ("SWIFT") is a private international communications network formed in 1973 by 240 large North American and European banks to provide a secure system of international communication links.

[D] Check Clearing

The United States payments system processes approximately 64 billion checks each year with a total value of $75 trillion.[11] Check clearing is performed by the Federal Reserve System, which handled 15.5 billion checks in 1995, and by approximately 150 private check clearing house associations including the California Bankers Clearing House ("CBCH") serving over 100 depository institutions, the Chicago Clearing House Association ("CCH") serving over 260 depository institutions, and the New York Clearing House Association ("NYCHA") serving over 140 depository institutions. CBCH, CCH, and NYCHA processed, respectively, 1.6 million, 563 million, and 336 million checks in 1995.[12]

---

[10] *Id.*

[11] Statement of Alice Rivlin, Vice Chairman, Board of Governors of the Federal Reserve System, on the Federal Payments System, before the House Subcommittee on Domestic and International Monetary Policy, 1997 WL 14150817.

[12] *Id.*

Although at one time it was thought that paper checks would be replaced by ACH payments and electronic cash, this development has not occurred. As Federal Reserve Chairman Greenspan has stated, "[a]s we look forward, the Federal Reserve recognizes that whatever innovations develop, the check will likely be with us for many years." [3] Chairman Greenspan noted that the Federal Reserve is "testing new systems for truncating and electronically presenting checks, which include capturing and storing the image of checks and enabling institutions to make payment decisions in real time by accessing these images through the Internet.[14]

§ 5.03 PAYMENTS SYSTEM RISK

Payments system risk entails credit, systemic, legal, and other risks that can cause or result from the failure of payments to be properly transferred or settled.[15] The major risks of payment system failure generally are born by the participating depository institutions and/or the Federal Reserve System. Consumers also bear some risk, including the risk of lost or unauthorized payment instruments and errors in processing transactions. The risks to consumers generally are limited by the Uniform Commercial Code, Electronic Funds Transfer Act, and other consumer protection laws.

In 1986, the Federal Reserve Board implemented a Payment System Risk Reduction program designed to manage intraday credit exposure on large dollar U.S. payments systems through caps on daylight overdrafts and other measures.

The Federal Reserve has not viewed the risks posed by emerging stored value payment products or "e-cash" to be materially different from existing payments system risks. The Board has stated that such products "give rise to the same types of risk that other payment instruments do, although the degree of any particular risk may vary because of differences in operating characteristics among the payment instruments."[16]

---

[13] Remarks by Chairman Alan Greenspan before the National Automated Clearinghouse Association Annual Meeting, Apr. 10, 2000.

[14] *Id.*.

[15] *See generally* Comptroller's Handbook for National Bank Examiners § 410.1—Payment Systems and Funds Transfer Activities (June 1994).

[16] Board of Governors of the Federal Reserve System, *Report to the Congress on the Application of the Electronic Fund Transfer Act to Electronic Stored-Value Products* (Mar. 1997).

§ 5.04 NEW ELECTRONIC PAYMENTS SYSTEMS

The new electronic banking devices appearing in the financial marketplace are new forms of payments systems. Electronic cash and stored value cards in particular have as their primary function the transfer of payments. Electronic data interchange and electronic bill payment systems also are forms of payments systems, as are business-to-business information and transaction systems.

To the extent these new systems operate outside of the banking framework, they may raise policy issues concerning the operational soundness and security of such systems, the applicability of the existing regulatory scheme to such systems, and the impact on bank competitiveness.

With respect to competition, nonbank information technology companies such as Microsoft and various Internet providers have significant competitive capabilities in the business of transferring secure information, which is the fundamental function of a payments system. As one commentator has noted: "In the competition for information services, banks hold no inherent advantages in the processing of payments information."[17] The development of new financial applications by information technology companies thus poses a significant competitive issue for banks:

> The key question is whether banks will be effective in marshaling the technological prowess of other competitors, such as Microsoft, without losing their role in clearing transactions and serving as the primary contact with businesses and consumers in providing financial services.
>
> * * *
>
> The rapid expansion of computer and telecommunications networks has demonstrated anew that payments transactions fundamentally are the transfer of information. However, banks are not often thought of as the originators of innovations in information technology. Other corporations, such as Microsoft, First Data Corporation, and Fiserv, have significant advantages over banks in the development of new systems for the safe and secure movement of information. All that they lack to mount a major challenge to banks' role in the payments system are direct access to trusted clearing services, such as those presently offered to insured depository institutions by the Federal Reserve, and the liquid assets used to settle payments transactions. Both are readily available

---

[17] Michael Krimminger, "Banks and the Future of the Payments System—Part Two," E-Money, Vol. 1, No.2 (June 1998).

> through acquisition of an insured depository institution, if this is legally permitted through enactment of financial modernization legislation, or now through contractual relationships with a bank or thrift. Once a technology or software corporation develops the interface through which customers interact with their financial accounts ostensible held by the "captive" bank or thrift, customers' loyalty will almost certainly lie with the interface and its creator.[18]

In view of the rapid development of new electronic payments systems and the increasing participation of nonbank institutions in these systems, the American Bankers Association ("ABA") established a task force to study the future role of banks in the payments system. The ABA's Task Force on the Payments System in 1996 issued a report entitled "The Role of Banks in the Payments System of the Future."[19] Issues considered by the ABA's Task Force included:

- What steps are necessary to protect the integrity of the payments system?
- Who should be allowed to participate in the various lines of business that are being developed, and under what type of regulatory oversight?
- What actions should the industry take to assure that customers' rights and privacy are protected?
- What standards should be followed, and how should those standards be determined?
- What are the implications for the competitiveness of markets?
- What level of government involvement is necessary or desirable?
- What are the risks of government intervention in terms of technological development?

---

[18] *Id.*

[19] American Bankers Association, *The Role of Banks in the Payments System of the Future: A Report and Recommendations of the Payments System Task Force* (Oct. 1996). The Task Force included 11 bankers representing large and small institutions from different areas of the country.

The Task Force raised concerns that the participation of nonbank entities in the offering of new electronic payments services will adversely affect the integrity of the existing payments system and recommended that only insured depository institutions be permitted to access to the payments system:

> [A] safe and reliable payments system is absolutely critical to a modern economy. Electronic payment instruments like stored value cards and Internet payment products are money by any of the usual definitions. So the key policy question is: Who should be allowed to issue electronic liabilities that can be used to make payments to third parties, and under what conditions?
>
> * * *
>
> [T]he failure of an issuer has the potential to disrupt the payment system by derailing the final settlement of thousands of transactions. Thousands of consumers could be left with devalued or worthless payment instruments. This disruption, while perhaps not causing an overall system failure, would shake public confidence in the payment system.
>
> * * *
>
> A key conclusion of our task force is that any issuer of third-party instruments must meet high standards of financial soundness and responsibility. Banks, by the nature of their charters and the extensive system of regulation and supervision, clearly meet the test.
>
> * * *
>
> The bank model relies primarily on a complicated system of supervision and regulation to ensure the underlying financial stability of the issuer. This model doesn't translate well to nonbanks. How could we assure that regulations would be applied equally across banks and nonbanks? Would a parallel system of examination and supervision be necessary? What about differences in assets between banks and nonbanks? Bank assets are typically very liquid, whereas a commercial firm's assets are dominated by inventory, plant, and machinery. How would capital standards be applied and what would the organizational structure be?
>
> * * *
>
> There's any number of combinations and permutations of these models that may work. But we already have a system in place to protect the integrity of the payment system. And until we have more experi-

> ence with the ins and outs of electronic retail payments, it seems reasonable to use the system we have.[20]

For its part, the Federal Reserve Board has indicated that it does not view the new electronic payments devices as a threat to the integrity of the existing payments system. Apart from concerns regarding the soundness of payments system operators, the Board deems it unlikely that the new electronic payment products will have an adverse impact on the payments system in the near future:

> The U.S. payment system is well developed and comprises a number of competing products, including cash, checks, money orders, credit cards, "debit cards," and travelers checks. Electronic stored-value products are a recent innovation in payments systems technology that has the potential to increase the efficiency of the retail payment system. Nonetheless, although these products may provide benefits to both consumers and merchants, their introduction seems unlikely to change the fundamental nature of our current payment system in the near future. Electronic stored-value products, if successful, will add one more option to the set of payment technologies available to participants in retail transactions; they will compete with existing alternatives that are firmly entrenched among both consumers and merchants. If experience with the introduction of debit cards can serve as a guide, widespread public acceptance of stored-value products, if it occurs at all, will likely develop slowly over many years.[21]

The Administration's policy regarding new electronic payment systems similarly is one of nonintervention for the present:

> At this early stage in the development of electronic payment systems, the commercial and technological environment is changing rapidly. It would be hard to develop policy that is both timely and appropriate. For these reasons, inflexible and highly prescriptive regulations and

[20] Testimony of John M. Lewis, on behalf of the American Bankers Association, to the Interagency Consumer Electronic Payments Task Force (June 9, 1997).

[21] Board of Governors of the Federal Reserve System, *Report to Congress on the Application of the Electronic Fund Transfer Act to Electronic Stored Value Products* (Mar. 1997), 1-2. *See also* Remarks by Chairman Alan Greenspan before the National Automated Clearinghouse Association Annual Meeting. Apr. 10, 2000 ("Yet in the retail payments system, we have tended to underestimate the size of the hurdles confronting a shift away from paper.").

> rules are inappropriate and potentially harmful. Rather, in the near term, case-by-case monitoring of electronic payment experiments is preferred.
>
> For a longer term perspective, however, the marketplace and industry self-regulation alone may not fully address all issues. For example, government action may be necessary to ensure the safety and soundness of electronic payment systems, to protect consumers, or to respond to important law enforcement objectives.
>
> * * *
>
> As electronic payment systems develop, governments should work closely with the private sector to inform policy development, and ensure that governmental activities flexibly accommodate the needs of the emerging marketplace.[22]

§ 5.05 THE ROLE OF THE FEDERAL RESERVE

Maintaining the soundness of the payments system is a major goal of federal banking regulation and is frequently cited by the Federal Reserve Board as a basis for excluding nonbank institutions from the realm of banking and preserving the separation of banking and commerce, and for preserving its role as a banking supervisor.

In view of the major technological changes affecting the payments system, the Federal Reserve Board in 1996 created a Committee on the Federal Reserve in the Payments Mechanism. The Committee was assigned to review the retail payments services provided by the Federal Reserve System, including check collection and ACH operations, with a view to assessing what role the System should play in the payments system in the future.

The Committee considered five different scenarios under which the Federal Reserve would: (1) cease providing payments services, (2) privatize its payments services, (3) provide limited payments services, (4) take measures to increase the efficiency of the interbank retail payments system, and (5) expedite the movement to an electronic-based retail payments system by an active operational presence and creating incentives for commercial electronic payments system providers.

Based on extensive discussions with industry participants, academics, trade groups, consumers, and other governmental officials, the Federal

[22] The White House, *A Framework for Global Electronic Commerce*, posted at ⟨⟨*http://www.iif.nist.gov/eleccomm/ecomm.htm*⟩⟩.

Reserve Committee issued a report summarizing the input it received.[23] The report determined that, because the Federal Reserve is a key provider of check collection and ACH services, its withdrawal from the payments system "could cause significant short-term disruption with questionable benefits over the long run." In addition, the report concluded that, because of the scope of its operations and regulatory role, the Federal Reserve is viewed as playing a leadership role in working with other retail payments system participants to foster the transaction to an electronic payments system.

According to the report, while a few large banks and clearing houses favored withdrawal of the Federal Reserve from check collection and ACH services, the majority view favored a continued role for the Federal Reserve due to concern about payments system disruptions and the lack of a "service provider of last resort" during banking crises.

The Bankers Roundtable in May 1998 announced the release of its report on "The Role of the Federal Reserve and the Banking Industry in the Retail Electronic Payments Systems of the Future." The report recommended that the private sector, rather than the Federal Reserve, assume responsibility for operating the new retail electronic payments system, with the Federal Reserve serving an oversight role.

In 1999, the Federal Reserve Board created the Payments System Development Committee to advise on the medium- and long-term public policy issues surrounding developments in the retail payments system.[24] The Committee will serve as a forum for the analysis of technological and market trends, provide a mechanism for consulting with payments system providers and users, and advise the Board on the need for Board action on payment system topics.

---

[23] Federal Reserve System, Committee on the Federal Reserve in the Payments Mechanism, *Summary of Input from Payments System Forums* (Sept. 1997), Board Press Release (Oct. 7, 1997).

[24] Federal Reserve Board, Press Release (dated July 20, 1999).

CHAPTER 6

ELECTRONIC MONEY

§ 6.01 IN GENERAL

The nature of money has evolved over time to include gold and silver coins, paper notes, checks, and now, as a result of modern computer technology, electronic digital impulses. The emergence of electronic money as a medium of monetary exchange has far-reaching implications for banks, their customers, and the economy as a whole.

Electronic money offers potentially greater cost efficiencies, convenience, and security than paper money by facilitating paperless transactions. It also raises questions as to the nature of "money" and to what extent money in electronic form is different from money in paper form for regulatory purposes.

The term "electronic money" or "e-money" encompasses a variety of existing and emerging payment devices that provide recognized monetary value by electronic means. In general, there are two forms of electronic money: stored value cards and payments via an on-line device such as the Internet. Examples of the former include metro fare cards, prepaid telephone calling cards, and student meal tickets. Examples of the latter include a variety of proprietary products called "e-cash," "cybercash," "digital cash," and "e-money." Stored value cards generally are intended to be used for off-line transactions, whereas e-cash is more likely to be used for online large dollar transactions as well as "micro" payments.

Although the average electronic transaction could save an estimated 75 cents per transaction over paper checks, electronic money and payment systems have not developed as fast as some analysts had predicted.[1] Federal Reserve Chairman Greenspan has explained the persistence of paper money mainly as a function of consumer habit:

> [T]he average consumer is exceptionally conservative and traditional when it comes to money, which as a profoundly important role in day-to-day living. . . . To many, it is the embodiment of their life's work. Tampering with money has always had profoundly political implications. Much of American politics of the late nineteenth century, for example, was about the gold standard and the free silver movement. Our history vividly affirms that the average person is far more sensitive to what form our money—our store of value and

---

[1] *See generally* Hearings on "The Future of Electronic Payments: Roadblocks and Emerging Practices" before the House Subcomm. on Domestic and International Monetary Policy (Sept. 19, 2000).

medium of exchange—takes than we payments system specialists have readily understood. It took many generations for people to feel comfortable accepting paper in lieu of gold or silver. It is taking almost as long to convince them that holding money and making payments in ephemeral electronic form is as secure as using paper.

There is, of course, more to the tenacity of paper than a deep psychological connection between money and tangible wealth. Paper instruments also are perceived to have a greater degree of privacy than electronic payments, although there have been experiments with electronic money and other instruments that would provide relatively high levels of privacy. But confidence in such arrangements may take quite awhile to emerge. Currency, and to a large degree checks, are currently perceived to offer significant advantages in privacy over electronic payment systems that entail centrally maintained databases with elaborate records of individual transactions.

Perhaps an even more important dimension influencing our behavior regarding money and payments is convenience. Currency and checks do not require the users to travel to special locations, dial the number of a special machine, or maintain special equipment to originate payments. This is not to deny that automation has played an important role in reducing risks and increasing efficiency in handling currency and checks. Rather, the issue is that traditional paper instruments allow the users themselves, within a structured format, to have significant control over when, where, and how to make payments.[2]

§ 6.02 TYPES OF ELECTRONIC MONEY

[A] Electronic Cash

Electronic cash or "e-cash" refers to stored value in digital form that can be accessed through a personal computer, automated teller machine ("ATM"), television cable connection, enhanced telephone, or other telecommunications device. It also may be used with or without a stored value card or smart card. E-cash is designed primarily to facilitate online transactions on the Internet or "e-commerce" and is not yet widely used.

E-cash is not merely the electronic transfer of money. It is different from wire transfer or automatic debit devices such as debit cards that move money from one account to another. E-cash represents actual eco-

[2] Remarks by Chairman Alan Greenspan before the National Automated Clearinghouse Association Annual Meeting, Apr. 10, 2000.

nomic value and functions as the equivalent of cash. It has no physical manifestation, however, it cannot be physically counted. It does not require a vault for storage and protection. Yet, it is accepted as having monetary value based on liability assumed by the issuer.

While electronic cash is a substitute for paper money, it depends on paper money to exist. Electronic cash generally must be "bought" using conventional paper money. Unlike paper cash, e-cash generally cannot be used again once it is transferred to another party, although it may be designed for re-use under some systems.

[B] Stored Value Cards

A stored value card is a plastic card that looks like a credit card but has an embedded integrated circuit or chip that contains economic value that can be "spent" by transferring the value to a receiving device. The card allows cardholders to make cashless payments for the purchase of goods and services in a manner similar to the use of paper money and coins.

Some stored value cards have enhanced capabilities that allow them to function as "micro-computers" that can store and manipulate data and programs. Referred to as "smart cards," such cards may be used to retain customers' records of transactions as well as of frequent flyer miles, medical payment information, and other personal information.[2.1]

Although store value cards function like cash, they do not have the finality of cash. A stored value transaction generally must move through a complex payment system before payment is final. The card merely transfers the right to obtain cash from the cardholder to a payee.[2.2] Stored value cards may be used in connection with electronic payment systems such as the Mondex system, discussed below.

Two basic stored value card systems have been developed: closed systems and open systems. Banks and bank holding companies have been permitted to offer both open and closed systems, as well as complex closed systems.[3]

In a closed system, cash must be deposited in a particular vendor's card-dispensing terminal and the card received from the terminal may be used only for purchases from that specific vendor. The card itself is

---

[2.1] *See generally* OCC Bulletin on Stored Value Cards 96-48 (Sept. 10, 1996).

[2.2] *See* FDIC General Counsel's Opinion No. 8, 61 Fed. Reg. 40,490 (1996), for a description of stored value cards.

[3] *See, e.g., Banc One Corp., et al.*, 79 Fed. Res. Bull. 1158 (1993).

disposable and the only account reconciliation necessary involves the vendor's own cash receipts, the amount of funds debited from the cards at turnstiles or other points of sale, and the amount of the vendor's liabilities stored on outstanding cards. Closed systems include both single-vendor stored value card systems and systems designed for single-site use, such as at a college or university.

In an open stored value system, a customer's debit card contains a computer chip capable of storing value for use in stored card transactions with multiple vendors at multiple sites. Value is placed on the card in one of several ways: at an ATM adapted to read and place value on the chip, at a limited purpose ATM-type machine whose only functions are to add value to the chip and to transfer stored value back to the customer's account, or at a cash-to-card machine or other value transfer device.

Once value is placed on a card in an open system, equivalent funds are transferred to the stored value system operator, which holds the funds for payment of stored value card transactions. Stored value leaves the chip when the customer purchases goods or services either at a point of service ("POS") terminal or at a vending machine, telephone booth, mass transit turnstile, or other unmanned reader terminals or when the customer transfers funds back to an account at a value terminal. Reader terminals generally are off-line devices not connected to an ATM or POS network. Instead of a direct electronic connection, a reader terminal retains, for a period of time, value representing the amount of customer purchases at the terminal. Then, at the vendor's convenience, the stored value operating company, the vendor, or a third party collects value from the reader terminals using specifically designed collection cards issued by the operating company. The collection cards are then submitted to the company so funds can be properly credited. Once these transactions occur, the company is responsible for making settlement by transferring funds to the accounts of participating merchants and other appropriate parties.

Different types of stored value cards have been designed. Stored value cards that are self-operative and contain all the information necessary to permit the cardholder to conduct a transaction without access to a central computer system are referred to as "off-line" cards. Most stored value cards are off line. An "on-line" stored value card is one in which the information necessary to conduct transactions is stored not on the card itself but at a central data facility.

Disposable stored value cards are stored with a fixed value and are designed to be discarded after the value is exhausted. Some stored value cards have the capacity to be reloaded with value. Reloadable cards can be reloaded by withdrawing funds from an account through a teller, ATM, or specially equipped telephone or personal computer. Some cards allow a cardholder to obtain value directly from another cardholder's card.

Stored value cards can be used as credit cards, debit cards, or both, and may have multiple issuers. Some cards can be used by whoever has possession of the card and some cards cannot be activated without a personal identification number ("PIN").

Stored value cards can be used in connection with electronic payment systems, such as the Mondex system, or for making payments over computer networks such as the Internet.

[C] Electronic Money Systems

A variety of electronic cash and stored value card systems are in various stages of development and use in the marketplace. Although none of them as yet has emerged as a dominant form of alternative money to cash and checking accounts, they have the potential for widespread use in the future. In addition to the following, other forms of e-money are being developed including IBM Micro Payments and eCoin.

[1] DigiCash Coins

DigiCash, a Netherlands' company, developed a system to allow a computer user to purchase digital "coins" from a bank in the form of digits representing a specific amount or denomination of monetary value. The electronic coins are stored on the customer's PC hard drive and can be transferred to a merchant for on-line purchases. When a customer effects a transaction using the coins, the bank's deposit liability to the customer is reduced and an e-cash liability is logged. After the customer transfers coins to a merchant, the merchant's software transfers the coins to the issuer bank, thereby reducing the customer's electronic coin liability.[4] Mark Twain Bank was licensed to use the DigiCash electronic coin system in 1996.

---

[4] *See* General Accounting Office, *Payments, Clearance, and Settlement: A Guide to the Systems, Risks, and Issues*, GAO-GGD-97-73, at 149.

[2] Cybercash

Cybercash is an on-line computer-based product developed by CyberCash, Inc., Reston, Virginia, to enable a user to load digital "coins" from a bank account or credit card into the user's personal computer. The Cybercash system would enable users to make purchases over the Internet through an encrypted security system, much like the DigiCash system described above.

[3] Mondex Money

Mondex is an electronic payments medium based on stored value maintained in an electronic "purse" and accessed through smart cards and other devices. The system is designed to facilitate cashless transactions between cardholders and merchants utilizing the Mondex stored value or "Mondex money." The system also allows cardholders to transfer Mondex money among themselves.

The U.S. Mondex system is operated by a limited liability company (the Mondex "originator") that creates, sells, and redeems Mondex money in exchange for dollars that it invests in U.S. government securities and cash. Another limited liability company acts as a licensing and servicing entity for the system (the Mondex "servicer"). The servicer licenses financial institutions as the exclusive issuers of Mondex cards, collects transaction data, and performs other services necessary for the functioning of the system.

The Mondex system was originated by National Westminster Bank PLC. In the United States, Mondex is owned by seven major financial institutions[5] that license other financial service firms to issue cards and recruit merchants.

[4] Visa Cash Cards

Visa Cash is a chip-based, prepaid stored value card that also functions as a substitute for cash. Visa Cash cards are issued by financial institutions that are members of the Visa system. Visa Cash cards are reloadable and do not require a PIN, signature, or authorization for use.

---

[5] These are AT&T Universal Card Services, Chase Manhattan, First Chicago/NBD, MasterCard, Michigan National Bank, NOVUS, and Wells Fargo as of 1997.

Each issuer is obligated to settle for transactions involving the cards it issues.

Visa Cash was first introduced in the United States at the 1996 Summer Olympic Games by First Union, Wachovia, and NationsBank. As of February 1997, approximately 3.7 million Visa Cash cards had been issued and approximately 1.9 million Visa Cash transactions had been completed worth approximately $8.5 million.[6]

[5] Visa TravelMoney

Visa TravelMoney is a disposable, replaceable, prepaid stored value card with PIN protection that a traveling cardholder may use to withdraw local currency from 250,000 Visa ATMs worldwide.

[6] Citibank Electronic Money System

Citibank has designed an Electronic Money System or "EMS" to provide secure, real-time transactions over any network using the Internet. EMS reportedly provides an audit trail that can track transactions but maintain the anonymity of the parties.[7]

§ 6.03 GOVERNMENT REGULATION OF E-MONEY

Electronic money by its nature is a prime candidate for government regulation. It raises a host of policy and consumer protection issues that are likely to ultimately require government intervention. As noted below, however, the United States government has avoided taking steps to regulate electronic money during the developmental phase, in contrast to European governments.

[A] U.S. Government Policy

The need for regulation of electronic money by the federal government was addressed by the Consumer Electronic Payments Task Force in a 1998 report.[8] Created by the Secretary of the Treasury in 1996, the Task Force was chaired by the Comptroller of the Currency and included agency heads from the Federal Reserve Board ("Federal Reserve" or

[6] Hearing by the Consumer Electronic Payments Task Force (June 9, 1997) (Testimony by Visa U.S.A. Inc. and Visa International).

[7] GAO Report, *supra*, at 149.

[8] The Report of the Consumer Electronic Payments Task Force (April 1998).

"Board"), Federal Deposit Insurance Corporation ("FDIC"), Federal Trade Commission ("FTC"), and Office of Thrift Supervision ("OTS").

The Task Force addressed the need for regulation primarily on consumer issues such as privacy, financial soundness of issuers, transparency of legal rules, and access to electronic money. Based on the perception that the e-money industry in the United States is at a stage of development and "not now a significant factor in our economy or payments system," the Task Force concluded that government regulation is neither necessary nor appropriate at present:

> The Task force also has recognized the particular risks of governmental regulation of a market at this stage of development. In light of our limited current knowledge about the nature of the market participants, the ways in which e-money products and systems will relate to their other businesses, the e-money products that will be developed and become successful, the manner in which consumers will use these products and value various features, and the extent and adequacy of self-regulatory efforts that may be undertaken on an industry-wide or firm-by-firm basis, comprehensive new regulation of e-money and/or its issuers could be counterproductive at this time. Such efforts, while premised on the best of intentions, could result in an inefficient scheme of rules with little relevance to the market that actually develops. Moreover, regulation at this stage risks quashing competition and innovation that could produce more effective operational rules. At worst, regulation could retard the development of a promising new industry that could introduce efficiencies to the nation's retail payments system. The Task Force also notes that regulation based on inadequate understanding of the relevant factors could increase the cost of new products unnecessarily. Such cost increases would impede access to these new products and systems.

Instead of government intervention, the Task Force recommended that those involved in the development of e-money undertake meaningful and effective self-regulation through policies and procedures addressing specific, identifiable areas of consumer concern, noting that the early stage of development is "especially well-suited for the flexibility of self-regulatory approaches."

The Task Force recommended that government action be limited to encouraging meaningful industry self-regulatory efforts, providing consumer financial education to help consumers become better educated and empowered to utilize electronic money products, and monitoring the development of e-money in the marketplace. Federal Reserve Chairman Greenspan has reiterated this view:

> The Federal Reserve also clearly recognizes the need to foster innovation in the private sector and to help remove barriers to the development and adoption of new payment services for electronic and traditional commerce. As I have often said, to continue to be effective, government's regulatory role must increasingly be focused on assuring that adequate risk management systems are in place in the private sector. As financial systems have become more complex, detailed rules and standards have become both more burdensome and less effective. If we wish to foster financial innovation, we must first be careful not to impose rules that inhibit it, and we must be especially watchful that we not unduly impede our increasingly broad electronic payments system.
>
> Thus, the private sector needs to play the pivotal role in determining what payment services consumers and businesses actually demand and in supplying those services. In a period of change and uncertainty there may be a temptation, and a desire by some market participants, to have the government step in and resolve the uncertainty, whether through standards, regulation, or other policies. In the case of electronic payment innovations, only consumers and merchants will ultimately determine what new products are successful in the marketplace. Government action can retard progress, but almost certainly cannot ensure it.
>
> One important role government can play, however, is to help identify and, where appropriate, help remove barriers to innovation.[8.1]

[B] Regulatory Policy Issues

E-money raises a host of policy issues that ultimately may need to be addressed by the government if it becomes a major factor in the financial system. The issuance and transfer of electronic money by regulated and unregulated entities has potentially broad implications for the integrity of the payments system, monetary policy, and the competitive balance within the financial system, as well as consumer protection. As e-money becomes more prevalent, these policy issues could result in government regulatory initiatives.

[8.1] Remarks by Chairman Alan Greenspan before the National Automated Clearinghouse Association Annual Meeting, Apr. 10, 2000.

[1] Should E-Cash Be Regulated Like Money?

The value in a stored value card or electronic money system, unlike cash, does not have status as legal tender because a counterparty has no legal obligation to accept it in payment for debts.[9] It is not legal currency because it is not backed by the full faith and credit of the United States. While electronic money thus technically is not legal "money," the question nevertheless arises as to whether it should be regulated like money and whether the issuers of electronic money should be regulated like banks.[10]

A key issue is whether the issuance of e-money is the equivalent of deposit-taking and whether e-money should be treated as a deposit for a variety of regulatory purposes. For example, under existing law, deposits and checking accounts are subject to regulations imposing disclosure requirements as to rates and rate computation,[11] limitations on brokered deposits,[12] reserve requirements,[13] requirements as to when deposited funds must be available for withdrawal,[14] and a prohibition on the payment of interest on corporate checking accounts.[15] Because e-money has not been deemed to be a "deposit," it is not subject to these regulations. If e-money becomes widespread, however, questions likely will arise as to whether

[*Next page is 6-11.*]

---

[9] Only United States coins and currency, including Federal Reserve notes, are legal tender by law and thus must be accepted by creditors for the discharge debts. 31 U.S.C. § 5103.

[10] For an excellent discussion of the legal status of electronic money, *See* ABA Task Force on Stored-Value Cards, "A Commercial Lawyer's Take on the Electronic Purse: An Analysis of Commercial Law Issues Associated with Stored-Value Cards and Electronic Money," 52 Bus. Law. 653 (1997); Henry H. Perritt, Jr., "Legal and Technological Infrastructures for Electronic Payment Systems," 22 Rutgers Computer & Tech. L.J. 1 (1996); David G. Oedel, "Why Regulate Cybermoney?," 46 Am. U. L. Rev. 1075 (1997).

[11] Truth-in-Savings Act regulations, 12 C.F.R. Part 230.

[12] 12 U.S.C. § 337.6.

[13] 12 C.F.R. Part 204.

[14] 12 C.F.R. Part 229.

[15] 12 C.F.R. Part 217.

it should be subjected to equivalent regulation as a matter of competitive equity and to fulfill the policies underlying these regulations. Questions also will likely be raised as to whether e-money should be eligible for deposit insurance coverage, an issue discussed below.

It is arguably within the existing regulatory authority of the federal banking regulators to find that e-money is a form of deposit and should be regulated as such. Such a determination likely would be taken only after a rulemaking proceeding by the federal banking regulators, however, with an opportunity for interested parties to comment. As noted above, federal regulators thus far have shown a disinclination to regulate.

[2] Who May Issue Electronic Money?

The issuance of stored value cards and other forms of e-money by nonbank entities outside the banking system raises the issue of whether the issuers and operators of these new payments systems are engaging in the business of banking without proper authorization and regulation.

As a legal matter, most states require an entity to be chartered and regulated as a bank in order to engage in the business of banking. In addition, it is unlawful under Section 21(a)(2) of the Glass-Steagall Act for any person or entity to engage in the business of receiving deposits without being regulated like a bank.[16]

It is not clear, however, that an entity that issues electronic money necessarily is required to have a bank charter under current state laws or the Glass-Steagall Act. Nonbank entities that issue retail deposit-like payment instruments, such as money orders and travelers' checks, and other money transmitters generally are not required to be chartered as banks, although they are subject to supervision and examination under state law.[17] Similarly, issuers of credit or debit cards, which many cardholders use to conduct retail transactions in place of checks or cash, are not deemed to be engaged in the business of banking for purposes of state law or the Glass-Steagall Act. Nor are securities firms that issue cash management accounts with check writing capability.

---

[16] 12 U.S.C. § 378(a)(2).

[17] Forty-three states license and regulate the business of check selling and money wires by nonbank entities. *See* Ezra C. Levine and Rosemary H. McEnery, "Electronic Benefits Transfers and the Role of Non-Bank Financial Intermediaries," Electronic Banking Law and Commerce Report (July/Aug. 1997).

Neither Congress nor the federal banking regulators have found cause thus far to subject electronic money to federal banking regulation. Because many electronic money systems to date appear to have been developed by banks or entities affiliated with banks through common ownership or joint ventures, the regulators may feel they have sufficient leverage to intervene if problems arise. If nonbank issuers of e-money or smart cards were to become so prevalent as to replace cash and checking accounts as the primary form of money, however, Congress and the regulators could be expected to act to assert jurisdiction over such entities.

As noted below, the European Commission initially proposed a regulatory framework under which only banks could issue e-money but has since indicated that it will allow nonbank issuers subject to prudential supervision by bank regulatory authorities.

[3] How Should Electronic Money Be Regulated?

Assuming that electronic money and issuers thereof eventually will need to be regulated, questions will arise as to how they should be regulated. These questions may include the following:

- At what stage in the process should electronic money be treated as a liability of the issuing entity? How is liability determined?
- Does state law govern? How would state regulation affect the flow of electronic money across state lines?
- Should the originator or the servicer of electronic money, or both, be regulated?
- Should use of "float" by an e-money issuer be regulated?
- What restrictions, if any, should be imposed on the investment of assets underlying e-money?
- What laws should govern redemption and other rights and obligations of the parties?
- What disclosure requirements should apply?
- What rules should govern the confidentiality and usage of customer account information?
- What guarantee or loss-sharing requirements should be imposed on electronic money issuers? Should federal deposit coverage be available?

- Should all or only some of the banking laws apply?
- What minimum capital standards should apply?
- Should the Community Reinvestment Act be applied to e-money issuers?
- Is e-money considered part of the banking line of commerce for purposes of antitrust analysis?
- Is e-money a deposit or a security?

So far, the SEC has not indicated any interest in regulating e-money as a security. Question may be raised, however, as to whether e-money is a deposit or a security for purposes of the antifraud and other provisions of the securities laws in certain contexts.

These are only a few of the many legal and regulatory issues that likely will be raised by electronic money as it gains greater usage in the marketplace.

[C] Regulatory Approval of E-Money Systems

The federal banking regulators generally view the issuance of electronic money as an appropriate activity for banks and have permitted banks and their affiliates to participate in the development and issuance of stored value cards and other electronic money systems. In permitting national banks to acquire interests in Mondex, for example, the Office of the Comptroller of the Currency ("OCC") stated that the "Mondex stored value system involves both advanced versions of well-recognized functions of the banking business, and integration into adjacent businesses that supply the technological expertise and resources for banks to engage in a segment of the payments system in a new way."[18] Several examples of e-money proposals approved by the regulators are described below.

In 1996, the OCC permitted a national bank to invest in a limited liability company ("LLC") that would develop, market, deliver, and maintain stored value and information systems for universities, hospitals, business centers, theme parks, military installations, and other self-contained

[18] OCC Conditional Approval No. 220 (Dec. 2, 1996).

geographic locations.[19] The activity approved by the OCC involved providing collection, processing, and recordkeeping services for stored value transactions, including loading of stored value on the cards. The LLC itself did not propose to hold the stored value funds or be the stored value obligor. These functions would be performed by a third-party bank or other entity agreed upon by the LLC and the customer and that entity would be responsible for the stored value. The LLC proposed to sell the cards to a system customer, which would distribute the cards to cardholders, and would not itself have any direct contractual relationship with the cardholder. Two kinds of cards were proposed to be offered: a card that could be loaded only by cash inserted at a cash revalue station or kiosk, and a card that could be loaded either by that method or by electronic funds transfer from an account at the bank. Either method would involve on-line communication with the LLC for purposes of authentication and loading of stored value. The LLC would be responsible for collecting cash from machines and forwarding appropriate amounts of funds to the bank or other stored value issuer. The LLC also would provide support services for merchants accepting the cards for stored value purchase transactions, including honoring cards and providing processing and settlement services for participating merchants.

The OCC also approved a pilot program at a college under which the bank would be the holder of funds and obligor on the stored value.[20] Under the pilot program, the stored card would serve as an identification card, building access control, library card, computer network access card, and meal plan card. The LLC's function in the pilot program would be to replace the card readers on existing systems with stored value card readers and program the new card readers.

The Federal Reserve Board has permitted bank holding companies to offer both open and closed stored value card systems and has approved flexible applications of stored value card technology.[21] For example, the Board authorized 15 bank holding companies to engage in a joint venture that, among other things, would operate a worldwide retail electronic funds transfer and automated teller machine ("ATM") network that could

---

[19] OCC Interpretive Letter No. 737 (Aug. 19, 1996). *See also* OCC Interpretive Letter No. 855 (Mar. 1, 1999).

[20] *Id.*

[21] *See, e.g., Banc One Corp., et al.*, 79 Fed. Res. Bull. 1158 (1993).

be assessed with stored value cards.[22] Customers could use their ATM cards at ATM terminals to withdraw funds from a bank account in the form of travelers checks or stage stamps with payment effected by a direct debit to the cardholder's depository account.

[D] FDIC Insurance

An important issue affecting consumer confidence in electronic money systems is whether and under what circumstances the value in e-cash or stored value cards is eligible for federal deposit insurance under the Federal Deposit Insurance Act.

In Federal Deposit Insurance Corporation ("FDIC") General Counsel's Opinion No. 8, the FDIC discussed the different types of stored value systems and addressed which ones involve "deposits" eligible for insurance.[23] Under the Opinion, most do not.

In order for funds in a stored value card system to be considered insurable "deposits," Opinion No. 8 states that the funds must represent an unpaid balance of money or its equivalent, received or held by a bank in the usual course of business, and either the bank must have given or be obligated to give credit to a commercial, checking, savings, time, or thrift account, or the funds must be held for a special or specific purpose. In addition, funds in a stored value system must constitute "hard earnings" and not represent merely a contingent liability to redeem electronic value. Most stored value cards would not be protected by deposit insurance under the opinion because the issuing institution typically maintains a single pooled account to hold the funds represented by all of their customers' stored value cards.

For purposes of analyzing this issue, the FDIC's general counsel categorized stored value systems into the following categories and concluded as follows:

> *Bank Primary—Customer Account Systems*
>
> In these systems, the funds underlying the stored value card remain in a customer's account until the value is transferred to a

[22] *The Bank of New York Co., et al.*, 80 Fed. Res. Bull. 1107 (1994). *See also Barnett Banks, Inc., et al.*, 83 Fed. Res. Bull. 131 (1997).

[23] 61 Fed. Reg. 40,490 (1996).

merchant or other third party, who in turn collects the funds from the customer's bank.[24]

The FDIC's general counsel concluded that funds in these systems are deposits because the funds are held by an institution, in the usual course of business, and remain credited to the customer's account until the payee makes a claim on the funds.

Bank Primary—Reserve Systems

In these systems, as value is downloaded onto a card, funds are withdrawn from a customer's account or paid directly by the customer and paid into a reserve or general liability account held at the institution to pay merchants and other payees as they make claims for payment.

The FDIC's general counsel concluded that funds in these systems are not deposits because the funds are not credited to or obligated to be credited to a commercial, checking, time, or thrift account, and are not held for a special or specific purpose.

Bank Secondary Systems

In these systems, the electronic value is created by a third party and the funds underlying the electronic value are ultimately held by the third party. Banks act as intermediaries in collecting funds from customers in exchange for electronic value. In these systems, the bank may have a contingent liability to redeem the electronic value from consumers and merchants. As such electronic value is redeemed, the bank exchanges the value for funds with the third party.

In some bank secondary systems, referred to in the general counsel's opinion as "bank secondary advance systems," the electronic value may be provided to the bank to have available for its customers. As customers exchange funds for electronic value, the funds are held for a short period of time and then forwarded to the third party. The FDIC's general counsel concluded that funds in these systems are not the customer's deposits because the deposit liability is owed by the bank to the third party for whom the institution is temporarily holding the funds. The funds thus would be deposits of the third party rather than the customer.

In other bank secondary systems, referred to as "bank secondary pre-acquisition systems," the bank will exchange its own funds for electronic value from the third party and in turn exchange electronic value for funds with its customers. The FDIC's general coun-

---

[24] The FDIC stated that it was unaware of any such systems under development.

> sel concluded that funds in these systems are not deposits because the funds are received or held by the third party, not the depository institution.

The general counsel also concluded that the funds held in a stored value system are not trust funds, cashier's checks, money orders, drafts drawn on the bank, or negotiable instruments.

The FDIC has authority to determine by regulation that an obligation of a depository institution is a deposit "by general usage."[25] In 1996, the FDIC requested public comment on whether it should exercise this authority to find that some or all of the stored value systems and other electronic banking systems give rise to a deposit liability.[26] The FDIC stated that, if stored value cards become a significant element of the money and payments system in the United States, "it may be that the FDIC should determine that public confidence in these payment systems is critical to the safety and soundness of the banking system, such that deposit insurance is warranted." The FDIC invited public comment on the following policy issues:

- Should the FDIC treat funds underlying store value card systems like funds held by a bank to meet letters of credit, which are treated as deposits?
- Should the FDIC treat stored value funds like money orders and cashiers' checks drawn on a bank, which are treated as deposits?
- What are the expectations of consumers with respect to whether stored value cards are insured products? To what extent should consumer expectations be a factor in determining whether stored value cards involve deposits?
- Should the FDIC distinguish between reloadable and disposable stored value cards or between single function and multiple function cards?
- Should the projected low dollar denominations for stored value cards be considered?

---

[25] 12 U.S.C. § 1813(l)(5). The FDIC must first consult with the OCC, OTS, and Federal Reserve Board.

[26] 61 Fed. Reg. 40,494 (1996).

- What types of disclosure should the FDIC require with respect to the insured or non-insured status of stored value cards?
- To what extent would banks be placed at a competitive advantage or disadvantage with respect to other issuers of stored value products if the FDIC were to find these products to involve deposits?
- Should the FDIC ask Congress to amend the FDI Act to either include or exempt stored value cards from the definition of deposit?
- What safety and soundness concerns are raised by the development of stored value cards and other electronic payment systems?

In June 1997, the FDIC announced that it had decided not to exercise its authority to find that stored value cards in general are deposits and stated that General Counsel's Opinion No. 8 would continue to govern. The FDIC stated that it expected insured depository institutions to "clearly and conspicuously" disclose to customers the insured or noninsured status of stored value card they offer.

[E] Applicability of Regulation E

In 1996, the Federal Reserve Board proposed amendments to Regulation E that would have largely exempted stored value cards from coverage under the regulation to the extent they operate as a substitute for cash.[27] Congress ordered the Board not to adopt the amendments and instead to report to Congress on the implications of government regulation.[28]

In its report, the Board indicated that government regulation could be premature and that non-regulatory approaches, such as consumer education and industry guidelines, might be more appropriate at the present time.[29]

---

[27] 61 Fed. Reg. 37,229 (1996).

[28] Economic Growth and Regulatory Paperwork Reduction Act, Pub. L. No. 104-208, 110 Stat. 3009.

[29] Federal Reserve Board, *Report to the Congress on the Application of the Electronic Fund Transfer Act to Electronic Stored-Value Products* (Mar. 1997).

[F] European Regulatory Framework

The European Commission in its 1997 "European Initiative in Electronic Commerce" ordered the development of a supervisory framework governing the issuance of electronic money. Among the stated objectives for the framework were to enhance consumer confidence in electronic payment instruments by providing clear information, allocating liabilities fairly between issuers of such instruments and holders, and providing simple and effective dispute resolution procedures.

In accordance with the 1997 European Initiative, the European Central Bank in 1998 proposed a framework for electronic money comprised of the following seven elements:[30]

(1) **Prudential Supervision.** Issuers of electronic money must be subject to prudential supervision.

(2) **Solid and Transparent Legal Arrangements.** The rights and obligations on the part of the respective participants (customers, merchants, issuers and operators) in an electronic money scheme must be clearly defined and disclosed. Such rights and obligations must be enforceable under all relevant jurisdictions.

(3) **Technical Security.** Electronic money schemes must maintain adequate technical, organizational and procedural safeguards to prevent, contain and detect threats to the security of this scheme, particularly the threat of counterfeits.

(4) **Protection Against Criminal Abuse.** Protection against criminal abuse, such as money laundering, must be taken into account when designing and implementing electronic money schemes.

(5) **Monetary Statistics Reporting.** Electronic money schemes must supply the central bank in each relevant country with whatever information may be required for the purposes of monetary policy.

(6) **Redeemability.** Issuers of electronic money must be legally obliged to redeem electronic money against central bank money at par at the request of the holder of the electronic money.

[30] European Central Bank, *Report on Electronic Money* (Aug. 1998).

(7) **Reserve Requirements.** The possibility must exist for central banks to impose reserve requirements on all issuers of electronic money.

In contrast to an earlier 1994 proposal that would have allowed the issuance of stored value cards only by deposit-taking banking institutions,[31] the European framework would permit nonbank entities to issue electronic money subject to reserve requirements and prudential supervision by banking regulators.

[G] Uniform Money Services Act

The National Conference of Commissioners of Uniform State Laws in 2000 approved for adoption by the states the Uniform Money Services Act. The Act provides a framework for safety and soundness regulation of entities other than banks that engage in money transmission and prohibits a person from engaging in money transmission without obtaining a license from the relevant state.

The term "money transmission" is defined in the Act to mean:

> To engage in the business of selling or issuing payment instruments, selling or issuing stored value, or receiving money or monetary value for transmission to a location within or outside the United States. The term does not include the provision of package delivery services, online services, network access, and telecommunications services, unless the provider receives compensation for the transmission of money, payment instruments, or stored value that is different from the compensation received for other transmissions.

The term "payment instrument" means a "check, draft, money order, traveler's check, or other instrument for the transmission or payment of money or monetary value, whether or not negotiable" but does not include a credit card voucher, letter of credit, or instrument that is redeemable by the issuer in goods or services.[32]

---

[31] Report to the EMI Council on Prepaid Cards (May 1994).

[32] *See* Chapter 4, **The Regulatory Framework,** § 4.03, for a more detailed decision of the Uniform Money Services Act..

§ 6.04 OTHER POLICY ISSUES

[A] Access to Electronic Money

Electronic money is expected to benefit low- and moderate-income individuals by increasing the availability, convenience, and security of transaction services. Concerns have been raised, however, as to whether low-income and uneducated individuals will share in the benefits of electronic money to the extent they lack access to and familiarity with ATMs, personal computers, and other electronic money access devices.

The implementation of electronic federal benefits transfer payments, which became mandatory in 1999, is expected to address many of these concerns by ensuring that every federal benefit recipient has access to a bank account.[33]

Certain types of stored value cards are readily available and in use by low- and moderate-income persons. The National Community Reinvestment Coalition has pointed out that most of the marketing of stored value cards has been to low- and moderate-income consumers in the form of mass transit cards and benefit entitlement cards.[34] The Coalition has urged that educational programs be implemented to further increase familiarity and awareness of stored value cards within low- and moderate-income communities. The Coalition also has urged increased availability of ATMs and POS terminals in low- and moderate-income business districts so that stored value cards can be used for economic commerce in those local areas.[35]

The American Association for the Advancement of Retired Persons has argued against mandating the use of stored value cards to access social security benefits because many older people lack familiarity with the cards or access to retailers that will accept payment from stored value cards.

[B] Customer Privacy

The privacy of customer information in e-money systems is a major concern due to the ease with which such information can be gathered,

---

[33] *See* Chapter 10, **Electronic Transfer of Federal Payments**.

[34] Statement of John Harshaw, Senior Vice President, National Community Reinvestment Coalition, before the Consumer Electronic Payments Task Force (June 9, 1997).

[35] *Id.*

stored, manipulated, and accessed. Customer privacy issues are addressed in Chapter 13, **Consumer Protection and Privacy**.

[C] Competitive Concerns

The involvement of major nonbank computer companies and telecommunications firms in designing home banking and electronic payment systems has caused some in the banking industry to fear that these companies will become lodged between banks and their customers and ultimately control the customer relationship. These competitive fears, along with concerns regarding the integrity of the payments system, have led bank trade associations to call for limits on payments system participation and the issuance of electronic money by nonbank institutions.

The American Bankers Association ("ABA") in 1996 issued a task force report addressing who should be permitted to issue liabilities that can be used to make third party payments and who should have direct access to Federal Reserve payments services.[36] The task force concluded that the issuance of third-party payment instruments should be limited to regulated depository institutions and that only regulated depository institutions should have direct access to Federal Reserve payments services. The report is discussed in Chapter 5, **The Payments System**.

The exclusion of nonbank institutions from the electronic payments system was addressed in a ruling by the U.S. Court of Appeals for the District of Columbia Circuit, which held that the U.S. Treasury Department must permit nonbank entities to participate in the bidding process for contracts to deliver federal benefits payments through electronic terminals.[37]

The unique role of banks in the payments system was reaffirmed by the Treasury Department in its regulation implementing the statutory requirement that all federal benefits payments be made electronically after January 1, 1999. The regulation generally requires all payment recipients to maintain an account at an insured depository institution.[38]

---

[36] American Bankers Association, "The Role of Banks in the Payments System of the Future, A Report and Recommendations of the Payments System Task Force" (Oct. 1996).

[37] *Transactive Corp. v. United States*, 91 F.3d 232 (D.C. Cir. 1996).

[38] 62 Fed. Reg. 48,714 (1997). *See* Chapter 10, **Electronic Transfer of Federal Payments**.

[D] Electronic Money Risks

An important object of prudential regulation is to minimize risk. Electronic money poses risks to both its users and issuers. The main risk to the user is the risk of default or nonredemption by the issuer due to insolvency or otherwise. This risk is a function of the financial health and stability of the issuer, quality of management, consumer confidence in the issuer, economic conditions, and the availability of insurance or some other form of guarantee of the electronic value. The risk of loss of a card containing stored value also is present, but this risk is basically the same as the risk of losing cash. Technology risk also may occur, such as inadvertent deletion of a customer's records, but this risk also exists with paper money.

Significant risks also are present from the issuer's standpoint. The OCC addressed some of these risks in a bulletin to national banks describing the potential pitfalls in the development and operation of stored value cards.[39] Among the risks cited by the OCC were transaction, strategic, reputational, compliance, credit, liquidity, interest rate, and foreign exchange risk. The OCC's bulletin did not establish any risk-management requirements but provided useful guidance to banks offering stored value cards.

The risks of electronic money may vary depending on the type of system in use. For example, a single-purpose prepaid stored value card that can be used only at specific reader terminals exposes the issuer and user to less risk than does a multi-purpose reloadable open card system where the user can access value at many reader terminals.

These and other risk factors will likely be considered in the development of any supervisory or regulatory framework governing electronic money.[40]

[E] Monetary Policy Implications

Stored value cards and other forms of electronic cash may be viewed as a type of private currency with the potential to eventually replace paper dollars and coin as the dominant currency in the United States.[41] This

---

[39] OCC Bulletin 96-48 (Sept. 10, 1996).

[40] *See also* Chapter 11, **System Security and Risk**.

[41] *See* ABA Task Force on Stored-Value Cards, "A Commercial Lawyer's Take on the Electronic Purse: An Analysis of Commercial Law Issues Associated with Stored-Value Cards and Electronic Money," 52 Bus. Law. 653 (1997).

eventuality would raise issues regarding the Federal Reserve Board's ability to conduct monetary policy by controlling the supply of money.

The Board so far has not been overly concerned about the impact of electronic money on monetary policy. In testimony before Congress, the Board's Vice Chairman stated with respect to a potential negative impact on monetary policy: "I can assure you that this is most unlikely."[42]

The Board's primary monetary policy tool is its open market operations in the government securities market that would not be affected by the issuance of electronic money. With respect to reserve requirements, a secondary monetary policy tool, the Board has noted that stored value issued by a *bank* would be deemed to be a transaction account subject to reserves. Although *nonbank* issuers of stored value cards would not be subject to reserve requirements, reserves are of only secondary importance in the conduct of monetary policy in any event. The Board already includes nonbank financial instruments such as money market mutual funds in the M1 monetary aggregate and presumably could include other financial instruments that have transaction capability, such as stored value cards.

In the event the Board's conduct of monetary policy were to be adversely affected by electronic money, the Board undoubtedly would take action under its existing powers or seek legislation to protect the efficacy of its monetary policy authority.

In contrast to the Federal Reserve, the European Central Bank believes that electronic money "is likely to have significant implications for monetary policy in the future" and, as noted above, has proposed a framework to establish rules under which electronic money can be issued.[43]

§ 6.05 OTHER ELECTRONIC PAYMENT MECHANISMS

A variety of other electronic payment mechanisms are in use on the Internet that are not electronic money *per se* but play a significant role in facilitating electronic commerce.

---

[42] *See* Testimony of Alan Blinder, Vice Chairman, Federal Reserve Board, at Hearings on "The Future of Money," before the House Subcommittee on Domestic and International Monetary Policy (Oct. 11, 1995), 1995 WL 10732104.

[43] European Central Bank, *Report on Electronic Money* (Aug. 1998).

[A] Credit Cards

The most prevalent form of "electronic" payment mechanism is the common credit card. Federal Reserve Chairman Greenspan has stated that "credit cards have rapidly become the payment instrument of choice for consumers."[44] Credit cards have gained widespread consumer acceptance not only because they are a form of consumer credit but because of the ease and convenience of using credit cards, the need to make only a single monthly payment, the receipt of a monthly statement summarizing transactions, and the consumer protections that limit liability of consumers under Regulation E.

Credit cards also can be used to transact business on the Internet and are the most prevalent form of payment in Internet transactions. Most major commercial Web sites, such as Amazon.com, have encrypted secure servers that afford a high degree of security of customer credit card information. Indeed, "the success of credit cards on the Internet leaves open the question of relevance for electronic cash schemes."[45]

As a payment mechanism, however, credit cards are an expensive alternative to pure electronic money. A merchant pays an average of 2–3 percent of the total transaction amount when it accepts a credit card as payment, a cost that ultimately finds its way back to consumers. Credit card systems also are inefficient in their operations when compared to electronic payment systems. For example, the flow of information is loosely connected and slow, there is redundancy in the value chain, and there is no properly functioning authentication system.[46]

[B] Person-to-Person Payments

Person-to-person or "P2P" payments have developed as a means of effecting transactions between individuals on the Internet. P2P services have greatly facilitated the development of electronic commerce through online auction sites such as eBay, for example.

---

[44] *Id.*

[45] "Digicash Idea Finds New Life in More Flexible eCash," Am. Banker, Apr. 6, 2000 (commenting on demise of Digicash); "Electronic Cash for the Net Fails to Catch On," The New York Times on the Web, Nov. 28, 1998.

[46] *See* Testimony of Deutsche Banc Alex. Brown on "The Future of Electronic Payments: Roadblocks and Emerging Practices," before the House Subcomm. on Domestic and International Monetary Policy (Sept. 19, 2000).

P2P payments initially were developed by nonbank institutions, such as eBay and Yahoo, to facilitate the sale of their electronic products and services. Whether to foster customer confidence or to avoid questions as to whether the institution should be subjected to banking regulation or to tap into bank payments processing expertise and financial resources, many online services providers have teamed up with banking organizations to offer P2P services. For example, eBay's payment subsidiary, Billpoint, entered into an alliance with Wells Fargo & Company in 2000 under which Wells Fargo initially acquired a 35 percent equity interest in Billpoint and entered into a long-term payment processing and "customer care" contract with Billpoint.[47]

Yahoo entered into an arrangement with Canadian Imperial Bank of Commerce ("CIBC") by which CIBC will provide banking and funds transfer services in connection with Yahoo's PayDirect service. Citigroup has a P2P arrangement with America Online called "AOL Quick Cash" and Bank of America has a P2P arrangement with Checkfree.

Several P2P formats are available in the marketplace. The most widely used format is credit-card based. Ebay has entered into a marketing agreement with Visa, for example, through which eBay sellers can securely accept Visa payments within minutes of enrollment. PayDirect offers a "Move Money" feature that allows an individual to move money into a PayDirect account from a credit card and then e-mail money to anyone with an e-mail address. PayDirect also features a "Request Money" service allowing an individual to request money that is owed and a "Group Billing" service allowing an individual to simultaneously request payments from a group of persons, such as dues payments from club members or ticket payments for an event.

ProPay is another P2P service by which a customer can set up a free account and choose from a variety of methods to accept or send payments. In the online payment method, a seller will send information to ProPay on the product to be sold. ProPay e-mails the buyer a form to enter his or her credit card number and the seller never sees the number. ProPay takes 3.5 percent of the total sale in addition to charging a processing fee of 35 cents. ProPay also provides ProPay accounts by which transacting parties can transfer money to each other and also will send funds to any bank.

---

[47] *See* Billpoint Press Release dated Mar. 1, 2000.

PayPal offers a P2P service whereby individual buyers and sellers can pay or receive payment using mobile phones or hand held devices.

Banks are also developing their own P2P services without using credit cards. Citigroup in 2000 launched its "c2it" service by which an individual may register at a Web site and e-mail money to another person. The sender merely types in the e-mail address of the person to whom funds are to be sent, indicates the amount to be sent, chooses the account from which the funds are to be debited, and clicks "send cash." The recipient is then asked by e-mail to select an account in which to deposit the money. Neither party needs to be a customer of Citibank. Bank One's WingspanBank.com has introduced a similar service called "eMoneyMail" which it plans to market through Internet service providers such as AOL and Lycos.[48]

Depending on how they are structured (and it often is difficult to tell), P2P services may raise issues as to whether and when the customer's money is protected by FDIC insurance if a bank is involved and whether the Regulation E limits on credit card liability apply at various stages of the service. If a nonbank entity is involved in holding funds en route, that entity may be deemed to be a "bank" or a "money transmitter" subject to banking or other regulation.

[C] Electronic Checks

Payment by electronic check is another type of payment service. Electronic checks are an available form of payment on eBay, for example. An eBay seller presents an electronic invoice to the winning bidder who in turn enters his checking account information which is transmitted to Billpoint. Billpoint transmits the information to Wells Fargo which then presents the transaction to the buyer's bank for settlement. After three business days, Billpoint will send an e-mail confirmation of the transaction, assuming the payment clears, and will deposit funds to the seller's bank account. Billpoint states that it "guarantees" transactions once they have cleared.

[D] Business-to-Business Payments

Business-to-business or "B2B" payments are another new form of payment mechanism enabling commercial enterprises to transact business online. The FTC described B2B services as follows:

---

[48] *See* "More Players (Now Citi) and Questions for P-to-P," Am. Banker Nov. 1, 2000.

> B2B electronic marketplaces are software systems that allow buyers and sellers of similar goods to carry out procurement activities using common, industry-wide computer systems. . . . One possible model allows firms to place purchase orders using a joint, industry-wide computer system, with competitors potentially able to aggregate their orders.
>
> B2B electronic marketplaces may create significant efficiencies. For example, the marketplaces could reduce transaction costs; generate volume-related scale economies by combining orders from multiple purchasers; improve inventory management; and facilitate bidding by a broad spectrum of potential suppliers.[49]

The Federal Trade Commission has expressed concern about the antitrust implications of B2B services and in 2000 released a report on the competitive implications of B2B electronic marketplaces based on a workshop held with designers, owners and B2B operators and users.[50]

[49] 65 Fed. Reg. 30,120, 30,121 (2000).

[50] Federal Trade Commission, "Entering the 21st Century: Competition Policy in the World of B2B Electronic Marketplaces," Oct. 2000. *See* Chapter 15, **Antitrust,** for a further discussion of the antitrust implications of B2B electronic marketplaces.

CHAPTER 7

AUTOMATED BANKING FACILITIES

§7.01 ATMs

Automated teller machines ("ATMs") were the first retail electronic payment devices to be used widely in the banking industry.[1] As of February 1997, approximately 119,000 ATMs were in use by 8600 banks, representing 75 percent of all banks in the United States.[2]

ATMs perform many of the tasks performed by bank tellers, including enabling customers to make withdrawals or transfers from their accounts, make loan and credit card payments, access lines of credit, and conduct other transactions. Among the advantages of ATMs is the enormous reduction in transaction costs derived from the use of automated technology. An ATM transaction costs about $0.25 whereas the same transaction would cost over $1.00 when conducted by a teller at a bricks and mortar facility.

Although ATMs have not played a major role in electronic commerce thus far, ATM debit cards are viewed as potentially the "perfect payment instruments for the Internet" and the "ultimate payment solution."[2.1]

To access an ATM, a customer must insert a magnetically coded card into the ATM terminal, enter his or her personal identification number or "PIN" and select the type and amount of transaction to be conducted. The ATM sends this information to a central processor that identifies the customer's bank, verifies the PIN number and the amount of the transaction, and transmits a message to the ATM either approving or denying the transaction. The transaction is posted to the customer's account and reflected in the monthly statement of account.

As noted below, many banks participate in ATM networks, allowing customers to access their bank accounts through shared ATMs at a wider range of locations than would be possible for a single bank to maintain.

At one time, ATMs were considered to be branches of banks subject to the prohibitions on branching under the National Bank Act and state law.[3] In 1996, Congress expressly excluded ATMs from the definition of

---

[1] For a history of ATMs, *see* Baker & Brandel, The Law of Electronic Funds Transfer System (Rev. Ed. 1996), § 6.04.

[2] General Accounting Office, Automated Teller Machines, GAO/GGD-97-90 (May 1997), at 2.

[2.1] *See* "ATM Networks Envision Role as Internet Players," Am. Banker (Sept. 20, 1999).

[3] *See Independent Bankers Ass'n of America v. Smith*, 534 F.2d 921 (D.C. Cir.), *cert. denied*, 429 U.S. 862 (1976).

"branch" in the National Bank Act.[4] National banks thus may establish ATMs without geographic restriction under federal or state law.[5]

§7.02 OTHER AUTOMATED FACILITIES

[A] Automated Loan Machines

An automated loan machine ("ALM") is a remote service unit that enables a consumer to apply for and receive a loan from a bank. Normally, ALM loans are small, ranging from $500 to $7,500. An ALM is considered to be an "ATM" or "remote service unit" for purposes of federal law and thus is exempt from treatment as a "branch" and may be operated by a national bank without geographic restriction.[6]

[B] Automated Financial Receiving Stations

An automated financial receiving station ("AFRS") is an automated, unstaffed facility that enables customers to physically deposit cash or checks into a customer's account at a bank using a coded card to record the transaction. An AFRS also is considered to be an "ATM" and not a branch and may be operated by a national bank without geographic restriction.[7]

§7.03 ATM NETWORKS

An ATM or EFT ("electronic funds transfer") network is an arrangement in which the ATMs of two or more depository institutions are connected by electronic or telecommunications means to one or more computers, processors, or switches for the purpose of providing ATM services to retail customers.

Early ATM networks typically were used for dispensing cash and were located in branches in local banking markets. ATM networks have consolidated in recent years in order to achieve "economies of ubiquity" and opportunities for technology research and development associated with large networks.

---

[4] Pub. L. No. 104-208, § 2205 (*codified at* 12 U.S.C. § 36(j)).

[5] *See* OCC Interpretive Letter No. 772 (Mar. 6, 1997).

[6] OCC Interpretive Letter No. 772 (Mar. 6, 1997); FDIC Letter dated July 8, 1997, from Robert C. Fick, Counsel, to Ross S. Delston. *See* Ross S. Delston, "Automated Loan Machines and Automated Teller Machines: How to Expand Geographically Without Really Branching," Electronic Banking Law and Commerce Report (Oct. 1997).

[7] *See* OCC Interpretive Letter No. 838 (April 15, 1998).

ATM networks raise competitive issues under the antitrust laws due to their collaborative nature.[8]

[*Next page is 7-5.*]

[8] *See* Chapter 15, **Antitrust Implications.** *See also* David Balto, "The Murky World of Network Mergers: Searching for Opportunities for Network Competition," Antitrust Bull. 79 (Winter 1997); Baker & Brandel, ch. 24; Congressional Budget Office,

The Office of the Comptroller of the Currency ("OCC") and Federal Reserve Board ("Federal Reserve" or "Board") have approved numerous proposals by banks and bank holding companies to form and/or participate in EFT networks. The Board has noted that networks enable smaller financial institutions to provide their customers with greater access to their deposit accounts and thereby compete for retail deposits against larger, multi-state organizations without the need to make a substantial economic investment in a proprietary ATM network. The public benefits of such networks include economies of scale and reduced costs, a portion of which the Board has stated it expects to be passed on to member financial institutions and consumers in the form of lower fees.[9] The Board has cited procompetitive network rules that allow all depository institutions to participate in a network on a nondiscriminatory basis and to join other regional networks.[10]

The Board in 1986 authorized Citicorp to acquire Northeast Exchange Ltd. and thereby engage in the installation of and provision of support services to ATMs in retail stores, and to engage in the ownership, construction, and management of an EFT switch that transmitted transactions performed on the ATMs to ATM networks and financial institutions.[11] In determining that the proposal would not result in unfair competitive practices or other adverse effects, the Board specifically relied on the fact that depository institutions would have nondiscriminatory access to membership in the ATM network operated by Citicorp and that the network would not use the "Citi" prefix or logo.

The OCC similarly has permitted national banks to participate in EFT networks and to own stock interests in companies that operate EFT networks.[12] The OCC stated that:

> the transfer of funds from one account to another, or from one financial institution to another, is a fundamental part of the basic business of banking and, as such, is clearly a permissible activity for national

---

"Competition in ATM Markets: Are ATMs Money Machines?," Report to the Senate Committee on Banking, Housing and Urban Affairs (July 1998).

[9] *See Barnett Banks, Inc.*, 83 Fed. Res. Bull. 131, 134 (1997).

[10] *Id.* at 132.

[11] *Citicorp (Northeast Exchange)*, 72 Fed. Res. Bull. 583 (1986).

[12] *See, e.g.*, OCC Interpretive Letter No. 289 (May 15, 1984); unnumbered OCC Interpretive Letter dated November 9, 1992, 1992 WL 486340 (OCC).

banks. Moreover, the use of an electronic device or an EFT network to effect a transmittal of funds does not change the nature of the underlying services or functions performed.[13]

§ 7.04 NETWORK INTERCHANGE SERVICES

The banking regulators have permitted banks and their affiliates to provide network interchange services in connection with ATM/EFT networks.

For example, the Board in 1984 approved a joint venture among bank holding companies that proposed to operate an EFT system for the interchange of financial transactions of depository institutions among different EFT networks—a type of network of networks.[14] Each of the bank holding companies operated proprietary ATM networks and some belonged to shared ATM networks that would interface with the joint venture EFT switch. As described in the Board's order, the system would operate as a neutral clearing house for electronic funds transfer, payment, and withdrawal transactions at ATMs operated by any participating institutions, and would enable customers of participating institutions to complete such EFT transactions at ATMs operated by any member of the system. The system would provide POS (point of sale) services involving the transfer of funds from the checking, savings, or credit card account of a participating institution's customer to a merchant's account at POS terminals owned and operated by the merchants.

In approving the joint venture, the Board relied on the fact that the co-venturers and all other participating institutions were free to join other switching networks and that all depository institutions would have equal access to membership in the switch.[15]

---

[13] *Id.*

[14] *Barclays Bank PLC and Barclays Bank International Limited, et al.*, 70 Fed. Res. Bull. 113 (1984). This joint venture involved Barclays, Chemical New York Corporation, National Westminster Bank PLC, Northeast Bancorp, Manufacturers Hanover Corporation, The Bank of New York Company, and Marine Midland Banks, Inc., among others.

[15] The Board has approved other similar EFT switch systems operated by bank holding companies in joint ventures subject to similar conditions. *See, e.g., First National Cincinnati Corporation, et al.*, 70 Fed. Res. Bull. 889 (1984); *First City Bancorp*, 70 Fed. Res. Bull. 735 (1984); *CB&T Bancshares, Inc., et al.*, 70 Fed. Res. Bull. 589 (1984).

§ 7.05 MERGERS OF ATM NETWORKS

Several major mergers of EFT networks have occurred in recent years, raising issues under the antitrust laws.[16] Two such mergers are discussed below.

[A] MAC Network

In 1995, the Federal Reserve Board authorized Banc One Corporation, CoreStates Financial Corp, PNC Bank Corp., and KeyCorp, to acquire certain data processing assets of National City Corporation through an existing joint venture, Electronic Payment Services, Inc. ("EPS"), which National City would join.[17] EPS provided data processing and transmission services to banks and retail merchants who were members of EPS's branded ATM and POS network ("MAC"). EPS was engaged in developing and providing a variety of electronic payment, benefit transfer, and data interchange services.

The transaction was protested on antitrust grounds by a competing EFT network, Money Station, and several banking organizations that operated in Ohio and adjacent states. The protestants alleged that consummation of the proposal would result in significant anticompetitive effects in the market for ATM services in the Ohio-Kentucky-Pennsylvania region.

The Antitrust Division of the Department of Justice earlier had issued a consent decree attacking the network's rules that had required smaller banks to have their ATMs driven by the network switch and exclusively routed through the network.[18]

In analyzing the competitive effects of the proposal, the Board identified three distinct services as constituting the relevant product markets:

- Network access (access to an ATM network identified by a common trademark or logo displayed on ATMs and ATM cards);

---

[16] *See* Chapter 15, **Antitrust Implications,** for a discussion of antitrust issues. *See also* Balto, *supra* note 8 *and* Donald Baker, "The Regulation of ATM Networks—Competition and Public Policy Considerations," Electronic Banking Law and Commerce Report (Oct. 1997).

[17] *Banc One Corporation, et al.*, 81 Fed. Res. Bull. 492 (1995).

[18] *United States v. Electronic Payment Services, Inc.*, 1994-2 Trade Cas. (CCH) ¶ 70,796 (D. Del. 1994) (consent decree); Proposed Final Judgment and Response of United States, 59 Fed. Reg. 44,757 (1994).

- Network services (the switching functions for the network); and
- ATM processing (the data processing and telecommunications facilities used to operate, monitor, and support a bank's ATMs).

With respect to the relevant geographic market, the Board concluded that the appropriate geographic market area for MAC's product lines was a region composed of several states, and that MAC had a competitively significant presence in the New England, Middle Atlantic, and Mideast regions. The Board did not find anticompetitive effects in either the relevant product or geographic markets.

Regarding the potential for undue concentration of resources, the Board noted that the BHC Act reflects Congress' concern that the combination of large banking and nonbanking organizations might be contrary to the public interest. The Board determined that the proposed transaction did not involve the combination of a large banking organization with a large nonbanking business or the merger of large regionally shared EFT networks, but instead would result in additional equity investments in a single regional data processing and transmission joint venture already owned by banking organizations.

Moreover, the Board stated that the significant size of a regional ATM network is not, standing alone, contrary to the public interest and that "network externalities, such as the economies of ubiquity, tend to promote consolidation of regional ATM networks." As a result, the Board noted, dominant ATM networks were emerging throughout the EFT industry. The Board cited a study indicating that the 10 largest regional networks accounted for 80 percent of all regional ATM network transactions in the United States and that, as a result of economic and market structure conditions, regions were likely to have one dominant ATM network.

Accordingly, the Board denied the protestants' request for a hearing and approved the proposal. On appeal, the Board's order was initially overturned, but the court subsequently vacated its order and dismissed the case.[19]

---

[19] *Money Station, Inc. v. Board of Governors*, 81 F.3d 1128, (D.C. Cir. 1996), *reh'g en banc granted, judgment vacated by* 94 F.3d 658, 320 (D.C. Cir. 1996).

[B] Southeast Switch

In another case, the Board approved a merger of EFT networks operated by large banking organizations in the southeast United States.[20] The Board stated that, in previously considering whether similar joint ventures would result in undue concentration of resources or unfair competition, the Board viewed the economic and market structure characteristics of the EFT industry as tending to favor establishing a dominant network to serve a multistate region.

The Board found that the proposed joint venture would provide services to affiliated and unaffiliated financial institutions under operating rules that promoted open access to the network. Moreover, the joint venture would afford smaller financial institutions the opportunity to provide their customers with greater access to their deposit accounts and thereby compete for retail deposit with larger, multistate organizations funds.

The Board noted that the network's operating rules would promote competition between the network and alternative providers of EFT-related services, including national ATM and POS networks, other regional networks, and third-party providers of EFT switching and processing services, thereby encouraging price and other competition. In addition, each of the applicants would be free to continue to operate its own proprietary network and to participate in other national and regional networks while participating in the proposed consolidated network. The Board specifically noted that the network's operating rules did not set prices that a member institution must charge its retail customers for ATM or POS transactions.

Moreover, the Board found that national networks offered an attractive alternative to regional networks for some financial institutions in the Southeast Region, and the national networks appeared to be increasing their competitive pressure on regional networks. Moreover, all depository institutions would be permitted to participate in the network on a nondiscriminatory basis and would be permitted to join other regional networks

[20] 83 Fed. Res. Bull. 131 (1997). As proposed, the joint venture was to be operated Barnett Banks, Inc., Crestar Financial Corporation, First Union Corporation, NationsBank Corporation, Southern National Corporation, and Wachovia Corporation, each of which would acquire or retain control of five percent or more of the voting shares of Southeast Switch, Inc. ("SES") after its mergers with Internet, Inc., Reston, Virginia (Internet), and Alabama Network, Inc., Birmingham, Alabama (Alabama Network).

and to cobrand their cards and ATM terminals. The Board noted that national network transactions initiated at a terminal in the proposed network would not be required to be routed through the network's switch. The combined entity would allow the use of third-party processors and would permit unbranded subswitching of transactions subject only to a royalty fee established to compensate the network for the use of its brand.

With respect to public benefits, the Board noted that consumers would benefit from the added account availability and convenience resulting from an ATM network with a larger number of financial institution members. Smaller financial institutions would have the opportunity to provide their customers with greater access to their deposit accounts and to compete with larger, multistate organizations for retail deposit funds without the necessity of making substantial investments in branch systems or their own proprietary ATM networks.

The Board found that the proposal would produce economies of scale and reduce average costs for the combined network, which the Board said it expected would be passed on to member financial institutions and consumers in the form of lower fees. The Board cited as a public benefit increased research and development expenditures and noted that the broader ownership base of the proposed consolidated network should improve the probability of success for new products by increasing the number of financial institutions that would be willing to introduce these products to consumers in earlier stages of development.

§ 7.06 ATM FEES

The Congressional Budget Office ("CBO") has determined that most ATM services involve five types of fees: membership, switch and interchange fees set by the ATM network; a fee set by the card issuer; and a surcharge fee set by the ATM owner.[21] According to the CBO, an ATM owner pays a fee to join the network; card-issuing banks pay a switch fee to the network and a surcharge fee to the ATM owner for each transaction made by their cardholders; and the cardholders pay a fee to their own banks when they use an ATM owned by another bank, and sometimes pay a surcharge fee to the ATM owner as well.

---

[21] Congressional Budget Office, "Competition in ATM Markets: Are ATMs Money Machines?," Report to the Senate Committee on Banking, Housing and Urban Affairs (July 1998).

The amount of fees charged to customers for using ATMs has been a subject of intense Congressional interest. Senator D'Amato, former chairman of the Senate Banking Committee, held several hearings and commissioned a GAO study on the practice of "double-billing" of ATM fees to ATM users.[22] The GAO found that approximately one-third of banks that operated ATMs in 1997 imposed surcharges ranging from $1.00 to $3.00 on users of their ATMs who did not maintain an account at the bank.[23]

Although legislation has been introduced to limit ATM surcharge fees, Congress has not enacted any restrictions on ATM fees to date.

---

[22] *See* "The Expanding ATM Market and Increased Surcharge Fees," Hearing before the Senate Committee on Banking, Housing, and Urban Affairs, S. Hrg. 105-287 (June 11, 1997); "Analysis of the Impact of ATM Double-Charges on Consumers and Competition," Hearing before the Senate Committee on Banking, Housing, and Urban Affairs, S. Hrg. 105-206 (July 29, 1997).

[23] General Accounting Office, Automated Teller Machines, GAO/GGD-97-90 (May 1997), at 2.

CHAPTER 8

INTERNET SERVICES

§ 8.01 THE INTERNET

The "Internet" is a nonproprietary electronic communications medium based on a global system of interconnected computer networks that transmits data over telephone lines, television cable, and satellite links. Originally developed for military use, the Internet now is an "information superhighway" used by students, researchers, shoppers, and pleasure seekers to access every conceivable type of information, merchandise, and entertainment. A court has described the Internet as "a unique and wholly new medium of worldwide human communication."[1] Increasingly, the Internet has become a means of commerce through which consumers, investors, and businesses can obtain financial products and services and conduct financial transactions.

The Office of the Comptroller of the Currency ("OCC") estimated that, as of 1996, over 40 million people worldwide had access to the Internet using home PCs and, in the United States, over 12 million households subscribed to commercial online Internet access services such as America OnLine, CompuServe, and Prodigy.[2] As of 1999, it was estimated that 140 million people utilized the Internet worldwide, 77 percent of which were in the United States, including 21 percent of all American households.[3] These numbers are expected to increase dramatically in the future.

By its nature, the Internet is not a secure communication channel, raising special concerns for use of the Internet to transfer financial data and information. The Internet is not governmentally regulated, although questions have been raised as to whether it should be.[4]

§ 8.02 INTERNET BANKING

In a study released in 1999, the OCC estimated that the number of Internet banking Web sites operated by banks and thrifts grew from 103

---

[1] *ACLU v. Reno,* 929 F. Supp. 824 (E.D. Pa. 1996).

[2] OCC Interpretive Letter No. 742 (1996) (Apollo Trust Company).

[3] *See* U.S. Securities and Exchange Commission, Statement Concerning the Effect of Technology on the Capital Markets by Laura S. Unger, Commissioner, before the House Subcommittee on Capital Markets, Securities, and Government Sponsored Enterprises (Mar. 25, 1999).

[4] *See* Thorsten Wichmann, "Do We Really Need an Information Highway Patrol Governing the Internet?," E-Money, Vol. 1, No. 6 (Oct. 1998).

at the end of 1997, to 258 by June 1998.[5] As of September 1999, the OCC reported that 541 national banks had transactional Web sites.[6] These Web sites allow customers to check account balances, transfer money among accounts, and make electronic bill payments.

Although the number of banks offering transactional Internet services is less than five percent, the OCC's study indicated that the banks offering such services account for 40 percent of all banking assets. Some bank Web sites also allow customers to retrieve digitized pictures of canceled checks.[7] Some Web banks offer online safe deposit services.[8]

A recent study found that 5.9 million people were "active Web bankers" (defined as those who conduct a banking transaction online at least once a month) and that 11.1 million people were using the Internet to access their account information.[9] The study predicted that nearly 50 million people will use the Internet to do some type of banking by 2003. The U.S. Department of Commerce reported in 1999 that over 40 percent of American households own computers, one-quarter of all households have Internet access, and the number of Americans connected to the nation's information infrastructure is "soaring."[10] An OCC staff study of Internet banking in 2000 found the following:

- Only 20 percent of national banks offered Internet banking in the third quarter of 1999 but these banks accounted for almost 90 percent of total national bank assets and 84 percent of total small deposit accounts.
- All of the largest national banks offered Internet banking but only about 7 percent of smallest banks offered it. Large banks offering Internet banking offered a wider range of services on the Internet.

---

[5] OCC, "Banking Over the Internet," Q. J. (1999), *reprinted at* ⟨⟨*www.occ.treas.gov/qj/qj17-4.pdf*⟩⟩.

[6] 65 Fed. Reg. 4895 (2000).

[7] *See* "Harris Savings Providing On-Line Check Images," Am. Banker (Oct. 13, 1999).

[8] "Net.Bank to Provide On-line Safe Deposit Service," Am. Banker (Aug. 27, 1999).

[9] "Has Web Banking Peaked? Surveys Suggest Yes, and No," Am. Banker (Feb. 17, 2000); "Projections: Web Banks' Clientele Is Expected to Triple and Then Some by '04," Am. Banker (Aug. 20, 1999).

[10] U.S. Department of Commerce, "Falling Through the Net: A Report on the Telecommunications and Information Technology Gap in America" (July 1999).

- Banks offering Internet banking services relied less on interest-yielding activities and deposits than other banks.
- Banks offering Internet banking services were more profitable than other banks, unless they were established de novo in which case they were less profitable and less efficient than non-Internet-based de novo banks.
- An estimated 45 percent of all national banks are expected to offer internet banking services by early 2001.
- Almost one-half of all national banks had no plans to offer Internet banking.
- Customer use of Internet banking is concentrated among a few large banks. The five banks with the greatest number of online customers account for almost 36 percent of all Internet banking users but represent only 20 percent of small deposit accounts.[10.1]

The OCC study found that approximately 89 percent of national banks offering Internet banking services offered balance inquiry and funds transfer capability, 78 percent offered bill paying capability, 50 percent offered credit applications, 37 percent offered new account set-up, 22 percent offered brokerage services, 16 percent offered cash management services, 12 percent offered fiduciary services, 11 percent offered bill presentment, and 5 percent offered insurance products.[10.2]

The OCC announced in 2000 that 32 percent of all national banks had transactional Web sites in July 2000 compared to 21 percent in September 1999, an increase of 52 percent. Thirty-eight percent of national banks had no Web sites at all, either transactional or informational.[10.3] The OCC also noted that "customer use of transactional Web sites at national banks is growing but remains at modest levels." Only about 5 percent of national banks with transactions Web sites reported that over 25 percent of their online customers were regular users of Internet banking services

---

[10.1] Furst, Lang, and Nolle, "Internet Banking: Developments and Prospects," OCC Economic and Policy Analysis Working Paper 2000-9 (Sept. 2000) at 2. *See also* Furst, Lang, and Nolle, "Who Offers Internet Banking?" OCC Special Studies on Technology and Banking.

[10.2] *Id.* at 13.

[10.3] OCC News Release 2000-84 (Oct. 27, 2000).

and overall the majority of national banks with such sites had less than 10 percent of their online customers as regular users.

The federal banking regulators have approved a variety of forms of Internet banking, including "PC banking," "virtual banking," and Internet credit cards.

[A] PC Banking

The term "PC banking" refers to the use by bank customers of personal computers ("PCs") to access their bank accounts. Sometimes called "home banking" or "online banking," PC banking enables customers to check their accounts from the convenience of their homes and to perform a variety of online banking transactions such as paying bills, reconciling accounts, and transferring money from one account to another. A customer must maintain a traditional bank account in order to utilize PC banking but is spared the inconvenience of traveling to a bank branch.

Although some forms of PC banking are conducted on proprietary systems that require the customer to dial into the bank's computer network,[11] many PC banking systems utilize the Internet.[12] The federal banking regulators regard PC banking as an accepted form of offering traditional banking services and have authorized banks to provide such services for themselves as well as to assist other financial institutions in providing such services.[13]

[B] Internet Banks

A "virtual bank" or "Internet bank" is a depository institution that delivers banking services primarily through electronic means via the Internet or other communication channel but has no physical banking location where customers can conduct banking business. Customers of such banks generally conduct banking transactions through automated teller machines (ATMs), transactional Web sites, and toll-free customer services

[11] *See also* Chapter 9, **Electronic Commerce and Related Applications**, for a discussion of home banking applications.

[12] *See, e.g.*, OTS P-97-2 (April 14, 1997).

[13] The OCC and Federal Reserve, for example, both have approved the Integrion Financial Network, LLC, owned by a consortium of banks and IBM to provide an electronic gateway for PC banking services via the Internet and other electronic channels. *See* OCC Conditional Approval No. 221 (Dec. 4, 1996). *See also* OCC Interpretive Letter No. 677 (June 28, 1995); *Cardinal Bancshares, Inc.*, 82 Fed. Res. Bull. 674 (1996).

lines. The bank may outsource to third-party service providers major components of its operations, including telephone customer services, the Internet banking platform, item processing, core data processing, bill payment services, card and check production, accounts receivable auditing, delinquent loan collection, legal, and internal audit.

The Office of Thrift Supervision ("OTS") has approved several virtual Internet banks.[14]

The OCC approved a national bank charter for such a bank called CompuBank in 1997.[15] The bank would not have any traditional banking offices. Rather, customers could communicate with the bank through personal computer, automated voice response system, customer service lines, and the mail. Deposits could be made by direct deposit, wire transfer, or mail, and withdrawals could be made using ATMs or debit cards. The OCC did not apply any special criteria in approving the charter but required a full functionality and security review of the bank's computer banking platform by an independent computer-security specialist.

An interesting issue arises in the case of a virtual bank as to what the bank's compliance obligation is under the Community Reinvestment Act ("CRA"). This issue has not been fully addressed by the regulators. In the *CompuBank* case, the bank proposed to invest its deposits in U.S. government securities rather than making loans and the OCC treated the bank as a limited purpose bank for CRA purposes.

In the *Aeorbank.com* case, the bank chose to be evaluated initially as a large bank for CRA purposes and proposed to help meet the credit needs of its assessment area(s) through its lending activities, qualified investments, and retail and community development banking services. The bank's assessment areas included the area of its main office and areas where it established deposit-taking ATMs.

The OCC has allowed Internet banks to provide customer access to third-party products and services through hyperlinks, both as a value-added service and to generate fee income through finders fees. The OCC requires banks to take reasonable steps to clearly distinguish between the bank's products and services and those of the third party: "Bank customers should be able to identify when they are dealing with the Bank and when they are not,

---

[14] *See, e.g.*, OTS P-97-2 (April 14, 1997).

[15] OCC Conditional Approval No. 253 (Aug. 20, 1997). *See also* OCC Conditional Approval No. 312 (May 8, 1999) (NextBank); OCC Conditional Approval No. 313 (July 9, 1999) (CIBC Bank); OCC Conditional Approval No. 347 (Jan. 29, 2000) (AeroBank.com).

and the Bank should indicate that it does not provide, endorse, or guarantee any of the products or services available through the third party Web sites."[16]

Some banks have elected to create separately identifiable Internet "bank" divisions rather than charter an Internet bank as a separate entity. Wingspan.com, a division of Banc One, and Citi f/i, a division of Citibank, are examples of such "banks."[17]

[C] Internet Credit Cards

The OCC in 1999 approved a charter for a national bank that proposed to operate solely online and limit its activities to providing Internet credit cards.[18] The bank would offer on its Web site the "First True Internet VISA" card, which could be used primarily for online transactions but offline transactions as well. Cardholders would have access to an Internet-based account management system including online account statements, the ability to download transactions into personal financial management software, and online customer service. Online shopping and rewards programs would be included.

The bank would not have any traditional banking offices and would interact with its customers through its Internet Web site. The bank would obtain funding for its credit activities through wholesale certificates of deposit in amounts greater than $100,000 and would securitize its credit card portfolios. The OCC treated the bank as a limited purpose bank for purposes of the Community Reinvestment Act.

[D] Internet Domain Names

All banks that maintain an Internet Web site have an Internet address by which customers can connect to their site. A bank can establish an Internet address by registering a domain name through a domain name registration authority. The registration authority typically does not impose restrictions on the registration of similar domain names but merely serves as a register of domain names and contact information.

---

[16] OCC Conditional Approval No. 47 (Jan. 29, 2000), n.6.

[17] *See* "With Little Fanfare, Citibank Rolls Out Internet-Based, Branchless Retail Bank," Am. Banker (Aug. 19, 1999).

[18] OCC Conditional Approval No. 312 (May 8, 1999) ("NextBank, N.A."). This application was the second approved by the OCC for a bank that would offer its services solely on the Internet.

The federal banking agencies have warned banks of the need to protect their Internet addresses and domain names, citing examples of customer confusion that resulted when banks had similar names with some customers transmitting confidential information to the wrong bank.[18.1] Among other things, the OCC recommended that banks register similar domain names, increase consumer education efforts and consider establishing trademarks for their domain names. A bank also may seek relief under the Anti-Cybersquatting Consumer Protection Act which prohibits registering or using a domain name that is confusingly similar to another name with the intent to profit.[18.2] The use of bank Web sites to promote financial fraud and computer crimes can be addressed under federal criminal laws.[18.3]

[E] Electronic Records and Signatures
(*See also* Chapter 16, Electronic Signatures)

The Electronic Signatures in Global and National Commerce Act, or "E-Sign Act"[18.4] eliminated legal impediments to the use of electronic records and signatures, subject to certain consumer consent requirements, thereby facilitating electronic banking and other services. The Federal Reserve Board has authority under the Act to exempt specific disclosures from the consumer consent requirements if the exemption is necessary to eliminate a substantial burden on electronic commerce and will not increase the material risk of harm to consumers. The Board has requested comment on whether it should consider exercising this authority and also whether other regulatory changes are needed to adapt current requirements to online banking and lending to facilitate the electronic deliver of consumer financial services.[18.5]

The Board suggested that it might modify the periodic statement requirements under Regulations E (Electronic Funds Transfer Act), Z (Truth-in-Lending Act) and DD (Truth-in-Savings Act):

> As an example, under Regulations E, Z, and DD, periodic statements inform consumers about their account activity over a period time,

---

[18.1] *See* OCC Alert 2000-9 (July 19, 2000); FDIC Bank Technology Bulletin (Nov. 8, 2000).

[18.2] 15 U.S.C. § 1125(d).

[18.3] *See* 18 U.S.C. § 1101 (fraud and false statements), § 1030 (fraud in connection with computers), and § 1343 (wire fraud).

[18.4] Pub. L. No. 106-229, *codified at* 15 U.S.C. § 7001.

[18.5] 66 Fed. Reg. __ (2001).

> typically monthly. The beginning and ending dates of the cycle determine account balances and other information that must be disclosed. In addition, transmittal of the periodic statement triggers important consumer protections such as error resolution procedures. Online banking, however, can provide consumers with up-to-date information about their accounts on a continuing basis. Such information is a helpful supplement to—but does not comply as a substitute for—periodic statements. Should the rules for periodic statements be modified for online banking, and if so, how could the rules be crafted to maintain for consumers (1) a perspective of the activity of an account over time, and (2) protections for resolving errors or liability for unauthorized transactions?[18.6]

The Board noted that the comments received would assist the Board in future efforts to update its regulations and also would be helpful in connection with a study by the federal banking agencies of banking regulations that affect the electronic delivery of financial services that was required by the Gramm-Leach-Bliley Act. That Act requires the agencies to submit to Congress by November 12, 2001, a report recommending any legislative changes needed to facilitate online banking and lending.

§ 8.03 INTERNET ACCESS

As an incident to Internet banking, banks may provide general Internet access to bank customers as well as to individuals with whom they do not have a banking relationship in the bank's service area.[19] In analyzing the permissibility of such services by national banks, the OCC stated:

> [F]ull Internet access service is permissible under national banks' incidental authority to provide electronic products or services that can be used for both banking and non-banking functions as part of a package of banking related products or services where the full function products or services are not an excessive amount of the total package.
>
> * * *
>
> In this case, the full access service adds virtually nothing to the cost of providing Internet home banking and does not dominate the Bank's home

[18.6] *Id.*

[19] OCC Interpretive Letter No. 742 (1996) (Apollo Trust Company). *See also* OCC Conditional Approval No. 221 (Dec. 4, 1996).

> banking package. Even assuming that the Bank could separate its home banking functions from Internet access, it is impracticable to do so. Once the customer has entered his/her password and gained access to the Bank's BBS, the customer has accessed the Internet.
>
> * * *
>
> Here, the full Internet access service is needed to successfully provide and market the Bank's Internet banking service. Limiting the Bank's gateway services, to block non-banking use, would create a hobbled home banking product unlikely to meet consumer demand.
>
> * * *
>
> A national bank, under its incidental authority, may market and sell excess electronic capacities acquired or developed by the bank in good faith for banking purposes. . . . A bank that has in good faith acquired excess Internet access capacity need not allow the excess capacity to go unused.
>
> * * *
>
> Providing Internet access does not present a unique risk to a bank. Guarding against unauthorized access to bank records and processes is a risk banks have faced historically in their roles as safekeepers of customers' assets and sensitive information. Today's banks, in addition to facing assaults on physical assets, also must protect their data processing systems from unauthorized access to information systems—the modern repositories of a customer's wealth—through the erection of electronic "firewalls" or other mechanisms.[20]

The Federal Reserve Board ("Federal Reserve" or "Board") has permitted bank holding companies to provide customers with access to the Internet in connection with electronic gateway and home banking systems.[21] In approving such a proposal, the Board noted that the Internet contains significant amounts of data that are not financial, banking, or economic in nature. The Board nevertheless viewed Internet access as a permissible incident to permissible data processing when the service was offered as an accommodation service to customers in order to enhance the marketability of permissible data processing services and to permit bank holding companies to compete more effectively with nonbank financial service providers, provided it constitutes a small part of the overall data processing and transmission activities.

---

[20] *Id.*

[21] *Royal Bank of Canada, et al.*, 83 Fed. Res. Bull. 135 (1997); *Cardinal Bancshares*, 82 Fed. Res. Bull. 674 (1996).

§ 8.04 SUPERVISORY CONCERNS

The federal banking regulators have expressed concerns that transactions conducted over the Internet pose greater risk than transactions performed through other more established technologies:

> [T]he use of an electronic channel such as the Internet to deliver products and services introduces unique risks due to the increased speed at which systems operate, user anonymity, and broad access in terms of geography, user groups, applications, databases, and peripheral systems."[22]

The Federal Reserve Board has cautioned that Internet banking activities could expose banks, their customers, information, and transactions to electronic interception, interference, or fraud.[23] Nonetheless, the Board allowed that no software product or security system can provide "absolute" protection against these risks and that the nature of these risks is not different from those to which more traditional banking operations are exposed in other forms. The Board warned banking organizations contemplating Internet services to carefully analyze the risks of such services, particularly relating to the security of customer information and other data.[24]

In order to avoid the possibility that consumers would view the Board's approval of Internet banking services by a bank holding company as a government endorsement or guarantee, the Board has required applicants to commit that they will not make any representations in any marketing materials that the Board's approval constitutes an endorsement by the Federal Reserve System or that the Federal Reserve System has approved, assured, or endorsed the security, functionality, or effectiveness of products or services to be offered.

The OCC in 1999 issued an Examination Handbook on Internet Banking.[25] The handbook outlines procedures for the examination of Internet banking activities of national banks. In 2000, the OCC stated that it "attaches a high priority to the supervision of national bank internet activity" and announced that approximately 300 examiners had received

---

[22] 62 Fed. Reg. 65,673, 65,678 (1998).

[23] *Cardinal Bancshares, Inc.*, 82 Fed. Res. Bull. 674 (1996).

[24] *Id.*

[25] Office of the Comptroller of the Currency, *Examination Handbook—Internet Banking* (Oct. 14, 1999).

Internet banking training, including 95 specialists in information technology systems.[25.1] In 2001, the OCC issued a new section of its Corporate Manual on Internet banking.[25.2]

The OCC in 1998 issued supervisory guidance to national banks on PC banking.[26] The OCC noted that PC banking on the Internet often increases a bank's reliance on third-party service providers and requires appropriate due diligence in evaluating their reputation, financial status, and viability. A primary concern is maintaining control over the products and services provided by third-party vendors. The OCC noted that risk controls are needed to address the additional transaction risk resulting from weaknesses in design, implementation, and monitoring of the PC banking infrastructure. The OCC provided guidance for additional controls addressing strategic, reputation, and compliance risks raised by PC banking. In addition, the OCC noted, PC banking requires special measures to address issues of customer identification, authentication, and transaction verification as well as the security of customer information and transaction data. The OCC's guidance discusses security measures such as passwords, firewalls, encryption, virus protection, and intrusion detection. With respect to strategic risk, the OCC advised banks to address potential issues such as vendor incompatibility, system capacity problems, and ongoing maintenance costs. The OCC also stated that its examiners will evaluate the compatibility of a bank's PC banking system with its strategic goals, business tactics and overall risk tolerance.

The federal banking agencies have imposed special requirements on newly chartered Internet banks that must be met before the bank is allowed to commence business, including the following, for example:

- The bank must submit to the OCC for review and approval a complete description of the bank's final information systems and operations architecture as well as the information systems risk assessment and management plan. This should include a schematic drawing and discussion of the following items:

[25.1] OCC News Release 2000-84 (Oct. 27, 2000).

[25.2] OCC, The Internet and the National Bank Charter—Comptroller's Corporate Manual (Jan. 2001).

[26] OCC Bulletin 98-38 (Aug. 24, 1998), included in the Appendix. *See also* OCC Bulletin 98-03, "Technology Risk Management" (1998).

—Vendor due diligence and contracts;
—Electronic banking security mechanisms and policies;
—Personnel;
—Internal controls;
—Audit plans;
—Operating policies and procedures including, but not limited to, vendor management, customer authentication, privacy, and disaster recovery and business resumption plans.

- The bank must have performed an independent security review and test of its electronic banking platform. The scope of the review should encompass all access points, including the Internet, Intranet, or remote access. The bank must have this review performed regardless of whether the platform is operated in-house or by one or more third-party service providers. If the bank outsources the technology platform, it can rely upon testing performed for the service provider to the extent that it satisfies the specified scope and requirements.
- The review must be conducted by an objective, qualified, independent reviewer. The scope of the review must cover the adequacy of physical and logical protection against unauthorized internal and external access including individual penetration attempts, computer viruses, denial of service and other forms of electronic access. By written report, the reviewer must confirm that the security measures, including the firewall, have been satisfactorily implemented and tested. The report must critique the effectiveness of security policies and controls and confirm, with reasonable certainty, that unauthorized internal or external data and network access or access attempts will be detected and recorded.
- As part of its decision to grant final charter approval, the OCC will consider the results of the report as well as any subsequent actions by the bank or service provider to implement any recommendations or to remedy any noted security or control deficiencies.
- The operating plan, including any revisions, will provide the context for the supervisory review at the pre-opening

> examination. Major deviations from the plan or changes in the composition of the board of directors, ownership, or chief executive officer that the OCC has not approved may result in withdrawal of preliminary approval.[26.1]

The OTS and Federal Deposit Insurance Corporation ("FDIC") have issued similar guidance.[27] In 1998, the OTS adopted a rule requiring savings associations to provide advance notice to the OTS when they establish transactional Web sites in order to address the risks of Internet banking.[28]

In a 1999 report to Congress, the General Accounting Office found that Internet banking heightens traditional banking risks.[29] A review of 81 depository institutions' examinations by the GAO showed that approximately 44 percent of the institutions examined had not completely implemented risk-management steps that regulators said were needed to limit online banking risks. Some of the shortcomings included lack of approval of strategic plans by bank boards of directors and a lack of policies and procedures at some institutions for Internet banking operations.[30]

The solicitation of deposits on the Internet also may raise supervisory concerns. In 1997, the Idaho Department of Finance issued a cease and desist order against a West Indies bank to prevent it from soliciting deposits in Idaho on the Internet. The bank was accused of violating an Idaho law making it unlawful for any person to engage in banking by soliciting deposits without a bank charter.[31]

[*Next page is 8-11.*]

[26.1] *See, e.g.,* OCC Conditional Approval No. 427 (Nov. 17, 2000) (Bridge Bank of Silicon Valley, N.A.). *See also* Office of Thrift Supervision Order No. 2000-40, approving federal savings bank charter for Bank of Internet USA (Apr. 25, 2000).

[27] OTS, "Statement on Retail On-Line Personal Computer Banking" (1997); FDIC, "Security Risks Associated with the Internet," FIL-131-97 (Dec. 18, 1997).

[28] 62 Fed. Reg. 65,673 (1998).

[29] General Accounting Office, *Electronic Banking: Enhancing Federal Oversight of Internet Banking Activities,* GAO/T-GGD-99-91 (July 6, 1999).

[30] *See also* Chapter 11, **System Security and Risk,** *infra.*

[31] *See* Idaho Department of Finance, Press Release (dated May 30, 1997).

ELECTRONIC COMMERCE AND RELATED APPLICATIONS

§8.05 HOSTING INTERNET WEB SITES

The OCC has authorized a national bank to host Internet Web sites for its small business customers and thereby participate in electronic commerce on the Internet.[32]

§8.06 OTHER INTERNET-BASED SERVICES

The federal banking agencies have permitted banking organizations to offer a variety of other services via the Internet. For example, the OCC authorized Barnett Bank to acquire an interest in an electronic vehicle remarketing company that would enable used car sellers to market their inventory to interested buyers on the Internet.[33] The OCC viewed the activity as a permissible "finder" activity, stating:

> The OCC has long recognized the finder function as a permissible banking activity that includes, "without limitation, identifying potential parties, making inquiries as to interest, introducing or arranging meetings of interested parties, and otherwise bringing parties together for a transaction that the parties themselves negotiate and consummate."[34]

The OCC stated that "national banks may provide finder services via the Internet."

The OCC also approved a national bank proposal to place customer funds in foreign currency time deposits with foreign banks through an interactive Internet site linked to the bank's Internet site.[35]

§8.07 INTERNET SECURITIES TRANSACTIONS

The Internet provides a new media for the sale of securities as well as banking products by financial institutions. The GAO has estimated that approximately 22 percent of all securities transactions were conducted over the Internet in 1998 whereas no such transactions occurred as recently

[32] OCC Interpretive Letter No. 856 (March 5, 1999) (Fleet Financial Group). This letter is included in the Appendix and discussed in Chapter 9, **Electronic Commerce and Related Applications.**

[33] *Id.*

[34] *Id.*, citing 12 C.F.R. § 7.1002.

[35] OCC Interpretive Letter No. 778 (Mar. 20, 1997).

as 1995.[36] Online brokerage services via the Internet are increasingly seen as a cost-effective way for small community banks to offer brokerage services to their customers by avoiding the necessity of hiring, training, and compensating a dedicated securities salesperson.[37]

The federal banking agencies have authorized banking organizations to utilize the Internet for securities brokerage services and to provide related support services. In 1997, for example, the Federal Reserve Board authorized a bank holding company to develop and sell to broker-dealers and other financial institutions computer software that would allow brokerage customers to purchase and sell securities over the Internet by means of personal computers.[38] The proposed software systems would permit retail customers to have computer access to their securities brokerage accounts, and allow broker-dealers and financial institutions to integrate customer-generated electronic brokerage transactions with their backoffice operations. The software would be maintained on a host computer operated by a broker or the broker's service provider and would be available for use by customers after accessing the Internet through an unaffiliated Internet service provider. The software would enable customers to initiate transactions and to obtain information concerning their securities brokerage accounts. Additionally, the applicant proposed to provide software maintenance and product support. In discussing the public benefits of the proposal, the Board stated that it would enable securities brokerage customers to initiate transactions and communicate with their brokers using personal computers during business and non-business hours, and provide broker-dealers and financial institutions with additional means of making their securities brokerage services available to the public and thereby produce additional sources of transaction volume and resulting fee income. The Board noted that the proposal would increase competition among existing providers of similar software products.

Some banks offer online securities brokerage services through links to their affiliated broker-dealers on their Web sites.[39]

---

[36] Statement of Richard J. Hillman, Associate Director, Financial Institutions and Markets Issues, General Government Division, General Accounting Office, before the Senate Permanent Subcommittee on Investigations, "Securities Fraud: The Internet Poses Challenges to Regulators and Investors" (Mar. 22, 1999).

[37] *See* "For Small Banks, Internet Is Fast Lane to Offering Securities Trading Services," Am. Banker (Oct. 11, 1999).

[38] *Toronto-Dominion Bank*, 83 Fed. Res. Bull. 335 (1997).

[39] *See* "Mellon Expands Web Site to Include On-Line Trading," Am. Banker (Aug. 20, 1999).

The use of the Internet for securities transactions has resulted in major structural changes in the securities and futures markets:

> Electronic trading systems are replacing floor trading at exchanges around the world. The ultimate role of intermediaries in these new systems is not yet clear. Moreover, instantaneous international communication and transactional capabilities are creating truly global markets.[40]
>
> * * *
>
> In a way, the Internet is the wild card that makes it difficult to predict what the securities market will look like five or ten years from now.[41]

The Internet has enhanced the ability of individual investors to participate in the securities markets by dramatically reducing commissions, making readily available real-time quotes and market research. According to the SEC, approximately 30 percent of the volume traded on the NASDAQ and New York Stock Exchange is transacted over the Internet.[42] The SEC has cited estimates that 21 million people will have online brokerage accounts by the year 2003.[43]

Use of the Internet for securities transactions has posed new regulatory challenges for securities regulators. The Internet provides a new medium for securities fraud, for example, by making it easier for fraudulent operators to communicate electronically and inexpensively with a vastly larger audience of potential investors. In 1998, the SEC created an Office of Internet Enforcement to coordinate and oversee its regulatory efforts relating to the Internet. This office supervises a 125-person "cyberforce" devoted to "surfing the Internet looking for questionable securities-related activities."[44] The SEC reported in 1999 that it had brought 66 Internet-related cases since 1995.[45] Congress has held hearings on securities fraud

---

[40] Testimony of Brooksley Born, Chairperson, Commodity Futures Trading Commission, before the House Subcommittee on Capital Markets, Securities, and Government Sponsored Enterprises (Mar. 25, 1999).

[41] U.S. Securities and Exchange Commission, Statement Concerning the Effect of Technology on the Capital Markets by Laura S. Unger, Commissioner, before the House Subcommittee on Capital Markets, Securities, and Government Sponsored Enterprises (Mar. 25, 1999).

[42] *Id.*

[43] *Id. See also* "Seats on NYSE Lose Prestige, Value in Computer Age," Wash. Post, April 25, 2000 A1 (reporting a decline in the value of a seat on the New York Stock Exchange—"Soon the electronic networks will even be able to trade NYSE stocks.")

[44] *Id.*

[45] *Id.*

on the Internet but has taken no legislative action specifically addressing Internet securities fraud.[46]

Several studies have been conducted on online brokerage, discussing such issues as customer expectations and risk management and how online brokers can fulfill their obligations to recommend only suitable products and obtain the best execution for their customers.[47]

The Internet also has facilitated the development of alternative trading systems that the SEC has found sometimes function as private securities exchanges. In 1998, the SEC adopted a regulatory framework to govern such systems, noting that the current regulatory framework, designed more 60 years ago, did not envision many of the new electronic trading systems.[48]

In September 1998, the Cantor Financial Futures Exchange became the first fully electronic-based exchange in the United States for futures contracts on U.S. Treasury bonds and notes. FutureCom has applied with the Commodity Futures Trading Commission ("CFTC") to become the first Internet-based futures exchange in the world. As described by the CFTC, the exchange would have a unique structure:

> FutureCom, as proposed, would be structured unlike any existing exchange. All its members would be clearing members, would have their trading accounts held by the exchange and would be directly liked to the trading system. Members' account balances and positions would be updated in real-time, and members would be prevented from entering any orders for which they did not have the requisite margin in their accounts. Each FutureCom member would be directly financially responsible to FutureCom for its own trades. FutureCom would not be owned by its members, as all U.S. exchanges other than CFFE are, but would instead be organized as a limited partnership among the organizers of the exchange and would be run on a for-profit basis.
>
> FutureCom's use of the Internet and its membership structure would create a new model for participation in U.S. future exchanges.

---

[46] Hearings before the Permanent Subcommittee On Investigations of the Senate Committee On Governmental Affairs on "Securities Frauds on the Internet and Current Issues Concerning Online Trading" (March 23, 1999).

[47] *See, e.g.*, SEC Commissioner Laura Unger, "On-Line Brokerage: Keeping Apace of Cyberspace" (Nov. 22, 1999); New York Attorney General's Office, "From Wall Street to Web Street: A Report on the Problems and Promise of the Online Brokerage Industry" (1999).

[48] 63 Fed. Reg. 70,844, 70,845 (1998).

> Using the Internet to transmit trade and financial information would facilitate direct access by the public and would result in the elimination of a significant role for intermediaries. Since each FutureCom member would provide for its own access to the Internet and thus to FutureCom, functions traditionally performed by a futures commission merchant ("FCM") would not be needed by a member to access and trade on FutureCom. The radically different proposed structure of FutureCom has presented the Commission with the challenge of how best to apply laws and regulations designed for an intermediated, open outcry trading environment to an electronic direct access system.[49]

The Federal Reserve Board has authorized a bank holding company to operate an electronic securities exchange called the "Tradepoint Stock Exchange."[50] As described by the Board, Tradepoint is a screen-based electronic market that provides securities trade matching, execution, and related services to U.S. and foreign market-makers, broker-dealers, and institutional investors that become members of the Exchange. Terminals linked to the Exchange can be located anywhere in the world. The Board noted that Tradepoint would not take a principal position in securities, clear or settle the securities, or assume any principal risk for securities executed on the Exchange, and was under no obligation to guarantee a member's trades.

The SEC in 1998 issued a statement on how investment advisers, broker-dealers, mutual funds, and issuers of securities can use Internet Web sites to solicit offshore securities transactions and clients without triggering registration requirements under the federal securities laws.[51] The statement clarified when the posting of solicitation materials on the Internet would not be considered activity occurring "in the United States."

The NASDR has issued guidance as to when a broker-dealer will be deemed responsible for the content and filing of material on Web sites to which the broker-dealer's Web site is hyperlinked.[52] A broker-dealer is not responsible for ongoing hyperlinks that are continuously available

---

[49] Testimony of Brooksley Born, Chairperson, Commodity Futures Trading Commission, before the House Subcommittee on Capital Markets, Securities, and Government Sponsored Enterprises (Mar. 25, 1999).

[50] *J.P. Morgan & Co. Incorporated,* 86 Fed. Res. Bull. 61 (2000).

[51] 63 Fed. Reg. 14,806 (1998).

[52] *See* Letter dated November 11, 1997, to Craig S. Tyle, General Counsel, Investment Company Institute, from Thomas Selman, NASDR.

to investors from the broker-dealer's Web site and the broker-dealer has no discretion to alter the information on the linked site. The broker-dealer may not establish a link to a site that the broker-dealer knows or has reason to know contains false or misleading information about the broker-dealer's products or services. A broker-dealer also is not responsible for information provided on a hyperlinked site that is used by the public for general reference and educational purposes and does not refer to the broker-dealer. A broker-dealer will be held responsible in certain situations, however, such as for links to the home page of an investment newsletter that contains a misleading article about a broker-dealer's products.

The North American Securities Administrators Association ("NASAA") in 1997 adopted a model interpretive order to govern the activities of broker-dealers on the Internet.[53] The interpretive order provides that a broker-dealer or investment adviser advertising on the Internet will not be deemed to be transacting business in a state for purposes of state registration requirements if the following conditions are met:

- The Internet communication contains a legend stating that the broker-dealer or investment adviser may transact business in the state only if it is registered;
- Any follow-up individualized responses to persons in the state will not be made absent compliance with state broker-dealer or investment adviser registration requirements;
- The Internet communication contains technical "firewalls" to ensure that, prior to any subsequent direct communication with prospective customers in the state, the broker-dealer or investment adviser is first registered;
- The Internet communication does not involve affecting or attempting to affect transactions in securities or the rendering of personalized investment advice for compensation but is limited to the dissemination of general information on products and services;

[53] NASAA, *Interpretive Order Concerning Broker-Dealers, Investment Advisers, Broker-Dealer Agents and Investment Adviser Representatives Using the Internet for General Dissemination of Information on Products and Services* (adopted April 27, 1997).

- In the case of a representative of a broker-dealer or investment adviser, the representative acts within the scope of authority granted by the broker-dealer or investment adviser with which the representative is affiliated and the broker-dealer or investment adviser reviews and approves the content of any Internet communication and authorizes dissemination of information via the Internet.

The SEC staff has granted no-action relief permitting America Online, CompuServe, Microsoft, and other online service providers to connect their customers to the Web site of Charles Schwab & Co., Inc. for securities transactions without registering as broker-dealers.[54] The SEC allowed the online service providers to receive a nominal, flat fee per order from Schwab for each securities order sent by their subscribers to Schwab through the online service. The online services may not, among other things, recommend specific securities, take part in the financial services offered by Schwab (other than by routing messages), answer questions or engage in negotiations involving securities accounts or transactions, accept or route orders, handle customer funds or securities, extend credit to customers in connection with securities transactions, or receive any fee from Schwab other than a flat fee per order transmitted. The fee may not vary depending on the number of shares or value of the securities included in the order, or whether the order results in an executed trade.

In 1997, the SEC issued a concept release on ways to update the federal regulatory framework to address recent changes in the U.S. securities markets resulting from technological advances. The concept release invited public comment on the rapid growth in electronic trading systems that present alternatives to traditional exchange trading and the development of technology that allows U.S. investors to trade directly on foreign markets from the United States.

[54] *Charles Schwab & Co., Inc.* (pub. avail. Nov. 27, 1996).

CHAPTER 9

ELECTRONIC COMMERCE AND RELATED APPLICATIONS

A variety of electronic banking applications have been approved for banks and their affiliates by federal banking regulations. Many of these applications involve banks directly in the channels of electronic commerce.[1]

Banks are particularly well equipped to serve as "engines of electronic commerce." In their role as financial intermediaries, banks have developed core competencies in many of the operational aspects needed to support electronic commerce. Banks are experts in managing large databases of financial information, in archiving and retrieving data, providing information security, assessing financial risks, and acting as "finders" in linking merchants and customers.

§ 9.01 HOME BANKING SERVICES

[A] Home Banking Systems

Home banking services enable customers to perform a variety of banking transactions from their homes using personal computers and, in some systems, enhanced screen telephones. Home banking customers can use their home banking software to pay bills, transfer funds between accounts, obtain information about account balances and checks paid, apply for a loan, and purchase certificates of deposit or securities. The General Accounting Office estimated that approximately 50 percent of all U.S. banks will offer some form of online banking by the end of 1998.[1.1]

The Federal Reserve Board ("Federal Reserve" or "Board") has permitted bank holding companies to offer home banking services since at least 1982, when it authorized Citicorp to provide consumers with the capability to access banking and financial services through packaged electronic data processing and data transmission systems including software and hardware.[2] Citicorp offered desktop automated teller machines to consumers for home use that would enable consumers to instruct their bank to pay bills, receive financial information, such as money market rates and stock prices, and to perform limited budget and accounting functions.

In 1996, the Board authorized Royal Bank of Canada to acquire 20 percent of the voting shares of MECA Software and thereby engage in the

---

[1] *See* "Banks Have What It Takes for E-Commerce," Am. Banker (Jan. 25, 2000).

[1.1] General Accounting Office, *Electronic Banking: Experiences Reported by Banks in Implementing On-line Banking*, GAO/GGD-98-34 (Jan. 1998), at 4. *See also* Chapter 8, **Internet Services.**

[2] *See, e.g., Citicorp (Citishare)*, 68 Fed. Res. Bull. 505 (1982).

development, production, and provision of home banking, personal financial management, and other computer software.[3] MECA's products included its principal software product, "Managing Your Money," a computer program that permits customers to conduct basic banking transactions and personal financial management using personal computers. Managing Your Money enables customers to pay bills, view and reconcile checking account registers, gain access to their checking and savings account statements, transfer funds between accounts, receive stock quotations, and engage in tax and financial planning. The Office of the Comptroller of the Currency ("OCC") also permitted national banks to acquire interests in MECA.[4]

[B] Home Banking Gateway Services

The federal banking regulators permitted a consortium of banking organizations to acquire voting interests in the Integrion Financial Network, ILC, a joint venture with a subsidiary of International Business Machines Corporation, to design, develop, and operate a data processing and transmission system through which depository institutions and their affiliates may make available home banking and other financial services to their respective customers.[5] As proposed, Integrion itself would not provide home banking or other financial services but would provide a data processing and data transmission "gateway" system to serve as a switch or interface to electronically connect member depository institutions with their customers. Customers connect to the gateway using a variety of devices, including personal computers ("PCs"), touchtone telephones, or other electronic communication devices. Once a customer connects to the gateway, Integrion electronically routes and connects the customer to the appropriate member depository institution, using software developed by Integrion to facilitate communications between the customer's PC or other device and the depository institution's hardware and software. Customers can access remote banking services, bill payment functions, and stock quotations.

The Integrion gateway also provides access to the Internet and third-party service providers. The OCC stated that the linkage to third-party

---

[3] *Royal Bank of Canada*, 82 Fed. Res. Bull. 363 (1996).

[4] OCC Interpretive Letter No. 677 (June 28, 1995) (Bank of America and NationsBank joint venture).

[5] *Royal Bank of Canada, et al.*, 83 Fed. Res. Bull. 135 (1997); OCC Conditional Approval No. 221 (Dec. 4, 1996).

vendors' Web sites is part of the "business of banking" because it is a use of modern technology to provide a recognized banking function—acting as a "finder."

[C] Home Shopping and Travel Planning

The Federal Reserve Board's staff in 1984 allowed a bank holding company to participate in a pilot research program that would offer home shopping, travel planning, and general news and information in connection with home banking services. As proposed, these services were to be offered through general purpose hardware provided to 100 household customers for 12 months.[6] The staff opinion stated that the activities were not permissible for a bank holding company under Regulation Y. The staff allowed the bank holding company to participate in the pilot program for research purposes, however, and not for the purpose of establishing a permanent, profit-making home shopping system. The Board's staff stated that the bank holding company would be required to file an application under Regulation Y if it wanted to offer such services on other than an experimental basis in the future.

The Board has declined to allow a bank holding company to provide a software program allowing customers to receive airline and hotel information and make airline and hotel reservations online.[7] The Board stated that the program was not related to the provision of banking, financial, or economic data and was similar to travel agency services which the Board determined are not "closely related" to banking. Such a program would appear to be permissible under recent OCC interpretations,[8] however, and a change in the Board's position in the future is not inconceivable.

Indeed, in 2000, the Board amended Regulation Y to authorize financial holding companies to act as "finders" and thereby operate "electronic marketplaces" through which consumers can shop and purchase

---

[6] Board Staff Opinion of August 31, 1984; F.R.R.S. 4-472. The bank holding company receiving the staff opinion was Barnett Banks of Florida, Inc.

[7] *Citicorp (Quotron Systems, Inc.)*, 72 Fed. Res. Bull. 497 (1986). As described in *Citicorp*, Quotron engaged in a variety of data processing and data transmission activities for customers such as securities and commodities exchanges, brokerage firms, commercial banks, S&Ls, insurance companies, and investment managers.

[8] *See, e.g.*, OCC Interpretive Letter No. 856 (Mar. 5, 1999), included in the Appendix.

goods and services. *See* Chapter 9, **Electronic Commerce and Related Applications,** § 9.17.

§ 9.02 ELECTRONIC BILL PRESENTMENT AND PAYMENT

Electronic bill payment systems are in effect in many banks through "Quicken" and other home banking software services. Such systems allow a bank customer to send electronic instructions to his or her bank to pay designated amounts to various merchants and service providers from whom the customer has received a paper bill in the mail.

Electronic bill presentment allows a merchant or other biller to send a bill to the customer and the customer's bank through the Internet. Using a personal identification number ("PIN"), the customer can access the bill on the bank's Web site and pay the bill through an automated clearing house ("ACH") transfer. A number of banks have begun to offer electronic presentment and payment services through Integrion and other consortia.

The Banking Industry Technology Secretariat ("BITS") and national automated Clearing House Association ("NACHA") announced a joint project in 1998 for the development of an open, vendor-neutral platform-independent standard that will enable the electronic delivery of a bill from any biller to any consumer and the electronic payment of the bill independent of the service provider and vendor.[9]

Among the key vendors of electronic bill presentment and payment services are the Integrion Financial Network, LLC (a consortium of banks, IBM and Visa USA), The Exchange (owned by Chase Manhattan, First Union, and Wells Fargo), CheckFree Holdings Corporation, and TransPoint LLC (a joint venture of Microsoft and First Data with Citibank as a minority investor). Bill paying services do not require a bank charter and thus nonbanking companies also may offer such services in competition with banks.

The Council for Electronic Billing & Payment in 1999 released "Electronic Bill Payment/Presentment Business Practices" to create a framework for security, privacy, timeliness, swift error resolution, and effective communication in the electronic bill payment process.[9.1]

---

[9] NACHA Press Release (Aug. 12, 1998).

[9.1] *See* Robert Y. Wood III, "Banks Wading Into the EBPP Tsunami," Electronic Banking Law and Commerce Report (Sept. 1999), at 14; *see also* July/August issue of Electronic Banking Law and Commerce Report devoted to Electronic Bill Presentment and Payment.

In 1999, the OCC authorized Chase Manhattan Bank, First Union National Bank, and Wells Fargo Bank to engage in electronic bill presentment services over the Internet through a joint venture limited liability company called "Spectrum."[9.2] Spectrum would develop a switch through which bank customers and others could receive bills electronically from various merchants and service providers. Spectrum would develop standards for electronic presentation of billing information, create a biller file and biller direc-

[*Next page is 9-7.*]

[9.2] OCC Conditional Approval No. 332 (Oct. 18, 1999).

tory, and enter into arrangements with a variety of entities in order to receive bills from billers and route bills to a large number of customers.

§9.03 ELECTRONIC DATA INTERCHANGE

Electronic data interchange ("EDI") refers to business-to-business transactions conducted through the ACH and Fedwire networks. EDI links purchasers and sellers of goods and services, allowing business and trading partners to electronically communicate purchase orders and sales transactions in place of paper purchase orders, invoices, shipping notices, payment orders, remittance advices, and other commercial documents.[10] EDI has vastly increased the efficiency of commercial transactions and reduced costs.

Banks generally are allowed to provide EDI services. The OCC has authorized national banks to invest in companies providing EDI services. In one such case, the OCC authorized a national bank to invest in a nonbanking company engaged in the design, development, marketing, and maintenance of an EDI network for the transaction of electronic commerce and the marketing of software products for use on its world-wide electronic commerce network.[11] As described by the OCC, the network was designed to enable subscribing business customers to send and receive purchase and sales orders and payments to and from any company worldwide. The bank would recruit business customers as network end-users and would derive fee income based on the number of transactions moving through the network.

Another example of EDI is the automated purchasing, payment and claims processing system developed by Banc One that utilizes the Internet to enable major academic, medical and corporate libraries to electronically order publications from electronic catalogues of scientific, technical, and medical journals with over 20,000 titles.[12]

Chase Manhattan Corporation reportedly has created an online business-to-business purchasing community allowing the bank's 350,000 business customers to sell products directly to one another via a Chase Web site.[12.1]

---

[10] *See* Scott Knudson, Jack Walton, & Florence Young, "Business-to-Business Payments and the Role of Financial Electronic Data Interchange," 80 Fed. Res. Bull. 269 (1994).

[11] *See, e.g.*, OCC Interpretive Letter No. 732 (May 10, 1996).

[12] *See* Congressional Testimony of Richard J. Moorman and Richard R. Rowe, Banc One Corporation (July 11, 1996), 1996 WL 10829747.

[12.1] *See* "Big Banks Grapple with Moving Corporate Services On-line," Am. Banker (Oct. 6, 1999).

§9.04 DISPENSING ALTERNATIVE MEDIA

The OCC has permitted a national bank to dispense from customer bank communication terminals ("CBCT") or automated teller machines ("ATMs") alternative media such as public transportation tickets, event tickets, gift certificates, and prepaid telephone cards.[13] The OCC also authorized a bank-owned EFT network to operate scrip terminals that dispense a cash equivalent, such as a voucher, that can be redeemed for merchandise at designated retailers.[14]

The OCC addressed whether the dispensing of prepaid gift certificates would involve the bank in the sale of goods or services on behalf of the participating merchants and thus exceed the bank's powers. The OCC reasoned that the media being sold were certificates of value rather than merchandise and the bank's function was analogous to the issuance of a credit card to a bank customer who uses the card to purchase merchandise. Instead of a credit card, the customer used a gift certificate. The OCC also analogized the activity to a bill payment function in which the bank transfers funds from the customer's account to the merchant's account and concluded that the activity was a "logical outgrowth of the recognized bill payment and funds transfer functions of national banks."[15]

The Federal Reserve Board has approved a joint venture between bank holding companies to provide data processing services to owners of ATMs to enable the owners to distribute through their ATMs tickets, gift certificates, prepaid telephone cards, and other documents evidencing prepayment for goods and services, including mutual fund shares or insurance policies where permitted by applicable law.[16] The joint venture would provide the software and telecommunications channels necessary to transmit cardholder requests and card issuer authorizations and related switching and account reconciliation services.[17]

---

[13] OCC Interpretive Letter No. 718 (Mar. 14, 1996).

[14] OCC Interpretive Letter No. 854 (Feb. 25, 1999), n.10.

[15] OCC Interpretive Letter No. 718 (Mar. 14, 1996).

[16] *Banc One Corp./CoreStates Financial Corp./PNC Bank Corp./KeyCorp/National City Corp.*, 82 Fed. Res. Bull. 848 (1996).

[17] These services would include terminal driving services such as maintaining an electronic link between an ATM and a telecommunications switch to transmit cardholder requests and card issuer authorizations and operating the feature and function displays on an ATM screen using computer software to permit an ATM to dispense various products in addition to currency. The joint venture also would provide switching services and transaction processing to transmit account debiting, transaction authorization, and settlement between the ATM owner or its bank and the cardholder's bank.

In a typical transaction, an ATM cardholder would select a particular product from a menu offered at an ATM, electronic commands transmitted by the network operator would verify that the deposit account or line of credit designated by the cardholder had sufficient funds to make the purchase and, after the authorization was received, the ATM would dispense the product and a receipt in accordance with the Board's Regulation E (Electronic Fund Transfers). The card-issuing bank would then debit an amount equal to the cost of the purchase from the cardholder's designated account and transfer the funds to the account of the merchant or ATM deployer, as appropriate, using settlement procedures established by the ATM network.

In addressing the public benefits of the proposal, the Federal Reserve Board stated that the proposed activities would allow consumers to purchase products at additional locations and during non-business hours, facilitate convenient payment for such products, enhance the ability of merchants to distribute products through new channels, provide ATM deployers with additional sources of transaction volume and resulting fee income, and increase competition among existing providers of the services.

The Board also has approved data processing services related to the dispensing of travelers' checks and postage stamps from ATM machines.[18]

§9.05 MEDICAL PAYMENT SERVICES

Banc One Corporation obtained Board approval to operate a network for the processing and transmission of medical payment data between health care providers (such as physicians, hospitals, and pharmacies) and entities responsible for providing medical benefits (such as health insurers, health maintenance organizations, and preferred providers).[19] As proposed, the network would operate in a manner similar to existing automated-teller-machine ("ATM") and point of sale ("POS") networks. Health care providers would enter claims information into the network with a request for payment, and health claim payers would authorize electronic fund transfers in full or partial payment of the claims.

In addition, the company proposed to furnish software for use in the medical payments network, including adjudication software that would automate the determination of what claims should be paid and the amount of the claim. The company also proposed to provide by-products of its data

[18] *The Bank of New York, et al.*, 80 Fed. Res. Bull. 1107 (1994).

[19] *Banc One Corp.*, 80 Fed. Res. Bull. 139 (1994).

processing activities, including statistical information derived from the data transmitted through the payment network, and to the additional related services that resulted from its research and development efforts. As proposed, the medical data submitted by health care providers would include only information required to assess the appropriateness, validity, and amount of a claim for payment, or otherwise necessary to authorize payment for a claim, and the providers would not transmit data for general medical use.

The OCC has permitted national banks to offer similar services.[20] For example, the OCC authorized NationsBank to acquire an interest in a company called Electronic Health Services that would offer to health care providers a package of integrated banking and information services designed to communicate billing and payment-related information to insurance carriers responsible for providing medical benefits.[21] The service ultimately would afford a single online point of referral for all parties to a health care transaction, including patients, providers, and insurance carriers, providing access to information such as insurance status and coverage, payment records, patient data and history, and medical data necessary to substantiate and evaluate medical claims. Health care providers and insurers would use the service for case management, member verification, referrals to other physicians, managed care claims analysis, insurance claim processing, and payment transfers.

The OCC also permitted a national bank to provide facilities for the collection of premiums and co-payments from participants in Medicare, Medicaid, and similar government health insurance plans and to remit the funds to the appropriate government agency.[22] The OCC also has permitted national banks to provide electronically medical insurance cost information and benefits counseling,[23] factoring of medical receivables including filing of related insurance claims,[24] and settlement and payment of medical claims.[25]

---

[20] *See, e.g.*, OCC Interpretive Letter No. 836 (Mar. 12, 1996), included in Appendix A8, *infra*. *See also* OCC Interpretive Letter No. 419 (Feb. 16, 1988).

[21] OCC Conditional Approval No. 282 (July 31, 1998).

[22] OCC Corporate Decision 98-13 (Feb. 9, 1998), included in the Appendix; OCC Letter from Horace Sneed, Senior Attorney (Dec. 6, 1993) (unpublished).

[23] OCC Corporate Decision 98-13.

[24] OCC Interpretive Letter No. 712 (Feb. 29, 1996).

[25] OCC Interpretive Letter No. 419 (1988).

§9.06 SHAREHOLDER, BANKRUPTCY, AND CLASS ACTION SERVICES

State Street Boston Corporation and The First National Bank of Boston were permitted to enter into a partnership for the performance of data processing services in connection with certain trust activities.[26] The partnership proposed to provide shareholder services to corporations and other securities issuers, including limited partnerships, closed-end investment companies, and issuers of American Depository Receipts, and to provide stock option processing, recordkeeping and account maintenance, restricted securities processing and recordkeeping, stock watch services, dividend reinvestment and employee stock purchase plan administration, annual meeting services, and reorganization services. For example, the partnership would process proxies from shareholders, create and update shareholder databases, maintain accounts for dividend reinvestment and other stock purchase plans, process changes of address, and scan shareholder correspondence in connection with providing the proposed shareholder services.

In addition, the partnership proposed to provide processing services for government allotment programs in which participating government employees would have a designated portion of their paychecks withheld by their employer and invested in employee-selected investment vehicles.

The State Street/Bank of Boston partnership would also provide claims processing and disbursement services in connection with bankruptcy and class action judgments or settlements. In conducting such activities, the partnership would be retained to provide accounting, recordkeeping, and remittance services in connection with the distribution of judgment or settlement proceeds to the bankrupt party's creditors or class action plaintiffs. For example, the partnership would calculate the amount to be remitted from a judgment or settlement to each creditor or class action plaintiff based on data provided by a third party, provide an accounting of such payments to the court or defendant, and remit payments to creditors or plaintiffs entitled to such distributions. The partnership would not make a determination as to whether a creditor or plaintiff was entitled to participate in any judgment or settlement. The Board viewed these activities as functionally equivalent to the types of accounts receivables processing and remittance services that the Board previously had

[26] 81 Fed. Res. Bull. 1049 (1995).

determined to be permissible for bank holding companies to provide to nonfinancial customers.

§9.07 ELECTRONIC TOLL COLLECTION SYSTEM

The OCC has permitted a national bank to contract with a public authority to operate an electronic toll collection system.[27]

As described by the OCC, the bank would contract with a public authority acting on behalf of itself and a consortium of other public authorities to implement the "E-Z Pass" toll collection throughout the roadways and facilities operated by the consortium. The toll system would allow drivers to use a transponder tag attached to their vehicles to be scanned by reader equipment while the vehicles pass through reader-equipped toll lanes. The contract required the bank to design, furnish, and install the toll collection equipment and to design, implement, and operate a customer service center to manage E-Z Pass accounts of participating drivers. The E-Z Pass system permitted identification of participating vehicles and the automatic debiting of the prepaid balance in their E-Z Pass accounts.

The E-Z Pass accounts were maintained by the bank as agent for and on behalf of the consortium and the accounts were not treated as deposits but rather as representing a record of prepaid tolls collected and held by the bank on behalf of the consortium. Under the terms of the E-Z Pass system, a driver's prepaid balance would be reduced or debited each time the driver passed through a reader equipped toll plaza and drivers could periodically replenish their prepaid balances for their E-Z Pass accounts. The collected funds were deposited in or transmitted to a bank account for the consortium.

The OCC noted that the contract also required the bank to perform toll plaza infrastructure and toll lane traffic flow modifications in order to implement the E-Z Pass system and to integrate the toll data into existing toll audit systems. This would require furnishing and installing the toll collection equipment and computers, toll plaza signing, plaza/ramp striping plans, operational plans for plaza and ramp operation and disaster/equipment failure contingency plans, and providing a communications system. The OCC noted that the bank would subcontract through a wholly owned operating subsidiary and that the design, construction, and equipment installation would be performed by recognized and qualified subcontractors who would indemnify the

[27] OCC Interpretive Letter No. 731 (July 1, 1996).

bank and the subsidiary to the maximum extent for any claims attributable to the work of each of the subcontractors. In addition, the bank and the subsidiary would maintain general liability insurance as appropriate.

§9.08 MONEY TRANSMITTAL SERVICES

The Federal Reserve Board has approved "money transmittal" services as a permissible nonbanking activity for bank holding companies.[28]

As approved by the Board, a customer could place an order to transit funds to a third party by paying cash and a fee to a representative of the nonbank company. The representative would issue a receipt and deposit the customer's cash in a bank account maintained by the representative solely for the purpose of receiving funds in trust to be transmitted to third parties. The representative would not have any agreement to accept deposits on behalf of the bank in which it maintains its account. On a daily basis, the company would collect funds deposits in each representative's account through an ACH or similar transaction and deposit an amount equal to the amount to be transmitted into an account maintained by the company at a bank located near the third party receiving the funds. The third party would be notified that the money is available at a local disbursement site, which could be a bank branch or a nonbank office of a consumer finance company or check cashing office. The third party could collect its funds almost immediately by a check drawn on the company's account. The customer generally would not be permitted to leave money on deposit with the company but could use the service solely to transfer money to a third party.

The Board concluded that money transmission services do not involve the paying of checks because, although the third party would receive money by means of a check drawn on an account maintained by the company, the receipt of funds in check form is not the payment of a check. Similarly, the service did not involve lending money because only funds provided by the customer were transmitted to a third party.

While the Board did not specifically address whether the money transmission service involved the receiving of deposits, it did note that there would be no agreement between a customer and a bank to accept money in an account for use by the bank and that a customer could not use the service to transmit funds to any bank account maintained by the

[28] *Norwest Corp.*, 81 Fed. Res. Bull. 1130 (1995).

customer or a third party. Thus, the Board concluded that the service would not be used to collect deposits by banks affiliated with the company.

The OCC also has determined that a national bank can accept money from nonbank affiliates for the purpose of transmitting the funds to a foreign country.[29] The affiliates were not deemed to be receiving deposits and thus operating as branches of the bank.

§9.09 MERCHANT SERVICES

[A] Merchant Data Services

The Federal Reserve Board has authorized bank holding companies to provide electronic data interchange services by which a data processing company furnishes retail merchants with data collected from sales transactions consummated at the merchant's place of business.[30] In such services, the data is rendered through a retail merchant's POS terminals and provides information to the merchant showing specific items and quantities of products purchased by the customer as well as customer purchasing patterns over a period of time. The data is formatted so that it can be used by the merchant for inventory control, targeted marketing, and other purposes.

The OCC has authorized national banks to offer such services also.[30.1]

[B] Merchant Card Processing

The Federal Reserve Board approved a proposal by Banc One Corporation to acquire First USA and its subsidiaries engaged in credit card processing activities.[31] In connection with the proposal, the Board authorized Banc One to engage in merchant card processing consisting of three primary activities:

- Merchant contract acquisition;
- Front-end network processing; and
- Back-end merchant accounting.

---

[29] Unpublished Letter from Peter Liebesman, Assistant Director, Legal Advisory Services Division (May 15, 1990).

[30] *Banc One Corp., et al.*, 79 Fed. Res. Bull. 1158 (1993). *See also* § 9.03.

[30.1] OCC Interpretive Letter No. 732 (May 10, 1996).

[31] 83 Fed. Res. Bull. 602 (1997).

As described by the Board, merchant contract acquisition includes the marketing and sale of card transaction processing services to merchants. Front-end network processing includes card authorization at the time of a purchase and the electronic capture of sales drafts; back-end merchant accounting includes recording the number and amount of all sales drafts and credits submitted by each merchant, managing and reporting transaction information, resolving charge backs, and investigating fraudulent activity.

Banc One was authorized to acquire the following subsidiaries of First USA:

- First USA Merchant Services, Inc., engaged in processing credit and debit card transactions for merchants directly and indirectly through financial institutions and independent sales organizations, including card transaction authorization, processing of card transactions, settlement of card transactions, and arranging for deposit of funds in merchants' accounts.
- First USA Technology, Inc., engaged in serving as licensor for software provided to merchants in connection with credit and debt card processing activities.
- First Virtual Holdings Incorporated, engaged in providing merchants selling their products and services over the Internet with a payment system capable of verifying the identity of the purchaser and the seller to a credit card transaction, and in providing processing services, including authorization, capture, settlement, and merchant funds deposit activities for the credit card transaction; and operating a shared Web site on the Internet for sellers of information products by mangling all aspects of the selling process such as confirmation of purchases, distribution of information products, accounting, settlement, and collection and payment of proceeds.
- Gensar Technologies, Inc., engaged in providing certain credit and debit card transaction processing services and equipment for merchants directly and indirectly through financial institutions and independent sales organizations, and acting as licensor of personal computer-based software designed for the processing of financial data.

- Merchant Link Inc., engaged in providing specialized help-desk services only in connection with the operation of the bank card modules of certain integrated hotel, restaurant, and retail financial management systems, and specialized credit and debit card transactions processing services, including authorization, capture, settlement, and merchant funds deposit activities, and providing specialized personal computer-based software used by direct response merchants in connection with the entry of customer card data and card transaction processing.

[C] Customer Tracking Services

The OCC has permitted a national bank to operate a computerized system allowing automobile dealers to track information on customers and to generate market statistics such as buying trends and cycles.[32]

[D] Merchant Web Sites

Hosting merchant Web sites has become a profit-making activity for a number of banks.[32.1] The OCC has permitted a national bank to host Web sites for retailers and offer other services designed to enable its small business customers to establish a retail sales presence on the Internet.[33]

As described by the OCC, the bank would assign a retailer an Internet Web address and register the address with major Internet search engines. The Web address could include the bank's URL (*e.g., http://www.Bank.com/yourbusinessname*). The Web site would reside on Internet servers controlled by the bank, which would maintain the Web site for the retailer. The retailer would design its own Web site using software provided by the bank. The bank would maintain the data necessary for the Web site to operate, including product descriptions, images, and pricing information, and would provide the functions by which customers visiting the

---

[32] OCC Interpretive Letter No. 741 (Aug. 19, 1996).

[32.1] *See* "Wells Fargo Markets One-Stop Service Package for Businesses Going On-Line," Am. Banker (Sept. 21, 1999).

[33] OCC Interpretive Letter No. 856 (Mar. 5, 1999) (Fleet Financial Group). This letter is included in the Appendix.

Web site could select products, communicate their product selection and shipping instructions to the retailer, and pay for products using their credit cards. The bank would provide monthly reports to the retailer on site "hits" and transaction volume. As compensation for its services, the bank would charge a monthly fee for maintaining the Web site and also would collect merchant discounts on credit card processing.

In considering the legality of the Web site services, the OCC concluded that the activity was a form of "finder" activity permissible for national banks. Under the OCC's regulations, a national bank may engage in "without limitation, identifying potential parties, making inquiries as to interest, introducing or arranging meetings of interested parties, and otherwise bringing parties together for transactions that the parties themselves negotiate and consummate."[34] Citing this regulation, the OCC determined that banks may conduct finder activities on the Internet by providing potential customers with information about a retailer's goods and services and performing data processing and storage functions to facilitate any resulting transactions. The hosting of a Web site does not involve a bank in negotiations between buyer and seller, said the OCC, and thus the activity is within the scope of permissible finder activities.

[E] Merchant Hyperlinks

The OCC has permitted, as a finder activity, a national bank to provide hypertext links between the bank's retail banking Web site and the Web sites of third parties interested in selling products or services to the bank's customers.[35] For example, the OCC authorized a national bank to maintain and operate an Internet Web site to provide information to support potential buyers of pre-owned automobiles as a finder activity for a customer.[36]

Chase Manhattan Corporation reportedly has created an online business-to-business purchasing community allowing the bank's 350,000 business customers to sell products directly to one another via a Chase Web site.[36.1] The Web site presumably provides hyperlinks to facilitate the service.

---

[34] 12 C.F.R. § 7.1002.

[35] OCC Conditional Approval No. 221 (Dec. 4, 1996).

[36] OCC Corporate Decision No. 97-60 (July 1, 1997).

[36.1] "Big Banks Grapple with Moving Corporate Services On-line," Am. Banker (Oct. 6, 1999).

Some banks are using Web sites of merchants to advertise their services.[36.2] For example, Banc One reportedly advertises auto loans on an online dealership Web site that allows customers to research, order, finance, and take delivery of a vehicle. The bank was the sole lender on the site.[36.3]

The OCC has allowed national banks to provide hyperlinks both as a value-added service and to generate fee income through finders fees.[36.4] The OCC requires a bank offering such hyperlinks to take reasonable steps to clearly distinguish between the bank's products and services and those of the third party: "Bank customers should be able to identify when they are dealing with the Bank and when they are not, and the Bank should indicate that it does not provide, endorse, or guarantee any of the products or services available through the third-party Web sites."[36.5]

The OCC has stated that a national bank may negotiate arrangements with linked merchants to provide reduced rates to the bank's customers consistent with its role as a "finder."[36.6]

[F] Virtual Malls

In 1999, the OCC approved a proposal by a national bank to invest in a company that would operate a "virtual mall" by providing merchants a package of electronic services designed to facilitate consumer purchases on interlinked merchant Web sites and the bank's Web site.[36.7] The proposed activity involved building Web sites for merchants, processing payments resulting from customer orders received through such sites, providing monthly reports on transaction volume, including the number and types of products sold, and calculation of sales taxes owed by merchants.

[36.2] *See* "Banks on Web Rush into Deals for Pricey Portal Real Estate," Am. Banker (Aug. 10, 1999) (noting that Banc One's WinspanBank.com Internet banking department signed a multiyear cobranding agreement with Lycos worth up to $135 million and Banc One itself is paying Excite@Home up to $125 million to be the exclusive banking center at the Excite site).

[36.3] *See* "Auto Finance: Internet Auto Sites Attract Big Money," Am. Banker (Aug. 13, 1999).

[36.4] OCC Conditional Approval No. 347 (Jan. 29, 2000), n.6.

[36.5] *Id.*

[36.6] OCC Conditional Approval No. 347 (Jan. 29, 2000), n.7.

[36.7] OCC Interpretive Letter No. 875 (Oct. 31, 1999).

§9.10 TELECOMMUNICATIONS APPLICATIONS

[A] In General

Banks and their affiliates are extensive users of telecommunications services for their own operations. Large banks frequently lease telecommu-

[*Next page is 9-17.*]

nication lines in order to obtain high levels of capacity and security for transmitting data between branches as well as to and from ATM networks and PCs used for home banking services.

Banking organizations are not permitted to own or control telecommunications companies unless such companies are limited to providing services for financial institutions. Although banks sometimes resell telephone time, they risk being deemed common carriers under the Federal Communications Act.[37] A common carrier generally is an entity that offers communications services to the public for profit. A general common carrier business has not been found to be part of the business of banking for purposes of the National Bank Act or closely related to banking for purposes of the Bank Holding Company Act ("BHC Act").

Citicorp reportedly applied with the Federal Communications Commission in 1982 to become a common carrier but the FCC rejected its application on grounds that the proposal was beyond Citicorp's authority under the BHC Act.[38]

[B] Excess Telecommunications Capacity

The OCC has permitted a national bank to sell excess capacity in long-line telecommunications equipment when the excess capacity was acquired for anticipated future needs in a private telecommunications network created to link the bank's branches and affiliated banks.[39]

[C] "Smart Phones"

The OCC permitted a national bank to utilize computerized telephones or "smart phones" designed to enable its customer to communicate with the bank for the purpose of performing banking transactions.[40] The smart phone was developed by AT&T and could be used as a normal telephone as well. The phone device had a visual, touch-sensitive screen enabling a caller to access the bank's computers. The OCC determined that the smart phone was merely a convenient way for bank

---

[37] 47 U.S.C. §§ 201-228.

[38] *See* Kalpak S. Gude, "The Integration of Banking and Telecommunications: The Need for Regulatory Reform," 46 Fed. Comm. L.J. 521, 530 (1994).

[39] Unpublished Letter by Stephen B. Brown, OCC Attorney (Dec. 20, 1989), *cited in* OCC Interpretive Letter No. 742 (1996).

[40] OCC Interpretive Letter No. 611 (Nov. 23, 1992), *reprinted in* Fed. Banking L. Rep. (CCH) ¶ 83,449.

customer's to conduct banking transactions and therefore was within the scope of the business of banking notwithstanding its use as a normal phone as well.

[D] Mobile Telephone Services

The Federal Reserve Board has permitted a banking organization to provide an integrated software program for operators of digital mobile telephone networks to perform billing and account-related services for the operator's customer accounts.[41] The Board noted that the program would not be a part of an operator's network operating and switching system and would be operated on dedicated hardware separate from the hardware and software that ran the network.

As proposed, the program would calculate an operator's customer bills based on data provided by the operator's network operating system after customers' calls are completed, additional data provided by the operator concerning the terms of customer service contracts, and individual account balances. Based on this data, the operator would produce billing statements to be sent by the operator to its customers for payment directly to the operator. The system was designed to perform general accounting services, such as making summary entries in the operator's general ledger reflecting payments and changes in accounts receivable and payable, recording payments automatically, and making preauthorized debits directly from customers' bank or credit card accounts. To facilitate these billing functions, the program would store basic information (names, addresses, and telephone numbers) necessary to identify a customer when a new account is opened.

§ 9.11 FINANCIAL INSTITUTION BACK OFFICE SERVICES

A variety of back office services may be performed by banks and their affiliates for other financial institutions using electronic banking technology.

The Board has authorized bank holding companies to provide comprehensive data processing services needed in the operation of a financial institution.[42] Such services may relate to opening and closing customer accounts; calculation of account balances, fees, and interest payments;

---

[41] *Compagnie Financiere de Paribas*, 82 Fed. Res. Bull. 348 (1996).

[42] *BNCCORP*, 81 Fed. Res. Bull. 295 (1995).

preparation of account statements; issuance of certificates of deposit; credit analysis and financial modeling; monitoring of data processing costs; access to financial and economic data bases; bill payments and other home banking transactions; check collection and processing; loan processing and documentation; trade finance; cash management; bank retail operations; tax documentation; signature verification; lockbox operations; securities recordkeeping; and general recordkeeping. The Board also authorized the provision of online data processing and transmission services; data processing services with computer output to optical digital disks, and related storage, retrieval, processing, and transmission capabilities; and on-site data processing and transmission facilities. As an incident to these activities, the Board authorized the purchase, sale, rental, and maintaining of electronic equipment used to perform permissible data processing and transmission services.[43]

In connection with these activities, the Board permitted the processing of nonfinancial data, such as personnel information, for financial institutions in their internal operations. The Board stated that such services may be provided as part of a larger package of data processing services to a financial institution, and may not be offered on a stand-alone basis or to customers other than financial institutions.[44]

In approving such activities, the Board noted that financial institutions must process some nonfinancial information to support their internal operations and that these data typically represent a relatively small percentage of the data processing activities of financial institutions. The Board stated that processing of nonfinancial data is a necessary part of providing general data processing services to financial institutions and that the proposed activity was incidental to permissible data processing activities.

The Board stated that it was not authorizing the provision of management assistance or advice to any financial institution or other customer. For example, in providing data processing services for loan processing and credit analysis, a bank holding company was not authorized to make lending or credit decisions for other financial institutions, process loan or credit applications using the underwriting or credit standards of its

[43] *Id.*

[44] The data processing authority in Regulation Y was broadened by the Board in 1997 to include nonfinancial data processing provided that the total annual revenue derived from such activities does not exceed 30 percent of the company's total annual revenues derived from data processing and transmission activities. 12 C.F.R. § 225.28(b)(14).

own affiliated banks, or provide software incorporating the underwriting or credit standards of any affiliated bank.

In approving Citicorp's acquisition of Quotron Systems, Inc.,[45] the Board permitted Quotron to offer a variety of financial back office services, including a broker portfolio system; an automated client bookkeeping system that analyzed and maintained the value of clients' financial assets based on current market prices; a spreadsheet service which permitted financial calculations, forecasting and analysis; business graphics, allowing customers to plot and analyze financial information; and electronic mail and word processing systems. While the Board noted that the word processing and electronic mail components of the services were capable of being used for nonfinancial applications, the Board approved these services based on Citicorp's commitment that the services would be offered pursuant to a written contract that described and limited the services to the transmission and processing of banking, financial, or economic data. The Board noted that, while Quotron provided its customers with the capacity to access information stored in the customer's own databases, it was likely that such information would be financial data given the nature of Quotron's customers. Because customers would be required to subscribe to Quotron's financial information and database service, the Board concluded that a customer would not be likely to subscribe to the Quotron service merely to obtain word processing capability.

§ 9.12 NONFINANCIAL INSTITUTION AND INFORMATION SERVICES

The Board revised Regulation Y in 1997 to authorize bank holding companies to engage in nonfinancial data processing services provided that the revenue from such services does not exceed 30 percent of a bank holding company's total annual revenues from data processing activities.[46]

Prior to this change in Regulation Y, the Board authorized the provision of nonfinancial data processing services on a limited basis. For example, the Board permitted a bank holding company to provide data

---

[45] *Citicorp (Quotron Systems, Inc.)*, 72 Fed. Res. Bull. 497 (1986). As described in *Citicorp*, Quotron engaged in a variety of data processing and data transmission activities for customers such as securities and commodities exchanges, brokerage firms, commercial banks, S&Ls, insurance companies, and investment managers.

[46] 12 C.F.R. § 225.28(b)(14)(ii).

processing services to nonfinancial institution customers in the following areas:

- billing and payroll;
- accounts receivable and payable;
- inventory;
- accounting and bookkeeping;
- economic forecasting; and
- access to financial and economic databases.[47]

In connection with digital mobile telephone network billing services, the Board approved the transmission of customer identification and account information to the operator's verification files and the generation of certain reports based on these data to detect possible fraudulent use of the network.[48]

In connection with data processing services for financial institutions, the Board authorized a bank holding company to process certain nonfinancial data necessary for the internal operations of a financial institution, such as personnel information.[49]

In approving a bank holding company proposal to acquire an interest in MECA Software, the Board noted that MECA had previously developed several nonfinancial software products, including games, a computer security program, a medical reference library, and a program providing basic legal forms.[50] The Board allowed MEECA to retain these activities based on the applicant's representations that MECA would not dedicate any employees or resources exclusively to the development or marketing of nonfinancial software, revenues from the separate sale of nonfinancial software accounted for only approximately seven percent of MECA's 1994 revenues, and MECA had no intention to develop any new nonfinancial software or to upgrade, enhance, or promote its nonfinancial programs. The Board also noted that it was expected that this portion of MECA's business would diminish over time.

---

[47] *BNCCORP*, 81 Fed. Res. Bull. 295 (1995).

[48] *Compagnie Financiere de Paribas*, 82 Fed. Res. Bull. 348 (1995).

[49] *BNCCORP*, 81 Fed. Res. Bull. 295 (1995).

[50] *Royal Bank of Canada*, 82 Fed. Res. Bull. 363 (1996).

§ 9.13 STOCK QUOTATION AND DATABASE SERVICES

The Federal Reserve Board approved Quotron's financial information service, consisting of online transaction and quotation data regarding stocks, bonds, options, mutual funds, commodities, and a variety of other financial data.[51] The Board approved the provision by Quotron of access to a library of financial and economic databases prepared by third-party database services, including financial information extracted from SEC reports, business and economic news, commentary and forecasts, and advisory services.

The Board and other federal banking regulators have since permitted banking organizations to offer Internet-based securities brokerage services. *See* Chapter 8, **Internet Services,** § 8.07 Internet Securities Transactions.

§ 9.14 COMPUTER NETWORK CONSULTING

The Board has authorized bank holding companies to provide advice and assistance to unaffiliated insured depository institutions in the design, selection, acquisition, installation, and operation of computer networks.[52] Such activities may consist of:

- Evaluating the client's needs in processing banking, financial, or economic data and determining what hardware and software are available to satisfy these needs;[53]
- Recommending combinations of hardware and software that could be assembled to perform the required data processing and transmission functions;

---

[51] *Citicorp (Quotron Systems, Inc.)*, 72 Fed. Res. Bull. 497 (1986).

[52] *First National of Nebraska, Inc*., 82 Fed. Res. Bull. 82 (1996).

[53] Such needs may involve deposit account processing (including account opening, calculating deposits, withdrawals, interest and fees, and generating statements and reports); loan processing (including preparing application forms and disclosures and calculating advances, payments, interest, and fees); item processing; check imaging; lockbox processing; safe deposit box accounting; asset/liability monitoring and management; credit bureau reporting; collecting call report data; geographic activity tracking; application tracking and consumer compliance monitoring; large cash transaction reporting; general ledger accounting; fixed asset accounting; tax accounting and producing customer tax forms; analyzing bank and branch profitability; automated clearing house transactions; wire transfers; telephone and electronic funds transfers initiated by customers.

- Developing a plan for the orderly and timely acquisition and assembly of computer network components by the client, and assisting the client in acquiring these components;
- Setting up individual personal computers and other work stations, such as teller stations and personal banker stations, on the client's computer network; connecting these components to the computer network; installing and testing software components of the computer network; and training the client in the use of the computer network; and
- Providing telephone support to help the client resolve computer network operating problems; isolating and identifying hardware or software defects in the computer network; and helping the client obtain service for these computer network defects from the appropriate vendor or other maintenance provider.

In connection with these activities, the Board permitted the provision of advice and assistance in obtaining and operating facilities for the processing and transmission of nonfinancial data. The Board noted that computer networks operated within insured depository institutions typically are used for processing and transmitting nonfinancial data that the institutions use in their internal operations (such as personnel information), as well as for nonfinancial functions that support the financial data processing and transmission needs of these institutions (such as word processing and electronic mail).

In response to an applicant's argument that, for purposes of marketing, customer service, and technological reasons, it was necessary that the computer networks perform these related nonfinancial functions in addition to its primary financial functions, the Board allowed the company to provide advice and assistance related to the processing and transmission of nonfinancial data, but only as a relatively small part of a larger package of services to insured depository institutions, and not on a stand-alone basis or to customers other than insured depository institutions.

The OCC has authorized similar services for national banks.[54]

[54] OCC Interpretive Letter No. 754 (Nov. 6, 1996).

§ 9.15 OTHER DATA PROCESSING FUNCTIONS

[A] Key Entry Services

Key entry services involve the conversion of non-machine readable source documents obtained from customers into a form that is machine readable without substantively altering the data. The Board at one time denied permission for bank holding companies to provide key entry services.[55] The Board determined that key entry services were neither a data processing activity nor reasonably necessary to permissible data processing activities. Such services now are permissible under Regulation Y.

[B] Computer Output to Microfilm

At one time, the Federal Reserve Board did not allow bank holding companies to offer computer output to microfilm ("COM") services. In 1987, the Board began allowing such services, including reading computer data from magnetic tape, disk or diskette and, through the use of software, microcomputers and recorders, transferring the data to microfilm or microfiches.[56] Such activities now are permissible under Regulation Y.

§ 9.16 COMPUTER HARDWARE

Regulation Y provides that data processing hardware may be offered only in conjunction with permissible software (*i.e.*, the software may be used to process only financial, banking, or economic data).[57] The 30 percent leeway authority under Regulation Y, however, may allow bank holding companies flexibility to offer hardware for use with impermissible software.[58]

[A] Special Purpose Hardware

"Special purpose hardware" is hardware that generally cannot be used for general data processing purposes and is limited to specific applica-

---

[55] *Orbanco*, 66 Fed. Res. Bull. 666 (1980).

[56] *MCorp (Kalvar Corp.)*, 73 Fed. Res. Bull. 933 (1987). The data to be processed were financial, banking, or economic data.

[57] 12 C.F.R. § 225.28(b)(14).

[58] 12 C.F.R. § 225.28(b)(14)(ii).

tions for the processing and transmitting of banking, financial, and economic data.[59]

The OCC has permitted national banks to provide special purpose computer hardware in connection with permissible data processing services, such as card readers for stored value cards[60] and medical information systems.[61]

[B] General Purpose Hardware

"General purpose hardware" is hardware that may be used for purposes other than data processing services relating to banking, financial, and economic data. For example, a personal computer that enables the user to perform general word processing functions is considered to be general purpose hardware. For bank holding companies, the provision of general purpose hardware may be permissible as incidental to a closely related activity, provided its cost is limited to 30 percent of any packaged offering.[62]

The OCC has permitted national banks to offer general purpose hardware that can be used for processing purposes other than, and in addition to, those relating to banking, financial, or economic data. For example, the OCC has permitted a national bank to provide hardware and software capacities to enable customers to use a smart card system to support ancillary functions—such as serving as an identification card, building access control, library card, computer network access device, and meal plan card—as well as the stored value function.[63]

The OCC has stated that a determination that such multi-purpose hardware is permissible must be made on a case-by-case basis taking into consideration such factors as cost, expected revenues, and the expected life of the hardware relative to other aspects of the hardware.[64] The nonbanking functions must be necessary for the banking services to be offered and must not be an excessive part of the service offered. If the multipurpose hardware enables the bank to offer a package of related services required to satisfy customer needs and to successfully market a banking

59 *See Citicorp/Quotron*, 72 Fed. Res. Bull. 497, 499 (1986).

60 OCC Interpretive Letter No. 737 (Aug. 19, 1996).

61 OCC Conditional Approval No. 282 (July 31, 1998).

62 *See Citicorp/Quotron*, 72 Fed. Res. Bull. 497, 499 (1986).

63 OCC Interpretive Letter No. 737 (Aug. 19, 1996).

64 *Id.*

product, the hardware is deemed to be necessary.[65] The OCC has stated that the Regulation Y standard that the cost of hardware may not constitute more than 30 percent of the cost of the total package of services is one means of demonstrating that the sale of the hardware is incidental to the permitted banking service.[66]

[C] Hardware Design and Assembly

In the past, the Board has not generally considered the design and assembly of hardware to be permissible for bank holding companies. In approving Citicorp's acquisition of Quotron,[67] for example, the Board ruled that Citicorp had not demonstrated that the design and assembly by Quotron of hardware used in conjunction with Quotron's software was necessary to Quotron's provision of permissible data processing services and thus could not be considered incidental to the approved activities. The Board noted that hardware of the type provided by Quotron was available and marketed by companies providing services similar to those of Quotron's. The Board allowed Citicorp a two-year period, however, in which to submit arguments to the Board demonstrating that design and assembly of hardware were necessary components of Quotron's services.

[D] Computer Hardware Inventory

The Federal Reserve Board has allowed a bank holding company, as an incident to providing computer networking consulting, to maintain a small inventory of computer hardware that it would make available to its clients as "loaners" to replace defective computer network hardware on a temporary basis. The Board noted that the company's clients would acquire hardware and software directly from third parties and the company would not be a vendor or distributor of any hardware or software or an agent of any third-party provider of hardware or software.[68]

---

[65] *Id.*

[66] OCC Interpretive Letter No. 345 (1985), *reprinted in* Fed. Banking L. Rep. (CCH) ¶ 85,515. *See also* OCC Interpretive Letter No. 516 (1990), *reprinted in* Fed. Banking L. Rep. (CCH) ¶ 83,220.

[67] *Citicorp (Quotron Systems, Inc.)*, 72 Fed. Res. Bull. 497 (1986).

[68] *First National of Nebraska, Inc.*, 82 Fed. Res. Bull. 82 (1996).

§ 9.17 ELECTRONIC MARKETPLACE AND OTHER FINDER ACTIVITIES

Banking organizations are authorized to engage in a wide range of "electronic marketplace" activities through their authority to act as "finders." The federal banking agencies have interpreted the finder authority to allow banking organizations to participate in electronic commerce in diverse ways. Many of the merchant and other services discussed in previous sections were authorized by the OCC as finder activities.

Until recently, bank holding companies were not authorized to engage in finder activities to the same extent as national banks. In 2000, however, the Federal Reserve Board amended its regulations to authorize bank holding companies that become financial holding companies to engage in broad finder activities.[69] Under this new authority, a financial holding company may act as a "finder" in bringing together buyers and sellers of any product or service for transactions that the parties themselves negotiate and consummate. The authority is not limited to financial transactions and would allow a financial holding company, for example, to host a auction site such as that of eBay.

Regulation Y defines the scope of finder activities to include:

- Identifying potential parties, making inquiries as to interest, introducing and referring potential parties to each other, and arranging contacts between and meetings of interested parties;
- Conveying between interested parties expressions of interest, bids, offers, orders and confirmations relating to a transaction; and
- Transmitting information concerning products and services to potential parties in connection with such activities.

Regulation Y gives the following examples of the kinds of services that may be provided by a financial holding company acting as a finder:

- Hosting an electronic marketplace on the financial holding company's Internet Web site by providing hypertext or similar links to the Web sites of third party buyers or sellers.

[69] Fed Reg. 80,735 (2000); *codified at* 12 C.F.R. § 225.86.

- Hosting on the financial holding company's servers the Internet Web site of:
  —A buyer (or seller) that provides information concerning the buyer (or seller) and the products or services it seeks to buy (or sell) and allows sellers (or buyers) to submit expressions of interest, bids, offers, orders and confirmations relating to such products or services; or
  —A government or government agency that provides information concerning the services or benefits made available by the government or government agency, assists persons in completing applications to receive such services or benefits from the government or agency, and allows persons to transmit their applications for services or benefits to the government or agency.
- Operating an Internet Web site that allows multiple buyers and sellers to exchange information concerning the products and services that they are willing to purchase or sell, locate potential counterparties for transactions, aggregate orders for goods or services with those made by other parties, and enter into transactions between themselves.
- Operating a telephone call center that provides permissible finder services.

Regulation Y imposes certain limitations on finder activities. For example, a financial holding company acting as a finder may act only as an intermediary between a buyer and a seller and may not bind any buyer or seller to the terms of a specific transaction or negotiate the terms of a transaction on behalf of a buyer or seller. The financial holding company may, however, establish rules of general applicability governing the use and operation of the company's finder services and arrange for buyers to receive preferred terms from sellers on a general basis. The company may not take title to own any product or service offered through the finder service or provide distribution services. The company also may not own or operate any real or personal property used for the purpose of manufacturing, storing, transporting, or assembling physical products offered or sold by third parties, or that serves as a physical location for the physical purchase, sale or distribution of products or services offered by third parties. In addition, a finder must provide appropriate disclosures distinguishing its products and services from those of third parties.

In adopting these restrictions, the Federal Reserve Board stated that it would review these limits in light of developments in technology, the financial services industry, and the market for finder services to determine whether they continue to be necessary or appropriate. The Board stated that it recognizes "that technological developments in communications, computing, and the Internet have made the intermediary function more important and that further developments in these areas may alter the methods and manner of providing finder services.[70]

Although the finder activity is limited to financial holding companies at present, the Board issued a separate proposal under which bank holding companies that are not financial holding companies could engage in similar activities.[71]

§ 9.18 ACCOUNT AGGREGATION SERVICES

Account aggregation is a service by which consumer account data is gathered from a variety of Web sites, using customer-provided user-names and passwords, and presented to the consumer in a consolidated format. This process sometimes is referred to as "screen scraping." Account aggregation services may be offered with respect to banking accounts, credit cards brokerage accounts, and other types of personal accounts.

A number of large banks and other financial institutions offer account aggregation services, including Citigroup, Wells Fargo, Chase Manhattan, and Morgan Stanley Dean Witter & Co.[72] Banks face major competition from large Internet portals—including AOL, Yahoo, and Microsoft Network—that also offer account aggregation services. Some observers believe that the portals have a competitive advantage over banks because they can aggregate more types of information, including news services, favorite shopping sites, and other information.[73] Recent bank regulatory decisions expanding the activities of banks to engage in "finder" activities should allow banks to offer similar services.[74]

---

[70] 65 Fed. Reg. 80,738 (2000).

[71] 65 Fed. Reg. 80,384 (2000).

[72] *See* "Citi Aggregation Service Called a Hit," Am. Banker, Nov. 30, 2000.

[73] *See* "The New Bankers: Aggregation Pits Banks Against Web Portals," Am. Banker, Dec. 8, 2000.

[74] *See* § 9.17 *supra*.

The federal banking regulators view account aggregation services as a means by which banks can "expand and deepen their customer relationships by leveraging their position as trusted intermediaries."[75] The regulators nevertheless have cautioned banks as to certain risks posed by account aggregation services and have issued supervisory guidance.[76] Among other things, the OCC has cautioned banks that the Web sites from which they access customer information may change or have data integrity or compatibility problems resulting in the collection of inaccurate or incomplete information that could result in customer confusion, loss of reputation and other risks. The OCC advised banks to clearly distinguish between their products and services and those that are offered by third parties and to state that the bank does not provide, endorse or guarantee any of the products or services available through hyper-linked Web sites. In addition, compliance with the federal privacy regulations is required.

Regulation E Implications. The OCC also has warned that disclosures may be required under Regulation E implementing the Electronic Fund Transfer Act if the aggregator issues a card, PIN or other access device to the consumer and agrees to provide electronic fund transfer services with respect to accounts at other institutions.[77]

In 2000, the Federal Reserve Board solicited public comment on how account aggregation services operate and whether account aggregators are financial institutions subject to Regulation E:

> Comment is solicited on how these services that aggregate consumer financial information operate or plan to operate. Are aggregators providing or planning to provide bill-payment or other EFT services (in addition to information services)? To what extent do agreements exist between aggregators and account-holding institutions, governing matters such as procedures for access to information and for electronic transfers?
>
> In addition, comment is solicited on the implications of a determination that aggregators are or are not financial institutions for purposes of Regulation E generally or under § 205.14. Typically, only one access device is contemplated to initiate an EFT to or from a consumer's account. Nevertheless, if a consumer enters a security code issued by the aggregator to access information on the aggregator's web site and the consumer initiates an EFT using a security

[75] *See* OCC Bulletin 2001–12 (Feb. 28, 2001).

[76] *Id.*

[77] *Id.*

> code provided by the account-holding institution, the security code issued by the aggregator arguably meets the definition of an "access device." Two access codes (the one provided by the aggregator and the other by the account-holding institution) are needed to initiate electronic transfers from the consumer's account from the aggregator's web site. Thus, the aggregator would be a financial institution for purposes of Regulation E.
>
> If the aggregator is not a financial institution and an unauthorized EFT occurs through an aggregator's service, comment 2(m)-2 could be read to suggest that a consumer who has given the aggregator access to the consumer's account assumes liability for the transfers. The guidance in the comment, however, was not originally provided to address this situation.[78]

The Board did not take any final action but stated that it "will consider addressing these issues in a future proposal."[79]

---

[78] 65 Fed. Feg. 40,064 (2000).

[79] 66 Fed. Reg. 15,187, 15,188 (2001). *See also* Chapter 13, **Consumer Protection and Privacy,** for a discussion of Regulation E.

CHAPTER 10

ELECTRONIC TRANSFER OF FEDERAL PAYMENTS

§ 10.01 EFT DELIVERY OF FEDERAL PAYMENTS

In 1996, Congress required the conversion of federal payments from paper-based instruments to electronic funds transfer ("EFT").[1] After January 1, 1999, all payments by agencies of the federal government must be delivered electronically, with the exception of payments under the Internal Revenue Code, unless the Secretary of the Treasury grants a waiver.[2]

The conversion to EFT delivery is expected to save the federal government approximately $100 million each year by simplifying the dispersal process for the more than 850 million federal payments made by the Treasury each year.[3] The Treasury Department has noted that, whereas a check payment costs the government about 43 cents, including postage and labor costs, an EFT payment costs only about two cents.[4]

Approximately 53 percent of payments made by the U.S. Treasury were made by electronic funds transfer as of 1996.[5] The Treasury has estimated that recipients are 20 times less likely to have a problem with an electronic payment than with a paper check due to the reduced susceptibility of an EFT payment to damage, forgery, or theft.

The Treasury stated that, in implementing the EFT requirement, it hoped to "bring into the mainstream of the financial system those millions of Americans who receive Federal payments and who currently do not use the financial system to receive funds, make payments, save, borrow or invest."[6] The Treasury's goals in implementing the Act include "making certain that recipients have access to their funds at a reasonable cost; providing appropriate consumer protection; ensuring that the system deliv-

---

[1] Section 31001(x) of the Debt Collection Improvement Act of 1996.

[2] 31 U.S.C. § 3332. The law required all federal payments to be made electronically to newly eligible benefit recipients after July 26, 1996, unless the recipient did not have a bank account. As of January 1, 1999, no exception is provided for individuals without bank accounts, although the Treasury may grant waivers.

[3] 62 Fed. Reg. 48,714, 48,715 (1997). Of the 850 million payments, 585 million were made to individuals under various benefit programs such as Social Security.

[4] *Id.*

[5] 62 Fed. Reg. 48,714 (1997). The federal government uses Direct Deposit by which federal agencies make wage, salary, retirement, and other payments; Vendor Express, which transfers payments directly into the accounts of vendors and other commercial payees; and the Automated Standard Application for Payments ("ASAP") program, which delivers time-sensitive federal funds to payees, grant payments, and same-day payments to contractors.

[6] 62 Fed. Reg. 48,714 (1997).

ers payments and information accurately, conveniently, and in a timely manner; and significantly increasing participation by recipients in the country's financial system."[7]

§ 10.02 ELECTRONIC BENEFITS TRANSFER

Electronic benefits transfer or "EBT" refers to the electronic delivery of government benefits, such as food stamps and social security payments, through magnetic-stripe cards that can be used at ATMs or point-of-sale ("POS") terminals. The terminals may be part of existing bank ATM networks or, in the case of food stamps, may be located in grocery stores.

EBT systems provide faster, more convenient access to benefits, lower costs to recipients (no check cashing fees), and greater privacy and security of funds. EBT also lowers the government's cost of delivering benefits, facilitates the management of benefit programs, and reduces fraud.[8]

Under the 1996 law, benefit recipients are required to designate a "financial institution" or "authorized agent" to which federal payments are to be sent electronically and to provide the issuing agency with the information necessary to make the payments electronically. The term "financial institution" is defined in the Treasury's implementing regulations to mean an insured depository institution or an institution that is eligible to apply for deposit insurance. An "authorized payment agent" is defined to mean an individual or entity appointed as a representative payee or fiduciary of the recipient for purposes of receiving a federal payment under regulations of the Social Security Administration, Department of Veterans Affairs, Railroad Retirement Board, or other federal agency.

The Treasury may grant waivers from the EBT requirement in cases of hardship or other circumstances. The Treasury estimates that approximately 10 million individuals fall into the waiver category.

[A] Regulation E

The Federal Reserve Board ("Board") amended Regulation E in 1994 to expressly bring EBT programs within its coverage.[9] In 1996,

---

[7] *Id.*

[8] *See* 62 Fed. Reg. 43,467 (1997).

[9] 59 Fed. Reg. 10,678 (1994); 12 C.F.R. 205.15.

Congress enacted legislation exempting from Regulation E "needs-tested" EBT programs established or administered under state or local law, and the Board amended Regulation E accordingly.[10] A "needs-tested" program generally considers a recipient's income or other resources in determining the amount of benefits to which the recipient is entitled. Congress acted in response to concerns voiced by state and local officials regarding the costs of compliance with Regulation E.

The Board has specifically authorized bank holding companies to provide electronic benefit transfer services under the Bank Holding Company Act.[11] These activities consist of data processing and transmission services for the delivery of welfare payments and food stamps, and other government benefits through the POS and ATM terminals of participating merchants and banks.

[B] Treasury Regulation

In 1998, the Treasury adopted a final regulation to implement the requirement for federal payments by EFT.[12] Under the regulation, each recipient of federal payments who has an account with a financial institution is required to designate a financial institution through which the payment may be direct deposited and to provide the agency with information necessary to effect the payment.[13]

An individual who does not have an account with a financial institution may open a Treasury-designated electronic transfer account or "ETA^sm" at a federally insured financial institution. An ETA^sm account may be opened by any individual that receives federal payments, whether or not the individual has a bank account. An ETA^sm account can be opened only at a financial institution that offers ETA^sm s.

Financial institutions are not required to offer ETA^sm s but may elect to do so. An institution that so elects is required to enter into an ETA^sm Financial Agency Agreement with the Treasury and to be designated as the Treasury's Financial Agent.[14]

---

[10] *See* 62 Fed. Reg. 43,467 (1997).

[11] *See Banc One Corp., et al.*, 79 Fed. Res. Bull. 1158 (1994).

[12] 63 Fed. Reg. 51,490 (1998).

[13] 31 C.F.R. § 208.8.

[14] 31 C.F.R. § 208.5 ("Any Federally-insured financial institution shall be eligible, but not required, to offer ETA^sm as Treasury's Financial Agent.")

The EFT requirement is waived if an individual determines "in his or her sole discretion" that EFT payment would impose a "hardship due to a physical or mental disability or a geographic, language, or literacy barrier, or would impose a financial hardship."[15] For example, if it would cost more for a recipient to receive a payment electronically than by check, the individual may elect not to receive an electronic payment. The EFT requirement is also waived in certain cases involving payments to foreign countries, in disaster areas, to military personnel on active duty, or in cases involving a national security risk.

The regulation distinguishes between a direct deposit payment and an EBT payment by defining EBT as an electronic payment disbursed through a Financial Agent acting on behalf of the Treasury:

> In Direct Deposit, Treasury initiates an electronic payment to a recipient's account, but has no responsibilities with respect to the account or the nature or quality of the account services provided. In contrast, in an EBT program, the attributes of the account to which the Federal payments are sent are determined by Treasury, and the financial institution provides recipients access to their payments in the manner and on terms specified by Treasury. The financial institution holding the EBT account acts as Treasury's Financial Agent in establishing and maintaining the account for the recipient, and thus has a legal relationship with Treasury with respect to the account.[16]

An ETA^{sm} account may be opened only by an individual who receives a federal benefit, wage, salary, or retirement payment, thereby excluding government contractors or vendors with respect to contract payments from the government. Such contractors or vendors must open a direct deposit account with a federally insured financial institution.

An individual may designate an "authorized payment agent" to receive payments on his or her behalf at a financial institution under regulations of the Social Security Administration, Department of Veterans Affairs, or other agency making federal payments. Such an agent may be a broker-dealer that maintains an investment account on behalf of the recipient. In most cases, the federal payment must be made to an account in the name of the recipient but, in the case of an investment account,

---

[15] 31 C.F.R. § 208.4.

[16] 63 Fed. Reg. at 51,492.

the account may be in the broker-dealer's name.[17] The Treasury's initial proposal would have required an investment account to be structured so the recipient's interest is protected by deposit insurance, but this requirement was eliminated in the final rule in view of the costs of structuring such an arrangement and the protections afforded to investors under the securities laws.

Some recipients of federal payments utilize payment services of nonbank check cashers, currency exchanges, or money transmitters in rural or low- and moderate-income areas not served by banks but which have entered into EFT arrangements with banks. The Treasury voiced concerns that the lack of federal regulation of such nonbank payment service providers could raise the possibility that recipients would not be clearly informed of the fees involved, the applicability of deposit insurance, or the ETA^sm option.[18] Treasury noted that it has advised the federal bank regulatory agencies that banks should provide appropriate disclosures to customers when it participates in arrangements with nonbank providers of payment services with respect to federal payments and explain the applicability of federal deposit insurance. Treasury said it would monitor such arrangements and possibly issue regulations governing nonbank payment providers in the future.

In a separate action, the Treasury requested public comment on the attributes that would be required for an ETA^sm account.[19] As proposed, an ETA^sm account would:

- Be an individually owned account at a federally-insured financial institution;
- Be available to any individual who receives a federal benefit, wage, salary, or retirement payment;
- Accept only electronic federal benefit, wage, salary, and retirement payments;
- Be subject to a maximum price of $3.00 per month;
- Have a minimum of four cash withdrawals per month, to be included in the monthly fee, through (a) the financial institution's proprietary (on-us) ATMs, (b) over-the-counter

---

[17] 31 C.F.R. § 208.6.

[18] 63 Fed. Reg. at 51,498.

[19] 63 Fed. Reg. 64,820 (Nov. 23, 1998).

transactions at the main office or a branch of the financial institution, or (c) any combination of on-us ATM access and over-the-counter access at the option of the financial institution. (Financial institutions may provide additional withdrawals at no charge or for a fee.);

- Provide the same consumer protections that are available to other account holders at the financial institution, including, for accounts that provide electronic access, Regulation E protections regarding disclosure, limitations on liability, procedures for reporting lost or stolen cards, and procedures for error resolution;
- For financial institutions that are members of POS networks, allow POS purchases at no additional charge by the financial institution offering the ETA^sm, as well as cash withdrawals and cash back with purchases, consistent with current commercial practice;
- Require no minimum balance, except as required by federal or state law; and
- Provide a monthly statement.

Treasury requested comment on whether ETA^sm account balances should earn interest. Treasury noted that, while the payment of interest could encourage more individuals to use ETA^sm accounts, account balances in an ETA^sm account likely would be drawn down very quickly after deposit and thus interest earnings could be very small. Also, Treasury noted that there would be regulatory compliance costs associated with the offering of an interest bearing account under the Truth in Savings Act and 1099 tax reporting.[20]

In order to maximize the number of financial institutions that choose to offer ETA^sm s, Treasury proposed to pay each bank a one-time fee per account to offset the costs of setting up the account. The Treasury cited studies indicating that the cost would be approximately $13 per account and said that it might also compensate banks to offset marketing, training, and education costs relating to the offering of ETA^sm accounts.

In 1999, Treasury issued a notice of the following attributes of ETA^sm accounts under which such an account must:

---

[20] *Id.* at 64,824.

- Be an individually owned account at a federally insured financial institution;
- Be available to any individual who receives a federal benefit, wage, salary, or retirement payment;
- Accept electronic federal benefit, wage, salary, and retirement payments and such other deposits as a financial institution agrees to permit;
- Be subject to a maximum price of $3.00 per month;
- Have a minimum of four cash withdrawals and four balance inquiries per month, to be included in the monthly fee, through (a) the financial institution's proprietary (on-us) automated teller machines (ATMs), (b) over-the-counter transactions at the main office or a branch of the financial institution, or (c) any combination of on-us ATM access and over-the-counter access at the option of the financial institution;
- Provide the same consumer protections that are available to other account holders at the financial institution, including, for accounts that provide electronic access, Regulation E protections regarding disclosure, limitations on liability, procedures for reporting lost or stolen cards, and procedures for error resolution;
- For financial institutions that are members of an on-line point-of-sale (POS) network, allow on-line POS purchases, cash withdrawals, and cash back with purchases at no additional charge by the financial institution offering the ETA[sm]; require no minimum balance, except as required by federal or state law;
- At the option of the financial institution, be either an interest-bearing or a non-interest-bearing account; and
- Provide a monthly statement.[21]

A financial institution may provide additional withdrawals from an ETA[sm] or balance inquiries at no charge or for a fee.

---

[21] 64 Fed. Reg. 38,510 (1999).

CHAPTER 11

SYSTEM SECURITY AND RISK

§ 11.01 NEW TYPES OF RISK

The use of computer technology for nearly all aspects of banking operations exposes banks to new risks as well as opportunities. With electronic banking comes increased potential for loss or corruption of critical data, unauthorized access to sensitive information, and fatal system failure. These risks can result from human error, technological malfunctions, or criminal activity including "cyber-terrorism."

The use of the Internet for banking operations presents additional risks. As the federal banking regulators have warned:

> The broad geographic reach, ease of access, and anonymity of the Internet require close attention to maintaining secure systems, intrusion detection and reporting systems, and customer authentication, verification, and authorization.[1]

Whatever the cause, the potential for adverse operational, financial, reputational, and legal consequences affecting individual banks as well as the entire banking industry is greatly magnified by the use of electronic banking technology without proper security precautions and procedures. For this reason, the growing participation of banks in electronic banking has resulted in heightened supervisory concerns regarding the effectiveness of system security.

The Office of the Comptroller of the Currency ("OCC") in 1998, issued a bulletin to national banks on Technology Risk Management, focusing on transaction risk, strategic risk, reputation risk, and compliance risk.[1.1] The following is a summary of the OCC's description of these risks:

- *Transaction risk,* according to the OCC, is risk to earnings or capital due to problems in product or service delivery arising from deficiencies in hardware or software design, faulty implementation or maintenance, or incompatible internal and external systems or incompatible equipment and software. Transaction risk can increase when a bank outsources computer services to third-party vendors and when

[1] Federal Financial Institutions Examination Council, *Statement on Risk Management of Outsourced Technology Services* (Nov. 28, 2000) at 2.

[1.1] OCC Bulletin 98-3, *Technology Risk Management* (Feb. 4, 1998).

banks merge or acquire new businesses, due to the increased likelihood of incompatibility problems and lack of controls.

- *Strategic risk* arises when bank management fails to understand, support, or use technological processes or systems that are essential for the bank to compete or if management depends on a technology that is not outdated or reliable.
- *Reputation risk* may arise from negative public opinion caused by malfunctions, misuse of customer information, flawed security, or litigation resulting from the foregoing that can impair the bank's customer relationships.
- *Compliance risk* can arise when a bank's systems fail to ensure compliance with mandatory reporting or other requirements, such as credit scoring models used in automated lending systems that may result in lending patterns violative of the fair lending laws if not used correctly.

In its 1998 bulletin, the OCC outlined risk management review guidelines for bank examiners and indicated that technology risk will be an important focus of bank examinations in the future.

In a separate initiative, the OCC issued supplementary guidance on the risks associated with personal computer ("PC") banking.[2] The OCC cautioned that, in addition to the risks noted above, PC banking may present other types of risk including, for example, credit risk from Internet lending services which may pose problems in identification, authentication, and transaction verification. Poor data integrity or system unreliability also may pose liquidity, interest rate, market, price, and foreign exchange risk, according to the OCC.

The Basle Committee on Banking Supervision in 1998 released guidelines to assist banks and their supervisors in developing methods for identifying, assessing, managing, and controlling risks associated with electronic banking.[3] Among the types of risk addressed in the guidelines are:

- Legal risks of noncompliance due to uncertain or ambiguous laws.

---

[2] OCC Bulletin 98-38, *Technology Risk Management: PC Banking* (Aug. 24, 1998).

[3] Basle Committee on Banking Supervision, *Risk Management for Electronic Banking and Electronic Money Activities* (1998).

- Money laundering.
- Lawsuits by customers disputing transactions.
- Litigation for violations of customer privacy expectations.
- Litigation by customers defrauded by linked Web sites.
- Digital signature forgeries and fraud.

[*Next page is 11-5.*]

- Exposure to foreign jurisdictions alleging violations of foreign laws applicable to Internet transactions involving customers in other countries.

The Federal Reserve Board ("Federal Reserve" or "Board") has cautioned that Internet banking activities create the risk of electronic interception, interference, or fraud, but that no software product or security system can provide "absolute" protection against these risks. The Board stated that the nature of these risks is not materially different from those to which more traditional banking operations are exposed in other forms.[4] The Board warned banking organizations contemplating Internet services to carefully analyze the risks of such services.

In order to avoid the possibility that consumers would view the Board's approval of a bank holding company's application for Internet banking services as an endorsement or guarantee, the Board requires applicants to commit that they will not make any representations in any marketing materials that the Board's approval constitutes an endorsement by the Federal Reserve System or that the Federal Reserve System has approved, assured, or endorsed the security, functionality, or effectiveness of products or services to be offered.[5]

The Office of Thrift Supervision ("OTS") has taken a more cautious view of Internet banking, stating that it "does not agree that transactions conducted over the Internet pose no more risk than transactions performed through other more established technologies. While it is true that risks are inherent in all electronic capabilities, the use of an electronic channel such as the Internet to deliver products and services introduces unique risks due to the increased speed at which systems operate, user anonymity, and broad access in terms of geography, user groups, applications, databases, and peripheral systems."[6] In 1998, the OTS adopted a rule requiring savings associations to provide advance notice to the OTS when they establish transactional Web sites to address such risks.[7]

The federal banking agencies have noted that PC banking on the Internet often increases a bank's reliance on third-party service providers

---

[4] *Cardinal Bancshares, Inc.*, 82 Fed. Res. Bull. 674 (1996).

[5] *Id.*

[6] 62 Fed. Reg. 65,673, 65,678 (1998).

[7] *Id.*

and requires appropriate due diligence in evaluating their reputation, financial status, and viability.[8]

The General Accounting Office ("GAO") in 1999 issued a report on the oversight of Internet banking activities by the federal banking agencies.[9] The GAO reviewed 81 examinations of Internet activities and found that 44 percent of the depository institutions examined had not completely implemented risk-management steps recommended by regulators to limit online banking risks. The GAO cited lack of approval of strategic plans by bank boards of directors and policies and procedures at some institutions for Internet banking operations. The GAO noted that too few examinations had been performed at the time of GAO's review to identify the extent of any industry-wide Internet banking-related problems. The GAO found variations in the supervisory approaches used by the banking agencies.

§11.02 SYSTEM SECURITY

According to a 1996 survey by the Computer Security Institute and the Federal Bureau of Investigation ("FBI"), of 428 corporations, government agencies, financial institutions, and universities surveyed, 53 percent reported having been victims of computer viruses and 42 percent reported unauthorized use of their computer systems in the prior 12 months.[10]

On July 15, 1996, President Clinton signed Executive Order 13010 creating the President's Commission on Infrastructure Protection ("PCIP"). The PCIP's mission was to assess the nation's infrastructure vulnerabilities and to develop protection strategies for the future. Among the eight critical infrastructures identified by the PCIP as requiring review and assurance strategies was banking and finance.[11] The commission defined "an infrastructure threat," stating that it could be posed by anyone with the capability, technology, opportunity, and intent to do harm. Potential threats could be foreign or domestic, internal or external, state-

---

[8] *See, e.g.*, OCC Bulletin 98-38 (Aug. 24, 1998).

[9] General Accounting Office, *Electronic Banking: Enhancing Federal Oversight of Internet Banking Activities,* GAO/GGD-99-91 (July 6, 1999).

[10] *See* 63 Fed. Reg. 43,327 n.7 (1998) (OTS notice of proposed rulemaking).

[11] The other infrastructures were information and communications, electric power systems, oil and gas transportation and storage, transportation, water supply systems, emergency services, and government services.

sponsored, or a single rogue element and included terrorists, insiders, disgruntled employees, and hackers.

The banking and finance infrastructure was defined by the PCIP as composed of five principal sectors: banks, financial service companies, payment systems, investment companies, and securities and commodities exchanges. The PCIP's banking and finance team conducted a broad-based industry outreach effort, developed a profile of major participants, geographically mapped industry operations, assessed the level of vulnerability and defense within the financial system, and reviewed the analytic structures in use for such key industry processes as risk analysis and countermeasure investment decision-making. The PCIP's principal finding regarding the financial services sector was:

> [D]ue to its carefully structured mixture of public oversight and private initiative, the U.S. financial system is among the world's finest. The modern U.S. financial system never has suffered a debilitating catastrophe, and for that reason among others carries an extraordinarily high level of global confidence. Some observers go so far as to characterize it as shock proof.
>
> * * *
>
> The institutions comprising the financial services industry are further ahead than most in employing sophisticated and, in some cases, unique defenses against loss of assets and corruption of core data systems. Consequently, the U.S. financial system is unusually well protected at the national level, and is well prepared to confront a broad range of threats to its operations and integrity.
>
> * * *
>
> Managing risk is the principal business of financial institutions. They view protection against physical and cyber threats as a necessary cost of doing business, and they often position security as a competitive advantage and highlight it in advertising designed to attract new customers for such services as remote banking. Security is an integral component of institutional performance and accountability.

Nevertheless, the financial service sector has significant exposure to cyber risks and the industry and its regulators have taken substantial measures to guard against these risks.

On May 22, 1998, President Clinton signed Presidential Decision Directive (PDD) 63, Critical Infrastructure Protection, establishing government policy direction and goals to address issues and recommendations made by the FFIEC. A critical objective of PDD 63 was to assure the viability and continuity of the financial service sector against intentional acts that could significantly impact its ability to provide for the orderly functioning of the economy and the continued public confidence in the sector's ability to prevent, detect, and respond to infrastructure incidents. To implement this objective, the U.S. Treasury Department has held Financial Sector Critical Infrastructure Protection meetings with representatives from the private and public sectors. The meetings concluded that the threat of cyber attack is valid and that a cooperative effort between the public and private sectors was essential to guard against such attack. The meetings also determined that efforts must be made to create a process to identify and respond to cyber attack and recommended the creation of an Information Sharing and Analysis Center to screen and analyze problems in the financial service sector.

In 1998, the General Accounting Office reported a lack of adequate electronic banking security measures at a number of banks it surveyed in connection with a study of online banking activities. According to the GAO, 10 percent of the banks surveyed lacked firewalls restricting access between computer networks, 11 percent did not have such basic security features as detection software for computer viruses and worms, 38 percent had experienced lapses in service, 30 percent had experienced security problems, and 36 percent had experienced system operation difficulties.[12]

To assist bank management in adopting appropriate security measures the Federal Reserve Board's Division of Banking Supervision and Regulation in 1997 released "Sound Practices Guidance for Information Security for Networks."[13] The guidance does not have the force of a regulation but rather outlines prudent and effective measures to protect information and ensure its integrity, availability, and confidentiality. The guidance emphasizes the need for active board and management oversight, policies and procedures, and ongoing monitoring and internal controls. Among the measures discussed are encryption techniques, background checks on systems administrators and technology personnel, access controls, proper configuration of network servers, and crisis management procedures.

---

[12] General Accounting Office, *Electronic Banking: Experiences Reported by Banks in Implementing On-line Banking*, GAO/GGD-98-34 (Jan. 1998), at 3.

[13] Board of Governors of the Federal Reserve System, Division of Banking Supervision and Regulation, SR 97-32 (SUP) (Dec. 4, 1997).

The Federal Deposit Insurance Corporation ("FDIC") also has addressed security risks associated with use of the Internet.[14] Describing the Internet as "inherently insecure," the FDIC noted that the principal risks of Internet use are its global reach and open architecture, which also are its principal benefits. The FDIC pointed out that, unless otherwise protected, all data transfers over the Internet can be read and even altered by others and that the Internet is a means by which unauthorized access to a bank's internal information systems can be obtained and used to debilitate the system:

> The open architecture of the Internet also makes it easy for system attacks to be launched against systems from anywhere in the world. Systems can even be accessed and then used to launch attacks against other systems. A typical attack would be a denial of service attack, which is intended to bring down a server, system, or application. This might be done by overwhelming a system with so many requests that it shuts down. Or, an attack could be as simple as accessing and altering a Web site, such as changing advertised rates on certificates of deposit.[15]

The FDIC also warned against flaws and bugs in system software and hardware and other vulnerabilities that can compromise the integrity of an entire system, such as viruses and other malicious programs. The FDIC described appropriate risk controls for Internet use but avoided making specific recommendations, leaving to each bank's management the decision as to which security system is best suited to the bank's system design and objectives.

In 1997, the FDIC issued Electronic Banking Safety and Soundness Examination Procedures to provide a framework for banks and their examiners in assessing and managing the risks of electronic banking. The Procedures establish different levels of examiner review for information-only systems, electronic information transfer systems, and retail electronic payments systems that are viewed as posing different levels of risk. The Procedures also identify different types of risk that may arise including financial, strategic, and systemic risk, depending on the capacity in which a bank is acting.

In more recent guidance, the FDIC in 1999 issued a paper providing guidance on tools and practices designed to facilitate the online banking

---

[14] FDIC, "Security Risks Associated with the Internet," FIL-131-97 (Dec. 18, 1997).
[15] *Id.* at 4.

risk assessment process.[16] The FDIC emphasized three fundamentals of information security—prevention, detection, and response—and noted that a bank's information security program should be customized based on a comprehensive assessment of risk. The FDIC also recommended that banks adopt sound vendor management programs to address risk from third parties to whom they outsource operations.

In its 1998 issued guidance to national banks on PC banking,[17] the OCC noted that PC banking on the Internet often increases a bank's reliance on third-party service providers and requires appropriate due diligence in evaluating their reputation, financial status, and viability. A primary concern is maintaining control over the products and services provided by third-party vendors. The OCC noted that risk controls are needed to address the additional transaction risk resulting from weaknesses in design, implementation, and monitoring of the PC banking infrastructure. The OCC also provided guidance for additional controls addressing strategic, reputation, and compliance risks raised by PC banking. In addition, the OCC noted, PC banking requires special measures to address issues of customer identification, authentication and transaction verification as well as the security of customer information and transaction data. The OCC's guidance discusses security measures such as passwords, firewalls, encryption, virus protection, and intrusion detection.

The Federal Financial Institutions Examination Council ("FFIEC") in 1996 raised concerns regarding the decentralization of computer systems at many banks through so-called client/server systems, which have replaced mainframe computer systems with networks of individual computerized workstations using shared data and information processing systems.[18] The FFIEC noted that the diffusion of computing power throughout the network makes it more difficult to maintain security controls, creates the possibility of unauthorized modification of application programs, and increases vulnerability to usage incompatibilities, among other problems.

Several private industry initiatives have designed programs to provide security for electronic banking and commerce transactions. For example, MasterCard has developed the SET Secure Electronic Transaction™ standards for shopping on the Internet. SET uses a system of locks and

---

[16] Federal Deposit Insurance Corporation, *Risk Assessment Tools and Practices for Information System Security*, FIL-68-99.

[17] OCC Bulletin 98-38 (Aug. 24, 1998).

[18] FFIEC, "Risk Management of Client/Server Systems," FDIC FIL-82-96 (Oct. 8, 1996).

keys along with certified account IDs for both consumers and merchants and encrypts the information to provide a secure exchange of transaction data. The American Bankers Association has created a subsidiary called ABAecom to provide high-level encryption services for financial institutions as a means of facilitating secure electronic banking and commerce.

On the international level, the Organization for Economic Cooperation and Development ("OECD") has been active in considering policy and regulatory issues relating the development of secure information and communication infrastructures and technologies. The OECD has published several reports addressing infrastructure security.[19]

§11.03 SOUNDNESS OF SYSTEM OPERATORS

Apart from the issue of system security is the question of the financial soundness of the system operator. If an issuer of stored value cards runs into financial difficulty or fails, what is the status of the electronic money issued by the issuer? Can a customer still use his card or redeem it, and from whom? Should the government impose prudential requirements on electronic money issuers, such as liquidity and capital requirements, investment limitations, and reserve requirements? Should the government license and examine electronic money issuers?

The answer to these questions will depend on how prevalent electronic money systems become and whether they develop within or outside of the banking system. As of this writing, the government appears to have little interest in regulating electronic money issuers in view of the small scale of such systems at present.

§11.04 TECHNOLOGY RISK

Technology risk is the risk of operational failure due to unintentional technological malfunctions, such as software glitches or hardware design flaws causing computers to operate improperly or fail. Incompatibility of computer systems and obsolescence are other types of technology risk. Technology risk exposes banks to potential loss of valuable data, disruption

[19] *See* Organization for Economic Cooperation and Development, *Guidelines on the Securities of Information Systems* (1992); *Cryptography Policy* (1997); *Ministerial Declaration on Authentication for Electronic Commerce* (1998); *Inventory of Approaches to Authentication and Certification, Background Paper* (1998).

of operations, and loss of customer goodwill that can cost a bank millions of dollars.

The Year 2000 problem is an example of technology risk on a grand scale.[20]

Instances of technology risk at individual banks can also be costly and can have a ripple effect throughout the banking system. An often cited example of technology risk is a software failure that halted securities clearing operations at The Bank of New York in November of 1985, forcing the bank to incur $23 billion in overdrafts from the Federal Reserve System at a major cost to the bank.

With respect to strategic technology risk, the OCC has advised banks to address potential issues such as vendor incompatibility, system capacity problems, and ongoing maintenance costs, and stated that OCC examiners will evaluate the compatibility of a bank's PC banking system with its strategic goals, business tactics, and overall risk tolerance.[21]

The rapid pace of technological invention and the banking industry's critical dependence on computerized information and communications systems has made technology risk a major focus of supervisory concern.[22] In 1999, the FFIEC adopted a new Uniform Rating System for Information Technology ("URSIT") that replaces the former rating system for data processing operations and clarifies the supervisors' expectations as to how well banking organizations manage technology risk.[23] Under the proposed rating system, each bank will be assigned a composite rating from 1 to 5 based on four components: adequacy of the bank's information technology audit function; capability of information technology management; adequacy of systems development and programming; and quality, reliability, availability, and integrity of information technology operations.

Ongoing system maintenance and evaluation, testing, upgrades, computer training, and contingency planning are among the technology risk management techniques available to banks. The Federal Reserve has stated

---

[20] *See* Chapter 12, **Year 2000 Issues**, for a discussion of how this problem is being addressed in the financial sector.

[21] OCC Bulletin 98-38 (Aug. 24, 1998). *See also* OCC Bulletin 98-03, *Technology Risk Management* (Feb. 4, 1998).

[22] *See* Federal Reserve Division of Banking Supervision and Regulation, "Assessment of Information Technology in the Risk-Focused Frameworks for the Supervision of Community Banks and Large Complex Banking Organizations," SR 98-9 (Apr. 20, 1998).

[23] 64 Fed. Reg. 3109 (1999).

that technology risks must be managed by a bank for each of its significant business activities, as well as for the overall banking organization. The Federal Reserve has determined that all safety and soundness examinations of banking organizations conducted by its examiners should include an assessment and evaluation of information technology risks and risk management, and in 2000 eliminated the former frequency guidelines for information technology examinations.[24] The Board stated that the scope of the information technology assessment generally should be sufficient to assign a composite rating under the URSIT. With respect to banking organizations that outsource core processing functions, the Board stated that the URSIT rating may not be meaningful and thus the assessment of information technology activities should be incorporated directly into the safety and soundness rating rather than through a URSIT rating.[25]

§ 11.05 SYSTEMIC RISK

The increasing speed with which electronic payments can occur as a result of computer technology heightens the potential for systemic risk to the entire banking system due to the rapidity with which the ripple effect of a financial shock can be transmitted throughout the system. Systemic risk is the risk that problems at one institution will have a domino effect on other institutions and ultimately cause instability in the financial system as a whole.

Systemic risk can occur not only within the United States financial system but within the global system as a whole and can be difficult to contain across international borders.

§ 11.06 CRIMINAL ACTIVITY AND FRAUD

The possibility for criminal activity in the financial system, particularly money laundering and theft, is greatly increased by electronic payment systems that permit virtually anonymous transactions without any paper trail. It has been estimated that banking, insurance, and securities firms collectively lost more than $800 million in 1996 due to computer crimes.[26] The FBI has estimated that computer criminals cost United States businesses $7.5 billion a year.[27]

---

[24] Federal Reserve Board, SR 00-3 (SUP) (Feb. 29, 2000).

[25] *Id.*

[26] *See* 63 Fed. Reg. 43,327 n.7 (1998) (OTS notice of proposed rulemaking).

[27] *Id.*

The Department of Justice has warned of the dangers of increased money laundering:

> Some [stored value card] systems . . . would permit money launderers to obscure the origins of funds while avoiding the use of financial institutions entirely. These systems have no central registry of transactions which would allow the transactions to be reconstructed. A sophisticated launderer, using multiple cards, could create an intricate series of transfers that could not be unraveled, and that would circumvent almost all existing money laundering laws. Internet payment systems can similarly permit multiple transactions that could be next to impossible to trace, particularly if unscrupulous merchants cooperate with the criminals. This would mean, for example, that the chances of apprehending a criminal who successfully bilked consumers in fraudulent online transactions would be significantly reduced.[28]

Computer crimes are addressed in the federal criminal code at 18 U.S.C. § 1030 ("Fraud and Related Activity in Connection with Computers"). The statute prohibits any person from intentionally accessing a protected computer to obtain certain kinds of information without authority or in excess of authority, and specifically prohibits improper access to information contained in a "financial record" pertaining to a customer's relationship with a financial institution.[29] The statute also prohibits a person from knowingly using a protected computer with intent to defraud or obtain anything of value (*e.g.*, obtaining a home banking customer's password and fraudulently transferring funds from the customer's account).[30] Also prohibited is unauthorized access that results in damage to a protected computer (*e.g.*, introducing a virus or flooding a system with e-mail that disrupts the system).[31]

The federal banking regulators have issued guidance on the reporting of computer-related crimes by banks.[32] Developed with the FBI, the guidance is intended to facilitate timely and accurate reporting of apparent violations of 18 U.S.C. § 1030.

---

[28] Remarks of Peter J. Toren, Trial Attorney, Computer Crime and Intellectual Property Section of the Criminal Division of the U.S. Department of Justice, before the Federal Trade Commission (July 17, 1997).

[29] 18 U.S.C. § 1030(a)(2).

[30] 18 U.S.C. § 1030(a)(4).

[31] 18 U.S.C. § 1030(a)(5).

[32] *See* Federal Reserve Board, "Guidance Concerning the Reporting of Computer-Related Crimes by Financial Institutions," SR 97-28 (ENF) (Nov. 6, 1997).

Fraud on the Internet has become a focus of consumer protection actions by the Federal Trade Commission.[33] As of June 1998, the FTC had commenced over 35 enforcement actions alleging fraud using the Internet.[34]

The Check Fraud Task Force of the American Bankers Association ("ABA") concluded in a 1994 report that check fraud increased by over 100 percent from 1991-93 and attributed the increase in part to the proliferation of desktop publishing software and the use of laser printers to produce counterfeit checks.[35] The ABA stated that the fingerprinting of individuals who cash checks at a bank where they do not have an account has reduced check fraud significantly and that biometric techniques (*e.g.*, voice recognition, hand and face profile recognition, and iris and retina identification) have the potential to further reduce check fraud.

The FBI has warned of increased vulnerability of the nation's critical infrastructures, including banking, to computer attack designed to cause disruption and infrastructure breakdown. According to the FBI, the threat comes from a number of sources, including disgruntled insiders seeking revenge against employers, recreational "hackers," organized crime, domestic and international terrorist groups, foreign intelligence services seeking proprietary data and sensitive government information, and hostile nations.[36] The inherently open and accessible nature of the Internet and telecommunications systems, and the interdependency and interconnectivity of the nation's information infrastructure, have resulted not only in increased exposure to criminal activity, but also to the potential for harm on a more massive scale.

In a well-reported incident in 1994, foreign crime groups operating in several different countries gained access to Citibank's cash management

---

[33] *See, e.g., Federal Trade Comm'n v. Hare*, Civ. No. 98-8194 CIV HURLEY (M.D. Fla., filed Mar. 30, 1998) (alleged failure to deliver computers sold over the Internet).

[34] *See* Testimony of Associate Director Eileen Harrington, Division of Marketing Practices, Bureau of Competition, Federal Trade Commission, before the House Commerce Committee (June 1998); Harrington, "Protecting the Consumer in Cyberspace: The FTC's Perspective," Electronic Banking Law and Commerce Report, Vol. 3, No. 3 (July-Aug. 1998).

[35] *See* Testimony of John J. Byrne, Senior Counsel and Compliance Manager of the American Bankers Association, before the House Subcommittee on Financial Institutions and Consumer Credit (Sept. 18, 1997).

[36] *See* Testimony of Michael A. Vatis, Deputy Assistant FBI Director and Chief of the National Infrastructure Protection Center, before the Joint Economic Committee (Mar. 24, 1998).

system, compromised passwords to impersonate account holders worldwide, and attempted 40 transfers totaling $10 million from accounts as far away as Argentina and Indonesia to bank accounts in San Francisco, Finland, Russia, Switzerland, Germany, and Israel. Citibank detected the criminal activity and alerted the FBI, which was able to apprehend the criminals.

The vulnerability of the financial sector to computer attack was addressed in a 1997 House Banking Committee minority staff report.[37]

In 1998, the FBI established the National Infrastructure Protection Center with the mission to detect, deter, prevent, assess, warn, respond to, and investigate unlawful acts involving computer and information technologies and unlawful acts in cyberspace that threaten or target the nation's critical infrastructures. The head of the NIPC has stated that "an attack from a terrorist group, rogue nation, disgruntled former employee or hacker could destabilize the nation's economy unless there is closer cooperation among federal agencies and better coordination between private businesses and the [NIPC]."[38]

In 1999, the OCC issued a bulletin cautioning national banks against threats and vulnerabilities created by "cyber-terrorism" which the OCC defined as "the use of computing resources against persons or property to intimidate or coerce a government, the civilian population, or any segment thereof, in furtherance of political or social objectives."[39] Acts of commercial espionage and employee sabotage—the "ultimate threat" to computer security—are other forms of cyber-terrorism. The OCC's bulletin called for banks to establish intrusion detection systems and disaster recover plans, among other measures, to minimize the risks of cyber-terrorist attack on computer systems.

In 2000, the OCC issued guidance to banks on how to prevent, detect and respond to intrusions into bank computer systems.[40] The guidance recommends security strategies and plans, intrusion risk-assessment plans, controls, policies and procedures, and information sharing as means of addressing intrusions.

The OCC also issued an alert to banks cautioning them to protect their Internet addresses and domain names from inadvertent or deliberate

---

[37] House Banking Committee Minority Staff Report, *U.S. Financial Services Sector Vulnerable to Computer Attack* (Dec. 11, 1997).

[38] "FBI Warns of Cyber-Attack Threat," *Wash. Post,* Mar. 21, 2001, at A16.

[39] OCC Bulletin 99-9, *Infrastructure Threats from Cyber-Terrorists* (Mar. 5, 1999).

[40] OCC Bulletin 2000-14 (May 15, 2000).

usurpation by another bank or entity using the same or a similar name.[41] The OCC cited several instances when banks had discovered Internet Web sites with Internet addresses similar to their own which had resulted in customer confusion and some bank customers mistakenly transmitting confidential information to those other sites. Among other things, the OCC recommended that banks register similar domain names, increase consumer education efforts and consider establishing trademarks for their domain names.

The European Commission has proposed a European-wide framework for combating fraud in electronic banking at the international level, noting that unauthorized use and misuse of computers to defraud is not treated as a criminal activity in all jurisdictions.[42] The framework aims to ensure that fraud involving all forms of non-cash means of payment is recognized as a criminal offense and punishable by effective sanctions in all EU Member countries and calls for joint and coordinated prosecution and enforcement.

In 1998, the federal banking agencies, along with the FBI, Secret Service, Internal Revenue Service, and the Postal Inspection Service, issued a special alert to bankers regarding the practice of "pretext phone calling" by so-called "account information brokers."[43] These individuals or organizations gain illicit access to customers' confidential account information from public and nonpublic sources by posing as customers who have misplaced their account numbers or other pretext. They then sell it to various persons who are willing to buy it, including lawyers, debt collection services, private investigators, and identity thieves. The agencies advised banks to develop policies and procedures to guard against such abuses.

In 1999, Congress made it unlawful for any person to fraudulently obtain customer financial information.[44] The law makes it a violation of law for any person to obtain or attempt to obtain, or cause or attempt to cause to be disclosed to any person, customer information of a financial institution relating to another person:

(1) by making a false, fictitious or fraudulent statement or representation to an officer, employee, or agent of a financial institution;

---

[41] OCC Alert 2000-9 (July 19, 2000).

[42] European Commission, *A Framework for Action on Combating Fraud and Counterfeiting of Non-Cash Means of Payment* (July 1998).

[43] *See* FDIC FIL-98-98 (Sept. 2, 1998); OCC Advisory Letter 98-11 (Aug. 20, 1998).

[44] Pub L. No. 106-102, Title V, Subtitle B.

(2) by making a false, fictitious or fraudulent statement or representation to a customer of a financial institution; or
(3) by providing any document to an officer, employee, or agent of a financial institution, knowing that the document is forged, counterfeit, lost, or stolen, was fraudulently obtained, or contains a false, fictitious, or fraudulent statement or representation.

A person who knowingly and intentionally violates this prohibition may be fined or imprisoned for up to five years.

In 2000, the OCC issued a bulletin warning national banks of the threat of "distributed denial of service" ("DDoS") attacks involving the flooding of targeted Web sites and interruption of customer access to the Web sites.[45] The OCC noted that computer servers of unknowing entities, such as companies, government agencies, and universities may be commandeered and become unwitting participants in these attacks. The OCC instructed national banks to review and update their capacity for responding to these attacks and other emerging information security threats and urged banks to consider participating in information-sharing organizations such as the Financial Services Information Sharing and Analysis Center, Carnegie Mellon University's C'RT/CC, and the FBI's Infragard program. The OCC also instructed national banks that are victims of DDoS attacks to file Suspicious Activity Reports.

The FDIC has identified several fraudulent "banks" operating on the Internet without bank charters.[46] The FDIC has established a special Web site where individuals can report suspicious Internet banking activity.[47]

The Treasury Department's Financial Crimes Enforcement Network ("FinCEN") in 1997 proposed regulations to subject electronic banks and commerce to the Bank Secrecy Act.[48] Bank as well as nonbank entities participating in the "money services business" would be subject to the regulations. The regulations were intended to implement amendments enacted in the Money Laundering Suppression Act of 1994.[49] At Congres-

[45] OCC Alert 2000-1 (Feb. 11, 2000).

[46] *See* "Oh, What a Tangled Web: Cyberfraud Sullies Internet," Am. Banker (July 1, 1999).

[47] The Web site address is: ⟨⟨*http://www.fdic.gov/consumer/suspicious/*⟩⟩.

[48] 62 Fed. Reg. 27,890 (1997). The Bank Secrecy Act requires the reporting of transactions of over $10,000, recordkeeping on international funds transfers in excess of $3,000, and the reporting of "suspicious transactions" and "known or suspected criminal violations."

[49] 31 U.S.C. § 5330, *as added by* Title IV of the Riegle Community Development and Regulatory Improvement Act of 1994, Pub. L. No. 103-325.

sional hearings on the proposal, regulatory counsel for Mondex USA testified that the proposed regulation was premature and would stifle the development of the stored-value industry.[50] Nonbank money transmitters testified that such regulations, among other things, would place them at a competitive disadvantage relative to grocery and liquor stores and would be unduly burdensome.[51] They noted that nonbank wire funds transfers amount to less than $11 billion per year compared to the $1.2 trillion transferred through Fedwire each business day.

FinCEN's proposed regulations were adopted in 1999.[52] Under the new rule, each money services business must register with the Department of the Treasury and maintain a list of its agents. The term "money services business" includes currency dealers or exchangers; check cashers; issuers sellers or redeemers of traveler's checks, money orders, or stored value; and money transmitters, including any person engaged as a business in the transfer of funds. In 2000, FinCEN further amended its rules to require money services businesses to report suspicious transactions to the Department of the Treasury under the Bank Secrecy Act.[53]

Congress enacted the Money Laundering and Financial Crimes Strategy Act of 1998[54] to direct the Secretary of the Treasury to develop and submit to Congress a national strategy for combating money laundering and related financial crimes. The strategy must include research-based goals, prevention measures coordinated with other agencies, detection and prosecution initiatives, enhanced crime detection measures between financial service firms and law enforcement agencies, enhanced intergovernmental cooperation, and a description of geographical areas designated as high-risk money laundering and related financial crime areas. The Treasury adopted a "National Money Laundering Strategy for 1999" as the first in a series of five annual reports called for by the 1998 Act. The Treasury's 1999 Strategy committed Treasury to assuring that all types of financial institutions are subject to effective Bank Secrecy Act requirements and included the FinCEN initiatives noted above.

---

[50] Statement of Mark E. Plotkin, Regulatory Counsel for Mondex USA, before the House Subcommittee on General Oversight and Investigations (July 30, 1997).

[51] Statement of Ezra C. Levine on behalf of the Non-Bank Funds Transmitters Group, before the House Subcommittee on General Oversight and Investigations (July 30, 1997).

[52] 64 Fed. Reg. 45,438 (1999).

[53] 65 Fed. Reg. 13,683 (2000).

[54] Pub. L. No. 105-310, 105th Cong., 2d Sess. (1998).

§ 11.07 OUTSOURCING RISKS

As the FDIC has observed, financial institutions "are increasingly relying on outside firms for technology-related products and services to support an array of banking functions. Institutions of all sizes are using these products and services, as technology grows more complex and dynamic, creating a greater impetus to outsource."[55]

Outsourcing can result in operating efficiencies and enable a bank to obtain data processing expertise and services at reduced cost. Outsourcing of technology functions, however, also exposes banks to risks beyond their control. The federal banking agencies have expressed concern regarding the potential risks involved when a bank outsources key functions. The FDIC has noted in particular that "the emergence of new startup service companies with limited experience, resources and knowledge of the regulated financial services environment heightens the importance of effective risk-management practices at the financial institution."[56]

Regulatory Guidance. Acting through the Federal Financial Institutions Examination Council ("FFIEC"), the federal banking agencies have adopted guidance for banking institutions in managing the risks of outsourcing.[57]

Technology Service Providers. The guidance applies to outsourcing arrangements with "technology service providers" including affiliates and non-affiliates. This term encompasses a broad range of providers of the following services:

- Core processing;
- Information and transaction processing and settlement activities that support banking functions such as lending, deposit-taking, funds transfer, fiduciary, or trading activities;
- Internet-related services;
- Security monitoring;
- Systems development and maintenance;

---

[55] FDIC FIL-81-2000 (Nov. 29, 2000).

[56] *Id.*

[57] Federal Financial Institutions Examination Council, *Statement on Risk Management of Outsourced Technology Services,* Nov. 28, 2000.

- Aggregation services;
- Digital certification services; and
- Call centers.

The FFIEC guidance focuses on risk assessment, due diligence, contract issues, and oversight of service providers.

[A] Risk Assessment

The federal banking agencies expect a bank's board of directors and senior management to understand the risks associated with outsourcing arrangements for technology services and to ensure that effective risk management practices are in place. The board and management are expected to assess "how the outsourcing arrangement will support the institution's objectives and strategic plans and how the service provider's relationship will be managed." The agencies cautioned that outsourcing technology services "may be inconsistent with the institution's strategic plans, too costly, or introduce unforeseen risks."

Additional risk controls are expected when services involve the Internet:

> The broad geographic reach, ease of access, and anonymity of the Internet require close attention to maintaining secure systems, intrusion detection and reporting systems, and customer authentication, verification, and authorization. Institutions should also understand that the potential risks introduced are a function of a system's structure, design and controls and not necessarily the volume of activity.

[B] Due Diligence

A bank is expected to review the service provider's own due diligence process for any of its significant subcontractors and to hire or consult with qualified independent sources such as consultants, user groups, and trade associations. The extent of the due diligence analysis may vary depending on the "scope and importance of the outsourced services as well as the risk to the institution." The FFIEC Statement provides detailed guidance on due diligence factors and analysis a bank should consider when selecting a technology service provider:

[1] Technical and Industry Expertise

- Assess the service provider's experience and ability to provide the necessary services and supporting technology for current and anticipated needs.
- Identify areas where the institution would have to supplement the service provider's expertise to fully manage risk.
- Evaluate the service provider's use of third parties or partners that would be used to support the outsourced operations.
- Evaluate the experience of the service provider in providing services in the anticipated operating environment.
- Consider whether additional systems, data conversions, and work are necessary.
- Evaluate the service provider's ability to respond to service disruptions.
- Contact references and user groups to learn about the service provider's reputation and performance.
- Evaluate key service provider personnel that would be assigned to support the institution.
- Perform on-site visits where necessary to better understand how the service provider operates and supports its services.

[2] Operations and Controls

- Determine adequacy of the service provider's standards, policies and procedures relating to internal controls, facilities management (e.g., access requirements, sharing of facilities, etc.), security (e.g., systems, data, equipment, etc.), privacy protections, maintenance of records, business resumption contingency planning, systems development and maintenance, and employee background checks.
- Determine if the service provider provides sufficient security precautions, including when appropriate, firewalls, encryption, and customer identity authentication, to protect institution resources as well as detect and respond to intrusions.

- Review audit reports of the service provider to determine whether the audit scope, internal controls, and security safeguards are adequate.
- Evaluate whether the institution will have complete and timely access to its information maintained by the provider.
- Evaluate the service provider's knowledge of regulations that are relevant to the services they are providing (e.g., Regulation E, privacy and other consumer protection regulations, Bank Secrecy Act, etc.).
- Assess the adequacy of the service provider's insurance coverage including fidelity, fire, liability, data losses from errors and omissions, and protection of documents in transit.

[3] Financial Condition

- Analyze the service provider's most recent audited financial statements and annual report as well as other indicators (e.g., publicly traded bond ratings), if available.
- Consider factors such as how long the service provider has been in business and the service provider's market share for a given service and how it has fluctuated.
- Consider the significance of the institution's proposed contract on the service provider's financial condition.
- Evaluate technological expenditures. Is the service provider's level of investment in technology consistent with supporting the institution's activities? Does the service provider have the financial resources to invest in and support the required technology?

[C] Contracting with Service Providers

The FFIEC's Statement also provides guidance on contracting with service providers and suggests that contracts, in addition to clearly describing the rights and responsibilities of the parties, include the following considerations:

Scope of service

- Timeframes and activities for implementation and assignment of responsibility. Implementation provisions should take into consideration other existing systems or interrelated systems to be developed by different service providers (e.g., an Internet banking system being integrated with existing core applications or systems customization).
- Services to be performed by the service provider including duties such as software support and maintenance, training of employees or customer service.
- Obligations of the financial institution.
- The contracting parties' rights in modifying existing services performed under the contract.
- Guidelines for adding new or different services and for contract re-negotiation.

Performance standards

Institutions should generally include performance standards defining minimum service level requirements and remedies for failure to meet standards in the contract. For example, common service level metrics include percent system uptime, deadlines for completing batch processing, or number of processing errors. Industry standards for service levels may provide a reference point. The institution should periodically review overall performance standards to ensure consistency with its goals and objectives.

Security and confidentiality

The contract should address the service provider's responsibility for security and confidentiality of the institution's resources (e.g., information, hardware). The agreement should prohibit the service provider and its agents from using or disclosing the institution's information, except as necessary to or consistent with providing the contracted services, to protect against unauthorized use (e.g., disclosure of information to institution competitors). If the service provider receives nonpublic personal information regarding the institution's customers, the institution should notify the service provider to assess the applicability of the privacy regulations. Institutions should require the service provider to fully disclose breaches in security resulting in unauthorized intrusions into the service provider that may materially affect the institution or its customers. The service provider should report to the institution when material intrusions occur, the effect on the institution, and corrective action to respond to the intrusion.

Controls

- Internal controls to be maintained by the service provider.
- Compliance with applicable regulatory requirements.
- Records to be maintained by the service provider.
- Access to the records by the institution.
- Notification by the service provider to the institution and the institution's approval rights regarding material changes to services, systems, controls, key project personnel allocated to the institution, and new service locations.
- Setting and monitoring of parameters relating to any financial functions, such as payments processing and any extensions of credit on behalf of the institution.
- Insurance coverage to be maintained by the service provider.

Audit

The institution should generally include in the contract the types of audit reports the institution is entitled to receive (e.g., financial, internal control and security reviews). The contract can specify audit frequency, cost to the institution associated with the audits if any, as well as the rights of the institution and its agencies to obtain the results of the audits in a timely manner. The contract may also specify rights to obtain documentation regarding the resolution of audit disclosed deficiencies and inspect the processing facilities and operating practices of the service provider. Management should consider, based upon the risk assessment phase, the degree to which independent internal audits completed by service provider audit staff can be used and the need for external audits and reviews (e.g., SAS 70 Type I and II reviews).

For services involving access to open networks, such as Internet-related services, special attention should be paid to security. The institution may wish to include contract terms requiring periodic audits to be performed by an independent party with sufficient expertise. These audits may include penetration testing, intrusion detection, and firewall configuration. The institution should receive sufficiently detailed reports on the findings of these ongoing audits to adequately assess security without compromising the service provider's security. It can be beneficial to both the service provider and the institution to contract for such ongoing tests on a coordinated basis given the number of institutions that may contract with the service provider and the importance of the test results to the institution.

Reports

Contractual terms should discuss the frequency and type of reports the institution will receive (e.g., performance reports, control audits, financial statements, security, and business resumption testing reports). Guidelines and fees for obtaining customer reports should also be discussed.

Business resumption and contingency plans

The contract should address the service provider's responsibility for back up and record protection, including equipment, program and data files, and maintenance of disaster recovery and contingency plans. Responsibilities should include testing of the plans and providing results to the institution. The institution should consider interdependencies among service providers when determining business resumption testing requirements. The service provider should provide the institution with operating procedures the service provider and institution are to implement in the event business resumption contingency plans are implemented. Contracts should include specific provisions for business recovery timeframes that meet the institution's business requirements. The institution should ensure that the contract does not contain any provisions that would excuse the service provider from implementing its contingency plans.

Subsidiary-contracting and multiple service provider relationships

Some service providers may contract with third-parties in providing service to the financial institution. To provide accountability, it may be beneficial for the financial institution to seek an agreement with and designate a primary contracting service provider. The institution may want to consider including a provision specifying that the contracting service provider is responsible for the service provided to the institution regardless of which entity is actually conducting the operations. The institution may also want to consider including notification and approval requirements regarding changes to the service provider's significant subcontractors.

Cost

The contract should fully describe fees and calculations for base services, including any development, conversion, and recurring services, as well as any charges based upon volume of activity and for special requests. Cost and responsibility for purchase and maintenance of hardware and software may also need to be addressed. Any conditions under which the cost structure may be changed should be addressed in detail including limits on any cost increases.

Ownership and license

The contract should address ownership and allowable use by the service provider of the institution's data, equipment/hardware, system documentation, system and application software, and other intellectual property rights. Other intellectual property rights may include the institution's name and logo; its trademark or copyrighted material; domain names; Web sites designs; and other work products developed by the service provider for the institution. The contract should not contain unnecessary limitations on the return of items owned by the institution. Institutions that purchase software should consider establishing escrow agreements. These escrow agreements may provide for the following: institution access to source programs under certain conditions (e.g., insolvency of the vendor), documentation of programming and systems, and verification of updated source code.

Duration

Institutions should consider the type of technology and current state of the industry when negotiating the appropriate length of the contract and its renewal periods. While there can be benefits to long-term technology contracts, certain technologies may be subject to rapid change and a shorter-term contract may prove beneficial. Similarly, institutions should consider the appropriate length of time required to notify the service provider of the institutions' intent not to renew the contract prior to expiration. Institutions should consider coordinating the expiration dates of contracts for inter-related services (e.g., Web site, telecommunications, programming, network support) so that they coincide, where practical. Such coordination can minimize the risk of terminating a contract early and incurring penalties as a result of necessary termination of another related service contract.

Dispute resolution

The institution should consider including in the contract a provision for a dispute resolution process that attempts to resolve problems in an expeditious manner as well as provide for continuation of services during the dispute resolution period.

Indemnification

Indemnification provisions generally require the financial institution to hold the service provider harmless from liability for the negligence of the institution, and vice versa. These provisions should be reviewed to reduce the likelihood of potential situations in which the institution may be liable for claims arising as a result of the negligence of the service provider.

Limitation of liability

Some service provider standard contracts may contain clauses limiting the amount of liability that can be incurred by the service provider. If the institution is considering such a contract, consideration should be given to whether the damage limitation bears an adequate relationship to the amount of loss the financial institution might reasonably experience as a result of the service provider's failure to perform its obligations.

Termination

The extent and flexibility of termination rights sought can vary depending upon the service. Contracts for technologies subject to rapid change, for example, may benefit from greater flexibility in termination rights. Termination rights may be sought for a variety of conditions including change in control (e.g., acquisitions and mergers), convenience, substantial increase in cost, repeated failure to meet service levels, failure to provide critical services, bankruptcy, company closure, and insolvency.

Institution management should consider whether or not the contract permits the institution to terminate the contract in a timely manner and without prohibitive expense (e.g., reasonableness of cost or penalty provisions). The contract should state termination and notification requirements with time frames to allow the orderly conversion to another provider. The contract must provide for return of the institution's data, as well as other institution resources, in a timely manner and in machine readable format. Any costs associated with transition assistance should be clearly stated.

Assignment

The institution should consider contract provisions that prohibit assignment of the contract to a third party without the institution's consent, including changes to subcontractors.

[D] Oversight of Service Providers

The FFIEC Statement on Risk Management of Outsourced Technology Services provides guidance on the extent of oversight a bank must exercise over its external technology service providers. While the degree of oversight will vary depending on the nature of the services involved, the agencies expect banks to do the following:

Monitor financial condition and operations

- Evaluate the service provider's financial condition periodically.
- Ensure that the service provider's financial obligations to subcontractors are being met in a timely manner.
- Review audit reports (e.g., SAS 70 reviews, security reviews) as well as regulatory examination reports if available, and evaluate the adequacy of the service providers' systems and controls including resource availability, security, integrity, and confidentiality. (Regulatory reports are not a substitute for a financial institution's due diligence in oversight of the service provider.)
- Follow up on any deficiencies noted in the audits and reviews of the service provider.
- Periodically review the service provider's policies relating to internal controls, security, systems development and maintenance, and back up and contingency planning to ensure they meet the institution's minimum guidelines, contract requirements, and are consistent with the current market and technological environment.
- Review access control reports for suspicious activity.
- Monitor changes in key service provider project personnel allocated to the institution.
- Review and monitor the service provider's insurance policies for effective coverage.
- Perform on-site inspections in conjunction with some of the reviews performed above, where practicable and necessary.
- Sponsor coordinated audits and reviews with other client institutions.

Assess quality of service and support

- Regularly review reports documenting the service provider's performance. Determine if the reports are accurate and allow for a meaningful assessment of the service provider's performance.

- Document and follow up on any problem in service in a timely manner. Assess service provider plans to enhance service levels.
- Review system update procedures to ensure appropriate change controls are in effect, and ensure authorization is established for significant system changes.
- Evaluate the provider's ability to support and enhance the institution's strategic direction including anticipated business development goals and objectives, service delivery requirements, and technology initiatives.
- Determine adequacy of training provided to financial institution employees.
- Review customer complaints on the products and services provided by the service provider.
- Periodically meet with contract parties to discuss performance and operational issues.
- Participate in user groups and other forums.

Monitor contract compliance and revision needs

- Review invoices to assure proper charges for services rendered, the appropriateness of rate changes and new service charges.
- Periodically, review the service provider's performance relative to service level agreements, determine whether other contractual terms and conditions are being met, and whether any revisions to service level expectations or other terms are needed given changes in the institution's needs and technological developments.
- Maintain documents and records regarding contract compliance, revision and dispute resolution.

Maintain business resumption contingency plans

- Review the service provider's business resumption contingency plans to ensure that any services considered mission critical for the institution can be restored within an acceptable timeframe.

- Review the service provider's program for contingency plan testing. For many critical services, annual or more frequent tests of the contingency plan are typical.
- Ensure service provider interdependencies are considered for mission critical services and applications.

[E] Examination Procedures

The federal banking agencies have adopted procedures for examining and assessing the risks incurred when banks outsource information technology functions.[58] These risks include the same risks that a bank faces when it performs such services internally, including threats to system availability to support customer transactions and threats to the integrity or security of customer account information and the integrity of risk management information systems. The regulators expect banks to ensure that risk management controls pertaining to outsourced information and transaction processing activities are equivalent to those that would be implemented if the activities were performed internally.

The federal banking agencies have authority to examine technology companies that provide services to banks under the Bank Service Company Act.[59] Such examinations are conducted solely to support the supervision of banks. The risk assessment factors consider the inherent risk of the services provided along with mitigating factors and focus on material supervisory risks rather than on routine operating risks. Specific risk factors include:

- Evidence that the outsourced activity gives rise to risk of significant financial losses
- Significant internal control deficiencies, inadequate audit or reporting, or other concerns with the service provider identified during examinations of serviced institutions
- Evidence of inadequate oversight by the service provider's customers

[58] *See, e.g.*, Federal Reserve Board, SR 00-4 (SUP) (Feb. 29, 2000).
[59] 12 U.S.C. § 1867.

- Significant changes in management, staffing or services at the service provider that may adversely affect risk management
- Evidence that a service provider that is a nonbank subsidiary of a bank holding company poses significant risk to the holding company.[60]

The schedule for examination of service providers is at least once every two years for those providers that are considered to pose high risk.[61]

§ 11.08 ACH RISK

Banks that process automated clearing house ("ACH") debit entries initiated pursuant to an authorization obtained through the Internet to effect a transfer of funds from a customer account ("WEB entries") may incur risks due to the failure of their customers to meet ACH operating standards.

Effective March 16, 2001, the National Automated Clearing House Association ("NACHA") amended its operating rules to require originating banks to warranty compliance with NACHA's rules by their merchant and other customers that originate WEB entries. Originators of WEB entries are required to:

- Employ commercially reasonable fraudulent-transaction detection systems to screen the entries in order to minimize the risk of fraud related to Internet-initiated payments.
- Use commercially reasonable procedures to verify that routing numbers are valid.
- Establish a secure Internet session with each receiver prior to the key entry by the receiver of any banking information.
- Conduct an annual audit to ensure that the financial information obtained from receivers is protected by prescribed security practices and procedures. The first audit must be completed by December 31, 2001.

---

60 Federal Reserve Board, SR 00-3 (SUP) (Feb. 29, 2000).

61 *Id.*

Under the new NACHA rule, banks must ensure that their customers that originate WEB entries are in compliance with the above requirements on an ongoing basis and are deemed to warrant that originators have conformed to the new requirements. Banks also are required to establish the identity of the originator, monitor the originator's creditworthiness, establish and review exposure limits for originators, and monitor entries by each originator relative to its exposure limit across multiple settlement dates.

The OCC issued supervisory guidance to national banks concerning the potential liability of banks for losses that result from the NACHA rule change and urged banks to implement risk management measures to minimize the risk of such liability.[62]

§ 11.09 GUIDELINES FOR SAFEGUARDING INFORMATION

The Gramm-Leach-Bliley Act ("GLBA") required the federal banking agencies, the Federal Trade Commission and Securities and Exchange Commission to establish standards for financial institutions relating to the "administrative, technical, and physical safeguards for customer records and information."[63] The safeguards are required to:

- Insure the security and confidentiality of customer records and information;
- Protect against any anticipated threats or hazards to the security or integrity of such records; and
- Protect against unauthorized access to or use of such records or information that would result in substantial harm or inconvenience to any customer.

The agencies in 2001 promulgated joint guidelines to implement the safeguards.[64] The agencies determined to adopt guidelines instead of regulations, citing the "drawbacks of prescriptive requirements that could become rapidly outdated as a result of changes in technology."[65] Because the guidelines apply to a broad range of different types of institutions in addition to banks, the agencies drafted the guidelines to allow "a high

[62] OCC Advisory Letter 2001-3 (Jan. 29, 2001).
[63] Pub. L. No. 106-102 § 501 (1999).
[64] 66 Fed. Reg. 8616 (2001); 12 C.F.R. §§ 30, 208.3, 225.4, and 263.302.
[65] *Id.* at 8617.

degree of flexibility for each institution to design a security program that suits its circumstances" and to give each institution the "discretion to design an information security program that suits its particular size and complexity and the nature and scope of its activities."[66] The agencies noted that, because the guidelines were derived from security-related guidance previously issued by the agencies, in many cases "little or no modification to an institution's program will be required."

The guidelines require the board of directors of a bank (or other financial institution) or a committee thereof to approve a written information security program for the bank and oversee the development, implementation and maintenance of the program. Each bank is required to assess its own risks by doing the following:

- Identifying reasonably foreseeable internal and external threats that could result in unauthorized disclosure, misuse, alteration, or destruction of customer information or customer information systems;
- Assessing the likelihood and potential damage of these threats, taking into consideration the sensitivity of customer information; and
- Assessing the sufficiency of policies, procedures, customer information systems, and other arrangements in place to control risks.

Each bank is required to manage and control risks by designing an information security program "commensurate with the sensitivity of the information as well as the complexity and scope of the bank's activities." Each bank must consider whether the following security measures are appropriate and, if so, take steps to implement them:

- Access controls on customer information systems, including controls to authenticate and permit access only to authorized individuals and controls to prevent employees from providing customer information to unauthorized individuals who may seek to obtain this information through fraudulent means;

[66] *Id.*

- Access restrictions at physical locations containing customer information, such as buildings, computer facilities, and records storage facilities to permit access only to authorized individuals;
- Encryption of electronic customer information, including while in transit or in storage on networks or systems to which unauthorized individuals may have access;
- Procedures designed to ensure that customer information system modifications are consistent with the bank's information security program;
- Dual control procedures, segregation of duties, and employee background checks for employees with responsibilities for or access to customer information;
- Monitoring systems and procedures to detect actual and attempted attacks on or intrusions into customer information systems;
- Response programs that specify actions to be taken when the bank suspects or detects that unauthorized individuals have gained access to customer information systems, including appropriate reports to regulatory and law enforcement agencies; and
- Measures to protect against destruction, loss, or damage of customer information due to potential environmental hazards, such as fire and water damage or technological failures.

Each bank is required to train its staff to implement the bank's information security program and to regularly test key controls, systems and procedures. The agencies require testing to be conducted or reviewed by independent third parties or staff independent of the bank's employees who develop or maintain the security program.

With respect to third party service providers to the bank, the guidelines require each bank to exercise appropriate due diligence in selecting such providers and to require each service provider by contract to implement appropriate measures designed to meet the objectives of the guidelines. Where appropriate, the guidelines require banks to monitor service providers to confirm that they have satisfied their contractual safeguards and to review audits, summaries of test results or other equivalent evaluations. Contracts with service providers existing as of March 5, 2001 are grandfathered until July 1, 2003.

The Gramm-Leach-Bliley Act requires the safeguards to be implemented in the same manner as standards prescribed in the FDI Act, which authorizes the agencies to establish operational and managerial standards for insured depository institutions relative to internal controls, information systems, and internal audit systems, as well as such other operational and managerial standards as the agencies determine are appropriate.

CHAPTER 12

YEAR 2000 ISSUES

§12.01 THE Y2K PROBLEM

Apart from world wars, few global problems mobilized the world's resources to a single national and international effort as did the Year 2000 or "Y2K" problem. The problem arose because, until recently, nearly all computer software was written to process dates with two digits instead of four (*i.e.*, "99" for "1999") and without the ability to recognize the year 2000. Unless corrected, computers would have read "00" as the year 1900 and incapacitate critical operations around the world.

Doomsday scenarios were much exaggerated, but the problem could have caused major malfunctions in public utilities, transportation, health and safety, financial, business, and other functions that rely on computer technology, resulting in disruption, chaos, and potentially fatal economic consequences for some companies. The costs of correcting the problem were in the billions of dollars.[1] Because of the enormous effort devoted to correcting the problem, no significant disruptions occurred in the U.S. banking system as a result of the Y2K problem.[2]

Congress defined the Y2K problem as follows:

> [T]he term "Year 2000 computer problem" means, with respect to information technology, any problem which prevents such technology from accurately processing, calculating, comparing, or sequencing date or time data—
>
> (A) from, into, or between—
>
> (i) the 20th and 21st centuries; or
>
> (ii) the years 1999 and 2000; or
>
> (B) with regard to leap year calculations.[3]

In enacting legislation to address the Y2K problem, Congress made findings that:

> At least thousands but possibly millions of information technology computer systems, software programs, and semiconductors are not capable of recognizing certain dates in 1999 and after December 31, 1999, and will read dates in the year 2000 and thereafter as if

[1] Citigroup has estimated its Y2K costs to be $850-925 billion, for example. *See* "Year-2000 Expenses for 100 Largest U.S. Banks," Am. Banker (Dec. 18, 1999).

[2] *See* Joint Release by the federal banking agencies, "Insured Financial Institutions Operating Normally Following Century Date Change" (Jan. 1, 2000).

[3] Pub. L. No. 105-164, 105th Cong., 2d Sess. (1998), § 2(b)(5).

> those dates represent the year 1900 or thereafter or will fail to process those dates.
>
> The problem described in subparagraph (A) and resulting failures could incapacitate systems that are essential to the functioning of markets, commerce, consumer products, utilities, government, and safety and defense systems, in the United States and throughout the world.
>
> Reprogramming or replacing affected systems before the problem incapacitates essential systems is a matter of national and global interest.[4]

For banks in particular, the Y2K problem was of critical magnitude. Banks use dated computerized information in nearly all aspects of their business, including the computation of interest payments, loan due dates, amortizations, check clearance, and bank account statements. The nation's payments system is dependent on the flow of accurately dated information through banks. Banks handle billions of transactions each day that must be properly dated. Moreover, bank computers are linked with potentially hundreds of other computers outside the bank that must be able to read dated information accurately in order to be interoperable.

In enacting legislation to address the Y2K problem as it affects banks, Congress noted in its findings that:

> thousands of banks, savings associations, and credit unions rely heavily on internal information technology and computer systems, as well as outside service providers, for mission-critical functions, such as check clearing, direct deposit, accounting, automated teller machine networks, credit card processing, and data exchanges with domestic and international borrowers, customers, and other financial institutions."[5]

§12.02 THE ADMINISTRATION'S RESPONSE

[A] Executive Order 13073

President Clinton in 1998 issued an executive order declaring it to be Executive Branch policy that all federal agencies should give priority

[4] Pub. L. No. 105-271, 105th Cong., 2d Sess. (1998), § 2.

[5] Pub. L. No. 105-164, 105th Cong., 2d Sess. (1998), § 2.

attention to addressing the Y2K problem to assure that no critical federal program experiences disruption because of the Y2K problem.[6] The President also ordered all federal agencies to assist and cooperate with state and local governments, the private sector, and international bodies in addressing the problem.

[B] President's Council on Year 2000

In order to oversee and coordinate the Administration's Y2K response, Executive Order 13073 appointed the President's Council on Year 2000 Conversion. The Council was comprised of representatives from more than 30 federal government agencies.

Among its actions, the Council launched a "National Campaign for Year 2000 Solutions" to promote public and private sector action on the Y2K problem and foster information sharing about solutions. Part of the Campaign was a "National Y2K Action Week" from October 19-23, 1998, during which federal agencies conducted educational events and outreach activities designed to help managers of small- and medium-sized businesses address the Y2K problem.

The Council appointed various federal agencies to serve as "sector coordinators" to increase awareness of the Y2K problem and offer support to public and private sector organizations domestically and internationally. The Federal Reserve Board and the Office of the Comptroller of the Currency ("OCC") were sector coordinators for the banking industry.

§12.03 CONGRESSIONAL RESPONSE

The 105th Congress held numerous hearings on the Y2K problem generally and as it affected the banking and financial services industry in particular.[7] The Senate established a Special Committee on the Year 2000 Technology Problem that heightened the Congressional focus on this issue. In addition, Congress enacted several bills to address specific issues raised by the Y2K problem, including those discussed below.

---

[6] Executive Order 13073 (Feb. 4, 1998).

[7] *See* Hearings before the subcommittee on Financial Services and Technology of the Senate Committee on Banking, Housing, and Urban Affairs (July 30, 1997) Hearings on The Depository Institution Year 2000 Computer Problem Remediation Act before the House Committee on Banking and Financial Services (Feb. 5, 1998).

[A] Year 2000 Readiness for Financial Institutions Act

The Examination Parity and Year 2000 Readiness for Financial Institutions Act[8] was enacted in 1998 to enhance the examination authority of the federal banking agencies "to ensure that the safety and soundness of the Nation's financial institutions will not be at risk."

The Act required each federal banking agency to offer seminars to depository institutions on the implication of the Y2K problem for the safe and sound operations of depository institutions and transactions with other financial institutions. Each agency also was required to develop and make available to banks model approaches to common Y2K computer problems, such as model approaches with regard to project management, vendor contracts, testing regimes, and business continuity planning. The agencies were directed to develop a variety of approaches to correspond to the variety of depository institutions within their respective jurisdictions.[9]

[B] Year 2000 Information and Readiness Disclosure Act

The Year 2000 Information and Readiness Disclosure Act[10] was enacted in 1998 to address fears that the disclosure and exchange of information by companies for the purpose of addressing the Y2K problem would subject the disclosing party to litigation. Congress determined that:

> The prompt, candid, and thorough disclosure and exchange of information related to year 2000 readiness of entities, products, and services—would greatly enhance the ability of public and private entities to improve their year 2000 readiness; and is therefore a matter of national importance and a vital factor in minimizing any potential year 2000 related disruption to the Nation's economic well-being and security.
>
> The national interest will be served by uniform legal standards in connection with the disclosure and exchange of year 2000 readiness information that will promote disclosures and exchanges of such information in a timely fashion.[11]

---

[8] Pub. L. No. 105-164, 105th Cong., 2d Sess. (1998).

[9] *Id.*

[10] Pub. L. No. 105-271, 105th Cong., 2d Sess. (1998).

[11] *Id.* (statement of Congressional findings).

Accordingly, the purposes of the Act were:

(1) to promote the free disclosure and exchange of information related to Year 2000 readiness;
(2) to assist consumers, small businesses, and local governments in effectively and rapidly responding to Year 2000 problems; and
(3) to lessen burdens on interstate commerce by establishing certain uniform legal principles in connection with the disclosure and exchange of information related to Year 2000 readiness.

To accomplish these goals, the Act provided that no Y2K readiness disclosure would be admissible in any civil action arising under federal or state law against the company making the disclosure except as the basis for a claim for anticipatory breach or repudiation or a similar claim against the maker and when a court determined that the maker's disclosure amounted to bad faith or fraud or was otherwise unreasonable. Under the Act, a company that made a Y2K disclosure would not be liable for making a false, inaccurate, or misleading statement unless the claimant established that the statement was made with knowledge that it was such or with intent to deceive or mislead or with reckless disregard for its accuracy.

The Act also prohibited Y2K statements from being construed as an alteration of a contract or warranty; protected Y2K information that was voluntarily submitted to the government from disclosure under the Freedom of Information Act; and provided an antitrust exemption for conduct intended to facilitate Y2K corrective activities.

[C] Small Business Year 2000 Readiness Act

The Small Business Year 2000 Readiness Act[12] was enacted to address the need of small businesses for financial resources to correct their Y2K problems. The Act established a loan guarantee program under which small businesses may qualify for funding to purchase or repair software and obtain Y2K consulting services. The funds also could be used to compensate small businesses for economic injury caused by Y2K computer problems.

§12.04 FEDERAL BANKING AGENCY ACTIONS

The federal banking agencies issued numerous advisories to the banking industry providing guidance and establishing safety and sound-

[12] Pub. L. No. 106-8, 106th Cong., 1st Sess. (1999).

ness standards for bank Y2K preparedness. For the most part, the agencies acted jointly and uniformly through the Federal Financial Institutions Examination Council ("FFIEC") rather than adopting their own Y2K policies. Some of the joint agency FFIEC issuances are discussed below.

[A] Interagency Statement on Effect of Year 2000 on Computer Systems[13]

The agencies alerted financial institutions to the substantial risks to the industry posed by the Y2K problem and urged them to conduct Y2K risk assessments and develop Y2K action plans.

[B] Interagency Statement on Year 2000 Project Management Awareness[14]

In this interagency statement, the regulators emphasized the need for senior management involvement in the Y2K correction process and outlined a Y2K problem identification, planning, and implementation process for bank management. The agencies established a preliminary timetable for Y2K compliance, advising that mission critical applications should be identified and priorities set by the end of September 1997, code revisions and hardware upgrades largely completed by December 31, 1998, and testing well underway by December 31, 1998.

The agencies advised bank management to take a proactive approach in ensuring Y2K compliance by third-party vendors and indicated that banks should obtain certification of Y2K readiness from vendors. Bank management also was advised to review Y2K compliance in considering the creditworthiness of corporate borrowers and to consider the risks inherent in data exchanges with other financial institutions.

[C] Interagency Safety and Soundness Guidelines[15]

Noting that the Y2K problem "is much more than a technology issue; it is an enterprise-wide challenge," the regulators reiterated the responsibilities of senior management and the board of directors for ad-

[13] FFIEC, *The Effect of Year 2000 on Computer Systems* (June 1996).

[14] FFIEC, *Year 2000 Project Management Awareness* (May 5, 1997).

[15] FFIEC, *Safety and Soundness Guidelines Concerning the Year 2000 Business Risk* (Dec. 17, 1997).

dressing the business risks associated with the Y2K problem Among the measures required were quarterly status reports by bank management on Y2K progress.

The regulators revised their guidance on vendor compliance, stating formal certification was unnecessary but advising banks to implement internal testing and verification processes regarding vendor products and services to ensure proper Y2K functioning. The regulators also advised banks to develop contingency plans for all vendors that service mission critical applications and establish a trigger data for implementing alternative solutions should the vendor not complete its Y2K conversion efforts on schedule.

Noting the interdependencies of bank operational systems, the regulators encouraged banks to work together to find common solutions to Y2K compliance by sharing successful practices, common testing methodologies and other non-proprietary information.

[D] Interagency Statement on Year 2000 Impact on Customers[16]

The regulators described due diligence methods by which bank management should address the risks arising from the failure or inability of a bank's material customers to address their Y2K vulnerabilities. Noting that a bank could face increased credit, liquidity, or counterparty trading risk from non-Y2K-compliant customers, the agencies advised banks to establish a due diligence process by June 30, 1998, and by September 30, 1998, to have completed an assessment of the Y2K readiness of three categories of customers: funds takers (*e.g.*, bond issuers), funds providers (*e.g.*, large depositors), and capital market/asset management counterparties (*e.g.*, customers active in market trading or fiduciary activities).

[E] Interagency Statement on Service Providers and Software Vendors[17]

The regulators announced that they themselves would examine service providers for Y2K compliance.[18] While the agencies stated that they

[16] FFIEC, *Interagency Guidance Concerning the Year 2000 Impact on Customers* (Mar. 17, 1998).

[17] FFIEC, *Guidance Concerning Institution Due Diligence in Connection with Service Provider and Software Vendor Year 2000 Readiness* (Mar. 17, 1998).

[18] The agencies are authorized to conduct such examinations under the Bank Service Company Act of 1962. 12 U.S.C. §§ 1861 *et seq.*

would not certify service providers or software vendors as Y2K compliant, they would forward the results of examinations to banks that use their services. Banks nevertheless were told that they still would be expected to perform their own comprehensive Y2K due diligence review of third-party service providers and software vendors, but that they could collaborate with other banks using the same vendors in joint review and testing efforts. Banks also were told to develop contingency plans for each mission critical service and product and establish trigger dates for changing service providers if necessary.

[F] Interagency Statement on Testing for Year 2000 Readiness[19]

In this interagency advisory, the agencies described their expectations for Y2K testing and established the following schedule:

June 30, 1998	Completion of written testing strategies and plans.
September 1, 1998	Mission-critical testing commenced.
December 31, 1998	Testing of internal mission-critical systems substantially complete. Service providers ready to test with customers.
March 31, 1999	Testing of vendor-reliant mission-critical systems substantially complete. External testing with material third parties (customers, other banks, payment system providers, etc.) commenced.
June 30, 1999	Testing of mission-critical systems and implementation of Y2K readiness substantially complete.

[G] Interagency Statement on Year 2000 Customer Awareness Programs

The agencies advised banks to develop retail customer awareness programs to respond to customer questions about Y2K matters.[20] Such programs would include informational brochures or other written disclo-

[19] FFIEC, *Guidance Concerning Testing for Year 2000 Readiness* (April 10, 1998).
[20] FFIEC, *Guidance on Year 2000 Customer Awareness Programs* (May 13, 1998).

sures in account statements, toll-free hotlines for customer inquiries, seminars, and Internet sites to inform customers of their Y2K readiness efforts. The agencies recommended that banks consult with legal counsel before issuing information describing the status of their Y2K readiness.

The agencies advised banks to be prepared to address consumer inquiries concerning the safety of the money in their accounts, their ability to access their funds, whether they would receive proper credit for loan payments, and the like.

The agencies prepared a checklist of actions consumers can take to protect themselves in anticipation of the year 2000 date change.[21]

[H] Interagency Statement on Contingency Planning

The agencies provided guidance to banks on Y2K contingency planning, noting that "each financial institution must evaluate its own unique circumstances and environment to development a comprehensive plan to ensure its ability to continue as a functioning business entity after January 1, 2000."[22] The guidance outlined four phases of Y2K business resumption contingency planning:

(1) Organizational planning guidelines that define a strategy for continuing business operations;
(2) A business impact analysis assessing the potential impact of mission-critical system failures;
(3) A contingency plan with a timeline for implementation and action;
(4) A method of testing and validating the business resumption contingency plan.

The agencies noted that each bank is unique and management should determine the best testing strategies for its own organization, taking into account the size of the bank, the complexity of its operations, and the level of its business risk exposure to Y2K. The FFIEC estimated that testing would consume 50 to 60 percent of the time and resources needed to make banks Y2K ready.

---

[21] *See* Federal Reserve Board, "A Y2K Checklist for Customers," SR 99-9 (SUP) (April 29, 1999).

[22] FFIEC, *Guidance Concerning Contingency Planning in Connection with Year 2000 Readiness* (May 13, 1998).

[I] Guidance on Fiduciary Services

The agencies issued special guidance to banks with respect Y2K risks associated with fiduciary services.[23] Areas of potential concern included account and asset administration, third-party risk, counterparty risk, transfer agent services, and customer disclosures. Agency officials made clear in informal statements that they do not expect banks to liquidate equity portfolios held as trustee in response to Y2K fears.

[J] Interagency Rules for Year 2000 Compliance

The federal banking agencies codified much of the guidance set forth in the FFIEC's issuances in interim rules adopted in 1998.[24] The rules outlined mandatory steps to be taken by banks at the awareness, assessment, renovation, validation (testing), and implementation phases of their Y2K readiness programs. The adoption of the FFIEC guidance in rule form ensured that the agencies could require corrective action or take other enforcement measures if necessary to ensure compliance. The agencies rescinded their Y2K guidance in 2001, stating that "[s]ince the events for which these guidelines were issued have passed, the Agencies have concluded that the guidelines are no longer necessary."[25]

[K] Questions and Answers

The FFIEC issued further guidance on testing and contingency planning in a series of questions and answers.[26]

[L] Other Advisories

The individual banking agencies also issued separate guidance on Y2K-related topics.[27] For example, the Federal Reserve Board and OCC

---

[23] FFIEC, *Year 2000 Guidance on Fiduciary Services* (Sept. 2, 1998).

[24] 63 Fed. Reg. 55,479 (Oct. 15, 1998).

[25] 66 Fed. Reg. 8616 (2001).

[26] *See* FFIEC, *Questions and Answers on Testing* (Aug. 31, 1998); *Questions and Answers Concerning Contingency Planning* (Dec. 11, 1998); *Additional Questions and Answers Concerning Year 2000 Business Resumption Contingency Planning* (May 6, 1999).

[27] *See, e.g.*, Federal Reserve Board, "The Federal Reserve's Intensified Year 2000 Compliance Efforts," SR 98-3 (SUP) (Mar. 4, 1998); "Year 2000 Supervisory Review Plan—Phase II," SR 98-17 (SUP) (June 23, 1998); "Year 2000 Workprogram, Phase II," SR 98-19 (SUP) (July 14, 1998); "Phase IIII of the Federal Reserve's Year 2000 Supervision Program and Guidance Concerning Follow-up Enforcement Actions and Applications," SR 99-2 (SUP) (Jan. 29, 1999).

emphasized the need for banking organizations involved in mergers and acquisitions to address system integration issues, including software compatibility and hardware capacity and backup.[28] The OCC warned that inadequate planning or poor implementation for a systems consolidation could result in increased costs, lost revenues, loss of customer confidence, and "in worst-case scenarios, inability to operate the bank or bank failure."

The agencies indicated that Y2K readiness progress would be required as a condition to regulatory approval of expansion proposals.[29]

[M] Confidentiality of Y2K Ratings

The federal banking agencies reminded banks that Y2K compliance ratings assigned to banks in the examination process may not be publicly disclosed.[30] Apart from maintaining the confidentiality of examination reports, the regulators stated that Y2K ratings "cannot be used in any manner to suggest that the Federal Reserve or another bank supervisory authority certifies or warrants an organization's readiness for the century date change."[31]

[N] Y2K Enforcement Actions

The federal regulators took enforcement action against banking organizations that had inadequate Y2K readiness programs[32] as well as nonbank providers of mission-critical services to banks.[33]

§ 12.05 SECURITIES AND EXCHANGE COMMISSION

The Securities and Exchange Commission ("SEC") recognized the potential impact of the Year 2000 problem on securities firms and took

---

[28] Federal Reserve Board, SR 97-29; OCC Advisory Letter 98-1 (Jan. 20, 1998).

[29] *Id.*

[30] Federal Reserve Board, "Confidentiality of Examination Findings and Ratings and Disclosures Relating to Year 2000 Compliance Efforts," SR 98-21 (SUP) (Aug. 3, 1998).

[31] *Id.*

[32] *See, e.g.*, cease-and-desist orders, *In the Matter of Putnam-Greene Financial Corporation*, Docket No. 97-027-B-BHC; and *In the Matter of Farmers and Merchants Bank, Eatonton, Georgia*, FDIC-97-084b; FDIC Press Release 83-97 (Nov. 17, 1997), and Federal Reserve Press Release of the same date.

[33] *See* Joint Federal Banking Agency Press Release (Mar. 30, 1999), announcing written agreement with First Data Corporation ordering Y2K testing and implementation.

measures to address the Y2K readiness of broker-dealers, investment advisers, and transfer agents.[34]

[A] Year 2000 Reporting Requirements

[1] Broker-Dealers

The SEC required every broker-dealer to promptly notify the SEC of its failure to keep current books and records and advised broker-dealers that they may be deemed not to have accurate and current records in violation of the Securities Exchange Act if their computer systems had Y2K problems.[35]

In 1998, the SEC adopted a regulation requiring broker-dealers to file publicly available reports on their Y2K compliance status on Form BD-Y2K.[36] The SEC also adopted a rule requiring every broker-dealer with a net capital of $100,000 or greater to include in its April 30, 1999, Form BD-Y2K filing a report prepared by an independent public accountant regarding the broker-dealer's process for addressing Y2K problems.

[2] Investment Advisers

The SEC in 1998 also adopted a rule requiring SEC-registered investment advisers to file a report on Form ADV-Y2K addressing their Y2K preparedness.[37] The reporting requirement applied to individual portfolio advisers as well as to investment advisers to mutual funds.

---

[34] *See* Letter dated November 13, 1997, from SEC Chairman Arthur Levitt, to Investment Advisers and Letter dated November 3, 1997, to broker-dealers and transfer agents Regarding Year 2000 Compliance; Statement of the Commission Regarding Disclosure of Year 2000 Issues and Consequences by Public Companies, Investment Advisers, Investment Companies, and Municipal Securities Issuers (Aug. 4, 1998); Testimony of SEC Chairman Arthur Levitt Concerning the Readiness of the United States Securities Industry and Public Companies to Meet the Information Processing Challenges of the Year 2000, before the subcommittee on Financial Services and Technology of the Senate Committee on Banking, Housing and Urban Affairs (July 30, 1997); Second Report on the Readiness of the United States Securities Industry and Public Companies To Meet the Information Processing Challenges of the Year 2000 (June 1998).

[35] 63 Fed. Reg. 37,668 (1998).

[36] *Id.*

[37] 63 Fed. Reg. 54,308 (1998).

[3] Transfer Agents

Transfer agents similarly were required by the SEC to report on their Y2K readiness status[38] and to file a form prepared by an independent public accountant.[39] Bank transfer agents are exempt from SEC registration and thus were exempt from the SEC's reporting rule. At the request of the Office of Thrift Supervision, the SEC also exempted savings associations from the rule.[40]

[B] Operational Capability Requirements

In 1999, the SEC proposed a rule under which broker-dealers and transfer agents would be required to demonstrate sufficient operational capability to assure the prompt and accurate performance of their securities execution and processing functions.[41] Although broker-dealers and transfer agents already had this obligation under the antifraud provisions of the Securities Exchange Act, the SEC noted that the proposed rule would enable the SEC to take preventive measures to enforce compliance before operational problems harmed investors whereas without the rule the SEC could act only after customers are harmed.

[C] Enforcement Actions

The SEC in 1998 brought several enforcement actions against SEC registrants that did not file Year 2000 information required under SEC rules.[42]

§ 12.06 INTERNATIONAL Y2K INITIATIVES

Initiatives were taken at the international level to address Y2K concerns, including the following relating to financial institutions.

---

[38] 63 Fed. Reg. 37,688 (1998).

[39] 63 Fed. Reg. 58,630 (1998).

[40] 63 Fed. Reg. at 37,689 (1998).

[41] 64 Fed. Reg. 12,127 (1999).

[42] Proceedings Instituted Against Nine Transfer Agents for Failing to Make Timely Year 2000-Related Disclosure, Release Nos. 34-40894, 34-40899 (Jan. 7, 1999); Proceedings Instituted Against 37 Broker-Dealers for Failing to Make Timely Year 2000-Related Disclosure, Release Nos. 34-40574, 34-40573 (Oct. 20, 1998).

[A] Basle Committee

Among other actions, the Basle Committee on Banking Supervision in 1997 issued a paper addressing the need for a targeted, multifaceted action plan by bank management to address the Y2K problem.[43] The Basle Committee also issued a paper discussing the responsibilities of home and host country regulators for Y2K readiness of banks with an international presence and calling for cooperation between regulators on cross-border issues.[44]

In 1998, the Basle Committee jointly sponsored a Round Table on the Year 2000 with the International Association of Insurance Supervisors, the International Organization of Securities Commissions, and the Committee on Payment and Settlement Systems. As a result of the Round Table, the Joint Year 2000 Council was created, for which the Basle Committee served as secretariat.

[B] Joint Year 2000 Council

The Joint Year 2000 Council was created in 1998 to ensure a high level of global attention to the Y2K problem in banking and financial services and to serve as a point of contact for national and international private-sector initiatives. The Council provided a forum for the sharing of information on regulatory and supervisory strategies and approaches to the Y2K problem as well as discussion of possible contingency measures. The Council was sponsored jointly by the Basle Committee on Banking Supervision, the G-10 Central Bank Governors' Committee on Payment and Settlement Systems, the International Association of Insurance Supervisors, and the International Organization of Securities Commissions. Federal Reserve Governor Roger W. Ferguson chaired the Council.

In 1998, the Council issued supervisory guidance for use by international supervisors of insurance activities and securities markets in conducting independent assessments of financial institution Y2K readiness.[45] The

---

[43] Basle Committee on Banking Supervision, *The Year 2000: A Challenge for Financial Institutions and Bank Supervisors* (Sept. 1997).

[44] Basle Committee on Banking Supervision, *Supervisory Cooperation on Year 2000 Cross-Border Issues*, No. 38 (June 1998).

[45] Year 2000 Council, *Supervisory Guidance on the Independent Assessment of Financial Institution Year 2000 Preparations* (July 1998).

Committee also developed a reporting framework to be used by operators of payment and settlement systems to indicate the state of Y2K preparedness and testing.[46]

[C] Global 2000 Coordinating Group

The Global 2000 Coordinating Group was an informal group of 250 banks, securities firms, and insurance companies from 53 countries that joined together in coordinated initiatives to facilitate efforts by the global financial community to minimize the risks to global financial markets arising from the Y2K problem.

The Group's main initiative was the Year 2000 Self-Assessment program, which was intended to provide a common format for public disclosure of an institution's assessment of its Y2K readiness status at various stages.

§ 12.07 Y2K AFTERMATH

Following the transition to the new Millennium without major repercussions to the financial system due to the Y2K computer "bug," the federal banking agencies, through the FFIEC, issued a report on "Lessons Learned from the Year 2000 Project."[47] The report observed that the Year 2000 project was "one of the most expensive and resource-intensive information technology challenges ever faced by the financial service industry."

The report cited a number of benefits that resulted from the Y2K crisis prevention effort, including the following:

- The experience of senior management and directors in managing a comprehensive, corporate-wide compliance effort involving interdisciplinary teams.
- The development of comprehensive inventories of information technology systems and applications.

---

[46] *Id.*

[47] Federal Financial Institutions Examination Council, "Lessons Learned from the Year 2000 Project," (Mar. 21, 2000).

- Improved management of relationships with software vendors and other external providers of mission-critical functions.
- Effective technology testing strategies.
- Detailed contingency planning.
- Strengthened internal controls and security.
- Open information sharing among organizations across competitive lines and regulatory boundaries. "Financial institutions worked together in unprecedented fashion with other financial institutions, service providers, software vendors, trade associations, regulators, and other industries to share information and strategies and to respond to media reports or perceptions that could decrease public confidence in the financial services industry."
- Improved public relations.
- Greater involvement of legal counsel in reviewing technology contracts and developing consistent approaches to document retention and recordkeeping as a legal defense strategy for demonstrating due diligence.

CHAPTER 13

CONSUMER PROTECTION AND PRIVACY

§ 13.01 IN GENERAL

The ultimate success of electronic banking and commerce will require a high level of consumer confidence in the ability of banks and other financial service firms to conduct electronic financial transactions with the same or greater degree of security and consumer protection as is currently available for conventional financial services transactions.

Foremost among the consumer protection concerns raised by new electronic banking and commerce technologies is the privacy of customer information. Electronic banking systems and smart cards greatly increase the opportunities for gathering, storing, manipulating, and disseminating enormous volumes of customer information into commercially useful formats. They also significantly increase the possibilities for violation of consumer privacy expectations and misuse of confidential customer information.

Online stored value systems, for example, may have the ability to make consumer information available to the card issuer, participating retailers, and the stored value processor. Offline systems may enable the retailer to retain information on its terminal. Some systems store not only financial information but personal information, such as medical records. Users of the World Wide Web leave a stream of electronic markers at every site they visit, allowing each site to capture information about them. The Internet has exposed consumers to a new kind of invasion of privacy and created enhanced opportunities for criminals to unlawfully obtain personal identification information, such as social security numbers and credit card numbers, and to use it for criminal purposes, such as credit card fraud.

Privacy issues have long been a matter of congressional concern in the financial sector. Congress enacted the Fair Credit Reporting Act in 1970 to protect consumer credit information. After the United States Supreme Court held that there was no legitimate expectation of privacy with regard to checks and deposit slips,[1] Congress, in 1977, appointed the Privacy Protection Study Commission to review issues relating to personal privacy and since then has enacted a variety of consumer protection laws with privacy provisions. Congress has never deemed it necessary, however, to adopt a comprehensive privacy policy at the federal level.

---

[1] *United States v. Miller*, 425 U.S. 435 (1976).

Although many federal and state laws address discreet matters dealing with privacy,[1.1] no national privacy framework exists. The United States uses a "sectoral approach that relies on a mix of legislation, regulation, and self-regulation."[1.2]

The rapid growth of online databases of consumer information has led to a vigorous debate at the national and international levels concerning the need for privacy regulation which is likely to continue for the foreseeable future, notwithstanding the enactment of major privacy legislation governing the banking and financial services sector in 1999.[1.3]

§ 13.02 FEDERAL PRIVACY AND CONSUMER PROTECTION STATUTES

A number of federal statutes address privacy and consumer protection concerns, as discussed below.

[A] Fair Credit Reporting Act

The Fair Credit Reporting Act of 1970 ("FCRA")[2] governs the information handling practices of consumer reporting agencies, such as credit bureaus, and the use of consumer reports. Congress enacted FCRA based on the following findings:

(1) The banking system is dependent upon fair and accurate credit reporting. Inaccurate credit reports directly impair the efficiency of the banking system, and unfair credit reporting methods undermine the public confidence which is essential to the continued functioning of the banking system.

(2) An elaborate mechanism has been developed for investigating and evaluating the credit worthiness, credit standing, credit capacity, character, and general reputation of consumers.

[1.1] *See* 65 Fed. Reg. 45,666 (2000) (Department of Commerce letter to European Commission on Safe Harbor Privacy Principles) for an excellent discussion of state law mechanisms for enforcing common law and state law rights against invasion of privacy.

[1.2] *See* 65 Fed. Reg. 45,666, 45,667 (2000) (Department of Commerce letter to European Commission on Safe Harbor Privacy Principles).

[1.3] Title V of the Gramm-Leach-Bliley Act, 106-102, discussed *infra.*

[2] 15 U.S.C. §§ 1681 *et seq.*

(3) Consumer reporting agencies have assumed a vital role in assembling and evaluating consumer credit and other information on consumers.

(4) There is a need to insure that consumer reporting agencies exercise their grave responsibilities with fairness, impartiality, and a respect for the consumer's right to privacy.[3]

Under the Act, a "consumer report" is defined to mean:

> any written, oral, or other communication of any information by a consumer reporting agency bearing on a consumer's credit worthiness, credit standing, credit capacity, character, general reputation, personal characteristics, or mode of living which is used or expected to be used or collected in whole or in part for the purpose of serving as a factor in establishing the consumer's eligibility for—
>
> (A) credit or insurance to be used primarily for personal, family, or household purposes;
>
> (B) employment purposes; or
>
> (C) any other purpose authorized under [the Act].[4]

A "consumer reporting agency" is defined to mean:

> Any person which, for monetary fees, dues, or on a cooperative nonprofit basis, regularly engages in whole or in part in the practice of assembling or evaluating consumer credit information or other information on consumers for the purpose of furnishing consumer reports to third parties, and which uses any means or facility of interstate commerce for the purpose of preparing or furnishing consumer reports.[5]

FCRA subjects consumer reporting agencies to legal requirements for safeguarding consumer reports, including restrictions on the purposes for which consumer information may be distributed or sold. Consumer reporting agencies are required to give a consumer access to all information maintained by the agency about the consumer and to maintain procedures for correcting erroneous information.

A major issue for banking and other financial service organizations arises under FCRA when such institutions transfer consumer information

---

[3] 15 U.S.C. § 1681.

[4] 15 U.S.C. § 1681a(d).

[5] 15 U.S.C. § 1681a(f).

among affiliates for cross-marketing purposes. Prior to 1996, it was feared that such information sharing would cause a bank or its affiliate to become a consumer reporting agency subject to the legal requirements of FCRA. This issue took on increased significance in the 1990s as banks consolidated with other financial service firms and acquired separate securities and insurance brokerage affiliates.

In 1996, Congress amended FCRA to clarify when banks and their affiliates may share customer information without triggering compliance requirements under FCRA.[6] As amended, the Act exempts from the definition of "consumer report" so-called "experience information" and thereby allows banks to share such information with affiliates and third parties without triggering the Act's requirements. Experience information is derived from the bank's relationship with the customer and includes, for example, the customer's outstanding balances, the bank's delinquency experience with the customer, etc. In addition, the Act was amended to allow banks to share with their affiliates (but not third parties) so-called "non-experience information" provided the customer is given clear and conspicuous notice of the possibility of information sharing and an opportunity to instruct the bank not to share the information.[7]

The 1996 amendments to FCRA also impose on banks responsibility for the accuracy of customer data they submit to credit bureaus and require banks to inform customers who have been denied credit of their right to obtain information that was the basis for the action.

The Office of the Comptroller of the Currency ("OCC") in 1998 issued a banking bulletin summarizing the rights and responsibilities of national banks under FCRA when they share customer information with their affiliates.[8] The OCC noted that FCRA limits the authority of the federal banking agencies to examine for compliance with FCRA only in circumstances when an agency receives a complaint or if the agency otherwise has knowledge of a violation.

The OCC in 1999 issued an advisory letter to national banks providing examples of existing bank practices for complying with the customer opt-out provisions for the sharing of information with affiliates.[9] The OCC

[6] Title II of the Economic Growth and Regulatory Paperwork Reduction Act of 1996, Pub. L. No. 104-208, 110 Stat. 3009, *codified at* 15 U.S.C. §§ 1681 *et seq*.

[7] 12 U.S.C. § 1681a(d)(2)(A)(iii).

[8] OCC Bulletin No. 98-33 (Aug. 3, 1998).

[9] OCC Advisory Letter 99-3 (March 29, 1999).

noted that FCRA does not impose specific requirements for the placement or content of the opt-out notice.

The Gramm-Leach-Bliley Act authorized the federal banking agencies to develop regulations jointly to implement the provisions of FCRA.[9.1] The agencies in 2000 proposed joint regulations to promote consistency between the opt-out notice requirements of FCRA with those of the Gramm-Leach-Bliley Act.[9.2] The proposed regulations apply to the sharing with affiliates of consumer information other than transaction or experience information which, as noted, can be shared with affiliates as well as non-affiliates without giving the customer an opt-out notice.

[B] Electronic Funds Transfer Act of 1978

The Electronic Funds Transfer Act of 1978 ("EFT Act")[10] establishes the basic rights, liabilities and responsibilities of consumers and financial institutions in the use of electronic fund transfer services.[11] Among other provisions, the EFT Act requires financial institutions to provide written receipts of EFT transactions and limits a consumer's liability to $50 for unauthorized EFT transactions. The Act also requires financial institutions to give notice to customers of the circumstances when account information will be disclosed to third parties.[12] This disclosure may be made by electronic means.[13]

The EFT Act is administered by the Federal Reserve Board under the Board's Regulation E.[13.1] Under Regulation E, an "electronic fund transfer" is defined as follows:

> The term electronic fund transfer means any transfer of funds that is initiated through an electronic terminal, telephone, computer, or magnetic tape for the purpose of ordering, instructing, or authorizing a financial institution to debit or credit an account. The term includes, but is not limited to—
>
> (1) point-of-sale transfers;
> (2) automated teller machine transfers;

9.1 Pub. L. No. 106-102.

9.2 65 Fed. Reg. 63,120 (2000). *See* 13.02[M] *infra* for a discussion of the Gramm-Leach-Bliley Act privacy provisions.

10 15 U.S.C. §§ 1693 *et seq.*

11 *See* Chapter 4, **The Regulatory Framework**, for a further discussion of the EFT Act.

12 15 U.S.C. § 1693c(a)(9).

13 *See* 12 C.F.R. § 205.4(c)(2); 63 Fed. Reg. 14,528 (1998).

13.1 12 C.F.R. § 205.

(3) direct deposits or withdrawals of funds;
(4) transfers initiated by telephone; and
(5) transfers resulting from debit card transactions, whether or not initiated through an electronic terminal.[13.2]

This definition encompasses ATMs, automated clearinghouse (ACH) transactions, telephone bill-payment plans, and other forms of remote banking services.

Regulation E generally applies to "financial institutions" as defined to mean a bank, savings association, credit union, "or any other person that directly or indirectly holds an account belonging to a consumer or that issues an access device and agrees with a consumer to provide electronic fund transfer services."[13.3]

The provisions of Regulation E are triggered when a financial institution issues an "access device." An "access device" is defined to mean "a card, code, or other means of access to a consumer's account, or any combination thereof, that may be used by the consumer to initiate electronic fund transfers."[13.4]

The Board in 2001 clarified the means by which electronic delivery of Regulation E disclosures may be made in light of enactment of the Electronic Signatures in Global and National Commerce Act ("E-Sign Act").[13.5] Under the Board's interim final rule,[13.6] Regulation E disclosures may be sent by e-mail to an electronic address designated by the consumer or may be made available at an Internet Web site if consumers are sent a notice alerting them to the availability of the disclosures. Disclosures posted on a Web site must be available for at least 90 days to allow consumers adequate time to access them. With respect to electronic disclosures that are returned undelivered, a financial institution must make a good faith attempt to redeliver the disclosures.

In 2000, the Board solicited public comment on whether account aggregators are financial institutions subject to Regulation E.[13.7] Account aggregation is a service by which consumer account data is gathered from a variety of Web sites, using customer-provided usernames and passwords, and presented to the consumer in a consolidated format. This process

---

[13.2] 12 C.F.R. § 205.3(b).
[13.3] 12 C.F.R. § 205.2(i).
[13.4] 12 C.F.R. § 205.2(a)(1).
[13.5] 15 U.S.C. § 1693 *et seq.*
[13.6] 66 Fed. Reg. __ (2001).
[13.7] 65 Fed. Reg. 40,064 (2000).

sometimes is referred to as "screen scraping." Account aggregation services may be offered with respect to banking accounts, credit cards brokerage accounts, and other types of personal accounts.[13.8] In its request for public comment, the Board asked commenters to address the following issues:

> Are aggregators providing or planning to provide bill-payment or other EFT services (in addition to information services)? To what extent do agreements exist between aggregators and account-holding institutions, governing matters such as procedures for access to information and for electronic transfers?
>
> In addition, comment is solicited on the implications of a determination that aggregators are or are not financial institutions for purposes of Regulation E generally or under § 205.14. Typically, only one access device is contemplated to initiate an EFT to or from a consumer's account. Nevertheless, if a consumer enters a security code issued by the aggregator to access information on the aggregator's web site and the consumer initiates an EFT using a security code provided by the account-holding institution, the security code issued by the aggregator arguably meets the definition of an "access device." Two access codes (the one provided by the aggregator and the other by the account-holding institution) are needed to initiate electronic transfers from the consumer's account from the aggregator's web site. Thus, the aggregator would be a financial institution for purposes of Regulation E.
>
> If the aggregator is not a financial institution and an unauthorized EFT occurs through an aggregator's service, comment 2(m)-2 could be read to suggest that a consumer who has given the aggregator access to the consumer's account assumes liability for the transfers. The guidance in the comment, however, was not originally provided to address this situation.[13.9]

The Board did not take any final action as a result of the comments but stated that it "will consider addressing these issues in a future proposal."[13.10]

[13.8] *See* Chapter 9, § 9.18, for a discussion of account aggregation services.

[13.9] 65 Fed. Reg. 40,064 (2000).

[13.10] 66 Fed. Reg. 15,187, 15,188 (2001). *See* § 13.02[B] *supra* for a discussion of Regulation E.

[C] Fair Debt Collection Practices Act

The Fair Debt Collection Practices Act[14] protects the privacy of debtors by limiting intrusion on consumer privacy and prohibiting excessive and abusive collection practices.

[D] Fair Credit Billing Act

The Fair Credit Billing Act[15] authorizes consumers to challenge the accuracy of information in a creditor's files.

[E] Telephone Consumer Protection Act of 1991

The Telephone Consumer Protection Act of 1991[16] authorizes the Federal Communications Commission to adopt regulations protecting consumer privacy rights to avoid objectionable telephone solicitations.

[F] Telemarketing and Consumer Fraud and Abuse Prevention Act of 1991

This Act[17] protects consumers from deceptive and abusive telemarketing practices.

[G] Federal Trade Commission Act

The Federal Trade Commission Act[18] prohibits unfair or deceptive acts or practices in or affecting commerce.[19] While affiliates of banks are subject to regulation by the Federal Trade Commission ("FTC") under the Act, banks themselves are exempt from FTC regulation.[20] Nevertheless, the Act requires each of the federal banking agencies to establish a separate division of consumer affairs to handle consumer complaints regarding unfair or deceptive acts or practices by banks, including violations of

---

[14] 12 U.S.C. §§ 1601 *et seq.*

[15] 15 U.S.C. §§ 1666 *et seq.*

[16] 47 U.S.C. § 227.

[17] 15 U.S.C. §§ 6101 *et seq.*

[18] 15 U.S.C. §§ 41 *et seq., enforced under* 12 U.S.C. § 1818.

[19] 15 U.S.C. § 45(a)(1).

[20] 15 U.S.C. § 45(a)(2).

an institution's privacy policies and procedures.[21] Moreover, the FTC's decisions on unfair and deceptive acts and practices often influence the consumer protection standards applicable to bank activities.

[H] Right to Financial Privacy Act of 1978

The Right to Financial Privacy Act of 1978[22] protects personal financial data from unwarranted access by federal government agencies.

[I] Electronic Communications Privacy Act of 1986

The Electronic Communications Privacy Act of 1986[23] protects against unauthorized interception of electronic communications.

[J] Cable Communications Policy Act

The Cable Communications Policy Act, as amended by the Cable Television Consumer Protection and Competition Act of 1992,[24] establishes written consumer disclosure requirements for the collection and use of personally identifiable information and prohibits sharing of such information without the prior written or electronic consent of the customer. The Act also provides for customer inspection of information and error correction.

[K] Comprehensive Crime Control Act of 1984

The Comprehensive Crime Control Act[25] makes it a federal crime to access certain computer systems, including government and bank computers, and obtain information without authorization.

[L] Identity Theft and Assumption Deterrence Act of 1998

The Identity Theft and Assumption Deterrence Act of 1998[25.1] makes it unlawful for anyone to knowingly transfer or use, without lawful author-

---

[21] *See, e.g.*, Regulation AA, Unfair or Deceptive Acts or Practices, of the Federal Reserve Board, 12 C.F.R. Part 227.

[22] 12 U.S.C. §§ 3401 *et seq.*

[23] 18 U.S.C. §§ 2510 *et seq.*

[24] 47 U.S.C. §§ 551 *et seq.*

[25] 18 U.S.C. §§ 1030 *et seq.*

[25.1] Pub. L. No. 105-318, 95th Cong., 2d Sess. (1998).

ity, a means of identification of another person with the intent to commit, or to aid or abet, any unlawful activity in violation of federal law or that constitutes a felony under state law.[25.2] Among its provisions, the Act directs the Federal Trade Commission to establish procedures to receive complaints by individuals who believe that their identification has been assumed, stolen, or otherwise unlawfully acquired.

The FTC has taken several measures to implement the Act including establishing a toll-free telephone hotline that customers can call to report identity theft, an identity theft complaint database, and dissemination of comprehensive consumer education material for victims of identity theft.[26]

[M] Gramm-Leach-Bliley Act

[1] Subtitle A—Protection of Nonpublic Financial Information

Title V of the Gramm-Leach-Bliley Act, enacted on November 12, 1999, includes substantial provisions protecting the privacy of consumer financial information.

Congressional Policy. The new law states as a matter of Congressional policy that:

> It is the policy of the Congress that each financial institution has an affirmative and continuing obligation to respect the privacy of its customers and to protect the security and confidentiality of those customers' nonpublic personal information.[26.1]

In furtherance of the new privacy policy, Congress directed each financial institution regulatory agency to establish standards relating to "administrative, technical, and physical safeguards" to do the following:

(1) To insure the security and confidentiality of customer records and information;

[25.2] 18 U.S.C. § 1028(a)(7).

[26] *See* Testimony of Betsy Broder, Assistant Director for the Division of Planning and Information of the Bureau of Consumer Protection, Federal Trade Commission, before the House Committee on Banking and Financial Services (Sept. 13, 2000).

[26.1] Pub. L. No. 106-102, § 501.

(2) To protect against any anticipated threats or hazards to the security or integrity of such records; and
(3) To protect against unauthorized access to or use of such records or information which could result in substantial harm or inconvenience to any customer.[26.2]

Nondisclosure to Nonaffiliates. The new law provides that a financial institution may not disclose to a nonaffiliated third party any nonpublic personal information concerning a customer unless the institution provides or has provided to the consumer a notice containing the institution's policies and practices regarding disclosure of nonpublic customer information.[26.3]

Opt Out Provision. Moreover, no disclosure of such information to a third party is allowed unless the institution notifies the customer that such disclosure may be made, the customer is given an opportunity to direct that such disclosure not be made, and the customer is given an explanation of how he or she can exercise the nondisclosure option.[26.4]

Joint Agreement Exception. The prohibition against disclosure of customer information does not prevent a bank from disclosing nonpublic personal information to a nonaffiliated third party to perform services for or functions on behalf of the bank, including marketing of the bank's

---

[26.2] *Id.*

[26.3] Pub. L. No. 106-102, § 502.

[26.4] These prohibitions do not apply to the disclosure of information in certain circumstances, including:

- As necessary to affect, administer, or enforce a transaction requested or authorized by the consumer,
- With the consent of or at the direction of the customer,
- To persons acting in a fiduciary or representative capacity on behalf of the customer,
- In connection with servicing or processing a financial product or service requested or authorized by the customer,
- In connection with maintaining or servicing the customer's account with the bank,
- In connection with a proposed or actual securitization, secondary market sale (including sales of servicing rights), or similar transaction related to a transaction of the customer,
- To the extent specifically permitted or required under the Right to Financial Privacy Act of 1978,
- In connection with a proposed or actual sale, merger, transfer, or exchange of all or a portion of a business or operating unit if the disclosure of nonpublic personal information concerns solely consumers of such business or unit, or
- In order to comply with applicable legal requirements.

own products or services, or financial products or services offered pursuant to a joint agreement, if the bank fully discloses the providing of such information and enters into a contractual agreement with the third party that requires the third party to maintain the confidentiality of the customer information.[26.5] In furtherance of this exception, a joint employee is expressly excluded from the definition of a "nonaffiliated third party."[26.6]

Account Numbers. The new law specifically prohibits a financial institution from disclosing to any nonaffiliated third party an account number for a credit card, deposit, or transaction account for use in telemarketing, direct mail marketing, or other marketing through electronic mail to a consumer.[26.7]

Definition of "Financial Institution." A "financial institution" for purposes of the privacy provisions includes not only banks, but broker-dealers, investment advisers, mutual funds, insurance companies, and any institution "the business of which is engaging in financial activities" as defined in Section 4(k) of the Bank Holding Company Act.[26.8] The definition of financial institution is broad and arguably would cover travel agencies, real estate brokers, leasing companies, data processing companies, and other entities engaged in "financial activities" under Section 4(k) of the Bank Holding Company Act.

Disclosure of Privacy Policies and Practices. Title V requires a financial institution to disclose the institution's policies and practices regarding the disclosure of nonpublic personal information to affiliated and nonaffiliated third parties.[26.9] Such disclosure must be made at the time the customer relationship is established and not less than annually during the continuation of the relationship, and may be made in writing or electronic form. The policies and practices that must be disclosed

---

[26.5] Pub. L. No. 106-102, § 503(b)(2).

[26.6] Pub. L. No. 106-102, § 509(5). Information sharing pursuant to this exception nevertheless may be problematic under the Fair Credit Reporting Act ("FCRA"). That Act does not include a joint agreement exception, although it arguably would be possible to treat a joint employee as an affiliate under the FCRA to the extent such as employee is a person "affiliated by corporate control." As long as the information sharing is limited to "experience information," however, FCRA should not pose a problem.

[26.7] Pub. L. No. 106-102, § 502(d).

[26.8] Pub. L. No. 106-102, § 509(3). Institutions subject to the jurisdiction of the Commodity Futures Trading Commission and farm credit organizations are specifically excluded.

[26.9] Pub. L. No. 106-102, § 503.

include those relating to nonpublic personal information of persons who have ceased to be customers of the financial institution as well as existing customers.

Regulations. Regulations to implement the privacy provisions of the new law were to be adopted within six months by the federal banking agencies with respect to banks, the Securities and Exchange Commission with respect to broker-dealers and investment advisers, and the Federal Trade Commission with respect to other financial institutions. The agencies were required to consult with representatives of state insurance authorities.

Relationship to State Law. The Title V privacy provisions do not preempt state law except to the extent state law is inconsistent with the Title V privacy protections.[26.10] State laws that are more protective are not deemed to be inconsistent, thus encouraging the states to be more protective.

[2] Subtitle B—Fraudulent Access to Financial Information

Subtitle B of the Gramm-Leach-Bliley Act makes it unlawful for any person to obtain or disclose, or attempt to obtain or disclose, customer information of a financial institution relating to another person by false, fictitious, or fraudulent means.[26.11] A violator is subject to a criminal penalty of imprisonment for up to 5 years, or 10 years if the violation is part of a pattern of any illegal activity involving more than $100,000 in a 12-month period.

§ 13.03 GOVERNMENT POLICY AND INITIATIVES

[A] The Administration

The Clinton Administration in its *Framework for Global Electronic Commerce* supported private sector efforts to develop self-regulatory measures to protect privacy in online banking systems and other Internet applications rather than additional government action, but indicated that this policy will be reconsidered if necessary:

> We believe that private efforts of industry working in cooperation with consumer groups are preferable to government regulation, but

---

[26.10] Pub. L. No. 106-102, § 507.

[26.11] Pub. L. No. 106-102, § 521.

> if effective privacy protection cannot be provided in this way, we will reevaluate this policy.[27]

The Administration modified its position in favor of some government restrictions in the "Clinton-Gore Plan for Financial Privacy and Consumer Protection in the 21st Century."[28] Among other recommendations, the Plan recommended that Congress enact legislation to limit the sharing of consumer financial information within financial conglomerates, impose special restrictions on sharing of medical information within a financial conglomerate, and enhance the authority of the federal banking regulators to enforce compliance with the Fair Credit Reporting Act. As part of the Administration's Plan for Financial Privacy, a Chief Counselor for Privacy was established in the Office of Management and Budget to coordinate the government's privacy policy.

Vice President Gore articulated an "Electronic Bill of Rights" relating to online privacy:

(1) The right to choose whether one's personal information is disclosed.
(2) The right to know how, when and how much of that information is being used.
(3) The right to see that information themselves.
(4) The right to know if information is accurate and correct if it is not.[29]

[B] Information Infrastructure Task Force

In June of 1995, the Privacy Working Group of the United States Government Information Infrastructure Task Force ("IITF") issued a report entitled *Privacy and the National Information Infrastructure: Principles for Providing and Using Personal Information*. The report recommended a set of principles to govern the collection, processing, storage, and use of personal data.

---

[27] The White House, *A Framework for Global Electronic Commerce* (July 1, 1997).

[28] Released May 4, 1999.

[29] *See* U.S. Government Working Group on Electronic Commerce, First Annual Report (Nov. 1998), at 17.

The IITF's Privacy Principles built on the privacy guidelines of the Organization for Economic Cooperation and Development ("OECD")[30] that emphasize disclosure and afford consumers a means of limiting the use of personal information and provide that an individual's reasonable expectation of privacy with respect to his or her personal information should be assured, that personal information should not be improperly altered or destroyed, and that personal information should be accurate, timely, complete, and relevant for the purposes for which it is provided and used. Under these principles, consumers are entitled to redress if they are harmed by improper use or disclosure of personal information or if decisions are based on inaccurate, outdated, incomplete, or irrelevant personal information.

In 1997, the Information Policy Committee of the IITF issued a draft paper entitled *Options for Promoting Privacy on the National Information Infrastructure*. The paper surveyed information privacy practices in the United States and solicited public comment on the best way to implement the Privacy Principles.

[C] Department of Commerce

The Department of Commerce, through its National Telecommunications and Information Administration ("NTIA") and other bureaus, has played a key role in implementing the Administration's policy on privacy and consumer protection. The Department in 1997 issued a comprehensive paper on privacy addressing various models of government regulation and self-regulation of privacy.[31]

In 1998, the Department requested public comment on a draft paper entitled "Elements of Effective Self-Regulation for Protection of Privacy" in connection with a report to the President on industry efforts to establish self-regulatory regimes to ensure online privacy and to develop technological means of protecting information privacy.[32]

As noted below, the Department has taken the lead in negotiating with the European Union on safe harbor principles for privacy protection.[33]

---

[30] *See* § 13.05[A], *infra*.

[31] U.S. Department of Commerce, National Telecommunications and Information Administration, "Privacy and Self-Regulation in the Information Age" (June 1997).

[32] 63 Fed. Reg. 30,729 (1998).

[33] *See* § 13.05, *infra*.

[D] Federal Trade Commission

As noted above, the Federal Trade Commission Act[34] authorizes the Federal Trade Commission ("FTC") to protect consumers from unfair or deceptive acts or practices. A "deceptive practice" is defined as a representation, omission or practice that is likely to mislead reasonable consumers in a material fashion. The FTC takes the position that misrepresenting why information is being collected from consumers or how the collected information will be used constitutes a "deceptive practice."

Banks, savings associations and credit unions are exempt from the FTC's authority, but securities broker-dealers and investment advisers are not. Insurance companies are not specifically exempt but the FTC generally treats them as such under the McCarran-Ferguson Act.[34.1]

The FTC has been particularly active in addressing online consumer privacy concerns. The Commission held a series of workshops on privacy issues commencing in April 1995, followed by another workshop in June 1996, which examined Web site information collection practices, industry self-regulatory efforts and the role of government in protecting online information privacy.[35] The FTC held hearings in October and November 1995 on the implications of globalization and technological innovation for competition and consumer protection issues, including privacy.

The FTC has taken enforcement actions to protect consumers from unfair or deceptive practices via the Internet. In 1998, in the first action of its kind, the FTC commenced action against GeoCities based on allegations that GeoCities' Web site misrepresented the type of information collected from users and how the information was used.[36] In 1999, the FTC charged three individuals and eight businesses with fraudulently billing or debiting consumer credit card accounts for Internet entertainment services they had not ordered.[37]

The FTC as a matter of policy has supported industry self-regulatory measures aimed at privacy protection:

---

[34] 15 U.S.C. § 45(a)(2).

[34.1] *See* 65 Fed. Reg. 45,666, 45,676 (2000).

[35] *See* Federal Trade Commission, *Consumer Privacy on the Global Information Infrastructure*, Staff Report (Dec. 1996).

[36] *See* ⟨⟨*http:www.ftc.gov/os/9808/geo-cmpl.htm*⟩⟩.

[37] Federal Trade Commission Press Release (dated Jan. 12, 1999). *See also Federal Trade Commission v. Toysmart.com LLC,* D.Mass., No. 00-11341-RBS (consent judgment filed July 21, 2000).

> The Commission has encouraged industry to address consumer concerns through self-regulation. In the Commission's view, self-regulation in the first instance generally is more prompt, flexible, and effective than government regulation. Further, self-regulation can bring the accumulated judgment and experience of industry to bear on issues that may be difficult for the government to define with bright-line rules. Industry and consumers are well-situated to know what is needed and where immediate concerns lie.[38]

In 1998, the Commission requested public comment on the effectiveness of self-regulation as a means of protecting consumer information privacy online.[39] In June 1998, the Commission released a report based on the comments it received as well as an analysis of over 1,400 commercial Web sites, including 125 Web sites operated by financial service providers.[40] The report found that, while 97 percent of the sites collected personal information, only 17 percent of the sites contained appropriate disclosures such as a privacy policy notice or an information practice statement. The FTC's report raised questions as to whether the policy of relying on industry self-regulation on privacy is appropriate. The FTC issued a follow-up report in 1999 reporting on new survey results showing that, "despite the laudable efforts of industry leaders, the vast majority of even the busiest Web sites have not implemented all four substantive fair information practice principles of Notice/Awareness, Choice/Consent, Access/Participation, and Security/Integrity."[40.1] The FTC concluded nevertheless, because of industry efforts, that legislation to address online privacy issues was not appropriate.[40.2] In its third report on privacy, the FTC changed its view and concluded that "while self-regulatory efforts have achieved some real progress, the lack of broad-based implementation of such consumer protections online requires legislative action in order

---

[38] "Internet Privacy," Testimony of the Federal Trade Commission before the subcommittee on Courts and Intellectual Property of the House Judiciary Committee (Mar. 26, 1998).

[39] 63 Fed. Reg. 10,916 (1998).

[40] Federal Trade Commission, *Privacy Online: A Report to Congress* (June 1998), at 22, 24, 27. Posted at ⟨⟨*www.FTC.gov/reports/privacy3*⟩⟩.

[40.1] Federal Trade Commission, *Self-Regulation and Privacy Online: A Report to Congress,* (July 1999) at 6.

[40.2] *Id.* at 12.

to fully protect consumers' personal information and build public confidence in electronic commerce."[40.3]

The FTC has opined that the antitrust laws do not bar an industry trade association from requiring its members to abide by certain privacy protection measures, such as the requirement that members honor consumer requests that members not sell or transfer their personal information.[41]

The FTC has established a Privacy Information Web Site to educate consumers about the importance of personal information privacy.[42]

In addition to privacy issues, the FTC has taken a lead role in addressing other consumer protection matters.

In 1999, the FTC held a workshop on how to protect consumers in global electronic commerce,[43] addressing such issues as:

- **Conflicts of Law:** When a consumer does business with a foreign entity, which laws apply?
- **Electronic Contracts:** Do existing laws protect consumers engaged in electronic commerce abroad?
- **International Requirements:** What protections should be available to consumers in general in the electronic marketplace?
- **Law Enforcement Agencies:** What is their appropriate role in the electronic commerce world?
- **Industry:** How can consumer protections be adequately addressed in the global electronic marketplace?

The FTC released a report based on its workshop which, among other things, cautions against allowing online sellers to be governed only by their own country's laws and courts, or only by the laws they prescribe in their sales contracts.[43.1]

[40.3] Federal Trade Commission, "Privacy Online: Fair Information Practices in the Electronic Marketplace," May 2000.

[41] Letter dated September 9, 1997, from the Bureau of Competition, Federal Trade Commission, to counsel for the Direct Marketing Association.

[42] The Web site address is ⟨⟨*http://www.ftc.gov/privacy/index.html*⟩⟩.

[43] Federal Trade Commission, "Workshop on Consumer Protection in the Global Electronic Marketplace," (June 8–9, 1999). *See also* 63 Fed. Reg. 69,289 (1998), requesting academic papers and public comment.

[43.1] Federal Trade Commission, Bureau of Consumer Protection, "Consumer Protection in the Global Electronic Marketplace: Looking Ahead," 2000.

The FTC has brought charges under the FTC Act alleging that certain individuals and businesses billed or debited consumers' credit card accounts for unordered or fictitious Internet services.[43.2] The FTC alleged that the defendants obtained consumer credit and debit card numbers without the cardholders' knowledge or approval and used the cards to order entertainment and other services.

[E] Federal Banking Agencies

The Comptroller of the Currency established a Privacy Working Group in 1998 to develop guidance for national banks on consumer privacy issues.[44] The Working Group was directed to address disclosure of bank privacy policies, sharing of customer information, information security, and the problem of identity theft, and to draft model disclosures informing consumers about a bank's information sharing practices and the right of consumers to opt-out of information sharing between a bank and its affiliates under the Fair Credit Reporting Act.

In 1999, the OCC issued an advisory letter to national banks on privacy policies for bank Internet Web sites.[45] The guidance provided examples of effective practices for informing consumers who access bank Web sites about bank policies for the collection and use of personal information.

The OCC also issued an advisory letter alerting national banks to the practice of pretext phone calling by unauthorized individuals seeking access to confidential customer information.[46]

The Federal Deposit Insurance Corporation ("FDIC") in 1998 issued a letter to FDIC-insured institutions urging them to adopt and enforce meaningful disclosures of privacy policies and information practices.[47] The FDIC stated that it considers the privacy of customer personal information to be "an element of public trust and confidence" in banks and that its examiners would review a bank's information collection practices during bank examinations.

[43.2] *See* FTC Press Release (dated Jan. 12, 1999).

[44] *See* OCC Press Release 98-59 (June 12, 1998).

[45] OCC Advisory Letter 99-6, Guidance to National Banks on Web Site Privacy Statements (May 4, 1999), *posted at* ⟨⟨*www.occ.treas.gov/ftp/advisory/99-6.txt*⟩⟩.

[46] OCC Advisory Letter 98-11.

[47] FDIC, "Online Privacy of Consumer Personal Information," FIL 86-98 (Aug. 17, 1998).

The agencies in 1999 conducted a survey of the Web sites of the 50 largest banking institutions and 314 randomly selected financial institutions to ascertain the extent of privacy policy implementation.[47.1] The survey indicated that 64 percent of the Web sites surveyed collected personal information, 48 percent posted some type of privacy disclosure, 40 percent posted a privacy policy, 29 percent posted an information practice statement, and 21 percent posted both types of disclosures. Web sites that collected personal information were almost three times more likely to post a privacy policy than sites that did not. Of the 50 largest institutions' Web sites, 96 percent provided at least one privacy disclosure. All of these collected personal or demographic information and 94 percent were interactive.

In 2000, the banking agencies adopted privacy regulations to implement Title V of the Gramm-Leach-Bliley Act.[47.2]

[F] State Governments

Several states have constitutions expressly providing privacy rights. Courts in some states have recognized a common law right of financial privacy. Many states have enacted privacy statutes providing general privacy rights or more limited privacy protection in certain areas.[48] All fifty states have enacted so-called "mini-FTC statutes" that, like the Federal Trade Commission Act, are designed to prevent unfair or deceptive trade practices.[48.1]

§ 13.04 INDUSTRY SELF-REGULATION

[A] Banking Industry

The banking industry has argued that adoption of federal privacy legislation is unnecessary in view of the existence of numerous federal

---

[47.1] *See* Federal Reserve Board, Federal Deposit Insurance Corporation, Office of the Comptroller of the Currency, Office of Thrift Supervision, *Interagency Financial Institution Web Site Privacy Survey Report* (Nov. 1999).

[47.2] 65 Fed. Reg. 35,162 (2000).

[48] For a list of state privacy laws, *see* "Financial Privacy in America: A Review of Consumer Financial Services Issues" (June 1998), Appendix 1, prepared by the Consumer Bankers Association and the American Bankers Association.

[48.1] *See* 65 Fed, Reg, 45,666, 45,678 (2000).

and state laws in place that address privacy and in light of the extensive privacy protection practices employed by the industry.[49] The banking industry has undertaken major efforts to demonstrate its commitment to

[*Next page is 13-15.*]

[49] *See* "Financial Privacy in America: A Review of Consumer Financial Services Issues" (June 1998), prepared by the Consumer Bankers Association and other bank trade associations. For a contrary view, *see* Mark E. Budnitz, "Privacy Protection for Consumer Transactions in Electronic Commerce, Why Self-regulation is Inadequate," 49 S.C.L. Rev. 847 (1998).

consumer privacy in response to increased governmental interest in privacy issues as a result of the growth of electronic banking and commerce and the European Union Privacy Directive, discussed below.[50]

The Consumer Bankers Association, long interested in issues of consumer privacy, has developed uniform industry guidelines in conjunction with the American Bankers Association and The Bankers Roundtable. The guidelines provide as follows:

- Financial institutions should recognize and respect the privacy expectations of their customers and explain principles of financial privacy to their customers in an appropriate fashion.
- Financial institutions should collect, retain, and use information about individual customers only where the institution reasonably believes it would be useful (and allowed by law) to administer that organization's business and to provide products, services, and other opportunities to its customers.
- Financial institutions should establish procedures so that a customer's financial information is accurate, current and complete in accordance with reasonable commercial standards.
- Financial institutions should limit employee access to personally identifiable information to those with a business reason for knowing such information. Financial institutions should educate their employees so that they will understand the importance of confidentiality and customer privacy.
- Financial institutions should maintain appropriate security standards and procedures regarding unauthorized access to customer information.
- Financial institutions should not reveal specific information about customer accounts or other personally identifiable data to unaffiliated third parties for their independent use, except for the exchange of information with reputable information reporting agencies to maximize the accuracy and

---

[50] *See* § 13.05[B], *infra.*

security of such information or in the performance of bona fide corporate due diligence, unless (1) the information is provided to help complete a customer-initiated transaction; (2) the customer requests it; (3) the disclosure is required or allowed by law (*e.g.*, subpoena, investigation of fraudulent activity, etc.); or (4) the customer has been informed about the possibility of disclosure for marketing or similar purposes through a prior communication and is given the opportunity to decline (*i.e.*, "opt out").

- If personally identifiable customer information is provided to a third party, the financial institutions should insist that the third party adhere to similar privacy principles that provide for keeping such information confidential.
- Financial institutions should devise methods of providing a customer with an understanding of their privacy policies.[51]

[B] Smart Card Forum

The Smart Card Forum has adopted the following consumer privacy guidelines for smart cards issuers to follow:

- Identify, recognize, and respect the privacy expectations of consumers and make applicable privacy guidelines available to them.
- Establish procedures to ensure that consumer data—information directly related to the consumer's use of the card—is as accurate, up-to-date and complete as possible. Promptly honor requests from consumers for information the company has about them as a result of the consumers' use of their cards and provide a procedure for them to correct inaccurate personally identifiable information.

---

[51] *See* Testimony of Marcia Z. Sullivan, before the House subcommittee on Financial Institutions and Consumer Credit (Sept. 18, 1997). *See also* Consumer Bankers Association, "Best Practices: Use of Customer Information," included in Testimony of Marcia Z. Sullivan on behalf of the CBA, before the Consumer Electronic Payments Task Force (July 17, 1997).

- Limit the use, collection, and retention of information about consumers to what is necessary to administer their accounts, provide superior service and offer consumers new opportunities.
- If personally identifiable consumer information is to be provided to unaffiliated third parties for marketing or similar purposes, inform the consumer of that purpose and provide the consumer the opportunity to decline (*i.e.*, "opt out"). If personally identifiable consumer information is provided to a third party, require the third party to adhere to equivalent privacy standards with respect to that information. This would not apply to situations where information is disclosed in order to complete a transaction or pursuant to legal process, including the investigation of fraud or criminal activity.
- Provide a means for consumers to remove their names from the company's telemarketing, online, mailing, and other solicitation lists.
- Maintain appropriate security standards and procedures regarding access to personally identifiable consumer information.
- Implement policies and procedures to limit employee access to personally identifiable consumer information to a need-to-know basis. Educate employees about privacy standards and employees' responsibilities to protect consumer privacy and monitor employee compliance, and take appropriate disciplinary measures with employees who fail to adhere to such standards.[52]

[C] Insurance Industry

The National Association of Insurance Commissioners ("NAIC") in 1979 adopted a Model Insurance Information and Privacy Protection Act governing insurance information practices in the life, health, and property

[52] Smart Card Forum, "Guide to Responsible Consumer Information Practices," included in testimony before the Consumer Electronic Payments Task Force (July 9, 1997).

and casualty insurance sectors and to protect the privacy rights of insured individuals. The Model Act addresses data collection practices, an individual's right to access and correct information, permitted uses of personal information, and enforcement rights. Sixteen states have adopted privacy legislation based on the Model Act.

In June 1998, a group of 12 insurance trade associations submitted a report addressing the insurance industry's information practices and available legal protections.[53]

The NAIC is in the process of drafting a new Health Information Privacy Model Act for adoption by the states.

[D] Securities Industry

The securities industry generally relies on common law agency duties of loyalty and care and business conduct rules of the National Association of Securities Dealers ("NASD") as the source of privacy rights for securities customers, rather than on any model law or statutory provision.[54]

The NASD has proposed a rule governing the use of confidential customer information by broker-dealers.[55] The rule was originally aimed at bank-affiliated broker-dealers but was reproposed by the NASD to apply to all broker-dealers. The proposed rule addresses the release of information to a person other than a business affiliate, the release of information to a business affiliate, and the use of information received from an affiliate. Depending on the type of information, a broker-dealer would be required to obtain consent from the customer or provide the customer a meaningful opportunity to object to disclosure.

§ 13.05 INTERNATIONAL CONCERNS

Governments around the world have undertaken a number of initiatives to address the need for consumer protection in electronic banking and commerce.[56]

---

[53] American Insurance Association et al., *United States Insurance Information Practices and Available Legal Protections* (June 21, 1998).

[54] *See* Securities Industry Association, *Privacy Protection in the United States Securities Industry* (June 23, 1998).

[55] NASDR Rule 3121 (proposed).

[56] *See, e.g.*, OECD, Ministerial Declaration on Consumer Protection in the Context of Electronic Commerce (1998); OECD Guidelines on Consumer Protection in the Context of Electronic Banking, to be completed in 1999.

[A] OECD Privacy Guidelines

The OECD has long been concerned with the protection of personal privacy in electronic commerce and in 1980 issued Guidelines Governing the Protection of Privacy and Transborder Data Flow of Personal Data. These Guidelines have been the basis for recent approaches to privacy in the context of electronic banking and commerce in the United States and other countries. The OECD has indicated that the Guidelines should be reaffirmed in the context of electronic commerce and has determined that it is unnecessary to revise them.[57]

The Guidelines include the following basic principles, among others:

- Personal data should be relevant to the purposes for which they are to be used and, to the extent necessary for those purposes, should be accurate, complete and kept up-to-date.
- The purposes for which personal data is collected should be specified not later than at the time of data collection and the subsequent use limited to the fulfillment of those purposes or such others as are not incompatible with those purposes and as are specified on each occasion of change of purpose.
- Personal data should not be disclosed, made available, or otherwise used for purposes other than those specified.
- Personal data should be protected by reasonable security safeguards against such risks as loss or unauthorized access, destruction, use, modification, or disclosure of data.
- There should be a general policy of openness about developments, practices, and policies with respect to personal data.
- An individual should have the right to:
  —obtain from a data controller confirmation of whether or not the data controller has data relating to him;
  —have communicated to him data relating to him within a reasonable time, at a charge, if any, that is not excessive,

[57] OECD, *Implementing the OECD "Privacy Guidelines" in the Electronic Environment: Focus on the Internet* (May 1998); *Ministerial Declaration on Protection of Privacy on Global Networks* (Oct. 1998); *Protection of Privacy on Global Networks*, OECD Background Report (1998).

in a reasonable manner, and in a form that is readily intelligible to him;
—be given reasons if a request for this information is denied and to be able to challenge such denial; and
—challenge data relating to him and, if the challenge is successful, to have the data erased, rectified, completed, or amended.

With respect to the international transfer of personal information, the OECD Guidelines provide that countries should take steps to ensure that transborder flows of personal data are uninterrupted and secure and that a country should not restrict transborder flows of personal data except where another country does not substantially observe the protections in the Guidelines. The Guidelines also provide that countries should encourage and support self-regulation in the area of privacy protection.

[B] European Privacy Directive

In 1995, the European Union ("EU") adopted a Directive on the Protection of Personal Data ("Privacy Directive").[58] The Directive requires EU countries to adopt laws governing the processing of personal data and prohibits a company operating in the European Union from transferring data outside EU borders unless an "adequate level of protection" is provided. The EU member states were required to have enacted implementing legislation by October 24, 1998.[59]

Many U.S. banks and other financial institutions have European credit card and other banking operations that require a continual flow of personal data outside of the EU to their headquarters in the United States and thus are required to comply with the Directive. The Directive's restriction on the transfer of personal data outside of the European Union is problematic for U.S. institutions because of the vague "adequate level of protection" standard. An "adequate level of protection" is to be determined on a case-by-case basis "in light of all the circumstances surrounding a

---

[58] Council Directive 95/46/EC, 1995 O.J. (L 281). For an excellent overview of the Directive, see Kimberly B. Kiefer, "The E.U. Data Directive: A Potential Disruption to Transborder Data," E-Money, Vol. 1, No. 4 (Aug. 1998).

[59] Most EU countries had not enacted such legislation by the implementing date nor did they have public privacy boards to enforce compliance as required by the Directive.

data transfer operation," including "the rules of law, both general and sectoral, in force in the third country in question and the professional rules and security measures which are complied with in that country."[60]

Under the Directive, a company may transfer personal data to a country that does not have a national privacy law if the customer consents to the transfer, the transfer is necessary for the performance of a contract, or appropriate contractual provisions exist to provide adequate safeguards and the EU member state authorizes the transfer. The cost of obtaining consent from existing customers generally is prohibitive. Accordingly, banks are relying on contractual provisions and industry privacy standards.

Prior to the enactment of federal privacy regulations in 2000 pursuant to the Gramm-Leach-Bliley Act, the absence of a federal privacy statute in the United States made it difficult for U.S. banks to demonstrate that data transferred into the United States would be adequately protected under U.S. law. Although the European Union initially demanded that the United States adopt a comprehensive privacy regime comparable to that of the EU, the EU modified its position after high level talks with the U.S. government. After U.S. officials threatened to take the matter to the World Trade Organization, the EU agreed that effective industry self-regulation through the implementation of industry guidelines and model contract clauses may be sufficient to comply with the Directive. The EU announced its intention to avoid disrupting data flows to the United States as long as the U.S. engaged in good faith negotiations with the EU.

The U.S. Department of Commerce in 1998 commenced a dialogue on privacy with the European Commission "in an effort to find ways to bridge differences in our approaches to privacy" and proposed the concept of a safe harbor for U.S. companies that voluntarily adhere to certain privacy principles.[61] Such companies would be presumed to be in compliance with the European Privacy Directive. The Department requested comment on the safe harbor principles in November of 1998, and again in March of 1999.[62]

The Consumer Bankers Association, American Bankers Association, and Financial Services Roundtable filed a joint comment letter requesting

[60] European Privacy Directive, Art. 25(1) and (2).

[61] *See* Letter dated November 4, 1998, from Under Secretary of Commerce David L. Aaron, to industry representatives.

[62] *See* "International Safe Harbor Privacy Principles," draft dated April 19, 1999, posted at *www.ita.doc.gov/ecom/shprin.html*.

that the banking industry be deemed automatically within the safe harbor, stating:

> The U.S. and European Union, for cultural and other reasons, not only treat and use information differently, but also conduct business differently. Despite the fact that the Safe Harbor Principles are intended to apply only to information originating in European member states, there is reluctance in this country to adopt a safe harbor when the ultimate effect could be to dictate domestic policy and corporate practices for U.S. companies.
>
> The U.S. banking industry is a heavily regulated industry with significant legal and regulatory controls that adequately protect personal data already in place. The European Commission repeatedly fails to acknowledge this fact and we hope to continue working with you to convey this message. No U.S. industry is as highly regulated as the financial services sector with such a high level of statutory privacy protections, regulatory oversight and case law. In addition, our industry-wide self-regulatory efforts provide added protection and demonstrate the due care taken by the banking industry with respect to personal data. We strongly believe that our current framework, though somewhat different, protects consumers as effectively as the European regime.[63]

The final Safe Harbor Privacy Principles were transmitted to the European Commission in 2000.[63.1] The European Commission responded that the Principles are adequate for purposes of the European Privacy Directive.[64] The Safe Harbor principles are based on general principles of notice, choice, onward transfer protection, security, data integrity, access, and enforcement. Banks are not exempt from the Safe Harbor provisions.

Under the Safe Harbor, a U.S. organization may "self-certify" that it qualifies for the Safe Harbor principles by filing with the Department

---

[63] Letter dated May 17, 1999, from the Consumer Bankers Association, American Bankers Association, and Financial Services Roundtable, to David L. Aaron, Under Secretary of Commerce for International Trade, posted at *www.ita.doc.gov/ecom/CBA.htm*. The Securities Industry Association, Investment Company Institute and insurance trade associations filed similar letters.

[63.1] *See* 65 Fed. Reg. 45,666 (2000).

[64] Letter from John Mogg, Director DG Internal Market, European Commission, to the Under Secretary for International Trade, U.S. Department of Commerce.

of Commerce a letter stating that it adheres to the Safe Harbor principles and describing the organization's privacy policy for personal information.

The U.S. Department of Commerce in 1998 issued a paper on "Elements of Effective Self-Regulation for Protection of Privacy" to assist in the development of industry privacy policies to satisfy the European Directive.

The International Chamber of Commerce ("ICC") has issued draft "Model Clauses for Use in Contracts Involving Transborder Data Flow," which are intended to comply with the EU Privacy Directive

§ 13.06 PRIVACY OF MEDICAL INFORMATION

As part of the Health Insurance Portability and Accountability Act of 1996, Congress required the Secretary of Health and Human Services to adopt standards governing the privacy of individually identifiable health information transmitted in connection with the electronic exchange of health care transactions.[65] The law also directs the Secretary to submit recommendations for privacy standards addressing the rights of an individual who is the subject of such information, procedures for the exercise of such rights, and the uses and disclosures of such information that should be authorized or required.

Every state has enacted some form of privacy protection for medical information and at least 21 states have laws that expressly govern the confidentiality of medical information.[66] As noted above, the NAIC is drafting a Health Information Privacy Model Act for adoption by the states.

In approving NationsBank's proposal to establish an operating subsidiary to acquire an interest in Electronic Health Services ("EHS"), the OCC noted with approval NationsBank's commitments with respect to the privacy of customer medical information, including the following:

- Employees of the bank and its operating subsidiary would not have access to patient health, financial, and personal information collected and stored by EHS, except with respect to the provision of services to EHS pursuant to a contract including express confidentiality provisions.

[65] Pub. L. No. 104-191, Title II, § 262(a).

[66] American Insurance Association *et al.*, "United States Insurance Information Practices and Available Legal Protections" (June 21, 1998), at 50.

- Confidential information acquired by EHS would not be transmitted through the bank's data processing systems except when "integral to the provision of banking services" governed by express contractual provisions regarding confidentiality, access, and security.
- EHS would maintain systems to protect the privacy and security of confidential information transmitted via EHS systems and would be designed with a limited access feature. EHS clients would have access only to accounts, data, and information relating to their specific business operations and individual employee access would be provided only upon specific request by EHS clients.
- Security features such as user identification numbers and restricted access levels would be implemented.
- Internet access would be restricted through the use of digital certificates.
- EHS would develop internal guidelines for the treatment of confidential information.[67]

The OCC also noted that, as a transmitter of Medicare payments, EHS would be subject to privacy regulations of the federal Health Care Financing Administration.[68]

Congress has considered, but not adopted, legislation to augment the privacy provisions in the Gramm-Leach-Bliley Act by adding provisions relating to the privacy of medical information.[68.1] The proposed legislation would require a customer's affirmative consent to "opt in" before a financial institution could disclose individually identifiable health information to an affiliate or non-affiliated third party. In addition, a financial institution would not use such information in making credit decisions without express consent of the borrower. Information relating to mental health would be singled out for particular protection with separate and specific customer consent required before such information could be disclosed.

---

[67] OCC Conditional Approval No. 282 (July 31, 1998), n.3.

[68] 42 C.F.R. Parts 401(k) and 405.

[68.1] *See* Hearings before the House Committee on Banking and Financial Services on H.R. 4585, "Medical Financial Privacy Protection Act," 106th Cong., 2d Sess. (2000).

§ 13.07 DISCLOSURE ISSUES

Because electronic banking technology creates new obligations and liabilities, it is important for banks to protect themselves and their customers by giving complete and accurate information regarding the usage of new electronic banking devices. The federal banking regulators have provided guidance in this regard.

With respect to stored value cards, for example, the OCC has encouraged national banks to provide disclosures regarding the following:

- How to use the card;
- Where and how the cardholder can increase the value on the card;
- All fees charged;
- The name of the issuing entity and the extent of its obligation to redeem the card;
- Whether the cardholder is protected in the event the card is lost or stolen;
- Whether the value on the card is FDIC insured;
- Where liability lies for a failed transaction;
- What happens to electronic cash that is abandoned or expires;
- How to resolve disputes;
- The circumstances under which information contained on the card may be disclosed to third parties.[69]

Other disclosure items with respect to stored value cards include whether or not the card is redeemable for cash or nonrefundable, the expiration date of the card, where the card can be used, a customer service toll-free number, the address of the card issuer, and any limits or restrictions on the use of the card.[70] When and how the disclosures should be given may vary depending on the type of card being used.

---

[69] OCC Bulletin No. 96-48, *Stored Value Card Systems* (Sept. 10, 1996).

[70] *See* Statement of American Express, before the Consumer Electronic Payments Task Force (June 9, 1997).

Some consumer groups have called for nationally uniform disclosure requirements to reduce customer confusion regarding stored value cards.[71] The consumer groups complain about widespread confusion regarding the differences between stored value, credit, and debit cards and cite instances of misleading advertisements that imply that stored value cards are better than cash without disclosing that the cards are not legal tender.

Issuers of stored value cards have argued that it would be inappropriate for federal or state governments to impose uniform disclosure requirements due to differences in how the various programs are structured and marketed. They argue that the industry is self-imposing effective disclosures and that the regulators should wait for consumer experience with these new products to develop before acting.[72]

The Federal Reserve Board has allowed financial institutions to deliver electronically a host of consumer disclosures required under the Equal Credit Opportunity Act, Electronic Funds Transfer Act, Truth in Lending Act, Truth in Savings Act, and other consumer protection laws.[73]

See also discussion of electronic disclosures in Chapter 16, **Electronic Signatures.**

---

[71] *See* Statement of the American Association of Retired Persons, before the Consumer Electronic Payments Task Force (June 9, 1997).

[72] *See, e.g.*, Testimony by representatives for Mondex USA, VISA USA, and VISA International, at the June 9, 1997, meeting of the Consumer Electronic Payments Task Force.

[73] 65 Fed. Reg. ___ (2001).

CHAPTER 14

JOINT VENTURES AND STRATEGIC ALLIANCES

§14.01 IN GENERAL

Because of the substantial costs of acquiring data processing technology, banking organizations frequently engage in data processing activities through partnerships, joint ventures, strategic alliances, service agreements, or other arrangements with other banking organizations or third parties as a means of sharing costs and achieving economies of scale. Electronic funds transfer ("EFT") and automated teller machine ("ATM") networks typically are operated as joint ventures among banking organizations for this reason.

Such arrangements raise practical operational issues, such as who will have the primary relationship with the customer, who will be responsible for marketing, pricing, regulatory compliance, indemnification, information security, and how to unwind the arrangement, among others.[1] Joint ventures and strategic alliance agreements also raise a number of regulatory issues, including the legal authority of banks to participate in joint ventures, the ability of banking regulators to supervise the jointly owned entity, and competitive considerations, among others.[1.1]

§14.02 REGULATORY ISSUES

[A] National Banks

The authority of a national bank to enter into a partnership or joint venture is limited under a 1906 ruling of the Supreme Court holding that it is *ultra vires* for a national bank to become a general partner and thereby subject itself to unlimited liability for the acts of others.[2] The Office of the Comptroller of the Currency ("OCC") has read the Court's ruling not to impose an unconditional prohibition on partnership investments in the

---

[1] For a discussion of various business arrangements and practical issues. *See* Robert E. Zahler and Jennifer P. Clasby, "Structuring Relationships Between Banks and Technology Providers Entering the Electronic Banking Market," *Electronic Banking Law and Commerce Report* (Oct. 1996). *See also* John L. Douglas, "Structuring Relationships Between Banks and Technology Companies: Pitfalls from the Perspective of the Banking Lawyer," *Electronic Banking Law and Commerce Report* (Jan. 1998).

[1.1] *See* Dwight C. Smith III, "Federal Regulation of Electronic Commerce: Joint Ventures Involving Banks and Thrifts," Electronic Banking Law and Commerce Report (May 1999), at 15.

[2] *Merchants National Bank v. Wehrmann*, 202 U.S. 295 (1906).

National Bank Act, however, but rather to preclude them from making investments that result in unlimited liability.[3]

Accordingly, the OCC has permitted national banks to enter into partnerships when the activities of the partnership are limited to those permissible for national banks under the National Bank Act and when the potential liability of the bank is limited.[4] The means of limiting the bank's liability may include entering into the partnership through a separately incorporated operating subsidiary or as a limited partner.

The authority of a national bank to enter into a joint venture also is limited under Section 16 of the Glass-Steagall Act which states, "nothing herein contained shall authorize the purchase by [a national bank] for its own account of any shares of stock of any corporation."[5] The OCC has interpreted this section as not barring a national bank from owning the stock of an operating subsidiary[6] or stock in a membership corporation or limited liability company formed to provide services to the bank or its customers.[7] This exception is based on the rationale that a subsidiary of a bank generally functions as a division of the bank and is an organizational convenience. For this reason, it was initially presumed that a bank was limited to owning no less than 100 percent of the stock of a subsidiary.

Because joint ventures with other entities generally require a bank to own less than 100 percent of the stock, the question arose in the 1990s (when joint ventures became increasingly common) as to whether a national bank could acquire a less than a 100 percent stock interest in a joint venture company. In 1996, the OCC adopted a rule authorizing national banks to invest in operating subsidiaries where the bank owns more than 50 percent of the entity's voting stock, or even a smaller interest if the bank controls the entity and no other party controls more than 50 percent of the entity's voting stock.[8]

The OCC has authorized national banks to acquire minority interests (less than 50 percent) in joint venture companies subject to the following four criteria:

---

[3] *See* OCC Interpretive Letter No. 289 (May 15, 1984).

[4] *See, e.g.*, OCC Interpretive Letter No. 381, *reprinted in* Fed. Banking L. Rep. (CCH) ¶ 85,605; OCC Interpretive Letter No. 382, *reprinted in* Fed. Banking L. Rep. 85,606.

[5] 12 U.S.C. § 24(Seventh). The OCC does not treat a partnership interest as an investment in stock for purposes of this section. *See* OCC Interpretive Letter No. 435 (June 30, 1988), *reprinted in* Fed. Banking L. Rep. (CCH) ¶ 85,659.

[6] 12 C.F.R. § 5.34.

[7] *See* OCC Interpretive Letter No. 419 (Feb. 16, 1988); OCC Interpretive Letter No. 677 (June 28, 1995).

[8] 12 C.F.R. § 5.34(d)(2).

(1) The activities of the enterprise must be limited to activities that are part of, or incidental to, the business of banking;
(2) The bank must be able to prevent the enterprise from engaging in activities that do not meet the foregoing standard, or be able to withdraw its investment;
(3) The bank's loss exposure must be limited, as a legal and accounting matter, and the bank must not have open-ended liability for the obligations of the enterprise; and
(4) The investment must be convenient or useful to the bank in carrying out its business and not a mere passive investment unrelated to the bank's banking business.[9]

The OCC has stated that the first and second requirements do not require the investing bank to have veto power over the entity's activities and that the requirements may be satisfied by provisions in the entity's articles of incorporation or bylaws limiting its activities to those permissible for national banks.

The OCC has stated that a bank may satisfy the third requirement by investing in a joint venture through a legally separate operating subsidiary and by accounting for the investment using the cost method of accounting (used for equity interests of less than 20 percent) under which losses recognized by the investor will not exceed the amount of the investment shown on the investor's books.

The last requirement is intended to address the Glass-Steagall Act concern that banks not make speculative investments in stock. A bank thus must demonstrate that a minority investment is convenient or useful to the bank in conducting its banking business and that the investment is not a mere passive or speculative investment made solely for the purpose of earning an investment return. This requirement may be satisfied if the bank has a contractual relationship with the joint venture entity relating to the bank's business, such as to provide services to the bank or its customers.

[B] State Member Banks

State members banks do not have as much flexibility as national banks to acquire joint venture interests inasmuch as the Federal Reserve

[9] *See* OCC Interpretive Letter No. 697 (Nov. 15, 1995), *reprinted in* Fed Banking L. Rep. (CCH) ¶ 81,013; OCC Interpretive Letter No. 732 (May 10, 1996).

Board ("Board") generally still requires state member banks to wholly own their operating subsidiaries.[10]

In certain instances, however, the Board's staff has followed the OCC's suit in allowing state member banks to acquire less than 100 percent interests in limited liability companies ("LLCs") provided the bank's liability exposure is limited to the amount of the bank's investment and the LLC engages only in activities permissible for the bank to engage in.[11]

[C] Bank Holding Companies

Bank holding companies generally are permitted to acquire controlling and noncontrolling interests in joint ventures through partnerships and jointly owned entities.[12] A joint venture in which a bank holding company is a participant may not engage in any activities impermissible for bank holding companies under the BHC Act.

The Board closely scrutinizes such joint ventures to ensure that they will not result in adverse effects, such as a lessening of competition that might result if the co-venturers abstain from entering into each other's markets, preferential extensions of credit by affiliated banks to the nonbank venturer, conflicts of interest or tie-ins, or unsafe and unsound practices.[13] In the past, the Board has expressed concern that joint ventures between bank holding companies and nonbanking firms may "lead to a matrix of relationships between co-venturers that could break down the legally mandated separation of banking and commerce."[14] To prevent such results, the Board imposes limitations on business relationships between a bank holding company and its co-venturers and requires the bank holding

---

[10] 12 C.F.R. § 250.141(c). *See also* 12 C.F.R. § 225.22(e).

[11] *See, e.g.*, Letter dated December 19, 1996, from the Board's associate general counsel, to The Depository Trust Company (joint venture with National Securities Clearing Corporation); Memorandum dated October 10, 1996, from the Board's general counsel, to Reserve Bank general counsels.

[12] A limited partnership interest generally is not deemed to be a voting security for purposes of the Bank Holding Company Act provided that the voting rights attached to the interest are restricted and the interest represents a passive investment and does not provide a means for controlling the partnership. 12 C.F.R. § 225.2(o)(2).

[13] *See, e.g., Maryland Nat'l Corp.*, 65 Fed. Res. Bull. 271 (1979); *First Interstate Bancorp*, 70 Fed. Res. Bull. 449 (1981).

[14] *Amsterdam-Rotterdam Bank, N.V.*, 70 Fed. Res. Bull. 835 (1984); *Deutsche Bank AG*, 67 Fed. Res. Bull. 449 (1981); *Maryland Nat'l Corp.*, 65 Fed. Res. Bull. 271 (1979).

company to commit that it will not solicit business on behalf of any co-venturer or their affiliates.

In general, the Board has not found data processing joint ventures to result in decreased competition or undue concentrations of resources, but rather views such ventures as a means by which banking organizations can achieve economies of scale and efficiencies through the sharing of costs and pooling of resources. The Board tends to view such ventures as offering significant public benefits by facilitating the development and availability of banking services and making these services available in new ways.

The Board has allowed bank holding companies to form joint ventures for electronic banking and Internet services[15] and interbank clearinghouses, such as for multilateral netting of foreign exchange transactions.[16]

[D] Sections 23A and 23B

A joint venture entity in which a bank or bank holding company has a controlling interest generally is treated as an affiliate of a bank for purposes of Sections 23A and 23B of the Federal Reserve Act.[17]

§ 14.03 JOINT VENTURES AMONG BANKING ORGANIZATIONS

The banking agencies have approved numerous joint ventures among banks and their affiliates involving electronic banking activities. ATM networks, discussed in Chapter 7, **Automated Banking Facilities**, are the most common example. Other examples are discussed below.

[A] Multinet International Bank

The Federal Reserve Board approved a joint venture among seven bank holding companies and/or foreign banks that proposed to form a clearinghouse for multilateral netting of foreign exchange transactions.[18] Each joint venture participant would own up to 13.3 percent of the

---

[15] *See, e.g., Royal Bank of Canada, et al./Integrion Financial Network, LLC*, 83 Fed. Res. Bull. 135 (1997); *Cardinal Bancshares, Inc.*, 81 Fed. Res. Bull. 674 (1996).

[16] *Bank of Montreal, et al./Multinet International Bank*, 83 Fed. Res. Bull. 127 (1997).

[17] 12 U.S.C. §§ 371c and 371c-1.

[18] *Bank of Montreal, et al.*, 83 Fed. Res. Bull. 127 (1997).

proposed bank, which was not FDIC-insured and was not treated as a "bank" for purposes of the Bank Holding Company Act.

The purpose of the joint venture was to address the risks inherent in foreign exchange clearing and settlement by providing a clearinghouse with rules governing the netting of spot and forward foreign exchange contacts between worldwide participants in the clearinghouse. The Board stated that the clearinghouse would reduce the volume of settlement payments among participants and have the potential to significantly reduce the credit, liquidity, and other risks and transaction costs associated with clearing and settling of foreign exchange contracts.

[B] InfiNet Payment Services, Inc.

The Board approved a proposal by 13 banking organizations to engage, through a joint venture corporation, InfiNet Payment Services, Inc., in the following activities related to the operation of EFT/ATM networks:[19]

- ATM services permitting customers to make withdrawals, obtain cash advances, make deposit account inquiries, make transfers between accounts, make deposits, and receive account statements; terminal driving services; and ownership of ATM terminals to the extent permitted by applicable state and federal law;
- Point of sale services permitting permit customers to use their ATM cards to purchase goods and services;
- Point of banking services permitting customers to conduct transactions similar to those available at ATM terminals, but with the help of a third party;
- Scrip services, in which a customer receives a voucher (scrip) that is redeemable for cash at a retail register;

[19] *The Bank of New York, et al.,* 80 Fed. Res. Bull. 1107 (1994). The joint venture participants included The Bank of New York, Baybanks, Chase Manhattan, Chemical Banking Corporation, Citicorp, Fleet Financial Group, HSBC Holdings PLC, Marine Midland Banks, Banco de Santander, First Fidelity Bancorporation, Bank of Boston Corporation, Shawmut National Corporation, and National Westminster Bank PLC.

- Gateway services, by which the joint venture company would provide routing of transaction requests between the company's network and other EFT networks;
- Home banking and bill payment services, in which customers could use a telephone, personal computer, or interactive cable television to conduct a variety of banking transactions such as transferring money between accounts, opening and closing accounts, and paying bills, as well as accessing banking, financial and economic databases from the home or office;
- Purchasing and reselling or renting electronic equipment used to perform EFT services subject to the specific limits in Regulation Y;
- Electronic benefit transfer services, in which recipients of government benefits such as food stamps and other recurring types of government transfer payments could access their benefits at ATM and point of sale ("POS") machines through use of a card issued by a government agency;
- Providing services in connection with stored value cards, which are capable of having value assigned to them by use of a magnetic strip or computer chip;
- Electronic data capture and electronic data interchange services, in which merchants are provided with information relating to inventory and the buying patterns of customers;
- Providing data processing and related services in connection with dispensing travelers checks and postage stamps from ATM terminals; and
- Check verification services for retailers.

The Board approved the following incidental activities:

- Group purchasing, in which the joint venture company would purchase EFT-related supplies such as signage, statement stuffers, and terminals, for the benefit of the financial institution participating in the network;
- Incidental terminal driving services, such as hardware maintenance and maintaining the cash stock in ATM terminals;

- Card production and issuance, including ordering and embossing cards, establishing cardholder records, and assigning personal identification numbers;
- Data processing services in connection with dispensing travelers checks and postage stamps from ATM terminals; and
- Check verification services for retailers.

The Board noted that the proposal would increase transaction volume, thereby producing economies of scale and reducing average costs, and would improve service to retail merchants through increased POS services. In addition, the Board noted that the larger number of ATM terminals would increase the convenience of EFT transactions for retail customers and facilitate the introduction of additional EFT related products in the future.[20]

[C] NationsBank/Bank of America

The OCC authorized operating subsidiaries of NationsBank and Bank of America to form a jointly owned limited liability company to engage in the development and distribution of home banking and financial management software and data processing services by acquiring MECA Software, Inc. and its Managing Your Money software program.[21] The joint venture would enter into licensing and distribution arrangements with banking and financial service companies enabling them to offer home banking services to their customers using the Managing Your Money program purchased through retail outlets and other channels. The Federal Reserve Board also approved investments in MECA by banking organizations under the Bank Holding Company Act.

[D] State Street/Bank of Boston

The Federal Reserve Board approved a partnership joint venture between State Street Corporation and Bank of Boston for the performance of data processing relating to shareholder services for securities issuers.[22]

---

[20] *See also Barnett Banks, Inc., et al.*, 83 Fed. Res. Bull. 131 (1997).

[21] OCC Interpretive Letter No. 677 (June 28, 1995), included in Appendix.

[22] *See also State Street Boston Corp.*, 81 Fed. Res. Bull. 1049 (1995) (joint venture with the First National Bank of Boston), included in Appendix. *See also* Chapter 9, **Electronic Commerce and Related Applications**.

The activities included recordkeeping and account maintenance, stock option processing, restricted securities processing, stock watch services, dividend reinvestment and employee stock purchase plan administration, annual meeting services, proxy processing, and the maintenance of shareholder databases.

In addition, the joint venture proposed to provide claims processing and disbursement services in connection with bankruptcy and class action judgments or settlements whereby the partnership would calculate the amount to be remitted to each creditor or class action plaintiff, provide an accounting of such payments to the court or defendant, and remit payments to creditors or plaintiffs entitled to such distributions.

§ 14.04 JOINT VENTURES WITH NONBANK COMPANIES

The following are examples of electronic banking joint ventures between banking and nonbanking organizations that have been approved by the regulators.

[A] Integrion/IBM

The federal banking regulators permitted a consortium of banks, along with a subsidiary of IBM, to form an entity to act as an electronic distribution channel or "gateway" for financial institutions to provide home banking and other electronic financial services to their customers through access devices such as personal computers, telephones, interactive televisions, and other electronic devices. The system also would provide gateway access to the Internet and to third-party service providers.

The joint venture entity, called Integrion Financial Network, LLC, proposed to design, develop, and operate a data processing and transmission system through which depository institutions and their affiliates would make available home banking and other financial services to their respective customers.[23] Integrion itself would not provide home banking or other financial services. Rather, it would provide a data processing and data transmission "gateway" system to serve as a switch or interface to electronically connect member depository institutions with their customers. Customers would connect to the gateway using a variety of devices, including personal computers ("PCs"), touchtone telephones, or other electronic

[23] *See Royal Bank of Canada, et al.*, 83 Fed. Res. Bull. 135 (1997); OCC Conditional Approval No. 221 (Dec. 4, 1996).

communication devices. Once connected to the gateway, Integrion would electronically route and connect the customer to the appropriate member depository institution, using software developed by Integrion that would facilitate communications between the customer's PC or other device and the depository institution's hardware and software. Customers could access remote banking services, bill payment functions, and stock quotations. The gateway also would provide access to the Internet.

[B] Exclaim

The OCC in 1988 authorized a joint venture called "Exclaim" between national banks and health insurance companies.[24] The joint venture proposed to operate an electronic funds transfer system linking health care providers, health care insurers, patients, and their banks to facilitate the settlement and payment of health insurance claims. As described by the OCC, Exclaim would transmit claims eligibility information, receive and transmit information for claims entry and payment, operate a data base, accomplish payment, and develop and license appropriate software programs to enable health care providers to participate.

[C] Citicorp/Dow Jones and AT&T

The Board permitted Citicorp, through its then subsidiary Quotron, to engage in joint ventures with subsidiaries of the Associated Press and Dow Jones & Company, Inc. for the purpose of marketing Quotron's services overseas and with AT&T as a means of developing, marketing, and operating the financial information products of both parties. The Board required the services with the AT&T joint venture to be provided pursuant to a written agreement describing and limiting the data to be furnished or processed to banking, financial, or economic data.[25]

[D] Deutsche Bank/Fiat

The Board approved a data processing joint venture between Deutsche Bank and Fiat in the United States involving data processing and bookkeeping for Fiat dealers to develop and maintain detailed dealer

---

[24] OCC Interpretive Letter No. 419 (Feb. 16, 1988).
[25] 72 Fed. Res. Bull. 497, 500-01 (1986).

and inventory data.[26] The Board denied other parts of the joint venture involving finance, loan servicing, leasing, and insurance activities, stating that a joint venture involving large banking and commercial organizations engaged in a broad range of financial activities was inconsistent with the purposes of the BHC Act. The Board's position in this regard likely would be different in today's financial marketplace.

[E] Sovran/Giant Foods

The Board authorized Sovran Financial Corporation to operate an ATM network with a subsidiary of Giant Foods, Inc.[27] The Board specifically noted that depository institutions would have nondiscriminatory access to membership in the ATM network.

---

[26] *Deutsche Bank AG,* 68 Fed. Res. Bull. 449 (1981).

[27] *Sovran Financial Corp.*, 72 Fed. Res. Bull. 347 (1986).

CHAPTER 15

ANTITRUST

by David A. Balto*

*Mr. Balto is a partner with White and Case in Washington, D.C. He was the Assistant Director for Policy and Evaluation in the Bureau of Competition in the Federal Trade Commission until 2001.

§ 15.01 INTRODUCTION*

This chapter addresses the antitrust concerns that may arise as banks and other financial service firms compete in new markets of electronic banking and commerce. These concerns are most likely to arise when financial service firms pool resources and share risks through joint ventures. Hence, much of this chapter deals with the antitrust implications of joint ventures.

As noted in the preceding chapter, many of the new competitors in emerging electronic banking and commerce markets are joint ventures. Joint ventures have played a critical role in the development of banking and financial service networks, such as credit card systems, automated teller machines ("ATM") networks, and clearing houses. Because joint ventures involve collaboration among competitors, they have been prone to government antitrust investigations and in some cases private antitrust challenges. The major credit card and ATM networks have particularly spawned antitrust litigation, because ATM and other networks pose a paradoxical dilemma: the more participants a network has, the more valuable it is to consumers (because customers of any one participant enjoy many more locations whence to withdraw cash or conduct other transactions than the participants could furnish individually), but the fewer rivals are left to compete on price, service, marketing, and otherwise, to the possible detriment of consumers. To the extent that joint ventures continue to play a major role in the development of banking and commerce, antitrust concerns will continue to be relevant.[1]

The chapter closes with a description of banking mergers and acquisitions and their treatment under the antitrust laws.

§ 15.02 THE ANTITRUST STATUTES

The purpose of the antitrust laws is to guard against practices that may substantially lessen competition or tend to create monopolies. The symptoms of such practices are an increase in price and a correspondent

---

* The author gratefully acknowledges the assistance of Bruce Ellis Fein, clerk to Hon. Morton I. Greenberg of the United States Court of Appeals for the Third Circuit and soon to return as an associate to Sullivan and Cromwell in Washington, D.C., in preparing the 2001 update to this chapter.

[1] For a further discussion of the network joint venture issues discussed in this paper, *see* David A. Balto, "The Problem of Interchange Fees: Costs Without Benefits?" 2000 E.C.L.R. 215 (2000); David A. Balto, "Networks and Exclusivity: Antitrust Analysis to Promote Network Competition," 7 George Mason L. Rev. 523 (1999); Donald I. Baker & Roland E. Brandel, The Law of Electronic Fund Transfer Systems, Chapters 21, 23 (3d ed. 1996).

reduction in output. Several antitrust statutes seek to prevent these effects, enforced mainly by the Department of Justice Antitrust Division ("DOJ") and the Federal Trade Commission ("FTC"), as well as the Federal Reserve Board.

[A] Sherman Antitrust Act

Section 1 of the Sherman Antitrust Act provides that "every contract, combination . . . or conspiracy, in restraint of trade or commerce . . . is declared to be illegal."[2] Read literally, Section 1 would prohibit all agreements among two or more persons or entities that restrict any person's business freedom. However, since virtually every agreement restrains business freedom to some degree, the Supreme Court has construed Section 1 to proscribe only "unreasonable" restraints of trade.[3]

Section 2[4] of the Sherman Antitrust Act prohibits monopolization, attempts to monopolize, and conspiracies to monopolize trade or commerce. Section 2 comprehends solo as well as joint action, whereas Section 1 bans only concerted action by two or more parties.

[B] Clayton Act

Section 7 of the Clayton Act prohibits mergers and acquisitions where "in any line of commerce or in any activity affecting commerce in any section of the country, the effect of such acquisition may be substantially to lessen competition, or to tend to create a monopoly."[5]

The Clayton Act was enacted in 1914 at the height of government concern with the perceived "evils of corporate bigness" and was strengthened in 1950 in response to the "rising tide of economic concentration." The purpose of the Act is to reach anticompetitive trends outside the scope of the Sherman Act by "arresting mergers at a time when the trend to a lessening of competition in a line of commerce still in its incipiency."[6]

---

[2] 15 U.S.C. § 1.

[3] *See, e.g., Standard Oil v. United States,* 246 U.S. 231, 238 (1918).

[4] 15 U.S.C. § 2.

[5] 15 U.S.C. § 18.

[6] *See United States v. E. I. Du Pont de Nemours & Co.,* 353 U.S. 586, 589 (1957); *Brown Shoe Co. v. United States,* 370 U.S. 294, 317-318 (1962) ("Congress saw the process of concentration in American business as a dynamic force; it sought to assure the Federal Trade Commission and the courts the power to brake this force at its outset and before it gathered momentum.").

Because the Clayton Act is intended to "nip monopoly in the bud"[7] by attacking mergers and acquisitions that merely "tend" to create a monopoly, whereas Section 2 of the Sherman Act requires a showing that a monopoly or conspiracy to monopolize actually exists, it is easier for the antitrust enforcement agencies to challenge business combinations under the Clayton Act.

Section 7 has been used to challenge the creation of joint ventures as well as mergers between joint ventures.[8]

[C] Federal Trade Commission Act

The Federal Trade Commission Act,[9] enforced by the FTC, prohibits unfair or deceptive acts or practices in or affecting commerce.[10] Banks and other financial institutions are exempt from the Act.[11] Nevertheless, the consumer affairs divisions of the federal banking regulators often draw on the FTC's policies with respect to unfair and deceptive practices.[12]

Although the Antitrust Division of the DOJ has taken the lead in policing mergers and acquisitions of financial institutions, the FTC also plays an important role, particularly in the area of payment systems such as consumer money transfers and merchant processing. In 1995, for example, the FTC challenged the merger of acquisition of First Financial Management Corp. by First Data Corp., charging that the acquisition would reduce competition in consumer money transfers.[13]

[D] Hart-Scott-Rodino Act

The Hart-Scott-Rodino Antitrust Improvements Act of 1976 ("HSR Act")[14] requires parties to certain mergers or acquisitions to file premerger

---

[7] *Transamerica Corp. v. Board of Governors of the Federal Reserve System*, 206 F.2d 163, 169 (3d Cir. 1953).

[8] *See, e.g., United States v. Penn-Olin Chemical Co.*, 378 U.S. 158 (1964).

[9] 15 U.S.C. §§ 41 *et seq.*

[10] 15 U.S.C. § 45(a)(1).

[11] 15 U.S.C. § 45(a)(2).

[12] *See, e.g.,* Regulation AA, Unfair or Deceptive Acts or Practices, of the Federal Reserve Board, 12 C.F.R. Part 227.

[13] *See In the Matter of First Data Corp.*, FTC File No. 951-0107 (Aug. 28, 1995) (settling charges that the acquisition of First Financial Management Corp. by First Data Corp. would reduce competition in consumer money transfers; requiring divestiture of either Western Union or the MoneyGram network).

[14] 15 U.S.C. § 18a.

notification forms with the FTC and the DOJ and to observe a waiting period before consummating the transaction. In general, an acquisition of voting securities of a company having a market value of $15 million or more, or constituting 15 percent or more of the outstanding voting securities of the company, will trigger the HSR Act notification and waiting period requirements, subject to certain exemptions.

Acquisitions of nonbank companies by bank holding companies are exempt from the notification requirement under the HSR Act, which exempts transactions that require agency approval under Section 4 of the Bank Holding Company Act if copies of all information and documentary material filed with the Board are filed with the DOJ and FTC at least 30 days prior to consummation. This exemption does not apply to acquisitions by nonbank subsidiaries that are owned directly by banks rather than bank holding companies.

[E] Bank Holding Company Act

The Bank Holding Company Act ("BHC Act")[15] allows acquisitions of banks and nonbank entities, that the Sherman or Clayton Acts would otherwise proscribe, where "the anticompetitive effects of the proposed transaction are clearly outweighed in the public interest by the probable effect of the transaction in meeting the convenience and needs of the community to be served."[16]

Acquisitions of nonbank entities by bank holding companies are subject to review under Section 4 of the BHC Act. Section 4(c)(8) permits a bank holding company to acquire, with prior Federal Reserve Board approval, more than five percent of the shares of any company engaged in activities that are "closely related to banking" provided that certain conditions are met.[17] In considering proposed transactions under Section 4(c)(8), the Board is required to apply the so-called "public benefits test" under which it considers whether the transaction:

> Can reasonably be expected to produce benefits to the public, such as greater convenience, increased competition, or gains in efficiency, that outweigh possible adverse effects, such as undue concentration

---

[15] 12 U.S.C. §§ 1841 *et seq.*

[16] 12 U.S.C. §§ 1828(c) and 1842(c).

[17] 12 U.S.C. § 1843(c)(8). Acquisitions of less than five percent do not require prior Board approval and are not subject to the "closely related to banking" requirement.

of resources, decreased or unfair competition, conflicts of interests, or unsound banking practices.[18]

A bank holding company that acquires five percent or more of an interest in a joint venture entity would be required to obtain prior Board approval subject to this public benefits test.

The introduction of a new product or service, lower fees, and improved service (such as one-stop shopping and greater access to financial expertise) are considered public benefits under the test.[19]

The courts have held that Section 4(c)(8) contemplates "a more searching inquiry than the usual antitrust considerations"[20] and the Board has disapproved transactions on the basis of undue concentration of resources without finding a violation of the antitrust laws.[21] At least one court has indicated confusion in distinguishing "undue concentration of resources" from "decreased competition" under the Section 4(c)(8) public benefits test.[22]

Section 4(c)(8) does not require the Board to apply the Sherman or Clayton Act standards to transactions involving nonbank subsidiaries of a bank holding company. Such standards nevertheless may be applied by the FTC or DOJ.

[F] Anti-Tying Restrictions

Section 106 of the Bank Holding Company Act Amendments of 1970 generally prohibits a bank from conditioning the availability of, or varying the consideration charged for, any product or service, on the condition or requirement that the customer obtain an additional product or service from the bank or an affiliate or provide some additional product or service to the bank or affiliate.[23]

---

[18] *Id.*

[19] *Alabama Ass'n of Insurance Agents v. Board of Governors,* 533 F.2d 224 (5th Cir. 1976); *modified* 588 F.2d 729 (5th Cir. 1977), *cert. denied,* 435 U.S. 904 (1978).

[20] *See Citicorp v. Board of Governors,* 589 F.2d 1182, 1190-1191 (3d Cir. 1978), *cert. denied,* 442 U.S. 929 (1979).

[21] *See Citicorp/Advance Mortgage,* 64 Fed. Res. Bull. 321 (1978), *upheld in Citicorp v. Board of Governors,* 589 F.2d 1182 (2d Cir. 1979), *cert. denied,* 442 U.S. 929 (1979).

[22] *Id.* at 228 ("It is not immediately clear to us the extent to which the factor of undue concentration differs from the factor of 'decreased or unfair competition.'").

[23] 12 U.S.C. §§ 1971 *et seq.*

The Section 106 anti-tying provisions were adopted because Congress concluded that the perceived unique economic power of banks to extend credit warranted tighter restrictions on tying than generally applicable antitrust law. The purpose of Section 106 is "to prohibit anti-competitive practices which require bank customers to accept or provide some other service or product or refrain from dealing with other parties in order to obtain the bank product or service they desire."[24]

The restrictions imposed by Section 106 are broader than those under the antitrust laws. The tying practices prohibited by Section 106 are prohibited *per se* (meaning that they cannot be justified by procompetitive or other benefits, and market power vel non is irrelevant). Moreover, unlike the antitrust laws, Section 106 imposes treble damages for violations.

The statutory provisions of Section 106 do not apply directly to bank holding companies. Although the Federal Reserve Board by regulation in 1971 applied Section 106 to bank holding companies and their nonbank subsidiaries as if they were banks, the Board rescinded that regulation in 1997.[25] Section 106 also does not generally apply to credit card companies.[26]

Tying arrangements can also be challenged under the Sherman Act.

[G] State Antitrust Statutes

In addition to the federal antitrust statutes, the states also have antitrust laws that are similar to the federal laws and can also be used to challenge business combinations involving electronic banking and financial services.[27]

[H] Guidelines

The FTC and DOJ have published guidelines outlining how they will analyze joint ventures and mergers in two publications, "Antitrust Guidelines for Collaborations Among Competitors" (the "Joint Venture

---

[24] S. Rep. No. 1084, 91st Cong. 2d Sess. 17 (1970).

[25] 62 Fed. Reg. 9290 (1997).

[26] 12 U.S.C. § 1841(c)(2)(f).

[27] *See generally* 6 Trade Reg. Rep. (CCH) ¶¶ 30,000 *et seq.* (listing of antitrust laws by state).

Guidelines") and "1992 Horizontal Merger Guidelines, With 1997 Amendments" (the "Merger Guidelines").[28] These are exceptionally useful guides to the enforcement agencies' review process. Also useful is the FTC Staff Report "Entering the 21st Century: Competition in the World of B2B Electronic Marketplaces" (the "B2B Report").[29]

§ 15.03 ANTITRUST ANALYSIS OF JOINT VENTURES

[A] In General

Joint ventures generally have received more hospitable treatment in recent years than in the past in recognition that they may increase efficiency, facilitate entry into new markets or create productive capacity that would otherwise be unavailable.[30] Joint ventures nevertheless may raise antitrust concerns.

Joint ventures generally will be reviewed by the antitrust enforcement agencies and courts under the so-called "rule of reason" to determine:

- whether the *formation* of the venture is likely to be anticompetitive or procompetitive [see §15.04, *infra*];
- whether the venture has adopted any unreasonable restraints, including any restraints on access, exclusivity, or pricing [see §§15.05–15.07, *infra*]; and
- whether there are any "spillover effects" such as improper information exchanges [see §15.08, *infra*].

Each of these concerns is addressed below.

The Joint Venture Guidelines have carved a "safety zone" for joint ventures comprising less than 20 percent of a market: "Absent extraordinary circumstances, the Agencies do not challenge a competitor collaboration when the market shares of the collaboration and its participants collectively account for no more than twenty percent of each relevant market in which competition may be affected. The safety zone, however,

---

[28] These publications are available at the FTC Web site, *http://www.ftc.gov/bc/guidelin.htm.*

[29] This can be found at the FTC Web site, *http://www.ftc.gov/bc/b2b/index.htm.*

[30] *Northwest Wholesale Stationers, Inc. v. Pacific Stationery & Printing Co.*, 472 U.S. 284 (1985); *NCAA v. Board of Regents*, 468 U.S. 85 (1984) ("*NCAA*"); *Broadcast Music, Inc. v. CBS*, 441 U.S. 1 (1979) ("*Broadcast Music*").

does not apply to agreements that are *per se* illegal," or that are clearly anticompetitive, "or to competitor collaborations to which a merger analysis is applied."[31]

[B] *Per Se* Illegality and the Rule of Reason

Under the antitrust laws, an agreement or practice will be either classified as per se illegal, or analyzed under the "rule of reason." *Per se* illegal agreements or practices are regarded as so likely to be anticompetitive that they are illegal notwithstanding any business or other justification that might be proffered. This category generally includes "naked" restraints of competition *with no ancillary business integration,* such as price-fixing, bid-rigging, setting output levels, dividing markets by allocating customers, suppliers, territories, or lines of commerce.[32] Other agreements generally fall under the rule of reason, with all relevant surrounding facts examined to determine whether the agreement or practice restrains competition.[33]

In practice, the *per se* category is not rigid. Restrictions on rivalry (such as price or output coordination, geographical division of markets) are far more likely to be regarded as *per se* illegal when not ancillary to other business arrangements. Business integration is a shoehorn into rule-of-reason analysis.

[1] *Per Se* Illegality

Thirty years ago, joint venture agreements were often found to be *per se* illegal under the *per se* rule based on a perception of such ventures as cartel-type arrangements.[34] These cases typically involved arrangements between existing or potential competitors that attempted to regulate competition by assigning territories or customers.

---

[31] Joint Venture Guidelines § 4.2.

[32] *See id* § 3.2.

[33] *See id.* § 3.3. An agreement that is not *per se* illegal, but has obvious anticompetitive effects, may receive only a "quick look" before antitrust condemnation. *See, e.g., California Dental Association v. Federal Trade Commission,* 526 U.S. 756, 769-770 (1999) (holding that advertising restrictions agreed to by competitors warranted an in-depth rule-of-reason analysis, not just a quick look).

[34] *See, e.g., United States v. Topco Assocs.,* 405 U.S. 596 (1972); *United States v. Sealy, Inc.,* 388 U.S. 350 (1967) (territorial and price restraints); *Timken Roller Bearing Co. v. United States,* 341 U.S. 593 (1951) (arrangement to divide markets).

More recently, courts have been reluctant to apply the *per se* rule in reviewing joint ventures. "[C]ourts have been very careful to confine *per se* treatment to conduct of the type that is almost always actually or potentially anticompetitive and has no redeeming benefits (e.g., reduced costs, increased competition) worthy of being weighed against the negative effects. Joint venture enterprises . . . unless they amount to complete shams are rarely susceptible to per se treatment."[35]

Certain factors are considered particularly important in determining whether joint venture agreements among competitors will be subject to the *per se* rule or the rule of reason. First, courts consider the degree of integration between the members of the joint venture.[36] The higher the degree of integration, the less likely the *per se* rule will be applied. Second, if restraints are necessary for the marketing of the product, the rule of reason will usually be applied.[37] If a product could not be marketed absent the restraint, then the agreement effectively does not restrain competition. Finally, a court may refrain from applying the *per se* rule when reviewing practices or industries with which the courts have had little experience.[38]

---

[35] *Addamax Corp. v. Open Software Foundation, Inc.,* 152 F.3d 48, 51-52 (1st Cir. 1998) (citations omitted).

[36] *See, e.g., Arizona v. Maricopa Medical Soc'y,* 457 U.S. 332, 356-57 (1982) (applying the *per se* rule because the level of integration was not substantial); *National Bancard Corp. v. VISA U.S.A., Inc.,* 596 F. Supp. 1231 (S.D. Fla. 1984), *aff'd,* 779 F.2d 592, 599 (11th Cir.) ("BMI's underlying teaching therefore appears to be that courts should look to whether the restraint at issue potentially could create an efficiency enhancing integration to which the restraint is ancillary."), *cert. denied,* 479 U.S. 923 (1986) ("*NaBanco*").

[37] *See, e.g., NCAA,* 486 U.S. at 101 (college football telecasts are "an industry in which horizontal restraints on competition are essential if the product is to be available at all"); *NaBanco,* 779 F.2d at 601 (issuer reimbursement fee necessary to the existence of the network); *but see United States v. Topco Associates, Inc.,* 405 U.S. 596 (1972) (allocations of exclusive territorial licenses among association of small grocers who developed a joint brand in order to economize on advertising and compete with larger brands *per se* illegal).

[38] *See, e.g., Broadcast Music,* 441 U.S. at 10 (declining to apply the *per se* rule since the court had little familiarity with the antitrust implications of the practice of licensing copyrighted materials); *Worthen v. National Bank Americard,* 485 F.2d 119, 126 (8th Cir. 1973) ("*Worthen*")(rejecting application of *per se* rule because of lack of experience with credit cards), *cert. denied,* 415 U.S. 918 (1974). *But see Arizona v. Maricopa County Medical Soc'y,* 457 U.S. 332 (1982) (rejecting argument that court should not apply the *per se* standard simply because the judiciary had little experience in the health care industry).

As long as a joint venture is considered legitimate, the rule of reason is generally applied to all agreements composing the venture, including any ancillary agreements. Even activities typically characterized as horizontal price-fixing and group boycotts, which otherwise would be treated be as *per se* violations, have been found reasonable when the joint venture did not possess market power and the restraints were found reasonably necessary to fulfill the venture's legitimate objectives.[39]

Section 3.2 of the Joint Venture Guidelines further discusses *per se* illegality.

[2] The Rule of Reason

Joint ventures involving banks and financial service firms generally have been analyzed under the rule of reason.[40]

The rule of reason is a flexible inquiry and the particular burdens of proof in a trial may vary depending upon the restraint at issue. Generally, in a rule of reason case, the plaintiff must prove that the challenged restraint has a significant anticompetitive effect in the relevant product and geographic markets. As part of this burden, the plaintiff generally must make some showing that the joint venture possesses market power—*i.e.*, the power to affect price or output.[41] This showing typically involves a complex and fact-intensive inquiry. In some cases, the plaintiff may dispense with the burden of showing market power

---

[39] *See, e.g., NaBanco,* 596 F. Supp. 1231 (S.D. Fla. 1984) (upholding interchange fee established by credit card joint venture), *aff'd,* 779 F.2d 592 (11th Cir.), *cert. denied,* 479 U.S. 923 (1986).

[40] *See NaBanco,* 779 F.2d 592 (interchange fee upheld under rule of reason); *Worthen,* 485 F.2d 119, 126 (rejecting application of *per se* rule to anti-duality rule); *National Bank of Canada v. Interbank Card Ass'n,* 507 F. Supp. 1113 (S.D.N.Y. 1980) (exclusivity provisions evaluated under the rule of reason), *aff'd,* 666 F.2d 6 (2d Cir. 1981); *In re Arbitration between First Texas Sav. Ass'n & Financial Interchange, Inc.,* 55 Antitrust & Trade Reg. Rep. (BNA) 340, 350 (Aug. 25, 1988) ("*Financial Interchange*") (arbitration decision by Professor Thomas Kauper, former Assistant Attorney General for Antitrust, U.S. Department of Justice).

[41] *See, e.g., Rothery Storage & Van Co. v. Atlas Van Lines, Inc.,* 792 F.2d 210, 229 (D.C. Cir. 1986), *cert. denied,* 479 U.S. 1033 (1987); *General Leaseways v. National Truck Leasing Ass'n,* 744 F.2d 588, 596 (7th Cir. 1984); *Financial Interchange,* 55 Antitrust & Trade Reg. Rep. (BNA) at 350.

through evidence that the restraint at issue is likely to have anticompetitive effects.[42]

The burden will then shift to the defendant to justify the restraint, the key question being whether the challenged restraint is reasonably necessary to achieve the joint venture's legitimate business purposes. As part of that analysis, the court may examine whether the legitimate business purposes can be achieved through a less restrictive alternative.[43] If a particular joint venture rule or practice has the potential for both enhancing and restricting competition, the court must then weigh the procompetitive effects against the anticompetitive effects.

The balancing required under a rule of reason approach is often difficult to apply in "network industries" such as ATM networks because the cooperation that is required to achieve a joint venture's efficiencies may also tend to suppress competition:

> Unlike many industries, atomistic competition just does not work well in network industries. Some co-operation among competitors may be essential for efficiency in a network but such co-operation is precisely opposite to the way economists usually think about generating efficient behavior. The logical underpinnings of antitrust laws are based on the economist's belief in the desirability of competition. Applying traditional antitrust concepts to network industries creates the potential for endless litigation and confusion.[44]

[3] Relevant Markets

A starting point in the antitrust analysis of joint ventures or other business combinations or competitive activity is the delineation of the relevant markets where competition will be affected. The rule of reason

---

[42] *FTC v. Indiana Fed'n of Dentists,* 476 U.S. 447, 458-59 (1986); *Law v. NCAA,* 134 F.3d 1010, 1019 (10th Cir.), *cert. denied,* 119 S. Ct. 65 (1998) (truncated rule of reason applied to horizontal price fixing restraint involving limit on compensation of men's basketball coaches).

[43] *See, e.g., United States v. Realty Multi-List, Inc.,* 629 F.2d 1351, 1374-75 (5th Cir. 1980); *NaBanco,* 596 F. Supp. at 1265.

[44] Dennis W. Carlton, The Economics of Co-operation and Competition in Electronic Service Network Industries, in Electronic Services Networks: A Business and Public Policy Challenge 77, Margaret Guerin-Calvert and Steven S. Wildman (eds.) (1991).

looks at both the relevant product market and the relevant geographic market.

A joint venture or merger is more likely to pass antitrust muster if the product and geographic markets are large and have many competitors than if the markets are narrowly circumscribed and have few competitors. In its market analysis for purposes of competitive analysis, the Federal Reserve Board has stated that the relevant markets "must reflect commercial and banking realities and must consist of the local area where customers practicably can turn for alternatives."[45]

In the age of electronic banking and commerce where "cyber-competition" defies traditional geographic bounds and new "cyber-products" appear weekly, traditional market definitions may no longer reflect market realities. As antitrust concerns are raised, market analysis in the electronic marketplace will pose new challenges for antitrust enforcers and the courts.

[i] Product Market

The product market is determined by reference to the "line of commerce" in which the competitors that are parties to a transaction compete.

In the case of banks, the Supreme Court has held that the relevant product market is the "cluster of products and services" offered by banking institutions, including checking accounts, loans, and other services traditionally offered by banks.[46] Although the federal banking agencies generally adhere to the "cluster" approach when reviewing bank mergers and acquisitions, the DOJ disaggregates the product market.[47] In some cases, the banking agencies will include in the banking product market financial firms such as full-service brokers and finance companies in recognition that these institutions compete with banks.

The product market for financial services other than banking is more closely defined by specific product characteristics and usage in the marketplace. The antitrust enforcement agencies and the courts traditionally have defined the boundaries of the relevant market for related products by determining the cross-elasticities of demand and supply. That is, the

---

[45] *See, e.g., Norwest Corporation,* 82 Fed. Res. Bull. 580, 581 (1996).

[46] *United States v. Philadelphia Nat'l Bank,* 374 U.S. 321 (1963); *United States v. Connecticut Nat'l Bank,* 418 U.S. 656 (1974).

[47] *See, e.g., United States v. Fleet/Norstar Financial Group, Inc.,* Notice of Proposed Final Judgment, 56 Fed. Reg. 33,458 (1991).

agencies look at the degree to which a change in price will cause a change in the quantity of related products demanded and supplied.

Specifically, the inquiry asks whether a hypothetical monopolist could profitably institute a "small but significant and nontransitory" increase in price.[48] If a change in price causes insufficient reaction in other goods thought to be substitutes to defeat the price increase, then those goods are deemed not part of the product market. Relevant facts include evidence that buyers have shifted purchases in response to price changes, evidence that sellers base business decisions on the prospect of buyer substitution in response to relative price changes, and the timing and costs of switching products.

The approach to product market definition has become more sensitive to the competitive problems raised by network competition. In the early 1980s, the courts and enforcement agencies defined the retail market broadly as a market of all payment systems, such as credit cards, checks, and ATMs. That was the approach taken in the *NaBanco* case involving a disputed credit card interchange fee.[49]

With respect to the wholesale market (i.e., the market in which banks are consumers), the early cases emphasized the data processing functions of bank ATM networks. For example, in *The Treasurer,*[50] the court defined the relevant product market as "electronic data processing to all ATMs *plus* all of those institutions which have unaffiliated ATM systems and those institutions which do not currently have ATMs but have the capacity to install them and utilize market technology to its fullest.'[51] In other words, the market included all firms capable of performing the electronic communication function performed by an ATM network.

In more recent decisions and enforcement actions, fact finders have defined more narrow markets, focusing primarily on demand side factors. For example, in the *Financial Interchange* arbitration involving ATM network interchange fees, the arbitrator rejected proposed retail markets of "all payment systems" and "all means of obtaining cash" similar to the markets defined in *NaBanco* and *The Treasurer*. Instead, it identified a narrow market of "ATM services" on the ground that "there is a significant group of ATM users who value the characteristics of

[48] Merger Guidelines § 1.11.

[49] *NaBanco, supra.*

[50] *The Treasurer, Inc. v. Philadelphia Nat'l Bank,* 682 F. Supp. 269 (D.N.J.), *aff'd mem.,* 853 F.2d 921 (3d Cir. 1988).

[51] 682 F. Supp. at 279 (emphasis in original).

ATMs and for whom other means of obtaining cash are not reasonable substitutes."[52]

In addition, the arbitrator identified a wholesale market for "network switching," and concluded that the PULSE network had market power because "existing subnetworks, regional networks and national networks do not presently provide a reasonable substitute for the [switching] service PULSE provides to its members."[53] In the *Electronic Payments Services* monopolization case, the DOJ took a similar approach, albeit focusing on the wholesale side of the market.[54] It defined a market for "regional ATM service" based on the needs of banks to provide depositors "ubiquitous access to their accounts" and a second market for ATM processing.

The Federal Reserve Board, in approving the acquisition by Electronic Payments Services (a joint venture owned by bank holding companies) of certain data processing assets, defined the relevant product market as threefold:

- network access (access to an ATM network identified by a common trademark or logo displayed on ATMs and ATM cards);
- network services (the switching functions of the network); and
- ATM processing (the data processing and telecommunications facilities used to operate, monitor, and support a bank's ATMs).[55]

The critical element in the analysis of the relevant network market, at least in the wholesale market, is the weight accorded to the value of the network trademark. If one looks only to the *data processing* function of shared ATM networks, it may be plausible to conclude, as did the court in the *Treasurer* case, that the market is one of data processing and that market

---

[52] *In re Arbitration Between First Texas Savings Ass'n and Financial Interchange, Inc.*, 55 Antitrust & Trade Reg. Rep. (BNA) 340 (Aug. 25, 1988) ("*Financial Interchange*") (arbitration decision by Professor Thomas Kauper, former Assistant Attorney General for Antitrust).

[53] *Id.* at 355.

[54] *United States v. Electronic Payments Services, Inc.*, No. 94-208 (D. Del. Apr. 21, 1994), 59 Fed. Reg. 24,711 (May 12, 1994).

[55] *See Banc One Corporation et al.*, 81 Fed. Res. Bull. 492, 494 (1995).

is unconcentrated, that there are numerous alternatives available to financial institutions to perform their data processing, and that a network—even a dominant regional network—does not have market power. On the other hand, if the network is viewed not so much as a vendor of undifferentiated data processing services, but rather as the purveyor of a *unique branded product* marketed under the network logo, the fact finder may reach a very different conclusion.

[ii] Geographic Market

The geographic market is defined with reference to a specific product or service market. Markets have been defined as national, regional, or local depending on the product involved.

The Supreme Court has ruled that the geographic market for banking is local.[56] The local banking market generally is defined as the area in which the cluster of products and services provided by banking competitors involved in a transaction and the area in which purchasers of banking products and services seek to obtain them.[57] The Federal Reserve Board and the DOJ do not always agree on the bounds of the relevant geographic market for banking.[58] In recent bank acquisition cases, the Board has tended to draw the "local" geographic market more broadly whereas the DOJ, because it focuses on the small business loan market which is local, tends to view the geographic market more narrowly.

Joint ventures among banks frequently do not involve "banking" and thus other product markets may be relevant for purposes of defining the geographic market. A back office network switching market, for example, may be regional or national. A nonbanking retail market defined from the perspective of consumers is probably local.

---

[56] *United States v. Philadelphia Nat'l Bank,* 374 U.S. 321 (1963).

[57] *See Chemical Banking Corp.,* 82 Fed. Res. Bull. 239 (1996).

[58] The federal banking agencies generally measure geographic market presence by deposits. The DOJ is more likely to measure the level of commercial loan activity in the market, although it does not treat loans as a substitute for deposit data. DOJ officials have noted that "deposit data historically have been more reliable and loan data have not necessarily reflected lending capability or the full competitive significance of a commercial bank in the market." *See* "Bank Mergers—Antitrust Trends," Address before the Association of the Bar of the City of New York by Constance K. Robinson, Director of Operations, Antitrust Division, U.S. Dep't of Justice, Sept. 30, 1996 WL 623106 (D.O.J.).

The antitrust enforcement agencies generally believe that the geographic market should be defined narrowly. The appropriate geographic market for most ATM funds generally is no larger than a region of the United States.

To date, there is little precedent on how the agencies and the courts will define the geographic market in a case involving Internet banking and commerce. However, in light of the Internet's nationwide (indeed global) accessability, the geographic market for Internet banking may well encompass the whole country.

§15.04 FORMATION OF A JOINT VENTURE

In reviewing joint venture formations, the courts and enforcement agencies generally apply the rule of reason and carefully examine both the procompetitive efficiencies and anticompetitive effects that may flow from the joint activity.

A joint venture generally does not raise the same level of competitive concern as a merger since it may have a less restrictive effect on the independent decision-making of joint participants with respect to price and output than would an outright merger. Hence, a joint venture may be "unlikely to facilitate the exercise of market power in circumstances [where a] complete merger would be likely to do so."[59] In addition, the parties may be able to structure their joint venture to include operational safeguards that eliminate or reduce any threat to competition.

Joint ventures in electronic banking and commerce generally have raised few antitrust concerns to date. Even though many of these ventures are owned by relatively large firms, the presence of many firms available to create alternative ventures has mitigated antitrust concerns. Only when the firms forming the venture are so large, or control some vital elements of competition, have antitrust concerns been raised.

[A] Is the Joint Venture Legitimate or a Sham?

The threshold inquiry in reviewing the formation of a joint venture under the rule of reason is whether the venture represents an efficiency-enhancing integration of economic functions or a thinly veiled effort to restrict output without any redeeming efficiency consequences. As the Supreme Court has explained, the inquiry begins by asking whether the arrangement "facially

[59] U.S. Dep't of Justice, Antitrust Enforcement Guidelines for Int'l Operations § 3.3 ("International Guidelines"), 4 Trade Reg. Rep. (CCH) ¶ 13,109 (1988).

appears to be one that would always or almost always tend to restrict competition and decrease output" or is designed to "increase economic efficiency and render markets more, rather than less, competitive."[60]

Simply labeling an agreement as a "joint venture" will not immunize it from antitrust scrutiny.[61] Where a so-called "joint venture" does not involve any integration of resources or efficiencies and is really no more than an attempt by horizontal competitors to restrict competition, the courts and enforcement agencies have condemned the joint activity as a "naked restraint of trade" and invalidated it as unlawful *per se*.

Three principal factors have been recognized by the courts as indicative of integrative efficiencies: (1) the joint venture leads to the creation of a new product or is a prerequisite to marketing that product; (2) the joint venture is necessary to engage in risk sharing; or (3) the joint venture involves a pooling of resources to achieve economies of scale and scope.[62] Each of these factors focuses on the existence of efficiencies

[1] New or Better Product

The courts and agencies consider whether the venture may enable the participants to purvey a product or service that they could or would not provide individually,[63] or to supply the product or service more quickly, cheaply, or conveniently; whether it may enable small firms to compete with larger firms by pooling resources;[64] whether it will combine the participants' complementary capabilities in synergy; whether it will facilitate economies of scope or scale; in sum, whether it will facilitate greater economic efficiency.[65]

---

[60] *Broadcast Music,* 441 U.S. at 19-20.

[61] Joint Venture Guidelines, § 3.2; *Timken Roller Bearing Co. v. United States,* 341 U.S. 593, 598 (1951) (arrangement to divide markets held illegal *per se*). See *Brunswick Corp.,* 94 F.T.C. 1174, 1266 (1979) ("A price-fixing scheme or other cartel-like behavior cannot be insulated from review simply by fixing the 'joint venture' label to a device used to engage in behavior inherently pernicious to competition."), *modified,* 96 F.T.C. 151 (1980), *aff'd sub nom. Yamaha Motor Co. v. FTC,* 657 F.2d 971 (8th Cir. 1981), *cert. denied,* 456 U.S. 915 (1982).

[62] ABA Section of Antitrust Law, 1 Antitrust Law Developments (Fourth) 395-96 (1997).

[63] *See Broadcast Music,* 441 U.S. at 20-23 (economies of scale from blanket licenses).

[64] *See, e.g., Northrop Corp. v. McDonnell Douglas Corp.,* 705 F.2d 1030, 1052-53 (9th Cir.) (new Navy aircraft), *cert. denied,* 464 U.S. 849 (1983); *Worthen,* 485 F.2d 119 (national credit card system).

[65] *See* Joint Venture Guidelines §§ 2.1, 3.36.

[2] Risk Sharing

Businesses often form joint ventures to share operational and other risks. Examples of joint ventures that have been formed by financial institutions to spread risks include reinsurance syndicates, loan participations, and underwriting syndicates. Risk-spreading ventures have seldom been struck down on antitrust grounds.[66]

[3] Pooling of Resources

A joint venture may permit a group of firms to achieve economies of scale and scope that no single firm could achieve on its own. This factor is particularly important in networks in high technology markets where research and development costs are substantial. Joint ventures also may enable firms to make more effective use of complementary resources among firms that have expertise in different areas. These factors help to insulate a joint venture from antitrust challenge.

Credit card joint ventures and ATM networks are obvious examples of products that can be provided more efficiently by pooling of resources and risk sharing through joint ventures and thus these arrangements have been considered legitimate and not *per se* illegal.

[B] Is the Joint Venture Too Large?

Another inquiry is whether a joint venture is too large and whether the size of the joint venture would unreasonably deter the development or competing ventures. Even in new product joint ventures, such as bank card networks, there may be a concern that the venture is too large—*i.e.,* that it includes so many competitors that the potential development of competing ventures is unduly inhibited.

In general, the antitrust enforcement agencies are concerned about the anticompetitive effects of a joint venture when it is overinclusive—that is, when it restricts competition among competitors that account for a large portion of sales (or capacity) in the market, thereby creating, enhancing, or facilitating the exercise of market power. The basic analysis applied is similar to that applied to horizontal mergers, the concern being

---

[66] *See United States v. Morgan,* 118 F. Supp. 621, 689 (S.D.N.Y. 1953) (court rejected challenge to creation of underwriting consortium formed by 17 banks).

that the venture may decrease actual or potential competition among its members.[67]

The fundamental question in analyzing questions of size is whether the venture is so large, or controls such critical inputs, that sufficient alternative networks cannot be formed. While there is no "bright line" test, competitive concerns typically are not raised when a joint venture possesses less than 20 percent of the market.

In the context of a network joint venture, the "size" issue is frequently outweighed by resulting efficiencies. Mergers among ATM networks generally were unchallenged in the 1980s for this reason. The Justice Department believed that "economies of ubiquity" and resulting consumer benefits achievable by widespread sharing of ATMs benefited consumers by increasing the available ATMs in a single network, among other things. Similarly, increasing the number of cardholders increased the deployment of ATMs.[68] As a result, the consolidation of ATM networks has left only a handful of ATM networks dominating large regions of the country. As described below, however, the Department's nonintervention policy was largely reversed in the 1990s.

[C] Antitrust Challenges to Joint Ventures

The two cases discussed below demonstrate how antitrust considerations have been applied to financial service joint ventures.

[1] Entrée Case

Visa and MasterCard in the 1980s created a joint venture to issue online debit cards, known as Entrée. Although the Justice Department chose not to challenge the formation of the venture, a group of 13 state attorneys general challenged the Entrée debit card under state antitrust laws.[69]

---

[67] *See* Joint Venture Guidelines, § 3.33; B2B Report, Executive Summary, pp. 4-5; *see generally* Merger Guidelines.

[68] *See* "Antitrust Analysis of Joint Ventures in the Banking Industry: Evaluating Shared ATMs," A-142-43, Remarks by Charles F. Rule, Acting Assistant Attorney General, Antitrust Division, Department of Justice, before the Federal Bar Ass'n and American Bar Ass'n (May 23, 1985) ("Rule"), *reprinted in* Baker & Brandel, Appendix F, *supra.*

[69] *See State of New York v. Visa U.S.A., Inc.*, 1990-1 Trade Cas. (CCH) ¶ 69,016 (S.D.N.Y. 1990).

The states alleged that the two credit card associations had violated state antitrust laws through their joint development of the Entrée debit program and their respective acquisitions of interests in CIRRUS and PLUS (the national debit card networks) and Interlink, a California debit card network. The states claimed that by forming Entrée and acquiring the ATM networks, Visa and MasterCard intended to retard the development of online debit, a payment system that they feared would compete with and erode the profitability of credit cards. Entrée, the states alleged, was a combination of the five most likely entrants into the debit card market. The states further alleged that as part of the joint venture, MasterCard and Visa had agreed not to introduce their own separate systems to compete with Entrée. The states challenged the fact that participation in the venture was limited to banks that were members of both associations, thereby excluding nonbanks such as Discover Card and American Express from participating.

The states effectively claimed that Entrée was a sham endeavor whose purpose was not to enter the market but rather to acquire the most likely entrants and thereby deter or retard the creation of the online debit market. In fact, although Entrée had been operating for several years at the time of the challenge, it had issued very few cards and signed up only a handful of merchants.

The complaint sought divestiture of CIRRUS by MasterCard and of PLUS and Interlink by Visa, as well as an injunction against the implementation of Entrée. In 1990, Visa and MasterCard agreed to abandon the Entrée joint venture and have since created their own independent online debit card networks—Interlink (owned by Visa) and Maestro (owned by MasterCard). The online debit market has grown significantly since then, primarily through the development of online systems by regional ATM networks.[70]

[2] Visa-MasterCard Duality Case

The most recent example of antitrust concerns raised by overinclusive joint ventures is the Justice Department's October 1998 suit against Visa and MasterCard alleging that the dual control of Visa and MasterCard by the same banks ("duality") stifles network competition.[71]

---

[70] *See* David A. Balto, "Can the Promise of Debit Cards be Fulfilled?" 53 Bus. Law. 1093 (May 1998).

[71] *United States v. Visa U.S.A., Inc. et al.*, 98 Civ. No 7076 (BSJ) (S.D.N.Y.) (documents available on the DOJ's Web site at *http://www.usdoj.gov/atr/cases/indx57.htm*).

Under both Visa and MasterCard rules, a member bank in each association has the right to issue cards in either card association. More importantly for the Justice Department's case, the association's rules enable individual card issuers to effectively govern both associations simultaneously. Although individual banks cannot sit on the boards of directors of both networks, the DOJ's complaint alleges that almost all of the large card issuing banks have representatives on one of the association board of directors as well as representatives on the important committees that influence policy for each network.

The Justice Department alleges that, under duality, Visa and MasterCard are at most amicable competitors. The theory underlying the case suggests that it is not in the interests of the member banks of either organization to permit active network rivalry. Dual members have little interest in actively differentiating the products of the two networks or spending money to do so because, the DOJ argues, they will not benefit by convincing customers to switch networks. In addition, duality creates a problem of access to competitively sensitive information among competitors. The Department's complaint alleges that neither association enforces the safeguards necessary to prevent each association from learning competitive information about the other.

The Department's complaint presented five examples of how duality allegedly restrains competition between Visa and MasterCard:

(1) Duality lessens each association's incentives to compete against each other. Since a number of the governing banks issued a large volume of cards in each of the networks, those banks have rejected investments in and implementation of competitive initiatives that might lead consumers to switch from one network to another.

(2) Both Visa and MasterCard top executives have admitted that duality restrained competition.

(3) There were several occasions where the respective staffs of Visa and MasterCard recommended rolling back duality and these recommendations were rejected.

(4) Duality dampened product promotion, since there is no comparative advertising between Visa and MasterCard in the United States.

(5) Duality dampened innovation such as the promotion and development of smart cards, commercial cards and secure transactions over the Internet.

The DOJ seeks, among other things, to enjoin Visa and MasterCard from permitting any issuer to serve on their boards or governing committees unless (a) that issuer has agreed to issue new cards exclusively on either Visa's or MasterCard's network, and (b) by 2003, 80 percent or more of the issuer's total issuing volume was on the chosen network. It also seeks to force Visa and MasterCard to stop prohibiting their issuers from issuing debit cards on other networks, and to treat American Express and Discover the same way they treat each other. The case remains pending as of this writing.

§ 15.05 RESTRAINTS ON ACCESS

[A] In General

One of the most controversial antitrust issues that new electronic banking and commerce joint ventures will face is the question of "access"—that is, which companies can belong to the joint venture or have access to its services. If a joint venture does not limit access, it may become too large and acquire market power—thus becoming a victim of its own success. On the other hand, if it denies access, an excluded party may sue the network and its joint venture members, contending that its exclusion constitutes an unlawful group boycott and/or that the facility operated by the venture is an "essential facility" to which it is entitled to access on reasonable and nondiscriminatory terms.[72]

Access issues in the emerging world of electronic commerce were addressed by FTC Chairman Robert Pitofsky:

> Although some may seek to restrict access to the new world of electronic commerce, those restrictions should be imposed only where necessary to protect a well defined interest. For example, regulators or private networks can impose restrictions to assure that participants are financially sound or capable of providing the necessary services. Those restrictions should not be overbroad. In some cases, groups of competitors have imposed restrictions on rivals to deter or delay

[72] This issue is extensively discussed in Donald I. Baker, "Compulsory Access to Network Joint Ventures Under the Sherman Act: Rules or Roulette?," 1993 Utah L. Rev. 999 (*"Compulsory Access"*) and David A. Balto, "Access Demands and Payment Systems Joint Ventures," 18 Harv. J.L. & Pub. Pol'y 624 (Spring 1995). *See also* Joint Venture Guidelines, §§ 3.33, 3.34(a), 3.35; B2B Report, Executive Summary pp. 3-4, and Part 3 pp. 10, 16-22.

competition. The antitrust laws disfavor the creation of artificial barriers to entry. Thus, the presumption should be that access is available to all who seek to compete for consumers business, and therefore that a general prohibition based on the class of competitor should be carefully scrutinized.[73]

[B] Essential Facility and Group Boycott Cases

The standards governing compulsory access to an essential facility have evolved through two related lines of cases: essential facility cases and traditional group boycott cases. The cases have so evolved that the standards applied under each have converged.

Generally, the "essential facility" or "bottleneck monopoly" issue arises when a joint venture is so dominant or successful that access to it offers a major competitive advantage and no reasonable substitute exists. Under this doctrine, courts have required the joint venture to provide access to an excluded competitor when the facility is of significant competitive importance.

The general rule is that those who control access to an essential joint venture facility must grant access on reasonable and nondiscriminatory terms. The rule has been applied to transportation facilities, local produce markets, and a worldwide news information system.[74]

The earliest essential facility cases in the bank joint venture area involved the exclusion of thrifts from bank-dominated automated clearinghouse associations ("ACHs"). In 1977, the Justice Department filed complaints against two bank-controlled ACHs, seeking to compel the banks to grant full access to thrift institutions.[75] While thrifts had already been given "pass-through" access to the ACHs, the Department argued that the lack of full access placed the thrifts at a competitive disadvantage. Further, they argued that the Federal Reserve subsidy of ACH operations rendered other

---

[73] "Competition and Consumer Protection Concerns in the Brave New World of Electronic Money," Remarks by Robert Pitofsky, Chairman, FTC, before the United States Department of the Treasury Conference, Toward Electronic Money & Banking: The Role of Government, Washington, D.C., Sept. 19, 1996 at 12.

[74] *See United States v. Terminal R.R. Ass'n,* 224 U.S. 383 (1912); *Gamco, Inc. v. Providence Fruit & Produce Bldg., Inc.,* 194 F.2d 484 (lst Cir.) (local produce markets), *cert. denied,* 344 U.S. 817 (1952); *Associated Press v. United States,* 326 U.S. 1 (1945).

[75] *See United States v. Rocky Mountain Automated Clearing House Ass'n,* No. 77-391 (D. Colo.) *dismissed* (Nov. 17, 1977); *United States v. California Automated Clearing House Ass'n,* No. 77-1643-LTZ (C.D. Cal.) *dismissed* (Oct. 28, 1977).

competitive alternatives economically infeasible, thereby justifying compulsory access. The two cases were dismissed after the defendant ACHs agreed to cease excluding thrift institutions. Other ACHs that had not already admitted thrift institutions shortly began to do so.

Group boycotts, also known as "concerted refusals to deal," refer to agreements among two or more firms at the same level of market structure to refuse to deal with particular suppliers or customers, often for the purpose of disciplining or disadvantaging a competitor. As with the law involving the formation of joint ventures and their collateral restraints, evaluation of group boycotts has evolved from *per se* condemnation to a rule of reason analysis that recognizes the procompetitive benefits that can be derived from joint action.

This change came about in the Supreme Court's decision in *Northwest Wholesale Stationers, Inc. v. Pacific Stationery & Printing Co.,*[76] which involved a wholesale purchasing cooperative whose membership consisted of office supply retailers in the Pacific Northwest states. When the cooperative expelled one of its members without any explanation, notice or hearing, the member sued, alleging that the expulsion without procedural protections was a group boycott that inhibited its ability to compete and was therefore *per se* illegal. The Supreme Court held that the expulsion was not within the categories of activities conclusively presumed to be anticompetitive so as to mandate *per se* invalidation of the co-op's action. It remanded the case for a rule of reason determination, explaining that the *per se* rule should only be applicable where:

> the cooperative possesses market power or exclusive access to an element essential to effective competition . . . Absent such a showing with respect to a cooperative buying arrangement, courts should apply a rule-of-reason analysis.[77]

The Court also noted that a rule of reason analysis might appropriately inquire into the cooperative's motive for expelling a member: "If the cooperative's action were not substantially related to the efficiency-enhancing or procompetitive purposes that otherwise justify the cooperative's practices, an inference of anticompetitive animus might be appropriate."[78] Since *Northwest Wholesale Stationers,* many lower courts have

---

[76] 472 U.S. 284 (1985).

[77] *Id.* at 296-97 (footnotes omitted) (emphasis added).

[78] *Id.* at 296 n.7.

applied a rule of reason analysis to group boycott claims. Typically, when the venture does not clearly possess market power, the exclusionary rules have been upheld.[79]

[C] Banking Joint Ventures

It is possible that no single industry has been subject to as many antitrust access claims and private litigation as the credit card and ATM network industries. The spate of litigation is due to a variety of factors, including uncertainty in the law and the economic characteristics of networks. The significant efficiencies that arise from greater size in these networks may suggest that the most efficient network is a single network. If that is true, requiring open access and forbidding exclusionary membership rules would seem a likely antitrust goal. However, whether ATM and credit card networks are natural monopolies to which open access should be compelled has been hotly debated. If there is the potential for multiple competing networks, requiring access may dampen the incentives of firms to create alternative networks.

The following are examples of cases raising the issue of access.

[1] The *Worthen* Case

When national credit card joint ventures were first formed in the 1960s, their memberships were distinct and network competition was vigorous. Card issuing banks belonged to either the National BankAmericard network (the predecessor to Visa) or the MasterCharge network (the predecessor to MasterCard). The credit card ventures had "anti-duality" rules that prohibited banks from issuing both National BankAmericard and MasterCharge cards.

In the early 1970s, Visa's anti-duality rules faced a private antitrust challenge from Worthen Bank, which sought to issue both Visa and Mastercards. Visa justified its anti-duality restriction as necessary to maintain network competition between the two bank card ventures. In particular, it argued that the two networks competed in the development of technology, especially with regard to interchange and authorization networks, that this competition affected both interest rates and discount rates of member

[79] *See, e.g., National Ass'n of Review Appraisers & Mortgage Underwriters v. Appraisal Found.*, 64 F.2d 1130 (8th Cir. 1995) (exclusion resulting from legitimate criteria not unlawful under rule of reason analysis).

banks by affecting their costs, and that if duality were permitted, network competition would be eliminated.

The litigation was settled in 1974. In order to protect itself from further private litigation (and the risks of treble damages), Visa sought approval from the DOJ for a revised anti-duality rule. The DOJ declined to grant approval. It suggested that a prohibition on duality among card-issuing banks might be permissible but declined to approve a restriction on merchant bank duality, primarily because insufficient information was available to determine the competitive effects of the rule.[80] National BankAmericard, faced with an ambivalent DOJ and the continuing threat of private litigation, reversed course and completely abandoned its anti-duality rule in mid-1976. With the rule removed, banks rushed to join both associations and by the end of the 1970s duality was pervasive.

[2] The *National Bank of Canada* Case

Six years after *Worthen*, MasterCard's anti-duality rule for its Canadian licensees was challenged in *National Bank of Canada v. Interbank Card Ass'n.*[81] MasterCard was a late entrant into the Canadian market and, like Visa, had an anti-duality rule. When Provincial Bank (a MasterCard issuer) merged with National Bank of Canada (a Visa issuer), MasterCard exercised the anti-duality rule and gave the bank a choice: either to withdraw from Visa or cease being a member of MasterCard. MasterCard terminated the bank and National Bank of Canada brought an antitrust suit in a U.S. court.

As in *Worthen*, the court rejected the claim that the anti-duality rule was *per se* illegal and chose to apply the rule of reason, focusing primarily on the effects on network competition. In this respect the court found the rule to be largely procompetitive: the "underlying purpose of the exclusivity provision was to enhance competition in the Canadian credit card market by introducing a new product, MasterCard."[82] The court also relied on the carefully tailored nature of the rule: it was adopted when MasterCard entered the market, it was necessary to protect the new members' start-up costs in the venture, and it was for a limited period of time (*i.e.,* eight years based on anticipated recovery of start-up costs). Thus, the rule was not an unlawful restraint.

---

[80] *See* Business Review Letter to National BankAmericard, Inc. (Oct. 7, 1975).

[81] 507 F. Supp. 1113 (S.D.N.Y. 1980), *aff'd,* 666 F.2d 6 (2d Cir. 1981).

[82] *Id.* at 1123.

The anti-duality rule was upheld on appeal, primarily on jurisdictional grounds.[83] Thus, in Canada, unlike the United States, membership in the credit card joint ventures has remained quite distinct. Because of the distinct membership, competition between MasterCard and Visa is far more vibrant in Canada than in the United States.[84]

[3] The Visa-Discover Dispute

Discover Card entered the credit card market in the mid-1980s and was the first card network to successfully enter for over two decades. It adopted a low price strategy, unlike that of most of the major Visa and MasterCard card issuers, offering consumers no annual fee cards with relatively low interest rates and also offering merchants a lower interchange fee.

In 1988, Visa responded to the increased competitive threat by adopting a rule that denied membership to any institution that issued Discover cards, American Express cards, or "any other card deemed competitive by the Board of Directors."

In 1991, an institution affiliated with the issuer of the Discover Card wanted to issue a "Prime Option" Visa card. Discover anticipated that the Prime Option card would be very popular and that Discover would quickly become one of the largest Visa card issuers. As a major card issuer, Discover could have demanded a seat on the Visa board of directors.

When Visa refused to permit the bank to issue Visa cards, Discover Card charged that the Visa rule violated the antitrust laws, and filed suit.[85] Visa filed a counterclaim alleging that Discover Card's admission into Visa would violate Section 7 of the Clayton Act by effectively merging the two credit card systems.

After several years of litigation, the court of appeals ruled against Discover Card. The court found that the Visa rule was not an antitrust violation for two reasons. First, the rule did not adversely affect competition. To

---

[83] 666 F.2d 6 (2d Cir. 1981).

[84] "Compulsory Access," 1993 Utah L. Rev. at 1065-68 (describing how credit card competition is more aggressive in Canada than in the United States).

[85] *SCFC ILC, Inc. v. Visa U.S.A*, 819 F. Supp. 956 (D. Utah 1993), *rev'd*, 36 F.3d 958 (10th Cir. 1994), *cert. denied*, 115 S. Ct. 2600 (1995). Discover Card also filed suit against MasterCard. *MasterCard Int'l Inc. v. Dean Witter, Discover & Co.*, 1993-2 Trade Cas. (CCH) ¶ 70,352 (S.D.N.Y. 1993). For a lengthy description of the litigation and the policy issues raised *see* David A. Balto, "Access Demands and Payment Systems Joint Ventures," 18 Harv. J.L. & Pub. Pol'y 624 (Spring 1995).

the extent there could be competitive harm, it would be in the market for credit card *issuance*, a market that appeared competitive in the view of the court because it was not very concentrated. Second, the rule was a legitimate response to potential free riding. Visa claimed that the purpose of the rule was to protect its property from network competitors (such as Discover) that sought to free-ride on its efforts. It also claimed that, because of the small number of network competitors, admitting Discover might harm network competition and eventually lead to government regulation of Visa as a possible monopolist. The court appeared to accept that the rule was a reasonable response to this free-riding concern.

With respect to Visa's counterclaim, the lower court found that network competition was important and helped "promote innovation in the development of transactional processing systems and merchant base expansion, thereby benefiting consumers."[86] Network competition would likely be harmed because Discover would not compete as vigorously with Visa after it issued its Prime Option card and Discover would have access to Visa's confidential information. Moreover, there was evidence that Discover wanted to dampen Visa's anti-Discover Card campaign. Despite these findings, the court declined to enter judgment on the counterclaim for Visa because it did not believe that the likely harm to competition would be significant in light of Discover's expressed intention to continue to market Discover Card vigorously. Therefore, the court dismissed the Section 7 counterclaim.

[4] ATM Networks

ATM networks have also been subject to private suits involving access claims. For example, in *BayBanks, Inc. v. New England Network, Inc.*,[87] the operator of the largest proprietary ATM network in New England, sued Yankee 24, a shared ATM network, seeking access for some of its ATMs in Yankee 24. In March 1988, the parties agreed to settle the case and the plaintiff joined Yankee 24.

Similar access issues have been raised by nonbank banks seeking access to ATM networks. These cases have been settled with the admission of the nonbank banks seeking access to ATM networks.[88]

In 1995, Canada's Bureau of Competition Policy required the Interac ATM network, which has a near monopoly, to provide access to small banks

---

[86] 819 F. Supp. at 995.

[87] No. 86-3532-K (D. Mass. filed Dec. 9, 1986).

[88] 682 F. Supp. 269, 280 (D.N.J.), *aff'd mem.*, 853 F.2d 921 (3d Cir. 1988).

and nonbanks on a non-discriminatory basis. Interac is an ATM and point of service ("POS") network. After several years of investigation, the Bureau entered into a consent agreement with Interac, Inc. and its owners. The Bureau argued that access to the network was essential for financial institutions and increasingly essential for non-financial institutions in order to compete in markets such as retail banking and credit cards. The consent decree required Interac to open its network to new members on a nondiscriminatory basis, although Interac may provide that only regulated financial institutions may issue cards that access the network. Interac agreed to stop assessing new member entry fees based on card issuance and to stop prohibiting its members from charging cardholders of other members for ATM use (and thus "depriving consumers of ATM deployment determined by market forces"). Interac also agreed to end its prohibition on pass-through accounts (accounts that permit access to accounts held by, or credit from, parties that are not members of Interac). The consent was approved by the Canadian Competition tribunal.[89]

[D] Tying as a Condition of Access: Visa/MasterCard Debit

A private class action was filed in 1996 by large retailers objecting to the requirement imposed by Visa and MasterCard that any retailer that accepts a credit card must accept the corresponding Visa Check or Mastermoney debit card.[90] The action claims treble damages for tying in violation of the Sherman Act. The case remains pending as of the time of this writing.

§ 15.06 EXCLUSIVITY RESTRAINTS

[A] In General

Some joint ventures prohibit their members from joining or participating in competing ventures. In some cases, only the "founding" members of the network are so restricted; in others, the restraint extends to the nonproprietary members as well. The legality of such exclusivity requirements depends on a variety of factors, including the market power of the venture

[89] *See Director of Investigation and Research v. Bank of Montreal, et al.*, CT 95-02 (Canadian Competition Tribunal, Dec. 14, 1995).

[90] *In re Visa Check / Mastermoney Antitrust Litigation,* No. 96-CV-5238 (E.D.N.Y.).

imposing the restraint, the duration of the exclusivity commitment, and the extent of market foreclosure resulting from the rule.[91]

In the mid-1980s, the Justice Department appeared to take the position that an exclusivity rule imposed by a dominant ATM network would be suspect, but that such a rule imposed by a non-dominant network could promote competition:

> When exclusivity requirements are employed by non-dominant systems that lack market power, anticompetitive effects are likely to be insignificant. . . . In a world of dominant shared systems, however, exclusivity could be used to impede the entry of competing systems. This in turn would reinforce the market power of the dominant system in the market for switching services.[92]

Courts have been particularly wary of arrangements that preclude the joint venture members from competing with the venture or from accomplishing the objectives of the venture independently (*e.g.*, by selling independently rather than through the venture).[93]

[B] Enforcement Actions

Several enforcement actions have been brought by the Justice Department challenging exclusivity provisions in bank ATM and credit card joint ventures, as described below.

[1] MAC ATM Network

In April 1994, the DOJ challenged the exclusivity rules of the MAC ATM network, the largest ATM network in the U.S., as illegal tying and

---

[91] For a general discussion of these factors, *see* David A. Balto, "Networks and Exclusivity: Antitrust Analysis to Promote Network Competition," 7 George Mason L. Rev. 523 (1999).

[92] Remarks by Charles Rule, *supra,* at A-148.

[93] *See, e.g., NCAA v. Board of Regents,* 468 U.S. 85 (1984); *Buffalo Broadcasting Co. v. ASCAP,* 744 F.2d 917, 924-28 (2d Cir. 1984) (whether there is restraint of trade depends in part on whether joint venture members offer realistic alternative to blanket copyright license), *cert. denied,* 468 U.S. 1211 (1985); *CBS v. ASCAP,* 620 F.2d at 936-39 (2d Cir. 1980) (blanket licensing was not restraint of trade in part because composers retained the right to license compositions independently); *NaBanco,* 596 F. Supp. at 1254-55 (there were no legal, practical, or conspiratorial impediments for members to make alternative arrangements).

monopolization under Sections 1 and 2 of the Sherman Act.[94] MAC was operated by Electronic Payments Services, Inc. ("EPS"), at the time a joint venture of four bank holding companies: CoreStates Financial Corp., Banc One Corp., PNC Bank Corp., and Society Corp. The MAC network had approximately a 90 percent market share in Pennsylvania and a strong position in adjacent mid-Atlantic states. The Department alleged that MAC barred its network banks from buying data processing service from third parties and used its control over ATM processing to prevent its network banks from connecting with competing networks.

Until 1992, MAC generally did not permit its customers to participate in rival ATM networks while also participating in MAC. Although the rule against multiple affiliations was formally dropped in 1992, the Department looked at the exclusionary effect of other practices.

In its suit, the Department alleged that a rule that required banks either to obtain ATM driving from the defendant or to provide ATM driving in-house as intercept processors (which is prohibitively expensive for many smaller banks, thrifts, and credit unions) effectively made it impossible for these smaller institutions to belong to rival networks while belonging to MAC. MAC generally prohibited its network customers from obtaining ATM driving from any of the several data processing firms that provide driving service in a national market. The MAC rules and practices, the DOJ alleged, "prevent willing buyers and sellers from conducting business at competitively determined prices and terms." In addition, by preventing banks from obtaining ATM driving from others, MAC effectively prevented these banks from participating in other ATM networks, thereby maintaining its monopoly position.

The tying claim alleged that "regional ATM network access" and "ATM processing" are separate products and that MAC's rules and practices effectively forced its customers to purchase ATM processing from MAC. The monopolization claim alleged that MAC willfully maintained its monopoly power in the market for regional ATM network access in the affected states through exclusionary practices.

The consent decree required MAC to open its network to independent ATM processors on a non-discriminatory basis. MAC was permitted to provide volume discounts, but only on a non-discriminatory basis. MAC also was required to sell its network services "at prices that will not vary

[94] *United States v. Electronic Payments Services, Inc.*, No. 94-208 (D. Del. Apr. 21, 1994), 59 Fed. Reg. 24711 (May 12, 1994).

with the process selected" and to provide a more open environment for third-party processors. In addition, MAC was limited in the extent to which it could keep banks from displaying symbols of other ATM networks on their ATMs and ATM cards.

[2] Visa/MasterCard Exclusivity Rules

As noted earlier, the Justice Department in October 1998 challenged the exclusivity rules of Visa and MasterCard that prevent their members from issuing the cards of competing networks including American Express and Discover Card. The Department alleged that the exclusivity rules prevent American Express and Discover from effectively competing and raise barriers to entry and expansion in the network markets, noting that access to banks is particularly important in a network industry

> where increased usage leads to increased merchant acceptance, which in turn leads to increased usage, in a continuing cycle that economists call 'network effects.' In other words, because the number of merchants and consumers using a network greatly affects its success, any method that succeeds in materially reducing those numbers is anticompetitive because it negatively affects the growth and ability of a network competitor to compete.[95]

In addition to the exclusivity rule, the complaint identified other rules that allegedly impeded the ability of other networks to enter and develop. These include rules that deter the ability of alternative networks to sign up merchants and impede the ability of other networks to provide cash advances to consumers through their ATM networks.

§ 15.07 PRICE AND OUTPUT RESTRAINTS

Restraints on pricing and output imposed by a joint venture are typically evaluated under the rule of reason. In assessing the legality of such restrictions, the courts focus on the extent to which the pricing restraint is necessary to achieve the joint venture's objectives—that is, whether it is truly ancillary to the venture's ability to function efficiently.

---

[95] Justice Department Memorandum Regarding Discovery and Scheduling Issues (Jan. 4, 1999).

[A] In General

From an antitrust perspective, the most problematic type of pricing involves the prices charged directly to consumers. If a joint venture restricts the interest rate, annual fee, or transaction fee charged by members of the venture, those restrictions likely would be illegal, perhaps even under the *per se* rule.[96]

Although credit card joint ventures have faced challenges alleging interest rate price-fixing, however, such challenges have not prevailed to date.[97]

The types of credit card fees that are more commonly the source of antitrust litigation are fees charged between the financial institution members of the joint venture. Credit card and ATM joint ventures set an internal fee—the interchange fee—that is fixed collectively by the venture's board of directors but is paid by one member to another. In the credit card ventures, the fee is paid by the merchant bank to the card-issuing bank in order to compensate the card-issuer for fraud and other similar losses. In the ATM environment, it flows from the card-issuing member to the ATM member (the acquirer) and is designed to compensate the acquirer for its ATM costs and to create an incentive for it to bring

---

[96] *See* Department of Justice Business Review Letter to Mortgage-Backed Securities Dealers Ass'n (June 25, 1979) (DOJ declined to issue a favorable business review for the code of self-regulation of the association of securities dealers, in part because of requirement that dealers impose certain uniform margin requirements on their consumers); Department of Justice Business Review Letter to New Jersey Wholesalers Credit Bureau, (June 3, 1976) (DOJ announced intention to sue credit bureau that proposed to restrict terms under which credit could be extended).

[97] *See Weit v. Continental Illinois Nat'l Bank & Trust Co.*, 641 F.2d 457 (7th Cir. 1981) (parallel interest rates and mere opportunity to conspire were insufficient to create a reasonable inference of conspiracy); *Fisher v. First Nat'l Bank of Omaha*, 548 F.2d 255, 262 (8th Cir. 1977) (observing that credit card joint venture "promotes and facilitates, rather than restrains' competition); *Brown v. Visa U.S.A.*, 674 F. Supp. 249 (N.D. Ill. 1987) (dismissing complaint for lack of standing and other grounds); *cf. Wilcox Dev. Co. v. First Interstate Bank, NA*, 605 F. Supp. 592 (D. Or. 1985) (claim of conspiracy to fix prime rate), *aff'd in part and reversed in part*, 815 F.2d 522 (9th Cir. 1987); *Biljac v. Interstate Bank of Oregon, NA*, 1990 Cal. App. LEXIS 542 (Cal. Ct. App. Mar. 22, 1990) (conspiracy to set and manipulate variable interest rate on loans to commercial customers).

its terminals into the network. It is this interchange fee that has been the source of a number of challenges under the antitrust laws.[98]

[B] Private Litigation

[1] *NaBanco*

A Visa credit card interchange fee charged to merchants by card issuers was upheld against antitrust challenge in *National Bancard Corp. (NaBanco) v. Visa USA.*[99] The fee was challenged by one of Visa's largest merchant processors, which alleged that the fee constituted *per se* illegal price-fixing.

The court rejected the *per se* characterization since the fee was not mandatory, and instead analyzed the restraint under the rule of reason. In doing so, it rejected NaBanco's contention that Visa had market power in a narrowly defined market of "credit card processing" and instead defined the market broadly as "all payment services."[100] It then examined Visa's justification for the fee. The court accepted the rationale for an interchange fee flowing to the card issuer, which bore the burden of educating consumers with an unfamiliar product, carrying the float costs and bearing most of the fraud losses. Visa had commissioned a Big Eight accounting firm to do careful cost studies of the issuer costs. Thus, the court treated the interchange fee as "a cost-related mechanism" for encouraging card issuers to participate in the venture and found that the interchange fee:

> eliminates the costly uncertainty and prohibitive time and expense of 'price negotiations at the time of the exchange' between the thousands of Visa members [and that] transaction costs in this type of system would no doubt be high and stultifying since each and every bank would have to somehow contract each and every bank with which it might have some card business contact.[101]

[98] For a thorough examination of antitrust concerns relating to interchange fees, *see* David A. Balto, "The Problem of Interchange Fees: Costs Without Benefits?" 2000 E.C.L.R. 215 (2000).

[99] 596 F. Supp. 1231 (S.D. Fla. 1984), *aff'd,* 779 F.2d 592 (11th Cir.), *cert. denied,* 479 U.S. 923 (1986).

[100] 596 F. Supp. at 1257-59.

[101] *Id.* at 1259-61.

Viewing the interchange fee as an internal accounting procedure between the joint venture members, the appellate court upheld the lower court's broad market definition and also found that, even if Visa did have market power, the fee on balance was procompetitive. On the latter point, it explained that "the 'fundamental economic interdependence' between the card-issuing and merchant-signing banks demonstrate that redistribution of revenues or costs [was] a must for the continued existence of the product."[102] Hence, the court concluded that collectively set interchange fees were necessary for Visa to offer its joint product, and upheld the fee as " 'reasonably ancillary to [A] procompetitive efficiency creating endeavor'."[103]

[2] *Financial Interchange* Arbitration

At issue in the 1988 *Financial Interchange* arbitration proceeding[104] was a PULSE network ATM interchange fee charged by ATM owner-banks to card-issuing banks whose customers used PULSE network ATMs. When PULSE attempted to lower the interchange fee in order to make the network more attractive to card-issuing banks, one member, First Texas Savings Association, alleged a violation of Section 1 of the Sherman Act.

First Texas presented two arguments. First, it claimed that *any* setting of interchange fee (whatever the level) was a horizontal price-fixing agreement among competing buyers and sellers that unreasonably restrained trade in violation of Section 1 of the Sherman Act. Next, it argued that, even if collective fee-setting was lawful, PULSE's planned reduction in the interchange fee for off-premise ATMs violated Section 1 because the fee schedule was not based on neutral and objective criteria but rather was part of a "buyers' cartel" that favored the majority of PULSE's members who were "net purchasers" of ATM transactions.

The centerpiece of First Texas' argument was a "free market" proposal under which all interchange fees would be eliminated and the ATM owner would charge consumers directly for use of its ATMs by electronically debiting the cardholder's account. With compensation to the ATM-owner limited to the interchange fee, First Texas contended, output (in terms of the number of ATMs) was restricted and consumers did not

---

[102] 779 F.2d at 605.

[103] *Id.* at 602.

[104] *In re Arbitration Between First Texas Savings Ass'n and Financial Interchange, Inc.*, 55 Antitrust & Trade Reg. Rep. (BNA) No. 1380, at 340 (Aug. 25, 1988).

receive the full range of ATM availability, quality, and convenience that would be achievable in a free market environment.[105]

Despite First Texas' contention that it did not have to show that PULSE had market power, the arbitrator concluded that it did. However, he further found that PULSE had market power in both a narrowly defined wholesale "network switching" market and a retail "ATM services" market.

The burden then shifted to PULSE to establish that the fee was reasonably necessary for the efficient functioning of the network. PULSE pointed to the inefficiency and impracticality of separate bilateral agreements between the network's many members. PULSE also identified a number of external costs that would be imposed on the network and its membership if the free market proposal were adopted, including loss of members, possible price gouging, customer confusion, substantial technical conversion costs, inability to interconnect with other networks, and the need for additional customer education.

The arbitrator agreed in part with First Texas' argument: "Simply put, the ATM owner is in the best position to identify and respond to consumer demand. Consumer choice is generally enhanced through a maximization of price/quality/convenience options." Although the arbitrator considered the venture's business justification arguments, he nevertheless concluded that PULSE's fixed interchange fee would violate the Sherman Act unless it adopted the "less restrictive" alternative of allowing its ATM owning members to impose surcharges or rebates at their ATMs: "where the benefits of a competitive market can be obtained without a substantial impairment of efficiency, the restraint cannot be viewed as reasonable."

Because of this decision, the practice of setting uniform interchange fees and prohibiting surcharges has become controversial.

[3] *Valley Bank/PLUS*

Shortly after the PULSE arbitration was concluded, a surcharge prohibition imposed by PLUS, one of the national ATM networks, was challenged by Valley Bank. The antitrust issues in the case were never fully litigated. Nevada passed a statute prohibiting bans on surcharges,

---

[105] For an in-depth description of the First Texas proposal *see* Steven C. Salop, "Evaluating Network Pricing Self-Regulation" in Guerin-Calvert and Wildman (eds.), *supra,* at 88.

and Visa's contention that the statue violated the Commerce Clause was unavailing.[106]

[4] *Southtrust/PLUS*

In 1995, an ATM network finally prevailed in an antitrust case involving ATM surcharges.[107] Southtrust, an Alabama bank, sought to assess surcharges and challenged the PLUS network surcharge prohibition. The court held that the PLUS network surcharge prohibition did not violate the antitrust laws but rather was "designed to enhance economic efficiency, and render markets more . . . competitive" and "enhanced consumer welfare" and reduced consumer search costs.[108] In particular, the court observed that, since the PLUS network most likely would handle the transactions of travelers far from home who were the most vulnerable to opportunistic behavior, PLUS had a legitimate basis for protecting its card holders. In addition, the court followed the NaBanco precedent and defined the market broadly as all payment systems. In this market, the anti-surcharge rule could have no anticompetitive effect.

[C] Congressional Scrutiny

After the *Southtrust* decision, the national ATM networks changed course and eliminated their anti-surcharge policies. With the abandonment of these policies, the vast majority of banks began imposing surcharges, leading to an outcry by consumer groups and small banks against these practices. Congress has considered but not yet adopted legislation to ban surcharges or to impose other consumer protection provisions, except to require that ATM's disclose transaction fees to consumers.[109]

---

[106] *See Valley Bank of Nevada v. PLUS System, Inc.*, 749 F. Supp. 223 (D. Nov. 1989), *aff'd, Valley Bank of Nevada v. PLUS System, Inc.* 914 F.2d 1136 (9th Cir. 1990).

[107] *Southtrust Corp. v. PLUS System, Inc*, 1995-2 Trade Cas. (CCH) ¶ 71,219 (N.D. Ala. Aug. 10, 1995).

[108] *Id.* at 75,906.

[109] 15 U.S.C. § 1693b(d)(3). For a description of the debate and the proposed legislation *see* David Balto, "ATM Surcharges: Panacea or Pandora's Box?," 12 Rev. of Banking & Financial Services (Oct. 9, 1996); Paul M. Horvitz, "ATM Surcharges: Their Effect on Competition and Efficiency," 18 Journal of Retail Banking Services 57 (1996).

[D] Government Views

The Department of Justice has expressed concern about fixed interchange fees imposed by shared ATM networks:

> [A uniform interchange fee] eliminates the need to negotiate independent fees between each pair of members and avoids the breakdowns of universal sharing that would result if some such negotiations were unsuccessful. Thus, uniform fees could increase the efficiency of contracting among members and increase the overall reliability and value of the system to consumers.
>
> On the other hand, uniform fees may be set at a non-competitive level, thereby generating a misallocation of resources. If the shared system enjoys market power at the switching level and is controlled by institutions that are either predominantly card issuers or ATM owners, it may have an incentive to increase the profits of controlling members by setting the interchange fee at a non-competitive level. For example, suppose the shared system is controlled by card-issuing banks that are net purchasers of wholesale ATM services from pure ATM owners such as retailers.
>
> If the ATM owners have no practical alternative to interconnection with the shared system for the purpose of gaining access to cardholders, the card-issuing banks might set the interchange fee below the competitive level. This practice would discourage the efficient placement of ATMs in non-bank locations.
>
> Because of the controlling tendencies of uniform fees, it is not possible to say on *a priori* grounds whether uniform fees enhance or harm consumer welfare. However, certain restrictions that fall short of uniform fees, such as the establishment of maximum and minimum fees, may provide the same benefits without incurring the same economic detriments.[110]

Notwithstanding these concerns, the DOJ has not taken any action to prohibit the practice.

§ 15.08 SPILLOVER EFFECTS

A final concern in joint venture analysis is the potential for "spillover effects" in the form of anticompetitive conduct that goes beyond the scope of the venture.

---

[110] *See* Remarks of Charles Rule, *supra,* at A-147-48.

The most serious spillover effect is that a joint venture may facilitate collusion in other areas. Since joint ventures are combinations of competitors, the opportunity exists for these firms to collude in markets other than the one the joint venture participates in. The treatment of information exchanges illustrates these concerns.

[A] Information Exchanges

The DOJ recognizes that "the exchange of information among competitors often serves to promote the efficiency of markets and the competitiveness of firms selling in those markets."[111] However, the DOJ also recognizes that under certain circumstances, information exchanges may have anticompetitive effects by facilitating implicit or explicit agreements among competitors to raise prices or decrease output. For example, in a less-than-competitive market, a firm may be reluctant to compete by lowering its price or increasing output if its competitors can easily detect that conduct and respond to it quickly. Similarly, an information exchange may enable a group of competitors to act in unison in raising prices or decreasing output.

In evaluating the competitive effect of an information exchange, the DOJ initially evaluates market structure and related factors to determine whether the market is conducive to collusion. The DOJ begins by defining the relevant market, identifying competitors and assigning market shares. Where the market in which the information exchange participates is unconcentrated and the members of the exchange have a relatively small share of the market, competitive concerns will not be significant.[112]

Where concentration is high and the likelihood of new entry is low, however, the DOJ may decline to approve the information exchange. For example, in an information exchange involving the Georgia Bankers Association, market concentration and entry were critical in the DOJ's decision to approve the exchange in metropolitan markets. The result might have been different if the exchange had expanded into rural markets. The DOJ noted:

> [M]any rural bank markets in Georgia are characterized by high concentration and thus are more structurally susceptible to collusion, as a general matter, than urban markets, which tend to have a larger

[111] Business Review Letter to Georgia Bankers Ass'n (Sept. 13, 1988).

[112] *See* Business Review Letter to Kreitz Motor Express, Inc. (Dec. 18, 1988).

number of financial service providers. Moreover, the likelihood of entry into some of those rural markets may be sufficiently low that entry would not prevent successful collusion in those markets.[113]

In order to determine whether certain characteristics of the market make it conducive to collusion, the DOJ evaluates such factors as:

- the ease of entry into the market;
- the ease with which firms can expand supply;
- the homogeneity or heterogeneity of the products involved;
- the pricing and marketing practices employed by firms in the market;
- the availability of information concerning market conditions;
- whether the participants have in the past coordinated prices or output; and
- the complexity of prices.[114]

Where the structure of the market is such that an information exchange may be conducive to collusion, the DOJ considers the extent to which the information exchange program may enable firms to detect any competitive initiatives by its rivals. Thus, the DOJ considers a number of factors, including whether current, prospective or historical data is gathered, how the data is disseminated (*e.g.,* on a firm-specific or aggregated basis) and whether a competitor or independent third party controls the data.

[B] Operational Safeguards

Competitive concerns regarding information exchanges may be alleviated by operational or procedural safeguards that may substantially eliminate any risk of anticompetitive spillover effects. For example, the International Guidelines suggest that in order to avoid such spillover effects, an information exchange may require that competitively sensitive

---

[113] Letter of September 8, 1988, at 3.

[114] *See* Guidelines for the Issuance of Export Trade Certificates of Review, 50 Fed. Reg. 1795 (Jan. 11, 1985); *see also* Joint Venture Guidelines, § 3.34(e).

data be aggregated or disclosed only through neutral third parties, that counsel monitor meetings of the information exchange or that accurate records of the discussions in the meetings be compiled.[115]

Other useful safeguards include:

- limiting the data to past transactions, not present or future prices or costs;[116]
- providing data on list prices rather than actual sales prices or discounts;[117]
- supplying the data provided by individual companies to an independent third party for aggregation and analysis;[118]
- reporting the data in composite form and keeping the data supplied by individual companies confidential.[119]

§ 15.09 MERGERS AND ACQUISITIONS

Mergers and acquisitions involving firms engaged in electronic banking and commerce also may raise antitrust considerations. Such transactions may be challenged under Section 1 of the Sherman Act, Section 7 of the Clayton Act, or Section 4 of the Bank Holding Company Act. These statutes seek to prevent the accumulation of market power that will result in higher prices or less output and overall lower consumer welfare. To date there has not been a great deal of antitrust enforcement activity aimed at electronic commerce mergers.

---

[115] International Guidelines at § 3.43. *See also* Joint Venture Guidelines § 3.34(e); General Motors, 103 F.T.C. 374, 385 (1984) (consent decree required parties to record exchanges of information on a wide range of topics); Business Review Letter to Electronic Power Research Institute, Inc. (October 2, 2000) (approving exchange of information among electric power companies to combat cyber-threats, in part because the companies were prohibited from discussing competitively sensitive information such as prices, capacity, or future plans, specific prices for equipment, electronic information or communications systems, and participation was non-discriminatory).

[116] *See* Business Review Letter to Experience Information Bureau Inc. (Jan. 14, 1992).

[117] *See* Business Review Letter to Hyatt, Imler, Ott & Blount, P.C. (June 12, 1992).

[118] *See* Business Review Letter to RMJ Securities Corp., *et al.* (Mar. 29, 1989).

[119] *See* Business Review Letter to the Association of Ship Brokers and Agents (U.S.A.) Inc. (Oct. 23, 1992).

[A] Competitive Analysis

Analysis of mergers and acquisitions focuses on four basic issues:

(1) What are the relevant product and geographic markets?
(2) Does the increased size of the merged firm create a likelihood of anticompetitive effects?
(3) Is entry sufficiently likely to eliminate these anticompetitive effects?
(4) Are there efficiencies from the merger that will benefit consumers and overcome any anticompetitive effects?

The ultimate question is the likelihood of anticompetitive effects. As Judge Posner has observed:

> Section 7 does not require proof that a merger or other acquisition has caused higher prices in the affected market. All that is necessary is that the merger create an appreciable danger of such consequences in the future. A predictive judgment, necessarily probabilistic and judgmental rather than demonstrable . . . is called for.[120]

Because merger analysis is prospective, the probability of anticompetitive effects must be inferred from other evidence, most importantly the level of concentration in the relevant market and the post-merger increase in that concentration. If the post-merger concentration is high enough, and has increased enough, the merger is presumed to be anticompetitive. On the other hand, if post-merger concentration is low or the merged firm has a relatively modest market share (*e.g.*, below 20 percent), the acquisition probably will pass scrutiny.

A presumption of anticompetitive effects is rebuttable by a showing that the structural characteristics of the markets make post-merger collusion or the ability to unilaterally wield market power unlikely. The presumption can be strong or weak and a variety of evidence is relevant to the ultimate question of whether a merger is likely to lessen competition. A number of market characteristics make the presumption stronger, including high barriers to entry, low level of product differentiation, relatively inelastic demand for industry output at competitive price levels, a large number of small buyers, and a high degree of transaction frequency and visibility.

---

[120] *Hospital Corp. of Am. v. FTC,* 807 F.2d 1381, 1389 (7th Cir. 1986), *cert. denied,* 481 U.S. 1038 (1987).

Among the industry characteristics that may rebut a presumption of anticompetitive effects is the absence of barriers to entry. Where entry is easy, post-merger firms are unlikely to be able to abuse market power, either collusively or unilaterally, because such entry likely will deter or counteract the anticompetitive effects.[121] The surest evidence of actual entry conditions is often the experience of recent entrants. In order to rebut an anticompetitive presumption, entry must be timely, likely, and sufficient.[122]

Another important factor in merger analysis is efficiency. Mergers and acquisitions often can generate significant efficiencies by enabling firms to combine and better utilize assets to achieve lower costs and higher quality. The antitrust enforcement agencies will consider these efficiencies in exercising prosecutorial discretion. Efficiencies must be verifiable, quantifiable, and merger specific. They will "almost never justify a merger to monopoly or near-monopoly."[123]

Merger analysis in the area of electronic commerce tends to focus on the issues of entry and efficiency. One important factor is the existence of network externalities. A network typically enjoys economies of scale or scope in demand. The value of a network to a consumer depends on the total number of users and the identities of other specific users. The larger the network, the greater the number of consumers who will join it and conversely, the smaller the network, the less attractive it will be to consumers. These increasing returns in consumption are called "network externalities."

These network externalities suggest that entry barriers are far more formidable when a network is involved. The antitrust enforcers thus have traditionally found significant entry barriers involving ATM networks. However, network externalities also suggest that the merger of two networks can lead to greater efficiencies. Former Antitrust Division Assistant Attorney General Charles Rule discussed this factor in a 1985 speech about ATM networks. Rule stated that the Division was focusing more on the "economies of ubiquity" and the resulting consumer benefits achievable by widespread sharing of ATMs. Rule observed that the consolidation of ATM networks benefits consumers by, among other things, increasing the available ATMs in a single network; similarly, increasing the number of cardholders tends to increase the deployment of ATMs. Thus, Rule

[121] Merger Guidelines § 3.0.

[122] Merger Guidelines § 3.1.

[123] Merger Guidelines § 4.

indicated that the Division would not challenge the creation or merger of shared ATM networks based on size alone.[124]

In the 1990s, that approach was modified as the enforcement agencies looked more critically at the potential for anticompetitive effects in these mergers.

[B] Merger and Acquisition Cases

The following are examples of recent enforcement actions involving mergers and acquisitions of firms engaged in electronic banking and commerce.

[1] Microsoft-Intuit Case

The most prominent antitrust challenge to a merger proposal involving electronic banking was the Justice Department's 1995 challenge to Microsoft's acquisition of Intuit.[125] In April 1995, the DOJ filed suit against Microsoft's planned $2 billion acquisition of Intuit, Inc., the dominant producer of personal finance/checkbook software. At the time of the suit, Intuit and Microsoft accounted for more than 90 percent of the personal finance software sales in the United States.

The Department alleged that allowing Microsoft to buy a dominant position in such a highly concentrated market would result in higher prices and a lessening of innovation. In addition, the Department alleged that Microsoft's control of the personal finance software market would give it a cornerstone asset that could be used with its existing dominant position in operating systems for personal computers to seize control of markets of the future, including PC-based home banking.

The Department rejected Microsoft's proposed "fix" in which some but not all of its "Money" personal finance software assets would have been transferred to Novell Inc. since the Department believed that Novell would not be as effective a competitor with "Money" as was Microsoft. The acquisition was abandoned on the eve of trial.

---

[124] *See* Rule, *supra,* at A-142-43.

[125] *United States v. Microsoft Corp.,* No. C 95 1393 WHO (N.D. Cal. filed Apr. 27, 1995). For a description of the home banking market and the theory behind the case, *see* Paul M. Horvitz, "Efficiency and Antitrust Considerations in Home Banking: the Proposed Microsoft-Intuit Merger," 41 Antitrust Bull. 427 (1996),

[2] Payment Systems Mergers

The only enforcement action brought against a payment systems merger was the FTC's challenge to the acquisition of the Western Union consumer money transfer system (owned by First Financial Management Corp.) by First Data Corp., the owner of the MoneyGram system.[126] Consumer wire money transfer systems involve one-way money transfers, typically between two consumers.

Western Union has been the dominant firm in the market and had been a regulated monopoly until the late 1970s. MoneyGram, which was originally owned by American Express, entered in the late 1980s and was able to compete in part because it could rely on the trade name and agent base of American Express. After several years of losses, MoneyGram overcame the entry barrier posed by Western Union's monopoly power and introduced competition in a market in which a monopolist had dictated annual price increases.

At the time of the FTC's action, Western Union had approximately a 90 percent market share. According to the complaint, MoneyGram and Western Union were the only two services in the U.S. consumer money market transfer market and it would be very difficult for new companies to enter the market. The complaint noted that First Data's acquisition of Western Union would create a monopoly in the market. Further, the FTC contended that entry was unlikely because of the difficulty of gaining brand name recognition and establishing a nationwide network of retail outlets. Thus, absent the settlement, the FTC alleged that the acquisition would increase the likelihood that consumers, among other things, would be forced to pay higher fees and receive less service and that agents would be forced to accept reduced commissions. The complaint was resolved through a settlement that permitted First Data to acquire Western Union as long as it divested either the MoneyGram or Western Union consumer money wire transfer business.

From a preliminary perspective, the FTC's enforcement action appears to have led a stronger competitor and lower prices to consumers. Following this consent agreement, MoneyGram advertised a promotional price that undercut Western Union's prices by as much as seven percent.[127]

---

[126] *First Data Corp.*, FTC C-3436 (Sept. 21, 1995).

[127] *See* "The Dollars and Sense of Antitrust Enforcement," Remarks by William J. Baer, Director, Bureau of Competition, FTC, before the Antitrust Section of the New York State Bar Association (Jan. 25, 1996) (available on FTC Web site).

Moreover, MoneyGram's market share, at least in the short term, increased somewhat. In November 1996, MoneyGram became an independent firm and competes directly with Western Union.

[3] ATM Network Mergers

The Federal Reserve Board reviewed several ATM network mergers during the 1990s. In these cases, the Board recognized the impact of network externalities both on efficiency and entry barriers. In many cases, the Board mitigated competitive concerns by requiring the combined network to adopt rules that reduced entry barriers by enabling network members to participate in alternative networks.

In the NYCE/Yankee 24 merger, for example,[128] both networks were head-to-head competitors in New England. The most interesting aspect of the Board's order approving the merger was the requirement that the network commit to an "open architecture" structure. The critical factor from the Board's perspective was the new operating rules offered by the network that permitted all non-equity members to "bypass" the network and enter into arrangements with alternative networks or third-party processors. The network's operating rules permitted: (1) third-party processors to participate in the network, (2) members to participate in other networks, (3) card issuers determine routing, and (4) institutions to participate on a nondiscriminatory basis.[129]

The first and second of these rules provide network banks with possible alternatives to the network services, including processing and ATM-operating services from major third-party sources and ATM switching services from other networks. The third and fourth rules provide mechanisms by which small institutions can enhance their ability to obtain competitively-priced services from the network.

Of particular importance may be the card-issuer routing rule, which would permit banks to choose lower cost networks if the new network attempted to raise prices.[130] Where both the card and ATM belong to

---

[128] *Bank of New York Co.,* 80 Fed. Res. Bull. 1107 (1994).

[129] The parties also agreed that if the if a bank chose to bypass the network, it would not have to pay a royalty or bypass fee. *See* Application of Infinet Payment Services, Inc. (June 6, 1994), at 29.

[130] For discussion of the importance of card-issuer routing rules, *see* Karen L. Grimm & David A. Balto, "Consumer Pricing for ATM Services: Antitrust Constraints and Legislative Alternatives," 4 Ga. St. U. L. Rev. 839 (Spring 1993).

multiple networks, the bank that controls routing will choose which network to "send" or "route" the transaction. In an ATM network, the card-issuer pays the fees of every transaction (an interchange and switch fee). In most ATM networks, the ATM owner determines routing. The card-issuer will seek the network with the lowest fees; the ATM owner will seek the network with the highest fees.

A card-issuer routing rule gives the card-issuing bank the ability to search for lower cost alternatives. If the network attempts to exercise its market power by increasing its fees, a card-issuer routing rule will permit the card-issuing bank to choose a lower cost network (if one is available). Absent a card-issuer routing rule, a bank may have little alternative to paying the higher fees.

[4] Implications of Mergers Outside of Electronic Banking Mergers

[i] MCI/WorldCom

The expansion and development of the Internet has heightened interest in network competition analysis. The most significant Internet merger enforcement action to date involved the merger of MCI and WorldCom.[131] Each company owned a significant portion of the Internet backbone, the large-scale communications network over which most Internet traffic travels. The combined firm would have had more than 50 percent of the Internet backbone market. Supporters of the transaction argued that this level of concentration was not worrisome, pointing to network externalities and efficiencies based on the assumption that the larger the network the greater the benefits for consumers. Moreover, they argued that few, if any, barriers existed to entry or expansion in the Internet backbone market.

U.S. and European regulators determined that the transaction posed a threat to competition, focusing on borders and barriers. As to borders, MCI argued that the relevant market included Internet service providers who provide retail consumer services as well as backbone service providers. The Federal Communications Commission ("FCC") rejected that claim, finding that smaller Internet service providers do not offer the same

---

[131] *WorldCom, Inc.*, 13 F.C.C.R. 18,025 (1998).

service as backbone providers—transmission of traffic between all Internet users—and that good substitutes for backbone services did not exist.

The most difficult and hotly contested issue was whether there were significant barriers to entry into the Internet backbone market. Technically and financially, the barriers seemed formidable but not insurmountable. Constructing an Internet backbone network would cost millions of dollars and involve a great deal of technical talent, customer support and sales staff, and other back office systems. But these financial and technical barriers were not the crucial element of the analysis.

Internet backbone providers are dependent upon one another to interconnect in order to offer consumers near universal access to Internet service providers and customers. After the acquisition, MCI and WorldCom would have controlled over 50 percent of the market and would have been substantially larger than remaining competitors. Instead of a market with several moderately sized competitors that were equally dependent on one another to provide connections, a single network would have enjoyed much greater network externalities. This diminished dependence on other networks would have given MCI leverage to dictate the terms, conditions, and pricing of interconnection with other Internet backbone providers. Smaller backbone providers, including new entrants, would have been dependent on interconnection with MCI in order to effectively compete. This asymmetric relationship would have left small providers, including new entrants, without any leverage and subject to whatever terms and conditions MCI dictated. Indeed, the FCC found that, following the merger, MCI's huge disparity in size would have given it the incentive, ability, and power to increase the costs to or degrade the quality of interconnection for smaller rivals, and that once it did, entry barriers would be solidified.

Ultimately, the regulators used the "first-best" solution of structural relief and required MCI to divest its entire Internet business to Cable & Wireless in what was the largest government ordered divestiture in history.

[ii] AOL/Time Warner

The FTC imposed various conditions on the merger of America Online ("AOL"), the nation's largest Internet service provider ("ISP"), and Time Warner, the nation's largest cable provider, to protect competition in various electronic businesses. The merged entity, AOL Time Warner, must open its cable system to competing ISPs on a nondiscriminatory basis, may not interfere with their content, may not enter exclusive arrangements with other cable companies or ISPs, and must market and offer high-speed internet DSL access to subscribers at the same price and manner everywhere (in other words, it may not charge higher prices in areas where it faces no broadband competition from other cable companies).[132]

---

[132] FTC Docket No. C-3989 (documents available at the FTC Web site, *http://www.ftc.gov/opa/2000/12/aol.htm*).

CHAPTER 16

ELECTRONIC SIGNATURES

§ 16.01 IN GENERAL

A digital signature is a form of electronic authentication used to verify the identity of the sender of an electronic message through a string of characters relying on cryptography.[1] Authentification is needed not only for the protection of the sender of electronic information but for the recipient as well. Digital signatures are a means of overcoming some of the security problems of electronic banking and are essential to the ultimate success of electronic banking and commerce as accepted modes of transacting business.

Digital signatures require a trusted third party or other means to certify the validity of the signature. Some systems rely on the issuance of a digital certificate by a certification authority ("CA") to verify a digital signature. A variety of CA systems with different features are in various stages of development and usage.

§ 16.02 ELECTRONIC SIGNATURE ACT

Congress in 2000 established the validity of electronic signatures in the Electronic Signatures in Global and National Commerce Act, or "E-Sign Act."[2] The Act will facilitate electronic banking and commerce and greatly reduce the paperwork burden associated with traditional paper-based transactions by allowing commercial contracts to be formed, documented and stored electronically.[3]

The Act does not require any person to use or agree to use electronic signatures, but provides that an electronic signature may not be denied legal effect or enforceability merely because it is in electronic form. Effective as of October 1, 2000, in any transaction involving interstate or foreign commerce:

- a signature, contract, or other record relating to such transaction may not be denied legal effect, validity, or enforceability solely because it is in electronic form; and

[1] *See* OCC Conditional Approval No. 339 (Nov. 16, 1999), n.4.

[2] Pub. L. No. 106-229, *codified at* 15 U.S.C. § 7001.

[3] For an excellent overview of the Act and its implications for electronic commerce, *see* Roland Brandel and Veronica McGregor, "The E-Sign Act: A Federal Foundation for E-Commerce," Electronic Banking Law and Commerce Report, Vol. 5, No. 4 (Sept. 2000).

- a contract relating to such transaction may not be denied legal effect, validity, or enforceability solely because an electronic signature or electronic record was used in its formation.

Congress enacted the E-Sign Act to remedy the lack of consistent national rules governing the use of electronic signatures which Congress found was "one of the greatest barriers to the growth of Internet commerce."[4] Congress noted that more than forty states had enacted electronic authentication laws, no two of which were the same, and that this inconsistency deterred businesses and consumers from using electronic signature technologies in contracts and transactions in interstate commerce.

[A] Definitions

The term "electronic signature" is defined in the Act to mean "an electronic sound, symbol, or process, attached to or logically associated with a contract or other record and executed or adopted by a person with the intent to sign the record." The term "electronic" is defined to mean "relating to technology having electrical, digital, magnetic, wireless, optical, electromagnetic, or similar capabilities."

The Act generally applies to commercial and consumer "transactions" in personal and real property. The term "transaction" is defined to mean "an action or set of actions relating to the conduct of business, consumer, or commercial affairs between two or more persons, including any of the following types of conduct: (A) the sale lease, exchange, licensing, or other disposition of (i) personal property, including goods and intangibles, (ii) services, and (iii) any combination thereof; and (B) the sale, lease, exchange, or other disposition of any interest in real property, or any combination thereof." This definition of "transaction" allows electronic mortgages, among other electronic transactions.

[B] Exemptions

The E-Sign Act does not apply to contracts or records relating to wills or testamentary trusts, divorce, adoption, court orders, notices of cancellation of utility services, notices of default and foreclosure or eviction regarding a primary residence, cancellation of health insurance or

---

[4] S. Rep. No. 106-131, 106th Cong. 1 (1999).

life insurance other than annuities, recall notices for products endangering health or safety, documents relating to toxic substances, and the Uniform Commercial Code other than Article 1-107 (waiver or renunciation of claim or right after breach).

[C] Consumer Transactions

In the case of consumer transactions where a consumer is required to be given information relating to a transaction in writing, the E-Sign Act allows the use of an electronic format if certain consent and disclosure requirements are met as follows:

(A) the consumer has affirmatively consented to such use and has not withdrawn such consent;

(B) the consumer, prior to consenting, is provided with a clear and conspicuous statement—

(i) informing the consumer of (I) any right or option of the consumer to have the record provided or made available on paper or in non-electronic form, and (II) the right of the consumer to withdraw the consent to have the record provided or made available in an electronic form and of any conditions, consequences (which may include termination of the parties' relationship) or fees in the event of such withdrawal;

(ii) informing the consumer of whether the consent applies (I) only to the particular transaction which gave rise to the obligation to provide the record, or (II) to identified categories of records that may be provided or made available during the course of the parties' relationship;

(iii) describing the procedures the consumer must use to withdraw consent as provided in clause (i) and to update information needed to contact the consumer electronically; and

(iv) informing the consumer (I) how, after the consent, the consumer may, upon request, obtain a paper copy of an electronic record, and (II) whether any fee will be charged for such copy;

(C) the consumer—

(i) prior to consenting, is provided with a statement of the hardware and software requirements for access to and retention of the electronic records; and

(ii) consents electronically, or confirms his or her consent electronically, in a manner that reasonably demonstrates that the consumer can access information in the electronic form that will be used to provide the information that is the subject of the consent; and

(D) after the consent of a consumer in accordance with subparagraph (A), if a change in the hardware or software requirements needed to access or retain electronic records creates a material risk that the consumer will not be able to access or retain a subsequent electronic record that was the subject of the consent, the person providing the electronic record—

(i) provides the consumer with a statement of (I) the revised hardware and software requirements for access to and retention of the electronic records, and (II) the right to withdraw consent without the imposition of any fees for such withdrawal and without the imposition of any condition or consequence that was not disclosed under subparagraph (B)(i); and

(ii) again complies with subparagraph (C).

Electronic disclosure agreements made with consumers prior to October 1, 2000 are exempt from these requirements but may be subject to rules issued by the Federal Reserve Board.

Under the E-Sign Act, the federal banking agencies and other government agencies are authorized to interpret the Act's provisions and exempt by regulation particular categories of disclosures from the Act's consumer consent requirements. The Federal Reserve Board has requested public comment on how the Act's consumer consent requirements apply for purposes of the laws administered by the Board, such as the Electronic Funds Transfer Act and Regulation E thereunder and whether the Board should exercise its authority in future rulemakings to interpret the consumer consent provisions as they affect the Board's consumer protection regulations:

> Comment is requested on whether the statutory provisions relating to consumer consent are sufficient, or whether additional guidance is needed. For example, is interpretive guidance needed concerning the statutory requirement that consumers confirm their consent electronically in a manner that reasonably demonstrates they can access informa-

tion in the form to be used by the financial institution? Is clarification needed on the effect of consumers' withdrawing their consent, or on requesting paper copies of electronic disclosures? Institutions must also inform consumers of changes in hardware or software requirements if the change creates a material risk that the consumer will not be able to access or retain the disclosure. The Board solicits comment on whether regulatory standards are needed for determining a "material risk" for purposes of Regulation E and other financial services and fair lending laws administered by the Board, and if so what standards should apply.

Under section 104(d) of the E-Sign Act, the Board is authorized to exempt specific disclosures from the consumer consent requirements of section 101(c) of the E-Sign Act, if the exemption is necessary to eliminate a substantial burden on electronic commerce and will not increase the material risk of harm to consumers. The Board requests comment on whether it should consider exercising this exemption authority.[5]

[D] Preemption of State Law

The E-Sign Act generally preempts state law unless the state law constitutes an enactment of the Uniform Electronic Transactions Act as approved and recommended for enactment in all of the states by the National Conference of Commissioners on Uniform State Laws in 1999. *See* § 4.11 for a discussion of the Uniform Act. State law also may govern if it specifies alternative procedures or requirements for the use or acceptance of electronic records or electronic signatures to establish the legal effect of contracts or records if such procedures or requirements "do not require, or accord greater legal status or effect to, the implementation or application of a specific technology or technical specification for performing the functions of creating, generating, receiving, communicating, or authenticating electronic records or electronic signatures."

[E] Studies

The Secretary of Commerce is required to conduct an inquiry regarding the "effectiveness of the delivery of electronic records to consumers using electronic mail as compared with the delivery of written records via the United States Postal Service and private express mail services" and report to Congress within one year. In addition, the Secretary of Commerce and the Federal Trade Commission are required to report to

---

[5] 66 Fed. Reg. __ (Apr. 2001).

Congress within one year on the benefits and burdens to consumers of the consent requirements of the Act and whether the benefits outweigh the burdens and whether the absence of the consent procedure would increase the incidence of fraud against consumers.

[F] Promotion of International Electronic Commerce

The E-Sign Act requires the Secretary of Commerce to "promote the acceptance and use, on an international basis, of electronic signatures." The Secretary is required to take all actions necessary to "eliminate or reduce, to the maximum extent possible, the impediments to commerce in electronic signatures, for the purpose of facilitating the developing of interstate and foreign commerce" in a manner consistent with the following principles:

- Remove paper-based obstacles to electronic transactions by adopting relevant principles from the Model Law on Electronic Commerce adopted in 1996 by the United Nations Commission on International Trade Law.
- Permit parties to a transaction to determine the appropriate authentication technologies and implementation models for their transactions, with assurance that those technologies and implementation models will be recognized and enforced.
- Permit parties to a transaction to have the opportunity to prove in court or other proceedings that their authentication approaches and their transactions are valid.
- Take a nondiscriminatory approach to electronic signatures and authentication methods from other jurisdictions.

§ 16.03 STATE LAWS

A number of states have adopted digital signature laws to give legal effect to computerized signatures and minimize forgery.[6] Under

[6] *See, e.g.,* California Senate Bill 1124, signed into law July 28, 1999; Oregon House Bill 3041 and Senate Bill 240, signed into law July 14, 1999; Arkansas Bill 1631, signed April 6, 1999; Colorado House Bill 1079, signed June 2, 1999; Connecticut House Bill 6592, signed June 23, 1999; Iowa House Bill 624, signed May 19, 1999; Louisiana House Bill 1587, signed June 16, 1999; Missouri House Bill 795; signed July 9, 1999; Montana House Bill 188, signed April 20, 1999; Nevada Assembly Bill 674, signed May 29, 1999; Texas House Bill 806, signed June 19, 1999; Washington Senate Bill 5962, signed May 13, 1999.

the typical digital signature law, a CA certifies that the information about the sender and the sender's public key is accurate and assumes liability if it is not. States generally have avoided imposing specific rules for digital signatures or imposing liability or licensing regimes and instead have adopted generalized enabling and supporting legislation that endorses the use of digital signatures. This non-regulatory approach appears to be supported by international bodies that have issued guidance on digital signature laws.

Utah was the first state to adopt a legal framework for digital signatures. The Utah Digital Signature Act of 1995[7] provides a framework for the use of cryptography for authentication and integrity purposes. Contrary to the prevailing approach, Utah requires certification authorities to be licensed, requires a certification authority to maintain a surety bond or letter of credit to cover any liability incurred, and provides for annual auditing by the state Division of Corporations.

The standards of care applicable to CAs are not uniform among the various statutes. Under the Utah statute, for example, a CA is not liable for false or forged digital signatures.

The National Conference of Commissioners on Uniform State Laws in 1999 adopted a draft model Uniform Electronic Transactions Act ("UETA") for adoption by the states. The final draft limits UETA to electronic records and signatures in commercial transactions, including transactions with consumers.[8] California has adopted UETA effective January 1, 2000, and at least 27 state legislatures are expected to consider UETA in 2000.[9] UETA provides, *inter alia*, that a record or signature may not be denied legal effect or enforceability under state law solely because it is in electronic form and, if a state law requires a signature, an electronic signature satisfies the law. UETA applies only when the parties agree to conduct a transaction electronically.

The Information Security Committee of the American Bar Association's Section on Science and Technology has issued Digital Signature

---

[7] Utah Code Ann. §§ 46-3-101 *et seq.* (1995), as amended by 1996 Utah Laws 188. *See also* Washington Digital Signature Act, Wash. Rev. Code §§ 19.34.010 *et seq.*; Mississippi Digital Signature Act of 1997, 1997 Miss. Laws 329.

[8] The draft is available at ⟨⟨*www.law.upenn.edu/library/ulc/uecicta/etaam99.htm*⟩⟩.

[9] *See generally* Robert Ballen and Thomas Fox, "The New Uniform Electronic Transactions Act: A Framework for Electronic Commerce," Electronic Banking Law and Commerce Report (Sept. 1999), at 8.

Guidelines.[10] While nonbinding, the guidelines are available for use by states considering digital signature legislation.

§ 16.04 REGULATORY INITIATIVES

The OCC has permitted national banks to act as certification authorities in verifying digital signatures.[11] Such activities may involve acting as a repository maintaining a database of certificate information, transmitting digital signatures, and providing related software. The OCC viewed the activity as similar to a notary service, noting that such activity has been upheld as part of the business of banking by the courts.[12] Moreover, said the OCC, "one of the core competencies of banks is verification of identity and the authentication of transactions based upon that verification." The OCC stated that a bank need not have fiduciary powers to provide key escrow services when acting as a certification authority. Among the risk management measures that the OCC noted should be used by a bank acting as a certification authority is conformance with relevant standards established by the American National Standards Institute, National Institute of Standards and Technology, and National Security Agency. The OCC also indicated that the system's architecture should be accredited by the National Voluntary Laboratory Accreditation Program.

The OCC also has authorized national banks to conduct research and development in connection with the establishment of an identity certification service based initially on digital signature technology.[13] The OCC in 1999 issued a bulletin describing the elements of certification authority and the role of banks in such systems, and addressing risk-management issues.[14] The OCC advised banks that wish to participate in certification authority systems to first consult with the agency's legal or licensing staff to determine whether a legal interpretation or regulatory filing is necessary.

The OCC has authorized Bank of America, Citibank, and a consortium of other banks to establish and operate a global, interoperable network of participating financial institutions that will operate as certification

---

[10] ABA Information Security Committee, *Digital Signature Guidelines: Legal Infrastructure for Certification Authorities and Secure Electronic Commerce* (1996).

[11] OCC Conditional Approval No. 267 (Jan. 12, 1998) (Zions First National Bank).

[12] *Transamerica Ins. Co. v. The Valley Nat'l Bank*, 11 Ariz. App. 121, 462 P.2d 814 (1969).

[13] OCC Conditional Approval No. 301 (Jan. 15, 1999).

[14] OCC Bulletin 99-20, Certification Authority Systems (May 4, 1999), posted at ⟨⟨*www.occ.treas.gov/ftp/bulletin99-20*⟩⟩.

authorities.[15] Under the proposal, each participant would issue digital certificates to commercial customers and their employees based on a set of uniform system rules, minimum operating standards, and common business practices. The Federal Reserve Board also approved investments by several bank holding companies in the network.[16]

The National Association of Securities Dealers, Inc. has allowed broker-dealers to utilize electronic signatures in complying with a rule requirement that broker-dealers maintain, for each new customer account, a signature of the registered representative introducing the account and the signature of the manager who accepts the account.[17]

§ 16.05 INTERNATIONAL INITIATIVES

On the international level, a number of international bodies and individual countries have addressed the need for digital signature laws.[18] Germany was the first country to adopt a Digital Signature Act.[19]

In 1998, the United Nations Commission on International Trade Law ("UNCITRAL") presented a draft of uniform rules on electronic signatures.[20] The draft rules are intended to provide a basis for harmonizing the growing diversity of digital signature laws based on the principle of media-neutrality. Although public key cryptography is the predominant technique for digital signatures, the uniform rules are drafted so as not to discourage the use of other authentication techniques. The uniform rules do not impose any minimum standards for certification authorities. The United States government has proposed an International Convention on Electronic Transactions to discuss the uniform rules as well as UNCITRAL's draft Model Law on Electronic Commerce.[21]

---

[15] OCC Conditional Approval No. 339 (Nov. 16, 1999).

[16] *Bayerische Hypo- und Vereinsbank AG, et al.*, 86 Fed. Res. Bull. 56 (2000).

[17] *See* Letter dated November 26, 1997, to American Express Financial Corporation, from David A. Spotts, Office of General Counsel, NASD Regulation.

[18] *See* Organization for Economic Cooperation and Development, *Cryptography Policy* (1997); *Ministerial Declaration on Authentication for Electronic Commerce* (1998); *Inventory of Approaches to Authentication and Certification, Background Paper* (1998).

[19] For an excellent article on the German law, *see* Hanno Beck, "An Overview of the German Digital Signature Law," E-Money, Vol. 1, No. 5 (Sept. 1998).

[20] UNCITRAL, *Draft Uniform Rules on Electronic Signatures*, presented at the 39th Session of the Commission (July 1998).

[21] UNCITRAL, *Draft International Convention on Electronic Transactions*, U.S. Proposal to the Working Group on Electronic Commerce (July 1998).

The OECD has issued guidelines identifying issues that countries should take into consideration in the development of cryptography policies.[22] The OECD also has provided a report summarizing laws and regulations in OECD member countries relating to cryptography techniques, focusing on domestic controls and import/export restrictions.

The European Commission has proposed a European directive on a common framework for electronic signatures.[23] The framework is based on the following conclusions:

- The increasing legislative activity in this area in several Member States emphasizes the urgent need for a harmonized legal framework at the European level so as to avoid the development of serious obstacles to the functioning of the Internet Market.
- While there is much discussion and work on digital signature technologies that employ public key cryptograph, a Directive at the European level should be technology-neutral and should not focus only on these kinds of signatures. Since a variety of authentication mechanisms is expected to develop, the scope of this Directive should be broad enough to cover a spectrum of "electronic signatures," which would include digital signatures based on public-key cryptography as well as other means of authenticating data.
- In order to ensure the functioning of the Internal Market and to support the rapid development of the market in terms of user demand and technological innovation, prior authorization has to be avoided. As a means to gain the confidence of consumers, voluntary accreditation schemes for certification service provider aiming at providing enhanced levels of security is considered to be useful. As far as such measures are required by the market, they could give a clearer or more predictable level of legal security for both the certification service provider and the consumer.

---

[22] OECD, *Guidelines on Cryptography Policy* (1997).

[23] European Commission, *Proposal for a European Parliament and Council Directive on a Common Framework for Electronic Signatures* (May 13, 1998).

- Electronic signatures used within closed groups, for example, where contractual relationships already exist, should not automatically fall within the scope of this Directive. Contractual freedom should prevail in such a context.
- Ensuring legal recognition—in particular across borders—of electronic signatures and of certification services is regarded as the most important issue in this area. This involves clarifying the essential requirements for certification service providers, including their liability.
- Industry is supposed to take the lead with standardization bodies in developing internationally agreed standards for electronic signatures. These standards should focus on establishing an open environment for interoperable products and services. The role of the Commission will be to support this process.
- Ongoing activities at the international level should be taken into account in the implementation of a legal framework at the European level.

The proposal noted that a number of European countries have commenced drafting of digital signature and certification laws taking different approaches and that "divergent rules concerning the legal effect attributed to electronic signature are particularly detrimental to the further development of electronic commerce and, for this reason, to economic growth and employment in the [European] Community. Further uncertainty results from different liability rules and the risk of uncertain jurisdiction concerning liability where services are provided among different Member States."[24]

[24] *Id.*

Appendices

LAW OF ELECTRONIC BANKING

Appendices

APPENDICES SUMMARY OF CONTENTS

Appendix B4 OCC Conditional Approval No. 254 (Aug. 21, 1997) (authorizing Citibank to become a member of the MECA Software venture)

Appendix B5 OCC Conditional Approval No. 289 (Oct. 2, 1998) (authorizing a group of national banks to acquire CheckFree Corporation and thereby provide electronic commerce services)

Appendix C1 OCC Corporate Decision 97-60 (July 1, 1997) (approving Internet-based finder activities related to sales of used automobiles)

Appendix C2 OCC Corporate Decision 98-13 (Feb. 9, 1998) (authorizing national bank to operate the Smart Telephone Agent Referral and Response System for tracking telephone call topics, callers, and responses in connection with medical premium collection and disbursement services)

Appendix D1 *Banc One Corp., et. al.,* 79 Fed. Res. Bull. 1158 (1993) (authorizing bank holding companies to engage in electronic benefit transfer services, stored value card services, and electronic data interchange services)

Appendix D2 *Banc One Corp.,* 80 Fed. Res. Bull. 139 (1994) (authorizing bank holding company to operate a network for processing and transmission of medical payment data between physicians, hospitals, and pharmacies and health insurers)

Appendix D3 *The Bank of New York Co., et al.,* 80 Fed. Res. Bull. 1107 (1994) (authorizing bank holding companies to provide ATM services, including scrip services enabling customers to receive vouchers redeemable for cash at a retail location)

Appendix D4 *State Street Boston Corp./First National Bank of Boston,* 81 Fed. Res. Bull. 1049 (1995) (approving joint venture engaged in providing electronic shareholder and bankruptcy services to securities issuers)

Appendix D5 *Norwest Corp.,* 81 Fed. Res. Bull. 1130 (1995) (authorizing bank holding company to money transmission services)

Appendix D6 *First National of Nebraska, Inc.,* 82 Fed. Res. Bull. 82 (1995) (authorizing bank holding company to provide advice to other financial institutions in the design, selection, acquisition, installation, and operation of computer networks)

Appendix D7 *Compagnie Financiere de Paribas,* 82 Fed. Res. Bull. 348 (1996) (authorizing billing and account-related services through an integrated software program for operators of digital mobile telephone networks)

Appendix D8 *Banc One Corp., et al.,* 82 Fed. Res. Bull. 848 (1996) (authorizing ATM distribution of tickets, gift certificates, prepaid telephone cards, etc.)

Appendix D9 *Royal Bank of Canada, et. al.,* 83 Fed. Res. Bull. 135 (1997) (approving bank holding company ownership of Integrion Financial Network)

Appendix E1 FDIC General Counsel's Opinion No. 8 (Stored Value Cards) (1996)

Appendix A1
OCC Interpretive Letter No. 677 (June 28, 1995)

Patrick S. Antrim
Senior Counsel
Bank of America N.T. and S.A.
555 California Street
San Francisco, CA 94104

Gerald P. Hurst
Assistant General Counsel
NationsBank, N.A. (Carolinas)
101 South Tryon Street
Charlotte, NC 28255

Dear Messrs. Antrim and Hurst:

This is in response to your letter of May 12, 1995, providing notice to the OCC concerning the proposed establishment of operating subsidiaries by your two Banks to engage through a joint venture in the development and distribution of home banking and financial management software and data processing services. For the reasons given below, we conclude that the proposed activities are permissible and, pursuant to 12 C.F.R. 5.34, approve the operating subsidiary applications subject to the conditions specified.

Description of the Proposal

The operating subsidiaries plan to enter into a joint venture arrangement by forming a Delaware limited liability company ("LLC") to acquire the stock of MECA Software, Inc. ("MECA") through a cash forward merger transaction, with the LLC being the surviving entity. Each of the operating subsidiaries will own 50 percent of the LLC. Following the acquisition of MECA, the LLC will be renamed MECA Software, LLC. By acquiring MECA through the use of a joint venture, the costs associated with the acquisition and ongoing operation of the entity may be shared by the Banks. It is expected that in the future a limited number of other banks and technology companies will become members of the LLC.

MECA currently develops and markets computer software products, including the Managing Your Money personal financial management program, designed to assist individuals and small businesses manage their finances. Using Managing Your Money as the basis for a home banking service, MECA has entered into several licensing and distribution arrangements with banking and financial service companies. The personal finance software is distributed directly to customers through retail sales by retailers, mail order companies and other retail outlets, and indirectly through financial institutions.

The Banks' proposed joint venture through the LLC will continue the majority of the existing activities of MECA utilizing existing management, personnel and facilities of MECA. Specifically, the joint venture will engage in those activities related to the provision of home banking and financial management services through the development, production, marketing and distribution of computer software and related services. The joint venture will not engage in non-financial computer software development and distribution except to the extent the activities are a result of utilization of excess data processing, production, and distribution capacity.

The Banks believe that PC-based home banking is an important delivery channel for providing financial services to banking customers and that the services can be provided to customers in the most effective and efficient manner by providing them through the use of bank-focused computer software. Currently, there is no bank-focused entity that provides the needed services and, in the opinion of the Banks, the absence of such a provider could prove detrimental to banks that wish to provide PC-based home banking services to their customers in the future.

The acquisition of MECA will provide the Banks with important expertise in the development of PC-based home banking software and form the basis for development of a standard bank-focused home banking and financial management system. The software is critical to the transaction processing and electronic information handling requirements for home banking. The Banks' joint venture will provide the products and services indirectly to consumers through their banks, other financial institutions, networks and bank card associations, and directly through retail distribution to consumers, both individual and small business. With respect to providing the software and home banking services directly to their customers, the Banks expect to provide the products and services primarily in the principal geographic areas served by the Banks and their subsidiary and affiliated organizations.

Legal Analysis

The OCC has on several recent occasions allowed a national bank to engage in permissible activities through use of an LLC. See, e.g., Interpretative Letter No. 657, March 31, 1995, reprinted in [Current] Fed. Banking L. Rep. (CCH) para. 83,605; Interpretive Letter No. 645, April 29, 1994, reprinted in [1994

Transfer Binder] Fed. Banking L. Rep. (CCH) para. 83,554; Unpublished Letter of Senior Deputy Comptroller Maguire, Oct. 14, 1994. The Maguire Letter approved of a national bank's holding of a 50 percent interest in an LLC through an operating subsidiary of the bank, the precise structure proposed in your notice. The pertinent conditions set forth in this Letter required that the documentation establishing the LLC specify that it would engage only in activities permissible for national banks under 12 U.S.C. 24(Seventh), that the LLC agreement provide that the operating subsidiary could withdraw from the LLC if the latter engaged in impermissible activities, and that the bank would be shielded from unlimited liability for the acts of other partners and joint venturers. You indicate in your notice that the Banks will comply with these conditions.

The notice in an appendix explains that MECA software programs consist essentially of home banking, tax estimation, financial planning, and investment analysis components, and ancillary services relating thereto, including the furnishing of checks and other financial forms for the use of customers. All of these types of activities or services have been approved for national banks and their subsidiaries. See, e.g., Interpretive Letter No. 611, Nov. 23, 1992, reprinted in [1992-93 Transfer Binder] Fed. Banking L. Rep. (CCH) para. 83,449 (home banking for customers of the bank itself and for customers of other financial institutions using the bank's data processing equipment and program); Interpretive Ruling 7.7430, 12 C.F.R. 7.7430 (assistance in preparing tax returns); Interpretive Letter No. 367, Aug. 19, 1986, reprinted in [1985-87 Transfer Binder] Fed. Banking L. Rep. (CCH) para. 85,537 (financial planning and counselling); and Interpretive Letter No. 386, June 19, 1987, reprinted in [1988-89 Transfer Binder] Fed. Banking L. Rep. (CCH) para. 85,610 (investment analysis and advice). These approvals and others which might be cited allow the mentioned services to be provided to customers whether or not data processing equipment and programs are utilized.

Interpretive Ruling 7.3500, 12 C.F.R. 7.3500, "Use of data processing equipment and furnishing of data processing services" (1994), makes clear that a national bank may use data processing equipment and technology to perform for itself and others all services which are part of or incidental to the business of banking. An earlier version of this ruling gave an example of permissible data processing: "For example, as part of its banking business and incidental thereto, a national bank may collect, transcribe, process, analyze, and store for itself and others, banking, financial, or related economic data", Interpretive Ruling 7.3500, 39 Fed. Reg. 14195 (Apr. 22, 1974). Although in its 1984 revision of the ruling the OCC deleted this example because it believed that "specific examples are inappropriate given the imprecision of terms and rapid pace of change in the data processing industry", 49 Fed. Reg. 11157 (Mar. 26, 1984), the "analytical framework" embodied in the ruling remained the same, id.

A long line of OCC interpretations have permitted national banks in a variety of circumstances to collect, process, analyze, etc. for their customers banking, financial, or related economic data. In some instances the banks have sold relevant data processing equipment and software programs as an incident to the services being provided to their customers. See, e.g., Letter by Deputy Chief Counsel Shockey, Sept. 17, 1975 (economic analysis and forecasts, including security data and stock and bond prices); Letter by BOSD Director Pohn, Nov. 19, 1975 (processing of claims, accounts, billings, and financial reports for banks, retailers, insurance agents, and doctors); Interpretive Letter No. 345, July 9, 1985, reprinted in [1985-87 Transfer Binder] Fed. Banking L. Rep. (CCH) para. 85,515 (sale of computer hardware as part of a package of bank services provided through data processing); Interpretive Letter No. 346, July 31, 1985, id. at para. 85,516 (joint venture providing electronic information and transaction services in connection with commodities trading; the electronic information provided subscribers with banking, financial and related economic data relevant to commodities); Letter by District Counsel O'Keefe, July 13, 1987 (sale and licensing of computer software and related hardware to other financial institutions is permissible so long as the hardware does not "dominate" the permissible data processing services involved); Letter by Law Dept. Assistant Director Glidden, Feb. 16, 1988 (development and operation of data processing system linking health care providers, insurers, patients, and their depository institutions); Interpretive Letter No. 449, Aug. 23, 1988, reprinted in [1988-89 Transfer Binder] Fed. Banking L. Rep. (CCH) para. 85,673 (bank can provide software applications and systems for other financial institutions' backroom operations, allowing them, for example, to secure funds transfers, sort and process exception transactions, research and retrieve customer account information, prepare forms and monetary adjustments, and engage in recordkeeping and tracking services); Interpretive Letter No. 611, supra (bank can use "smart phone" developed by AT&T to offer a variety of data processing services to financial institutions and their customers, including balance inquiries, account transfers, transaction information, bill paying, financial planning, investments and stock market information and transactions, electronic checkbook, and electronic tax filing).

Interpretive Letter No. 284, March 26, 1984, reprinted in [1983-84 Transfer Binder] Fed. Banking L. Rep. (CCH) para. 85,448 allowed a bank to acquire a data processing company as an operating subsidiary and to use the software which had been developed by the company for the bank's own data processing activities, and for the data processing activities of the bank's customers, thereby providing those customers with access to the bank's banking, financial and economic data bases. This letter reserved for further consideration the question of whether the software could be marketed on a stand-alone basis to third parties generally as a by-product of the bank's other permissible data processing activities, noting that in the past the OCC had taken the position that programs marketed as by-products should be developed in-house, not acquired from third parties. Interpretive Letter No. 449, supra, allowed the bank to acquire a data processing company as an operating subsidiary, and to sell the company's software on a stand-alone basis to the bank's financial institution customers. It distinguished Interpretive Letter No. 284 as involving the marketing of software to third parties which were not financial institutions or financial institution customers.

You make two points in support of your Banks being able to market the MECA software which has been developed to date on a stand-alone basis to third parties generally, not limiting the marketing to financial institutions and financial institution customers. First, you observe that most of the software is banking and finance-related, and therefore should be able to be marketed as a permissible incidental-to-banking services package. In effect, this software is not a "by-product" at all, and should be able to be marketed to anyone. Second, you state that with respect to any software that is not banking and finance-related, the Banks were intimately involved in the development of MECA software as a whole. In this sense, the software "by-products" should be considered as having been developed by the Banks in-house, not as being merely acquired from some unrelated third party. These two points appear to be correct based upon the factual descriptions provided and are consistent with the OCC precedents. Moreover, subsequent to the publication of Interpretive Letter No. 284, supra, OCC staff took the position in an internal memorandum, dated August 17, 1984, that some software acquired from a company which the bank was acquiring as an operating subsidiary could be marketed as a by-product if this seemed appropriate in the circumstances. In the situation presented, the OCC decided that the data processing company was being acquired for its entire operation, not primarily to obtain the software in question.

Finally, your notice and a follow-up communication request approval for the continued use of MECA's excess capacity in equipment, personnel and facilities for the producing and distribution of some software products that are non-financial in nature. In 1994 financial software accounted for approximately 75 percent of the units of software produced and non-financial software accounted for the remaining 25 percent; 93 percent of MECA's revenues were generated from the financial software. You anticipate that in 1995 a similar percentage of excess capacity will be involved, and that in future years the excess capacity usage will be reduced. This is an acceptable current and future use of excess capacity. Until its revision in 1984, the OCC's data processing ruling expressly stated that, "incidental to the banking business, a national bank may (1) market a by-product (e.g., program, output, etc.) of [a permissible] data processing activity; and (2) market excess time on its data processing equipment so long as the only involvement by the bank is furnishing the facility and necessary operating personnel." In dropping this language from the ruling in 1984, as mentioned above, the OCC intended no substantive change. The "analytical framework" of Interpretive Ruling 7.3500 remained the same. In a variety of circumstances before and after 1984 OCC interpretations have allowed banks and their subsidiaries to utilize excess capacity in their permissible data processing activities. See, e.g., Letter by Law Dept. Director Fitzgerald, Mar. 22, 1978 (records management system manual, and supply catalog and purchasing manual, may be marketed as by-products of the bank's permissible data processing activity to banks and other institutions); Letter by Law Dept. Assistant Director Liebesman, Dec. 13, 1983 (bank may acquire equipment with excess capacity if, for example, this will meet the bank's projected needs for itself and its customers, or the "most practical equipment" available has an excess capacity); Letter by Attorney Brown, Dec. 20, 1989 (bank can resell excess capacity of its long line telecommunications and data processing equipment and perform related services for unrelated third parties, noting that the authority to market excess time is analogous to a bank's right to lease to tenants the excess portion of its bank premises property). The last letter cited also noted that the 1984 ruling change was not intended to be substantive in nature.

In sum, your Banks may go forward with their plan to engage through a joint venture in the development and distribution of home banking and financial management software and data processing services subject to the following conditions: (1) The articles of organization and Operating Agreement must specifically state that the LLC will engage only in activities which are legally permissible for national banks; (2) the articles of organization and Operating Agreement must acknowledge that the Banks have the authority to veto or withdraw from the LLC in the event that the LLC engages in activities otherwise impermissible for national banks; and (3) the articles of organization and Operating Agreement must provide that the Banks, as members of the LLC, will not be liable for the debts, obligations or liabilities of the other members.

If you have any questions, please contact Richard Erb, Licensing Manager, at (202) 874-4610.

Sincerely,

Frank Maguire
Senior Deputy Comptroller
Corporate Activities and Policy Analysis

APPENDIX A2
OCC Interpretive Letter No. 712 (Feb. 29, 1996)

Comptroller of the Currency
Washington, DC 20219

Release Date: March 1996

Re: [Material Deleted in Original] /Factoring of Medical Receivables

This is in response to your February 7, 1996 letter to William Glidden, Assistant Director, Bank Activities and Structure Division, in which you inquired whether certain activities in which your client, [Material Deleted in Original] ("Bank"), wishes to engage are permissible for national banks.

According to your letter, the Bank proposes to set up a division within the Bank to engage in two different activities. The first would involve the factoring of medical receivables for doctors, clinics, and medical facilities. In connection with these services, the Bank would purchase the medical receivables and file insurance claims to collect the amounts owed. In the second, the Bank would provide billing, filing and collection services to non-factoring clients for a fee. The Bank anticipates that the activities performed for non-factoring clients would amount to no more than thirty percent of the total services to be rendered by this new division.

Both of these are permissible activities for national banks. With respect to the first, factoring involves the direct purchase of a customer's accounts receivable without recourse, including the assumption of the risks and responsibilities of making collection. Factoring is permitted for national banks under *12 U.S.C. § 24(7)* and Interpretive Ruling 7.1105, 12 C.F.R. § 7.1105. Interpretive Ruling 7.1105, "Purchase of open accounts," specifically provides that

> The purchase of open accounts is a part of the business of banking and

> within the power of a national bank. Such accounts need not in every case represent an evidence of debt.[1]

The purchase of another party's accounts is therefore a permissible activity. It is subject to the lending limits as an indirect advance of funds to the seller under 12 C.F.R. § 32.2(a). Further, the Bank should be aware that a factor's ability successfully to purchase receivables without recourse is predicated on the factor's ability to make sound credit judgments, and to follow prudent safety and soundness principles in engaging in such activity.

With respect to the second proposed activity, the providing of billing services to physicians and clinics, it is well established that national banks may provide billing services to their customers as an activity incidental to the express authority to process payment instruments for customers. The OCC's position on this issue was clearly stated in a 1985 letter which opined that national banks may "[bill] persons for fees owed to doctors, hospitals, and other service providers." Letter from Peter Liebesman, Assistant Director, Legal Advisory Services Division (August 27, 1985) ("Liebesman Letter"). That letter noted that the OCC has traditionally looked to the usual and necessary functions banks undertake in collecting their own loans as a guide to the OCC's determination of whether a particular activity is a permissible means of "servicing" debts owed to others. Since it is both usual and necessary for banks to undertake collection activities with respect to their own delinquent loans, it is permissible for national banks to collect delinquent loans on others' behalf. Further, the OCC recognizes that banks may provide billing services to collect amounts due in repayment of money lent and in payment of other forms of receivables. Since billing activities form an integral part of the means by which debts are collected by banks, it has been the OCC's position that banks may provide billing services to collect amounts due to others.

As discussed in the Liebesman Letter, the billing service you describe falls within the scope of the incidental powers clause of *12 U.S.C.* § *24*(7). Its permissibility for national banks has been reiterated in subsequent OCC letters. See Letter from Coreen Arnold, Senior Attorney (June 30, 1988); Letter from Horace Sneed, Senior Attorney (December 6, 1993) ("Sneed Letter"). The Sneed Letter also considered the issue whether national banks may fill out and submit insurance claim forms, and stated that such a service is permissible because it is substantially equivalent to the billing services already approved. Its reasoning, which still represents the OCC view, was as follows:

> The Bank's physician customers look to the insurance companies as potential

---

[1]The OCC has recently revised a number of interpretive rulings, including I.R. § 7.1105, as part of a regulatory review program to update and streamline OCC regulations. These revised rulings were published in the Federal Register on February 9, 1996 (*61 F.R. 4849*) and will become effective April 1, 1996. On that date, *I.R. 7*.1105 will be replaced with new *I.R. 7*. 1020, which is essentially the same as the present interpretive ruling.

> third-party payors for the services provided to the patients. To obtain payment, the physicians submit claim forms identifying the patient, date of service, the patient's insurance identification number, the services rendered, and the amount charged for those services. This is substantially the same information that national banks would deal with in providing billing services to physicians. Moreover, the process of filling out claim forms according to the physicians' instructions is similar to preparing bills. Therefore, I believe that preparing the insurance forms is simply a variation of previously approved billing services and a permissible activity for national banks.

Both of the services you describe are permissible activities to be performed by national banks. Please contact me at (202) 874-5300 if you have any further questions.

I trust that this has been responsive to your inquiry.

Sincerely,

/s/

Sue E. Auerbach
Senior Attorney
Bank Activities and Structure Division

APPENDIX A3
OCC Interpretive Letter No. 718 (March 14, 1996)

Comptroller of the Currency
Washington, DC 20219

Release Date March 14, 1996

Re: * * * and * * * Request to Confirm Authority to Undertake Certain Activities

This is in response to your letter dated January 16, 1996 and February 20, 1996. You have requested, on behalf of * * * and its affiliate * * * (collectively, the "Banks"), confirmation that the Banks may dispense "alternate media" from all of their approved CBCT branches. You define the term "alternate media" to include any medium of value, receipt or document that is not coin or currency and specifically refer to the following: (1) public transportation tickets, (2) event and attraction tickets, (3) gift certificates, (3) prepaid phone cards, and (5) similar forms of alternate media, such as promotional and advertising materials, electronic benefits transfer ("EBT") script, and credit and debit cards. We conclude that the Banks may, under the authority of 12 U.S.C. § 24(7), dispense the "alternate media" listed in your letter from their approved CBCT branches

Description of the Proposed Activity

The Banks currently operate CBCT branches in the states of * * * and * * *. The Banks propose to expand upon the routine services currently offered at the CBCTs. Specifically, the Banks propose to dispense from those CBCTs "alternate media," i.e., public transportation tickets, event and attraction tickets, gift certificates, prepaid phone cards, promotional and advertising materials, EBT script and credit and debit cards.

The proposed new activities are described as follows in your letter. When the ATM cardholder inserts his or her card into the ATM, the cardholder will be able to select the alternate media purchase option, select the associated dollar amount and supply any other necessary information relating to the specific alternate medium. Electronically, the cost of the alternate medium will be debited to the cardholder's deposit account. The ATM will dispense the alternate medium with a receipt that complies with Regulation E. Daily posting to a settlement of the cardholder's account will follow the same procedures that apply to a typical point-of-sale ("POS") transaction. The financial institution that issued the ATM card ("Issuer") will transfer to the appropriate Bank (whose ATM dispensed the alternate medium) funds equal to the full amount of the cardholder's debit. Settlement between the Banks and the Issuer will be processed by * * * ("* * *")[1] or a third-party POS processor.

The Banks intend to dispense from the CBCT branches public transportation tickets in the form of passes denominated in fixed dollar amounts or fixed number of trips. The passes would be used for transportation on public rail and bus lines. The CBCTs would also dispense tickets for events and attractions, such as museums, zoos, amusement parks, shows and sporting events. The Banks propose to dispense fixed denomination gift certificates issued by or for the account of a specific merchant or group of merchants.

The certificates will serve as evidence of a prepayment credit, existing in favor of the certificate's bearer, which will be honored by the merchant. The Banks also intend to dispense prepaid phone cards. Like a gift certificate, the prepaid phone card will represent a prepayment credit, in favor of the holder of the card, that will be honored by a long-distance carrier or its agent. The other alternate media which the Banks are considering dispensing include advertising and promotional material, similar to statement "stuffers," postage stamps, travelers' checks, money orders, license renewals and registration, EBT script and credit and debit cards.

The merchants will bear sole responsibility for setting the price of the media or underlying product or service. The Banks will determine the amount of any fees it may charge the cardholder or the merchant for providing the media dispensing function.

Legal Analysis

National banks are authorized under the National Bank Act, 12 U.S.C. § 24(7), to exercise . . . all such incidental powers as shall be necessary to carry on the business of banking; by discounting and negotiation of promissory notes, drafts, bills of exchange, and other evidences of debt; by receiving deposits; by buying and selling exchange, coin, bullion; by loaning money on personal security; and by obtaining, issuing, and circulating notes according to the provisions of [this chapter].

The Supreme Court has recently confirmed that the powers included within the "business of banking" are not limited to the powers enumerated in 12 U.S.C. § 24(7) and that the Comptroller has discretion, within reasonable bounds, to authorize activities beyond those specifically enumerated. See NationsBank v. Variable Annuity Life Ins. Co., 115 S.Ct. 810 (1995) ("VALIC"). VALIC and

[1][* * *] is a corporation which provides ATM and POS support services to financial institutions. [* * *], the parent bank holding company of [* * *] the Banks, is a shareholder of [* * *].

the cases which preceded it reflect three factors that the courts have applied in analyzing whether activities fall within the business of banking: (1) whether the activity is the functional equivalent to or a logical outgrowth of a recognized banking activity, (2) whether the activity benefits bank customers or is convenient or useful to banks, and (3) whether the activity presents risks of a type similar to those already assumed by banks. See, e.g., VALIC, 115 S.Ct. at 811-12; Am. Ins. Ass'n v. Clarke, 865 F.2d 278 (D.C. Cir. 1988); M&M Leasing Corp. v. Seattle First Nat'l Bank, 563 F.2d 1377 (9th Cir. 1977); Arnold Tours, Inc. v. Camp, 472 F.2d 427 (1st Cir. 1972). Moreover, a national bank may use electronic data processing equipment and technology to perform any authorized activity. See 12 C.F.R. § 7.3500; see also 61 Fed. Reg 4849, 4865 (final rule amending 12 C.F.R. § 7.3500, to be codified at 12 C.F.R. § 7.1019, effective Apr. 1, 1996) (national bank may perform, provide or deliver any authorized activity, function, product or service through electronic means).

Many of the activities that the Banks propose to engage in from their CBCT branches have long been held to be part of or incidental to the business of banking. Specifically, national banks have been permitted to sell postage stamps, see 12 C.F.R. § 7.7482, travelers' checks, see Arnold Tours, 472 F.2d at 438, money orders, see 12 C.F.R. § 7.7500, and act as an agent for the state in selling and renewing license plates and license tags, see Corbett v. Devon Bank, 299 N.E.2d 521, 529 (Ill. App. Ct.1988); Letter from Stephen B. Brown, Attorney (Dec. 13, 1989) (unpublished). The OCC also has allowed national banks to distribute advertising and promotional information about non-banking products. See OCC Interpretive Letter No. 316, reprinted in [1985-87 Transfer Binder] Fed. Banking Law Rep. (CCH) ¶ 85,486. National banks are authorized to disperse food stamps and government welfare checks (the paper equivalent of EBT script). See Philadelphia Check Cashiers Assoc. v. Heimann, No. 79-1318 (D. Pa. March 12, 1980) (unpublished decision). National banks have been issuing credit and debit cards under their section 24(7) authority to maintain loan and deposit relationships with customers and to enable the customers to make payments to and withdrawals from those accounts.

Accordingly, the Banks may engage in these same activities by electronic means through their CBCT branches.

The four remaining proposed activities, i.e., the dispensing of public transportation tickets, event and attraction tickets, gift certificates, and prepaid phone cards, are similar to each other in that the alternate media being dispensed represent the cardholder's prepayment for a merchant's goods or services. The Banks, in dispensing these four media (collectively referred to herein as the "prepayment media"), are essentially performing a bill payment function by transferring funds from the cardholder's account to the merchant's account. The transfer of funds from one account to another is a fundamental part of the business of banking. See Letter from Robert B. Serino, Deputy Chief Counsel (Nov. 9, 1992) (unpublished) (participation in an EFT system which operates POS terminals is part of or incidental to the business of banking and therefore permissible for national banks); see also OCC Interpretive Letter No. 419, reprinted in [1988-89 Transfer Binder] Fed. Banking Law Rep. (CCH) ¶ 85,643 (national banks may participate as limited partners in a joint venture which facilitates settlement and payment of health insurance claims through the use of EFT technology); Letter from Horace G. Sneed, Senior Attorney (Dec. 6, 1993) (unpublished) (collection, processing and deposit to appropriate accounts of payments from patients and insurance companies is incidental to the business of banking and permissible for national banks). Accordingly, to the extent the proposed activities represent bill payment functions, that activity is permissible for the Banks via their CBCT branches.

The Banks' role in dispensing prepayment media is analagous to aspects of two separate but related functions performed by banks generally in the payments system. First, the proposed activity is similar to a bank's ("Issuing Bank") issuance of a credit card to a bank customer, who will use the card to purchase goods or services from participating merchants. The credit card is a vehicle to allow payments to be made by bank customers to the businesses with whom they deal. Second, the proposed activity is akin to credit card sales draft clearing services provided by a bank ("Merchant Clearing Bank") to those participating merchants. In a typical credit card transaction, the bank customer purchases goods or services from a merchant by charging those items on an Issuing Bank's credit card. The merchant then submits the credit card sales drafts (physically or electronically) to a Merchant Clearing Bank. The Merchant Clearing Bank wires funds in the amount of the sale, less any applicable discount, to the merchant's bank for the merchant's account. The Merchant Clearing Bank receives payment the next day from the Issuing Bank. The Issuing Bank then debits the customers's credit card account for the sales amount. The customer reimburses the Issuing Bank each month, or uses the credit card relationship as a line of credit to be paid back over time. The role of both Issuing Bank and Merchant Clearing Bank in this scenario is essentially a payments service provider and intermediary. The process generally follows this order: customer purchase—credit to merchant account—debit to customer account—customer payment.[2]

Under the instant proposal, the Banks would fulfill the role of both Issuing Bank and Merchant Clearing Bank, although the steps in the process would

[2]POS transactions generally follow a similar process. In a POS transaction, the customer purchases an item with a debit card. The POS terminal captures the necessary information and sends the sales amount electronically through a POS processor to the merchant's bank and customer's bank for recordation. The customer's deposit account is debited for the sales amount; the merchant's account is credited for the sales amount, less any applicable discount or fee. See Barcley Clark, The Law of Bank Deposits, Collections and Credit Cards p 10.7[1] (rev. ed. 1981). The order of processing is: customer purchase-customer payment-debit to customer account-credit to merchant account. OCC Inter. Ltr. 718, Fed. Banking L. Rep. ¶ 81,033, 1996 WL 223691 (O.C.C.)

follow a different order. For example, when a customer purchases a gift certificate from a merchant through an ATM machine, that customer first makes his or her payment to the Bank that dispensed the certificate ("Dispensing Bank"). The bank that issued the ATM card will transfer funds to the Dispensing Bank to cover the customer's payment. The Dispensing Bank will then transfer those funds, less any fees, to the merchant's bank for credit to its account. The customer subsequently purchases goods or services from the merchant with the certificate. The gift certificate is the analogue of the credit card; the gift certificate, rather than the credit card, will be used by the customer as the "payment vehicle." The Dispensing Bank is like the Issuer Bank in the credit card scenario in that it issues the "payment vehicle" to and receives payments from the customer. The Dispensing Bank is like the Merchant Clearing Bank in that it transfers funds to the merchant's bank. The order of this process is generally the reverse of the credit card process: customer payment—debit to customer account—credit to merchant account—customer purchase. The distinctions between the credit card and gift certificate scenarios are procedural, not substantive. In the gift certificate example, as in the credit card scenario, the bank's role will be that of an intermediary, effecting the payment from customer to merchant by transferring funds from one to the other. In this respect, the dispensing of prepayment media is a new way of conducting the old bill payment and funds transfer business of banks.

Unlike a traditional credit card transaction, however, the "sale" under this proposal will occur at the CBCT branch rather than at the merchant's facility. Thus, for those transactions involving a specific merchant or group of merchants, the proposal involves more than just the transfer of funds from one account to another. This aspect of the proposal raises the issue of whether, by dispensing from their CBCT branches the prepayment media on behalf of the merchants, the Banks would be engaged in the sale of goods or services on behalf of the participating merchants, not authorized under section 24(7). See, e.g., OCC No Objection Letter No. 89-02, reprinted in [1989-90 Transfer Binder] Fed. Banking Law Rep. (CCH) ¶ 83,014, at 71,122.

Under the present proposal, the prepayment media that will be dispensed by the Banks' CBCT branches are not the merchants' goods or services. Those media are the documents or devices which evidence a form of value defined in the contracts between the cardholders and the merchants. See, e.g., Vogel v. Saenger Theatres, Inc., 22 So.2d 189, 192 (La. 1945) (theater ticket is only evidence of the fact that the customer has contracted for admission and has fulfilled his part of the agreement); Greenfield v. Maryland Jockey Club of Baltimore, 57 A.2d 335, 336-37 (Md. 1948) (ticket to place of amusement is merely a revocable license, creating a contract but not an interest in land). The media will evidence that the cardholder has paid an appropriate amount for the evidence of value and the merchant has agreed to provide a good or service, e.g., transportation, admission to an event, or a fixed amount of long-distance phone time, in exchange for it. The transaction will not be consummated until the cardholder uses the media to obtain the merchant's goods or services. Thus, the Banks would not be selling the merchants' products or services by dispensing the media.

Making the prepayment media available through the Banks' CBCT branches would provide benefits to both cardholders and to participating merchants. Cardholders would be given an alternative means of obtaining these items. The proposed activity would benefit the participating merchants by providing their customers with greater access to their products and services, and by offering a convenient and reliable method of revenue collection. In sum, by dispensing the prepayment media from their CBCT branches, the Banks will be providing a convenience to their customers, and to the cardholder customers of other banks, in connection with the performance of a core banking activity-the transfer of funds from cardholder to merchant accounts through established ATM/POS settlement procedures. Moreover, this activity does not pose any type of risk that is not already present in traditional payment and funds transfer services offered by national banks.

In sum, the proposed activity is a logical outgrowth of the recognized bill payment and funds transfer functions of national banks. Moreover, it provides a benefit to the Banks' customers and poses no unusual risks to the Banks. Thus, this activity is within the authority of a national bank under 12 U.S.C. § 24(7) to engage in the business of banking and to provide products and services incidental thereto. Accordingly, the Banks are authorized under 12 U.S.C. § 24(7) to dispense from their CBCT branches, in the manner described in your letter, public transportation tickets, event and attraction tickets, gift certificates, prepaid phone cards, promotional and advertising material, postage stamps, travelers' checks, money orders, EBT script and bank debit and credit cards.

If you have any questions regarding this letter, please call me at (312) 360-8805.

Very truly yours,

/s/

Christopher G. Sablich
Senior Attorney

Appendix A4
OCC Interpretive Letter No. 731 (July 1, 1996)

Published in Interpretations and Actions July 1996

12 U.S.C. 24(7)14

[ ]

Re: Authority of [*Bank*] to Bid on The E-Z Pass System and to Perform the Contract by Means of an Operating Subsidiary

Dear [ ]:

This responds to your letter, dated May 31, 1996, requesting confirmation of telephone conversations you had with attorneys on my staff regarding the referenced issue. Specifically, you discussed whether the bank would be authorized to enter into a contract with a public authority to operate on behalf of the public authority an electronic toll collection ("ETC" or "E-Z Pass") system. At this time, the bank has been pre-qualified as one of the bidders to obtain this contract. After the submission of the bid on July 15, 1996, but prior to executing a contract, the bank intends to file an operating subsidiary notification with the OCC. Because the bank is obligated to proceed with the contract, in the event the bank is the winning bidder, you requested confirmation in writing that the proposal is legally permissible for the bank and the operating subsidiary.

I. THE PROPOSAL

The bank would enter into a contract with a public authority that is acting on behalf of itself and other public authorities (the "Consortium" who are also members of the E-Z Pass Interagency Group) to implement the ETC system throughout the roadways and facilities operated by the Consortium. The bank would not be involved in financing the project, which is to be funded by the Consortium, nor would the bank own the facilities and equipment. The ETC system would allow toll road patrons to use a transponder tag attached to the vehicles to be scanned by reader equipment for patron account identification while the vehicles pass through reader-equipped toll lanes. The contract specifies the transponder and reader equipment manufacturer but the bidder is required to design, furnish and install the ETC equipment at modified toll plazas. The winning bidder is also required to design, implement and operate a customer service center ("CSC") to manage toll road patron "E-Z Pass accounts" for all Consortium members. The ETC system is intended to interact with the ETC systems of the E-Z Pass Interagency Group, including the road agencies of other states in the region, so as to introduce and standardize ETC in the region. The E-Z Pass system permits identification of toll road patron vehicles and the automatic debiting of the prepaid balance in their "E-Z Pass accounts" by means of information transmitted to and received from the CSC. The toll road patrons' "E-Z Pass accounts" are maintained by the bank as agent for, and on behalf of, the Consortium. The winning bidder is required to provide the CSC computer system as a complete operational system with all necessary hardware and software components required for operation. As winning bidder, the bank would be expected to operate the CSC for an initial period of seven years.

The CSC must consist of a processing center and an adequate number of walk-in facilities to administer the "E-Z Pass accounts" (*e.g.*, inquiries, new enrollments, payments, account statements), interface with Consortium and non-Consortium members' ETC systems (*e.g.*, ETC toll transactions and exception and audit information), provide marketing services (*e.g.*, deposits, return items, investments, reconciliations), and provide violation enforcement imaging processing. The CSC will handle customers by attended telephone, automated voice/response, mail, facsimile, and in person. In addition to operating the separate processing center, the bank intends to use its branches for walk-in facilities to provide information about the system, distribute "E-Z Pass account" applications, enroll customers and issue tags, accept payments, issue tag replacements, provide account balances and status information, and resolve disputed items. In the performance of these activities, particularly accepting payments for the "E-Z Pass accounts", the bank is acting as agent for the Consortium and not as principal. "E-Z Pass accounts" are not bank deposit accounts for the toll patrons, but instead represent a record of prepaid tolls collected and held by the bank on behalf of the Consortium. Under the terms of the E-Z Pass system, the toll patron's prepaid balance is reduced or debited each time the patron passes through a reader equipped toll plaza. Toll road patrons will periodically replenish their prepaid balances for their "E-Z Pass accounts." The collected funds are deposited in or transmitted to a bank account for the Consortium.

In addition to the requirement to design, arrange for construction of and operate the CSC, the winning bidder is required to perform toll plaza infrastructure and toll lane traffic flow modifications in order to implement the E-Z Pass system and to integrate the ETC data into existing toll audit systems. This will require furnishing and installing the ETC equipment and computers, toll plaza and advance signing, plaza/ramp striping plans, operational plans for plaza and ramp operation and disaster/equipment failure contingency plans, and providing a communications system. Finally, the bank may also propose as part of its bid the technology to issue and use Smart Cards as an optional identification device for toll road patrons that would operate as a substitute for the transponder tags and trigger a debit of the patron's prepaid balance in the "E-Z Pass account."

Should it be the winning bidder, the bank proposes to assign the contract to, if permitted by the Consortium, or have the contract performed under subcontract by, a wholly-owned operating subsidiary of the bank. Required design, construction and equipment installation would be performed by recognized and qualified subcontractors who would indemnify the bank and the subsidiary to the maximum extent for any claims attributable to the work of each of the subcontractors. In addition, the bank and the subsidiary will maintain general liability insurance as appropriate under the circumstances. The primary value to the bank in bidding on the contract is the operation of the CSC for the initial seven-year period which would be conducted by the bank and/or the subsidiary and the possibility of issuing and utilizing Smart Card technology.

II. LEGAL ANALYSIS

Permissibility

The National Bank Act, in relevant part, provides that national banks shall have the power:

> [t]o exercise . . . all such incidental powers as shall be necessary to carry on the business of banking; by discounting and negotiating promissory notes, drafts, bills of exchange, and other evidences of debt; by receiving deposits; by buying and selling exchange, coin, and bullion; by loaning money on personal security; and by obtaining, issuing, and circulating notes . . .

12 U.S.C. 24(Seventh).

The Supreme Court has held that the powers clause of 12 U.S.C. 24(Seventh) is a broad grant of power to engage in the business of banking, including but not limited to the enumerated powers and the business of banking as a whole. *See NationsBank of North Carolina, N.A. v. Variable Life Annuity Co.*, 115 S.Ct. 810 (1995) ("*VALIC*"). Judicial cases reflect three general principles used to determine whether an activity is withing the scope of the "business of banking": (1) is the activity functionally equivalent to or a logical outgrowth of a recognized banking activity; (2) would the activity respond to customer needs or otherwise benefit the bank or its customers; and (3) does the activity involve risks similar in nature to those already assumed by banks. *See, e.g., Merchants' Bank v. State Bank,* 77 U.S. 604, 648 (1871)(certification of checks has grown out of the business needs of the country and involves no greater risk than a bank giving a certificate of deposit); *M&M Leasing Corp. v. Seattle First Nat. Bank,* 563 F.2d 1377, 1382-83 (9th Cir. 1977), *cert. denied,* 436 U.S. 987 (1978) (personal property lease financing is "functionally interchangeable" with the express power to loan money on personal property); *American Insurance Association v. Clarke,* 865 F.2d 278, 282 (D.C. Cir. 1988) (standby credits to insure municipal bonds is "functionally equivalent" to the issuance of a standby letter of credit). Further, as established by the Supreme Court in *VALIC,* national banks are authorized to engage in an activity if it is incidental to the performance of the five enumerated powers in section 24(Seventh) *or* if it is incidental to the performance of an activity that is part of the business of banking.

It is well-established that a national bank or its operating subsidiary <**NOTE:** Such activities that are part of or incidental to the business of banking may also be carried out by means of an operating subsidiary. 12 C.F.R. 5.34(c).> may provide data processing to perform services expressly or incidentally authorized to national banks. *See* OCC Interpretive Letter No. 677 (June 28, 1995) *reprinted in* [1994-1995 Transfer Binder] Fed. Banking L. Rep. (CCH) 83.625. Moreover, the recent revision and renumbering of the OCC Interpretive Ruling stating this authority, 12 C.F.R. 7.3500 (1995), recognizes the rapid advancement of technology and authorizes a national bank to "perform, provide, or deliver through electronic means and facilities any activity, function, product, or service that it is otherwise authorized to perform, provide or deliver." *See* the new regulation at 12 C.F.R. 7.1019 (1996).

The collection and processing activities that the bank proposes to perform for the Consortium are clearly part of the business of banking. The Supreme Court has established that 12 U.S.C. 24(Seventh) permits a national bank to "do those acts and occupy those relations which are usual or necessary in making collections of commercial paper and other evidences of debt" for its customers. *Miller v. King,* 223 U.S. 505, 510 (1912) (finding that a national bank may collect a judgment for its customer, and may also sue the bank's attorney in order to recover misused proceeds of the judgment). The activities associated with the operation of the CSC and the activities conducted at the walk-in facilities (including toll road patron tag issuance and "E-Z Pass account" initiation, processing payments and account management on behalf of the Consortium, and the possible issuance of the alternate identification and debit system by means of a Smart Card) essentially are financial management services for a customer (the Consortium) involving collection and remittance of funds. In effect, the bank/subsidiary in operating the CSC is acting as agent for the Consortium in collecting prepaid tolls from the toll road patrons who obtain the tags and set up "E-Z Pass accounts".

Moreover, the described activities are similar to those upheld in *Corbett v. Devon,* 12 Ill. App.3d 559, 299 N.E.2d 521 (App. Ct. 1st Cir. 1973), where the court found that national banks' participation in Illinois' program for motor vehicle license validation and renewal and the distribution of license plates, remitting fees to the state, was not ultra vires. The court stated that banks "are assisting in the performance of a public service, a large part of which is intimately connected with the ordinary and traditional banking function of collecting and remitting funds for other parties." *Corbett,* 299 N.E.2d at 529.

Similarly, the bank's or subsidiary's operation of the CSC and the use of the bank's branches as walk-in facilities to conduct the ETC system activities are part of its banking business and, therefore, legally permissible. Under any of the three general standards for determining the scope of the business of banking, collection and remittance activities are permitted to be performed, provided and delivered through electronic means and facilities by the new regulation. First, these activities are clearly functionally equivalent to or a logical outgrowth of recognized banking functions, as acknowledged by the judicial precedent. *See Miller v. King* and *Corbett v. Devon supra.* Second, the bank's performance of these activities will benefit the bank and its customers, both the Consortium and the toll road patrons who can use the bank's many branches to enroll in and use the E-Z Pass system. The bank will benefit from a new source of revenue for operating the CSC and may develop new customer relationships among enrolled E-Z Pass users for its own banking products and services. Finally, the risks to the bank in operating the CSC are the same risks associated with permissible collection and remittance operations the bank performs for other customers, *e.g.,* lockbox operations in which the bank collects funds for crediting to the customers' accounts. Accordingly, these activities are within the scope of the business of banking, may be performed by electronic means and facilities, and, thus, are legally permissible.

Incidental to these permissible banking activities is the ability to arrange for, by means of subcontracting, the one-time design, construction, and installation of facilities and equipment necessary to conduct the activities. As part of the bid package required by the Consortium, and in order to obtain the contract to operate the ETC system at least for seven years, the bank is required to arrange for the one-time design, construction and installation of the facilities and equipment necessary to render the ETC system operational. Consequently, the ability of the bank to arrange for others to perform the nonbanking activities is integral to the bid process to obtain the contract for operation of the banking-related activities. At no time will the bank perform these engineering and construction activities; instead, the bank will arrange for the performance of these activities by qualified subcontractors pursuant to agreements by which the bank and the subsidiary are indemnified to the extent permitted by law. Accordingly, these latter nonbanking activities, undertaken only as part of the bidding process, would be authorized as incidental to the bank's operation of the CSC, should the bank be the winning bidder.

Finally, under 12 U.S.C. 24(Third), a national bank or its operating subsidiary may enter into contracts. Accordingly, the bank can execute a contract to provide the specified banking services to the Consortium and to the toll road patrons using the ETC system by operating the CSC and performing certain activities at the branches ("walk-in facilities"). It can also execute contracts with subcontractors to perform the required design, construction, and installation of facilities and equipment to facilitate the accomplishment of the operational banking activities.

Conclusion

For the foregoing reasons, we conclude that the bank's proposal as described above would be legally permissible for a national bank and its operating subsidiary. This analysis is based on the facts presented and different circumstances may affect the legal analysis. In addition, this position reflects the application of current law and may be subject to revisions as future developments warrant. Finally, should the bank be the winning bidder, the bank is expected to ensure that these activities would be conducted in a safe and sound manner, adhering to sound prudential banking principles, including appropriate risk management.

If you have any further questions, please do not hesitate to contact either Senior Counsel Madonna Starr or me.

Sincerely,

/s/

Jonathan H. Rushdoony
District Counsel

Appendix A5
OCC Interpretive Letter No. 732 (May 10, 1996)

Published in Interpretations and Actions July 1996

12 U.S.C. 24(7)23C

[ ]

Dear [ ]:

This is in response to your letter of March 29, 1996, requesting confirmation that [ ] ("Bank"), may lawfully acquire and hold a minority interest in [ ] ("Company"), which offers electronic data interchange services. <**NOTE:** The Company currently is in the process of changing its corporate name to "[ ]."> For the reasons set forth below, I agree with your conclusion.

BACKGROUND

The Bank intends to acquire a 5.5% interest <**NOTE:** This percentage calculation is based on all presently owned Company voting shares (both common and preferred). The percentage calculation is 7.8% if based solely on presently owned common shares.> in the Company, which is engaged in the design, development, marketing and maintenance of a network for electronic funds transfers and electronic data interchange, including transacting electronic commerce and marketing software products for use on its world-wide electronic commerce network. Through the network, subscribing businesses, using appropriate Company-developed software, can send and receive payments worldwide, send and receive invoices electronically involving other subscribing companies, send purchase orders electronically to other subscribing companies and receive sales orders electronically from any company world-wide. The Company's marketing activities involve the recruitment of banks as submarketers and the recruitment of businesses as network end-users by such banks. The Bank and the Company have entered into a contractual arrangement whereby the Bank is acting as the recruiter of major banks as submarketers for the network and its associated software. The submarketers will recruit businesses as network end-users. The Bank also will offer the network's services to its own customers. The Bank's fee income from these efforts will be based on the number of transactions moving through the network. This contract will expire in two years unless the Bank invests in the Company and, thereby, becomes the sole owner of the Company's Series B Common stock.

The Company has two series of common stock and two series of preferred. There are eight holders of the almost 5 million shares of Series A common outstanding. These shareholders are company principals and various capital investors. The Bank intends to acquire 400,000 shares of Series B Common and obtain warrants for the remaining 400,000 shares. Series A Preferred has 625,000 shares outstanding, held by 21 holders. Series B Preferred has almost 2 million shares outstanding held by 33 holders. As a holder of the Series B Common, the Bank will be entitled to elect one member of the Company's board of directors and to vote, along with all other common and preferred shareholders, on all matters not specifically requiring voting by class or series.

A number of provisions governing the relationship between the Company and the Bank will cause the Company to restrict its activities to those permissible for national banks:

- The articles of incorporation of the Company will be restated to limit its activities to those permissible for national banks.
- If the Bank decides at any time that the Company is engaging in activities impermissible for national banks, it may demand redemption of the Series B Common Stock.
- As holder of Series B Common, the Bank will be entitled to vote by series on (and effectively veto) changes in, among other things, the rights or number of Series B Common or Series A Preferred and Series B Preferred, the creation of new classes or series of shares having preferences superior or equal to those of Series B Common or Series A Preferred and Series B Preferred shares, and any change in the provision of the articles of incorporation according such voting rights.

ANALYSIS

The Bank's plan to purchase a 5.5% interest in the Company initially raises the issue of the authority of a national bank to hold a minority interest in a corporation. A recent OCC interpretive letter extensively analyzed the authority of national banks under 12 U.S.C. 24(Seventh) to own stock, and reviewed OCC precedents on the ownership of stock in amounts less than that required for an operating subsidiary, *i.e.*, non-controlling stock investments. Interpretive Letter No. 697, [Current] Fed. Banking L. Rep. (CCH) 81-013 (Nov. 15, 1995). That letter concluded that ownership of a non-controlling interest in a corporation is permissible provided that four standards, drawn from OCC precedents, are satisfied. They are:

1) The activities of the enterprise in which the investment is made must be limited to activities that are part of, or incidental to, the business of banking;
2) The bank must be able to prevent the enterprise from engaging in activities that do not meet the foregoing standard, or be able to withdraw its investment;
3) The bank's loss exposure must be limited, as a legal and accounting matter, and the bank must not have open-ended liability for the obligations of the enterprise; and
4) The investment must be convenient or useful to the bank in carrying out its business and not a mere passive investment unrelated to *that bank's* banking business.

Each of these factors is discussed below and applied to your proposal.

1. The activities of the enterprise in which the investment is made must be limited to activities that are part of, or incidental to, the business of banking.

Our precedents on minority stock ownership have recognized that the enterprise in which the bank takes an equity interest must confine its activities to those that are part of or incidental to the conduct of the banking business. *See, e.g.*, Interpretive Letter No. 380, [1988-1989 Transfer Binder] Fed. Banking L. Rep. (CCH) 85,604 n.8 (Dec. 29, 1986) (since a national bank can provide options clearing services to customers, it can purchase stock in a corporation providing options clearing services); Letter from Robert B. Serino, Deputy Chief Counsel (Nov. 9, 1992) (since the operation of an ATM network is "a fundamental part of the basic business of banking," an equity investment in a corporation operating such a network is permissible).

You have represented that the Company's activities will involve the design and development of a network for electronic transfers of funds and financial information, along with the development and marketing of related software. The OCC previously has approved the activities the Company will perform.

OCC Interpretive Ruling 7.1019, Furnishing of products and services by electronic means and facilities, 61 Fed. Reg. 4849, 4865 (1996) (to be codified at 12 C.F.R. 7.1019), permits national banks to provide permissible services by electronic means. The OCC has permitted a national bank to participate in a communications link between subscribers and their banks as well as permitted subscribers to communicate with each other. Interpretive Letter No. 346, [1985-

1987 Transfer Binder] Fed. Banking L. Rep. (CCH) 85,516 (July 31, 1985). The OCC also has approved electronic data interchange services for financial information, Interpretive Letter No. 653, [1994-1995 Transfer Binder] Fed. Banking L. Rep. (CCH) 83,601 (Dec. 22, 1994) (informational and payments interface). National banks may use automated data processing to provide billing services and accounts receivable services for itself and others, Interpretive Letter No. 419, [1988-1989 Transfer Binder] Fed. Banking L. Rep. (CCH) 85,643 (Feb. 16, 1988), and engage in data processing related to funds transfer and cash management, *id.* (funds transfer); Letter from Peter Liebesman, Assistant Director, Legal Advisory Services Division (Dec. 13, 1985) (cash management); Interpretive Letter No. 611, [1992-1993 Transfer Binder] Fed. Banking L. Rep. (CCH) 83,449 (Nov. 23, 1992) (cash management, funds transfer).

Thus, the activities to be performed by the Company are activities that are part of or incidental to the business of banking, and the first standard is satisfied.

2. The bank must be able to prevent the enterprise from engaging in activities that do not meet the foregoing standard, or be able to withdraw its investment.

The activities of an enterprise in which a national bank invests must be part of or incidental to the business of banking not only at the time the bank initially purchases stock, but they must remain so for as long as the bank has an ownership interest. However, minority shareholders in a corporation do not possess a veto power over corporate activities as a matter of corporate law. One way to assure continuing compliance with the first standard is for the corporation's articles of incorporation or bylaws to limit its activities to those that are permissible for national banks. *See, e.g.,* Letters from Peter Liebesman, Assistant Director, Legal Advisory Services Division (January 26, 1981 and January 4, 1983).

You have stated that the Company's articles of incorporation will be amended to limit its activities to those permissible to national banks. Also, several other provisions, described in the "Background" section above, provide additional avenues for the Bank to ensure that while it has an investment in the Company, the Company's activities will remain permissible. These provisions assure that the Company will not engage in any activity that is not permissible for a corporation having a national bank shareholder. The Bank effectively will be able to prevent the Company from engaging in any impermissible activity as long as it continues to own shares in the Company. Thus, the second standard is satisfied.

3. The bank's loss exposure must be limited, as a legal and accounting matter, and the bank must not have open-ended liability for the obligations of the enterprise.

A primary concern of the OCC is that national banks should not be subjected to undue risk. Where an investing bank will not control the operations of the entity in which the bank holds an interest, it is important that a national bank's investment not expose it to unlimited liability. Normally, this is not a concern when a national bank invests in a corporation, for shareholders are protected by the "corporate veil" from liability for the debts of the corporation. 1 William M. Fletcher, Fletcher Cyclopedia of the Law of Private Corporations 25 (perm. ed. rev. vol. 1990). In the present case, both the Company and the Bank will be separate corporations, with their own capital, directors, and officers.

Further, the Bank has advised that the appropriate treatment for its investment in the Company will be the cost method of accounting. Under this method, which is used for equity interests of less than 20 percent in corporations, losses recognized by the investor will not exceed the amount of the investment (including extensions of credit or guarantees, if any) shown on the investor's books. *See generally,* Accounting Principles Board, Op. 18, 19 (1971).

Therefore, for both legal and accounting purposes, the Bank's potential loss exposure should be limited to the amount of its investment. Since that exposure will be quantifiable and controllable, the third standard is satisfied.

4. The investment must be convenient or useful to the bank in carrying out its business and not a mere passive investment unrelated to that bank's banking business.

Twelve U.S.C. 24(Seventh) gives national banks incidental powers that are "necessary" to carry on the business of banking. "Necessary" has been judicially construed to mean "convenient or useful." *Arnold Tours, Inc. v. Camp,* 472 F.2d 427, 432 (1st Cir. 1972). The provision in section 24(Seventh) relating to the purchase of stock, derived from section 16 of the Glass-Steagall Act, was intended only to make it clear that section 16 did not authorize speculative investments in stock. Interpretive Letter No. 697, *supra.* Therefore, a consistent thread running through our precedents concerning minority stock ownership is that such ownership must be convenient or useful to the investing bank in conducting its banking business. The investment must benefit or facilitate that business, and cannot be a mere passive or speculative investment. *See, e.g.,* Interpretive Letter No. 543, [1990-1991 Transfer Binder] Fed. Banking L. Rep. (CCH) 83,255 (Feb. 13, 1991); Interpretive Letter No. 427, [1988-1989 Transfer Binder] Fed. Banking L. Rep. (CCH) 85,651 (May 9, 1988); Interpretive Letter No. 421, [1988-1989 Transfer Binder] Fed. Banking L. Rep. (CCH) 85,645 (Mar. 14, 1988).

As set forth in the "Background" section, the Bank and the Company already have a contractual relationship relating to the Company's business which is limited to two years unless the Bank becomes and remains sole owner of the Series B Common stock. Thus, the proposed investment will facilitate the Bank's continued participation in the network. As discussed, the Bank is using participation in the network as a means to offer its customers and correspondent banks a range of electronic banking services that the Bank could not as economically offer directly. It is clear that the Company's services will provide the Bank and other banks involved in the network with the opportunity to offer electronic data interchange without establishing separate systems and maintaining them themselves. Thus, the investment is "necessary" to the continuation of those services. This investment also will provide the Bank a more favorable fee treatment in its recruiting role, in accordance with the agreement between the Company and the Bank. Where, as here, a bank uses a third party to make services available to its customers and correspondents, the bank normally will receive a higher level of the profits from the referred business if it is an owner of the servicing company rather than a mere contractor. Thus, a minority investment enables the bank to increase the profitability of its business. Also, you indicate that by having a seat on the Company's board of directors, the Bank will be able to monitor and influence the development of the network in ways best adapted to the needs of the Bank's customer base. In this way, a minority investment enhances the Bank's ability to serve and preserve its customer and correspondent relationships.

You note that the Series B Common is restricted in its transferability. Once acquired by the Bank, Series B Common shares may not be sold to a third party unless they have been offered to the Company at the same price. Thus, the Bank will not be able to dispose of its stock as freely as a shareholder merely interested in a passive investment.

For these reasons, the proposed investment is convenient and useful to the Bank in carrying out its business and is not a mere passive investment. Thus, the fourth standard is satisfied.

CONCLUSION

Based upon the representations made on behalf of the Bank and for the reasons outlined above, we conclude that the Bank's investment in the Company would satisfy the four standards the OCC has applied to non-controlling minority investments, provided the Bank complies with the following conditions:

1) the Company may engage only in activities that are part of, or incidental to, the business of banking;
2) the Company's articles of incorporation will limit its activities to those permissible for national banks;
3) the Company will be subject to OCC supervision and examination; and

4) the Bank will account for its investment in the Company under the cost method of accounting.

These conditions are conditions imposed in writing by the OCC in connection with its action on the request for a legal opinion confirming that the proposed investment is permissible under 12 U.S.C. 24(Seventh) and, as such, may be enforced in proceedings under applicable law.

Sincerely,

/s/

Julie L. Williams
Chief Counsel

Appendix A6
OCC Interpretive Letter No. 737 (Aug. 19, 1996)

Published in Interpretations and Actions September 1996

12 U.S.C. 24(7)

E. Jay Finkel Esq.
Porter, Wright, Morris & Arthur
1233 20th Street, N.W.
Washington, DC 20036-2395

Re: Huntington National Bank, Columbus, Ohio—Acquisition of Minority Interest in a Limited Liability Company Providing Stored Value Systems

Dear Mr. Finkel:

This responds to your letter of June 14, 1996, requesting confirmation that The Huntington National Bank, Columbus, Ohio ("Bank") may lawfully acquire and hold a minority interest in a joint venture to be formed as a for-profit Delaware limited liability company (the "LLC") with Battelle Memorial Institute, Columbus, Ohio ("Battelle") and the Student Loan Marketing Association, Washington, D.C. ("Sallie Mae"). <**NOTE:** Initial membership interests will be 33-1/3 percent for each of the members. [ ]> The LLC will develop, market, deliver and maintain stored value and information systems for universities, hospitals, business centers, theme parks, military installations, and other self-contained geographic locations (hereinafter: "System Customers"). The LLC's systems will use a smart card technology. <**NOTE:** A "smart card" is a plastic card with an embedded integrated circuit that looks like a credit card. A smart card is essentially a mini-computer that can store both data and programs. Depending on the capacity of the integrated circuit, the smart card may hold only limited information, or may have the capability of performing more complex computing functions. For stored value smart cards, an electronic device is used to load (add) or deduct value stored on the computer chip.> Based on the information and representations provided and for the reasons set forth below, I conclude that the proposed investment is permissible for a national bank.

A. The Proposal

The systems to be developed and supported by the LLC will serve two functions. The first function is a stored value system enabling cardholders to make cashless payments to System Customers and participating merchants. The second function is an information system for retrieving and exchanging data on the smart card; System Customers will use the cards with their data and systems for such institutional purposes as security access to buildings and computer systems, student meal plans, health care plan monitoring, and customer loyalty tracking in retail stores and supermarkets. The LLC proposes to test a prototype system in a pilot program that will be conducted with Ohio Dominican College ("ODC") this Fall. The specific role of the LLC in these two functions is described below.

1. Role of LLC in Stored Value Functions

The primary function of the LLC in the stored value systems will be to provide collection, processing and record keeping services for stored value transactions. The LLC will not itself hold the stored value funds nor be the stored value obligor. Instead, the funds from the sale of stored value will be held by and in the name of a bank or other entity agreed upon by the LLC and the System Customer, and that entity will be financially responsible for the stored value (hereinafter: the "issuer"). In the ODC pilot, the Bank will be the holder of funds and the obligor on the stored value. <**NOTE:** The Bank's request pertains only to the permissibility of its investment in the LLC. Thus, this letter does not address the permissibility of the activities of the Bank in the ODC pilot program. At this time, the precise role of the Bank in stored value systems is undetermined and many points of structure and process are still under development. Moreover, it is likely that the Bank will make changes in its role and functions based upon its experience with the ODC pilot. Thus, at this stage, the Bank's activities in stored value systems are not yet ripe for a formal opinion by the OCC and no such opinion has been requested. However, the OCC will review and monitor the Bank's activities in developing and operating the pilot program.> The LLC will not in the ODC pilot or in any other future system act as the issuer of the stored value and, thus, that value will in no way depend upon the financial soundness of the LLC. <**NOTE:** The Bank states that the maximum level of stored value that can be loaded on its System cards at any one time will initially be set at $50 and that no plans exist for a higher level. Under the proposed amendment to Regulation E, 12 C.F.R. 205, stored value cards (like those proposed by Bank) with a maximum load of $100 or less will be exempt from the requirements of the Regulation, including initial disclosures. 61 Fed. Reg. 19696 (May 2, 1996). However, as will be discussed, the LLC will ensure that certain disclosures are made to cardholders. The Bank has not yet determined whether the stored value in the ODC pilot will be covered by Federal deposit insurance. See Federal Deposit Insurance Corporation General Counsel Opinion No. 8, 61 Fed. Reg. 40494 (August 2, 1996).>

The LLC will arrange to have the cards produced and properly programmed for the System Customer. <**NOTE:** The cards will be produced by an outside card fulfillment company that currently produces various types of cards for banks. Additionally, some card production will be done locally to replace lost, stolen or damaged cards. The production, transit, storage and utilization of card stock will be in accordance with established security procedures. For cards with ATM or point of sale ("POS") functionality, the required information will be provided by Bank.> The LLC will sell the cards to the System Customer (and, perhaps, the issuer) who will distribute the cards to cardholders. <**NOTE:** The System Customer will provide cardholders written disclosures complying with applicable laws and regulations either as part of the cardholder agreement given when the card is issued or on the card itself. Even if applicable law requires no disclosures, the LLC will generally require the System Customer to disclose fundamental contract terms to the cardholder, such as the identity of the stored value issuer, cardholder liability for unauthorized use or lost or stolen cards, phone numbers or addresses to use for problems with the card, expiration dates for the card, and other basic terms.> In the ODC pilot, two parties will enter agreements with cardholders regarding the cards: ODC for college-provided functions and Bank for Bank-provided functions. This will probably also be true with other future Service Customers. The LLC itself will have no direct contractual relationship with the cardholder; the LLC's contractual relations will be with the System Customer and the Bank or other stored value issuer. The names of the System Customer and the Bank (or other issuer) will appear on the cards.

The LLC will also have functions regarding the loading of stored value on the cards. All load transactions will be done at on-line cash revalue stations or kiosks that will be secure devices to protect any cash they receive as a result of cash-to-card load transactions. Two types of cards will be offered initially: (i) a card that can be loaded only by cash inserted in a "cash revalue station" ("CRS"); and (ii) a card that can be loaded either by cash inserted in a CRS or by an electronic funds transfer from an account with the Bank using a "kiosk." <**NOTE:** With the second type of card, the cardholder would also be required to open a bank account at the Bank. The LLC will not be involved in opening bank accounts. Regulation E will apply to transactions where a cardholder transfers funds from a bank account to load stored value on a card.> The LLC will own and maintain the CRS and the kiosks. Both types of devices will be on-line to the LLC so the LLC can authenticate the card at the time of any load transaction and upgrade it with any new functionality. <**NOTE:** The cards will be protected by available encryption technology. The system will have multiple levels of security which reduce the risk of counterfeiting. [ ].> The LLC will continuously monitor all on-line CRS and kiosks to determine the status of the device.

When value is loaded by a CRS, the LLC will be responsible for collecting the cash from the machines and forwarding the appropriate amount of funds to the Bank (or other value issuer) with the related information so the issuer can adjust its records. <**NOTE:** The Bank anticipates that in the ODC pilot it will, as stored value issuer, deposit funds representing the proceeds from sale of stored value into an interest-free general liability pooled account. However, the precise details of this aspect of the program are still being developed.> When value is loaded from a Bank account using a kiosk, the transaction will be handled by the LLC's platform [ ]. The LLC's platform receives data from the kiosk, authenticates the transaction, then electronically forwards the transaction to an outside third party POS processor. The third party processor then electronically forwards the transaction through the settlement network to the Bank (or other issuer).

Finally, the LLC will provide support services for merchants accepting the cards for stored value purchase transactions. <**NOTE:** It is contemplated that where the cardholder maintains a deposit account with the Bank, the smart cards may also function as an ATM/POS card for that account. [
].> In the payment function, the LLC will contract directly with merchants who agree to honor the card as participants in the stored value system. The LLC will provide processing and settlement services to merchants participating in the stored value function of the card. <**NOTE:** Cards that are also Bank ATM/POS cards could also be used to make purchases using the POS function instead of the stored value function, and the POS function would settle through the existing POS arrangements with Bank.> [
]. The Bank expects that it (or another issuer) will also be a party to the merchant contracts as the funding bank, since the LLC will not hold the stored value pooled account or be liable for payments to merchants.

The LLC will provide the following specific products and services to participating merchants in order to facilitate the processing and settlement of transactions: (1) smart card readers to be used when the stored value cards are presented by cardholders for purchase transactions with the merchant; [Hardware and software that enable Merchants to store transaction data and transmit it to the LLC].

Once the LLC's platform receives the merchant transaction data, the LLC will issue automated clearing house transactions that will debit the stored value pooled account at the Bank (or other issuer) and credit the merchant's account at the merchant's bank with the amount of the transactions being processed.

Finally, the LLC will provide certain auditing and record keeping functions relating to the stored value transactions. The system's transactions will be auditable and the LLC will keep records of transactions. The LLC will provide the Bank (or other issuer) with periodic reports so the issuer can reconcile the total balance in the stored value pool account [ ]. The LLC will also maintain information that can be used to audit individual card transactions. <**NOTE:** [ ].>

[ ]. The LLC will archive all records of all stored value transactions and has no immediate plans to dispose of the archives.

2. Role of the LLC in Information Related Functions

The LLC will have a very limited role with respect to the information related functions that will mostly be provided and supported by the Service Customer. In the ODC pilot, the smart card will serve as an identification card, building access control, library card, ODC computer network access, and meal plan control. These functions will *not* involve any manipulation or processing of data by or through the LLC platform. The LLC's role with respect to these functions will be limited to two general activities: First, the LLC will replace the card readers of ODC's existing systems with card readers that will, upon insertion of a smart card, emulate the magnetic stripe access signals required for activation of ODC's existing systems. Second, the LLC will see that the smart cards are programed so that the new card readers can read and use them with ODC's existing data systems. ODC's data processing system will do all data processing on the information related functions. The LLC will play a similar limited role with respect to information related functions in any future systems it develops for other System Customers.

B. Legal Analysis

Your letter raises the issue of the authority of a national bank to make a non-controlling investment in a limited liability company. In a variety of circumstances the OCC has permitted national banks to own, either directly, or indirectly through an operating subsidiary, a minority interest in an enterprise. The enterprise might be a limited partnership, a corporation, or in more recent examples, a limited liability company. In two recent interpretive letters, the OCC concluded that national banks are legally permitted to make a minority investment in an LLC provided four criteria or standards are met. See Interpretive Letters No. 692 (Nov. 1, 1995), *reprinted in* [Current] Fed. Banking L. Rep. (CCH) 81,007, and No. 694 (Dec. 13, 1995), *reprinted in* [Current] Fed. Banking L. Rep. (CCH) 81,009.

These standards, which have been distilled from our previous decisions in the area of permissible minority investments for national banks and their subsidiaries, are: (1) the activities of the enterprise in which the bank invests must be limited to activities that are part of or incidental to the business of banking; (2) the bank must be able to prevent the enterprise from engaging in activities that do not meet the foregoing standard, or be able to withdraw its investment; (3) the bank's loss exposure must be limited, as a legal and accounting matter, and the bank must not have open-ended liability for the obligations of the enterprise; and (4) the investment must be convenient or useful to the bank in carrying out its business and not a mere passive investment unrelated to that bank's banking business. For the reasons discussed, I conclude that the proposed investment by Bank in the LLC satisfies these four criteria.

1. The activities of the LLC must be limited to activities that are part of or incidental to the business of banking.

The National Bank Act, in relevant part, provides that national banks shall have the power:

> [t]o exercise . . . all such incidental powers as shall be necessary to carry on the business of banking; by discounting and negotiating promissory notes, drafts, bills of exchange, and other evidences of debt; by receiving deposits; by buying and selling exchange, coin, and bullion; by loaning money on personal security; and by obtaining, issuing, and circulating notes . . .

12 U.S.C. 24(Seventh).

The Supreme Court has held that the powers clause of 12 U.S.C. 24(Seventh) is a broad grant of power to engage in the business of banking, including but not limited to the enumerated powers and the business of banking as a whole. *See NationsBank of North Carolina, N.A. v. Variable Life Annuity Co.,* 115 S.Ct. 810 (1995) ("*VALIC*"). Judicial cases reflect three general principles used to determine whether an activity is withing the scope of the "business of banking": (1) is the activity functionally equivalent to or a logical outgrowth of a recognized banking activity; (2) would the activity respond to customer needs or otherwise benefit the bank or its customers; and (3) does the activity involve risks similar in nature to those already assumed by banks. *See, e.g., Merchants' Bank v. State Bank,* 77 U.S. 604, 648 (1871) (certification of checks has grown out of the business needs of the country and involves no greater risk than a bank giving a certificate of deposit); *M&M Leasing Corp. v. Seattle First Nat. Bank,* 563 F.2d 1377, 1382-83 (9th Cir. 1977), *cert. denied,* 436 U.S. 987 (1978) (personal property lease financing is "functionally interchangeable" with the express power to loan money on personal property); *American Insurance Association v. Clarke,* 865 F.2d 278, 282 (D.C. Cir. 1988) (standby credits to insure municipal bonds is "functionally equivalent" to the issuance of a standby letter of credit). Further, as established by the Supreme Court in *VALIC,* national banks are authorized to engage in an activity if it is incidental to the performance of the five enumerated powers in section 24(Seventh) *or* if it is incidental to the performance of an activity that is part of the business of banking.

It is well established that a national bank may use electronic or data processing technology to perform services expressly or incidentally authorized to national banks. *See* OCC Interpretive Letter No. 677 *reprinted in* [1994-1995 Transfer Binder] Fed. Banking L. Rep. (CCH) 83,625. As noted in the recently revised OCC Interpretive Ruling recognizing this authority, a national bank may "perform, provide, or deliver through electronic means and facilities any activity, function, product, or service that it is otherwise authorized to perform, provide or deliver." *See* 12 C.F.R. 7.1019 (1996). The functions of the LLC in the proposed smart card systems are part of or incidental to the business of banking.

OCC Interpretive Letter #737, Part 2

Published in Interpretations and Actions September 1996

a. *Functions Relating to Stored Value*

The primary function of the LLC relating to stored value will be to provide for the collection, processing, and settlement of payments in the stored value system. Clearly, these activities are part of the business of banking.

When acting for merchants in the collection and settlement of stored value transactions, the LLC will be performing a recognized banking activity. The Supreme Court has established that 12 U.S.C. 24(Seventh) permits a national bank to "do those acts and occupy those relations which are usual or necessary in making collections of commercial paper and other evidences of debt" for its customers. *Miller v. King,* 223 U.S. 505, 510 (1912) (finding that a national bank may collect a judgment for its customer, and may also sue the bank's attorney in order to recover misused proceeds of the judgment). *See also,* OCC Interpretive Letter No. 731 (July 1, 1996) (national banks may enter into a contract with a public authority to operate on behalf of the authority an electronic toll collection system); OCC Interpretive Letter No. 732 (May 10, 1996) (national banks may provide electronic data interchange services that, among other things, provide for payments by EFT); and OCC Interpretive Letter No. 419, *reprinted in* [1988-1989 Transfer Binder] Fed. Banking Law. Rep. (CCH) 85,643 (national bank may provide a service that facilitates settlement and payment of health claims using EFT technology).

Similarly, when the LLC dispenses stored value to cardholders on behalf of the issuer, it will be performing the established banking functions of bill payment and dispensing of third party payment instruments. *See* OCC Interpretive Letter No. 718 (March 14, 1996) (national banks may dispense "alternative media" from their CBCT branches, including public transportation tickets, event tickets, gift certificates, and prepaid phone cards). *See also, Arnold Tours, Inc. v. Camp,* 472 F.2d 427, 438 (1st Cir. 1972) (national banks may sell travelers checks).

A secondary function of the LLC will be to provide record keeping services on the stored value transactions. This is also a function that is clearly part of the business of banking. An earlier version of 12 C.F.R. 7.1019 states that "as part of its banking business and incidental thereto, a national bank may collect, transcribe, process, analyze, and store for itself and others, banking, financial, or related economic data." Interpretive Ruling 7.3500, 39 Fed. Reg. 14195 (Apr. 22, 1974). Although in its 1984 revision of the ruling the OCC deleted this statement because it believed that "specific examples [of permissible electronic activities] are inappropriate given the imprecision of terms and rapid pace of change in the data processing industry", 49 Fed. Reg. 11157 (Mar. 26, 1984), the "analytical framework" embodied in the ruling remained the same, *id.* There was no intent to narrow or restrict the substantive effect of the rule. OCC Interpretive Letter No. 677, *supra*. *See also,* OCC Interpretive Letter No. 653 *reprinted in* [1994-1995 Transfer Binder] Fed. Banking L. Rep. (CCH) 83,601 (national bank may maintain records when acting as an informational and payments interface between insurance underwriters and general insurance agents); OCC Letter No. 346 [1985-1987 Transfer Binder] Fed. Banking Law. Rep. (CCH) 85,516 (national banks may maintain records on commodities transactions).

In connection with these payments and record keeping functions, the LLC will also provide system participants with certain hardware and software that will be used for the stored value functions. The LLC will provide System Customers with preprogramed smart cards and card readers for payment sites (e.g., at campus copy machines or laundromats). Participating merchants will receive card readers and associated software and hardware that will allow them to acquire and present stored value for settlement.

In analyzing the extent to which national banks may provide hardware and software, the OCC has distinguished between limited purpose and general purpose items:

> When the hardware is such that it is not to be used for uses beyond the [bank services], it may well be considered literally an indistinguishable part of the [banking services]. Accordingly, a national bank's sale of such hardware is permissible as a part of the [service] permitted under 12 U.S.C. 24(7), just as the bank's sale of checkbooks to its customers is a permissible part of offering checking accounts.

OCC Interpretive Letter No. 345, *reprinted in,* [1985-1987 Transfer Binder] Fed. Banking Law. Rep. (CCH) 85,515.

The hardware and software the LLC will provide to the merchants can only be used to support the stored value function and, thus, it is permissible as part of the business of banking. The hardware and software being provided to System Customers can serve a dual function of supporting the stored value system and also the information related functions and, thus, will be discussed below in connection with those functions.

b. Functions Relating to Other Information

As noted, the LLC will have a very limited role in the information related functions of the smart card systems. The LLC will provide certain hardware and software capacities so that System Customers will be able to use the smart card system to support certain ancillary information processing as well as a stored value function. For purposes of this letter, we will assume, without deciding, that the ancillary information could be characterized as not banking financial, or related economic data that would fall within the business of banking. Nevertheless, we conclude that the LLC's limited role in the information function is a permissible exercise of a national bank's incidental powers. There are two reasons for this conclusion.

First, while this is a determination that must be made on a case-by-case basis, the multi-function capacity that the LLC will provide Service Customers appears to be necessary for the banking services provided (*i.e.,* stored value system support) and not to be an excessive amount of the total stored value service package. The test was well summarized in OCC Interpretive letter No. 345, *supra:*

> [Unlike hardware limited to banking purposes,] hardware which can be used for purposes beyond the [banking] services is no longer merely part of the permitted services. The sale of such hardware . . . as part of its services package is permissible for national banks as incidental to the permitted services when the inclusion of the hardware is necessary, convenient, or useful to providing the permitted services in the package taken as a whole. The determination that hardware is subordinate within the total package can only be done on a case-by-case basis, taking into consideration factors such as cost, expected revenues, and the expected life of the hardware relative to other aspects of the package. Regulation Y's standard that the cost of the hardware 'not constitute more than 30 percent of the cost of any packaged offering,' *see* 12 C.F.R. 225.25(b)(7)(iii), is one means of demonstrating that the sale of the hardware is incidental to the permitted banking service. There may be other means as well.

See also, Letter from Michael J. O'Keefe, District Counsel, Midwestern District dated July 13, 1987 (unpublished) (distribution of software and hardware to banks permissible if full function hardware does not "dominate" permissible data processing services involved); OCC Interpretive Letter No. 516, *reprinted in* [1990-1991 Transfer Binder] Fed. Banking L. Rep. (CCH) 83,220 (hardware permissible when necessary and convenient to information services and where sale of such incidental hardware does not exceed 30% of total cost of the package). *Cf., Association of Data Processing v. Board of Governors,* 745 F.2d 677 (D.C. Cir. 1984).

Here, as noted, the LLC will provide no manipulation or processing of the System Customer's non-banking data. Further, a substantial portion of the system hardware and software (specifically, that provided to the merchants and that provided to System Customers which will be used exclusively for payments purposes) is limited to banking functions. The Bank states that the manufacturing cost of the multi-function smart cards is small and not a significant economic factor in relation to the total stored value system. Thus, it appears that the "multi-function" hardware and software the LLC will provide System Customers will not be an excessive part of the entire package. Moreover, the LLC has committed in the LLC Operating Agreement to engage only in activities that are permissible for national banks and, thus, to operate the "multi-function" aspects of its program in conformance with the standard described above.

Second, under the facts of this case, the providing of multi-function smart cards and card readers is incidental to the business of banking because it enables the LLC to create a package of related services required to satisfy customer needs and to market successfully its stored value system. National banks under their incidental powers may provide ancillary non-banking services when those ancillary services are needed to successfully package and to promote other permissible banking services. OCC Interpretive Letter No. 611, *reprinted in* [1992-1993 Transfer Binder] Fed. Banking L. Rep. (CCH) 83,449 (national banks selling home banking service may also provide customer access to non-banking services "to increase the customer base and the usage of the program"); OCC Interpretive Letter No. 653, *supra* (national banks may offer non-banking products as part of larger product or service when necessary, convenient and useful to bank permissible activities).

Here, the LLC needs to provide hardware and software related to the information functions to market successfully its stored value smart card system to institutions such as universities that need to use the cards for multiple purposes, some of which may not involve banking, financial, or economic data that national banks may process as part of the "business of banking." Smart cards are essentially mini-computers that can perform many useful data storage functions beyond just stored value systems. Systems Customers will undoubtedly be reluctant to purchase smart card systems from national banks (or the LLC) if those systems must be limited to preforming only stored value functions. As one authority has noted:

> While stored value is likely to be a popular smart card application and of great interest to bankers, the extraordinary data storage and processing capabilities of modern microchip technology allow multiple applications to be provided on the same card. For example, a smart card could store personal information such as medical insurance data, health records, and financial data. The cardholder could use the same card in a consumer loyalty program.

Wright, "Smart Cards: Legal and Regulatory Challenges," *Bankers Magazine,* March/April 1996 at p. 24. *See, generally,* Fancher, "Smart Cards,' *Scientific American,* August 1996. In many cases, bank-provided smart card systems will need to permit their system customers to utilize and enjoy this multi-functionality potential of smart card systems.

Where, as here, the System users purchase the smart cards from LLC, <**NOTE:** If the LLC retained ownership of the cards, there might be an argument that the additional information functions could be provided under an "excess capacity" theory. In most smart card stored value systems, the stored value function is not expected to consume the entire programing and data capacity of the smart cards. As recognized in 12 C.F.R. 7.1019, "[a] national bank may also, in order to optimize the use of the bank's resources, market and sell to third parties electronic capacities acquired or developed by the bank in good faith for banking purposes." However, this theory does not apply where, as here, the bank does not retain ownership of excess capacity.> they will want to be able to make full use of the cards and, thus, will need to have the cards programed to permit the System users to perform additional non-banking functions using the cards. Similarly, System Customers will need to have card readers connected to their data systems so that the readers can be used for both banking and non-banking functions. The additional card programing and reader connections needed to permit these non-banking functions are ancillary and incidental to the primary stored value function being provided by the LLC and, thus, permissible.

2. The Bank must be able to prevent the LLC from engaging in activities that do not meet the foregoing standard.

This is an obvious corollary to the first standard. It is not sufficient that the LLC's activities are permissible at the time the bank initially purchases LLC membership shares; they must also remain permissible for as long as the bank retains an ownership interest in the LLC.

Section 2.3 of the LLC's Operating Agreement provides that the LLC will only engage in activities permissible for national banks. In addition, the consent of all members through their representatives on the Board of Managers will be required before the LLC may engage in any new activities. Thus, Bank can prevent proposed new activities not permissible for national banks. Also, any amendment to the LLC Operating Agreement to change the LLC's purposes or permissible activities or to change any of the voting or consent requirements would require Bank's consent. As a result, Bank will be able, on an ongoing basis, to prevent the LLC from engaging in new activities that may be impermissible for national banks.

3. The Bank's loss exposure must be limited, as a legal and accounting matter, and the Bank must not have open-ended liability for the obligations of the enterprise.

a. Loss exposure from a legal standpoint

A primary concern of the OCC is that national banks should not be subjected to undue risk. Where an investing bank will not control the operations of the entity in which the bank holds an interest, it is important that a bank's investment not expose it to unlimited liability. This is the case here. <**NOTE:** As noted, this opinion does not address any *direct* activities of the Bank with regard to the stored value systems. See footnote 3, supra. Such direct activities could, of course, involve exposure of the bank in other aspects and, accordingly, will be subject to OCC monitoring and review even during the pilot program.> As a legal matter, investors in a Delaware LLC will not incur liability beyond their investment in the LLC because of being a member or manager of the LLC—even if they actively participate in the management or control of the business Del. Code Ann. Tit. 6, 18-303(a) (1994). Additionally, the LLC Operating Agreement does not expose the Bank to unlimited liability due to its investment in the LLC.

b. Loss exposure from an accounting standpoint

In assessing a bank's loss exposure as an accounting matter, the OCC has previously noted that the appropriate accounting treatment for a bank's 20-50 percent ownership share or investment in an LLC is to report it as an unconsolidated entity under the equity method of accounting. Under this method, unless the bank has extended a loan to the entity, guaranteed any of its liabilities or has other financial obligations to the entity, losses generally are limited to the amount of the investment shown on the investor's books. *See generally,* Accounting Principles Board, Op. 18 19 (1971) (equity method of accounting for investments in common stock). Interpretive Letter 692, *supra.* Bank's investment will amount to a one-third ownership interest in the LLC; therefore, it may rely on the equity method.

4. The investment must be convenient or useful to the Bank in carrying out its business and not a mere passive investment unrelated to that Bank's banking business.

A national bank's investment in an enterprise or entity that is not an operating subsidiary of the bank also must satisfy the requirement that the investment have a beneficial connection to the *bank's* business, i.e., be convenient or useful to the investing bank's business activities, and not be a mere passive investment unrelated to that bank's business activities, "Necessary" has been judicially construed to mean "convenient or useful." *See Arnold Tours, Inc. v. Camp, supra,* 472 F.2d at 432. The provision in 12 U.S.C. 24(Seventh) relating to the purchase of stock, derived from section 16 of the Glass-Steagall Act, was only intended to make it clear that section 16 did not authorize speculative investments in stock. *See* OCC Interpretive Letter No. 697, *reprinted in* [Current Transfer Binder] Fed. Banking L. Rep. (CCH) 81-102. Therefore, a consistent thread running through our precedents concerning stock ownership is that it must be convenient or useful to the bank in conducting that bank's banking business. The investment must benefit or facilitate that business and cannot be a mere passive or speculative investment.

That requirement is met in this case. Bank is actively engaged in many aspects of electronic banking and has become known as an innovator in the field. The basic function of the LLC is to effectuate transfers of financial value, and this will provide opportunities, particularly within Bank's market area, for Bank to provide account services for the holders of smart cards. In fact, Bank may serve as the issuer of the stored value used in the LLC's system. As has been shown in the discussion set forth above, the investment by Bank in LLC is designed to contribute to customer convenience in using the system for cashless payments; expand Bank's customer base; permit better use of Bank's data processing capacity and technical personnel; expand the number of Bank's contacts with universities and other entities using the system, with the potential for offering additional cash management and deposit processing services; and expand the Bank's merchant customer base as vendor capabilities. Additionally, existing customers of Bank's core banking and other services, who can use a stored value system, are increasingly looking to Bank to provide such a system and the ability of Bank to provide such a system to such customers will be a factor in Bank's being able to retain these existing customers for core banking and other services. Finally, the use of a joint venture vehicle to develop the stored value system gives the Bank access to technology owned by Battelle and Sallie Mae that might otherwise be unavailable to the Bank.

C. Conclusion

Based upon the information and representations you have provided, and for the reasons discussed above, Bank's investment in the LLC satisfies the four standards for a national bank's majority and minority, noncontrolling investment in a LLC. Therefore, the investment is approved subject to the following conditions:

1. the LLCs may engage only in activities that are part of or incidental to the business of banking;
2. the Bank will have veto power over any activities and major decisions of the LLC that are inconsistent with condition number one, or will withdraw from the LLC in the event its engages in an activity that is inconsistent with condition number one;
3. the Bank will account for the investment in the LLC under the equity method of accounting; and
4. the LLC will be subject to OCC supervision, regulation, and examination. <**NOTE:** In the future, the nature and scope of the LLC's activities might be so substantially enhanced that the methodology the OCC uses to compute the Bank's assessment will need to be adjusted to cover adequately the expense of supervising and examining the LLC.>

Please be advised that all conditions of this approval are "conditions imposed in writing by the agency in connection with the granting of any application or other request" within the meaning of 12 U.S.C. 1818.

Sincerely,

/s/

Julie L. Williams
Chief Counsel

Appendix A7
OCC Interpretive Letter No. 742 (Aug. 19, 1996)

Published in Interpretations and Actions September 1996

12 U.S.C. 1831a(d)
12 U.S.C. 24(7)

Lisa Detwiler Esq.
Schnader, Harrison, Segal & Lewis
1600 Market Street, Suite 3600
Philadelphia, PA 19103-4252

Re: Apollo Trust Company, Apollo, Pennsylvania

Dear Ms. Detwiler:

This responds to your request of June 25, 1996, that the Office of the Comptroller of the Currency (the "OCC") confirm that a national bank subsidiary may provide home banking services via a direct and Internet connection to the bank's home banking system and, incidental to that service, may also provide Internet access to customers and non-bank customers in the bank's service area. Apollo Trust Company, Apollo, Pennsylvania (the "Bank"), a state chartered bank, seeks the OCC's opinion in connection with its request for Federal Deposit Insurance Corporation (the "FDIC") approval under 12 U.S.C. 1831a(d) to establish a wholly owned subsidiary. <**NOTE:** Section 303 of the Federal Deposit Insurance Corporation Improvement Act of 1991, 12 U.S.C. 1831a(d), provides that a subsidiary of an insured state-chartered bank, such as the Bank, may not engage as principal in any type of activity that is not permissible for a subsidiary of a national bank unless, the FDIC determines that the activity poses no risk to the Insurance Fund and the bank meets applicable capital standards.> The Pennsylvania Department of Banking previously approved the Bank's application to establish the proposed Internet banking subsidiary, finding the provision of such electronic banking services permissible under Pennsylvania Law. *See* Pa. Stat. Ann. tit. 7, 201(a)(vi). Based on the information and representations provided, and for the reasons discussed below, I conclude that the proposed activity is permissible for a national bank subsidiary.

BACKGROUND

The Bank is a community bank located in rural Apollo, Pennsylvania, approximately 35 miles northeast of Pittsburgh, Pennsylvania. The Bank currently operates a proprietary Bulletin Board System ("BBS"); maintains a Home Page on the Internet <**NOTE:** The "Internet" is an electronic communications medium based on a global system of interconnected computer networks of over 6.5 million computers world-wide. This system of computer networks transmits data over telephone lines, television cable and satellite links. Over 40 million people access the Internet using their home PCS to reach mainframes worldwide. In the U.S. alone, there are over 12 million households which subscribe to commercial online services such as America OnLine, CompuServe, and Prodigy that provide access to the Internet. Commerce over the Internet, including banking, represents a relatively small but growing percentage of all Internet traffic. An "Internet access service", such as that proposed by the Bank, provides an electronic gateway by which service subscribers may connect their personal computers to the Internet using a modem and telephone line.> and provides banking services to its customers via the Bank's Home Page. These banking services include transferring funds between accounts, applying for loans and viewing account balances.

Using the Bank's BBS, customers and non-customers in the Bank's local service area may access the Internet with a local call. The Bank presently offers Internet access to its customers and to non-customers in its service area. Many community groups use the Bank's Internet service including local libraries, schools, local county governments and other public organizations. The Bank provides the least costly means of Internet access in the Bank's market area, as other service providers involve potentially costly toll calls.

To establish its Internet banking platform, the Bank acquired several server computers solely dedicated to the Bank's home banking and Internet services and has established a dedicated phone line connecting the Bank with its Internet access provider. The Bank represents that it will not incur any additional costs to use this equipment to provide Internet access to non-customers.

All users who contract to receive Internet access from the Bank's Internet banking subsidiary are required to sign a user agreement before accessing the Bank's Home Page. The user agreement outlines the rights and obligations of persons who choose to access the Internet via the Bank's BBS and limits the Bank's liability to the amount paid for such access.

The Bank represents that its home banking operation contains state-of-the-art security safeguards. The Bank's home banking operation is physically separate from the Bank's internal information systems. Customer transaction information is transmitted daily in batch form between the home banking servers and the

Bank's internal information systems. The Bank represents that such a system minimizes the risk of unauthorized access to customers' financial information housed in the Bank's internal information systems.

Currently, 840 individuals subscribe to the Bank's Internet services. Approximately 525 are bank customers who also subscribe to the Bank's home banking services and 315 local residents who subscribe solely for Internet access. To access the Bank's services, a local area subscriber dials into the Bank's dedicated Bulletin Board server. Once subscribers have accessed the Bank's Bulletin Board server, they may choose to transact their banking business directly or to access the Internet for banking and non-banking purposes. The Bank's logo appears on the subscriber's computer screen from the moment the customer accesses the Bank's BBS until they connect to the Internet. Customers located outside the Bank's local area and those already in an Internet session may connect to the Bank's home banking services via its Home Page on the Internet. <**NOTE:** The Bank, by providing access to the Internet, does not provide an information service *per se,* but rather it acts as a communications gateway service enabling users to connect electronically with the Internet. The Bank's role is strictly that of an electronic interface between the customer and the Internet. It does not exercise any control over information content or web sites users access on the Internet.>

DISCUSSION

Statutory Framework

The National Bank Act provides that national banks shall have the power:

> [t]o exercise . . . all such incidental powers as shall be necessary to carry on the business of banking; by discounting and negotiating promissory notes, drafts, bills of exchange, and other evidences of debt; by receiving deposits; by buying and selling exchange, coin, and bullion; by loaning money on personal security; and by obtaining, issuing, and circulating notes . . . .

12 U.S.C. 24(Seventh).

The Supreme Court has held that this clause is a broad grant of the power to engage in the business of banking including, but not limited to, the five specifically recited powers and the business of banking as a whole. *See NationsBank of North Carolina, N.A. v. Variable Life Annuity Co.,* 115 S. Ct. 810 (1995) ("*VALIC*"). Many activities that are not included in the enumerated powers are also part of the business of banking. Judicial precedent reflects three general principles used to determine whether an activity is within the scope of the "business of banking": (1) is the activity functionally equivalent to or a logical outgrowth of a recognized banking activity; (2) would the activity respond to customer needs or otherwise benefit the bank or its customers; and (3) does the activity involve risks similar in nature to those already assumed by banks. *See, e.g., Merchants' Bank v. State Bank,* 77 U.S. 604 (1871); *M & M Leasing Corp. v. Seattle First National Bank,* 563 F.2d 1377, 1382 (9th Cir. 1977), *cert. denied,* 436 U.S. 956 (1978); *American Insurance Association v. Clarke,* 865 F.2d 278, 282 (2d Cir. 1988).

Further, as the Supreme Court established in the *VALIC* decision, national banks are also authorized to engage in an activity if that activity is incidental to the performance of the five specified powers in 12 U.S.C. 24(Seventh) *or* incidental to the performance of an activity that is part of the business of banking. Before *VALIC,* the standard often considered in determining whether an activity was incidental to banking was that advanced by the First Circuit Court of Appeals in *Arnold Tours, Inc. v. Camp,* 472 F.2d 427 (1st Cir. 1972) ("*Arnold Tours*"). The *Arnold Tours* standard defined an incidental power as one that is "convenient or useful in connection with the performance of one of the bank's established activities pursuant to its ***express*** powers under the National Bank Act." *Arnold Tours* at 432 (emphasis added). Even before *VALIC,* the *Arnold Tours* formula represented the narrow interpretation of the "incidental powers" provision of the National Bank Act. OCC Interpretive Letter No. 494 *reprinted in* [1989-1990 Transfer Binder] Fed. Banking L. Rep. (CCH) 83,083 (Dec. 20, 1989). The *VALIC* decision, however, established that the *Arnold Tours* incidental power formula includes those activities that are convenient and useful to the "business of banking," as well as activities incidental to the express powers specifically enumerated in 12 U.S.C. 24(Seventh). *See Norwest Bank Minn., N.A. v. Sween Corp.,* 916 F. Supp. 1494 (D. Minn. 1996).

Internet Banking Is Part of the Business of Banking

Providing facilities to enable customers to conduct banking activities via the Internet clearly satisfies each of the three general principles that we look to in evaluating whether an activity is part of the business of banking.

First, the Bank's proposal to provide banking services to its customers either by a direct telephone connection or by the Internet is simply the use of new electronic technology to provide recognized banking services. It is well established that a national bank may use electronic means to perform services expressly or incidentally authorized to national banks. *See* OCC Interpretive Letter No. 677, *reprinted in* [1994-1995 Transfer Binder] Fed. Banking L. Rep. (CCH) 83,625 (June 28, 1995); OCC Interpretive Letter No. 284, *reprinted in* [1983-1984 Transfer Binder] Fed. Banking L. Rep. (CCH) 85,448 (Mar. 26, 1984), OCC Interpretive Letter No. 449, *reprinted in* [1988-1989 Transfer Binder] Fed. Banking L. Rep. (CCH) 85,673 (Aug. 23, 1988). The OCC Interpretive Ruling setting forth this authority was recently revised, in recognition of the rapid advancement of technology, to authorize a national bank to "perform, provide, or deliver through electronic means and facilities any activity, function, product, or service that it is otherwise authorized to perform, provide or deliver." 61 Fed. Reg. 4849 (1996) codified at 12 C.F.R. 7.1019. Thus, national banks may provide personal computer home banking services to their customers, enabling such customers to obtain account information, transfer balances, and conduct other banking transactions, using telephone lines as the access device. *See* OCC Interpretive Letter No. 677, *supra* (national bank may acquire software development personnel, equipment and facilities to develop home banking software), and OCC Interpretive Letter No. 611, *reprinted in* [1992-1993 Transfer Binder] Fed. Banking L. Rep. (CCH) 83,449 (Nov. 23, 1992) (national bank may provide banking services using specially designed computerized "smart phone").

Second, customers, who once could only access a bank's home banking servers through dedicated phone lines, will now have the option of connecting to the bank via the Internet. Providing bank services in the manner proposed by the Bank responds to customer needs. Bank customers will no longer be constrained to conduct their banking business during business hours but may do so whenever they choose through their personal computers. The Bank's system also gives customers dual means to access the Bank's home banking server to conduct their home banking activities. Customers can access the Bank directly when they are in the local calling area. When they are outside the Bank's local calling area, customers may connect to the Bank via the Internet. Local area customers who have connected to the Internet may also conduct their banking business during an Internet session without having to end the Internet session to connect directly to the Bank.

The Bank's proposal potentially benefits the Bank, as well as its customers. By providing home banking services to its customers, the Bank can increase the flexibility and responsiveness of its home banking services. The use of less costly electronic distribution channels also enables the bank to better compete with larger institutions.

Third, the risks a national bank confronts in providing home banking services in the manner proposed by the Bank are similar to the risks associated with the permissible activities of providing banking services via electronic means generally. To connect to the Bank's home banking servers, customers must enter their password to gain access to their account information. This information is then encrypted and transmitted to the Bank. This process serves both as an authentication mechanism and to protect the customers' confidential financial information from being intercepted and compromised when it travels across the telephone line used. Conducting the business of banking over an open system such as the Internet raises special security issues requiring systems and controls to manage these risks.

Internet Access for Bank Customers Is Incidental to the Business of Banking

Providing its customers full Internet access, in the manner proposed by the Bank even though customers may use that access for non-banking purposes, is incidental to the power of a national bank as part of the "business of banking" to provide Internet home banking services to its customers under 12 U.S.C. 24(Seventh).

In a variety of contexts, the OCC has concluded that a national bank under its incidental authority may provide electronic gateway and communications services, enabling its customers to conduct the business of banking. *See* OCC Interpretive Letter No. 346, *reprinted in* [1985-1987 Transfer Binder] Fed. Banking L. Rep. (CCH) 85,516 (July 31, 1985) (national banks may provide gateway service when service is electronic delivery means of banks' services); OCC Interpretive Letter No 419, *reprinted in* [1988-1989 Transfer Binder] Fed. Banking L. Rep. (CCH) 85,643 (Feb. 16, 1988) (national bank providing customers with a permissible electronic transactional information service may provide software to enable customers to participate in service); OCC Interpretive Letter No. 513, *reprinted in* [1990-1991 Transfer Binder] Fed. Banking L. Rep. (CCH) 83,215 (June 13, 1990) (national banks permitted to establish an electronic network for transmission of visual, voice and data communications). National banks may, incidental to the business of banking, own the means of distribution and communication to provide services to their customers. *Oklahoma v. Bank of Oklahoma,* 409 F. Supp. 71, 90 (N.D. Okla. 1975). National banks may therefore own Internet servers, the technology that enables the actual connection to the Internet, so that they may deliver banking services to their customers over the Internet. While the Bank proposes to provide full Internet access which will enable customers to use the Internet for non-banking as well as banking purposes, full Internet access service also is permissible in this case for three reasons.

First, the full Internet access service is permissible under national banks' incidental authority to provide electronic products or services that can be used for both banking and non-banking functions as part of a package of banking related products or services where the full function products or services are not an excessive amount of the total package. OCC Interpretive Letter No. 611, *supra,* (sale of computerized telephone "smart phone" is incidental to banking even though the phone can be used for non-banking functions). *See also* OCC Interpretive Letter No. 345, *reprinted in* [1985-1987 Transfer Binder] Fed. Banking L. Rep. (CCH) 85,515 (July 9, 1985) (permitting a national bank to provide full function computer hardware as part of package of banking and financial data processing services); Letter from Michael J. O'Keefe, District Counsel, Midwestern District dated July 13, 1987 (unpublished) (distribution of software and hardware to banks permissible so long as full function hardware does not "dominate" permissible data processing services involved); OCC Interpretive Letter No. 516, *reprinted in* [1990-1991 Transfer Binder] Fed. Banking L. Rep. (CCH) 83,220 (July 12, 1990) (hardware permissible when necessary and convenient to information services and where sale of such incidental hardware does not exceed 30% of total cost of package); *cf., Association of Data Processing v. Board of Governors,* 745 F. 2d 677 (D.C. Cir. 1984).

In this case, the full access service adds virtually nothing to the cost of providing Internet home banking and does not dominate the Bank's home banking package. Even assuming that the Bank could separate its home banking functions from Internet access, it is impracticable to do so. Once the customer has entered his/her password and gained access to the Bank's BBS, the customer has accessed the Internet. From this connection, the customer is then automatically sent to the Bank's Home Page. The screen that the customers view is identical no matter whether they access it through the Bank's dedicated phone line or from the Internet.

Second, providing full Internet access creates a package of related services needed to satisfy consumer demand and enable the Bank to successfully market its home banking services. OCC precedent has established that the provision of such ancillary non-banking services is permissible as incidental to the business of banking when needed to successfully package and promote other permissible banking services. OCC Interpretive Letter No. 611, *supra,* (bank selling home banking service can also provide customer access to non-banking services "to increase the customer base and the usage of the program"); OCC Interpretive Letter No. 653, *reprinted in* [1994-1995 Transfer Binder] Fed. Banking L. Rep. (CCH) 83,601 (Dec. 22, 1994) (national banks may offer non-banking products as part of larger product or service when necessary, convenient and useful to bank permissible activities). *Cf., National Courier Ass'n v. Board of Governors,* 516 F. 2d 1229, 1240 (D.C. Cir. 1975) (incidental powers of holding companies to provide specialized courier services when service necessary to obtain full benefit of data processing services).

Here, the full Internet access service is needed to successfully provide and market the Bank's Internet banking service. Limiting the Bank's gateway services, to block non-banking use, would create a hobbled home banking product unlikely to meet consumer demand. Customers in the midst of an Internet session wanting to view their account information would need to end the Internet session, then connect directly to the Bank. Such a cumbersome structure would not fully meet customer needs, causing them to search for more useful banking products offered by other institutions.

Third, in the Bank's situation, a national bank would be permitted to provide customers with full Internet access as a permissible use of its excess capacity acquired in good faith. A national bank, under its incidental authority, may market and sell excess electronic capacities acquired or developed by the bank in good faith for banking purposes. 12 C.F.R. 7.1019. *See also* OCC Interpretive Letter No. 677 (national bank that acquired software development personnel, equipment and facilities for legitimate banking and financial related software may use some excess capacity to develop non-banking products). The acquisition of equipment and its attendant excess capacity will be in good faith if it is done in order to meet the needs of the bank and its customers for data processing activities that are part of the business of banking. This can occur where, as here, due to characteristics of the data processing equipment available on the market, the capacity of the most practicable optimal equipment available to meet the bank's needs may also exceed its precise needs. *See e.g.*, Letter from Peter Liebesman, Asst. Director, Legal Activities and Services Division, dated Dec. 13, 1983 (unpublished).

A bank that has in good faith acquired excess Internet access capacity need not allow the excess capacity to go unused. The realities of Internet access and gateway systems technology demonstrate that the Bank would not incur additional costs to provide Internet access to its customers and non-bank customers located in the Bank's service area. The technological specifications of the equipment used to establish the Bank's Internet banking platform would legitimately have capacity in excess of that required to provide banking services over the Internet. Providing Internet access to its customers enables the Bank to benefit from the excess capacity resulting from the establishment of the Bank's Internet banking platform. *See* Letter from Stephen B. Brown, Attorney dated Dec. 20, 1989 (unpublished) (national banks may sell excess capacity in long-line telecommunications equipment where capacity acquired for anticipated future needs in private telecommunications network created to link branches and affiliated banks).

Providing Internet access does not present a unique risk to a bank. Guarding against unauthorized access to bank records and processes is a risk banks have faced historically in their roles as safekeepers of customers' assets and sensitive information. Today's banks, in addition to facing assaults on physical assets, also must protect their data processing systems from unauthorized access to information systems—the modern repositories of a customer's wealth—through the erection of electronic "firewalls" or other mechanisms.

The Bank represents that it has taken many steps to address this risk. Its Internet activities are performed on servers solely dedicated to these functions. No electronic connection is maintained between these systems and the Bank's internal information systems. Therefore, even if an individual was to obtain unauthorized access to the Bank's Internet servers, the Bank's information systems would not be compromised. Moreover, the Bank represents that it has provided banking services over the Internet since January 1995 and, therefore, has some familiarity with the risks presented by conducting electronic banking services.

Internet Access for Non-Customers in the Manner Proposed Is also Incidental to the Business of Banking

Finally, I conclude that providing Internet access to non-bank customers, in the manner proposed by the Bank, is incidental to the power of a national bank to provide Internet home banking services to its customers under 12 U.S.C. 24(Seventh).

National banks, like any other business, may engage in activities to establish their reputation as a good corporate citizen in the community, and to promote and advertise their goods and services. *See, e.g., Franklin Nat'l Bank of Franklin Square v. New York,* 347 U.S. 373 (1954) (national bank has power to advertise bank services); OCC Interpretive Letter No. 690, *reprinted in* [Current Transfer Binder] Fed. Banking L. Rep. (CCH) 81-005 (Oct. 2, 1995) (national bank may provide promotional merchandise bearing its logo so long as it engages in the activity primarily to market its banking services, not to make a significant profit on the merchandise itself). To that end, national banks may, to a limited extent, offer non-banking services to attract the public to its premises "in the hope of expanding their goodwill and thereby their banking business." *Corbett v. Devon Bank,* 299 N.E. 2d 521, 12 Ill App. 3d 559 (1973) (finding a national bank may sell motor vehicle licenses in its branch offices to attract customers).

Here, the Bank will offer Internet access to establish goodwill, and to promote and advertise its goods and services in its service area. Non-customer users of the Bank's Internet access include local libraries, schools and local governmental units. Providing Internet access to non-customers also specifically and effectively advertises the Bank's Internet banking services and increases the number of Internet banking customers. The Bank's Internet access service creates a class of active Internet users in the Bank's service area who are more likely to become customers of the Bank's home banking services.

Also, providing Internet access to non-bank customers in the Bank's service area is a valid and incidental distribution of excess capacity. As discussed earlier, a national bank may under its incidental authority distribute for non-banking purposes and uses its good faith excess capacity. 12 C.F.R. 7.1019. *See also* OCC Interpretive Letter No. 677 and OCC Interpretive Letter No 611, discussed above. It is well established that national banks are authorized to provide non-banking products developed through the utilization of such excess capacity to persons that have no banking relations with the institution. OCC Interpretive Letter No. 677, *supra.* Accordingly, the Bank may distribute its excess Internet capacity to non-customers.

CONCLUSION

Based upon the foregoing facts and analysis, and the representations made by the Bank in connection with its request, I conclude that the proposed activity is permissible for a national bank.

Sincerely,

/s/

Julie L. Williams
Chief Counsel

APPENDIX A8
OCC Interpretive Letter No. 836 (Mar. 12, 1996)

Comptroller of the Currency
Administrator of National Banks

Washington, DC 20219

March 12, 1996

12 U.S.C. 24(7)

Dear [ ]:

This is in response to your letters of January 10, 1996 and February 9, 1996, requesting confirmation that [ ], [*City, State*] ("Bank"), may lawfully acquire and hold a minority interest in [ ] ("Company"), which is engaged in medical claims processing. The Company currently is owned by [ ] ("Holding Company") and [ ] ("Individual"). For the reasons set forth below, I agree with your conclusion.

BACKGROUND

The Bank intends to acquire a 49% interest in the Company, which will use automated data processing and electronic data interchange facilities to assist hospitals and physicians ("Providers") in communicating billing and payment-related information, including abbreviated diagnosis and treatment information, to entities responsible for providing medical benefits (government agencies, health maintenance organizations, and insurance carriers) ("Payers"), determining how much of the patient's bill is owed by the patient and how much is owed by the Payer, billing the Payer and the patient as appropriate, and facilitating payment by the patient and the patient's Provider, through funds transfer and credit card processing services, including the use of Bank-issued special purpose medical credit cards, when requested by patients.[1]

[1] Currently, the Company's medical claims processing, handled through its own self-developed software system, would be considered an information exchange network, since the Company is not a financial institution and cannot provide actual funds transfer services from Payers to Providers.

The Company will store, process, and retrieve documents and information needed to substantiate the medical claims being submitted and collect on past-due accounts owed to hospitals and physicians. It also will continue to maintain and operate the electronic data processing ("EDP") facilities of a hospital owned by an affiliate of the Company ("Hospital"). This activity will not generate more than 5% of the Company's gross revenues and will be done in conformity with the OCC's Interpretive Ruling 7.3500, 12 C.F.R. § 7.3500, as revised at 61 Fed. Reg. 4849, 4865 (1996) (to be codified at 12 C.F.R. § 7.1019) (effective April 1, 1996).

The Company's two shareholders, the Holding Company and the Individual, currently own 98.25% and 1.75% of the Company's stock, respectively. The Individual owns all the issued and outstanding stock of the Holding Company. The Bank,[2] the Holding Company and the Individual have entered into a Shareholders' Agreement ("Agreement') that includes the following provisions:

- The initial Board of Directors of the Company will consist of five directors. Two directors will be elected by the Holding Company, and two will be elected by the Bank. The fifth director position will be filled by the Company's chief executive officer, who will be mutually agreed upon by the Company and the Bank. Thereafter, the Board of Directors will be increased in multiples of two. The Bank and the Company shall have equal representation on the Board so long as each owns directly or indirectly 80% of the shares they will hold on the effective date of the Agreement.

- Major Decisions of the Company must be agreed to by the directors representing the Holding Company and the Bank. The term "Major Decision" includes amendments to the Articles of Incorporation or By-Laws of the Company; a merger or other business combination with another corporation whose assets or net worth is more than 33% of the assets or net worth of the Company; the acquisition of the Company by any other person; the acquisition by the Company of any other corporation or business whose assets or net worth are more than 33% of the assets or net worth of the Company; the sale of substantially all of the assets of the Company; the liquidation or voluntary dissolution of the Company; the selection of a Chief Executive Officer; and the registration of shares of the Company with the Securities and Exchange Commission for sale of such shares to the public.

- Directors representing the Holding Company and the Bank must adopt an annual business plan which, among other things, will assure that the Company will not do anything to jeopardize the Bank's compliance with regulatory requirements and that the

---

[2] The Bank was not an initial signatory to the Agreement but was assigned all the rights under the Agreement by a wholly-owned subsidiary of the Bank's parent company which did sign the agreement.

Company will not engage in any line of business which would necessitate the Bank's divestiture of its ownership in the Company, or the Company's divestiture of any significant activity or line of business of the Company. The Bank and the Holding Company also agree that the annual business plan will restrict the Company's business to the extent necessary to assure that the Company will qualify for pooling-of interests accounting treatment under then current accounting provisions.

- Two primary provisions by which control of the Company may change subsequent to the closing are a put and call provision ("Put and Call") and a buy-sell provision ("Buy Sell"). The Put and Call permits the Bank to exercise a call option on an additional 18% of the Holding Company's stock in the Company under certain conditions. It also permits the Holding Company to cause the Bank to purchase 18% of those shares under certain conditions. You advise that the Put and Call would not necessarily increase the Bank's ownership because the Bank has the right to cause additional stock purchases to be made by its nominee or designee and because one of the primary purposes of the Put and Call is to prevent or minimize dilution, for example, upon the subsequent merger of the Company with another entity. The Buy Sell is applicable only so long as the Company and the Bank own at least 80% of what they own at closing and only if the parties cannot reach agreement on a Major Decision, as described above. Again, nominees are available to make the purchases.

ANALYSIS

The Bank's plan to purchase a 49% interest in the Company initially raises the issue of the authority of a national bank to hold a minority interest in a corporation. A recent OCC interpretive letter extensively analyzed the authority of national banks under 12 U.S.C. § 24(Seventh) to own stock, and reviewed OCC precedents on the ownership of stock in amounts less than that required for an operating subsidiary, *i.e.*, non-controlling stock investments. Interpretive Letter No. 697, [Current] Fed. Banking L. Rep. (CCH) ¶ 81-013 (Nov. 15, 1995). That letter concluded that ownership of a non-controlling interest in a corporation is permissible provided that four standards, drawn from OCC precedents, are satisfied. They are:

1) The activities of the enterprise in which the investment is made must be limited to activities that are part of, or incidental to, the business of banking;

2) The bank must be able to prevent the enterprise from engaging in activities that do not meet the foregoing standard, or be able to withdraw its investment;

3) The bank's loss exposure must be limited, as a legal and accounting matter, and the bank must not have open-ended liability for the obligations of the enterprise; and

4) The investment must be convenient or useful to the bank in carrying out its business and not a mere passive investment unrelated to *that bank's* banking business.

Each of these factors is discussed below and applied to your proposal.

1. The activities of the enterprise in which the investment is made must be limited to activities that are part of, or incidental to, the business of banking.

Our precedents on minority stock ownership have recognized that the enterprise in which the bank takes an equity interest must confine its activities to those that are part of or incidental to the conduct of the banking business. *See, e.g.*, Interpretive Letter No. 380, [1988-1989 Transfer Binder] Fed. Banking L. Rep. (CCH) ¶ 85,604 n.8 (Dec. 29, 1986) (since a national bank can provide options clearing services to customers, it can purchase stock in a corporation providing options clearing services); Letter from Robert B. Serino, Deputy Chief Counsel (Nov. 9, 1992) (since the operation of an ATM network is "a fundamental part of the basic business of banking," an equity investment in a corporation operating such a network is permissible).

The Company's activities will involve automated data processing services to facilitate accounts receivable collections, billing, and related funds transfers for Providers. The OCC previously has approved the activities the Company will perform. The following summarizes our precedents.

National banks may use automated data processing to provide billing services and accounts receivable services for itself and others, Interpretive Letter No. 419, [1988-1989 Transfer Binder] Fed. Banking L. Rep. (CCH) ¶ 85,643 (Feb. 16, 1988) ("Letter 419"), and engage in data processing related to funds transfer, cash management, and credit extensions, *id.*, (funds transfer); Letter from Peter Liebesman, Assistant Director, Legal Advisory Services Division (Dec. 13, 1985) (cash management); Interpretive Letter No. 611, [1992-1993 Transfer Binder] Fed. Banking L. Rep. (CCH) ¶ 83,449 (Nov. 23, 1992) (cash management, funds transfer); Letter from Peter Liebesman, Assistant Director, Legal Advisory Services Division (Aug. 15, 1983) (credit extensions). The OCC also has approved electronic data interchange services for financial information, Interpretive Letter No. 653, [1994-1995 Transfer Binder] Fed. Banking L. Rep. (CCH) ¶ 83,601 (Dec. 22, 1994) (informational and payments interface) and credit card processing, Interpretive Letter No. 689, [Current] Fed. Banking L. Rep. (CCH) ¶ 81-004 (Aug. 9, 1995).

The OCC, on several occasions, has found health insurance claims processing and related activities to be permissible. *See* Letter from Gail W. Pohn, Director, Bank Organization and Structure Division (Nov. 19, 1975) (providing doctors with an accounts receivable and billing system with inquiry and input capabilities); Letter 419 (settlement and payment of health insurance claims through the use of shared electronic funds transfer technology by linking health care providers, insurers, recipients, and their respective depository institutions, transmitting claim eligibility information, receiving and transmitting information for claims entry and payment, operating a data base, accomplishing payment, and developing and licensing appropriate software programs to health care providers to permit their participation);[3] Letter from Jeanne N. Devine, Senior Attorney (May 26, 1994) (collection services are permissible).

The Company's continued maintenance, operation, and management of the EDP facilities of the Hospital will include patient accounting, medical records, payroll, general ledger, accounts payable, employee time and attendance, scheduling the provision of services, and fixed assets. The contract between the Company and the Hospital will produce less than 5% of the total projected gross revenues of the Company. Many of the services involve data processing which is permissible under the above analysis. To the extent some activities may fall outside that analysis, they properly may be considered "excess capacity." The Bank's acquisition of its interest in the Company is being done in good faith, not to engage in such activities. *See generally* 12 C.F.R. § 7.3500 *supra.*; Preamble discussion of 12 C.F.R. § 7.1019, 61 Fed. Reg. 4853-4854 (1996); Interpretive Letter No. 677, [1994-1995 Transfer Binder] Fed. Banking L. Rep. (CCH) ¶ 83,625 (June 28, 1995) (national banks permitted to acquire interests in a software company where 7% of its revenues are derived from nonfinancial software production and distribution); Interpretive Letter No. 345, [1985-1987 Transfer Binder] Fed. Banking L. Rep. (CCH) ¶ 85,516 (July 31, 1985) (sale of computer hardware usable for nonfinancial purposes as well as financial purposes approved where hardware does not exceed 30% of cost of entire package of banking and financial data processing services).

Thus, the activities to be performed by the Company are activities that are part of or incidental to the business of banking, and the first standard is satisfied.

2. The bank must be able to prevent the enterprise from engaging in activities that do not meet the foregoing standard, or be able to withdraw its investment.

The activities of an enterprise in which a national bank invests must be part of or incidental to the business of banking not only at the time the bank initially purchases stock, but they must remain so for as long as the bank has an ownership interest. However, minority shareholders in a corporation do not possess a veto power as a matter of corporate law. One way to address this problem is for the corporation's articles of incorporation or bylaws to limit its activities to

---

[3] Letter 419 found that the transfer of funds from one account to another or from one institution to another is a fundamental part of the business of banking. The transmission of treatment information was found to be an integral part of and a proper incident to performing the funds transfer service.

those that are permissible for national banks. *See, e.g.*, Letters from Peter Liebesman, Assistant Director, Legal Advisory Services Division (January 26, 1981 and January 4, 1983).

Contractual solutions also are feasible. In the present case, the Bank, the Holding Company and the Individual have entered into a Shareholders' Agreement to address this concern. According to your letter, among other things, the Agreement provides that all Major Decisions must be approved by the affirmative vote of two-thirds of the directors, in absolute number. You have explained that this means the Bank and the Holding Company would have to approve all Major Decisions. Also, the Agreement requires that the Board adopt an annual business plan (among the items considered Major Decisions) which, among other things, includes actions to assure that the Company does not do anything to jeopardize the Bank's compliance with regulatory requirements and to assure that the Company will not engage in any line of business which would necessitate the Bank's divestiture of its ownership in the Company or the Company's divestiture of any significant activity or line of business.

These provisions assure that the Company will not engage in any activity that is not permissible for a corporation having a national bank shareholder. The Bank effectively will have a veto power over any impermissible activity as long as it continues to own shares in the Company. Thus, the second standard is satisfied.

3. The bank's loss exposure must be limited, as a legal and accounting matter, and the bank must not have open-ended liability for the obligations of the enterprise.

A primary concern of the OCC is that national banks should not be subjected to undue risk. Where an investing bank will not control the operations of the entity in which the bank holds an interest, it is important that a national bank's investment not expose it to unlimited liability. Normally, this is not a concern when investing in a corporation, for shareholders are protected by the "corporate veil" from liability for the debts of the corporation. 1 William M. Fletcher, Fletcher Cyclopedia of the Law of Private Corporations § 25 (perm. ed. rev. vol. 1990). In the present case, both the Company and the Bank will be separate corporations, with their own capital, directors, and officers.

Further, the Bank has been advised by its accountants, who have discussed the issue of limited loss exposure with the OCC's Office of the Chief Accountant, that the appropriate accounting treatment for its investment in the Company will be the equity method of accounting. Under this method, which is used for equity interests of 20 to 50 percent in corporations, losses recognized by the investor will not exceed the amount of the investment (including extensions of credit or guarantees, if any) shown on the investor's books. *See generally*, Accounting Principles Board, Op. 18, § 19 (1971) (equity method of accounting for investments in common stock).

Therefore, for both legal and accounting purposes, the Bank's potential loss exposure should be limited to the amount of its investment (plus, potentially, the amount of any extensions of credit that remain outstanding). Since that exposure will be quantifiable and controllable, the third standard is satisfied.[4]

4. The investment must be convenient or useful to the bank in carrying out its business and not a mere passive investment unrelated to that bank's banking business.

Twelve U.S.C. § 24(Seventh) gives national banks incidental powers that are "necessary" to carry on the business of banking. "Necessary" has been judicially construed to mean "convenient or useful." *Arnold Tours, Inc. v. Camp*, 472 F.2d 427, 432 (1st Cir. 1972). The provision in section 24(Seventh) relating to the purchase of stock, derived from section 16 of the Glass-Steagall Act, was intended only to make it clear that section 16 did not authorize speculative investments in stock. Interpretive Letter No. 697, *supra*. Therefore, a consistent thread running through our precedents concerning stock ownership is that such ownership must be convenient or useful to the investing bank in conducting its banking business. The investment must benefit or facilitate that business, and cannot be a mere passive or speculative investment. *See, e.g.*, Interpretive Letter No. 543, [1990-1991 Transfer Binder] Fed. Banking L. Rep. (CCH) ¶ 83,255 (Feb. 13, 1991); Interpretive Letter No. 427, [1988-1989 Transfer Binder] Fed. Banking L. Rep. (CCH) ¶ 85,651 (May 9, 1988); Interpretive Letter No. 421, [1988-1989 Transfer Binder] Fed. Banking L. Rep. (CCH) ¶ 85,645 (Mar. 14, 1988).

The Bank seeks the relationship with the Company in order to develop new financial data processing customers in the health care industry, which has proven difficult for the Bank to do on its own. The health care industry is an important sector of business within the Bank's market area, and it is doubtful the Bank would be able to develop a separate system in a timely and reasonably priced way. With its investment in the Company, the Bank will have access to the Company's successful payment processing business which can be integrated with other banking services provided by the Bank. The Bank also hopes, through its participation in the Company, to build relationships with Providers and insurance companies, and thereby obtain opportunities for cross-selling of banking products. The availability to the Company's customers of the Bank's funds transfer and credit card processing facilities will be convenient to them and should result in the development of a strong customer base for the Bank in the health care industry. Thus, this activity will be useful to the Bank in carrying out its banking business, and the fourth standard is satisfied.

---

[4] Whether exercising the Put and Call or the Buy Sell provisions of the Agreement would have an impact on the Bank's loss exposure as a legal or accounting matter cannot be determined unless such provisions are exercised. We do note your representation that the Bank's ability to designate nominees to purchase additional shares in the event these provisions are acted upon should enable it to avoid being placed in control of the Company against its wishes.

CONCLUSION

For the reasons outlined above, the Bank's investment in the Company would satisfy the four standards the OCC has applied to non-controlling minority investments. Our conclusion is conditioned upon the conditions listed below and compliance by the Bank with commitments made in connection with its request for a legal opinion:

1) the Company may engage only in activities that are part of, or incidental to, the business of banking;

2) the Bank will have veto power over any activities and Major Decisions of the Company that are inconsistent with condition 1), or the Bank will withdraw its investment in the Company if it proposes to engage in an activity that is inconsistent with condition 1);

3) the Company will be subject to OCC supervision and examination; and

4) the Bank will account for its investment in the Company under the equity method of accounting.

These commitments and conditions are conditions imposed in writing by the OCC in connection with its action on the request for a legal opinion confirming that the proposed investment is permissible under 12 U.S.C. § 24(Seventh) and, as such, may be enforced in proceedings under applicable law.

I hope that this has been responsive to your inquiry.

Sincerely,

/s/

Julie L. Williams
Chief Counsel

APPENDIX A9
OCC Interpretive Letter No. 856 (Mar. 12, 1996)

Comptroller of the Currency
Administrator of National Banks

Washington, DC 20219

March 5, 1999

12 USC 24(7)

William W. Templeton
Senior Counsel
Legal Department
Fleet Financial Group
50 Kennedy Plaza
Providence, RI 02903

Dear Mr. Templeton:

This responds to your request for an opinion on whether a national bank may offer certain connected Internet services and payments services to its small business banking customers pursuant to the authority in 12 U.S.C. § 24(Seventh) of the National Bank Act. Specifically, Fleet National Bank (the "Bank") wishes to offer a package of services that will include enabling its small business banking customers ("Retailers") to establish a retail sales presence on the Internet. Based upon the information and representations provided, I conclude that the proposed activity, as described in detail below, is permissible for a national bank.

BACKGROUND

The Bank proposes to offer its small business customers a package of electronic services (hereafter referred to as the "Product") that bundles traditional merchant credit card banking services with the software, hardware and technical support necessary for a small business to have its own retail web site that is able to accept credit card payments in a secure environment.[1] The package also includes monthly reports relating to activity on a Retailer's web site.

[1] A retail enabled web site will be able to accept credit card purchases on-line. This service will allow Retailers to create and maintain a web site that can also use the Bank's secure payments service. Bank is currently offering a web site credit card enabling service as a stand-alone service to retailers with web sites either established or in development. This particular product offering has, thus far, generally been directed at larger companies with their own established web sites.

To purchase the Product, a Retailer must: (i) already be, or qualify to be, a credit card merchant customer of the Bank, and (ii) have, or establish, a business checking account with the Bank. The Bank will provide authorization and processing services for credit card payments received through a Retailer's web site and will deposit the proceeds in the Retailer's checking account with the Bank.

In exchange for a one-time set up fee,[2] a Retailer is assigned a unique Internet web site address,[3] which the Bank registers with the major Internet search engines. The web site address can either include or not a reference to the Bank's URL, (e.g., "http://www.Bank.com/yourbusinessname" or http://www.yourbusinessname) depending upon the Retailer's choice.[4]

The Retailer's web site resides on Internet servers that are controlled by the Bank but not connected to any of the Bank's mainframe accounting or internal systems processing servers. The Retailer also is given access to the web site's "storebuilder wizard"-- a menu-driven software that enables the Retailer to build a catalog of product descriptions, pricing, delivery information and order forms. The Retailer works independently to build the web site to its satisfaction subject only to the limitation that the site cannot list more than 500 products. The product database (representing the Retailer's online catalog) is maintained and stored on the Bank's server.

Once the Retailer has established a business checking account, obtained credit underwriting approval to be a credit card merchant customer, and completed construction of the web site, the site is activated so that potential retail customers can access the site. After activation, the Bank

---

[2] Bank will charge a one time set up fee and a monthly maintenance fee for the Product. The web site Product (with related system support) is not available as a separate product offering and cannot be purchased without the entire package of associated banking products and services, such as the checking account and merchant credit card relationship. Although the Product will generate revenues from several sources, the Bank expects that the revenues from the associated traditional bank products will greatly exceed those relating only to the web site services.

[3] This address will be a Universal Resource Locator ("URL").

[4] The use of part of the Bank's name in the Retailer's URL could under some circumstances create a risk that the public will identify the Bank with the web site of its Retailer customers. However, that risk is mitigated here by the Bank's commitment to take all appropriate measures to limit its reputation risk associated with the Retailer's web site. Once activated, the Retailer's web site "store" will not carry any indication that it is carried on the Bank's servers or supported by Bank, aside from the URL that may be used by some Retailers (and the concomitant URL registration information that is publicly available). No Bank logo or any other reference to the Bank will appear within a Retailer's web site store, except as may be necessary to effect the payments processing component. Bank will also limit its reputation risk by reserving the right to prohibit offensive or indecent material from hosted sites.

This retail web hosting activity does not carry the same risks of bank customer confusion that can arise when a bank links its retail web site to sites of third parties so that bank customers are transported from a bank site to a non-bank site, *e.g.*, a bank sponsored "virtual or Internet mall." *Compare*, OCC Conditional Approval No. 221, *supra*. However, these risks could arise if the Bank began to link its retail banking web site to the Retailer sites it hosts. Bank has not indicated any intention to do this and, thus, we do not address it here.

provides ongoing maintenance and support of the web site's host servers and monthly reports on empirical data such as site "hits" and transaction volume.

The Bank servers maintain all the data associated with the web site, including product descriptions, images, and pricing.[5] The Bank also provides functions[6] by which customers of a Retailer select products, communicate their selection to the Retailer, and pay for products. Payments are made through a credit card, for which the Bank provides the payment authorization and processing.[7]

The Bank's retail web site hosting service also, via the Internet, provides an electronic communications pathway between the Retailer and its potential customers through which product orders and payment information flow. When a visitor to a Retailer's site submits a potential purchase order, the Bank captures and processes the necessary payments-related information and forwards an electronic message to the Retailer with the associated product and shipping order information. The Retailer is also able to electronically confirm payment authorization before shipping any goods.[8] Payment proceeds are deposited into the Retailer's business checking account with the Bank.

To maintain the site, the Retailer pays the Bank a monthly maintenance fee for the web site. In addition, all credit card purchases made through the site are assessed a credit card processing fee as a percentage of the amount, called a "merchant discount." The business checking account carries a fee as well. The Retailers will be cross-marketed other Bank products and banking services tailored to small business in an attempt to win other aspects of their retail banking business.

---

[5] Each Retailer is responsible to maintain and update the store and product information contained on their web site.

[6] The ordering function is a web page that lists all products selected by the visitor to the site. The paying function page allows the visitor to enter their credit card number, address, and shipping location in association with their potential purchase. These functions are applications that provide temporary storage of information relating to items selected for purchase as well as necessary payment and shipping information. Upon purchase authorization by the visitor, the application requests credit authorization and provides notification to the buyer and Retailer when authorization is received so the purchase may be completed if the parties elect to do so.

[7] Traditional merchant banking services are those services that enable retailers to collect the funds from credit card payments for goods and services sold. Once a retailer is approved through the credit underwriting process, the merchant bank provides the retailer with a card-accepting device for authorizing and recording credit card transactions. The merchant bank then provides services to clear and settle the credit card payments to the retailer, depositing funds collected in the retailer's account.

[8] The Bank also provides sales tax calculations for the Retailer using information on the product sold, the merchandise receiving location, and the identified state in which the Retailer operates. When constructing their web sites, the Retailers are responsible to identify the product codes and to identify their state of operation. In their agreement with the Bank, the Retailers acknowledge that they are responsible for the accuracy, collection, and submission of all appropriate and applicable sales taxes.

OCC recognizes that the proposed activity exposes the Bank to risks associated with accepting retail credit card payments on the Internet and conducting the activities necessary to clear and settle the payments received. The risks associated with credit underwriting, payment authorization, and processing are the same risks that banks already assume when providing merchant credit card processing services for business customers.[9] The risks associated with accepting and authorizing payments through the Retailer's website are identical to those already assumed when the Bank enables an established website to receive credit card orders. These risks include maintaining the accessibility, integrity, and confidentiality of the information systems necessary to complete the retail transactions through the website.[10] To the extent that the Bank contracts with other service providers, notably technology firms, to provide any of the necessary products and services to offer the Product to small business customers, the Bank will manage its indirect risk exposure to the activities of the service providers. Accordingly, the Bank has the necessary skills and expertise to effectively manage the risks.

DISCUSSION

The Product offered by the Bank to Retailers has three component services: retail web site hosting, retail payments processing, and business checking accounts. As each of these components is part of the business of banking, the Product is part of the business of banking and, thus, permissible for national banks under 12 U.S.C. § 24(Seventh).[11]

---

[9] As with other merchant credit card customers, applicants for the proposed product will be subject to a credit underwriting review by the Bank's merchant credit card division.

[10] Through an addendum to its merchant credit card agreement with its customers, the Bank will limit its legal liability for security breaches and systems failures.

[11] Assuming arguendo that the retail web hosting service was not part of the business of banking, an alternative grounds for permitting the activity would be that the Bank's web hosting activity is incidental to two traditional banking services: merchant credit card processing and business checking account services. The Bank has provided information indicating that provision of the web hosting service will significantly enhance the utility and desirability of these established banking services to the Bank's retail merchant customers and to allow the Bank to meet competition from non-banking firms that provide a similar package of services. See, e.g., OCC Conditional Approval No. 221, supra, and OCC Interpretive Letter No. 742, supra, (national banks providing home banking services via the internet may also provide internet access service to the banking customers as a product incidental to Internet home banking). Further, information provided by the Bank establishes that the anticipated level of revenue from the Bank's retail web site hosting component relative to the revenue from the associated business deposit account and merchant processing services would likely meet the subordination requirement for non-banking services incidental to banking services. OCC has said an incidental product may not dominate its connected banking service, but that where the gross profits generated by an incidental product provided in a package with a banking service do not exceed thirty percent of the total gross profits from the entire service package, the sale of the incidental product meets the subordination requirement. OCC Conditional Approval No. 221, (Dec. 4, 1996); OCC Interpretive Letter No. 754, reprinted in [1996-1997 Transfer Binder] Fed. Banking L. Rep. (CCH) ¶ 81,118 (November 6, 1996) (national bank operating subsidiary may sell general purpose computer hardware to other financial institutions as part of larger product or service when necessary, convenient, and useful to bank permissible activities). However, it is unnecessary to address that issue here because we conclude that the Bank's web site hosting activity is part of, rather than incidental to, the business of banking, and thus is not subject to scope limitations that apply to some incidental activities.

Retail web site hosting, as proposed by the Bank, is a form of finder activity authorized for national banks. The OCC has long recognized the finder function as a permissible banking activity that includes, "without limitation, identifying potential parties, making inquiries as to interest, introducing or arranging meetings of interested of parties, and otherwise bringing parties together for transactions that the parties themselves negotiate and consummate." 61 Fed. Reg. 4863 (Feb. 9, 1996) (codified at 12 C.F.R. 7.1002(b)).[12] Finder activities are part of the business of banking. OCC Interpretive Letter No. 824, *reprinted in* [1997-1998 Transfer Binder] Fed. Banking L. Rep. (CCH) ¶ 81-273 (February 27, 1998); OCC Corporate Decision No. 97-60 (July 1, 1997); and OCC Conditional Approval Letter No. 221, *supra.*[13]

The OCC has also recognized that banks may use new technology to conduct the finder activity. We have said:

> The means that national banks use to act as finders for their customers have evolved due to technological advancements. Where banks once performed this service for their customers via newsletters and personal contacts, they presently conduct the activity with computer technology.

Id. See also, OCC Interpretive Letter No. 516, *reprinted in* [1990-1991 Transfer Binder] Fed. Banking L. Rep. (CCH) ¶ 83,220 (July 12, 1990) (national banks may provide electronic

---

[12] 12 CFR § 7.1002 provides in its entirety:

> (a) General. A national bank may act as a finder in bringing together a buyer and seller.
> (b) Qualification. Acting as a finder includes, without limitation, identifying potential parties, making inquiries as to interest, introducing or arranging meetings of interested parties, and otherwise bringing parties together for transactions that they themselves negotiate and consummate. Acting as a finder does not include activities that would characterize the bank as a broker under applicable federal law.
> (c) Advertisement and fee. Unless otherwise prohibited, a national bank may advertise the availability of, and accept a fee for, the services provided pursuant to this section.

Earlier OCC decisions regarding finder activities cite 12 CFR § 7.7200. OCC interpretive rulings at 12 CFR Part 7 were revised and renumbered effective April 1, 1996. Interpretive ruling § 7.1002 (1996) replaced former interpretive ruling § 7.7200. The Bank has committed that its finder activities will be conducted in accordance with the provisions of 12 C.F.R. 7.1002.

[13] See also, Letter from J.T. Watson, Deputy Comptroller of the Currency, February 26, 1969 (unpublished); Letter from John M. Miller, July 26, 1977 (unpublished); Letter from Paul Allan Schott, Chief Counsel, May 5, 1988 (unpublished); Letter from Elizabeth Corey, May 18, 1989 (unpublished); OCC Interpretive Letter No. 238, *reprinted in* [1983-1984 Transfer Binder] Fed. Banking L. Rep. (CCH) ¶ 85,402 (Feb. 9, 1982); OCC Interpretive Letter No. 472, *reprinted in* [1989-1990 Transfer Binder] Fed. Banking L. Rep. (CCH) ¶ 83,008 (Mar. 2 1989); Letter from Lee Walzer, Attorney, Securities, Investments and Fiduciary Practices Division, August 24, 1992 (unpublished); and OCC Interpretive Letter No. 741, *reprinted in* [1996-1997 Transfer Binder] Fed. Banking L. Rep. (CCH) ¶ 81-105 (Aug. 19, 1996); and OCC Conditional Approval No. 220 (October 2, 1996). Cf. Norwest Bank v. Sween Corp., 118 F.3d 1255 (8th Cir. 1997).

communications channels for persons participating in securities transactions) and Letter from Julie L. Williams, Chief Counsel, October 2, 1996 (unpublished) (national bank as finder could use electronic means to facilitate contacts between third party providers and potential buyers).

Clearly, one of the Product's most significant functions for the Retailers is to provide potential customers, via the Internet, with information about the Retailers' goods and services. The OCC has concluded that "[p]roviding information [to prospective buyers about the products or services of prospective sellers] is one of the fundamental activities of a finder," and that as part of the finder function national banks may "make inquiries as to interest, arrange a meeting of the interested parties, and provide information pertinent to the meeting of the buyer and seller." OCC Interpretive Letter No. 653, *reprinted in* [1994-1995 Transfer Binder] Fed. Banking L. Rep. (CCH) ¶ 83,601 (Dec. 22, 1994). The function of finder involves the "conveying of information about available products or services to potential markets for them…." OCC Interpretive Letter No. 741, *supra*. *See also*, OCC Corporate Decision 98-13 (February 9, 1998) (national bank finder, as a benefits counselor, could provide potential buyers with information on benefits programs available); OCC Interpretive Letter No. 824, *supra*, (banks participating in a finder program would provide brochures, leaflets, and other literature informing customers on the availability of products and services from the potential seller); OCC Interpretive Letter No. 630, *reprinted in* [1993-1994 Transfer Binder] Fed. Banking L. Rep. (CCH) ¶ 83,513 (May 11, 1993) (finder banks may distribute informational brochures); OCC Interpretive Letter No. 593, *reprinted in* [1992-1993 Transfer Binder] Fed. Banking L. Rep. (CCH) ¶ 83,418 (July 1, 1992) (finder banks providing information on third party brokerage services); and Letter from Julie L. Williams, Chief Counsel, October 2, 1996 (unpublished) (national bank as part of finder function could provide marketing materials and information about third party service providers to potential buyers).

Maintaining or providing an Internet web site for Retailers is one device that national banks may use as finders to provide or make available information to potential buyers. Thus, in Corporate Decision 97-60, *supra*, the OCC found that a national bank conducting finder activities to support sales of pre-owned automobiles could maintain and operate an Internet web site which provided information to potential buyers on the vehicles offered.[14]

It also follows that to perform its finder function of providing information, a national bank must store and retrieve the information to be provided. Thus, in OCC Interpretive Letter No. 741, *supra*, the OCC found that under the finder authority, a national bank could operate a call center facility which provided access to bank-maintained database on new or used vehicles offered for sale. A similar finding is also implicit in OCC Corporate Decision No. 97-60, *supra*. Thus, it is permissible for the Bank, when hosting an Internet web site as a finder, to store and retrieve

[14] Accordingly, we also find that the Bank may, as part of its finder service, register a Retailer's web site with search engines. This is merely an additional device to serve the finder function of making information available to potential buyers.

electronically on its servers the data set for the Retailer's on-line catalog as part of the finder function.

There is no need to analyze whether the data set storage and retrieval functions in this case are "incidental" to the permissible finder activity because, for the reasons discussed, the data functions are actually part of the finder service, not a separate product or service. The OCC has distinguished incidental products, which support business of banking activities, from products like the data set functions here that, although arguably distinct from a related banking product, really are so closely connected to the banking product that the banking product cannot be provided without it. In other words, the other product is effectively merged with and becomes part of the banking product and, hence, becomes itself part of the business of banking. OCC has said:

> In analyzing the extent to which national banks may provide hardware and software, the OCC has distinguished between general purpose items, which can be used for purposes beyond banking services, and limited purpose items, which can be used solely for banking services. Limited purpose hardware is considered an indistinguishable part of banking services and, thus, part of the business of banking.

OCC Interpretive Letter No. 754, *supra*. *See also* OCC Interpretive Letter No. 737, *reprinted in* (1996-1997 Transfer Binder) Fed. Banking L. Rep. (CCH) ¶ 81,101 (August 19, 1996)(where a national bank was providing a closed stored value system to an institutional customer, the bank could as part of that service also provide system participants with certain hardware and software to be used for the stored value functions; the equipment was not viewed as a separate product or service) and OCC Interpretive Letter No. 345, *reprinted in*, [1985-1987 Transfer Binder] Fed. Banking L. Rep. (CCH) ¶ 85,515 (July 9, 1986).[15]

Another significant finder function is to bring together potential buyers and sellers. The OCC has found that one approach to this communication function is for the finder bank to provide an electronic medium to support communications between potential buyers and sellers so they can arrange their transactions. Thus, in OCC Conditional Approval No. 221, *supra*, the OCC found that, as part of the finder function, a national bank could provide hypertext links between the bank's retail banking web site and the web sites of third parties interested in selling products or services to the bank's customers. We said: "By providing links to third party vendors' web sites, the [LLC] merely introduces two parties who then engage in a transaction." *See also*, OCC Interpretive Letter No. 611, *reprinted in* [1992-1993 Transfer Binder] Fed. Banking L. Rep.

---

[15] The OCC said:

> When the hardware is such that it is not to be used for uses beyond the [bank services], it may well be considered literally an indistinguishable part of the [banking services]. Accordingly, a national bank's sale of such hardware is permissible as a part of the [service] permitted under 12 U.S.C. § 24(Seventh), just as the bank's sale of checkbooks to its customers is a permissible part of offering checking accounts.

(CCH) ¶ 83,449 (Nov. 23, 1992) (national bank linking non-bank service providers to its communications platform of smart phone banking services was within its authority as a finder "in bringing together a buyer and seller") and Letter from Julie L. Williams, Chief Counsel, October 2, 1996 (unpublished). For this reason, the Bank may communicate to its Retailers the offers to buy that result from their Bank hosted web sites as part of its Product.

Finally, by hosting the web site, the Bank does not become involved in the negotiations of the parties and thereby exceed its proper role as finder, *i.e.*, merely bringing parties together for a transaction that the parties themselves negotiate and consummate. The courts are likely to view retail web sites as inviting potential buyers to make an offer to the seller to buy the goods advertised on the site. Thus, in this case, the Retailers would retain the ability to reject a potential Internet buyer's offer of any potential purchases that might arise from the web site hosted by the Bank. *See, generally*, W. A. Effross, "The Legal Architecture of Virtual Stores: World Wide Web Sites and the Uniform Commercial Code," 34 *San Diego L. Rev.* 1263 (1997) at 1329-1331.

Accordingly, the retail web site hosting component to the Bank's Product is part of the business of banking and, thus, permissible for national banks. We now turn to several other aspects of the Product.

As noted, the Bank will provide Retailers with access to software that will enable the Retailers to design their web sites and software that enables the Retailer to build a catalog of product descriptions, pricing, delivery information and order forms. This is permissible. OCC has found a national bank can provide access to software that will enable bank customers to use or receive electronic banking services from the bank such as a specialized payment service or informational services. The software is "necessary" to use or fully enjoy the permissible service and, thus, is either part of the service (if limited function) or incidental thereto (if full function). Thus, in Conditional Approval No. 221, *supra*, the OCC found that providing full-function web browser software is a permissible incidental activity when a national bank is offering a home banking system based on web server technology using "Internet compatible" browser software. The fact that the customer might use the browser software for other non-banking purposes did not preclude the sale.[16]

The Bank will also process payments resulting from orders received from a Retailer's web site. Clearly, payments processing and handling of accounts receivable is part of the business of banking. OCC Conditional Approval No. 289 (October 2, 1998) (national banks may acquire a minority interest in a firm that, among other things, provides accounts receivable processing and

---

[16] *See also*, OCC Interpretive Letter No. 516, *supra* (national bank that is providing customers with a permissible database service of information relating to financial instruments can also provide software that enables the customers to download and analyze the information) and OCC Interpretive Letter No. 419, *reprinted in* [1988-1989 Transfer Binder] Fed. Banking L. Rep. (CCH) ¶ 85,463 (Feb. 2, 1988) (national bank that is providing customers with a permissible electronic transactional and information service can provide software that enables customers to participate in the system).

accounts payable processing); OCC Conditional Approval No. 282 (July 7, 1998) (national bank may acquire an interest in a firm that would, among other things, engage in payments processing for the health care firms); and OCC Interpretive Letter No. 731, *reprinted in* [1995-1996 Transfer Binder] Fed. Banking L. Rep. (CCH) ¶ 81,048 (July 1, 1996) (national banks as part of the banking business may collect and process accounts in relating to an electronic toll collection system).

The Bank will provide its Retailers with monthly reports on empirical data such as site "hits" and transaction volume arising from their web sites, including number and types of products sold. To the extent that these reports involve the processing and transmittal of information relating to specific payment transactions the Bank handles for the Retailer, it is part of the payment processing function and not a separate service.[17] OCC Interpretive Letter No, 731, *supra* and OCC Interpretive Letter No. 732, *reprinted in* [1995-1996 Transfer Binder] Fed. Banking L. Rep. (CCH) ¶ 81,049 (May 10, 1996) (design, development, marketing, and maintenance of a network for electronic funds transfer and electronic data interchange permissible for a national bank). Cf. Letter from Julie L. Williams, Chief Counsel, October 2, 1996 (unpublished) (national bank acting as finder could maintain a database of transactions resulting from its finder activities was "integral" to the finder function).

As for the more general information and reports, the OCC has long held that as part of the business of banking, national banks may collect, transcribe, process, analyze, and store for itself and others banking, financial, or related economic related data. The general reports will involve the processing of banking, financial, or related economic data and, thus, are part of the business of banking.

An earlier version of 12 C.F.R. § 7.1019 stated that "as part of its banking business and incidental thereto, a national bank may collect, transcribe, process, analyze, and store for itself and others, banking, financial, or related economic data."[18] Although in its 1984 revision of the ruling, the OCC deleted this statement because it believed that "specific examples [of permissible electronic activities] are inappropriate given the imprecision of terms and rapid pace of change in the data processing industry, the "analytical framework" embodied in the ruling remained the same.[19] There was no intent to narrow or restrict the substantive effect of the rule.[20]

---

[17] Under its agreements with its Retailers, the Bank will have an obligation to maintain the confidentiality of the transaction specific data, e.g., that relating to specific purchases by customers of a Retailer, that the Bank will acquire by offering the Package.

[18] Interpretive Ruling 7.3500, 39 Fed. Reg. 14195 (Apr. 22, 1974).

[19] 49 Fed. Reg. 11157 (Mar. 26, 1984).

[20] OCC Interpretive Letter No. 677, *reprinted in*, [1994-1995 Transfer Binder] Fed. Banking L. Rep. (CCH) ¶ 83,625 (June 28, 1995). *See also*, OCC Interpretive Letter No. 737, *supra* (national bank may provide transaction and information processing services to support an electronic stored value system); OCC Interpretive Letter No. 653, *supra* (national bank may act as an informational and payments interface between insurance underwriters and general insurance agents); and OCC Interpretive Letter No. 346, *reprinted in* (1985-1987 Transfer Binder) Fed. Banking L.

Thus, OCC has concluded that national banks may keep financial and other records of its customer's sales and disbursements arising from finder banking services provided by the bank. *See* OCC Interpretive Letter No. 653, *supra* (national bank acting as a finder for insurance could also keep financial and other records relating to the client agency sales, receipts and disbursements). *See also,* OCC Interpretive Letter No. 741, *supra* (national bank acting as finder for automobile dealers may also maintain a comprehensive system that allows dealers to track information on customers referred and to generate market statistics such as buying trends and cycles).[21]

Finally, as part of the Product, the Bank will calculate the sales taxes owed by its Retailers on their Internet sales. This activity is incidental to the retail web hosting and payments processing services and is thus permissible. In *Clement Nat'l Bank,*[22] the Supreme Court held that a national bank, incidental to its deposit services, could compute, report, and pay the state tax levied upon the interest earned by bank customers on their deposits.

CONCLUSION

Rep. (CCH) ¶85,516 (July 31, 1985) (national banks may maintain records on commodities transactions).

Case authority strongly supports the OCC precedent. In Ass'n of Data Processing v. Board of Governors, 745 F.2d 677 (D.C. Cir. 1984), the D.C. Circuit Court of Appeals upheld a Federal Reserve Board finding that data processing and database services were closely related to banking (and thus a proper activity for bank holding companies) if the "data to be processed ... are financial, banking or economic...." In reaching this conclusion the court said: "The record of this proceeding amply demonstrates, if any demonstration is needed, that banks regularly develop and process for their customers large amounts of banking, financial and economic data, and that they do so (and will presumably continue to do so) through the most advanced technological means." 745 F.2d at 689. Moreover, the court indicated that "economic data" would include: "agricultural matters, retail sales matters, housing matters, corporate profits matters, and anything of value in banking and financial decisions." 745 F.2d at 691.

[21] In National Retailers Corp. v. Valley Nat'l Bank, 411 F. Supp. 308 (D. Ariz 1976), *aff'd,* 604 F.2d 32 (9th Cir. 1979), a national bank was held not to have the authority to offer a data processing service to retailers involving the collection and compilation of information relating to their retail sales that had been collected by a special cash register. The district court held that no express provision of the National Bank Act authorized national banks to publicly market a retail information service ("RIS") and concluded that, since the RIS was not within the enumerated powers, the determining issue was whether the RIS was within the bank's "incidental powers." 411 F. Supp. at 313. Thus, by implication, the court held that the "business of banking" includes only the enumerated powers. This position has since been superceded by the Supreme Court's ruling in NationsBank v. Variable Life Annuity Co., 513 U.S. 251 (1995), that the "business of banking" is not limited to the enumerated powers. The *National Retailers* court failed to consider that non-enumerated informational services can come within the "business of banking" and specifically that the processing of banking, financial and related economic data is part of the business of banking. Ass'n of Data Processing, supra. In light of these defects, the holding of *National Retailers* is not entitled to much weight. Moreover, it is distinguishable from the Bank's proposed retail data reporting services that are to be offered in connection with its finder services which, for the reasons discussed above, are clearly part of the business of banking.

[22] Clement Nat'l Bank v. Vermont, 231 U.S. 120 (1913).

Based upon the foregoing facts and analysis, and the representations made by the Bank in connection with its request, I conclude that the proposed activity is permissible for a national bank.

Sincerely,

/s/

Julie L. Williams
Chief Counsel

Appendix B1
OCC Conditional Approval No. 220 (Dec. 2, 1996)

Published in Interpretations and Actions December 1996

Mark J. Welshimer, Esquire
Sullivan & Cromwell
125 Broad Street
New York, N.Y. 10004-2498

Re: Notices of Wells Fargo Bank, N.A., Michigan National Bank, First National Bank of Chicago, and Texas Commerce Bank of Intent to Establish an Operating Subsidiary Pursuant to 12 C.F.R. § 5.34 to Become a Member of Limited Liability Companies Operating a Stored Value System - Application Control Nos. 96-WO-08-0012, -0013, -0025, and -0026

Dear Mr. Welshimer:

This is in response to the operating subsidiary notices pursuant to 12 C.F.R. § 5.34, (**NOTE:** The OCC recently amended its operating subsidiary rule, 12 C.F.R. 5.34, as part of general revision to Part 5 ("Rules, Policies and Procedures for Corporate Activities") under the OCC's Regulation Review Program. See 61 Fed. Reg. 60342 (November 27, 1996). However, the amended rule does not take effect until December 31, 1996. Accordingly, this application was decided under the current rule. 48 Fed. Reg. 48454 (October 19, 1983) as amended at 50 Fed. Reg. 1440 (January 11, 1985); 53 Fed. Reg. 18547 (May 24, 1988); and 55 Fed. Reg. 997 (January 11, 1990).) submitted on behalf of Wells Fargo Bank, N.A.("Wells Fargo"), Michigan National Bank ("MNB"), First National Bank of Chicago, and Texas Commerce Bank, N.A. (collectively, the "Banks"), to establish operating subsidiaries to acquire membership interests in two Delaware limited liability companies (the "LLCs" or the "Companies") that will operate a stored value card system known as "Mondex." Each of the operating subsidiaries will be wholly owned by its parent Bank and will engage in no activities other than holding membership interests in the Companies.

For the reasons discussed below, we approve, subject to certain conditions, the establishment of such operating subsidiaries by the Banks because we find that national banks may under 12 U.S.C. § 24(Seventh) engage in the business of developing and operating a stored value system. Please note that our response is solely directed to the question stated above. We do not address how other federal and state laws and regulations will or might apply to the Banks' activities in connection with the Companies, or to the Companies's operations. Similarly, at this time, we do not address the important consumer protection and supervisory considerations that will arise when the Companies actually commence operations. (**NOTE:** At this time, many significant details of the Mondex stored value system are still to be determined. However, as part of its active supervision of the Mondex system, the OCC will provide guidance to the Banks and the LLCs on the implementation of the stored value system operations. This guidance will address supervisory, compliance and consumer protections issues. *See, e.g.*, OCC Bulletin 96-48 (September 10, 1996) on stored value systems. Among other things, the OCC will review the consumer disclosures provided by the Mondex system. The OCC will also develop supervisory procedures as the Mondex operations evolve.)

BACKGROUND

1. The Product

Mondex stored value is intended to serve as an electronic payments medium. The Mondex system will employ specially designed computer chips capable of storing and transferring the electronic stored value ("ESV") and other data in a secure manner. The computer chip and related software is referred to as a "Purse" and the devices containing a Purse are referred to as "Purse Carrier Devices" ("PCDs"). The most common PCD will be plastic cards ("Mondex Cards") issued to individuals ("Consumers") by institutions licensed to do so ("Members"). Retailers licensed by Members to participate in the Mondex System will have special Purses referred to as "Retailer PCDs."

2. The Mondex Entities

Rights relating to the Mondex concept are held by a U.K. limited liability company, Mondex International Limited ("Mondex International") that has authority to license institutions in various countries to develop and operate Mondex in their respective countries. (**NOTE:** Mondex International Limited is currently owned by 17 major organizations (collectively, the "Global Founders"): Nat West; Midland Bank; The Hong Kong and Shanghai Banking Corporation Limited; Canadian Imperial Bank of Commerce; Royal Bank of Canada; Australia and New Zealand Banking Group Limited; Commonwealth Bank of Australia; National Australia Bank Limited; Westpac Banking Corporation (Australia); ANZ Banking

Group Limited; Bank of New Zealand; Countrywide Banking Corporation Limited; the National Bank of New Zealand Limited; ASB Bank Limited; Westpac Banking Corp (New Zealand); Wells Fargo Bank; and AT&T Universal Card Services. National Australia Bank Limited ("NAB") is the parent of Michigan National Bank. Investing participants will have franchise rights to exploit Mondex in their respective geographical markets. MasterCard International, under a recent a letter of intent with the Global Founders, will acquire 51% of Mondex International; the Global Founders will own 49%.) Wells Fargo, AT&T Universal Bancorp Services, Inc. (AT&T Universal"), (**NOTE:** AT&T Universal manages the third largest credit card program in the United States with more than 18 million accounts.) NOVUS Services, Inc. ("NOVUS"), (**NOTE:** NOVUS Services, Inc. is a Delaware corporation that operates the NOVUS Card Network.) and NAB (collectively the "U.S. Founders") currently have the rights from Mondex International to operate the Mondex system in the United States. (**NOTE:** However, in the near future the list of US Founders will change, through a series of transactions, to include the following firms: AT&T, NOVUS, MasterCard, Wells Fargo, MNB, Texas Commerce Bank N.A., and First National Bank of Chicago.)

The U.S. Founders propose to establish two de novo Delaware limited liability companies that will implement the Mondex system in the United States: the LLCs. One LLC, Mondex USA Originator Limited Liability Company (the "OLLC"), will create, sell and redeem Mondex ESV in exchange for dollars. The other LLC, Mondex USA Services Limited Liability Company (the "SLLC"), will act as a licensing and servicing entity for the Mondex USA services. The U.S. Founders will own the equity in both LLCs in the following percentages: AT&T (10%), NOVUS (10%), MasterCard (10%), Wells Fargo Bank (30%), MNB (10%), Texas Commerce Bank N.A. (20%), and First National Bank of Chicago (10%).

3. Mondex Operations

The OLLC will perform the functions of creating and selling the ESV to Members in return for dollars and holding those dollars pending redemption of the ESV. The Banks commit that the OLLC will invest those dollars in U.S. government securities and, to the extent necessary to satisfy short-term liquidity needs, cash and certain cash equivalents. (**NOTE:** The Banks also commit that the OLLC will develop and implement asset/liability management policies and procedures (the "ALM Policies") to ensure that it is able to purchase the ESV tendered by Members. The ALM Polices will address both the nature and maturities of the assets in which the OLLC may invest, considered in light of the fact that the OLLC is obligated to purchase its ESV upon demand by Members. The OLLC's ALM Policies will likely evolve over time as the OLLC develops experience concerning the level of daily sales and purchases of Mondex Dollars. The Banks anticipate that the OLLC's assets will be limited to (i) U.S. government securities (including agency securities supported by the full faith and credit of the U.S. government) that, during at least the early stages of the OLLC's operations, will be limited to short-term maturities, and (ii) in order to provide the short-term liquidity necessary to enable the OLLC to purchase Mondex Dollars upon the demand of Members, cash and certain cash equivalents (for example, interbank deposits and over-night repurchase agreements with respect to U.S. government securities). The Banks commit to using their best efforts to assure that the LLC's policies and standards on reserves and portfolio quality and liquidity will be consistent with safe and sound banking practices. The Banks also anticipate that the OLLC will pledge the U.S. government securities (and other assets) purchased by it with the proceeds of the creation and sale of Mondex Dollars to secure the OLLC's obligation to purchase Mondex Dollars tendered by members upon demand. Such pledge will be effected by causing such U.S. government securities (and other securities constituting cash equivalents) to be held by a trust department of a commercial bank acting as collateral trustee for the benefit of holders of Mondex Dollars.) The OLLC will also perform the function of purchasing the ESV at par when tendered by Members. Members, in turn, will sell ESV to (and purchase the ESV from) Consumers and participating retailers in accord with their respective agreements.

The Banks commit that the OLLC, in conjunction with the SLLC, will implement a risk management system that will provide effective devices to control the risk of fraud and counterfeiting. Both LLCs will play important roles in the risk management system that will provide an important service to Member banks, helping them to control their risk exposures from the Mondex system.

The SLLC, as the licensing and servicing entity, will also perform all functions necessary to implement the Mondex USA system that are not performed by the OLLC. Thus, the SLLC will enter into licensing agreements with Members giving those Members the rights to issue Mondex Cards to Consumers and PCDs to retailers. SLLC will coordinate the purchase of necessary equipment from third party manufacturers. Finally, the SLLC will collect, assemble and evaluate transaction data generated by the Mondex system. The Banks commit that both the OLLC and SLLC will develop appropriate policies and procedures to ensure that consumer specific information is not used in a manner that violates the privacy of Consumers and that the Consumers will receive full disclosure of the uses that may be made of Consumer-specific information and the limitations on those uses.

As noted, Members will be the exclusive channel by which Consumers and retailers can purchase and redeem Mondex ESV. The Banks and AT&T Universal will be Members. Both depository and non-depository institutions are eligible to become Mondex Members. It is anticipated that the Member License Agreement will impose a restriction on each Member's maximum Mondex ESV exposure based upon appropriate financial standards.

Consumers and retailers that contract with a Member will receive a PCD used to receive and store ESV. Consumer PCDs will have the ability to transfer ESV to retailer PCDs and to other Consumer PCDs; retailer PCDs will, subject to certain limited exceptions, be able only to transfer ESV to a Member for redemption. Funds resulting from the redemption of ESV will be transferred to a linked depository account that may or may not be maintained at a Consumer's or retailer's related Mondex Member. Similarly, funds used to purchase ESV will normally be debited from the linked deposit account.

4. Material Terms of the LLC Agreements

As investors in the LLCs, the Banks' operating subsidiaries will enter into a LLC agreement for each LLC (the "LLC Agreements"). The LLC Agreements will describe the scope of business of each LLC, and will provide that in no case shall the LLC engage in any activity not permissible for a national bank. The LLC Agreement for the OLLC will provide that the LLC will invest the proceeds of the issuance of Mondex Dollars in accordance with the asset and liability management polices of the Company adopted by the Board.

Under Delaware law, unless provided otherwise in a LLC agreement, no member of a Delaware limited liability company is obligated for the debts, obligations and liabilities of the LLC, whether arising in contract, tort, or otherwise. (**NOTE:** Del. Code Ann. Tit. 6, Section 18-303(a) (1994).) The LLC Agreements will contain provisions that confirm no investor in the LLCs will have liability for the debts, obligations, and liabilities of the LLCs.

The LLC Agreements will require Members of the applicable LLC to make contributions to capital or loans to such LLC to the extent provided in the "Annual Budget" thereof. Under each LLC Agreement, the LLC Board of Managers can also adopt an "Annual Budget" for the applicable LLC containing a "Material Financial Item." A "Material Financial Item" will be defined in each LLC Agreement to include a request for a contribution to capital or a loan to the LLC exceeding, in the aggregate, the pre-approved "Required Funding Amount" for such LLC for such fiscal year. However, the LLC Agreement for the SLLC will provide that notwithstanding any other provision of the LLC Agreement for the SLLC, no Member that is a national bank (or controlled by a national bank) will have a "Required Funding Amount" for any "Budget Period" [ ]. The LLC Agreement for the OLLC will provide that, notwithstanding any other provision of the LLC Agreement for the OLLC, no Member that is a national bank (or controlled by a national bank) will have a "Required Funding Amount" for any "Budget Period" [].

Finally, the LLC Agreements will contain express provisions to implement OCC Conditions 1.a. and 1.b. (set out at the end of this letter) acknowledging that the performance of the services provided by the LLCs to national banks, including the sale and redemption of ESV, is subject to regulation, supervision, and examination by the OCC; and that for purposes of 12 U.S.C. §§ 1813 and 1818, the LLCs are "institution affiliated parties" with respect to all national banks that invest in the LLCs.

DISCUSSION

A national bank may engage in activities that are part of or incidental to the business of banking by means of an operating subsidiary. 12 C.F.R. § 5.34(c). Your letter raises the issue of the authority of a national bank to make indirectly a non-controlling investment in a limited liability company. (**NOTE:** The OCC has previously approved indirect investments by national banks in limited liability companies through an operating subsidiary structure. *See, e.g.,* OCC Conditional Approval Letter No. 219 (July, 15, 1996). Such investments are permissible if they meet the requirements for direct minority investments by national banks.) In a variety of circumstances the OCC has permitted national banks to own, either directly, or indirectly through an operating subsidiary, a minority interest in an enterprise. The enterprise might be a limited partnership, a corporation, or in more recent examples, a limited liability company. In two recent interpretive letters, the OCC concluded that national banks are legally permitted to make a minority investment in an LLC provided four criteria or standards are met. *See* OCC Interpretive Letter No. 692, *reprinted in* [Current] Fed. Banking L. Rep. (CCH) ¶ 81,007 (November 1, 1995) and OCC Interpretive Letter No. 694, *reprinted in* [Current] Fed. Banking L. Rep. (CCH) ¶ 81,009 (December 13, 1995). These standards, which have been distilled from our previous decisions in the area of permissible minority investments for national banks and their subsidiaries, are: (1) The activities of the enterprise in which the investment is made must be limited to activities that are part of or incidental to the business of banking. (2) The bank must be able to prevent the enterprise from engaging in activities that do not meet the foregoing standard, or be able to withdraw its investment. (3) The bank's loss exposure must be limited, as a legal and accounting matter, and the bank must not have open-ended liability for the obligations of the enterprise. (4) The investment must be convenient or useful to the bank in carrying out its business and not a mere passive investment unrelated to that bank's banking business. We conclude, as discussed below, that the proposed indirect investment by national banks in the Mondex LLCs satisfies these four criteria.

1. The activities of the enterprise in which the investment is made must be limited to activities that are part of or incidental to the business of banking

The National Bank Act, in relevant part, provides that national banks shall have the power:

> [t]o exercise . . . all such incidental powers as shall be necessary to carry on the business of banking; by discounting and negotiating promissory notes, drafts, bills of exchange, and other evidences of debt; by receiving deposits; by buying and selling exchange, coin, and bullion; by loaning money on personal security; and by obtaining, issuing, and circulating notes . . .

12 U.S.C. § 24(Seventh).

The Supreme Court has held that the powers clause of 12 U.S.C. § 24(Seventh) is a broad grant of power to engage in the business of banking, including the enumerated powers and the business of banking as a whole. *See NationsBank of North Carolina, N.A. v. Variable Life Annuity Co.,* 115 S.Ct. 810 (1995) ("*VALIC*"). Judicial cases reflect three general principles used to determine whether an activity is within the scope of the "business of banking": (1) is the activity functionally equivalent to or a logical outgrowth of a recognized banking activity; (2) would the activity respond to customer needs or otherwise benefit the bank or its customers; and (3) does the activity involve risks similar in nature to those already assumed by banks. *See, e.g., Merchants' Bank v. State Bank,* 77 U.S. 604, 648 (1871) (certification of checks has grown out of the business needs of the country and involves no greater risk than a bank giving a certificate of deposit); *M&M Leasing Corp. v. Seattle First Nat. Bank,* 563 F.2d 1377, 1382-83 (9th Cir. 1977), *cert. denied,* 436 U.S. 987 (1978) (personal property lease financing is "functionally interchangeable" with the express power to loan money on personal property); *American Insurance Association v. Clarke,* 865 F.2d 278, 282 (D.C. Cir. 1988) (standby credits to insure municipal bonds is "functionally equivalent" to the issuance of a standby letter of credit) ("*AMBAC*"). Further, as established by the Supreme Court in *VALIC,* national banks are authorized to engage in an activity if it is incidental to the performance of the five enumerated powers in section 24(Seventh) or if it is incidental to the performance of an activity that is part of the business of banking.

It is well established that a national bank may use electronic or data processing technology to perform services expressly or incidentally authorized to national banks. *See* OCC Interpretive Letter No. 677, *reprinted in* [1994-1995 Transfer Binder] Fed. Banking L. Rep. (CCH) ¶ 83,625 (June 28, 1995). As noted in the recently revised OCC Interpretive Ruling recognizing this authority, a national bank may "perform, provide, or deliver through electronic means and facilities any activity, function, product, or service that it is otherwise authorized to perform, provide or deliver." *See* 12 C.F.R. § 7.1019 (1996).

Banks are the most important institutional participants in the nation's payments system. They deal with cash, issue, process, clear and settle checks and similar monetary instruments, administer credit card and debit card programs for consumers and merchants, and transfer funds electronically in a variety of situations and circumstances. Although the largest number of payment transactions in the United States continue to involve individual consumers utilizing currency and checks, most of the dollar value transferred in the economy on a regular basis is accomplished by electronic means among institutions. (**NOTE:** During the early 1990's, while most transactions involved currency (300 billion annually) and checks (60 billion annually), electronic payments accounted for "more than 80 percent of the total *dollar value* of all financial transactions." R. Miller and D. VanHoose, *Modern Money and Banking* 389-91 (3d ed. 1993). Most of this 80 percent of value moved electronically through the privately-owned and operated Clearing House Interbank Payment System ("CHIPS"), or through Fedwire, which is owned and operated by the Federal Reserve System. CHIPS links about 140 large depository institutions, and transmitted an average of roughly $1 trillion in payments every day. All depository institutions that hold reserves at the Federal Reserve have access to Fedwire, and this system made more individual funds transfers than CHIPS, although it accounted for a slightly-smaller dollar volume of $950 billion in payments per day, *id.* 390-91. For other similar discussions of the Nation's payment system, including the growing use of sophisticated technology and communications to support or substitute for the use of currency and checks, *see, e.g.,* T. Mayer, J. Duesenberry, and R. Aliber, *Money, Banking and the Economy,* chs. 1, 6, 7, and 13 (5th ed. 1993); D. Friedman, *Money and Banking,* ch. 5, "Bank Operations and the Payments Mechanism" (2d ed. 1989), and R. Miller and D. VanHoose, id. 390.)

When the Mondex stored value card (and the system supporting it) is fully operational, it will become a new element of the nation's payment system by substituting ESV for cash and small checks in some consumer purchase transactions with retail merchants. Accordingly, national banks that participate in the Mondex program as owners or licensed users will be involving themselves in an additional facet of the payments system. For the reasons discussed below, the functions and activities of the Mondex LLCs are part of or incidental to the business of banking.

a. *Issuance and Redemption of Electronic Stored Value*

As noted above, 12 U.S.C. § 24(Seventh) provides that national banks shall have the power to carry on the business of banking by, among other things, "obtaining, issuing and circulating notes." The issuance, circulation and redemption of notes was one of the principal reasons Congress established the national banking system. The National Currency Act of 1863, re-enacted as the National Bank Act a year later, was intended to provide a more stable currency in the form of bank notes backed by government bonds. *See, e.g.,* R. Robertson, *The Comptroller and Bank Supervision,* chs. 2-3 (1995 rev. ed.); T. Mayer, J. Duesenberry, and R. Aliber, *supra* 86-88. Although that mode of operation became obsolete when the Federal Reserve System was created a half-century later, in 1913—Federal Reserve notes replaced bank notes as the Nation's currency—this example nevertheless demonstrates that the issuance, circulation, and redemption of ESV contemplated by the Mondex program is intimately connected with core banking as originally conceived and currently conducted. (**NOTE:** In 1994, Congress repealed the provisions in the National Bank Act dealing with the issuance of post notes by national banks (previously codified at 12 U.S.C. 101, et seq.) because they believed that those provisions were obsolete. H.R. Conf. Rep. No. 103-652, 103rd Cong., 2d Sess., *reprinted in* 1994 U.S. Code Cong. & Ad. News 2035. Thus, the repeal did not indicate a congressional intent to restrict national bank powers. Rather, more modern substitutes for currency, such as travelers checks, cashiers checks, and other bearer instruments issued or sold by banks, have developed as components of the payments system and as part of the business of banking.) In other words, just as the automobile leasing program approved for national banks in *M&M Leasing, supra,* represented a new way of conducting the business of making secured loans, the issuance and redemption of stored value represents a new way of conducting one aspect of the payments business of banks: issuing and circulating notes.

Similarly, the clearing and settlement functions regarding ESV which will be performed by the Mondex LLCs involve activities that are similar to those already being performed by banks in connection with the large volume of transactions using checks, drafts, travelers checks, credit cards, debit cards, and electronic transfers of funds within and through the payments system. Thus, the ESV clearing and settlement functions are also part of the business of banking. As the OCC recently noted:

> When acting for merchants in the collection and settlement of stored value transactions, the LLC will be performing a recognized banking activity. The Supreme Court has established that 12 U.S.C. § 24(Seventh) permits a national bank to "do those acts and occupy those relations which are usual or necessary in making collections of commercial paper and other evidences of debt" for its customers. *Miller v. King,* 223 U.S. 505, 510 (1912) (finding that a national bank may collect a judgment for its customer, and may also sue the bank's attorney in order to recover misused proceeds of the judgment).

OCC Interpretive Letter No. 737, to be published (August 19, 1996) (the collection, processing, and settlement of payments in a stored value system is part of the business of banking). *See also,* OCC Interpretive Letter No. 731, *reprinted in* [Current Transfer Binder] Fed. Banking Law. Rep. (CCH) ¶ 81,048 (July 1, 1996) (national banks may enter into a contract with a public authority to operate on behalf of the authority an electronic toll collection system); OCC Interpretive Letter No. 732, *reprinted in* [Current Transfer Binder] Fed. Banking Law. Rep. (CCH) ¶ 81,049 (May 10, 1996) (national banks may provide electronic data interchange services that, among other things, provide for payments by EFT); and OCC Interpretive Letter No. 419, *reprinted in* [1988-1989 Transfer Binder] Fed. Banking Law. Rep. (CCH) ¶ 85,643 (February 18, 1988) (national bank may provide a service that facilitates settlement and payment of health claims using EFT technology). (**NOTE:** The Federal Reserve Board has in approval orders under the Bank Holding Company Act determined that the development and operation of closed and open stored value card systems, including the provision of data processing and transmission services and electronic payment services relating thereto, are "so closely related to banking . . . as to be a proper incident thereto". This is the statutory standard which that agency administers under the Act for holding company investments, 12 U.S.C. § 1843(c)(8). *See Banc One Corporation,* 79 Fed. Res. Bull. 1158 (Dec. 1993); *The Bank of New York Company, Inc.,* 80 Fed. Res. Bull. 1107 (Dec. 1994).)

The functional equivalence and logical outgrowth lines of analysis which the courts have applied to current banking functions in the process of reviewing new activities of national banks can be multi-dimensional—the equivalence or outgrowth can involve both evolutionary advances in products and services as well as the integration of adjacent types of businesses that are useful to perform and deliver modern forms of banking and financial transactions. For example, in *M&M Leasing, supra,* the "new product" was a lease in substitution of a secured loan, the customer was a lessee rather than a borrower, the bank was an owner and lessor of a car rather than a lender, and yet in substance this amounted to an evolutionary expansion of the way in which the bank performed secured lending. By engaging in this activity, the bank was also becoming a participant in the personal property leasing industry, thereby integrating a new product delivery system into an existing functional line of business. It was reaching out to customers who preferred to lease a car rather than buy one, and accommodating them in this choice. In *AMBAC, supra,* the bank was not only offering a new product or service, municipal bond insurance, and thereby providing an advanced version of its traditional credit intermediation function, but it was also entering the adjacent business of municipal bond insurance.

The Mondex stored value system involves both advanced versions of well-recognized functions of the banking business, and integration into adjacent businesses that supply the technological expertise and resources for banks to engage in a segment of the payments business in a new way. Instead of banks dealing with regular cash or checks, as a traditional product or service, they will be issuing cards and loading them with ESV in substitution of cash and checks. The system will also clear and settle the ESV transactions. These aspects of the program represent an evolution of payments-related products and services traditionally offered by banks. The integration of adjacent businesses involves the utilization of electronic means and equipment, and bank alliance with several technology firms, to deliver and support the new payment medium of electronic stored value.

Moreover, if the business is properly conducted in the manner described in the Banks' submissions and in conformance with the OCC conditions and the commitments made by the Banks and others, there is no reason why the LLCs' issuance of stored value, the clearing and settlement of ESV obligations, and the other support functions should present risks that are different from those banks are accustomed to handling. The ability of the OCC to examine and supervise both LLCs provides additional assurance on this factor, particularly in light of commitments made by the Banks.

b. Supporting Activities for Stored Value System

The Mondex SLLC will provide record keeping, data analysis, and other support services for the stored value system. This is also a function that is clearly part of the business of banking. See OCC Interpretive Letter No. 737, *supra* (since as part of its banking business and incidental thereto, a national bank may collect, transcribe, process, analyze, and store for itself and others, banking, financial, or related economic data, the bank may also engage in record keeping for stored value systems.) *See also,* OCC Interpretive Letter No. 653, *reprinted in* [1994-1995 Transfer Binder] Fed. Banking L. Rep. (CCH) ¶ 83,601 (December 22, 1994) (national bank may maintain records when acting as an informational and payments interface between insurance underwriters and general insurance agents); OCC Interpretive Letter No. 346, *reprinted in* [1985-1987] Transfer Binder] Fed. Banking Law. Rep. (CCH) ¶ 85,516 (July 31, 1985) (national banks may maintain records on commodities transactions).

In connection with these payments and record keeping functions, the SLLC will also provide system participants with certain hardware and software that will be used for the stored value functions. Our understanding is that the hardware and software provided can be used solely for stored value functions. If so, the provision of that hardware and software is, itself, part of the business of banking. OCC Interpretive Letter No. 345, *reprinted in,* [1985-1987 Transfer Binder] Fed. Banking Law. Rep. (CCH) ¶ 85,515 (July 9, 1985). (**NOTE:** There the OCC said: When the hardware is such that it is not to be used for uses beyond the [bank services], it may well be considered literally an indistinguishable part of the [banking services]. Accordingly, a national bank's sale of such hardware is permissible as a part of the [service] permitted under 12 U.S C. 24(7), just as the bank's sale of checkbooks to its customers is a permissible part of offering checking accounts.) *See also,* OCC Interpretive Letter No. 737, *supra.*

2. *The bank must be able to prevent the enterprise from engaging in activities that do not meet the foregoing standard, or be able to withdraw its investment*

This is an obvious corollary of the first standard. It is not enough that the LLCs' activities are permissible at the time the bank acquires ownership; they must also remain permissible for as long as the bank retains an ownership interest.

Several provisions in the proposed LLC Agreements, copies of which were submitted to OCC, are designed to satisfy the requirement that national banks will participate as owners of the LLCs only so long as the Companies' activities remain permissible for national banks. Thus, both LLC Agreements provide that in no case shall the LLC engage in any activity not permissible for a national bank. These provisions are sufficient to ensure that the activities of the LLCs will remain permissible for the national bank owners so long as they are, directly or indirectly, involved in the enterprise.

3. The bank's loss exposure must be limited, as a legal and accounting matter, and the bank must not have open-ended liability for the obligations of the enterprise

A primary concern of the OCC is that national banks should not be subjected to undue risk. Where an investing bank will not control the operations of the entity in which the bank holds an interest, it is important that a bank's investment not expose it to unlimited liability. Such is the case here.

As members of a Delaware limited liability company, the liability of each of the Banks for the debts, obligations or liabilities of the company will be limited under Delaware law to the amount of each such bank's capital investment in the company. The LLC Agreements contain provisions that confirm no investor in the LLCs will have liability for the debts, obligations, and liabilities of the LLCs. Moreover, the LLC Agreements will contain absolute limits on the amount of additional funds that the Banks can be compelled to invest in the LLCs.

In addition, the OCC's Chief Accountant has advised that the appropriate accounting treatment for a bank's non-controlling ownership share or investment in an LLC is to report it as an unconsolidated entity under the cost or equity method of accounting, depending upon the circumstances. Under either the cost or equity method, unless the bank has extended a loan to the entity, guaranteed any of its liabilities or has other financial obligations to the entity, losses are generally limited to the amount of the investment shown on the investor's books. *See generally,* APB Opinion No. 18 (1971).

4. The investment must be convenient or useful to the bank in carrying out its business and not a mere passive investment unrelated to that bank's banking business

Mondex will develop and operate a new addition to the payments system, a stored value card which will allow the substitution of ESV for cash and checks in small retail merchant payment transactions by consumers. As such, the Banks will be conducting some of their payments business through these LLC vehicles, and not passively generating dividend income from an investment. The owner Banks, as opposed to those which are solely licensed users, will be more substantially involved in the adoption and monitoring of policies, procedures, and services provided in support of the payments system. The LLC interests will not be generally available to the public for purchase, which is another indication that the national banks which decide to acquire and hold an interest will do so as an aspect of carrying on their banking business. This standard is accordingly satisfied.

CONCLUSION

Based upon the notice and other materials submitted by the Banks and the commitments and representations contained therein, and upon the Banks' compliance with the supervisory conditions set forth below, the OCC concludes that the Banks' proposed investment in the Mondex LLCs through the operating subsidiaries would satisfy the four standards which the OCC has generally applied to non-controlling, minority investments. Therefore, the Banks' operating subsidiary notification is approved subject to the following special conditions:

1. The LLC Agreements signed by the Banks' operating subsidiaries will provide that:
   - the performance of the services provided by the LLCs to national banks, including the sale and redemption of ESV, is subject to regulation, supervision, and examination by the OCC; (**NOTE:** In the future, the nature and scope of the LLCs' activities might be so substantially enhanced that the methodology the OCC uses to compute the assessments of the Banks and other national banks participating in the Mondex system will need to be adjusted to cover adequately the expense of supervising and examining the LLCs.)
   - for purposes of 12 U.S.C. §§ 1813 and 1818, the LLCs stipulate that they are "institution affiliated parties" with respect to all national banks that invest in a LLC; and
   - the LLCs will notify the OCC and obtain the consent of the OCC before any material changes are made in the terms of the LLC Agreements mentioned in the section of this letter entitled "Material Provisions of the Agreements."
2. National banks investing in the LLCs will not account for their investment under the consolidated method of accounting.
3. A copy of this approval letter will be provided to all national banks proposing to invest in the LLCs.

Please be advised that all conditions of this approval are "conditions imposed in writing by the agency in connection with the granting of any application or other request" within the meaning of 12 U.S.C. § 1818.

Sincerely,

/s/

Julie L. Williams
Chief Counsel

Appendix B2
OCC Conditional Approval No. 221 (Dec. 4, 1996)

Comptroller of the Currency
Administrator of National Banks
Washington, D.C. 20219

December 4, 1996

Gerald P. Hurst, Esquire
Associate General Counsel
NationsBank Corporation
NationsBank Corporate Center
NC1-007-20-01
Charlotte, NC 28255

Re: Bank of America National Trust and Savings Association; NationsBank National Association; KeyBank National Association; Bank One, Columbus, National Association; Mellon Bank, N.A.; Barnett Bank, National Association; First Bank National Association; PNC Bank, National Association; Michigan National Bank; The First National Bank of Chicago; Comerica Bank - Ann Arbor, National Association; and Fleet National Bank: Notice of Intent to Establish Operating Subsidiaries Pursuant to 12 C.F.R. § 5.34 to Become a Member of a Limited Liability Company to Provide Data Processing for Home Banking and Other Electronic Financial Services. Application Control Numbers: 96-WO-08-0011 and 96-WO-08-0014 through -0024

Dear Mr. Hurst:

This is in response to your operating subsidiary notice pursuant to 12 C.F.R. § 5.34 [1] submitted on behalf of Bank of America, National Trust and Savings Association, Charter Number 13044 ("Bank of America"), NationsBank, National Association, Charter Number 14448 ("NationsBank"), KeyBank National Association, Charter Number 14761 ("KeyBank"), Bank One, Columbus, National Association, Charter Number 7621 ("Bank One"), Mellon Bank, N.A., Charter Number 6301 ("Mellon"), Barnett Bank, National Association, Charter Number 9049 ("Barnett"), First Bank National Association, Charter Number 710 ("First Bank"), PNC Bank, National Association, Charter Number 1316 ("PNC"), Michigan National Bank,

[1] The OCC recently amended its operating subsidiary rule , 12 C.F.R. 5.34, as part of general revision to Part 5 ("Rules, Policies and Procedures for Corporate Activities") under the OCC's Regulation Review Program. See 61 Fed. Reg. 60342 (November 27, 1996). However, the amended rule does not take effect until December 31, 1996. Accordingly, this application was decided under the current rule. 48 Fed. Reg. 48454 (October 19, 1983) as amended at 50 Fed. Reg. 1440 (January 11, 1985); 53 Fed. Reg. 18547 (May 24, 1988); and 55 Fed. Reg. 997 (January 11, 1990).

Charter Number 16660 ("Michigan National"), The First National Bank of Chicago, Charter Number 8 ("FNBC"), Comerica Bank - Ann Arbor, National Association, Charter Number 21527 ("Comerica"), and Fleet National Bank, Charter Number 1338 ("Fleet") (collectively, the "Banks") to establish new, or to engage in new activities in existing, operating subsidiaries (collectively, the "Operating Subsidiaries"). The purpose of the Banks' establishment of, or conduct of new activities within, the Operating Subsidiaries is to invest in a joint venture arrangement (the "Joint Venture") to form a Delaware limited liability company under the name of Integrion Financial Network, L.L.C. (the "LLC"), which will provide home banking and other electronic financial services.

For the reasons discussed below, we approve, subject to certain conditions, the establishment or expansion of such operating subsidiaries by the Banks because we find that the proposed investment by the operating subsidiaries in the LLC would be permissible for national banks under 12 U.S.C. § 24(Seventh). Please note that our response is solely directed to the question stated above. At this time, we will not address how other federal and state laws and regulations will or might apply to the Banks' activities in connection with the LLC, or to the LLC's operations, nor do we address the important supervisory or consumer protection considerations that will arise when the LLC actually commences operations. The LLC is still in the planning stage with some significant operational details still undecided. The OCC will work closely with the LLC so that supervisory and consumer matters are addressed, as appropriate, as the LLC's plans and actual operations develop.

A. Background

The LLC essentially will act as an electronic distribution channel for financial institutions to provide electronic financial services to their customers. More specifically, the LLC will establish an electronic "gateway" through which customers of the Banks will be able to obtain home banking and other financial services from their respective financial institutions through various electronic access devices, including telephone, personal computer, interactive television, etc. After the initial introduction of these home banking and other financial services, it is contemplated that other value-oriented services (such as stock quotations) will be offered to the financial institutions' customers by third party providers through the gateway. It is contemplated that the gateway eventually will be available, for a fee, to financial institutions that are not members of the LLC.

Each of the Banks (as well as several other financial institutions) [2] (collectively, the "Member Financial Institutions") has entered into a subscription agreement pursuant to which the Member Financial Institutions will make equal investments of up to [$$] in the LLC.

---

[2] The other financial institutions include Norwest Corp., Royal Bank of Canada, ABN AMRO North America, Inc. On December 2, 1996, the Board of Governors of the Federal Reserve granted the necessary regulatory approvals under section 4(c)(8) of the Bank Holding Company Act (12 U.S.C. 1843(c)(8)) for the investments by these institutions in the Integrion system. The Royal Bank of Canada, Montreal, Canada , __ Fed. Res. Bull. __, Order of December 2, 1996. See also, 61 Fed. Reg. 54441 (October 18, 1996). Washington Mutual, Inc., which is a thrift holding company regulated by the Office of Thrift Supervision ("OTS"), has filed with OTS its notice of intent to invest in the Integrion system.

International Business Machines Corporation ("IBM"), has entered into a substantially similar subscription agreement. The investment in the LLC by the Member Financial Institutions and IBM is pursuant to a Private Placement Memorandum, dated March 20, 1996, as amended (the "Private Placement Memorandum"). The Private Placement Memorandum contemplates that each investor enter into a Limited Liability Company Agreement (the "LLC Agreement") providing for the management and operation of the LLC upon receipt of all regulatory approvals and satisfaction of certain other conditions. [3]

Each of the Banks contemplates that its investment in the LLC will be made through its wholly owned Operating Subsidiary. The LLC will be a Delaware limited liability company. The purpose of the Banks' Operating Subsidiaries will be to own an interest in, and to participate in the management of, the LLC.

1. Proposed Activities of the LLC

In establishing and operating an electronic distribution channel for providing electronic financial services to customers of participating financial institutions, the LLC will design, develop, license and market services to financial institutions [4] (the "LLC Services") comprised of software[5], transaction processing, and direct network access that together will form an electronic gateway to the Member Financial Institutions, enabling the Member Financial Institutions to offer their customers a broad array of financial services delivered under individual financial institution brand names. Members using the LLC Services will be able to provide consumers full electronic access to their accounts through various devices, including personal computers, touch-tone telephones and, ultimately, other state-of the-art devices such as personal digital assistants, screen phones, and interactive television. The LLC will use the IBM Global Network ("IGN"), which provides users with levels of network, application and transaction security beyond that currently available on the public Internet. [6]

---

[3] Pursuant to the Private Placement Memorandum and the LLC Agreement, the total number of Member Financial Institutions may not exceed 18. To date, 16 financial institutions (i.e., each of the Banks, as well as Norwest Corp., Washington Mutual, Inc., ABN AMRO North America, Inc., and Royal Bank of Canada) have agreed to participate.

[4] The LLC will not itself provide any services directly to the customers of the Member Financial Institutions. Instead, the services will be provided to financial institutions. The LLC's role will be transparent to the customer and will be limited to establishing the electronic gateway through which the customers may obtain the LLC supported services from their respective Member Financial Institutions or from third parties.

[5] The LLC will provide a variety of software. For example, it will provide Member Financial Institutions with software to be distributed to customers so the customers can access and navigate the LLC's gateway. Because of the design of the LLC's system, the browser and dialer software required to access the LLC gateway is the same type of software required to access the public Internet. The LLC will provide other software to third party service providers that will enable a provider to gain access to, and operate within, the LLC gateway.

[6] Within the United States, electronic communications and host services will be provided by Advantis, a subsidiary of the IGN. In exchange for the LLC's agreement to certain usage commitments, IBM will grant the LLC certain exclusive domestic rights to a transaction processing platform (the "IFS Platform") that will serve as the basis for providing the LLC with transaction processing compatibility. The platform will facilitate

Initially, the LLC Services will be limited to facilitating certain banking services offered by the Member Financial Institutions to their customers. These core LLC Services will support traditional home banking and financial service activities, including remote banking and bill payment services, as well as certain customer service functions (such as check ordering, two-way customer service e-mail with the bank, and electronic statements).

Within one year, the Joint Venture intends to expand the scope of the LLC's Services to support additional home banking and financial service functions (such as on-line bill paying) through Internet protocol-style browsers (such as Netscape's Navigator), account access for inquiries and transfer, linkage to PC-based financial software (such as MECA's Managing Your Money, Microsoft's Money, and Intuit's Quicken), on-line statements, as well as enhanced customer service e-mail. Subsequent phase functions will include electronic bill presentment, interactive loan applications, and account opening services. Eventually, the LLC contemplates allowing customer access to other on-line services through the LLC's gateway. To the extent that these other on-line services are not permissible for a national bank, these on-line services would be made available through third party providers rather than by the Member Financial Institutions. [7] The LLC also contemplates that, eventually, the LLC's gateway function will be made available to other financial institutions.

Customers will be able to access the LLC gateway in two ways. First, customers who have a separate Internet access service provider will be able to access the LLC gateway through the Internet using the home page of a participating bank. Second, customers can access the LLC gateway through a private network using a local interface gateway ("LIG") that will be furnished to the LLC by IBM. [8] Financial institutions that subscribe to the LLC Services will also be able to use the LLC platform interface as a means of enabling their customers to access the public Internet for non-banking purposes. While the LLC will receive a modest fee

---

connections and compatibility between the customer's access device (e.g., a PC) and the bank's existing systems. It will consist of web servers for each participating financial institution. It will also contain certain core applications like bill payment and presentment. The Banks commit that in the agreement between the LLC and IBM, IBM will commit to preserve the confidentiality of bank customer information. The LLC Services performed for national banks directly or indirectly by the IGN or Advantis will be subject to OCC examination under 12 U.S.C. § 1867(c).

[7] Essentially, the LLC will provide a link via its web server to the Internet home page of the third party service provider. Specifically, the LLC will modify its web server architecture to link the customer directly with the party provider's Universal Reference Locator (i.e., Internet address) ("URL"). Thus, a customer desiring third party services will merely click on an icon on the LLC menu of services and will be connected with the third party's home page. The LLC will not provide any other form of data or transaction processing service to the third parties. The Banks will ensure that the appropriate disclosures are made by the third party vendors to make it clear that the nonbanking services are being offered by the nonaffiliated third party vendors and not by the Banks, and that the Banks are not responsible for such services. In addition, the Banks contemplate that the amount of nonbanking services made available through the LLC gateway will remain relatively small in relation to the amount of banking services.

[8] Eventually, the LLC will also enable customers to access the gateway using their own personal financial management software and third party online service providers (e.g., American On-line, Prodigy and CompuServe).

for enabling Internet access (in the form of hourly user fees and fees for the sale of browser and dialer software), the Banks assert that providing Internet access will entail little additional expense and that less than 10% of the LLC's total net income will be attributable to providing public Internet access.

2. *Structure of the LLC*

As noted above, pursuant to the subscription agreements, the Operating Subsidiaries (and IBM and the remaining Member Financial Institutions) will acquire, subject to regulatory approval, interests in the LLC. The Banks will contribute approximately [$$] in cash to each of their respective Operating Subsidiaries (unless the funds are currently available with respect to those Operating Subsidiaries that are already in existence). In turn, the Operating Subsidiaries will each invest the cash in the LLC. The other Member Financial Institutions and IBM also will, directly or indirectly, invest up to [$$] each in the LLC.

Pursuant to the Article III of the LLC Agreement, the LLC will be managed by a 13-member Board of Managers (the "Board"). The Chief Executive Officer of the LLC will be given a permanent seat on the Board, and IBM will be given a permanent right to appoint a Manager to the Board. For the first four years of operations, the remaining 11 Manager positions will be allocated as follows: (i) the nine "founding" financial institutions [9] will each be entitled to appoint a Manager to the Board; and (ii) two Managers will be "at-large" positions, selected for two-year terms by the remaining Member Financial Institutions not otherwise represented on the Board.

After the first four years, the nine Managers will be appointed by those nine Member Financial Institutions having the largest LLC revenue contribution, and will serve a term of four years. The other two "at large" Managers will be selected by the remaining Member Financial Institutions and will serve a term of two years. The LLC Board will appoint the executive management of the LLC and will oversee and approve the activities of the LLC in accordance with parameters set forth in the LLC Agreement.

3. *Other Material Terms of the LLC Agreement*

Under the LLC Agreement, the LLC may not engage in any activity that is not a permissible activity for a national bank or an operating subsidiary thereof and will cease any activity that the OCC formally opines to be an impermissible activity. Section 2.8(b). Further, the LLC will obtain OCC approval, to the extent required, prior to the commencement of any new activity. Id. Members may withdraw from the LLC without the consent of the other Members if, *inter alia*, the Member reasonably determines that the LLC is engaged in activities that are not permissible for a national bank or an operating subsidiary thereof. Section 8.2 Under the LLC Agreement, the interests in the LLC are subject to restrictions on transferability. Basically, a Member may not transfer all or a part of its interest without the

---

[9] The eight founding financial institutions include Bank of America, NationsBank, Key Bank, Bank One, Royal Bank of Canada, Barnett, FNBC, and Fleet.

prior written consent of a super majority of the Members and a majority of the members holding percentage interests. Id. After a Member is admitted, its mandatory additional capital contributions to the LLC cannot exceed an aggregate amount of [$$]. Section 4.2. Finally, the LLC Agreement acknowledges that the LLC will be subject to the examination, supervision and regulation by the OCC. Section 10.13.

B. Discussion

A national bank may engage in activities that are part of or incidental to the business of banking by means of an operating subsidiary. 12 C.F.R. § 5.34. Your letter raises the issue of the authority of a national bank to make indirectly a non-controlling investment in a limited liability company. In a variety of circumstances, the OCC has permitted national banks to own, either directly, or indirectly through an operating subsidiary, a minority interest in an enterprise.[10] The enterprise might be a limited partnership, a corporation, or in more recent examples, a limited liability company. In two recent interpretive letters, the OCC concluded that national banks are legally permitted to make a minority investment in an LLC provided four criteria or standards are met. See Interpretive Letter No. 692, reprinted in [Current] Fed. Banking L. Rep. (CCH) ¶ 81,007 (November 1, 1995), and OCC Interpretive Letter No. 694, reprinted in [Current] Fed. Banking L. Rep. (CCH) ¶ 81,009 (December 13, 1995). These standards, which have been distilled from our previous decisions in the area of permissible minority investments for national banks and their subsidiaries, are: (1) The activities of the enterprise in which the investment is made must be limited to activities that are part of or incidental to the business of banking. (2) The bank must be able to prevent the enterprise from engaging in activities that do not meet the foregoing standard, or be able to withdraw its investment. (3) The bank's loss exposure must be limited, as a legal and accounting matter, and the bank must not have open-ended liability for the obligations of the enterprise. (4) The investment must be convenient or useful to the bank in carrying out its business and not a mere passive investment unrelated to that bank's banking business. We conclude, as discussed below, that the proposed indirect investment by national banks in the LLC satisfies these four criteria.

1. The activities of the enterprise in which the investment is made must be limited to activities that are part of or incidental to the business of banking

The National Bank Act, in relevant part, provides that national banks shall have the power:

> [t]o exercise ... all such incidental powers as shall be necessary to carry on the business of banking; by discounting and negotiating promissory notes, drafts, bills of exchange, and other evidences of debt; by receiving deposits; by buying and selling exchange, coin, and bullion; by loaning money on personal security; and by obtaining, issuing, and circulating notes ...

---

[10] See, e.g., OCC Conditional Approval Letter No. 219 (July, 15, 1996). Such investments are permissible if they meet the requirements for direct minority investments by national banks.

12 U.S.C. § 24(Seventh).

The Supreme Court has held that the powers clause of 12 U.S.C. § 24(Seventh) is a broad grant of power to engage in the business of banking, including but not limited to the enumerated powers and the business of banking as a whole. See NationsBank of North Carolina, N.A. v. Variable Life Annuity Co., 115 S. Ct. 810 (1995) (" VALIC"). Judicial cases reflect three general principles used to determine whether an activity is within the scope of the "business of banking": (1) is the activity functionally equivalent to or a logical outgrowth of a recognized banking activity; (2) would the activity respond to customer needs or otherwise benefit the bank or its customers; and (3) does the activity involve risks similar in nature to those already assumed by banks. See, e.g., Merchants' Bank v. State Bank, 77 U.S. 604, 648 (1871) (certification of checks has grown out of the business needs of the country and involves no greater risk than a bank giving a certificate of deposit); M&M Leasing Corp. v. Seattle First Nat'l Bank, 563 F.2d 1377, 1382-83 (9th Cir. 1977), cert. denied, 436 U.S. 987 (1978) (personal property lease financing is "functionally interchangeable" with the express power to loan money on personal property); American Ins. Assoc. v. Clarke, 865 F.2d 278, 282 (D.C. Cir. 1988) (standby credits to insure municipal bonds is "functionally equivalent" to the issuance of a standby letter of credit)(" AMBAC"). Further, as established by the Supreme Court in VALIC, national banks are authorized to engage in an activity if it is incidental to the performance of the five enumerated powers in section 24(Seventh) or if it is incidental to the performance of an activity that is part of the business of banking.

In the present case, the LLC's activities will be limited to the development, licensing and marketing of services comprised of software development, data processing, and data transmission, enabling participating financial institutions to offer their customers the various services supported by the LLC through the LLC's electronic gateway. It is contemplated that the LLC gateway will enable customers of participating financial institutions to obtain other financially related services from third party provider firms. As will be developed below, these proposed activities are part of or incidental to the business of banking.

a. Providing an Electronic Gateway to Support the Provision of Home Banking and Financial services

The LLC will offer participating financial institutions an electronic gateway by which those institutions may provide their own customers with home banking and other electronic financial services. Initially, the gateway will support traditional home banking and financial services such as remote banking and bill paying. Eventually, the gateway will be expanded to support account inquiries and transfers, electronic bill presentment and on-line loan applications. To support these underlying consumer services, the LLC gateway will provide participating institutions with transaction and information processing, communications services, and supporting software. These are permissible activities for national banks.

It is well established that a national bank may use electronic means to perform services expressly or incidentally authorized to national banks. [11] The OCC Interpretive Ruling setting forth this authority was recently revised, in recognition of the rapid advancement of technology, to authorize a national bank to "perform, provide, or deliver through electronic means and facilities any activity, function, product, or service that it is otherwise authorized to perform, provide, or deliver." 61 Fed. Reg. 4849 (1996) codified at 12 C.F.R. § 7.1019.

The LLC's information and transaction processing for participating institutions will involve banking, financial, or related economic data and, thus, is part of the business of banking. An earlier version of 12 C.F.R. § 7.1019 stated that "as part of its banking business and incidental thereto, a national bank may collect, transcribe, process, analyze, and store for itself and others, banking, financial, or related economic data." Interpretive Ruling 7.3500, 39 Fed. Reg. 14195 (Apr. 22, 1974). Although in its 1984 revision of the ruling, the OCC deleted this statement because it believed that "specific examples [of permissible electronic activities] are inappropriate given the imprecision of terms and rapid pace of change in the data processing industry", 49 Fed. Reg. 11157 (Mar. 26, 1984), the "analytical framework" embodied in the ruling remained the same. Id. There was no intent to narrow or restrict the substantive effect of the rule. [12]

Similarly, the OCC has found that, as part of the business of banking, national banks may provide for the transmission of banking, financial, or related economic data and thereby establish communication or data networks that support banking and financial transactions. In OCC Interpretive Letter No. 732, reprinted in [Current] Fed. Banking L. Rep. (CCH) ¶ 81-049 (July 1, 1996), the OCC permitted a national bank to assume a minority ownership in a company engaged in the design, development, and marketing of a network for electronic funds transfer and electronic commercial data interchange. [13]

---

[11] See OCC Interpretive Letter No. 677, reprinted in [1994-1995 Transfer Binder] Fed. Banking L. Rep. (CCH) ¶ 83,625 (June 28, 1995); OCC Interpretive Letter No. 284, reprinted in [1983-1984 Transfer Binder] Fed. Banking L. Rep. (CCH) ¶85,448 (March 26, 1984); and OCC Interpretive Letter No. 449, reprinted in [1988-1989 Transfer Binder] Fed. Banking L. Rep. (CCH) ¶ 85,673 (August 23, 1988).

[12] OCC Interpretive Letter No. 677, supra. See also, OCC Interpretive Letter No. 737 (August 19, 1996) (to be published) (national bank may provide transaction and information processing services to support an electronic stored value system); OCC Interpretive Letter No. 653, reprinted in [1994-1995 Transfer Binder] Fed. Banking L. Rep. (CCH) ¶ 83,601 (December 22, 1994) (national bank may act as an informational and payments interface between insurance underwriters and general insurance agents); OCC Letter No. 346, reprinted in [1985-1987] Transfer Binder] Fed. Banking Law. Rep. (CCH) ¶ 85,516 (July 31, 1985) (national banks may maintain records on commodities transactions).

[13] See also, OCC Interpretive Letter No. 653, supra (national bank may establish a network to act as an informational and payments interface between insurance underwriters and their agents); OCC Interpretive Letter No. 516, reprinted in [1990-91 Transfer Binder] Fed. Banking L. Rep. (CCH) ¶83,220 (July 12, 1990) (national bank may provide electronic communications channels for persons participating in securities transactions); OCC Interpretive Letter No. 513, reprinted in [1990-91 Transfer Binder] Fed. Banking L. Rep. (CCH) ¶83,215 (June 18, 1990) (national bank may provide an electronic network for the transmission of visual, voice and data communications for other financial institutions); OCC Interpretive Letter No. 346, supra (national bank may establish an electronic gateway for financial settlement services).

Finally, the LLC will provide two types of software in connection with its gateway service. First, it will provide participating institutions with software to be distributed to customers so they can access and navigate the LLC's gateway. Second, the LLC will provide software to third party service providers that will enable a provider to gain access to, and operate within, the electronic gateway. Both are clearly incidental to the business of banking; the distribution of this software is necessary to the functioning of the LLC's gateway. A national bank can sell software where the software will enable the bank customer to receive or utilize other services from the bank such as a specialized payment service or informational services. [14] In this case, the software is a necessary adjunct to the gateway service and, thus, is incidental thereto. [15]

b. Providing Links to Third Party Vendor Websites

The LLC plans to allow customers of participating institutions to access the Internet home pages of other on-line services through an Internet link provided on the LLC's gateway. Providing links to third party vendors' websites, in the manner proposed by the LLC, is both part of the business of banking and, under the facts of this case, incidental to the business of banking.

The linkage to third party vendors' websites is part of the business of banking because it is a use of modern technology to provide a recognized banking function: acting as a "finder." The finder function is a well recognized banking activity that includes, "without limitation, identifying potential parties, making inquiries as to interest, introducing or arranging meetings of interested parties, and otherwise bringing parties together for a transaction that the parties

---

[14] See OCC Interpretive Letter No. 516, supra (a national bank that is providing customers with a permissible database service of information relating to financial instruments can also provide software that enables the customers to download and analyze the information) and OCC Interpretive Letter No. 419 reprinted in [1988-89 Transfer Binder] Fed. Banking L. Rep. (CCH) ¶85,643 (February 16, 1988) (a national bank that is providing customers with a permissible electronic transactional and information service can provide software that enables customers to participate in the system).

[15] The fact that the browser and dialer software provided by the LLC can also be used for other purposes, e.g., to access the public Internet, does not undercut this conclusion. The LLC's gateway system is based upon web server technology and, thus, uses "Internet-compatible" browser software. The OCC has long held that national banks have an incidental authority to provide electronic products or services that can be used for both banking and non-banking functions as part of a package of banking related products or services where the full function products or services are not an excessive amount of the total package. OCC Interpretive Letter No. 742 (August 19, 1996) (to be published) (Internet access service); OCC Interpretive Letter No. 611, reprinted in [1992-1993 Transfer Binder] Fed. Banking L. Rep. (CCH) ¶ 83,449 (Nov. 23, 1992) (sale of computerized telephone "smart phone" is incidental to banking even though the phone can be used for non-banking functions). The LLC will sell the dialer and browser software to the participating institutions at cost and, thus, it clearly will be a minor and incidental portion of the entire package. See OCC Interpretive Letter No. 754 (November 6, 1996) (to be published).

themselves negotiate and consummate." 61 Fed. Reg. 4849, 4863 (Feb. 9, 1996) (codified at 12 C.F.R. § 7.1002). [16]

Even though earlier OCC staff opinions sometimes characterized the finder function as an incidental powers activity, [17] it is actually part of the business of banking. Prior to VALIC, the courts and the OCC frequently blurred or combined the "business of banking" and "powers incidental to the business of banking" concepts. Under the now superseded Arnold Tours test,[18] all non-enumerated powers tended to be characterized as "incidental powers" even though some activities held to be incidental clearly fell within the "business of banking", e.g., an activity that is the functional equivalent of an established power such as lending. See, e.g., M & M Leasing, 563 F.2d 1382-83. Compare, American Ins. Assoc. v. Clarke, 656 F. Supp. 404 (D.D.C.), aff'd 865 F. 2d 278 (D.C. Cir. 1988). However, in light of VALIC, it is now clear that the incidental activities are activities that are permissible for national banks not because they are part of the "business of banking", but rather because they are "convenient" or "useful" to an activity that is part of the business of banking. In contrast, activities that are part of the business of banking are permissible without reference or connection to any other banking activity.

Clearly, the OCC has treated the finder activity as an activity that is permissible without reference to any other banking activity. OCC letters opining that the finder activity permissible have not been based upon any determination that the finder activity was somehow

[16] See also, Letter from J.T. Watson, Deputy Comptroller of the Currency, February 26, 1969 (unpublished); Letter from John M. Miller, July 26, 1977 (unpublished); Letter from Letter from Paul Allan Schott, Chief Counsel, May 9, 1988 (unpublished); Letter from Elizabeth Corey, May 18, 1989 (unpublished); OCC Interpretive Letter No. 238, reprinted in [1983-1984 Transfer Binder], Fed. Banking L. Rep. (CCH) ¶ 85,402 (February 9, 1982); OCC Interpretive Letter No. 472, reprinted in [1989-1990 Transfer Binder] Fed. Banking L. Rep. (CCH) ¶ 83,008 (March 2 1989); Letter from Lee Walzer, Attorney, Securities, Investments and Fiduciary Practices Division, August 24, 1992 (unpublished) and Letter from Julie L. Williams, Chief Counsel, October 2, 1996 (not yet assigned a number; to be published) .

[17] See e.g., Letter from Christopher Manthey, Senior Attorney, March 2, 1989 (unpublished) Letter from Elizabeth Corey May 18, 1989 (unpublished), Letter from Richard V. Fitzgerald, Director, May 29, 1979 (unpublished), Letter from Roberta Walsh Boylan, Assistant Director, October 17, 1980 (unpublished).

[18] Before VALIC, the standard used to determine whether an activity was "incidental" had been developed by the First Circuit Court of Appeals in Arnold Tours, Inc. v. Camp, 472 F.2d 427 (1st Cir. 1972). In Arnold Tours, the court held that "incidental" activities must be convenient or useful to one of the activities *expressly* enumerated or listed in 12 U.S.C. 24(Seventh). However, the VALIC decision clearly mandates that this aspect of the Arnold Tours test be modified to accommodate VALIC's flexible definition of the "business of banking." VALIC requires that the test be rephrased as follows: An activity is validly "incidental" if it is convenient or useful to the "business of banking" including, but not limited to, one of the powers specifically enumerated in the National Bank Act. Thus, we must distinguish analytically between activities that are part of the "business of banking" and those that are "incidental to the business of banking."

"necessary" to another banking activity. [19] Thus, the finder activity is more accurately characterized as part of the business of banking, rather than as incidental thereto.

The means that national banks use to act as finders for their customers have evolved due to technological advancements. Where banks once performed this service for their customers via newsletters and personal contacts, they presently conduct the activity with computer technology. [20] The LLC will merely use another new technology: the Internet and the LLC's web server architecture. Customers after having accessed their financial institution's webserver will be presented a menu and can select a third party vendor's icon appearing on screen to be linked to that vendor's URL. By providing links to third party vendors' websites, the LLC merely introduces two parties who may engage in a transaction. Any further negotiations will then occur between the customer and the vendor. At that point the LLC's role in the transaction is complete. Thus, the process of providing hypertext links in the manner proposed is acting as a finder and is a new way of conducting this aspect of the business of banking. See M&M Leasing Corp., 563 F.2d at 1382-1383.

Further, and independent of the prior analysis, the LLC's links to third party vendors' websites is incidental to the business of banking because it is a permissible use of the LLC's excess capacity acquired in good faith. It is well established that a national bank, under its incidental authority, may market and sell excess electronic capacities acquired or developed by the bank in good faith for banking purposes. 12 C.F.R. § 7.1019. See also OCC Interpretive Letter No. 742, supra, and OCC Interpretive Letter No. 677, supra. Thus, a national bank, under its incidental authority, may utilize the excess capacity inherent in the electronic media it uses to communicate with its customers. Banks have been permitted to include non-banking financial information as "statement stuffers" in envelopes containing a regularly scheduled mailings to customers. See OCC Interpretive Letter No. 316, reprinted in [1985-87 Transfer Binder] Fed. Banking Rep ¶85,486 (December 28, 1984). Providing links to non-banking vendors, in the manner proposed, is the use of a new technology to provide the equivalent of including written information in bank customers mailings since customers now receive the same information through links to the third party vendors' websites.

---

[19] See Letter from John D. Gwin, Deputy Comptroller of the Currency, May 22 1968 (unpublished) (national bank may act as a finder for target or acquiror industrial corporations); Letter from Kenneth W. Leaf, Chief National Bank Examiner, June 8, 1973 (unpublished) (national bank may act as finder for computer programs); Letter from James M. Kane, District Counsel, October 24, 1985 (unpublished) (permitting national bank to act as a finder for insurance products) OCC Interpretive Letter No. 472, supra (national banks may provide finder services for homeowners insurance); OCC Interpretive Letter No. 653, supra (national bank may act as finder for insurance products); Letter from Julie L. Williams, Chief Counsel, October 2, 1996, supra (permitting a national bank to conduct finder activities for a variety of third party products and services).

[20] See 12 C.F.R. § 7.1019. See also OCC Interpretive Letter No. 346, supra (national banks may act as a finder through electronic means for commodities transactions); OCC Interpretive Letter No. 516, supra (national banks may utilize computer channels to act as a finder for securities or other financial instruments); OCC Interpretive Letter No. 611, supra (national banks may provide finder service through connecting third party vendors to their home banking platform) and OCC Interpretive Letter No. 741 (August 19, 1996) (to be published) (permitting national banks to act as a finder for automobile sales and financing through database and call center services).

A bank that has in good faith acquired excess data processing capacity sufficient for website links need not allow that capacity to go unused. The specific server configuration necessary to provide banking services in the manner proposed by the LLC will legitimately have capacity in excess of that required to provide banking services. The LLC will establish logical separate webservers for each bank configured to permit URL links and possessing sufficient random access memory ("RAM") to tolerate varying customer banking traffic needs. Thus, this server architecture will have excess RAM sufficient for URL links to third party vendor's websites. Execution of these links, enabling customers to access other services, will require an insignificant amount of computer resources, and will not result in the LLC incurring additional costs. Providing links to other vendors' websites enables the LLC to benefit from the excess capacity resulting from the establishment of the banking webservers.

The LLC does not face significant additional risks by providing links to third party vendors in the manner proposed. The risks faced are similar to those associated with the permissible activities of providing banking services via electronic means generally. Acting as a finder does not pose any increased risks to the LLC since its role is limited to providing a link -- introducing the parties to the transaction. The links merely expedite users' navigation to other vendors websites.[21]

c. *Providing Internet Access*

Finally, the LLC will enable participating institutions to offer their customers access to the public Internet from the LLC platform. The LLC believes that the ability to enable participating banks to offer Internet access as part of package of home financial services is critical to the successful marketing of the package supported by the LLC. For the reasons below, we agree and therefore find that the LLC's wholesaling of Internet access to participating institutions is incidental to the business of banking.

In designing the package of consumer services to be supported by the LLC, some of the Banks and others conducted a survey in April 1996 of almost 600 consumers who either currently use or would consider using electronic financial services. This survey found that those consumers overwhelmingly demand public Internet access as part of a package of electronic financial management services. The survey, which rated consumer demand for more than 40 different services that might be included in a home financial services package, was based on a scale of 1 to 5 (with a "5" indicating that the consumer is extremely likely to use a service and a "1" indicating that the consumer is not at all likely to use the service). The consumer respondents assigned public Internet access a rating of 4.3, making it the second most important feature overall; 79.8% of the respondents rated Internet access as either a "4" or "5" in importance. Surprisingly, consumers rated public Internet access as more important than several traditional home banking functions such as account transfer and loan application functions. In light of this strong indicia of consumer demand, the LLC and participating

[21] The LLC will conduct this activity in conformance with 12 C.F.R. § 7.1002. Further, the Banks will ensure that third parties make the disclosures mentioned in footnote 6 and that the nonbanking services made available through the LLC gateway remain relatively small in proportion to the banking transactions conducted.

Banks assert that they need to include public Internet access as part of their package of consumer services in order to successfully market that package.

The marketplace apparently agrees. To enhance marketability, many consumer products and services are now being bundled with Internet access. Newspapers, which frequently post their content on Internet home pages, are now beginning to offer free and full Internet access service to their subscribers. See Mills, Newspapers Offer Free Internet to Subscribers, Washington Post, October 16, 1996 at C12, col. 2. Similarly, the largest telecommunications companies are offering their customers reduced cost Internet access as a marketing incentive for their telephone service. See Flanagan, AT&T Invades Internet with "Free" Service, 30 ASAP 5 (May 1996); Swett, MCI Matches AT&T Free Internet Offer, Sacramento Bee, March 19, 1996 at D1. Most significantly, the firms that will compete with the LLC in providing home banking networks also offer reduced cost public Internet service as part of their package of consumer financial services. Intuit, Inc., which will be one of the LLC's most significant competitors, operates the "Quicken Financial Network" ("QFN"), an area on the World Wide Web containing information on the Quicken financial software, the financial world, and the institutions that provide on-line financial services through Intuit. Users of the Quicken financial software gain free Internet access to the portion of the Internet housing the QFN. Intuit also offers its customers the option to purchase full Internet access at a reduced fee.[22]

Recently, the OCC determined that a national bank subsidiary may provide home banking services via an Internet connection to the bank's home banking system and, incidental to that service, may also provide Internet access to customers and non-bank customers in the bank's service area. OCC Interpretive Letter No. 742, supra (the "Apollo" letter). The OCC based this conclusion in part upon a finding that, under the facts of that case, providing full Internet access created a package of related services needed to satisfy consumer demand and enable the bank to successfully market its home banking services. The OCC said:

> OCC precedent has established that the provision of such ancillary non-banking services is permissible as incidental to the business of banking when needed to successfully package and promote other permissible banking services. [Citations omitted.]
>
> Here, the full Internet access service is needed to successfully provide and market the Bank's Internet banking service. Limiting the Bank's gateway services, to block non-banking use, would create a hobbled home banking product unlikely to meet consumer demand. Customers in the midst of an

---

[22] Intuit informs its customers that:

> [Y]ou can upgrade to full Internet access for a low monthly fee. This upgrade gives you access to the World Wide Web, electronic mail, and newsgroups. ... Full Internet access through QFN is economical. Our exclusive offer for Quicken users entitles you to very low access fees.

Intuit, Quicken User's Guide: Version 5 for Windows at p. 24 (1995).

> Internet session wanting to view their account information would need to end the Internet session, then connect directly to the Bank. Such a cumbersome structure would not fully meet customer needs, causing them to search for more useful banking products offered by other institutions.

OCC Interpretive Letter No. 742, supra. See also, OCC Interpretive Letter No. 611, supra, (bank selling home banking service can also provide customer access to non-banking services "to increase the customer base and the usage of the program"); OCC Interpretive Letter No. 653, reprinted in [1994-1995 Transfer Binder] Fed. Banking L. Rep. (CCH) ¶ 83,601 (December 22, 1994) (national banks may offer non-banking products as part of larger product or service when necessary, convenient and useful to bank permissible activities). Cf., National Courier Ass'n v. Board of Governors, 516 F. 2d 1229, 1240 (D.C. Cir. 1975) (incidental powers of holding companies to provide specialized courier services when service necessary to obtain full benefit of data processing services).

The facts in this case are somewhat different than in the Apollo letter. [23] Nevertheless, the LLC has made a strong showing of consumer demand for an Internet access feature in the package of services supported by the LLC. There is also clear evidence that competitors of the LLC will be offering such a feature. Finally, the Internet access feature will be only a minor part of the entire package offered by the LLC (less than 10% of total net income) [24] and will entail little additional expense for the LLC. Under these circumstances, we find the Internet access feature to be validly incidental to the other LLC Services.

2. *The Banks must be able to prevent the LLC from engaging in activities that do not meet the foregoing standard, or be able to withdraw their investment*

This is an obvious corollary to the first standard. It is not sufficient that the LLC's activities are permissible at the time the bank initially purchases LLC membership shares; they must also remain permissible for as long as the bank retains an ownership interest in the LLC.

---

[23] For example, here the LLC will not be using excess capacity to provide public Internet access.

[24] Full function products provided as an incidental part of a package of banking services cannot dominate the banking services being provided. *See* OCC Interpretive Letter No. 737, supra; OCC Interpretive Letter No. 516, supra; Letter from Michael J. O'Keefe, District Counsel, Midwestern District (July 13, 1987) (unpublished); OCC Interpretive Letter No. 345, [1986-1987 Transfer Binder] Fed. Banking L. Rep. (CCH) ¶ 77,799 (July 9, 1986). The OCC has two alternative tests for determining when sale of full function products as part of a package of banking services is "incidental" to those services. The older OCC test is whether the cost of the full function product is less than 30% of the cost of the entire package. OCC Interpretive Letter No. 742, supra. As an alternative to the cost test, a recent letter adopted a test based on the percentage of "gross profits" (sales less cost of goods sold) that is derived from the sale of the hardware. OCC Interpretive Letter No. 754, supra. Specifically, this letter held that where the gross profits generated by a full function product provided in connection with a banking service do not exceed thirty percent of the total gross profits from that service, the sale of the full function product is incidental to the permitted banking service. Here, the LLC has expressed the percentage in terms of net income rather than gross profits. However, under the facts in this case, the difference between gross profits and net income is not material.

The LLC Agreement provides that the LLC will only engage in activities permissible for national banks. In addition, Members may withdraw from the LLC without the consent of the other Members if, *inter alia*, the Member reasonably determines that the LLC is engaged in activities that are not permissible for a national bank or an operating subsidiary thereof. As a result, the Banks will be able, on an ongoing basis, to prevent the LLC from engaging in new activities that may be impermissible for national banks.

3. The Banks' loss exposure must be limited, as a legal and accounting matter, and the Banks must not have open-ended liability for the obligations of the enterprise

a. Loss exposure from a legal standpoint

A primary concern of the OCC is that national banks should not be subjected to undue risk. Where an investing bank will not control the operations of the entity in which the bank holds an interest, it is important that a bank's investment not expose it to unlimited liability. This is the case here. As a legal matter, investors in a Delaware LLC will not incur liability beyond their investment in the LLC because of being a member or manager of the LLC -- even if they actively participate in the management or control of the business. Del. Code Ann. Tit. 6, § 18-303(a) (1994). Additionally, the LLC Agreement does not expose the Banks to unlimited liability due to their investment in the LLC.

b. Loss exposure from an accounting standpoint

In assessing a bank's loss exposure as an accounting matter, the OCC has previously noted that the appropriate accounting treatment for a bank's less than 20 percent ownership share or investment in an LLC is to report it as an unconsolidated entity under the equity method or cost of accounting. Under the equity method of accounting, unless the investor has extended a loan to the entity, guaranteed any of its liabilities, or has other financial obligations, the investor's losses are generally limited to the amount of the investment shown on the investor's books.[25] Similarly, under the cost method of accounting, the investor records an investment at cost, dividends, or distributions from the entity are the basis for recognition of earnings, and losses recognized by the investor are limited to the extent of the investment. In sum, regardless of which accounting method is used, the investing bank's potential loss is limited to the amount of its investment. The Banks will meet this requirement.

---

[25] See generally, Accounting Principles Board, Op. No. 18 § 19 (1971). Under the equity method, the investor records the initial investment at cost and, then, adjusts the carrying amount to recognize the investor's pro rata share of subsequent earnings or losses in the LLC. When losses equal or exceed the carrying amount of the investment plus advances, the investment is reduced to zero value and no further losses need be recognized unless the investor has guaranteed obligations of the LLC or is otherwise committed to provide further financial support of the LLC. In contrast, under the cost method, the investor records the initial investment at cost and, then, adjusts the carrying amount to recognize dividends actually received. Operating losses are recognized if a series of losses or other factors indicate that a decrease in the value of the investment has occurred which is other than temporary. However, losses under the cost method are generally recognized only to the extent of the adjusted carrying amount of the investment.

4. *The investment must be convenient or useful to the Bank in carrying out its business and not a mere passive investment unrelated to that Bank's banking business*

A national bank's investment in an enterprise or entity that is not an operating subsidiary of the bank also must satisfy the requirement that the investment have a beneficial connection to the bank's business, i.e., be convenient or useful to the investing bank's business activities, and not be a mere passive investment unrelated to that bank's business activities. "Necessary" has been judicially construed to mean "convenient or useful." See Arnold Tours, 472 F.2d at 432. The provision in 12 U.S.C. § 24(Seventh) relating to the purchase of stock, derived from section 16 of the Glass-Steagall Act, was only intended to make it clear that section 16 did not authorize speculative investments in stock. See OCC Interpretive Letter No. 697, reprinted in [Current Transfer Binder] Fed. Banking L. Rep. (CCH) ¶ 81-102 (November 15, 1995). Therefore, a consistent thread running through our precedents concerning stock ownership is that it must be convenient or useful to the bank in conducting that bank's banking business. The investment must benefit or facilitate that business and cannot be a mere passive or speculative investment.

That requirement is met here. The LLC will be providing services to the investing Banks that will enable the Banks to offer their customers a competitive package of home banking and financial services.

C. Conclusion

On the basis of the representations specified in your notification letter and other submitted materials, the OCC finds that the Banks may operate subsidiaries that will invest in the LLC and that the notification should be and is approved subject to the following conditions:

1. the LLC may engage only in activities that are part of or incidental to the business of banking;

2. the Banks will withdraw from the LLC in the event it engages in an activity that is inconsistent with condition # 1;

3. the Banks will account for their investment in the LLC under the equity or cost method of accounting; and

4. the LLC will be subject to OCC supervision, regulation, and examination. [26]

Please be advised that all conditions of this approval are "conditions imposed in writing by the agency in connection with the granting of any application or other request" within the

[26] In the future, the nature and scope of the LLC's activities might be so substantially enhanced that the methodology the OCC uses to compute the Banks' assessment will need to be adjusted to cover adequately the expense of supervising and examining the LLC.

meaning of 12 U.S.C. § 1818.

Sincerely,

/s/

Julie L. Williams
Chief Counsel

Appendix B3
OCC Conditional Approval No. 253 (Aug. 20, 1997)

Comptroller of the Currency
Administrator of National Banks

Washington, DC 20219

**DECISION OF THE OFFICE OF THE COMPTROLLER OF THE CURRENCY
ON THE APPLICATION TO CHARTER
COMPUBANK, NATIONAL ASSOCIATION, HOUSTON, TEXAS**

AUGUST 20, 1997

I. DESCRIPTION OF THE PROPOSAL

On August 27, 1996, a group of individuals ("the Organizers") filed an application to charter a new national bank.[1] The proposed bank will be headquartered in Houston, Texas, and will be titled CompuBank, National Association ("Bank"). The application has been supplemented from time to time with additional or amended information. No comments were received from the public regarding this application.

This is the first charter proposal filed with the OCC for a national bank that will deliver products and services to customers primarily through electronic means. The Bank will not have any traditional banking offices. In addition to using the mail, customers will conduct their banking transactions by using a personal computer or by telephoning the automated voice response system or customer service line. Initially, the Bank does not plan to offer banking transactions via the Internet, but will likely add that delivery option in the near future. The Bank has applied to the Federal Deposit Insurance Corporation (FDIC) for deposit insurance and will become a member of the Federal Reserve System.

The Bank will focus exclusively on offering checking and savings accounts and electronic bill payment services. Bank customers will deposit funds into their accounts through direct deposit, wire transfers, or mail. Customers will use an ATM/debit card and existing ATM networks to make withdrawals. [

]

[1] The Organizers are Frank S. Goldberg, Edward J. Crawford, Joseph W. Kaplan, Irving Pozmantier, and Nathaniel C. Morgan. All of the Organizers with the exception of Mr. Morgan will serve on the Bank's board. Two non-Organizers with backgrounds in technology and information services will also serve on the Bank's board. They are Jeffrey D. Hoffman and Jonathan H. Lack.

The Bank will not make or purchase any loans. Instead, it will invest funds primarily in high-grade U.S. Treasury and U.S. Government-sponsored agency securities. All investments will be made pursuant to the OCC's Investment Securities Regulation (12 C.F.R. Part 1)

The initial primary service area for the Bank will be the metropolitan Houston market. The proposed Bank's use of technology, however, could allow its customer base to expand regionally and nationally. The Bank has defined its target market as individuals who are younger (age 18 to 49), own a personal computer, and frequently use ATMs. Its marketing strategy combines offering low- or no-fee electronic banking with more personalized customer service.

The Bank's main office, and initially its only office, will be situated in an office suite in Houston, Texas. The office will be designed as a "call center" reached primarily by telephone or computer, and it is not expected to have frequent walk-in customers. In the event that a customer chooses to visit the Bank's office, he or she will be able to make new account or customer service inquiries, but will not be able to conduct cash transactions. Bank staff will consist of a President/Chief Executive Officer, a Chief Technology Officer/Cashier, a computer systems administrator, and customer service representatives.

The Bank, similar to traditional community banks or those offering electronic banking products, will perform some key operational functions internally while contracting with third-party service providers for the provision of other functions. Bank staff will provide customer service, investment, cashier, and regulatory compliance functions. Internal and external audit functions will be provided by outside companies on a contract basis. With respect to technology, the Bank will employ a client/server network architecture and will license existing banking software customized for its own needs. The proposed architecture will offer the Bank the flexibility to conduct its electronic customer interface and core data processing either "in-house" or through an outside service bureau arrangement.[2] The Bank plans to contract with outside vendors to provide support for electronic bill payment services, ATM network services, and debit card operations.

II. LICENSING FACTORS

A. Policy Considerations

Under its Corporate Activities regulations (12 C.F.R. § 5.20), the OCC considers whether the proposed bank: (A) has organizers who are aware of, and understand, national banking laws and

[2]The electronic customer interface, or the "front-end," facilitates the interaction between the customer's computer and the Bank and that, in turn, allows the customer to perform tasks such as querying account balances, transferring funds between accounts, and paying bills. The core data processing, or "back-end," involves the Bank's posting of transactions to the appropriate accounts and to the general ledger and performing related functions such as internal reporting and customer account statement rendering.

regulations, and safe and sound operations and practices; (B) has competent management, including a board of directors, with ability and experience relevant to the types of services to be provided; (C) has capital that is sufficient to support the projected volume and type of business; (D) can reasonably be expected to achieve and maintain profitability; and (E) will be operated in a safe and sound manner.

In evaluating this charter proposal, the OCC performed a thorough analysis of the proposed operating plan. This included a field investigation with interviews of the proposed organizers, directors, and officers; evaluation of the Bank's proposed information system architecture and approach to security and controls; discussions with OCC examiners and other Federal banking agencies regarding their experience with existing financial institutions that have similar operational aspects; an on-site visit to a bank that delivers products via telephone; and a review of the OCC's ongoing research involving developments in electronic banking and payment systems technology.

The OCC's field investigation concluded that the Organizers are knowledgeable of, and understand, national banking laws and regulations and safe and sound operations. Three of the Organizers have served as either an officer, director, or principal shareholder of a national bank with combined banking experience totaling nearly 40 years. Each Organizer understands the roles and responsibilities of a national bank director, and is knowledgeable of banking concepts.

The proposed Bank has competent management, including a board of directors, with abilities and experience relevant to the types of services to be provided. The proposed President is an experienced banker who has the necessary attributes to implement the proposed operating plan, including a good working knowledge of bank technology. He formerly served as the founding President of a profitable *de novo* community bank in Houston, Texas. The Bank has also named an experienced individual to serve as Chief Technology Officer and has proposed two additional directors who will bring valuable technology-related experience to the board.

Proposed capital is sufficient to support the projected volume and type of business. The Organizers intend to capitalize the Bank with $5.0 million, net of all organizational and pre-opening expenses. Based upon the Bank's growth and earnings projections, this level of initial capital should ensure that the Bank's Tier 1 leverage ratio will exceed eight percent throughout the first three years of operations[3] However, as outlined below, the OCC has imposed a condition requiring the Bank to maintain this level of capital in the event that earnings or growth differ from the original projections. The Organizers have the financial capacity and business contacts to provide additional capital if needed.

The proposed Bank can reasonably be expected to achieve and maintain profitability. Its strategy is to minimize overhead -- fixed assets, equipment, management, and personnel -- while offering a limited product line focusing exclusively on deposits and payment related services. The

[3] See 12 C.F.R. part 3 for the definition of Tier 1 capital and the leverage ratio.

Organizers supported the profit prospects of this strategy by including an independent feasibility study in the application. The financial projections show the Bank becoming profitable within three years using reasonable growth assumptions. In this regard, there appears to be a rapidly growing market for on-line banking services. A recent study predicted that the number of on-line banking users in the United States will more than double, to approximately 2 million users, by the Year 2000. Other researchers have reported that the U.S. on-line banking market is already at that level and may rise to 10 million or more users by 2000.[4] Further, banks appear to be embracing the Internet. The OCC estimates that 840 U.S. banking organizations currently have Internet Websites, up from 440 sites only twelve months ago. While many of these Internet sites serve only as marketing tools at this time, the ability exists for banks to significantly increase the functionality of their sites. Surveys have also shown that on-line banking customers are some of banks' most profitable customers, using more products and carrying higher average balances.[5] The proposed Bank plans to attract this customer segment by offering its products and services with low or no fees and by providing more personalized customer service.

There are reasonable prospects that the Bank will attract its proposed customer base notwithstanding its limited product scope. The retail banking industry has experienced disintermediation in recent years with credit products such as automobile and credit card loans now being originated by focused, specialty banks or nonbanking companies. These loans often bear no relation to the consumer's depository institution. The Bank, by focusing only on the consumer's deposit and bill payment needs, will pursue a business strategy consistent with this industry trend. Further, until recently, this model would not have been economically viable, but the emergence of lower cost delivery channels such as personal computers, telephones, and ATMs, creates the potential for a profitable bank.

The OCC is satisfied that the Bank will be operated in a safe and sound manner. As part of the operating plan submitted to the OCC, the Organizers have outlined the proposed information system and operations architecture. This includes a draft schematic drawing and description of the system and discussion of the technology alternatives for each product/service line and the key requirements for the proposed security controls, internal controls, and audit procedures. Based upon our review of the plans, the OCC is satisfied with the controls being proposed to date, but will continue to monitor developments during the organizational phase of the Bank.

As is typical for a new bank charter proposal that has not yet received the OCC's preliminary approval, the Organizers and proposed management have not made the final hardware, software, and vendor selections and purchase commitments. The final information system and operations architecture will not be known until after the Bank makes these decisions. As a result, prior to receiving final charter approval, we are requiring the Bank to submit the final information system and operations architecture plans for the OCC's review and approval. In addition, before

[4] *The American Banker*, June 12, 1997, p. 18.

[5] *Consumer Demand for Internet Banking*, Booz-Allen Hamilton, Inc., July 1996.

implementation, the Bank's computer system must successfully undergo a full functionality and security review by an independent security firm, including attempts to gain unauthorized or undetected access. After this review has been completed and the Bank has satisfied all pre-opening requirements, the OCC will conduct a thorough pre-opening examination of the Bank and its information systems environment and will decide whether to grant final charter approval.[6] Once the Bank is opened, for the first three years and until it becomes profitable, we are requiring it to present to the OCC, for prior review and approval, any major changes in its strategic or operating plans, including, but not limited to, plans to offer banking services via the Internet.

The Organizers have made several representations regarding the proposed Bank's operations. They have represented that the Bank's internal systems will be Year 2000 compliant and that the proposed Bank will perform due diligence to ensure that any third-party data processing servicers or purchased applications or systems from software vendors will also be Year 2000 compliant.[7] In addition, each vendor will certify its Year 2000 compliance through convenants in the vendor contract. Finally, the Organizers represent that the Bank will not indicate in any of its marketing efforts or materials that the OCC has approved or endorsed the security, functionality, or effectiveness of the Bank's products or services.

Additionally, the OCC plans to issue by late 1997 guidance for national banks on remote banking. The guidance will lay out goals and objectives and communicate information to help national banks, including the proposed Bank, identify and manage the risks presented by electronic delivery channels. The primary focus will be on security precautions used to protect and verify customers' identification and transaction information, as well as to protect the system architecture. The OCC will expect the Bank to adhere to this future guidance.

Inclusive of the pre-opening requirements and supervisory conditions outlined below, the OCC believes that the Bank has a reasonable chance for success and can be adequately supervised using established safety and soundness and bank information system examination procedures.

B. Community Reinvestment Act Considerations

Under the Community Reinvestment Act (CRA) regulations, the OCC must take into account a proposed insured national bank's description of how it will meet its CRA objectives. (see 12 C.F.R. part 25). The Bank's operating plan includes such a description. Since the Bank

---

[6]The Bank's operating plan, including any future additions or revisions, will provide the context for the supervisory review during the pre-opening examination. The OCC will work closely with the Bank as its actual operations develop as part of the pre-opening examination process. Major deviations from the operating plan or changes in the composition of the board of directors, ownership, or executive officers that the OCC has not approved may result in withdrawal of preliminary conditional approval.

[7]For a discussion of bank regulatory concerns and guidelines for banks regarding Year 2000 system issues, see OCC Advisory Letter 97-6 (May 16, 1997) and the FFIEC Interagency Statement.

proposes to focus on offering deposit products and payment related services (i.e., electronic bill payment) with no lending products to be offered to the public or to be purchased from other institutions, it has requested to be designated as a limited purpose bank for evaluation under the CRA. Under the CRA regulation (12 CFR § 25.12(o)), a limited purpose bank is defined as "a bank that offers only a narrow product line (such as credit card or motor vehicle loans) to a regional or broader market. . . ."

The OCC assesses a limited purpose bank's record of helping to meet the credit needs of its assessment area under the community development test through its community development lending, qualified investments, and community development services. (see 12 C.F.R. § 25.25). The Bank plans to delineate the Greater Houston MSA as its assessment area, and to serve this community by making qualified investments and providing community development services as defined in the CRA regulations. Consistent with the Bank's alternative delivery channel approach, it plans to focus its CRA efforts in the areas of personal computer availability and access to on-line banking services for low- and moderate-income (LMI) individuals. The Bank's efforts will be centered upon making its services "responsive to the needs of low- and moderate-income areas and individuals." It will seek qualified investment and community development service opportunities relating to providing computers and computer literacy training through schools in LMI areas. It will also seek qualified investment and community development service opportunities such as Minority Enterprise Small Business Investment Companies, credit counseling, small business incubation projects, and special bonds designed to offer mortgage loans to LMI individuals within the assessment area.

Based upon a review of the proposed operating plan, the OCC has determined that the proposed Bank will not make loans which are traditionally evaluated under the CRA, and, accordingly, has approved the Bank's request for designation as a limited purpose bank for evaluation under the CRA.[8] Further, the activities that the Bank proposes as possible investments will likely meet the definition of qualified investments under the CRA Regulations (12 U.S.C. § 25.12). The OCC believes that the Bank's plan for meeting its CRA objectives is consistent with preliminary approval for this charter application.

C. Legal Considerations

The OCC charters a national bank under the authority of the National Bank Act of 1864, as amended, 12 U.S.C. § 1 *et seq.* There is no impediment under the National Bank Act to granting this preliminary charter approval.[9]

---

[8]The limited purpose bank designation will remain effective until the bank requests revocation or until one year after the OCC would notify the Bank that it has revoked the designation. The Bank would no longer qualify for such a designation if it begins to make loans which are traditionally evaluated under the CRA.

[9]The statutory requirements for chartering a national bank under the National Bank Act are as follows: articles of association and an organization certificate must be drafted and filed with the OCC, 12 U.S.C. §§ 21-23;

The Bank has indicated in its application that certain core functions of its internal operations as well as the operation of the computer interface with customers will be contracted out to various vendors. The process of subcontracting activities for which the bank would otherwise be responsible to perform itself implicates the requirements of the Bank Service Company Act, 12 U.S.C. § 1861 *et. seq*. In particular, 12 U.S.C. § 1867(c) states that

> [n]otwithstanding subsection (a) of this section, whenever a bank that is regularly examined by an appropriate Federal banking agency, or any subsidiary or affiliate of such bank that is subject to examination by that agency, causes to be performed for itself, by contract or otherwise, any services authorized under this chapter, whether on or off its premises - (1) such performance shall be subject to regulation and examination by such agency to the same extent as if such services were being performed by the bank itself on its own premises . . . .

Pursuant to this statute, services performed for the Bank by contract or otherwise, including but not limited to the provision of electronic customer interface processing, core data processing, electronic bill payment services, ATM network services, and debit card operations, will be subject to the examination and regulation of the OCC. The Bank has represented that it will notify potential vendors, in writing, of the OCC's examination and regulatory jurisdiction should they contract with the bank. This understanding regarding OCC jurisdiction will be included in all vendor contracts. Accordingly, subcontracting these functions to a vendor will not frustrate the OCC's ability to regulate all aspects of the bank that could affect its safe and sound operations.

III. PRE-OPENING REQUIREMENTS AND SUPERVISORY CONDITIONS

In all cases, following review of a new bank charter application, the OCC decides whether to grant preliminary approval, preliminary conditional approval, or disapproval to the request. Preliminary approval indicates permission to proceed with the organization of the bank according to the plan set forth in the application. The organizational steps of a new national bank generally include hiring management and staff, establishing premises, purchasing computers and other equipment, selecting vendors, developing and implementing policies, procedures, and controls, and raising capital. Preliminary approval is not an assurance, however, that the OCC will grant a new national bank charter. Once the OCC grants preliminary approval to a charter proposal, the organizing group must satisfy certain procedural requirements, and in some cases special requirements, before the OCC will grant final charter approval. In addition, the OCC sometimes imposes conditions that will remain in place after the bank opens.

---

the required amount of capital must be paid in, 12 U.S.C. § 53; certain requirements relating to directors must be satisfied, 12 U.S.C. §§ 71-73; and the OCC must be notified when these things have been accomplished, 12 U.S.C. § 26. As is typical with new charter proposals, these requirements will be satisfied after the OCC grants preliminary approval.

In this proposal, the OCC has decided to grant preliminary conditional approval subject to several pre-opening requirements and on-going supervisory conditions. These supplement the procedural requirements for a new national bank referenced in the attached transmittal letter to the Bank's spokesperson. The pre-opening requirements provide a framework for steps that the Organizers must successfully complete before the OCC can render a decision on final charter approval. The on-going supervisory conditions primarily establish certain checks and safeguards to ensure that the Bank, once open, will appropriately manage and control the relevant risks, maintain adequate capital, and operate in an overall safe and sound manner. The majority of the conditions will remain in place for the first three years of operation or until the Bank becomes profitable, whichever is later. After this time period, all but two of the conditions will expire. The OCC will monitor the Bank's future actions and performance through the normal supervisory process.

The following requirements must be satisfied before the OCC will grant final charter approval:

1. The Bank's initial Tier 1 capital, net of all organizational and pre-opening expenses, shall be no less than $5.0 million.

2. No later than 90 days before the Bank is scheduled to open, the Bank must submit to the OCC for review and approval a complete description of the Bank's final proposed information system and back office operations architecture. This should also include a discussion of the following items: proposed vendors; due diligence performed on the prospective third-party vendors; draft vendor contracts and draft notices pursuant to Supervisory Condition #3; operating processes; security controls; internal controls; and internal audit plans. This information must be considered satisfactory to the OCC before the Bank enters into final contracts and before the OCC will grant final charter approval.

3. The Bank, if it decides to implement an in-house core data processing system, shall name an individual to serve in a back-up role to the systems administrator.

4. The Bank shall cause to be performed an independent, full functionality and security review of its computer banking platform prior to initial implementation. This review must be conducted by an independent computer-security specialist, and the scope of the review must be pre-cleared by the OCC. The specialist should confirm by written report that the individual hardware and software components are well integrated and that the security measures set forth during the system design phase have been satisfactorily implemented and tested by various means to measure their effectiveness. Further, the report should confirm with reasonable certainty that the computer system allows neither unauthorized nor undetected access. The OCC will consider the results of the report as well as any subsequent actions by the Bank to implement recommendations or to remedy any noted security or control deficiencies, as part of its decision to grant final charter approval.

5. Prior to opening, the Bank must engage an independent, external auditor to perform an audit according to generally accepted auditing standards of sufficient scope to enable the

auditor to render an opinion on the financial statements of the Bank (or consolidated holding company), taken as a whole. The audit period must commence on the date that the organizing group forms a body corporate and may end on any calendar quarter-end no later than 12 months after the Bank opens. We expect that such audits will be performed on an annual basis for at least three years following commencement of operations. Engagement of an auditor will be verified during the pre-opening examination.

6. The Bank must receive all required regulatory approvals, including deposit insurance from the FDIC and membership in the Federal Reserve System.

Final approval will be subject to the following supervisory conditions:

1. During its first three years of operations, the Bank shall at all times maintain a ratio of Tier 1 capital to adjusted total assets, as defined in 12 C.F.R. § 3.2, in an amount that is equal to or greater than 8.0 percent.

2. During the Bank's first three years of operations or until it becomes profitable for two consecutive quarters, whichever is later, the Bank shall not make major changes in its strategic or operating plans without the prior approval of the OCC. This shall include, but not be limited to, offering banking services via the Internet, offering stored value card services, introducing loan products, and establishing bank premises for customer service. The Bank shall provide the Deputy Comptroller for the Southwestern District with a written request for OCC's prior approval of any such changes. The request shall include:

   - a general description of and reason for the change;
   - vendor contracts, if applicable;
   - a description of the security and internal controls governing the new activity;
   - the impact, if any, on staffing and operating expenses, and on the Bank's balance sheet, income statement, and regulatory capital ratios;
   - the impact on the Bank's CRA designation and plans, if applicable; and
   - a revised strategic plan that includes the proposed change.

   The OCC will act on the proposed change within 30 days of receipt of the written request, unless the OCC, in its sole discretion, decides that additional time is needed.

3. The Bank shall notify all potential vendors in writing of the OCC's examination and regulatory authority under 12 U.S.C. § 1867(c). The Bank must submit the draft notices to the OCC for its prior review and approval before disseminating the notices to vendors. All final vendor contracts shall stipulate that the performance of services provided by the vendors to the Bank is subject to the OCC's examination and regulatory authority.

4. Stock options issued to Bank organizers, directors, and executive officers must include the following legend:

If CompuBank, N.A.'s Tier 1 capital falls below the minimum requirements contained in 12 C.F.R. Part 3, or falls below a higher requirement as determined by the OCC in connection with a cease and desist order, consent order, formal written agreement, or Prompt Corrective Action directive (See 12 C.F.R. Part 6, Subpart B), the OCC may direct CompuBank, N.A. to require option holders to exercise or forfeit their options. CompuBank, N.A. will notify option holders within 45 days from the date the OCC notifies the bank in writing that option holders must exercise or forfeit their options. CompuBank, N.A. will cancel options not exercised within 21 days of CompuBank, N.A.'s notification. CompuBank, N.A. has agreed to comply with the OCC's request that CompuBank, N.A. invoke its right to require option holders to exercise or forfeit their options under the circumstances stated above.

The above listed conditions of this approval shall be deemed to be conditions "imposed in writing by the agency in connection with the granting of any application or other request" within the meaning of 12 U.S.C. § 1818(b)(1).

V. CONCLUSION

The charter proposal satisfies the applicable statutory requirements of the National Bank Act and the supervisory and general policy standards of the OCC, as set forth in 12 C.F.R. § 5.20. For the reasons set forth above, including the representations and commitments made by the applicants, it is my conclusion that this proposed national bank has a reasonable likelihood of success. Accordingly, the application is hereby preliminarily approved, subject to the requirements and conditions outlined in this Decision Document and the transmittal letter.

/s/
Julie L. Williams
Chief Counsel

08-20-97
Date

Application Control Number: 96-WO-01-0003

Appendix B4
OCC Conditional Approval No. 254 (Aug. 21, 1997)

Comptroller of the Currency
Administrator of National Banks

Washington, DC 20219

August 21, 1997

Mr. Jeffrey A. Watiker
Vice President Legal Affairs
Citibank, N.A.
425 Park Avenue
New York, NY 10043

Re: Application of Citibank, N.A., New York, New York ("the Bank") to Establish an Operating Subsidiary to Invest in and Become a Member of MECA Software, L.L.C.
Application Control Number 97-ML-08-0016

Dear Mr. Watiker:

This is in response to your operating subsidiary notice ("Notice") submitted pursuant to 12 C.F.R. § 5.34(e)(1) to establish an operating subsidiary to invest in and become a member of MECA Software, L.L.C., ("the LLC" or "MECA"). MECA is a Delaware limited liability company that provides home banking and financial management services through the development, production, marketing, and distribution of computer software and related services. For the reasons discussed below, we approve, subject to certain conditions, the establishment of such operating subsidiary by the Bank because we find that the proposed investment by the operating subsidiary in the LLC would be permissible for national banks under 12 U.S.C. § 24(Seventh).

A. Background

As described in the Bank's Notice, the Bank intends to establish an operating subsidiary, Citibank Strategic Technology, Inc. ("CSTI"), as a vehicle to invest in and become a member of the LLC.[1] The LLC's primary activities include: designing, marketing and supporting

[1] CSTI will be incorporated in Delaware as a wholly-owned subsidiary of Citibank. CSTI will be managed by a board of directors, each of whom is expected to be an employee of the Bank or one of its affiliates. CSTI's officers would consist of a President and a number of other executive officers, each of whom is also expected to be an employee of the Bank.

personal computer-based personal financial management and remote financial and insurance software for banks, other financial institution, insurance companies and other entities; and assisting such entities in the marketing of value-added electronic financial and insurance services to customers. The OCC previously authorized other national banks to become members of MECA by direct investment, and determined that MECA's activities are permissible joint venture activities for national banks. *See* Interpretive Letter No. 677, *reprinted in* [1994-1995 Transfer Binder] Fed. Banking L. Rep. (CCH) ¶ 83,625 (June 28, 1995).[2] MECA has since developed software products for Internet use, including products derived from its principal software product Managing Your Money. MECA's distribution strategy is now focused on selling products through financial institutions rather than selling products through retail channels. MECA is expected to continue to provide products and services indirectly to consumers through their banks, other financial institutions, networks and bank card associations, and directly through retail distribution to consumers, both individual and small business. Citibank might provide MECA's software and home banking services directly to Citibank's customers (or to the customers of its affiliates), in which case Citibank expects that it would provide the products and services in large part (though not necessarily exclusively) in the principal geographic areas served by Citibank and its affiliates, including the states of California, Connecticut, Florida, Illinois, Maryland, Nevada, New Jersey and New York and the District of Columbia.

MECA's governing documents specifically state that: the LLC will engage only in activities which are legally permissible for national banks; national bank members of the LLC will have authority to veto or withdraw from the LLC in the event that MECA engages in activities otherwise impermissible for national banks; and members of LLC are not liable for the debts, obligations or liabilities of the other members. The LLC's Operating Agreement ("the LLC Agreement") authorizes two membership classes -- Class A and Class B -- but Class B Members will not be entitled to vote or consent with respect to any action taken by the Class A Members. In general, actions of the members would require the affirmative vote or consent of at least a majority of the Class A Members. The Members would manage the business and affairs of the LLC through a Board of Managers. Each Class A Member would be entitled to designate one Manager. In addition, Class A Members could, by unanimous vote, designate two outside managers. The President of MECA would be a Manager and, if the aggregate "percentage interests" of all Class B Members equals or exceeds the "percentage interest" of any Class A Member, then one Manager could be designated by the Class B Members. Currently, there are six Class A Members of MECA and no Class B Members.[3] In its Notice,

---

[2] The letter stated that, "[i]t is expected that in the future a limited number of other banks and technology companies will become members of the LLC." Interpretive Letter No. 677 at 1.

[3] It is expected that in the future there could be a limited number of additional Class A and Class B Members.

the Bank seeks to be, at its discretion, either a Class B Member or Class A Member of MECA.[4]

The Bank has signed a letter of agreement with MECA that specifies that the Bank will, subject to OCC approval, pay MECA $3 million for a Class B membership. In addition, the LLC Agreement would give Citibank a right to convert its Class B membership to a Class A membership by making an additional capital contribution of $7.8 million to the LLC.[5] This conversion right would lapse after approximately one year from the date of the Bank's initial $3 million investment. Citibank expects to capitalize CSTI through capital contributions, including a cash contribution of approximately $3 million that will be used to purchase the Class B membership in MECA. If Citibank elects to switch its membership status from Class B to Class A, then an additional cash contribution of approximately $7.8 million would be required.

B. Discussion

A national bank may engage in activities that are part of or incidental to the business of banking by means of an operating subsidiary. 12 C.F.R. § 5.34(d)(1). Your application raises the issue of the authority of a national bank to make indirectly, through an operating subsidiary, a non-controlling investment in a limited liability company.[6] In a variety of circumstances the OCC has permitted national banks to own, either directly, or indirectly through an operating subsidiary, a minority interest in an enterprise. The enterprise might be a limited partnership, a corporation, or in more recent examples, a limited liability company. The OCC has concluded that national banks are legally permitted to make a minority

---

[4] If MECA continues to have six Class A Members and each of their total capital contributions remain unchanged and Citibank becomes a Class B Member that has contributed $3 million to MECA, then the Bank's "percentage interest" in MECA would be 4 percent and each Class A Member's percentage interest would be 16 percent. If Citibank chooses to become a Class A Member by making an additional capital contribution of $7.8 million to MECA, the Bank's "percentage interest" in MECA would increase from 4 to 14.28 percent, and the "percentage interest" of each of the other Class A Members would decrease from 16 to 14.28 percent.

[5] If Citibank converts its membership in MECA from Class B to Class A, then it would be entitled to designate one Manager and could participate in any votes by the Class A Members regarding the designation of the outside Mangers.

[6] The OCC has previously approved indirect investments by national banks in limited liability companies through an operating subsidiary structure. *See, e.g.*, OCC Conditional Approval Letter No. 219 (July 19, 1996). Such investments are permissible if they meet the requirements for direct minority investments by national banks.

investment in an LLC provided four criteria or standards are met. *See* OCC Interpretive Letter No. 692, *reprinted in* [Current] Fed. Banking L. Rep. (CCH) ¶ 81,007 (November 1, 1995) and OCC Interpretive Letter No. 694, *reprinted in* [Current] Fed. Banking L. Rep. (CCH) ¶ 81,009 (December 13, 1995). These standards, which have been distilled from our previous decisions in the area of permissible minority investments for national banks and their subsidiaries, are: (1) The activities of the enterprise in which the investment is made must be limited to activities that are part of, or incidental to, the business of banking. (2) The bank must be able to prevent the enterprise from engaging in activities that do not meet the foregoing standard, or be able to withdraw its investment. (3) The bank's loss exposure must be limited, as a legal and accounting matter, and the bank must not have open-ended liability for the obligations of the enterprise. (4) The investment must be convenient or useful to the bank in carrying out its business and not a mere passive investment unrelated to that bank's banking business. We conclude, as discussed below, that the proposed indirect investment by the Bank in MECA satisfies these four criteria.

1. *The activities of the enterprise in which the investment is made must be limited to activities that are part of, or incidental to, the business of banking.*

The National Bank Act, in relevant part, provides that national banks shall have the power:

> [t]o exercise...all such incidental powers as shall be necessary to carry on the business of banking; by discounting and negotiating promissory notes, drafts, bills of exchange, and other evidences of debt; by receiving deposits; by buying and selling exchange, coin, and bullion; by loaning money on personal security; and by obtaining, issuing, and circulating notes...

12 U.S.C. § 24(Seventh).

The Supreme Court has held that the powers clause of 12 U.S.C. § 24(Seventh) is a broad grant of power to engage in the business of banking, including, but not limited to the enumerated powers and the business of banking as a whole. *See NationsBank of North Carolina, N.A. v. Variable Life Annuity Co.*, 115 S.Ct. 810 (1995) ("VALIC").

It is well established that a national bank may use electronic means to perform services expressly or incidentally authorized to national banks. *See* OCC Interpretive Letter No. 677, *reprinted in* [1994-1995 Transfer Binder] Fed. Banking L. Rep. (CCH) ¶ 83,625 (June 28, 1995);OCC Interpretive Letter No. 284, *reprinted in* [1983-1984 Transfer Binder] Fed. Banking L. Rep. (CCH) ¶ 85,448 (March 26, 1984); and OCC Interpretive Letter No. 449, *reprinted in* [1988-1989 Transfer Binder] Fed. Banking L. Rep. (CCH) ¶ 85,673 (August 23, 1988). As noted in the recently revised OCC Interpretive Ruling recognizing this authority, a national bank may "perform, provide, or deliver through electronic means and facilities any activity, function, product, or service that it is otherwise authorized to perform, provide or deliver." *See* 12 C.F.R. § 7.1019 (1996).

Interpretive Letter No. 677 recognized that MECA's activities are permissible for national banks to engage in directly; thus, they are permissible for an operating subsidiary of a national bank. In addition, as discussed in the *Background* section, *supra*, the LLC Agreement provides that MECA will engage only in activities that are legally permissible for national banks, and national bank members of MECA have authority to veto or withdraw from the LLC in the event the LLC engages in activities otherwise impermissible for national banks. Thus, the first standard is satisfied.

2. *The bank must be able to prevent the enterprise from engaging in activities that do not meet the foregoing standard, or be able to withdraw its investment.*

The activities of the enterprise in which a national bank may invest must be part of or incidental to the business of banking not only at the time the bank initially purchases stock, but for as long as the bank has an ownership interest.

The LLC Agreement and the Letter of Agreement Citibank has signed with MECA contains certain safeguards to ensure that this standard is met. The LLC Agreement provides that the LLC will only engage in activities for national banks. Article II, section 2.8(b). In addition, national bank members have authority to veto or withdraw from the LLC in the event that MECA engages in activities otherwise impermissible for national banks. The LLC Agreement provides:

> Any Member may withdraw from the Company without the consent of the other Members if: (1) such Member reasonably determines on written advice from counsel that the Company is engaged or proposes to engage in activities which are not legally permissible (without necessary approvals, if any, being obtained) for a national bank, bank holding company, an insurance company or a non-bank or non-insurance company subsidiary thereof; (ii) at least sixty (60) days prior to such withdrawal, such Member notified the other Members of the activities which it deems to be impermissible and the reason such activities are believed to be impermissible; and (iii) the Company is continuing to engage or determines to engage in such activities notwithstanding such notice.

Article VIII, section 8.2(a).

Although the Bank, if it decides to become a Class B member, will not have be able to vote on LLC matters, it will still have the opportunity to withdraw from the LLC in the event MECA engages in activities otherwise impermissible for national banks. The Bank has stated that it will withdraw from MECA should the LLC engage in any impermissible activities for national banks. In addition, pursuant to the Letter of Agreement, if Citibank converts its Class B membership to MECA to a Class A membership, then it would be entitled to designate one Manager and could participate in any votes by Class A Members regarding the designation of the outside Managers. By these means, the Bank will be able to ensure that MECA engages only in activities that are part of, or incidental to, the business of banking.

Accordingly, the second standard is satisfied.

3. *The bank's loss exposure must be limited, as a legal and accounting matter, and the bank must not have open-ended liability for the obligations of the enterprise.*

a. *Loss exposure from a legal standpoint*

A primary concern of the OCC is that national banks should not be subjected to undue risk. Where an investing bank will not control the operations of the entity in which the bank holds an interest, it is important that a bank's investment not expose it to unlimited liability. Such is the case here.

As members of a Delaware limited liability company, the liability of the Bank for the debts, obligations or liabilities of the company will be limited under Delaware law to the amount of the Bank's capital investment in the company. The LLC Agreement contain provisions that confirm that no investor in the LLC will have liability for the debts, obligations, and liabilities of MECA. Article III, section 3.1(d).

b. *Loss exposure from an accounting standpoint*

In assessing a bank's loss exposure as an accounting matter, the OCC has previously noted that the appropriate accounting treatment for a bank's less than 20 percent ownership share of investment in a limited liability company is to report it as an unconsolidated entity under the equity method of accounting. Under this method, unless the bank has guaranteed any of the liabilities of the entity or has other financial obligations to the entity, losses are generally limited to the amount of the investment, including loans and other advances shown on the investor's books. *See generally,* Accounting Principles Board, Op. 18 § 19 (1971) (equity method of accounting for investments in common stock). Interpretive Letter No. 692, *supra.* Similarly, under the cost method of accounting, the investor records an investment at cost, dividends or distributions from the entity are the basis for recognition of earnings, and losses recognized by the investor are limited to the extent of the investment. In sum, regardless of which accounting method is used, the investing bank's potential loss is limited to the amount of the investment.

As proposed, the Bank will have either a 4 percent or 14.28 percent ownership share in MECA, depending upon whether it becomes a Class B or Class A Member.[7] The Bank has

---

[7] A member's "percentage interest" would be determined by a mathematical formula that takes into account the total capital contributions made by such member and whether the

stated that the appropriate accounting treatment for its investment is the cost method.[8] Thus, Citibank's loss from an accounting perspective will be limited to the cost of Citibank's investment and the Bank will not have any open-ended liability for the obligations of MECA.

In addition, as noted above, Delaware law limits members' losses to their capital investment. The LLC Agreement contains provisions that confirm that no investor in MECA will have liability for the debts, obligations, and liabilities of the LLC. Since the Bank will not have open-ended liability for the obligations of the LLC, the third standard is satisfied.

4. *The investment must be convenient or useful to the bank in carrying out its business and not a mere passive investment unrelated to that bank's banking business.*

A national bank's investment in an enterprise or entity must also satisfy the requirement that the investment have a beneficial connection to the *bank's* business, i.e., be convient or useful to the investing bank's business activities, and not constitute a mere passive investment unrelated to that bank's banking business. Twelve U.S.C. § 24(Seventh) gives national banks incidental powers that are "necessary" to carry on the business of banking. "Necessary" has been judicially construed to mean "convenient or useful". *See Arnold Tours, Inc. v Camp,* 472 F. 2d 427, 432 (1st Cir. 1972). The provision in 12 U.S.C. § 24(Seventh) relating to the purchase of stock, derived from section 16 did not authorize speculative investments in stock. *See* Interpretive Letter No 697 (November 15 1995), *reprinted in* [Current] Fed. Banking L. Rep. (CCH) ¶ 81,012. Therefore, a consistent thread running through our precedents concerning stock ownership is that it must be convenient or useful to that bank's banking business. The investment must benefit or facilitate that business and cannot be a mere passive or speculative investment. *See, e.g.,*Interpretive Letter No. 543, *reprinted in* [1990-1991 Transfer Binder] Fed. Banking L. Rep. (CCH) ¶ 83,225 (February 13, 1991) (national bank authorized to acquire nominal stockholding for membership in corporation of primary dealers in government securities); Interpretive Letter No. 427, *reprinted in* [1988-1989 Transfer Binder] Fed. Banking L. Rep. (CCH)

---

member is a account the total capital contributions made by each member and whether the member is a Class A or Class B Member.

[8] OCC's Chief Accountant has concluded that the Bank's investment in the LLC should be recorded as "Investments in unconsolidated subsidiaries and associated companies" on the Bank's Consolidated Reports of Condition and Income ("Call Reports"). Such classification is consistent with the Call Report Instructions. *See* Instructions to Schedule RC-M, item 8.b. Accordingly, any loss that may be realized by the LLC would not pass through to the books of the Bank other than to the extent that the value of the Bank's interest would thereby be reduced, in which case the amount of such loss would be limited to the amount of the Bank's investment in the LLC.

¶ 85,651 (May 9, 1988) (national bank permitted to buy Farmer Mac stock in nominal amounts); Interpretive Letter No. 421, *reprinted in* [1988-1989 Transfer Binder] Fed. Banking L. Rep. (CCH) ¶ 85,645 (March 14, 1988) (national bank permitted to invest in the Government Securities Clearing Corporation).

This requirement is met here. The LLC will be providing services to the investing Bank that will enable the Bank to offer its banking customers a competitive package of home banking and financial services. Citibank is investing in MECA in order to further its banking business. Through its investment in MECA, Citibank will, among other things, be able to participate (and gain important expertise) in the development, design, marketing and support of personal computer-based personal financial management and remote financial software for banks and other entities, including software design for Internet use. Moreover, Citibank might provide MECA's software and home banking services directly to Citibank's customers (or to the customers of its affiliates) which would provide a valuable service to those customers. The Bank's participation in MECA will enable Citibank to provide these services in a more efficient manner -- the costs associated with MECA can be shared with the other joint venturers -- thus permitting Citibank to conduct activities, gain expertise, and service its customers in ways that might well be cost-prohibitive if performed by Citibank alone.

For these reasons, the Bank's investment in MECA, through CSTI, is convenient and useful to the Bank in carrying out its business and is not a mere passive investment. Thus, the fourth standard is satisfied.

C. Conclusion

On the basis of the representations specified in your notification letter and other submitted materials, the OCC finds that the Bank may establish an operating subsidiary that will invest in MECA Software, L.L.C. ("the LLC") and that the notification is approved subject to the following conditions:

(1) The LLC will engage only in activities that are part of, or incidental to, the business of banking;

(2) The Bank will withdraw from the LLC in the event that the LLC engages in any activities that are inconsistent with condition number one;

(3) The Bank will account for the investment in the LLC under the cost method of accounting; and

(4) The LLC and CSTI will be subject to OCC supervision, regulation, and examination.

This approval is granted based on a thorough review of all information available including the representations and commitments made in the application, and by the Bank's representatives.

Please be advised that all conditions of this approval are "conditions imposed in writing by the agency in connection with the granting of an application or other request" within the meaning of 12 U.S.C. § 1818.

Sincerely,

/s/

Julie L. Williams
Chief Counsel

Appendix B5
OCC Conditional Approval No. 289 (Oct. 2, 1998)

Comptroller of the Currency
Administrator of National Banks

Washington, DC 20219

October 2, 1998

Mr. John L. Douglas
Alston & Bird LLP
1201 West Peachtree Street, N.W.
Atlanta, Georgia 30309

Re: Request of Operating Subsidiaries of Various National Banking Associations to Acquire Ownership Interests in CheckFree Corporation through Integrion Financial Network, L.L.C.
Application Control Nos. 98-WO-0006 through -0018 and -0021

Dear Mr. Douglas:

This is in response to the operating subsidiary application ("Application") submitted on behalf of Bank of America National Trust and Savings Association; Barnett Bank, National Association; NationsBank, National Association; Bank One, National Association; KeyBank National Association; Mellon Bank, N.A.; U.S. Bank National Association; PNC Bank, National Association; Michigan National Bank; The First National Bank of Chicago; Comerica Bank - Ann Arbor, National Association; Fleet National Bank; Citibank, N.A.; and First Union National Bank (collectively, the "Integrion Owner Banks" or "Applicant Banks").[1] Each of these banks owns a membership interest in Integrion Financial Network, L.L.C. ("Integrion") either directly or through direct or indirect wholly-owned operating subsidiaries.

---

[1] The OCC previously granted most of the Integrion Owner Banks approval to invest in Integrion through operating subsidiaries. OCC Conditional Approval No. 221 (December 4, 1996). Recently the OCC has granted approval to Citibank, N.A. (OCC Conditional Approval No. 273 (February 26, 1998)) and First Union National Bank (OCC Conditional Approval No. 271 (January 28, 1996)) to acquire their membership interest through an operating subsidiary. There are three other financial institution members of Integrion, ABN AMRO, Royal Bank of Canada, and Norwest Corporation, that either hold their interests in Integrion through bank holding company subsidiaries or are foreign banking organizations subject to the requirements of the Bank Holding Company Act (These approvals were granted by the Federal Reserve Bank of Chicago on March 10, 1998 (ABN AMRO), the Federal Reserve Bank of New York on March 27, 1998 (Royal Bank of Canada), and the Secretary of the Board of Governors on April 6, 1998 (Norwest Corporation).) One financial institution member, Washington Mutual, Inc., is a savings and loan holding company regulated by the Office of Thrift Supervision. Other members of Integrion are subsidiaries of International Business Machines Corporation and Visa U.S.A., Inc.

Integrion has entered into a series of agreements with CheckFree Corporation ("CheckFree") pursuant to which Integrion will obtain warrants to acquire shares of CheckFree common stock.[2]

This request is submitted pursuant to 12 C.F.R. § 5.34 and the representation set out in OCC Conditional Approval No. 221 (December 4, 1996) regarding the formation of operating subsidiaries for the purpose of investing in the Integrion Financial Network L.L.C., subsequently referred to as the First Integrion Letter. For the reasons discussed below, the application is approved, subject to the conditions set forth herein.[3] Please note that our response is solely directed to the investment in CheckFree and not to any other agreement and activities that Integrion may contemplate with CheckFree. It is also based upon the description of current CheckFree activities contained in the Application.[4]

A. *Background*

1. *Integrion.*

Integrion is a Delaware limited liability company, ("L.L.C.") formed in 1996 by sixteen of the nation's largest financial institutions and International Business Machines Corporation ("IBM").[5] In the First Integrion Letter, OCC approved direct and indirect investments in

---

[2] While Integrion is acquiring warrants, rather than stock in CheckFree, the Applicant Banks have asked that this notice be treated as if the warrants were fully exercised so that there is no need to seek further approval if the warrants are exercised. Under its agreements with CheckFree, Integrion has the right to distribute the warrants it may acquire, or the shares of CheckFree common stock it may acquire upon exercise of the warrants, to its owners.

[3] You have confirmed that this application seeks approval of Integrion's acquisition of CheckFree stock, i.e. a new activity of Integrion. Under the First Integrion Letter and subsequent approvals, OCC approved the direct and indirect acquisition of Integrion based on the activities it engaged in at that time. Therefore, this application implicitly requests approval of continued ownership interests in Integrion, notwithstanding its proposed ownership interest in CheckFree. Further, you have represented that if the Integrion Owner Banks desire to own the interests in CheckFree through their respective operating subsidiaries, or directly, they will seek OCC approval.

[4] If CheckFree should commence additional activities beyond those described in the Notice and approved in this letter, the Integrion Banks holding their Integrion interests in operating subsidiaries may need to file a new application under 12 C.F.R. § 5.34 depending on that nature of those new activities. Moreover, we are aware that Integrion and CheckFree contemplate a series of related agreements, described in the Application, that may further integrate the operations of both firms (the "Strategic Alliance"). In approving the investment in CheckFree, the OCC does not express its views upon the Strategic Alliance or any part of that relationship. The Alliance is still very much in the developmental phase with many important details to be worked out between the parties. Thus, it would be premature for the OCC at this time to express any opinion on Alliance. The OCC is, of course, willing to confer with the parties to the Alliance going forward to provide appropriate guidance.

[5] Subsequent to the formation of Integrion, a subsidiary of Visa U.S.A. acquired a non-voting membership interest in Integrion, and subsidiaries of First Union National Bank and Citibank, N.A. acquired voting membership interests.

Integrion to act as an electronic distribution channel for financial institutions to provide financial services to their customers. More specifically, the L.L.C. would establish an electronic "gateway" through which customers of the Banks will be able to obtain home banking and other financial services from their respective financial institutions through various electronic access devices, including telephone, personal computer, interactive television, etc.[6] After the initial introduction of these home banking and other financial services, it is contemplated that other value-oriented services (such as stock quotations) would be offered to the financial institutions' customers by third party providers through the gateway.[7] It was contemplated that the gateway eventually would be available, for a fee, to financial institutions that are not members of the L.L.C.[8]

[6] Integrion represents that its internal data processing systems will be year 2000 ready within the time frames specified in OCC Advisory Letter 97-6 and other subsequent OCC issuances. Further, Integrion represents that it will perform due diligence to ensure that any third-party data processing service providers or purchased applications or systems it uses, including those provided by CheckFree, will be year 2000 compliant in accord with OCC issuances. This due diligence process will enable Integrion, among other things, to monitor that the service provider or software vendor is taking appropriate action to achieve year 2000 readiness and to adopt contingency plans for mission-critical products and services. Moreover, pursuant to the First Integrion Letter, Integrion is subject to OCC supervision, examination, and regulation, including year 2000 readiness. The OCC has examination and regulation authority over CheckFree for services performed by contract or otherwise for Integrion or any national bank pursuant to 12 U.S.C. § 1867(c).

[7] In connection with the services it provides to financial institutions, Integrion may have access to personal information of a financial institution's customers. In this regard, Integrion has adopted a statement of policy concerning the treatment of personal customer information in the conduct of its business that recognizes the customer expectations for privacy and provides standards for the collection, retention and use of the customer's financial information. Under this statement, Integrion represents that it does not share customer information with unaffiliated parties except under limited circumstances. This includes where the customer or the customer's financial institution specifically consents, where it is necessary in order to complete a customer-initiated transaction, or in response to judicial subpoena. Subcontractors, processors, auditors or other third parties, including CheckFree, that provide services to Integrion are also required to abide by the confidentiality principles set forth in Integrion's statement of policy. Integrion represents that it will monitor compliance with this statement through its internal audit program and will take appropriate disciplinary measures to enforce the privacy responsibilities contained in the statement. Integrion further represents in this statement that it maintains security standards and procedures intended to preclude unauthorized access to or disclosure of customer information.

[8] A more complete description of the approved activities of Integrion is contained in the First Integrion Letter at pp. 2-5.

2. CheckFree.

CheckFree is a Delaware corporation, headquartered in Norcross, Georgia. CheckFree provides electronic commerce services, financial application software and related products. CheckFree provides home banking, bill payment and related services under contracts with more than 280 financial institutions in two distinct business segments, the electronic commerce segment and the financial application software segment. The electronic commerce segment includes electronic home banking, electronic bill payment, automatic accounts receivable collection, electronic accounts payable processing, investment portfolio management services and investment trading and reporting services. These services are primarily directed to the financial services industry and their customers. The financial application software segment includes reconciliation, wire transfer, mortgage loan origination and servicing, lease accounting and debt recovery software. These products and services are primarily directed to financial institutions and large corporations.

3. The Relationship between Integrion and CheckFree.

The relationship between Integrion and CheckFree is embodied in a series of agreements, discussed in the application relating to the Strategic Alliance. Among these is the "Warrant Agreement." Under the Warrant Agreement, dated January 8, 1998, Integrion will have the right to obtain warrants to acquire ten million shares of CheckFree common stock. Warrants for three million shares will be immediately exercisable; the remainder will be exercisable upon achievement of certain usage or revenue goals, measured at year-end 2000 and 2001. If exercised, the initial warrants (i.e., warrants for three million shares) would allow Integrion to own approximately 5.17% of CheckFree's outstanding shares. Were all warrants (i.e., warrants for the entire ten million shares) to be earned and exercised, Integrion would own approximately 15.38% of CheckFree's outstanding shares.

Because of CheckFree concerns about the risks of a block sale of its stock by Integrion, CheckFree insisted upon and the parties negotiated the "Stock Restriction Agreement."[9] The Stock Restriction Agreement, dated as of January 8, 1998, imposes certain restrictions on Integrion's ability to transfer the warrants or shares to protect CheckFree from facing a potentially large shareholder that was not its agreed-upon strategic partner. Generally, the warrants are not transferable except to Integrion's members; the shares are transferable subject to compliance with applicable securities laws. Integrion has agreed to hold the shares for a

---

[9] Although Integrion initially negotiated for the ability to sell its position immediately in the event of impermissible activities in connection with its various agreements with CheckFree, CheckFree was unable and unwilling to give Integrion the ability to place a large block of its stock in potentially unfriendly hands. CheckFree similarly was not willing to suffer the impact on its stock associated with the possibility of Integrion dumping a large block of stock on the market at one time. Accordingly, Integrion agreed to dispose of its interest in CheckFree gradually, and in a manner such that the ownership interest would likely be dispersed among a number of unrelated shareholders.

limited period, and has agreed to transfer the shares generally subject to the volume limitations imposed under Rule 144 of the Securities Act of 1933, as amended. Those volume limitations are increased under certain circumstances. The applicants represent that even under the most adverse circumstance, it could take Integrion approximately two years to fully dispose of its ownership position in CheckFree stock. Under the most likely scenarios, Integrion could dispose of its position within twelve months.

B. Analysis

A national bank may engage in activities that are part of or incidental to the business of banking by means of an operating subsidiary. 12 C.F.R. § 5.34. In a variety of circumstances, the OCC has permitted national banks to own, either directly, or indirectly through an operating subsidiary, a minority interest in an enterprise.[10] The OCC has concluded that national banks are legally permitted to make a minority investment in a company provided four criteria or standards are met.[11] These standards, which have been distilled from our previous decisions in the area of permissible minority investments for national banks and their subsidiaries, are:

(1) The activities of the enterprise in which the investment is made must be limited to activities that are part of or incidental to the business of banking.

(2) The bank must be able to prevent the enterprise from engaging in activities that do not meet the foregoing standard, or be able to withdraw its investment.

(3) The bank's loss exposure must be limited, as a legal and accounting matter, and the bank must not have open-ended liability for the obligations of the enterprise.

(4) The investment must be convenient or useful to the bank in carrying out its business and not a mere passive investment unrelated to that bank's banking business.

As noted, the OCC previously approved the investment by the national bank Integrion Owner Banks in the Integrion L.L.C. under these four standards. We conclude, as discussed below, that Integrion's proposed acquisition of CheckFree stock, and thus the continued indirect investment by the Applicant Banks in Integrion, satisfies these four criteria.

---

[10] See, e.g., OCC Conditional Approval Letter No. 219 (July, 15, 1996).

[11] See Interpretive Letter No. 692, reprinted in [1995 - 1996 Transfer Binder] Fed. Banking L. Rep. (CCH) ¶ 81,007 (November 1, 1995), and OCC Interpretive Letter No. 694, reprinted in [1995 - 1996 Transfer Binder] Fed. Banking L. Rep. (CCH) ¶ 81,009 (December 13, 1995).

1. The activities of the enterprise in which the investment is made must be limited to activities that are part of or incidental to the business of banking

The National Bank Act, in relevant part, provides that national banks shall have the power:

> [t]o exercise ... all such incidental powers as shall be necessary to carry on the business of banking; by discounting and negotiating promissory notes, drafts, bills of exchange, and other evidences of debt; by receiving deposits; by buying and selling exchange, coin, and bullion; by loaning money on personal security; and by obtaining, issuing, and circulating notes ...

12 U.S.C. § 24(Seventh).

The Supreme Court has held that the powers clause of 12 U.S.C. § 24(Seventh) is a broad grant of power to engage in the business of banking, including but not limited to the enumerated powers and the business of banking as a whole.[12] Judicial cases reflect three general principles used to determine whether an activity is within the scope of the "business of banking": (1) is the activity functionally equivalent to or a logical outgrowth of a recognized banking activity; (2) would the activity respond to customer needs or otherwise benefit the bank or its customers; and (3) does the activity involve risks similar in nature to those already assumed by banks.[13] Further, as established by the Supreme Court in *VALIC*, national banks are authorized to engage in an activity if it is incidental to the performance of the five enumerated powers in section 24(Seventh) or if it is incidental to the performance of an activity that is part of the business of banking.

We find that CheckFree's current activities as described in the Notice are permissible for national banks. CheckFree's most significant line of business is its bill payment operations under which CheckFree receives instructions from the customer of a financial institution to pay a specific bill. CheckFree then processes the information and undertakes the payment, either electronically or through a draft or other paper-based system. The OCC has held that such activities are clearly within the business of banking.[14]

---

[12] See *NationsBank of North Carolina, N.A. v. Variable Life Annuity Co.*, 513 U.S. 215 (1995) ("*VALIC*").

[13] See, e.g., *Merchants' Bank v. State Bank*, 77 U.S. 604, 648 (1871) (certification of checks has grown out of the business needs of the country and involves no greater risk than a bank giving a certificate of deposit); *M&M Leasing Corp. v. Seattle First National Bank*, 563 F.2d 1377, 1382-83 (9th Cir. 1977), cert. denied, 436 U.S. 987 (1978) (personal property lease financing is "functionally interchangeable" with the express power to loan money on personal property); *American Ins. Assoc. v. Clarke*, 865 F.2d 278, 282 (D.C. Cir. 1988) (standby credits to insure municipal bonds is "functionally equivalent" to the issuance of a standby letter of credit)("*AMBAC*").

[14] See, e.g., OCC Interpretive Letter No. 737, reprinted in [1996-97 Transfer Binder] Fed. Banking L. Rep. (CCH) ¶ 81,101 (Aug. 19, 1996)(national bank issuing stored value cards performing established banking

Similarly, CheckFree's other activities -- electronic home banking services, automatic accounts receivable collection, and electronic accounts payable processing services -- are also permissible activities for national banks.[15] Moreover, all these services relate to aspects of the payments systems that, as OCC recently noted, are central to banking.[16]

The financial application software programs that CheckFree provides, such as end-to-end reconciliation, wire transfer, mortgage loan origination and servicing, lease accounting, and debt recovery software are also permissible to the extent that they perform activities commonly performed by banks either directly for themselves or as part of servicing customers, or constitute the underlying software allowing the banks and their customers to perform these financially related services.[17] It is well established that a national bank may use electronic

---

function of bill payment and bill presentment); OCC Interpretive Letter No. 718, reprinted in [1995-96 Transfer Binder] Fed. Banking L. Rep. (CCH) ¶81,033 (March 14, 1996) (national bank ATMs dispensing alternative media performing permissible bill payment function); and OCC Interpretive Letter No. 419, reprinted in [1988-89 Transfer Binder] Fed. Banking L. Rep. (CCH) ¶ 85,643 (Feb. 18, 1988) (national banks may provide specialized electronic payments system for the collection, processing, and deposit of patient payments).

[15] See, e.g., OCC Interpretive Letter No. 742, reprinted in [1996-97 Transfer Binder] Fed Banking Law. Rep. (CCH) ¶81,105 (Aug. 19, 1996) (national banks may provide home banking services via dedicated phone lines and the Internet); OCC Interpretive Letter No. 677, reprinted in [1994-1995 Transfer Binder] Fed. Banking L. Rep. (CCH) ¶ 83,625 (June 28, 1995)(national bank may acquire software development personnel, equipment and facilities to develop home banking software); OCC Interpretive Letter No. 611, reprinted in [1992-1993 Transfer Binder] Fed. Banking L. Rep. (CCH) ¶ 83,449 (Nov. 23, 1992) (national bank may provide banking services using specially designed computerized "smart phone"); OCC Interpretive Letter No. 731, reprinted in [1995-96 Transfer Binder] Fed. Banking Law. Rep. (CCH) ¶ 81,048 (July 1, 1996)(national banks may initiate and process payments on behalf of a public authority to operate on behalf of the authority an electronic toll collection system); OCC Interpretive Letter No. 732, reprinted in [1995-96 Transfer Binder] Fed. Banking Law. Rep. (CCH) ¶ 81 049 (May 10, 1996)(national bank may design and develop a network for the processing of accounts receivable); and OCC Interpretive Letter No. 419, supra (national banks may use automated data processing to provide accounts receivable services).

[16] See OCC Conditional Approval Letter No. 220, 1996 OCC Letter. LEXIS 140 (Dec. 2, 1996) (the "Mondex Letter") ("Banks are the most important institutional participants in the nation's payment system. They deal with cash, issue, process, clear and settle checks and similar monetary instruments, administer credit card and debit card programs for consumers and merchants, and transfer funds electronically in a variety of situations and circumstances").

[17] See, e.g., First Integrion Letter, supra (national bank can sell software where the software will enable the bank customer to receive or utilize other services of the bank.); OCC Interpretive Letter No. 677, supra (national bank operating subsidiary may enter into a joint venture arrangement through a limited liability company to acquire a company that develops, produces, markets and distributes home banking and financial management software products designed to assist individuals and small business manage their finances through their personal computers) and OCC Interpretive Letter No. 756, reprinted in, [1996-97 Transfer Binder] Fed. Banking Law. Rep. (CCH) ¶ 81,120 (November 6, 1996)(national banks may provide cash management software to their customers).

means to perform services expressly or incidentally authorized to national banks.[18] In fact, the OCC Interpretive Ruling setting forth this authority was recently revised to authorize a national bank to "perform, provide, or deliver through electronic means and facilities any activity, function, product, or service that it is otherwise authorized to perform, provide, or deliver." 61 Fed. Reg. 4849 (1996) codified at 12 C.F.R. § 7.1019.[19]

Investment portfolio management and investment trading and reporting data processing services are also permissible activities for national banks.[20] These data processing services will involve the processing of banking, financial, or related economic data and, thus, are part of the business of banking. An earlier version of 12 C.F.R. § 7.1019 stated that "as part of its banking business and incidental thereto, a national bank may collect, transcribe, process, analyze, and store for itself and others, banking, financial, or related economic data."[21] Although in its 1984 revision of the ruling, the OCC deleted this statement because it believed that "specific examples [of permissible electronic activities] are inappropriate given the imprecision of terms and rapid pace of change in the data processing industry, the "analytical framework" embodied in the ruling remained the same.[22] There was no intent to narrow or restrict the substantive effect of the rule.[23]

---

[18] See, e.g., OCC Interpretive Letter No. 677; supra; OCC Interpretive Letter No. 284, reprinted in [1983-1984 Transfer Binder] Fed. Banking L. Rep. (CCH) ¶85,448 (Mar. 26, 1984); and OCC Interpretive Letter No. 449, reprinted in [1988-1989 Transfer Binder] Fed. Banking L. Rep. (CCH) ¶ 85,673 (Aug. 23, 1988).

[19] As CheckFree is a provider of services for financial institutions, its performance of those services is subject to examination by the various Federal banking agencies under provisions of the Bank Service Company Act. 12 U.S.C. § 1867(c). CheckFree is routinely examined by each of the federal banking agencies, as well as state banking authorities, and receives reports of examination as it is evaluated. We note that the services that CheckFree will perform for banks indirectly through Integrion will also be subject to examination and regulation under the Bank Service Company Act. Because several national banks own directly or indirectly an interest in CheckFree, the OCC will monitor its financial condition.

[20] See, e.g., OCC Interpretive Letter No. 346, reprinted in [1985-1987] Transfer Binder] Fed. Banking Law Rep. (CCH) ¶ 85,516 (July 31, 1985)(national bank may provide electronic information and transaction services for commodities transactions); and OCC Interpretive Letter No. 516, reprinted in [1990-1991 Transfer Binder] Fed. Banking Law Rep. (CCH) ¶ 83,220 (July 12, 1990)(national bank may provide electronic communication channels for persons participating in securities transactions).

[21] Interpretive Ruling 7.3500, 39 Fed. Reg. 14195 (Apr. 22, 1974).

[22] 49 Fed. Reg. 11157 (Mar. 26, 1984).

[23] OCC Interpretive Letter No. 677, supra. See also OCC Interpretive Letter No. 737, supra (national bank may provide transaction and information processing services to support an electronic stored value system); OCC Interpretive Letter No. 653, reprinted in [1994-1995 Transfer Binder] Fed. Banking L. Rep. (CCH) ¶ 83,601 (Dec. 22, 1994) (national bank may act as an informational and payments interface between insurance underwriters and general insurance agents); and OCC Letter No. 346, supra (national banks may maintain records on commodities transactions).

Thus, the first standard is satisfied.

> 2. *The Banks must be able to prevent the enterprise from engaging in activities that do not meet the foregoing standard, or be able to withdraw their investment*

This is an obvious corollary to the first standard. It is not sufficient that the entity's activities are permissible at the time a bank initially acquires its interest; they must also remain permissible for as long as the bank retains an ownership interest.

Minority shareholders in a corporation do not possess a veto power over corporate activities as a matter of corporate law. Accordingly, Applicant Banks and Integrion lack the ability to restrict the activities of CheckFree to only bank permissible activities. It has (or will have upon exercise of the warrants) a relatively small ownership interest, lacks representation on the board of directors, and has no contractual provision requiring CheckFree to conform its activities to only those that are bank permissible. However, Integrion can divest its shares of CheckFree stock subject to the Stock Restriction Agreement. For the reasons below, the OCC finds that under the facts of this case, this divestiture option is adequate to meet the second element.

In the present case, there is no doubt as to the ability of the Integrion to divest its investment in CheckFree should it commence impermissible activities; there are however restrictions as to the timing of this divestiture. Under the Stock Restriction Agreement, Integrion does not have the ability to immediately sell its interest in CheckFree if or when CheckFree commences to engage in an impermissible activity. Under the arrangements, Integrion has agreed to hold its ownership interests under the restrictions applicable under Rule 144 of the Securities Act of 1933 (basically requiring that Integrion hold its ownership interest for one year before disposition), and thereafter to dispose of its interest only subject to the volume limitations of Rule 144. As these limits apply to Integrion, it may take approximately two years to dispose of the entire interest were Integrion to earn and exercise all warrants. Integrion has certain registration rights, however, that accelerate the ability to dispose of the shares. Applicants state that under the most adverse circumstances Integrion would be able to dispose of its ownership interest within two years, and under most circumstances within one year.

Under the specific facts and circumstances of this request, we believe that the ability to divest the shares within two years is sufficient to protect Applicant Banks and Integrion and satisfy the policy concerns of the OCC in the event CheckFree commences impermissible activities. First, the limitation on divestiture is clearly the result of good faith negotiations and is not a subterfuge to avoid the activities limitations of the National Bank Act. Second, the longest period of time during which Integrion and the banks may be holding a non-conforming investment is two years. This is in accord with the OCC policy in other non-conforming holdings by national banks.[24] Third, the ownership interest in any non-conforming operation will not be large (less than 20% of CheckFree's outstanding shares if all warrants are earned and exercised), and Integrion will not be directly operating the business of CheckFree.

Thus, should CheckFree engage in impermissible activities, OCC will accept a delay in divesture of up to two years. However, the OCC expects Integrion to notify OCC immediately of any new CheckFree activities disclosed in a public securities filing or when Integrion otherwise acquires actual knowledge of such activities. As noted above, the investing banks may also be required to file an application under 12 C.F.R. 5.34 should CheckFree begin new activities.[25]

3. *The Banks' loss exposure must be limited, as a legal and accounting matter, and the Banks must not have open-ended liability for the obligations of the enterprise*

a. *Loss exposure from a legal standpoint*

A primary concern of the OCC is that national banks should not be subjected to undue risk. Where an investing bank will not control the operations of the entity in which the bank holds an interest, it is important that a bank's investment not expose it to unlimited liability. Typically, this is not a concern when a national bank invests in a corporations, for shareholders are not liable for the debts of the corporations, provided proper corporate separateness is maintained.[26] This is the case here.

The corporate structure contemplated insulates both the Integrion Owner Banks, their respective operating subsidiaries, and Integrion from liability or loss associated with their ownership interest in CheckFree. Not only does the arrangement have the protection of the corporate insulation, there is an actual remoteness between the Integrion Owner Banks and CheckFree. Each of the Integrion Owner Banks (other than PNC) holds its respective interest

[24] OCC policy allows a reasonable time period for a bank to bring newly acquired business into conformance by divesting nonconforming assets. See e.g. OCC Conditional Approval No. 259 (October 31, 1997). Similarly, the OCC generally requires a national bank to divest or conform nonconforming assets, or discontinue nonconforming activities, within a reasonable period of time following a business combination. See 12 C.F.R. § 5.33(e)(5); OCC Corporate Manual (Business Combinations). See also Corporate Decision 97-14 (March 4, 1997) "The OCC permits a reasonable divestiture period in these instances so that converting banks may be able to resolve nonconforming subsidiaries without hardship."; See also OCC Corporate Decision 97-41 (June 1, 1997).

[25] Moreover, OCC expressly reserves the authority to require Integrion to commence the divestiture process immediately any time that the revenue from new activities exceeds 30% of CheckFree's total revenues and the OCC concludes that the new activities are not part of or incidental to the business of banking.

[26] 1 W. Fletcher, Cyclopedia of the Law of Private Corporations, § 25 (rev. perm. ed. 1990).

in Integrion through a corporate operating subsidiary, which holds and owns its membership interest in Integrion (itself a limited liability company, which affords statutory protection for the owners against liabilities of the limited liability company), which in turn will hold and own the shares of CheckFree. This arrangement should more than adequately protect the Integrion Owner Banks, and Integrion, from any liability for the obligations of the enterprise.

b. Loss exposure from an accounting standpoint

In assessing a bank's loss exposure as an accounting matter, the OCC has previously noted that the appropriate accounting treatment for a bank's less than 20 percent ownership share or investment in a corporate entity is to report it as an unconsolidated entity under the equity or cost method of accounting. Under the equity method of accounting, unless the investor has extended a loan to the entity, guaranteed any of its liabilities, or has other financial obligations, the investor's losses are generally limited to the amount of the investment shown on the investor's books. Here, the investment of the Integrion Owner Banks in Integrion is reported under the equity or cost method of accounting. See First Integrion Letter at p.15. Similarly, Integrion's minority ownership interest in CheckFree will be reported under the equity method of accounting.

Accordingly, the third standard is satisfied.

4. The investment must be convenient or useful to the Bank in carrying out its business and not a mere passive investment unrelated to that Bank's banking business.

A national bank's investment in an enterprise or entity that is not an operating subsidiary of the bank also must satisfy the requirement that the investment have a beneficial connection to the bank's business, i.e., be convenient or useful to the investing bank's business activities, and not be a mere passive investment unrelated to that bank's business activities. "Necessary" has been judicially construed to mean "convenient or useful." See *Arnold Tours*, 472 F.2d at 432. Section 24(Seventh) does not authorize national banks to engage in speculative, investment banking activities with respect to stock.[27] Therefore, a consistent thread running through our precedents concerning stock ownership is that it must be convenient or useful to the bank in conducting that bank's banking business. The investment must benefit or facilitate that business and cannot be a mere passive or speculative investment.

---

[27] See OCC Interpretive Letter No. 697, reprinted in [1995 - 1996 Transfer Binder] Fed. Banking L. Rep. (CCH) ¶ 81-102 (November 15, 1995).

In this instance, the warrants and the share ownership are not merely evidences of a passive relationship, but are rather the results of the strategic business relationship created between Integrion and CheckFree as evidenced by the Strategic Alliance. Integrion and CheckFree plan to develop a fully-integrated bill payment system to be offered to Integrion's member banks and other customers.[28] As customers move to this integrated product, Integrion and its owner banks will be compensated for that movement through the warrants and potential share ownership. Integrion will cooperate with CheckFree in creating a mutually agreeable bill payment system and plans to market that system to its Owner Banks and other financial institutions. The ownership interests provide the method of involving Integrion and its member banks in the provision of the bill payment and related services contemplated by the strategic alliance, and of compensating Integrion for what it and its members bring to the strategic alliance.

C. Conclusion

Based upon the information and representations you have provided, and for the reasons discussed above, we conclude that the Applicant Banks may continue their investment in Integrion following Integrion's acquisition of an ownership interest in CheckFree, and that the application is approved subject to the conditions:[29]

1. CheckFree may engage only in activities that are part of, or incidental to, the business of banking;

2. In the event that CheckFree engages in an activity that is inconsistent with condition number one, the Integrion Owner Banks will either withdraw from the Integrion or, alternatively, Integrion will divest its interest in CheckFree in accord with Section B.2. of this letter;[30]

3. The Integrion Owner Banks will account for their investment in the Integrion (including their indirect investment in CheckFree) under the equity or cost method of accounting and, similarly, Integrion will account for its investment in CheckFree under the equity or cost method of accounting; and

---

[28] In connection with the processing of customer information, the OCC will require Integrion in its new relationship with CheckFree to conform to its existing commitment to preserve the confidentiality of bank customer information. See Note 6, supra; First Integrion Letter, Note 4, pp. 3-4.

[29] The conditions imposed in the First Integrion Letter still apply and are not modified by this letter.

[30] As noted, Integrion has requested up to two years to divest of its interest in CheckFree. Based on the representations and commitments you have provided, the OCC is willing to accept this divestiture period.

4. CheckFree will be subject to OCC examination.[31]

Please be advised that all conditions of this approval are "conditions imposed in writing by the agency in connection with the granting of any application or other request" within the meaning of 12 U.S.C. § 1818.

If you have any questions regarding this decision, please contact John W. Graetz, Licensing Expert (Financial Analyst), in Bank Organization and Structure at (202) 874-5060, or Kristina Whittaker, Assistant Director, Bank Activities and Structure at (202) 874-5300.

Sincerely,

/s/

Raymond Natter
Acting Chief Counsel

[31] This examination authority will be in addition to the authority vested in OCC by the Bank Service Company Act over CheckFree. 12 U.S.C. § 1867(c).

Appendix C1

OCC Corporate Decision 97-60 (July 1, 1997)

Comptroller of the Currency
Administrator of National Banks

Washington, DC 20219

July 1, 1997

Michael W. Briggs, Esq.
Regulatory Relations Attorney
Barnett Banks, Inc.
50 North Laura Street
Jacksonville, Florida 32202-3638

Re: Operating Subsidiary Application by Barnett Bank, National Association, Jacksonville, Florida, Application Control Number: 97-SE-08-0024

Dear Mr. Briggs:

This is in response to your letter of April 28, 1997, notifying the Office of the Comptroller of the Currency ("OCC") of the intent of Barnett Bank, National Association ("Barnett"), to expand the activities of an existing, indirect operating subsidiary and thereby engage in certain Internet-based finder activities related to sales of pre-owned automobiles. For the reasons set forth below, I find that these additional finder activities would be permissible for a national bank and its subsidiaries and would be conducted on a safe and sound basis. Accordingly, Barnett's operating subsidiary application is approved.

BACKGROUND

Description of the Parties

Barnett is the primary banking subsidiary of Barnett Banks, Inc. ("BBI"), a registered bank holding company. Barnett was formed on June 29, 1996, when 28 subsidiary banks of BBI, pursuant to an April 4, 1996, OCC approval order, merged with and into Barnett Bank of Jacksonville, N.A., under the name of Barnett. As part of this corporate reorganization, Barnett also acquired certain of BBI's nonbanking companies as operating subsidiaries, including Barnett Dealer Financial Services, Inc. ("BDFSI"). BDFSI engages in leasing of personal property and making, acquiring and servicing consumer loans, and ancillary activities.

On April 1, 1997, BBI acquired all of the outstanding stock of Oxford Resources Corp. ("Oxford"), a specialized automobile finance company. Immediately after this transaction was consummated, BBI contributed its 100% ownership interest in Oxford to Barnett. Oxford now operates as a wholly-owned operating subsidiary of Barnett. [1]

Prior to its acquisition by Barnett, Oxford acquired an 80% ownership interest in a start-up technology company, Electronic Vehicle Remarketing, Inc. ("EVRI"). EVRI was formed to develop technology that would enable sellers of used vehicles to market their inventory to interested buyers via an electronic marketplace. To that end, EVRI has developed and operates the Price Auto Outlet™ system ("PAO"). PAO is an interactive Internet-based used motor vehicle marketplace on which a consumer can locate specific models of used vehicles that are being offered for sale by Oxford.

Description of Proposed Activities

Currently, the PAO system only markets Oxford's pre-owned and off-lease vehicle inventory in certain states. However, the notification proposes that the PAO system be expanded to include both retail and wholesale components and, more significantly, to include vehicles owned by independent third parties as well as Oxford's inventory. In other words, the PAO would no longer be used only as a device to dispose of Barnett's off-lease and other vehicles acquired through auto leasing and lending activities; the PAO would also be used to market vehicles owned by third parties that have no other connection with the bank. This expansion will permit EVRI to earn fee income on the sale of the service to unaffiliated sellers and to enhance its opportunities to sell Oxford's financing products.

The proposed retail system, which could be accessed by consumers either through personal computers or at designated and strategically located PAO terminals, would work as follows: A consumer will access PAO either by a direct Internet connection to the EVRI website, or through a hyperlink connection from other websites with whom EVRI has arranged connections. Once on the PAO system, the consumer will be asked to provide information relating to the consumer's preferences.

As users of the PAO system review the subsidiary pages to this website, EVRI will provide all appropriate disclosures. These will include the identity of the owner of each vehicle and the party with whom the consigner will or would be contracting in the event a purchase selection is made. Thus, EVRI's role with respect to the selected vehicle will be disclosed. Specially, customers will be told whether EVRI (or Barnett or Oxford) [2] is the owner of the subject

---

[1] Barnett asserts that it operates Oxford as a subsidiary pursuant to its existing authority granted to Barnett at the time of its acquisition of BDFSI. See 12 C.F.R. § 5.33(e)(3).

[2] EVRI may or may not be the contracting party to sale transactions involving Oxford- or Barnett-owned vehicles.

vehicle and, thus, the contracting party to any sales transaction or, alternatively, whether EVRI is serving only as a finder for both purchasers and sellers and is neither a party to the transaction nor acting on behalf of either contracting party.

The listings will also provide the consumer with certain information about the vehicle including vehicle descriptions, photographs, the criteria used for an independent inspection and pricing information. Consumers will be able to print copies of all disclosures and application materials to maintain for their records.

After the consumer has selected one or more vehicles of interest, EVRI will transmit to the seller(s) (if other than Barnett or Oxford) the name, address and phone number of the consumer (a "purchase request") so that the dealer can contact the consumer and arrange for an appointment to visit the seller's location to view/purchase the vehicle.

Also, after a buyer/seller "match" has occurred, PAO will also make the following products and services available to customers: vehicle financing through Oxford/Barnett [3]; referrals to vendors of both short-term and extended-term warranties on selected vehicles; sale (as agent) of vehicle service contracts to PAO system customers who finance their vehicle purchases and leases through Oxford [4]; referrals for related insurance products, such as credit-life, Gap and road-service protection coverages [5]; and referrals to national auto service companies, such as Firestone, Jiffy Lube and other appropriate parties. EVRI would earn a fee for such referrals.

During the consumer's visit to the seller, and assuming the decision is made to purchase the vehicle, the purchase documentation will be completed between the seller and the consumer, including title paperwork showing the transfer of the ownership of the vehicle from the seller to the consumer (or lender as appropriate). [6]

---

[3] Customers would be given the option of securing the necessary financing through Barnett/Oxford. The use of the PAO service would in no way be tied to Barnett/Oxford financing.

[4] Barnett has committed that these sales will conform to existing OCC precedent and interpretative rulings, including OCC Interpretive Letter No. 671, reprinted in, [1994-1995 Transfer Binder] Fed. Banking Law Rep. (CCH) ¶ 83,619 (July 10, 1995).

[5] The OCC has previously addressed other types of situations where referral of bank customers to unaffiliated firms for insurance coverage has been found to be a valid finder activity. See, e.g., OCC Interpretive Letter No. 567, reprinted in [1991-1992 Transfer Binder] Fed. Banking Law Rep. (CCH) ¶ 83,337 (Oct. 29, 1991) and OCC Interpretive Letter No. 472, reprinted in [1989-1990 Transfer Binder] Fed. Banking Law Rep. (CCH) ¶ 83,008 (Mar. 2, 1989).

[6] With respect to vehicles owned by third parties, when Barnett/Oxford is not providing the financing, the third-party dealer and the financing source will provide any requisite disclosures to the consumer incident to the sale of such vehicles.

The wholesale side of the PAO system would include "electronic vehicle auctions," through which dealers would bid on listed cars for resale to consumers. Alternatively, dealers would be able to access PAO's electronic inventory of vehicles to identify specific vehicles of interest to that dealer's customers.

EVRI anticipates that the bulk of revenue will be derived from vehicle financing transactions initiated via the PAO system and from referral income derived from the sources outlined above. Neither Barnett nor Oxford would take title to any of the vehicles listed by such third parties. Neither EVRI nor Oxford would be adding to Oxford's existing inventory by purchasing additional vehicles from those third parties utilizing the PAO system. Rather, EVRI's role would be as a provider of the means that brings together unaffiliated sellers of used cars and interested buyers.

ANALYSIS

Essentially, this proposal entails the operation of an Internet-based referral system for sellers of used vehicles and for services connected with the purchase or ownership of such vehicles that will expand and supplement the financing business of Oxford/Barnett. We believe this is a permissible application of national bank's finder authority.

The OCC has long recognized the finder function as a permissible banking activity that includes, "without limitation, identifying potential parties, making inquiries as to interest, introducing or arranging meetings of interested parties, and otherwise bringing parties together for a transaction that the parties themselves negotiate and consummate." 61 Fed. Reg. 4849, 4863 (Feb. 9, 1996) (codified at 12 C.F.R. § 7.1002). [7] Such activities are part of the business of banking. OCC Conditional Approval Letter No. 221, (December 4, 1996) (hereinafter: "Integrion Letter").

Among other finder activities, the OCC has permitted national banks to bring together potential purchasers and sellers of automobiles. Specifically, in OCC Interpretive Letter No. 741, supra, the OCC permitted a national bank to operate a call center facility for new or used automobiles through which potential purchasers of vehicles could access databases containing information on the used and new vehicle inventories of dealers. In this program, consumers interested in automobiles would contact the call center facility and tell the center

[7] See also, Letter from J.T. Watson, Deputy Comptroller of the Currency, February 26, 1969 (unpublished); Letter from John M. Miller, July 26, 1977 (unpublished); Letter from Letter from Paul Allan Schott, Chief Counsel, May 9, 1988 (unpublished); Letter from Elizabeth Corey, May 18, 1989 (unpublished); OCC Interpretive Letter No. 238, reprinted in [1983-1984 Transfer Binder], Fed. Banking L. Rep. (CCH) ¶ 85,402 (Feb. 9, 1982); OCC Interpretive Letter No. 472, reprinted in [1989-1990 Transfer Binder] Fed. Banking L. Rep. (CCH) ¶ 83,008 (Mar. 2 1989); Letter from Lee Walzer, Attorney, Securities, Investments and Fiduciary Practices Division, August 24, 1992 (unpublished) and OCC Interpretive Letter No. 741, reprinted in [1996-1997 Transfer Binder] Fed. Banking L. Rep. (CCH) ¶ 81-105 (Aug. 19, 1996); and Letter from Julie L. Williams, Chief Counsel, October 2, 1996 (to be published).

representatives their pertinent information. The call center representative would then match the consumer with a dealer handling the desired vehicle and would telecopy the consumer data to the dealer as a qualified sales lead. The bank, which had no further role in the transactions, will be compensated by the dealers for the referrals. After reviewing its precedent on permissible finder activities, the OCC concluded that these listing and referral activities were "within the scope of activities of a finder contemplated by I.R. § 7.1002 and therefore are permissible activities for a national bank or its subsidiaries."

Barnett proposes to provide virtually the identical service with respect to used automobiles, except that the service would be delivered through the media of the Internet rather than a telephone call center. The use of a different technology to perform an otherwise permissible finder activity does not cause the activity to become impermissible; national banks may provide finder services via the Internet. Integrion Letter, supra. The other finder referral activities that Barnett proposes to engage in regarding related services, such as referrals to warranty firms, are likewise permissible. [8] Id.

As noted, the PAO will list vehicles owned by Barnett and Oxford [9] and by unaffiliated third parties. Thus, in some transactions resulting from the PAO, Barnett will be acting as principal (and seller) while in others it will be acting in the limited role of finder. However, to avoid consumer confusion over Barnett's role (and the potential liability that could arise from role confusion), Barnett commits that consumers choosing to initiate a vehicle purchase or lease transaction via the PAO will receive all required and appropriate disclosures. Specifically, such consumers will be advised online (and also in writing) when EVRI is acting as a principal in the sale of pre-owned and off-lease vehicles owned by Oxford and Barnett and, alternatively, when EVRI is serving as finder, providing only the link between seller and purchaser, as well as referrals to any financing or related products and services. Moreover, to assure that it will not be incurring any special obligations through this program, Barnett commits that EVRI, Oxford, and Barnett will not issue warranties on vehicles sold either by Oxford/Barnett or by third parties using the PAO system. [10] Finally, Barnett, Oxford, and EVRI will not offer any commitments to third party sellers of vehicles under which Barnett (or Oxford or EVRI) would agree to purchase those vehicles listed on the PAO system which have not sold within a certain time period.

---

[8] Barnett commits that the finder activities contemplated by the proposed expansion by EVRI will be conducted in accordance with the provisions of 12 C.F.R. § 7.1002.

[9] As noted previously, these vehicles are off-lease and other vehicles acquired as a result of the auto leasing and lending activities conducted by Barnett and Oxford.

[10] However, as noted above, interested consumers may be referred to vendors of warranty contracts with which Barnett or EVRI has referral agreements.

CONCLUSION

Based upon the foregoing facts and analysis, and the representations and commitments made by Barnett in connection with its request, the operating subsidiary application is hereby approved.

If you have any questions regarding this approval, please contact Senior Bank Structure Analyst John W. Graetz at (202) 874-5060 or Licensing Manager John Stein in our Southeastern District Office at (404) 588-4525.

Sincerely,

/s/

Julie L. Williams
Chief Counsel

APPENDIX C2
OCC Corporate Decision 98-13 (Feb. 9, 1998)

Comptroller of the Currency
Administrator of National Banks

Washington, DC 20219

February 9, 1998

Mr. William W. Templeton
Counsel
Legal Department
Fleet Financial Group
50 Kennedy Plaza
Providence, R.I. 02903

Re: Fleet National Bank, Providence, Rhode Island/Operating Subsidiary Notice

Dear Mr. Templeton:

This is in response to your December 5, 1997 letter to Richard Erb, Licensing Manager, requesting OCC approval of the proposal by Fleet National Bank, Providence, Rhode Island ("Fleet" or "Bank") to acquire and hold as an operating subsidiary Benova, Inc. ("Benova"), a company engaged in providing medical insurance cost information, benefits counseling, premium collection and disbursement, and related activities. Based on the information and representations you provided and the reasons discussed below, the Bank's request is approved.

FACTS

Benova is a closely held company based in Portland, Oregon. Fleet has entered into an agreement to acquire Benova, subject to OCC approval of this application. Under the terms of the agreement, Benova will be held as a wholly-owned subsidiary of an existing operating subsidiary, AFSA Data Corporation ("AFSA"). AFSA, in turn, is a wholly-owned subsidiary of Fleet which engages in student loan servicing and related activities.

As a benefits counselor, Benova contracts with the federal government through the Health Care Financial Administration ("HCFA") and with state governments to provide Medicare and Medicaid enrollment counseling to program beneficiaries. Benova works with the contracting agencies to identify individuals eligible to participate in these programs, and provides counseling to new participants by explaining the programs and the health plan choices available to them. Counseling, provided through the use of a toll-free number, includes explaining the differences between managed care and fee-for-service plans, identifying the specific plans available to the beneficiary and enrolling callers in the plans they select. These activities require staff possessing both a detailed knowledge of health insurance programs, including Medicare and Medicaid, and well-developed communications skills.

Recent changes in social security legislation have prompted plans to have Benova expand its activities to add premium collection and disbursement activities to the services it currently offers. In August 1997, Title XXI of the Social Security Act (added to existing law by the Balanced Budget Act of 1997, P.L. No. 105-33, sec. 4901, 111 Stat. 552 (1997)) expanded health insurance coverage for previously uninsured children. Unlike the Medicaid program, this new program for children contemplates cost sharing by the beneficiary. Therefore, the various state welfare agencies will probably design and implement programs under Title XXI that require beneficiaries to pay, on a sliding scale, a portion of the premium charged by health maintenance organizations. It is anticipated that the need for contractors who can provide assistance in handling these insurance premiums will grow as this new children's health insurance program is implemented nationwide. Benova plans to take advantage of this opportunity and expand its services to include the handling of premiums and disbursements on behalf of state government agencies.

The Bank also anticipates that the acquisition of Benova will facilitate the expansion of AFSA's technological capability. Although Benova and AFSA will continue to operate separately, Benova will be responsible for certain common automated systems. Chief among these is a personal computer-based system called Smart Telephone Agent Referral and Response System ("STARRS"), which will allow both AFSA and Benova to track telephone call topics, callers, and responses. Benova employees will be responsible for maintaining the information content and call center procedures for the STARRS system for both Benova and AFSA.[1]

DISCUSSION

The services proposed to be provided by Benova following the planned acquisition are all aspects of well-recognized banking activities previously approved by the OCC: (1) financial planning and counseling; (2) billing and claims processing; and (3) acting as a finder. National banks may engage in activities that are part of or incidental to the business of banking by means of an operating subsidiary. 12 C.F.R. § 5.34(d).

---

[1]As provided by OCC Interpretive Ruling No. 7.1019, "Furnishing of products and services by electronic means," a national bank may use electronic technology to perform any otherwise permissible banking activity. Therefore, to the extent that Benova's activities are otherwise permissible for national banks and their operating subsidiaries, the use of the STARRS system in furtherance of these activities is also permissible.

Financial Planning and Counseling

It is well established that national banks have the power to provide financial advice and counseling to their customers as part of or incidental to the business of banking pursuant to 12 U.S.C. § 24(Seventh). See, e.g., Interpretive Letter No. 137, reprinted in [1981-1982 Transfer Binder] Fed. Banking L. Rep. (CCH) ¶ 85,218 (Dec. 27, 1979); Letter from Judy Walter, Senior Deputy Comptroller for National Operations (July 17, 1986) (unpublished). In reliance on this authority, the OCC has also stated that it is permissible for national banks to offer employee benefit consulting services to corporations wishing to establish qualified benefit plans. Letter from William B. Glidden, Assistant Director, Legal Advisory Services Division (Oct. 6, 1987) (unpublished).

Benova is a health benefits counselor. As discussed above, Benova provides its callers with a variety of information about Medicare and Medicaid benefits and related programs. It provides specific information and advice that callers may use to assess their health care needs and related expenses. It answers questions regarding federal and state health insurance regulations. Some of the questions addressed, such as the eligibility requirements for entitlement programs and the different costs, benefits, copayments, and deductibles of managed care versus fee for service plans, can bear directly on a caller's budget and financial plans. Benova's expertise in Medicare and Medicaid benefits and enrollment requirements enables it to assists its clients in their own financial and retirement planning. Benova does not charge callers for answering these questions; it is compensated under a contract with the state or federal agencies that administer the programs.

Benova's activities in the area of health benefits counseling are aspects of the financial planning and employee benefit consulting services that have been previously deemed permissible for national banks and their subsidiaries. Since health care coverage and expenses are a significant and necessary component of an individual's financial and retirement planning, individuals planning their financial future will accordingly seek information regarding available health coverage options. Similarly, it is reasonable that national banks should wish to meet customer demand for comprehensive financial planning services by being in a position to answer customers' questions about a category of expenses common to nearly every individual's budget.

Payments and Claims Processing

It is well established that national banks may provide billing, collection and claims-processing services as an activity incidental to the express authority to process payment instruments for customers. Interpretive Letter No. 712, reprinted in [1988-1989 Transfer Binder] Fed. Banking L. Rep. (CCH) ¶ 81-027 (Feb. 29, 1996); Interpretive Letter No. 718, reprinted in [1995-1996 Transfer Binder] Fed. Banking L. Rep. (CCH) ¶ 81,033 (March 14, 1996). The OCC has stated that it is permissible for national banks to fill out and submit insurance claim forms because such an activity is substantially similar to providing billing services. For example, a 1993 letter stated:

> The Bank's physician customers look to the insurance companies as potential third-party payors for the services provided to the patients. To obtain payment, the physicians submit claim forms identifying the patient, date of service, the patient's insurance identification number, the services rendered, and the amount charged for those services. This is substantially the same information that national banks would deal with in providing billing services to physicians. Moreover, the process of filling out claim forms according to the physicians' instructions is similar to preparing bills. Therefore, I believe that preparing the insurance forms is simply a variation of previously approved billing services and a permissible activity for national banks. Letter from Horace Sneed, Senior Attorney (Dec. 6, 1993) (unpublished).

This precedent makes clear that the proposed Benova activities in collecting premiums or copayments from participants in Medicare, Medicaid, and similar government health insurance plans are recognized as incidental to banking and within the scope of permissible national bank activities. Collecting premiums from Medicaid users, for example, and remitting the funds to the appropriate governmental agency, is substantially similar to providing billing services on behalf of the private clients referred to in Interpretive Letter No. 712 and the precedents cited therein. The OCC's December 6, 1993 letter, quoted above, further made clear that the permissibility of such activities extends to the filling out and submission of insurance claim forms.

Finder Activity

As described above, Benova provides a toll-free telephone number for use by individuals who seek information about or wish to enroll in Medicare, Medicaid, or some other federal- or state-sponsored health insurance program. Benefit counselors respond to these telephone inquiries by providing a variety of information. If a caller wishes to enroll in a particular program, the counselor can provide instruction and assistance with the enrollment process, including help with the appropriate enrollment forms. The Benova counselors do not represent or act as agent for either the caller or the particular program. The caller does not pay for such services. Further, since Benova's contract with the relevant governmental agencies provides for compensation either as a fixed sum or on a per-caller basis, there is no incentive to enroll callers in any particular plan.

Benova's role in bringing callers together with providers of health care programs is properly characterized as a finder activity. The permissibility of a national bank acting as a finder to bring together buyers and sellers of various types of products and services is specifically set forth in Interpretive Ruling 7.1002, 12 C.F.R. § 7.1002. The OCC has confirmed the permissibility of national banks acting as finders in several interpretive letters. For example, in Interpretive Letter No. 653, reprinted in [1994-1995 Transfer Binder] Fed. Banking L. Rep. (CCH) ¶ 83,601 (Dec. 22, 1994), the OCC stated that a national bank, acting through an operating subsidiary, might act as finder with respect to certain insurance services. The OCC noted that it has "historically permitted national banks to make inquiries as to interest, arrange a meeting of the interested parties, and provide information pertinent to the meeting of the buyer and seller."[2] The OCC has approved national banks or their subsidiaries acting as finders in several other contexts. See, e.g., Interpretive Letter No. 567, reprinted in [1991-1992 Transfer Binder] Fed. Banking L. Rep. (CCH) ¶ 83,337 (Oct. 29, 1991) (finder services for personal property leasing); Interpretive Letter No. 566, reprinted in [1991-1992 Transfer Binder] Fed. Banking L. Rep. (CCH) ¶ 83,320 (Dec. 2, 1991) (finder services for insurance coverage); Interpretive Letter No. 437, reprinted in [1988-1989 Transfer Binder] Fed. Banking L. Rep. (CCH) at ¶ 85,661 (Jul. 27, 1988) (selling tax auditing representation services to customers).

CONCLUSION

Based upon the facts as described, I conclude that the activities proposed to be conducted by Benova following its acquisition by Fleet are permissible activities for a national bank and its operating subsidiaries. Accordingly, the Bank's application is approved.

Sincerely,

/s/

Julie L. Williams
Chief Counsel

ACN# 97 ML 08 0033

---

[2] See also Interpretive Letter No. 472, reprinted in [1989-1990 Transfer Binder] Fed. Banking L. Rep. (CCH) ¶ 83,008 (Mar. 2, 1989); Letter from James Kane, District Counsel, Central District Office (Oct. 24, 1985) (unpublished).

Appendix D1

Banc One Corp. et al., 79 Fed. Res. Bull. 1158 (1993)

Orders Issued Under Section 4 of the Bank Holding Company Act

Banc One Corporation, Columbus, Ohio
CoreStates Financial Corp, Philadelphia, Pennsylvania
PNC Financial Corp, Pittsburgh, Pennsylvania
Society Corporation, Cleveland, Ohio

Order Approving Applications to Conduct Certain Data Processing and Other Nonbanking Activities

Banc One Corporation, Columbus, Ohio ("Banc One"), CoreStates Financial Corp, Philadelphia, Pennsylvania ("CoreStates"), PNC Financial Corp, Pittsburgh, Pennsylvania ("PNC"), and Society Corporation, Cleveland, Ohio ("Society") (collectively, "Applicants"), bank holding companies within the meaning of the Bank Holding Company Act ("BHC Act"), have applied for the Board's approval under section 4(c)(8) of the BHC Act (*12 U.S.C.* § *1843*(c)(8)) and section 225.23(a) of the Board's Regulation Y (12 C.F.R. 225.23(a)) to engage de novo, through their joint venture corporation, Electronic Payment Services, Inc., Wilmington, Delaware ("Company"), in certain nonbanking activities, including data processing and data transmission activities pursuant to section 225.25(b)(7) of Regulation Y.

Applicants currently provide data processing and transmission services through Company to retail merchants using point-of-sale ("POS") terminals and to banks who are members of Company's automated teller machine ("ATM") network.[1] Applicants now propose to offer through Company certain data pro-

[1] On November 30, 1992, acting pursuant to delegated authority, the Federal Reserve Banks of Cleveland and Philadelphia approved a proposal by Applicants to form Company through the consolidation of their respective ATM and POS networks.

cessing and transmission services and electronic payment services that have not previously been considered by the Board. In particular, Company proposes to provide:

(1) Electronic Benefit Transfer Services. Data processing and transmission services required to permit the delivery of governmental program benefits (such as welfare payments and food stamps) through the POS and ATM terminals of participating merchants and banks ("Benefits services"). Under a Benefits services system, a benefit recipient would be issued a magnetically encoded card, similar to an ATM card, which could be used to obtain access to a government benefit account maintained on behalf of the recipient.

(2) Stored Value Card Services. Data processing and transmission services and electronic payment services related to stored value cards, which are cards similar to credit or debit cards to which funds could be credited through magnetic stripe or computer chip technology. These services would be provided in connection with both single-vendor stored value card systems and multiple-vendor systems currently in development.

(3) Electronic Data Interchange Services. The provision to retail merchants of data collected from sales transactions processed at the merchants' POS terminals ("Data services"). These data would relate to specific product purchases and customer purchasing patterns, and could be used by the merchants for inventory control, targeted marketing, and other purposes.

Applicants propose to engage in these activities throughout the United States.

Notice of these applications, affording interested persons an opportunity to submit comments, has been published *(57 Federal Register 44,571 (1992))*. The time for filing comments has expired, and the Board has considered the applications and all comments received in light of the factors set forth in section 4(c)(8) of the BHC Act.

Banc One, with $75.4 billion in total consolidated assets, is the eighth largest commercial banking organization in the United States, controlling $59.4 billion in deposits.[2] Banc One operates subsidiary banks in Ohio, Kentucky, Indiana, Michigan, Illinois, Wisconsin, Texas, Colorado, Arizona, California, Utah, and West Virginia, and engages directly and through its subsidiaries in a broad range of banking and permissible nonbanking activities.

---

[2] Asset and deposit data are as of June 30, 1993.

CoreStates, with $23.6 billion in total consolidated assets, is the 33d largest commercial banking organization in the United States, controlling $16.5 billion in deposits. CoreStates operates subsidiary banks in Pennsylvania, New Jersey, and Delaware, and engages through its subsidiaries in a broad range of banking and permissible nonbanking activities.

PNC, with $53.3 billion in total consolidated assets, is the tenth largest commercial banking organization in the United States, controlling $27.9 billion in deposits. PNC operates subsidiary banks in Pennsylvania, Ohio, Kentucky, Indiana, and Delaware, and engages directly and through its subsidiaries in a broad range of banking and permissible nonbanking activities.

Society, with $26 billion in total consolidated assets, is the 28th largest commercial banking organization in the United States, controlling $16.6 billion in deposits. Society operates subsidiary banks in Ohio, Indiana, and Michigan, and engages directly and through its subsidiaries in a broad range of banking and permissible nonbanking activities.

Closely Related to Banking Analysis

Section 4(c)(8) of the BHC Act provides that a bank holding company may, with Board approval, engage in any activity that the Board determines to be "so closely related to banking or managing or controlling banks as to be a proper incident thereto." An activity may be deemed to be closely related to banking if it is demonstrated that:

(1) Banks generally provide the proposed services; or
(2) Banks generally provide services that are operationally or functionally so similar to the proposed services as to equip them particularly well to provide the proposed services; or
(3) Banks generally provide services that are so integrally related to the proposed services as to require their provision in a specialized form. See *National Courier Association v. Board of Governors of the Federal Reserve System, 516 F.2d 1229, 1237 (D.C. Cir. 1975).*[3]

The Board has determined that certain data processing activities are closely related to banking and, therefore, permissible for bank holding companies under section 4(c)(8) of the BHC Act. Section 225.25(b)(7) of Regulation Y permits bank holding companies to provide data processing and data transmission services, facilities, data bases, or access to such services, facilities, or data bases by any

[3] In addition, the Board may consider any other basis that may demonstrate that the proposed activity has a reasonable or close connection or relationship to banking or managing or controlling banks. See Board Statement Regarding Regulation Y, *49 Federal Register 806 (1984); Securities Industry Association v. Board of Governors of the Federal Reserve System, 468 U.S. 207, 210-11 n. 5 (1984).*

technological means, so long as the data to be processed or furnished are "financial, banking, or economic" in nature.[4]

Electronic Benefit Transfer Services. Under a Benefits services program, a benefit recipient would have access to a benefit account maintained by a governmental agency or by the agency's transaction processor on behalf of the recipient. The account would be credited by the agency or transaction processor with the amount of benefits to which the recipient is entitled, such as for welfare payments or food stamps. The recipient would be issued a magnetic card, similar to an ATM card, which could be used (i) at ATM terminals to receive cash benefits from the account, and (ii) at POS terminals to pay for food or other in-kind entitlements, or to obtain cash benefits in the account.

The proposed Benefits services would be provided through Company's existing ATM and POS networks, and, in general, the system would operate like existing electronic fund transfer systems. As in the operation of an ATM or POS network, Company's primary activities would consist of processing and transmitting access requests and payment authorizations entered into the Benefits services system. In addition, Company may function as the transaction processor for one or more governmental agencies. In this role, Company would provide record maintenance and payment authorization services similar to those currently furnished to Company's financial institution customers.[5]

These activities represent the electronic payment of government benefits and are financial activities that are operationally and functionally similar to the electronic payment and data processing services provided by banks and bank holding companies in the operation of ATM and POS networks. In particular, the proposed Benefits services involve the processing of access and authorization requests submitted to, and electronic payments originating from, financial accounts on the same basis as transactions initiated with traditional debit and credit cards. Based on the record, the Board has concluded that the proposed Benefits services constitute financial data processing and transmission activities, are

---

[4] Regulation Y also requires that the services be provided pursuant to a written agreement, and places certain limitations on the facilities and hardware provided with the data processing services. See 12 C.F.R. 225.25(b)(7). See also *Association of Data Processing Service Organizations, Inc. v. Board of Governors of the Federal Reserve System, 745 F.2d 677 (D.C. Cir. 1984).* Applicants have represented that Company will provide the proposed services pursuant to a written agreement, and will provide facilities and hardware within the limitations established by Regulation Y. The hardware to be provided by Company consists of debit and credit access cards, the ATM and POS terminals that will be used in delivering the proposed services, and special terminals designed for use in a stored value card system.

[5] The eligibility of recipients of government benefits, and the eligibility of items for purchase under the food stamp program and other in-kind benefit programs, are currently decided by governmental agencies, with individual merchants making determinations as to the qualification of particular items at the point of sale. Company has indicated that it does not propose at this time to furnish software for, or provide other services relating to, any such determination of eligibility.

closely related to banking, and are permissible for bank holding companies under the BHC Act.

Stored Value Card Services. Company proposes to provide data processing and transmission services and electronic payment services related to stored value cards, which are cards similar to credit or debit cards to which funds could be credited through magnetic stripe or computer chip technology. Company's services would be provided in connection with both "closed" and "open" stored value card systems. "Closed systems" include both single-vendor stored value card systems and systems designed for single-site use, such as at a college or university. An "open system", by contrast, refers to a multiple-vendor, multiple-site stored value card system.

Closed Systems. Currently, open systems are in developmental stages only, while closed systems are in limited operation in the United States. In current closed systems, in general, cash must be deposited in a particular vendor's card-dispensing terminal, and the card received from the terminal may be used only for purchases from that specific vendor. The card itself is disposable, and the only account reconciliation that may be required would involve the vendor's own cash receipts, the amount of funds debited from the cards at turnstiles or other points of sale, and the amount of the vendor's liabilities stored on outstanding cards. Company does not intend to play a role in the operation of this basic type of closed system.

Company does propose to play a role in the development and operation of more complex closed systems. These systems would use a plastic card containing electronic technology such as a computer chip or magnetic stripe to which funds could be credited, and from which funds could be debited for an indefinite period of time. Company's primary activities would include the performance of accounting functions in such customer accounts, as well as the level of the vendor's stored value liabilities. In this capacity, Company also would be responsible for settlement and reconciliation of these customer and vendor accounts. Company also would perform other functions, such as embossing and issuing cards and arranging for funds collection.

Closed systems also may be developed—for example, in a university setting—in which pre-paid accounts are maintained by the vendor or some central party (in this example, the university) on behalf of a customer (in this case, a student or other member of the university community). In such a system, value could be placed on a stored value card either at a cash-to-card machine or through a direct electronic debit to one's pre-paid account. Such a direct debit would be made at an ATM-type machine specially adapted for that purpose ("value transfer machine"). Closed systems also may involve multiple vendors at a single site. For example, in the university case, the stored value cards could be used to pay charges at locations such as student centers, cafeterias, bookstores, and copy machines. In each case, however, Company's activities in connection with these more complex closed systems would be essentially the same as the accounting, settlement, and reconciliation functions and other activities described in the preceding paragraph. In addition, Company may operate value transfer machines used in these more complex closed systems.

Open Systems. Applicants anticipate that stored value cards eventually will operate in an open system similar to a POS network, so that value stored on the card could be used with a wide range of participating vendors. Applicants expect that Company's principal stored value card activities would involve the development and operation of such open systems.

In an open system, customers' debit cards would hold an integrated computer chip or comparable technology capable of storing value for use in stored value card transactions. Value could be placed on the card at an ATM adapted to read and place value on the chip, at a limited purpose ATM-type machine whose only functions would be to add value to the chip and to transfer stored value back to the customer's account, or at a cash-to-card machine or other value transfer device (collectively, "Value Terminals"). These Value Terminals would be operated, in at least some cases, by Company. Once value is placed on a card, equivalent funds would be transferred to Company, which would hold the funds for payment of stored value card transactions. Stored value would leave the chip when the customer purchases goods or services either at a POS terminal (which may be operated by Company) or at a vending machine, telephone booth, mass transit turnstile, or other unmanned delivery location (collectively, "Reader Terminals"), or when the customer transfers funds back to an account at a Value Terminal. Reader Terminals generally would be off-line devices, not connected to Company's ATM or POS networks. Instead of a direct electronic connection, a Reader Terminal would retain, for a period of time, value representing the amount of customer purchases at the terminal. Then, at the vendor's convenience, Company, the vendor, or a third party would collect value from the Reader Terminals using specially-designed collection cards issued by Company. The collection cards would then be submitted to Company so that funds can be properly credited. Once these transactions occur, Company would be responsible for making settlement by transferring funds to the accounts of participating merchants and other appropriate parties.

Closely Related to Banking Analysis. The Board believes that Company's activities in providing stored value card services, in both closed and open systems, are closely related to banking. These activities involve processing debits and credits to the stored value cards, and performing related accounting and settlement functions. This aspect of the proposal is a data processing activity in which financial balances are maintained and adjusted at POS and other terminals as the customer purchases various items, or adds value to the card, and constitutes the processing of banking, financial, or economic data within the meaning of Regulation Y. In addition, aspects of Company's stored value card services are functionally similar to the issuance and sale of consumer payment instruments such as travelers checks, which also are activities that banks conduct and that the Board has previously determined are closely related to banking within the meaning of the BHC Act.[6] For these reasons, and based on the record, the Board has concluded that Company's proposed services in connection with stored value cards, in either an open system or a closed system, are closely related to banking.

Electronic Data Interchange Services. Company also proposes to furnish retail merchants with data collected from sales transactions consummated at the merchant's place of business ("Data services").[7] The data collected and furnished would relate to specific items and quantities of products purchased by the customer, as well as customer purchasing patterns over a period of time. The data would be formatted so that it could be used by the merchant for inventory control, targeted marketing, and other purposes. Company's Data services generally would be furnished to merchants as an adjunct to Company's POS transaction processing services, and would be rendered through a retail merchant's POS terminals. Company does not intend to offer Data services on an independent basis. In addition, data collected by Company would be furnished only to the merchant that is party to the underlying sales transaction: that is, Company does not intend to provide such information to third parties.

Company's Data services would be limited to capturing, formatting, and furnishing data collected from sales transactions consummated at a particular merchant's place of business. In addition, the data collected would be furnished only to that merchant, and only in accordance with the merchant's specific instructions. Company does not intend to provide software or render advice or provide other services associated with the marketing or other uses of the data.[8] Applicants do anticipate, however, that Company could provide additional related functions, such as the issuance at POS terminals of store coupons or credits related to a merchant's marketing programs.

The Board believes that the sales data that would be processed under the proposed Data services are financial and economic data within the meaning of Regulation Y. In 1971, the Board determined that the processing of "banking, financial, or related economic data, such as performing payroll, accounts receivable or payable, or billing services", was an activity closely related to banking and therefore permissible for bank holding companies under the BHC Act. In 1982, the regulatory standard was expanded to include all types of economic data. This includes the processing of microeconomic data, such as data collected in the performance of accounts receivable and payable functions and inventory and sales analyses. On the basis of the record and these considerations, the

[6] See 12 C.F.R. 225.25(b)(12). See also Citicorp, *79 Federal Reserve Bulletin 42 (1993).*

[7] Ordinarily, the sales transaction and the related payment would be processed electronically through Company's POS network. However, Data services also could be furnished when cash payments are tendered, through the use of a merchant proprietary card held by the consumer.

[8] In addition, Company will not furnish software that provides broad-based marketing or demographic analysis.

Board has concluded that Company's proposed Data services, which involve the processing of financial and sales data, are within the range of financial and economic data processing activities contemplated by Regulation Y.

Other Enhanced ATM and POS Functions. Applicants have stated that Company will place significant emphasis on research relating to and the development and provision of new and enhanced ATM and POS services. For this reason, Applicants have requested authority for Company to provide such new or enhanced services (in addition to the activities discussed above) without further application, under a general authority to provide data processing services pursuant to Regulation Y. The Board believes that the enhanced functions that Applicants have specifically proposed, such as providing electronic access to additional government benefit programs, and developing the ability to cash checks, to allocate deposits, or to make loan payments at an ATM, as well as bill paying services and account maintenance functions such as check ordering, constitute the processing of banking, financial, or economic data, and are permissible under the BHC Act.[9]

Other Considerations

In every case involving a nonbanking acquisition by a bank holding company under section 4 of the BHC Act, the Board considers the financial condition and resources of the applicant and its subsidiaries and the effect of the transaction on these resources.[10] Based on all the facts of record, the Board concludes that financial considerations are consistent with approval of these applications. The managerial resources of each of the Applicants also are consistent with approval.

In order to approve these applications, the Board also must find that the performance of the proposed activities by Applicants through Company "can reasonably be expected to produce benefits to the public . . . that outweigh possible adverse effects, such as undue concentration of resources, decreased or unfair competition, conflicts of interests, or unsound banking practices." *12 U.S.C.* § *1843*(c)(8). The Board expects that the participation of Company in the market for the proposed data processing and electronic payment services would increase the level of competition among providers of those services. The Board also anticipates that Company's proposed activities would result in new products,

---

[9] Applicants have indicated that, in the future, Company may develop other data processing and transmission services that are not described in the applications, and are not discussed in this order. Applicants must consult with the Federal Reserve System before commencing any new activity not described in this order to ensure that the activity will satisfy the criteria set forth in the BHC Act and Regulation Y, and to allow the Federal Reserve System an opportunity to consider whether a separate application should be reviewed in any particular case.

[10] See 12 C.F.R. 225.24. See also The Fuji Bank, Limited, *75 Federal Reserve Bulletin 94 (1989)*; Bayerische Vereinsbank AG, *73 Federal Reserve Bulletin 155 (1987)*.

improved service, greater efficiencies, and increased convenience for consumers. In particular, the electronic delivery of government benefits offers opportunities for improving the delivery service to recipients, maximizing the efficiency of operations at state agencies, and minimizing costs for all parties.[11] The Board also notes that services rendered in connection with stored value cards would extend the benefits associated with electronic funds transfer systems to a greater range of consumer transactions.

In addition, there is no evidence in the record that consummation of the proposed activities would result in any significantly adverse effects, such as undue concentration of resources, decreased or unfair competition, conflicts of interests, or unsound banking practices.[12] Accordingly, the Board has concluded that the balance of the public interest factors that it is required to consider under section 4(c)(8) of the BHC Act is favorable.

In addition, the Board's approval is subject to the requirement that, to the extent the proposed activities are subject to state or federal laws relating to branching, deposit-taking and other matters, the activities will be conducted in conformity with all such legal requirements.

Based on all the facts of record, the Board has determined that the applications should be, and hereby are, approved. The Board's approval is specifically conditioned on compliance with the commitments made in connection with these applications and with the conditions referred to in this order. The Board's determination also is subject to all of the conditions set forth in Regulation Y, including those in sections 225.4(d) and 225.23(b) of Regulation Y, and to the Board's authority to require such modification or termination of the activities of a bank holding company or any of its subsidiaries as the Board finds necessary to ensure compliance with, and to prevent evasion of, the provisions of the BHC Act and the Board's regulations and orders issued thereunder. For purposes of this action, these commitments and conditions are deemed to be conditions imposed in writing by the Board in connection with its findings and decision, and, as such, may be enforced in proceedings under applicable law.

This transaction shall not be consummated later than three months after the effective date of this Order, unless such period is extended for good cause by the Board, or by the Federal Reserve Bank of Cleveland or the Federal Reserve Bank of Philadelphia, acting pursuant to delegated authority.

By order of the Board of Governors, effective October 28, 1993.

JENNIFER J. JOHNSON
Associate Secretary of the Board

---

[11] Electronic Transfer of Government Benefits, *77 Federal Reserve Bulletin 203 (1991).*

[12] In this regard, the Board notes that Applicants have committed to provide to the Federal Reserve System data regarding the aggregate balances being held by Company in connection with its stored value card activities. The Board's approval is subject to compliance with this commitment.

VOTE:

Voting for this action: Chairman Greenspan and Governors Angell, Kelley, LaWare, and Phillips. Absent and not voting: Governors Mullins and Lindsey.

Appendix D2

Banc One Corp., 80 Fed. Res. Bull. 139 (1994)

Order Approving Application to Conduct Certain Data Processing Activities

Banc One Corporation, Columbus, Ohio

Banc One Corporation, Columbus, Ohio ("Applicant"), a bank holding company within the meaning of the Bank Holding Company Act ("BHC Act"), has applied for the Board's approval under section 4(c)(8) of the BHC Act (*12 U.S.C. § 1843*(c)(8)) and section 225.23(a) of Regulation Y (12 C.F.R. 225.23(a)) to acquire all the voting shares of Croghan & Associates, Inc., Boulder, Colorado ("Company"), and thereby to engage de novo in certain data processing and data transmission activities pursuant to section 225.25(b)(7) of Regulation Y.

In particular, Applicant intends to operate, through Company, a network for the processing and transmission of medical payment data between health care providers (such as physicians, hospitals, and pharmacies) ("Providers") and entities responsible for providing medical benefits (such as health insurers, health maintenance organizations, and preferred provider organizations) ("Payers"). The network would operate in a manner similar to existing automated-teller-machine ("ATM") and point-of-sale ("POS") networks. In general, Providers would enter claims information into the network with a request for payment, and Payers would authorize electronic fund transfers in full or partial payment of the claims.

In addition, Company proposes to furnish Providers and Payers with software for use in the medical payments network, including claims adjudication software that would automate the determination of what claims should be paid and the amount of each claim that should be paid. Company also intends to provide by-products of its data processing activities, including statistical information derived from the data transmitted through the payment network, and to furnish additional related services that may result from its research and development efforts.[1]

Notice of the application, affording interested persons an opportunity to submit comments, has been published *(58 Federal Register 33,443 (1993))*. The time for filing comments has expired, and the Board has considered the application and all comments received in light of the factors set forth in section 4(c)(8) of the BHC Act.

Applicant, with $75.4 billion in total consolidated assets, is the eighth largest commercial banking organization in the United States, controlling $59.4 billion in deposits.[2] Applicant operates subsidiary banks in Ohio, Kentucky, Indiana, Michigan, Illinois, Wisconsin, Texas, Colorado, Arizona, California, Utah, and West Virginia, and engages directly and through its subsidiaries in a broad range of banking and permissible nonbanking activities.

Closely Related to Banking Analysis

Section 4(c)(8) of the BHC Act provides that a bank holding company may, with Board approval, engage in any activity that the Board determines to be "so closely related to banking or managing or controlling banks as to be a proper incident thereto." An activity may be deemed to be closely related to banking if it is demonstrated that:

(1) Banks generally provide the proposed services; or
(2) Banks generally provide services that are operationally or functionally so similar to the proposed services as to equip them particularly well to provide the proposed services; or
(3) Banks generally provide services that are so integrally related to the proposed services as to require their provision in a specialized form.[3]

The Board has determined generally that certain data processing activities are closely related to banking and therefore permissible for bank holding companies under section 4(c)(8) of the BHC Act. Section 225.25(b)(7) of Regulation Y

---

[1] The Board has relied on Applicant's commitment to consult with the Federal Reserve System before Company offers new data processing services or products not specifically discussed in the application to ensure that the activity will satisfy the criteria set forth in the BHC Act and Regulation Y, and to allow the Federal Reserve System an opportunity to consider whether a separate application should be reviewed in any particular case.

[2] Asset and deposit data are as of June 30, 1993.

[3] See *National Courier Association v. Board of Governors of the Federal Reserve System, 516 F.2d 1229, 1237 (D.C. Cir. 1975)*. In addition, the Board may consider any other basis that may demonstrate that the proposed activity has a reasonable or close connection or relationship to banking or managing or controlling banks. See Board Statement Regarding Regulation Y, *49 Federal Register 806 (1984); Securities Industry Association v. Board of Governors of the Federal Reserve System, 468 U.S. 207, 210-211 n. 5 (1984)*.

permits bank holding companies to provide data processing and data transmission services, facilities (including software), data bases, or access to such services, facilities, or data bases by any technological means, so long as the data to be processed or furnished are "financial, banking, or economic" in nature.[4] In addition, Regulation Y provides that bank holding companies may engage in incidental activities that are necessary to carry on an activity that is closely related to banking. See 12 C.F.R. 225.21 (a)(2). In the data processing context, such incidental activities include the provision of by-products of permissible data processing and data transmission services, so long as such by-products are not designed, or appreciably enhanced, for the purpose of marketability. See 12 C.F.R. 225.123(e)(2).

For analytical purposes, Applicant's proposal can be viewed in three parts:

(1) The basic operation of a medical payments network;
(2) The provision of claims adjudication software; and
(3) The provision of statistical and other information derived from the data flowing over the network.

(1) **Basic Network Services.** Under the medical payments system proposed by Company, Payer organizations would issue to their members a medical benefits card similar to a credit or debit card.[5] Before receiving health care services, a patient would present this medical benefits card to the relevant Provider. The Provider could then use the card to obtain access through Company to a central database containing information on patient eligibility, co-payment requirements, year-to-date deductible values, and other coverage data. After medical services are furnished, the Provider would transmit claim information to the relevant Payer through Company's medical payments network. This claim information would include the amount charged and a description of the services rendered that is sufficient to allow the Payer to determine the eligibility of the claim and the amount that should be paid. The Payer would then authorize electronic payment of the appropriate amount through Company and participating financial

[4] Regulation Y also requires that the services be provided pursuant to a written agreement, and places certain limitations on the facilities and hardware provided with the data processing services. In particular, the facilities must be designed, marketed, and operated for the processing and transmission of financial, banking, or economic data; hardware must be provided only in conjunction with permissible software; and general purpose hardware must not constitute more than 30 percent of the cost of any packaged offering. See 12 C.F.R. 225.25(b)(7). Applicant has committed that Company will provide the proposed services pursuant to a written agreement, and will provide facilities and hardware within the limitations established by Regulation Y.

[5] Company would perform embossing and encoding functions with respect to these medical benefits cards. Applicant expects that medical benefits cards may be developed with debit or credit card features, so that the cards could be used by consumers to obtain access to, and authorize medical payments from, their banking or other accounts.

institutions. Throughout this process, Providers would be able to ascertain the status of the claim and any related payment.[6]

Company's primary activities would include the routing and processing of medical payment transactions through direct connections between Company's computer switch and Payer and Provider terminals. Company also would perform the accounting functions necessary to settle the payments processed through the network, and would provide electronic transaction and settlement reports to participating financial institutions, Providers, and Payers. In addition, Company would provide other services analogous to functions performed by the operator of an ATM or POS network, including switching, gateway, and terminal driving services. These functions represent the processing of banking, financial, and economic data of the type previously approved for bank holding companies.[7]

In addition to banking, financial, and economic information, however, Company would process and transmit medical treatment data sufficient to allow Payers to make decisions regarding the legitimacy of a claim and the appropriate degree of coverage. Similarly, when Providers obtain access to the coverage information database, Company would transmit data relating to the terms of a particular Payer's medical coverage contract and the extent to which specific medical treatments would be covered by the patient's insurance policy.

While such medical and coverage data are not financial data, processing and transmitting this data are essential components in the transmission and processing of the medical payments and financial information in the network. For example, the medical data submitted by Providers as part of a claim (such as descriptions of a patient's symptoms and of medical procedures performed by the Provider) are necessary to the Payer's decision to authorize an electronic

[6] Alternative financial arrangements among Providers and Payers—for example, pricing based on the number of patients treated by a Provider, with payments to be made at regular intervals upon presentation of satisfactory documentation—also could be accommodated by the proposed network.

[7] Company also proposes to provide and maintain software and hardware used in the medical payments network. The hardware provided by Company would consist primarily of general purpose hardware which, together with operating system, database and network access, and network processing software, would comprise the basic operating environment for the medical payments network. The software provided by Company for use in the network would be an essential component in the operation of the medical payments system. Applicant has stated that Company would provide hardware and software only in accordance with the limitations established by Regulation Y. System software would constitute general purpose software and be considered part of the general purpose hardware of the system, subject to the 30 percent limitation in Regulation Y. Other software would include database and network access products, as well as network processing software similar to that used in the operation of ATM and POS networks. This software, together with the adjudication software discussed below, would be special purpose software designed to carry out the billing, accounts payable, and electronic fund transfer functions of the network.

funds transfer payment.[8] Similarly, a Payer must furnish insurance policy coverage information to a Provider in order to permit the Provider to calculate the payment reasonably to be expected from the Payer and the charges that should be allocated to the patient.

Moreover, the purpose of the data processing services rendered by Company in its operation of the network would be to permit the electronic transfer of funds from patient and Payer accounts to Provider accounts. The Board also notes that banking organizations transmit and process similar incidental data (though in less significant quantities) in connection with bill-paying services provided to consumers and accounts payable services rendered to corporate customers. In addition, the Office of the Comptroller of the Currency ("OCC") has permitted national banks to operate a medical payments network that processes a somewhat more limited amount of non-financial medical treatment and claims eligibility data.[9] For the foregoing reasons, the Board believes that Company's processing and transmission of medical and coverage data in connection with its operation of a payments network are permissible as incidental activities.[10]

Accordingly, and on the basis of all the facts of record, the Board has concluded that, although the operation of a medical payments network would involve the processing and transmission of medical and coverage data, as well as data of a financial, banking, or economic nature, Company's proposed operation of a medical payments network would constitute permissible data processing and data transmission activities under the BHC Act.

(2) **Adjudication Software.** In addition to the software used in the basic operation of the medical payments network, Company proposes to provide claims adjudication software to Payers. This software would represent an electronic version of the basic rules of a Payer's coverage contract, and would be designed for the processing of routine claims. In general, the claims adjudication software would automate a large portion of the process by which a Payer determines the extent to which a submitted claim should be paid.

---

[8] Applicant has represented that this medical data submitted by Providers would include only information required to assess the appropriateness, validity, and amount of a claim for payment, or otherwise necessary to authorize payment for a claim, and that Providers would not be transmitting data for general medical use.

[9] For example, the proposal approved by the OCC did not appear to include an adjudication mechanism (such as that discussed below) that permits an immediate analysis and payment of claims that fall within specifications set by the Payer. In many other respects, however, the network considered by the OCC involved the transmission of non-financial data, including medical treatment data, such as that at issue in this proposal, The OCC concluded that operation of the network was a permissible activity because it constituted the provision of a data processing system in connection with electronic fund transfers. See OCC Interpretive Letter No. 419 (February 16, 1988), reprinted in Federal Banking Law Reporter (CCH) ¶ 85,643 (May 27, 1988).

[10] See 12 C.F.R. 225.21(a)(2).

Company would not make decisions or render advice as to what portions, if any, of the claims adjudication process should be automated for any particular Payer, and each adjudication program developed by Company would contain only the information necessary to process submitted claims. In addition, Company would not play any role in determining the extent to which a claim would be covered: all parameters for payment of insurance claims would be set by the Payer, and questions, payment decisions, or disputes about the extent of coverage would be handled by the Payer (and not by Company).[11]

The claims adjudication process essentially involves the interaction of financial and banking data (the amount of a submitted claim and a request for an electronic funds transfer) and medical and coverage data (treatment information and the basic rules of a Payer's coverage contract). Claims adjudication is a central aspect of the authorization function in the proposed network, and is necessary to the consummation of an electronic funds transfer. For these reasons, claims adjudication is functionally similar to the payment authorization services rendered by operators of ATM and POS networks to their financial institution and other customers. In addition, the provision of claims adjudication software is an integral part of the accounts payable function Company proposes to provide to Payers.

Accordingly, the Board believes that the processing of medical and coverage data involved in claims adjudication is an integral part of, and therefore necessary to, the processing of related financial and banking information, and Company's processing of the underlying payment transactions. Hence, on the basis of all the facts of record, the Board has concluded that Company's provision of claims adjudication software that processes such medical and coverage data is permissible as an activity incidental to its provision of software for the processing of banking and financial data, and its operation of a medical payments network.[12]

(3) **Electronic Data Interchange.** Company also proposes to furnish participants in the medical payments system with statistical and other data derived from the information contained in Company's database.[13] Each customer would have on-line access to all the data it places in the system, and third parties designated by a Payer or Provider also could receive access to data owned by

---

[11] These limitations should ensure that Company does not become engaged in the provision of insurance-related services or advice. Company would only provide the electronic media and software for adjudication and payment of benefits, and would not be engaged in insurance agency activities or in the sale of medical insurance. In this regard, Applicant has committed that Company would not conduct any activity that would require it to be licensed as an insurance agent or broker under state law.

[12] See 12 C.F.R. 225.21(a)(2).

[13] Applicant has stated that these electronic data interchange services would be offered as part of a package of services purchased by a Payer or Provider. Company also would make these services available on an independent basis to potential customers of Company's network processing and claims adjudication services. Company would not, in any event, market these services to the general public.

such customer.[14] Applicant has indicated that the information comprising the database for these services would consist solely of medical claims data necessary for the authorization of payments, other data transmitted through Company's network, and similar claims and payment information provided to Company by actual and potential processing and adjudication customers.

The Board has stated that bank holding companies may provide by-products of permissible data processing and data transmission activities, so long as such by-products are not designed, or appreciably enhanced, for the purpose of marketability. 12 C.F.R. 225.123(e)(2). The Board has indicated that by-products include data, software, or data processing techniques that may be applicable to the data processing requirements of other industries. See Citicorp, *68 Federal Reserve Bulletin 505, 510-511 (1982).*

Company expects that, in most instances, raw data will be transmitted to a customer from the network's central computer upon the customer's electronic request, without any intervention by Company personnel. The customer would then analyze the data to suit its own particular needs. In some cases, however, pursuant to a customer's instructions, Company may perform limited selection, combination, and similar functions upon raw data so that it can be transmitted to the customer in a reorganized and more usable form.[15] Company also may design software that would enable customers to perform similar reorganization functions upon raw data. Company would not, however, render advisory or consulting services in connection with the provision or use of these electronic data interchange capabilities, and would not engage in any scientific, actuarial, or clinical research or analysis of the information contained in the database. Moreover, Company would not, under any circumstances, make data available to the general public.

On the basis of all the facts of record, including the limitations discussed in the application and the limitations discussed above, the Board has concluded that the proposed electronic data interchange services would constitute permissible by-products of Company's primary data processing activities, and that such services are, therefore, permissible as an incidental activity.

Other Considerations

In every case involving a nonbanking acquisition by a bank holding company under section 4 of the BHC Act, the Board considers the financial condition

[14] All data furnished by Company in rendering these services would be formatted so that individual Providers and patients could not be identified by persons not authorized to receive access to such information. In addition, such data would be furnished only to the extent permitted by relevant patient and other consent forms.

[15] See 12 C.F.R. 225.24. See also The Fuji Bank, Limited, *75 Federal Reserve Bulletin 94 (1989);* Bayerische Vereinsbank, AG *73 Federal Reserve Bulletin 155 (1987).*

and resources of the applicant and its subsidiaries and the effect of the transaction on those resources. Based on all the facts of record, the Board has concluded that financial and managerial considerations are consistent with approval of this proposal.

In order to approve this application, the Board also must determine that the performance of the proposed activities by Applicant through Company "can reasonably be expected to produce benefits to the public . . . that outweigh possible adverse effects, such as undue concentration of resources, decreased or unfair competition, conflicts of interests, or unsound banking practices." *12 U.S.C.* § *1843*(c)(8). The Board expects that the participation of Company in the market for the proposed data processing services would increase the level of competition among providers of those services. The Board also anticipates that Company's proposed activities would result in new products and services, greater efficiencies, and increased convenience for consumers. In addition, there is no evidence in the record that consummation of the proposed activities would result in any significantly adverse effects, such as undue concentration of resources, decreased or unfair competition, conflicts of interests, or unsound banking practices. Accordingly, the Board concludes that the balance of the public interest factors that it is required to consider under section 4(c)(8) of the BHC Act is favorable.

Based on all the facts of record, the Board has determined that the application should be, and hereby is, approved. The Board's approval is specifically conditioned on compliance with the commitments made in connection with this application and with the conditions referred to in this order. The Board's determination also is subject to all the conditions set forth in Regulation Y, including those in sections 225.4(d) and 225.23(b) of Regulation Y, and to the Board's authority to require such modification or termination of the activities of a bank holding company or any of its subsidiaries as the Board finds necessary to ensure compliance with, and to prevent evasion of, the provisions of the BHC Act and the Board's regulations and orders issued thereunder. For purposes of this action, these commitments and conditions are deemed to be conditions imposed in writing by the Board in connection with its findings and decision, and, as such, may be enforced in proceedings under applicable law.

This transaction shall not be consummated later than three months after the effective date of this order, unless such period is extended for good cause by the Board or by the Federal Reserve Bank of Cleveland, acting pursuant to delegated authority.

By order of the Board of Governors, effective December 22, 1993.

JENNIFER J. JOHNSON
Associate Secretary of the Board

VOTE:

Voting for this action: Chairman Greenspan, Vice Chairman Mullins and Governors Kelley, Lindsey, and Phillips. Absent and not voting: Governors Angell and LaWare.

APPENDIX D3

The Bank of New York Co., et al. 80 Fed. Res. Bull. 1107 (1994)

Orders Issued Under Section 3 of the Bank Holding Company Act
The Bank of New York Company, Inc., New York, New York
BayBanks, Inc., Boston, Massachusetts
The Chase Manhattan Corporation, New York, New York
Chemical Banking Corporation, New York, New York
Citicorp, New York, New York
Fleet Financial Group, Inc., Providence, Rhode Island
HSBC Holdings PLC, London, England
HSBC Holdings BV, The Netherlands
Marine Midland Banks, Inc., Buffalo, New York
Banco de Santander, S.A., Madrid, Spain
First Fidelity Bancorporation, Lawrenceville, New Jersey
The Bank of Boston Corporation, Boston, Massachusetts
Shawmut National Corporation, Hartford, Connecticut
National Westminster Bank PLC, London, England
NatWest Holdings, Inc., New York, New York

The Bank of New York Company, Inc., New York, New York; BayBanks, Inc., Boston, Massachusetts; The Chase Manhattan Corporation, New York, New York; Chemical Banking Corporation, New York, New York; Citicorp, New York, New York; Fleet Financial Group, Inc., Providence, Rhode Island; HSBC Holdings PLC, London, England; HSBC Holdings BV, The Netherlands; Marine Midland Banks, Inc., Buffalo, New York; Banco de Santander, S.A., Madrid, Spain; First Fidelity Bancorporation, Lawrenceville, New Jersey; The Bank of Boston Corporation, Boston, Massachusetts; Shawmut National Corporation, Hartford, Connecticut; National Westminster Bank PLC, London, England; and NatWest Holdings, Inc., New York, New York (collectively, "Applicants"), bank holding companies within the meaning of the Bank Holding Company Act ("BHC Act"), have applied for the Board's approval under section 4(c)(8) of the BHC

Act (*12 U.S.C.* § *1843*(c)(8)) and section 225.23(a) of the Board's Regulation Y (12 C.F.R. 225.23(a)) to engage through a joint venture corporation, InfiNet Payment Services, Inc., Hackensack, New Jersey ("Company"), in certain non-banking activities related to the operation of a retail electronic funds transfer ("EFT") and automated teller machine ("ATM") network, including data processing and data transmission activities pursuant to section 225.25(b)(7) of Regulation Y (12 C.F.R. 225.25(b)(7)). A complete list of the activities proposed to be conducted is contained in the Appendix to this order.

Company would be formed through the combination of NENI Corporation ("NENI"), which operates a retail EFT network under the tradename Yankee 24, and The New York Switch Corporation ("NY Switch"), which operates the NYCE EFT network under various tradenames.[1] Applicants propose to engage through Company in operating a retail EFT network and thereby providing point of sale ("POS") and ATM services, including electronic benefit transfer, stored value card, and electronic data capture and interchange services. Applicants propose to engage in these activities worldwide.[2]

The Board notes that deposit-taking and other activities of Company's network must be conducted in conformity with federal, state and other laws. Applicants have committed that Company will conduct its activities in accordance with applicable law, and that the operating rules of Company's network will require compliance with all applicable federal and state laws.

Notice of the application, affording interested persons an opportunity to submit comments, has been published *(59 Federal Register 35,347 and 46,047 (1994))*. The time for filing comments has expired, and the Board has considered the application and all comments received in light of the factors set forth in section 4(c)(8) of the BHC Act.

Applicants are large commercial banking organizations whose principal U.S. banking offices are located in New England, New York, or the Mid-Atlantic region. Applicants engage directly and through subsidiaries in a broad range of banking and permissible nonbanking activities in the United States.

---

[1] Applicants are those bank holding companies that would own, directly or indirectly, 5 percent or more of any class of Company's voting shares. Other current members of NENI also would own shares of Company.

[2] Applicants also propose to permit foreign banks, including affiliates of the domestic banks that participate in Company's EFT network, to participate in the network on either a "cards-only" basis or a "terminal" basis. Cards-only participation would permit cardholder customers of foreign bank participants to use the ATM terminals in Company's network, but the ATM terminals of those foreign banks would not be part of the network. Terminal participation would permit foreign banks to include their ATM terminals in Company's network. Applicants have stated that Company would not render services in connection with deposits made at foreign ATMs or deposits made by the customers of foreign banks at ATMs in the United States. The Board also notes that Applicants have not proposed to include POS terminals located abroad as part of Company's network.

Closely Related to Banking Analysis

Section 4(c)(8) of the BHC Act provides that a bank holding company may, with Board approval, engage in any activity that the Board determines to be "so closely related to banking or managing or controlling banks as to be a proper incident thereto." An activity may be deemed to be closely related to banking if it is demonstrated that:

> (1) Banks generally provide the proposed services; or (2) Banks generally provide services that are operationally or functionally so similar to the proposed services as to equip them particularly well to provide the proposed services; or (3) Banks generally provide services that are so integrally related to the proposed services as to require their provision in a specialized form.[3]

The Board has determined generally that certain data processing and check guaranty activities are closely related to banking and, therefore, are permissible for bank holding companies under section 4(c)(8) of the BHC Act. Section 225.25(b)(7) of Regulation Y permits bank holding companies to provide data processing and data transmission services, facilities (including software), data bases, or access to such services, facilities, or data bases by any technological means, so long as the data to be processed or furnished are "financial, banking, or economic" in nature.[4] Regulation Y also permits bank holding companies to provide check guaranty services, subject to certain limitations.[5] Applicants have proposed to conduct the activities that the Board has previously determined to be closely related to banking in accordance with applicable Board precedent. In

---

[3] See *National Courier Association v. Board of Governors of the Federal Reserve System, 516 F.2d 1229, 1237 (D.C. Cir. 1975).* In addition, the Board may consider any other basis that may demonstrate that the proposed activity has a reasonable or close connection or relationship to banking or managing or controlling banks. See Board Statement Regarding Regulation Y, *49 Federal Register 806 (1984); Securities Industry Association v. Board of Governors of the Federal Reserve System, 468 U.S. 207, 210-211 n. 5 (1984).*

[4] Regulation Y also requires that the services be provided pursuant to a written agreement, and places certain limitations on the facilities and hardware provided with the data processing services. In particular, the facilities must be designed, marketed, and operated for the processing and transmission of financial, banking, or economic data; hardware must be provided only in conjunction with permissible software; and general purpose hardware must not constitute more than 30 percent of the cost of any packaged offering. See 12 C.F.R. 225.25(b)(7). Applicants have committed that Company will provide the proposed services pursuant to a written agreement, and will provide facilities and hardware within the limitations established by Regulation Y.

[5] Section 225.25(b)(22) of Regulation Y permits a bank holding company to engage in authorizing a subscribing merchant to accept personal checks and purchasing from the merchant validly authorized checks that are subsequently dishonored. Company proposes to engage only in check authorization or verification activities, and Applicants have stated they would apply to the Board if they wish to expand this activity to include the purchasing of checks.

particular, Applicants have committed to conduct the proposed data processing and transmission activities and check guaranty services in conformity with sections 225.25(b)(7) and 225.25(b)(22) of Regulation Y. In addition, Applicants have committed to conduct the proposed electronic benefit transfer services, electronic data interchange services, and stored value card services in the same manner and subject to the same limitations established by the Board in prior cases determining that these activities are permissible for bank holding companies under section 4(c)(8) of the BHC Act.[6]

Applicants also propose to offer through Company certain data processing and transmission services that have not previously been considered by the Board. In particular, Company would provide data processing and related services that would permit customers to use their ATM cards at an ATM terminal to withdraw funds from a bank account in the form of travelers checks or postage stamps.[7] Payment by the customer would be effected by a direct debit to the cardholder's depository account, and the transaction would be processed as a withdrawal from the account. Company's primary activities would consist of processing and transmitting access requests and payment authorizations. Company also would provide terminal driving services, load ATM terminals with postage stamps and travelers checks, and market these products through the network.

This activity involves the processing of access and authorization requests submitted to depository accounts on the same basis as other transactions initiated with traditional debit cards. This activity is operationally and functionally similar to the data processing services provided by banks and bank holding companies in the operation of ATM and POS networks. In addition, banks traditionally have been permitted to sell and have engaged in the sale of both travelers checks and postage stamps.[8] Accordingly, the Board finds that providing the data processing and additional services described above in connection with processing withdrawals from an ATM terminal in the form of postage stamps or travelers checks is an activity that is closely related to banking for purposes of section 4(c)(8) of the BHC Act.[9]

---

[6] See Banc One Corporation, et al., *79 Federal Reserve Bulletin 1158 (1993).*

[7] These transactions would occur at ATM terminals that are not owned and operated by Company. Cardholders buying postage stamps or travelers checks at an ATM terminal would purchase these products from the bank owning the ATM. In addition, Company would not be an issuer of travelers checks. The decision concerning which travelers checks would be sold at a particular ATM terminal would be made by the bank that owns the ATM terminal.

[8] See *Arnold Tours, Inc., v. Camp, 472 F.2d 427,438 (9th Cir. 1972)* (travelers checks); 12 C.F.R. 7.7482 (postal substation). See also 12 C.F.R. 225.25(b)(12).

[9] Applicants have indicated that, in the future, Company may develop other data processing and transmission services that are not described in the application, and are not discussed in this order. Applicants have committed to consult with the Federal Reserve System before commencing any new activity not described in this order to ensure that the activity would satisfy the criteria set forth in the BHC Act and Regulation Y, and to allow the Federal Reserve System to determine whether an application should be submitted in any particular case.

Proper Incident to Banking Analysis

In order to approve this application, the Board also must determine that the performance of the proposed activities by Applicants through Company "can reasonably be expected to produce benefits to the public . . . that outweigh possible adverse effects, such as undue concentration of resources, decreased or unfair competition, conflicts of interests, or unsound banking practices" *12 U.S.C.* § *1843*(c)(8).

The NYCE and Yankee 24 ATM networks operate in the northeastern region of the United States.[10] In reviewing the competitive effects of this transaction, the Board believes that a number of factors should mitigate the loss of the Yankee 24 ATM network as an independent competitor. In particular, significant weight was given to Company's operating rules,[11] which are likely to promote competition and access to the network. The Board also considered that Company would compete in varying degrees with other providers of EFT services. This includes competition from third-party providers of terminal driving, switching, and other data processing services and competition from other regional networks and national ATM and POS networks.

The record in this case also indicates that consummation of this proposal should result in public benefits. For example, increased transaction volume under the particular circumstances of this case should allow Company to benefit from economies of scale and thereby reduce average costs. Company also should be able to improve service to retail merchants by increasing its ability to offer POS services. In addition, the larger number of ATM terminals available to consumers should increase the convenience of electronic transactions to retail customers. The record also indicates that this transaction should enable the combined organization to introduce additional EFT-related products more efficiently.

Based on the foregoing and all the other facts of record, the Board has determined that consummation of this proposal would not result in any significantly adverse effects, such as undue concentration of resources, decreased or unfair competition, conflicts of interests, or unsound banking practices, that are not outweighed by the benefits to the public that may reasonably be expected to result from this transaction. Accordingly, the Board has concluded that the balance

---

[10] Yankee 24 operates almost exclusively in New England. Although NYCE is concentrated in New York, it has recently entered New England and has expanded its service area to cover the entire Northeast.

[11] Certain Company operating rules, when taken together, promote competition:

> (1) Third party processors, subject to demonstrating certain technical capabilities, would be given access to Infinet; (2) Membership in multiple regional networks would be permitted; (3) With certain exceptions not applicable to smaller participants in the network, the electronic route to be used for a transaction would be determined by the bank that is obligated to pay the transaction fees; and (4) Depository institutions would be permitted to participate in the network on a nondiscriminatory basis.

of the public interest factors that it is required to consider under section 4(c)(8) of the BHC Act is favorable.

Other Considerations

In every case involving a nonbanking acquisition by a bank holding company under section 4(c)(8) of the BHC Act, the Board considers the financial and managerial resources of the applicants and their subsidiaries and the effect of the transaction on those resources.[12] Based on all the facts of record, the Board has concluded that financial and managerial considerations are consistent with approval of this proposal.

Based on all the facts of record, the Board has determined that the application should be, and hereby is, approved. The Board's approval is specifically conditioned on compliance with the commitments made in connection with this application and with the conditions referred to in this order. The Board's determination also is subject to all the conditions set forth in Regulation Y, including those in sections 225.7 and 225.23(b) of Regulation Y, and to the Board's authority to require such modification or termination of the activities of a bank holding company or any of its subsidiaries as the Board finds necessary to ensure compliance with, and to prevent evasion of, the provisions of the BHC Act and the Board's regulations and orders issued thereunder. For purposes of this action, these commitments and conditions are deemed to be conditions imposed in writing by the Board in connection with its findings and decision, and, as such, may be enforced in proceedings under applicable law.

This transaction shall not be consummated later than three months after the effective date of this order, unless such period is extended for good cause by the Board or by the Federal Reserve Banks of Boston, New York, or Philadelphia, acting pursuant to delegated authority.

By order of the Board of Governors, effective October 3, 1994.

JENNIFER J. JOHNSON
Deputy Secretary of the Board

VOTE:

Voting for this action: Chairman Greenspan and Governors Phillips and Yellen.
Absent and not voting: Vice Chairman Blinder and Governors Kelley and Lindsey.
Abstaining from this action: Governor LaWare.

---

[12] See 12 C.F.R. 225.24. See also The Fuji Bank, Limited, *75 Federal Reserve Bulletin 94 (1989);* Bayerische Vereinsbank AG, *73 Federal Reserve Bulletin 155 (1987).*

Order Approving Application to Conduct Certain Data Processing and Other Nonbanking Activities

(1) ATM services that will permit customers to make withdrawals, obtain cash advances, make deposit account inquiries, make transfers between accounts, make deposits, and receive account statements; terminal driving services; and ownership of ATM terminals to the extent permitted by applicable state and federal law; (2) Point of sale services that will permit customers to use their ATM cards to purchase goods and services; (3) Point of banking services that will permit customers to conduct transactions similar to those available at ATM terminals, but with the help of a third party; (4) Scrip services in which a customer receives a voucher (scrip) that is redeemable for cash at a retail register (Company would provide the data processing necessary to debit a customer's account when the customer obtains scrip); (5) Gateway services, by which Company will provide routing of transaction requests between Company's network and other EFT networks for participants in Company's network; (6) Home banking and bill payment services, in which customers could use a telephone, personal computer, or interactive cable television to conduct a variety of banking transactions such as transferring money between accounts, opening and closing accounts, and paying bills, as well as accessing banking, financial and economic databases from the home or office (any hardware provided in connection with this service would be subject to the specific limits in section 225.25(b)(7) of Regulation Y); and (7) Purchasing and reselling or renting electronic equipment used to perform EFT services subject to the specific limits in section 225.25(b)(7) of Regulation Y.

Data Processing Activities Approved in Banc One Corporation, *79 Federal Reserve Bulletin 1158 (1993):*

(8) Electronic benefit transfer services, in which recipients of government benefits such as food stamps and other recurring types of government transfer payments could access their benefits at ATM and POS machines through use of a card issued by a government agency; (9) Providing services in connection with stored value cards, which are capable of having value assigned to them by use of a magnetic strip or computer chip; and (10) Electronic data capture and electronic data interchange services, in which merchants are provided with information relating to inventory and the buying patterns of customers.

Activities Incidental to Data Processing Activities:

(11) Group purchasing, in which Company will purchase EFT-related supplies, such as signage, statement stuffers, and terminals, for the benefit of the

financial institution participants in Company's network; (12) Incidental terminal driving services, such as hardware maintenance and maintaining the cash stock in ATM terminals; and (13) Card production and issuance, including ordering and embossing cards, establishing cardholder records, and assigning personal identification numbers.

New Data Processing and Related Activities:

(14) Providing data processing and related services in connection with dispensing travelers checks and postage stamps from ATM terminals. Other Activities: (15) Check verification services for retailers pursuant to section 225.25(b)(22) of Regulation Y (12 C.F.R. 225.25(b)(22)).

APPENDIX D4

State Street Boston Corp./First National Bank of Boston, 81 Fed. Res. Bull. 1049 (1995)

81 Federal Reserve Bulletin 1049

November, 1995

Orders Issued Under Section 4 of the Bank Holding Company Act

State Street Boston Corporation Boston, Massachusetts

Order Approving Notice to Engage in Nonbanking Activities

State Street Boston Corporation, Boston, Massachusetts ("State Street"), a bank holding company within the meaning of the Bank Holding Company Act ("BHC Act"), has given notice pursuant to section 4(c)(8) of the BHC Act (*12 U.S.C.* § *1843*(c)(8)) and section 225.23 of the Board's Regulation Y (12 C.F.R. 225.23) to acquire, through its existing joint venture subsidiary, Boston Financial Data Services, Inc., Quincy, Massachusetts ("BFDS"), a controlling interest in Banc-Boston State Street Investor Services, L.P., Canton, Massachusetts ("Partnership"), a de novo joint venture with The First National Bank of Boston, N.A., Boston, Massachusetts ("FNBB"),[1] and thereby engage under the Board's Regulation Y in trust-related services pursuant to section 225.25(b)(3), in data processing activities in connection with these services, and in certain other data processing activities pursuant to section 225.25(b)(7) and in accordance with section 225.123(e).

Notice of this proposal, affording interested persons an opportunity to submit comments, has been published *(59 Federal Register 47,176 and 43,800 (1995))*. The time for filing comments has expired, and the Board has considered

---

[1] BFDS is equally owned by State Street and DST Systems, Inc., a nonbanking organization. BFDS and FNBB each would own a 49.5 percent limited partnership interest in Partnership, and two wholly owned subsidiaries of BFDS and FNBB would own a 0.5 percent general partnership interest in Partnership.

the notice and all comments received in light of the factors set forth in section 4(c)(8) of the BHC Act.

State Street, with total consolidated assets of approximately $25.6 billion,[2] operates one banking subsidiary, State Street Bank and Trust Company, Boston, Massachusetts ("SSBTC"). Through 32 offices worldwide, State Street also provides a broad range of financial asset services, such as corporate trusteeship, domestic and global custody arrangements, and portfolio accounting.

Proposed Trust-Related Services

Partnership proposes to act as agent or administrator in providing certain shareholder services to corporations and other securities issuers, including limited partnerships, closed-end investment companies, and issuers of American Depository Receipts.[3] In these capacities, Partnership would provide stock option processing, record-keeping and account maintenance, restricted securities processing and recordkeeping, stock watch services, dividend reinvestment and employee stock purchase plan administration, annual meeting services, and reorganization services.[4] Partnership also would provide investor communication services in its capacity as agent or administrator for a securities issuer or a stock purchase or option plan, which would include responding to oral or written inquiries by current or potential shareholders.[5] In addition, Partnership proposes to provide processing services for government allotment programs in which participating

[2] Asset data are as of June 30, 1995.

[3] For example, in providing shareholder services to corporations and securities issuers, Partnership would act as registrar, transfer agent, paying agent, dividend disbursing agent, employee stock purchase plan agent or administrator, stock option administrator, rights agent, tender agent, reorganization agent, and proxy agent or administrator. Partnership also might act as sub-agent or sub-administrator for another organization serving in any such role. When acting as sub-agent or sub-administrator, Partnership would provide only those shareholder services that Partnership may provide directly. Partnership would not provide shareholder services to open-end investment companies ("mutual funds") or unit investment trusts.

[4] Annual meeting services would include the printing, mailing, and processing of proxy cards and related materials for annual or special meetings of shareholders, and serving as inspector of elections at shareholder meetings. In providing reorganization services, Partnership would effect share exchanges in mergers and acquisitions, remit payments to shareholders in corporate reorganizations, and issue shares in subscription offerings.

[5] For example, in its capacity as transfer agent or dividend reinvestment plan agent, Partnership might distribute annual reports, proxies, dividend reinvestment statements and other similar information to persons who request such information. Partnership also might distribute such information in a scheduled or general mailing at the request of the securities issuer or plan. Partnership would not provide investment advice, marketing and advertisement services, or brokerage services to a securities issuer or plan for which Partnership acted as agent or administrator.

government employees have a designated portion of their paychecks withheld by their employer and invested in employee-selected investment vehicles.[6]

Under section 225.25(b)(3) of Regulation Y, a bank holding company may perform those functions or activities that may be performed by a trust company (including activities of a fiduciary, agency, or custodial nature) in the manner authorized by federal or state law, as long as the institution does not make loans or investments or accept deposits.[7] The Board previously has determined that the provision of corporate agency services and acting as trustee, paying agent, stock transfer agent, dividend disbursing agent and general transfer agent are functions or activities that may be performed by bank holding companies pursuant to and subject to the limitations contained in, section 225.23(b)(3) of Regulation Y.[8]

The record also indicates that annual meeting services, reorganization services, and proxy solicitation services are among the activities that a trust company providing full-service, general transfer agency functions may provide to securities issuers in connection with the trust company's traditional transfer agency functions. The Board notes that SSBTC, a Massachusetts-chartered bank and trust company, and FNBB, a national bank authorized to exercise fiduciary powers, currently provide shareholder services to securities issuers in connection with their agency and fiduciary functions, including annual meeting services reorganization services and stock watch services.

Moreover, trust companies that serve as transfer or paying agent for a securities issuer, or agent or administrator for a dividend, purchase, or investment plan, generally provide investor communication services regarding the securities or plan for which the trust company acts in an agency capacity. In providing these investor communication services, trust companies essentially perform a ministerial role on behalf of the securities issuer or plan, such as, for example, answering inquiries regarding a securities transaction or the terms of a plan. In addition, trust companies currently provide processing services in connection with government allotment programs and provide processing and administrative

---

[6] Funds would be deposited in savings accounts opened by Partnership in the name of the participating employee and invested in the vehicle selected by the employee. Partnership would not act as government allotment agent for payroll deduction programs that offered as investment vehicles mutual funds that were advised by, or primarily sold through, State Street, FNBB, or any of their affiliates, without prior approval of the Board.

[7] Section 225.25(b)(3) also provides certain exceptions from the general limitation on deposit-taking, investment and lending activities by a trust company. State Street has represented that Partnership will comply with the limitations contained in section 225.25(b)(3). In addition, Partnership proposes to establish a limited-purpose, federally chartered trust company that would perform transfer agency services on behalf of Partnership. This trust company subsidiary would be wholly owned by Partnership, would not be a "bank" within the meaning of section 2 of the BHC Act, and would be authorized to engage in only those activities in which Partnership may engage directly.

[8] See State Street Boston Corporation, *81 Federal Reserve Bulletin 297 (1995);* Bancorp Hawaii. Inc., *71 Federal Reserve Bulletin 168 (1985).*

services to similar types of employee benefit and profit sharing plans.[9] The Board also notes that FNBB has received approval to engage in these activities through Partnership from the Office of the Comptroller of the Currency ("OCC"), its primary federal supervisor.[10]

Based on these and other facts of record, the Board concludes that the proposed services are functions or activities that may be performed by a trust company in the manner authorized by federal or state law, and, therefore, the provision of these services as proposed is permissible under section 225.25(b)(3) of the Board's Regulation Y.

Proposed Data Processing Activities

Partnership would engage in data processing activities in connection with providing the proposed trust-related services.[11] Partnership also proposes to engage in data processing activities independently for customers not purchasing the proposed trust-related services. For example, Partnership proposes to optically scan and convert to an electronic database the customer signature cards or other banking-related data of financial institutions. In addition, Partnership proposes to provide claims processing and disbursement services in connection with bankruptcy and class action judgments or settlements.

The Board has concluded that the data processing activities that Partnership proposes to conduct in connection with providing trust-related services are incidental to providing those services.[12] In addition, the proposed optical scanning and data base preparation services for financial institutions would involve the processing of financial, banking, or economic data within the meaning of Regulation Y.[13]

In conducting data processing activities in a bankruptcy proceeding or class action lawsuit, Partnership would be retained to provide accounting, recordkeeping, and remittance services in connection with the distribution of a judgment or settlement proceeds to the bankrupt's creditors or class action plaintiffs.[14] No

---

[9] See, e.g., Bancorp Hawaii, Inc., *71 Federal Reserve Bulletin 168 (1985)* (recordkeeping agent and administrator for qualified employee benefit pension and profit sharing plans).

[10] See Letter from Ralph E. Sharpe, Deputy Comptroller, OCC, to Robert M. Klivans, FNBB, September 15, 1995.

[11] For example, Partnership would process proxies from shareholders, create and update shareholder data bases, maintain accounts for dividend reinvestment and other stock purchase plans, process changes of address, and scan shareholder correspondence in connection with providing the proposed shareholder services.

[12] See 12 C.F.R. 225.21(a)(2).

[13] See 12 C.F.R. 225.25(b)(7); BNCCORP, *81 Federal Reserve Bulletin 295 (1995).*

[14] For example, Partnership would calculate the amount to be remitted from a judgment or settlement to each creditor or class action plaintiff based on data provided by a third party, provide an accounting of such payments to the court or defendant, and remit payments to creditors or plaintiffs entitled to such distributions. Partnership would not make a determination as to whether a creditor or plaintiff was entitled to participate in any judgment or settlement.

services would be provided by Partnership until after a final judgment was rendered, or a final settlement of the action was proposed for ratification by the creditors or class action plaintiffs and a distribution of the settlement proceeds was expected by the court or defendant. These activities are functionally equivalent to the types of accounts receivables processing and remittance services that the Board previously has determined are permissible for bank holding companies to provide to nonfinancial customers.[15] State Street has committed that the Partnership will conduct its data processing and transmission activities in accordance with the requirements set forth in Regulation Y, including the limitation on the nature of the data to be processed or furnished.[16] Based on these and other facts of record, the Board concludes that the proposed claims processing activities involve the processing of financial, banking, or economic data consistent with the requirements of section 225.25(b)(7) of Regulation Y.[17]

In order to approve this notice, the Board also must find that the performance of the proposed activities by Partnership "can reasonably be expected to produce benefits to the public . . . that outweigh possible adverse effects, such as undue concentration of resources, decreased or unfair competition, conflicts of interests, or unsound banking practices." *12 U.S.C.* § *1843*(c)(8). The Board believes that

---

[15] See BNCCORP, *81 Federal Reserve Bulletin 295 (1995).* In some instances, Partnership may process data that are not financial but nevertheless are directly related to the payment of settlement proceeds. For example, Partnership would process and transmit data to creditors and plaintiffs for the purpose of obtaining their consent to a proposed settlement. The Board previously has recognized that processing non-financial data may be required in order to perform permissible data processing activities. See Banc One Corporation, *80 Federal Reserve Bulletin 139 (1994)* (permitting the transmission of limited medical data necessary to operate an electronic medical payments network). Partnership has stated that the non-financial data it proposes to transmit to creditors or plaintiffs would include only the information required to obtain approval of the proposed settlement, and that Partnership would not otherwise transmit non-financial data in connection with these activities. For the foregoing reasons, the Board believes that processing and transmission by Partnership of data necessary to obtain the ratification of a bankruptcy or class action settlement are permissible.

[16] See 12 C.F.R. 225.25(b)(7). Regulation Y also requires that data processing services be provided pursuant to a written agreement and places certain limitations on the facilities and hardware that may be provided with the data processing services. In particular, the facilities must be designed, marketed, and operated for the processing and transmission of financial, banking, or economic data; hardware must be provided only in conjunction with permissible software; and general purpose hardware must not constitute more than 30 percent of the cost of any packaged offering. See id.

[17] Partnership also proposes to use its excess data processing capacity to process data that are not financial, banking, or economic in nature. Partnership has made several commitments to ensure that these activities would be conducted in accordance with the Board's policy statement regarding the provision of excess data processing capacity. See 12 C.F.R. 225.123(e). State Street has committed that revenues from processing data that are not financial, banking, or economic in nature, or that is not incidental to the provision of Partnership's trust-related services, will not exceed 5 percent of Partnership's total revenues from providing permissible data processing and trust-related services. State Street also has committed that Partnership will process non-financial customer data (such as customer responses to a new product survey) only as an accommodation to Partnership's shareholder services clients, and that Partnership will not separately market these data processing services.

the performance of the proposed activities by Partnership can reasonably be expected to produce benefits to the public such as increased efficiency and greater convenience. State Street also has made certain commitments previously relied on by the Board to address potentially adverse competitive and other effects that may be presented by joint venture proposals. Based on these and other commitments, and all the facts of record, the Board finds that the public benefits of Partnership's proposed activities outweigh any adverse effects, and, therefore, that the activities are a proper incident to banking for purposes of section 4(c)(8) of the BHC Act.

Based on the foregoing and all the facts of record, including State Street's commitments and representations, and subject to all the terms and conditions set forth in this order, the Board has determined that the notice should be, and hereby is, approved. The Board's determination is subject to all the conditions set forth in Regulation Y, including those in sections 225.7 and 225.23(b)(3) and (b)(7) of Regulation Y (12 C.F.R. 225.7 and 225.25(b)(3) and (b)(7)), and to the Board's authority to require modification or termination of the activities of a bank holding company or any of its subsidiaries as the Board finds necessary to assure compliance with, and to prevent evasion of, the provisions of the BHC Act and the Board's regulations and orders issued thereunder. The Board's decision is specifically conditioned on State Street's compliance with the commitments and representations made in connection with this notice, including the commitments and conditions discussed in this order. The commitments, representations, and conditions relied on in reaching this decision shall be deemed to be conditions imposed in writing by the Board in connection with its findings and decision and may be enforced in proceedings under applicable law.

This transaction shall not be consummated later than three months after the effective date of this order, unless such period is extended for good cause by the Board or by the Federal Reserve Bank of Boston, acting pursuant to delegated authority.

By order of the Board of Governors, effective September 25, 1995.

WILLIAM W. WILES
Secretary of the Board

VOTE:

Voting for this action: Chairman Greenspan, Vice Chairman Blinder, and Governors Kelley, Lindsey, Phillips, and Yellen.

Appendix D5

Norwest Corp., 81 Fed. Res. Bull. 1130 (1995)

81 Federal Reserve Bulletin 1130

December, 1995

Orders Issued Under Sections 4 of the Bank Holding Company Act

Norwest Corporation, Minneapolis, Minnesota

Order Approving a Notice to Engage in the Activity of Transmitting Money within the United States

Norwest Corporation, Minneapolis, Minnesota ("Norwest"), a bank holding company within the meaning of the Bank Holding Company Act ("BHC Act"), and its subsidiary, Norwest Financial Services, Inc., Des Moines, Iowa ("NFS"), have filed notice under section 4(c)(8) of the BHC Act (12U.S.C. § 1843(c)(8)) and section 225.23 of the Board's Regulation Y (12 C.F.R. 225.23) to engage de novo through Orlandi Valuta, Los Angeles, California, and Orlandi Valuta Nacional, Boulder City, Nevada (collectively, "Companies"), in the activity of transmitting money for customers to third parties within the United States and its territories ("domestic money transmission services").[1] The proposed activity would be conducted at first through a network of approximately 1,200 "outside representative offices" located in California, Florida, Illinois, and Texas that are under contract with Companies to provide money transmission services.[2] Norwest proposes to engage in the proposed activity nationwide.

Notice of the proposal, affording interested persons an opportunity to submit comments, has been published *(60 Federal Register 46,281 (1995))*. The time for filing comments has expired, and the Board has considered the notice and

---

[1] The Board previously approved Norwest's acquisition of Orlandi to engage in the activity of transmitting funds to third parties in Mexico by using an unaffiliated foreign bank to make the cash payments. Norwest Corporation, *81 Federal Reserve Bulletin 974 (1995)* ("Norwest Order").

[2] Outside representative offices currently include grocery stores, travel agencies, pharmacies, and insurance agencies, and would be expanded to include Norwest's consumer finance offices.

all comments received in light of the factors set forth in section 4(c)(8) of the BHC Act.

Norwest, with total consolidated assets of approximately $61.8 billion, controls bank subsidiaries in 15 states.[3] Norwest also engages directly and through subsidiaries in a broad range of permissible nonbanking activities. Companies are corporations that currently engage in the business of money transmission to Mexico through representatives in California, Florida, Illinois, and Texas.

Domestic money transmission services would be provided in the following manner. A customer would contact Companies directly by means of a dedicated telephone located in the outside representative office to request Companies to transmit funds to a third party for a fee. The outside representative would collect cash and a fee from the customer, issue a receipt, and deposit funds in an account maintained by the outside representative solely for the purpose of receiving funds in trust to be transmitted to a third party. The outside representative may maintain this account at any bank, including a Norwest subsidiary bank, but would have no agreement with any bank to accept deposits on its behalf. Neither the outside representatives nor Companies would be FDIC-insured institutions.

Companies would collect funds deposited in an outside representative's account on a daily basis through an ACH or similar transaction and deposit an amount equal to the amount to be transmitted into an account maintained by Companies at a bank, which may include a Norwest subsidiary bank, located near the third party receiving the funds. The third party would be notified that money is available at a local disbursement site, which could include a Norwest bank subsidiary or consumer finance office, or an unaffiliated check cashing, finance, or other type of office. Funds would be made available to the third party by check drawn on Companies' account almost immediately after the transmission order is placed by the customer.[4]

A customer may not transmit funds to any bank account maintained by the customer or any third party. Thus, Norwest would not use this service to collect deposits for customers of Norwest's subsidiary banks or any other bank.

There is no agreement between a customer and a bank to accept money in an account for use by the bank in connection with the proposed domestic money transmission services. Companies and their outside representative would accept money from a customer for the sole purpose of transmitting funds to a third party. A customer would not give funds to Companies with the expectation that Companies would permit the customer to reclaim the funds on demand or after

[3] Asset data are as of March 31, 1995.

[4] Domestic money transmission services do not involve lending money because only funds provided by the customer would be transmitted to a third party. Moreover, the proposal does not involve the paying of checks because, although the third party receives money by means of a check drawn on an account maintained by Companies, the receipt of funds in check form is not the payment of a check. *Independent Bankers Ass'n of America v. Smith, 534 F.2d 921,943,5 (D.C. Cir. 1976).*

a period of time. Moreover, Companies would not maintain balances or pay interest on the money they receive, and would only hold funds long enough to transmit them to the designated third party.[5]

The Board previously has determined that money transmission abroad is closely related to banking.[6] The Office of the Comptroller of the Currency ("OCC") also has concluded that it is permissible for a national bank to accept money from nonbank affiliates for the purpose of transmitting the funds to a foreign country, and that a nonbank affiliate that participates with the national bank in transmitting money abroad would not become a branch of the bank.[7] Based on all the facts of record, and for the reasons discussed in this order and the Board's previous orders, the Board concludes that domestic money transmission services are closely related to banking, and would not cause Norwest or its banks to be engaged in illegal branching activities under federal law.

In determining whether an activity is a proper incident to banking, the Board must consider whether the activity "can reasonably be expected to produce benefits to the public, such as greater convenience, increased competition, or gains in efficiency, that outweigh possible adverse effects, such as undue concentration of resources, decreased or unfair competition, conflicts of interests, or unsound banking practices."[8] In weighing foreign money transmission services under the public benefits test, the Board relied on the fact that these companies are subject to licensing and examination by state authorities.[9] Companies have

---

[5] Many states permit companies that are not chartered as banks to transmit money without deeming this activity to involve the taking of deposits. Norwest must conduct the proposed activities in compliance with licensing and other requirements of relevant state law. Norwest operates several state chartered banks in Colorado, South Dakota, and Texas. The state chartered banks are subject to state law branching restrictions. The record in this case indicates that the proposed activities would not constitute branch banking under the laws of Colorado, South Dakota, and Texas. Colorado has established procedures for licensing money transmitters, and does not consider the proposed activities to constitute branch banking. Companies are licensed to conduct domestic money transmission services in Illinois and Texas and have applied for a license in Florida. California does not require a license to transmit money to locations within the United States. A "payments instruments" license, however, is required to issue checks at disbursements sites in California. Furthermore, although South Dakota has not established formal licensing requirements for money transmitters, the Office of the Director of Banking has indicated that the proposed activities would not constitute banking under South Dakota law. See S.D. Codified Laws Ann. § 51A-7-1 (1990).

[6] Norwest Corporation, supra; Philippine Commercial International Bank, *77 Federal Reserve Bulletin 270 (1991);* Bergen Bank A/S, *76 Federal Reserve Bulletin 457 (1990).*

[7] See Letter from Peter Liebesman, Assistant Director, Legal Advisory Services Division, May 15, 1990 (unpublished). Most of Norwest's banks are national banks, and the courts have determined that whether an entity would be a "branch" for purposes of the National Bank Act is a matter of federal law. First National Bank in *Plant City v. Dickinson, 396 U.S. 122 (1969).* The OCC has reasoned that non-bank offices that transmit funds through a national bank to a third party do not constitute "branches" under federal law.

[8] *12 U.S.C.* § *1843*(c)(8).

[9] This order is specifically conditioned on Norwest obtaining all necessary state licenses.

committed to comply with all applicable reporting requirements, including reporting all transactions over $10,000 to the Internal Revenue Service. Norwest also has committed to apply the internal controls currently in place at NFS to assure compliance with the Bank Secrecy Act.[10]

The record indicates that Norwest's de novo entry into this market can reasonably be expected to result in public benefits, including increased competition, greater convenience for customers, and gains in efficiencies in the operation of Companies and Norwest. In addition, there is no evidence in the record to indicate that the proposed activities would lead to any undue concentration of resources, unsound banking practices, or other adverse effects.

For these reasons, the Board believes that Norwest's proposal to engage in domestic money transmission, as described above, is not likely to result in significantly adverse effects that would outweigh the public benefits of Norwest's proposal. The financial and managerial resources of Norwest and NFS also are consistent with approval.

Based on the foregoing and all the facts of record, the Board has determined to, and hereby does, approve the notice. The Board's decision is specifically conditioned on Norwest's complying with all the commitments made in connection with this notice, and obtaining all necessary approvals from state regulators. The Board's determination also is subject to all the terms and conditions set forth in Regulation Y, including those in sections 225.7 and 225.23(b) of Regulation Y, and to the Board's authority to require such modification or termination of the activities of a bank holding company or any of its subsidiaries as the Board finds necessary to ensure compliance with, and to prevent evasion of, the provisions of the BHC Act and the Board's regulations and orders issued thereunder. For purposes of this transaction, these commitments and conditions shall be deemed to be conditions imposed in writing by the Board in connection with its findings and decision, and, as such, may be enforced in proceedings under applicable law.[11]

These activities shall not be commenced later than three months after the effective date of this order, unless such period is extended for good cause by the Board or by the Federal Reserve Bank of Minneapolis, pursuant to delegated authority.

---

[10] These procedures include a weekly review of all transactions over $10,000. In addition, Companies will require customer identification, including the customer's current address and occupation, for all transmissions above $3,000. Companies also will run a computer match of all remitters and recipients by name and social security number so that reporting requirements cannot be evaded by means of a series of transactions. At this time, Orlandi does not contemplate engaging in transactions over $9,000.

[11] This order is conditioned on Norwest consulting with the Federal Reserve System before commencing domestic money transmission services in any state which does not require examination and licensure to give the System the opportunity to consider whether a separate application should be submitted for Board review.

By order of the Board of Governors, effective October 17, 1995.

WILLIAM W. WILES
Secretary of the Board

VOTE:

Voting for this action: Chairman Greenspan, Vice Chairman Blinder, and Governors Kelley, Lindsey, Phillips, and Yellen.

APPENDIX D6

First National of Nebraska, Inc., 82 Fed. Res. Bull. 82 (1995)

82 Federal Reserve Bulletin 82

January, 1996

Orders Issued Under Section 4 of the Bank Holding Company Act

First National of Nebraska, Inc., Omaha, Nebraska

Order Approving Notice to Provide Computer Network Advice and Assistance to Insured Depository Institutions

First National of Nebraska, Inc., Omaha, Nebraska ("Applicant") a bank holding company within the meaning of the Bank Holding Company Act ("BHC Act"), has given notice under section 4(c)(8) of the BHC Act (*12 U.S.C.* § *1843*(c)(8)) and section 225.23(a) of the Board's Regulation Y (12 C.F.R. 225.23(a)) to engage de novo through its wholly owned subsidiary, First Technology Solutions, Inc., Omaha, Nebraska ("Company"), in providing certain data processing and data transmission services to insured depository institutions, such as banks and savings associations, nationwide, pursuant to section 225.25(b)(7) of Regulation (12 C.F.R. 225.25(b)(7)). In particular, Company would provide advice and assistance to unaffiliated insured depository institutions in the design, selection, acquisition, installation, and operation of computer networks as described in the Appendix.[1]

Notice of this proposal, affording interested persons an opportunity to submit comments, has been published *(60 Federal Register 54 503 (1995))*. The time for filing comments has expired, and the Board has considered the notice

[1] Company also proposes to provide this advice and assistance as an incidental activity, to affliates an insured depository institution if these services also are provided to the related insured depository institution, if the affiliates' use of the computer network constitutes a relatively small portion of the computer network's operations, and if it is not feasible to provide these services to the insured depository institution separately.

and all comments received in light of the factors set forth in section 4(c)(8) of the BHC Act.

Applicant, with approximately $5.7 billion in consolidaled assets, operates ten subsidiary banks in Nebraska, South Dakota, Kansas, and Colorado, and engages through its subsidiaries in a variety (if nonbanking activities.[2] Applicant is the largest commercial banking organization in Nebraska, controlling approximately $3.2 billion of deposits in the state.[3] Company hits received approval to engage in the development of software to process banking, financial, or economic data for insured depository institutions and other clients, pursuant to section 225.25(b)(7) of Regulation Y.

Section 4(c)(8) of the BHC Act provides that a bank holding company may, with Board approval, engage in any activity that the Board determines to be "so closely related to banking or managing or controlling banks as to be a proper incident thereto."[4] The Board previously has determined by regulation that certain data processing and transmission activities are closely related to banking and permissible for bank holding companies under section 4(c)(8) of the BHC Act. Regulation Y permits bank holding companies to provide data processing and data transmission services, facilities, data bases, or access to such services, facilities, or data bases by any technological means, if the data to be processed or furnished are "financial, banking, or economic" in nature.[5] Applicant would provide advice and assistance to support data processing and transmission activities of insured depository institutions.[6] Because of the specialized operations of insured depository institutions, these activities generally would involve data

[2] Asset data are as of June 30, 1995.

[3] Deposit data are as of June 30, 1994.

[4] *12 U.S.C.* § *1843*(c)(8).

[5] See 12 C.F.R. 225.25(b)(7). Regulation Y also requires that the services be provided pursuant to a written agreement and places certain limitations on the facilities and hardware provided with the data processing services. In particular, the facilities must be designed, marketed, and operated for the processing and transmission of financial, banking, or economic data; hardware must be provided only in conjunction with permissible software: and general purpose hardware must not constitute more than 30 percent of the cost of any packaged offering. Id. Applicant has committed to the Board that Company will comply with these limitations in providing services under this proposal. Company would maintain a small inventory of computer hardware that it would make available to its clients as "loaners" to replace defective computer network hardware on a temporary basis. The Board has determined that a bank holding company or its subsidiary may engage in any incidental activities that are necessary to carry on an approved nonbanking activity. The Board finds that providing computer hardware in this context would be incidental to Company's primary proposal to provide computer network advice and assistance, and, therefore, is permissible under section 4 of the BHC Act and Regulation Y. See 12 C.F.R. 225.21(a)(2); *National Courier Association v. Board of Governors, 516 F.2d 1229, 1239-41 (D.C. Cir. 1975).*

[6] Company's services would not include providing management advice or assistance to any unaffiliated insured depository institution, and Company would not make lending or credit decisions for its clients or provide software or services that incorporate the underwriting or credit standards of any affiliated bank.

that is financial, banking, or economic in nature and, therefore, would be permissible activities under section 4(c)(8) of the BHC Act and the Board's regulations.[7] In addition, as a result of Applicant's experience establishing and operating computer networks for its subsidiary banks, Applicant has particular expertise and knowledge of the specialized data processing and transmission requirements of insured depository institutions, which should equip it particularly well to provide the proposed services to unaffiliated insured depository institutions.

In connection with providing these services, Applicant also proposes to provide advice and assistance to insured depository institutions in obtaining and operating facilities for the processing and transmission of nonfinancial data. Specifically, computer networks that are operated within insured depository institutions may be used for processing and transmitting nonfinancial data, such as personnel information, that the institutions use in their internal operations, for nonfinancial functions, such as word processing and electronic mail, that support the primarily financial data processing and transmission needs of these institutions. Applicant contends that, for marketing, customer service, and technological reasons, computer networks that it provides to its clients must perform these related nonfinancial functions in addition to its primary financial functions. Applicant would provide advice and assistance related to the processing and transmission of nonfinancial data, however, only as a relatively small part of a larger package of services to insured depository institutions, and Applicant would not offer these services on a stand-alone basis or to customers other than insured depository institutions.

The Board previously has permitted a bank holding company to process and transmit electronic data for unaffiliated insured depository institutions. In BNCCORP, the Board recognized that, while data processing services for financial institutions relate largely to financial and banking data, financial institutions must also process some nonfinancial information to support their internal operations.[8] Because nonfinancial information represented a relatively small percentage of the data processed as part of the services provided by the bank holding company to unaffiliated insured depository institutions, the Board found that processing nonfinancial data was a necessary part of providing general data processing services to such institutions and, as such, was permissible under section 4 of the BHC Act and Regulation Y as an incidental activity.[9]

In this light, the Board concludes that the advice and assistance related to nonfinancial data processing and data transmission that Applicant proposes to provide are a necessary part of providing advice and assistance to insured depository institutions regarding the data processing requirements of such institutions. Accordingly, these aspects of Company's proposal are incidental to its primary

[7] See BNCCORP, Inc., *81 Federal Reserve Bulletin 295, 296 (1995)* ("BNCCORP").

[8] Id.

[9] Id.

activities, and, therefore, are permissible under section 4 of the BHC Act and Regulation Y.[10]

In order to approve this proposal, the Board also must determine that the proposed activity is a proper incident to banking that "can reasonably be expected to produce benefits to the public, such as greater convenience, increased competition, or gains in efficiency, that outweigh possible adverse effects, such as undue concentration of resources, decreased or unfair competition, conflicts of interests, or unsound banking practices."[11] The record indicates that Company's de novo entry into this market would enhance competition and provide greater services and convenience to insured depository institutions. There is no evidence in the record to indicate that the proposed activity would lead to any undue concentration of resources, conflicts of interests, unsound banking practices, or other adverse effects,[12] and financial and managerial considerations are consistent with approval.[13] Accordingly, the Board has determined that the balance of the public interest factors it is required to consider under the proper incident to banking standard of section 4(c)(8) of the BHC Act is favorable and consistent with approval of this notice.

Based on all the facts of record, the Board has determined that the notice should be, and hereby is, approved. The Board's approval is specifically conditioned on compliance with the commitments made in connection with this notice and with the conditions referred to in this order. The Board's determination also is subject to all the conditions set forth in Regulation Y, including those in sections 225.7 and 225.23(g) of Regulation Y, and to the Board's authority to require such modification or termination of the activities of a bank holding company or any of its subsidiaries as the Board finds necessary to ensure compliance with, and to prevent evasion of, the provisions of the BHC Act and the Board's regulations and orders issued thereunder. For purposes of this action, these conditions and commitments are deemed to be conditions imposed in writing by the Board in connection with its findings and decision, and, as such, may be enforced in proceedings under applicable law.

This transaction shall not be consummated later than three months after the effective date of this order, unless such period is extended for good cause

---

[10] See 12 C.F.R. 225.21(a)(2).

[11] *12 U.S.C.* § *1843*(c)(8).

[12] Applicant has committed that Company will not disclose any confidential information it may obtain concerning its clients and its clients' customers to Applicant or its affiliates without the client's express consent, or to any other person without the client's express consent, or as necessary to fulfill its contractual obligations to the client. Company also is prohibited by the Board's regulations from tying the provision of its services to an extension of credit or the sale or lease of any other product of service of its bank affiliates. See 12 C.F.R. 225.7.

[13] See 12 C.F.R. 225.24. See also The Fuji Bank, Limited, *75 Federal Reserve Bulletin 94 (1989);* Bayerische Vereinsbank AG, *73 Federal Reserve Bulletin 155 (1987).*

by the Board or by the Federal Reserve Bank of Kansas City, acting pursuant to delegated authority.

By order of the Board of Governors, effective November 27, 1995.

JENNIFER J. JOHNSON
Deputy Secretary of the Board

Appendix

List of Computer Network Services

(1) Evaluating the client's needs in processing banking, financial, or economic data, such as deposit account processing (including account opening, calculating deposits, withdrawals, interest and fees, and generating statements and reports); loan processing (including preparing application forms and disclosures and calculating advances, payments, interest, and fees); item processing; check imaging; lockbox processing; safe deposit box accounting; asset/liability monitoring and management; credit bureau reporting; collecting call report data; geographic activity tracking; application tracking and consumer compliance monitoring; large cash transaction reporting; general ledger accounting; fixed asset accounting; tax accounting and producing customer tax forms; analyzing bank and branch profitability; automated clearing house transactions; wire transfers; and telephone and electronic funds transfers initiated by customers; and determining what hardware and software are available to satisfy these needs;

(2) Recommending combinations of hardware and software that could be assembled to perform the required data processing and transmission functions, such as those described in paragraph (1) above;

(3) Developing a plan for the orderly and timely acquisition and assembly of computer network components by the client, and assisting the client in acquiring these components;[1]

(4) Setting up individual personal computers and other workstations, such as teller stations and personal banker stations, on the client's computer network; connecting these components to the computer network; installing and testing software components of the computer network; and training the client in the use of the computer network;[2] and

(5) Providing telephone support to help the client resolve computer network operating problems; isolating and identifying hardware or software defects in the computer network; and helping the client obtain service for these computer network defects from the appropriate vendor or other maintenance provider.

VOTE:

Voting for this action: Chairman Greenspan, Vice Chairman Blinder, and Governors Kelley, Lindsey, Phillips, and Yellen.

---

[1] Other than a limited amount of software that Company may develop for use in an individual client's computer network, Company's clients would acquire hardware and software directly from third parties. Company would not be a vendor or distributor of any hardware or software or an agent of any third party provider of hardware or software.

[2] Installation services would not include laying local area or wide area telecommunications cables.

Appendix D7

Compagnie Financiere de Paribas, 82 Fed. Res. Bull. 348 (1996)

82 Federal Reserve Bulletin 348

April, 1996

Orders Issued Under Section 4 of the Bank Holding Company Act

Compagnie Financiere de Paribas Paris, France

Order Approving Notice to Provide Mobile Telephone Billing Software

Compagnie Financiere de Paribas, Paris, France ("Paribas"), a bank holding company within the meaning of the Bank Holding Company Act ("BHC Act"), has given notice under section 4(c)(8) of the BHC Act (*12 U.S.C* § *1843*(c)(8)) and section 225.23(a) of the Board's Regulation Y (12 C.F.R. 225.23(a)) to engage de novo through a new United States subsidiary ("Company") in providing certain data processing and transmission services nationwide, under section 225.25(b)(7) of Regulation Y (12 C.F.R. 225.25(b)(7)).[1]

Paribas, through Company, would offer an integrated software program ("CABS") to operators of digital mobile telephone networks ("Operator") to perform billing and account-related services for the Operator's customer accounts. CABS would not be a part of an Operator's network operating and switching system, and it would be operated on dedicated hardware that is separate from the hardware and software that runs the network.

Notice of this proposal, affording interested persons an opportunity to submit comments, has been published *(60 Federal Register 62,092 (1995))*. The time for filing comments has expired, and the Board has considered the notice

---

[1] Paribas owns 50.1 percent and France Telecom, the French national telephone operating company, owns 49.9 percent of Financiere Sema, a French investment company that owns 41.6 percent of the voting shares of Sema Group plc, London, England ("Sema Group"). Sema Group developed the software described in this order and proposes to establish Company as a wholly-owned United States subsidiary to sell the described software in the United States.

and all comments received in light of the factors set forth in section 4(c)(8) of the BHC Act.[2]

Paribas, with $282.5 billion in consolidated assets, is the fifth largest commercial banking organization in France and the 29th largest commercial banking organization in the world, and it engages in a wide range of banking and nonbanking activities outside the United States.[3] Paribas operates branches in New York, New York, and Chicago, Illinois; agencies in Los Angeles, California, and Houston, Texas; and representative offices in San Francisco, California, and Dallas, Texas. Paribas also engages through its subsidiaries in the United States in a broad range of nonbanking activities.

Proposed Activities

CABS calculates an Operator's customer bills based on data provided by the Operator's network operating system after customers' calls are completed (such as the date, time, duration, and destination of the call); additional data provided by the Operator concerning the terms of customers' service contracts (such as subscription fees, applicable discounts, and special charges); and individual account balances. Based on these data, CABS produces the billing statements that the Operator sends to its customers for payment by customers directly to the Operator. CABS also performs general accounting services, such as making summary entries in the Operator's general ledger reflecting payments and changes in accounts receivable and payable, and recording payments automatically and making pre-authorized debits directly from customers' bank or credit card accounts. CABS also reports past due and closed accounts to the Operator. In addition, CABS can submit call data to a network clearing house and receive such data from a clearing house to ensure proper billing and account settlements for multi-network telephone calls.

To facilitate these billing functions, CABS stores basic information (such as name, address, and telephone number) necessary to identify a customer when a new account is opened.[4] CABS also stores information that identifies the services to be provided to the customer and the customer's handset. CABS transmits the latter information, and information about the payment status of each account and instructions for the issuance of personal identification numbers, to the Operator's caller and equipment verification files, for use by the Operator to limit access to the telephone network. The caller and equipment verification files are maintained by the Operator independently of CABS.

---

[2] The Board received one comment from another banking organization supporting this proposal.

[3] Asset data are as of June 30, 1995. Ranking data are as of December 31, 1994.

[4] Company would play no role in soliciting or contacting new or prospective customers. These functions would be handled by the Operator or a third party.

As noted previously, CABS is not part of and does not intervene in the operation of the Operator's network access or switching system.[5] CABS is operated on dedicated hardware that is separate from the hardware and software that runs the mobile telephone network itself.

Closely Related to Banking Analysis

Section 4(c)(8) of the BHC Act provides that a bank holding company may, with Board approval, engage in any activity that the Board determines to be so closely related to banking or managing or controlling banks as to be a proper incident thereto."[6] The Board has determined that certain data processing activities are closely related to banking and, therefore, permissible for bank holding companies under section 4(c)(8) of the BHC Act. Section 225.25(b)(7) of Regulation Y permits bank holding companies to provide data processing and data transmission services, facilities (including software), or data bases, or access thereto, by any technological means, so long as the data to be processed or furnished are "financial, banking, or economic" in nature.[7] Regulation Y also provides that bank holding companies may engage in incidental activities that are necessary to carry on an activity that is closely related to banking.[8]

In 1971, when data processing services were added to Regulation Y's list of activities deemed closely related to banking, the performance of billing services was specifically included in the rule as an example of processing "banking, financial, or related economic data".[9] The Board noted at that time that banks historically had performed certain types of billing services for nonfinancial cus-

---

[5] Data compiled by CABS for billing purposes may be reported by CABS to the Operator for use in identifying atypical usage patterns that indicate fraudulent use. All access determinations, including those based on usage patterns and customer and equipment identification and account data, are made by the Operator.

[6] *12 U.S.C.* § *1843*(c)(8). See *National Courier Association v. Board of Governors of the Federal Reserve System, 516 F. 2d 1229, 1237* (D.C. Cir. 1975) ("National Courier"). In addition, the Board may consider any other basis that may demonstrate that the proposed activity has a reasonable or close connection or relationship to banking or managing or controlling banks. See Board Statement Regarding Regulation Y, *49 Federal Register 806 (1984); Securities Industry Association v. Board of Governors of the Federal Reserve System. 468 U.S. 207, 210-211 n.5 (1984).*

[7] Regulation Y also requires that the services be provided pursuant to a written agreement and places certain limitations on the facilities and hardware provided with the data processing services. In particular, the facilities must be designed, marketed, and operated for the processing and transmission of financial, banking, or economic data: hardware must be provided only in conjunction with permissible software; and general purpose hardware must not constitute more than 30 percent of the cost of any packaged offering. See 12 C.F.R. 225.25(b)(7). Paribas has committed that Company will comply with these requirements and limitations in providing the proposed services.

[8] See 12 C.F.R. 225.21(a)(2); National Courier, 516 F.2d at 1239-41.

[9] Approved data processing activities included "storing and processing other banking, financial, or related economic data, such as performing payroll, accounts receivable or payable, or billing services." *57 Federal Reserve Bulletin 512 (1971).*

tomers,[10] and commenters had suggested that billing services (like the other services specifically mentioned) were integrally related to the "basic money transfer function" of banks.[11]

In 1982, the Board amended its data processing regulation to expand the types of services that could be performed by bank holding companies and the types of data on which data processing could be performed.[12] In particular, the types of permissible data were expanded to include all "financial, banking or economic" information.[13] This change permitted bank holding companies to process all types of economic data and eliminated the requirement that economic data be "related" to other banking or financial data.

In making this change, the Board deleted the reference to specific examples of permissible data processing functions, such as performing payroll, accounts receivable, and billing services. The Board stated, however, that it intended the changes to expand the delineation of permissible data processing services and types of data that could be processed by bank holding companies. On this basis, the Board has continued to approve data processing proposals to provide billing services for nonfinancial customers.[14]

The principal function of CABS is to collect data necessary to prepare and transmit bills for Operators. In light of the foregoing, the Board has determined that the performance of these billing functions—including opening customer accounts, preparing customer account statements, initiating payments by customers and other networks, recording payments and accounts receivable and payable in the Operator's general ledger, and reporting past due and closed accounts—is an activity that is closely related to banking and constitutes the processing and transmission of banking, financial, or economic data within the meaning of Regulation Y and prior Board decisions.

As described above, CABS also would perform certain limited nonfinancial data processing and transmission services in connection with its billing functions. These services are the transmission of customer identification and account information to the Operator's verification files; and the generation of certain reports based on these data that may be used by the Operator to detect possible fraudulent use of the network. The data that CABS processes and transmits to the Operator for access and security purposes consist of data that CABS stores and uses to perform its basic billing function.

---

[10] See Memorandum from Legal Division to Board of Governors (June 7, 1971) at 8.

[11] See Supplemental Statement of the American Bankers Association (April 30, 1971), at 6-7; see also BankAmerica Corporation, *66 Federal Reserve Bulletin 511 (1980).*

[12] See *47 Federal Register 37,368* (August 26, 1982); Memorandum from Legal Division to Board of Governors (August 12, 1982).

[13] The language of the 1982 amendment remains in the current version of Regulation Y. See 12 C.F.R. 225.25(b)(7).

[14] See, e.g., BNCCORP. INC., *81 Federal Reserve Bulletin 295, 297 (1995).*

Paribas has stated that CABS would not perform these functions apart from its billing services, and that these functions would be a relatively small part of its operation.[15] In light of the foregoing, the Board has concluded that the limited role to be played by CABS in an Operator's access and security functions appears to be incidental to the primary billing and account functions that would be provided to the Operator, and therefore permissible under Regulation Y and prior Board decisions.

Other Considerations

In order to approve this proposal, the Board also must determine that the proposed activity is a proper incident to banking, that is, that the proposal "can reasonably be expected to produce benefits to the public, such as greater convenience, increased competition, or gains in efficiency, that outweigh possible adverse effects, such as undue concentration of resources, decreased or unfair competition, conflicts of interests, or unsound banking practices."[16] As part of the Board's evaluation of these factors, the Board considers the financial and managerial resources of the notificant and its subsidiaries and the effect the transaction would have on such resources.[17] The record indicates that Company's de novo entry would enhance competition in the market for the proposed services. In addition, the experience of Sema Group in providing the described services abroad should assist it in making improved billing and account-related services available to Operators. Moreover, there is no evidence in the record to indicate that this proposal would lead to any undue concentration of resources, conflicts of interests, unsound banking practices, or other adverse effects that would outweigh the public benefits of this proposal.[18] Accordingly, the Board has determined that the balance of the public interest factors it is required to consider under the proper incident to banking standard of section 4(c)(8) of the BHC Act is favorable and consistent with approval of this notice.

Based on all the facts of record, the Board has determined that the notice should be, and hereby is, approved. The Board's approval is specifically conditioned on compliance with the commitments made in connection with this notice and with the conditions referred to in this order. The Board's determination also is subject to all the conditions set forth in Regulation Y, including those in

---

[15] Paribas indicates that it is likely that less than 5 percent of the data screens generated by CABS would consist of fraud detection and other network access information.

[16] *12 U.S.C.* § *1843*(c)(8).

[17] See 12 C.F.R. 225.24. See also The Fuji Bank, Limited, *75 Federal Reserve Bulletin 94 (1989)*; Bayerische Vereinsbank AG, *73 Federal Reserve Bulletin 155 (1987)*. The Board notes that Paribas's capital ratios satisfy applicable risk-based standards under the Basle Accord and are considered equivalent to the capital levels that would be required of a U.S. banking organization.

[18] Paribas also has made certain commitments previously relied on by the Board to address potentially adverse competitive and other effects that may be presented by joint venture proposals.

sections 225.7 and 225.23(g) of Regulation Y, and to the Board's authority to require such modification or termination of the activities of a bank holding company or any of its subsidiaries as the Board finds necessary to ensure compliance with, and to prevent evasion of, the provisions of the BHC Act and the Board's regulations and orders issued thereunder. For purposes of this action, these conditions and commitments are deemed to be conditions imposed in writing by the Board in connection with its findings and decision, and, as such, may be enforced in proceedings under applicable law.

This transaction shall not be consummated later than three months after the effective date of this order, unless such period is extended for good cause by the Board or by the Federal Reserve Bank of New York, acting pursuant to delegated authority.

By order of the Board of Governors, effective February 26, 1996.

JENNIFER J. JOHNSON
Deputy Secretary of the Board

VOTE:

Voting for this action: Chairman Greenspan and Governors Kelley, Lindsey, Phillips, and Yellen.

Appendix D8

Banc One Corp./CoreStates Financial Corp./PNC Bank Corp./ KeyCorp/National City Corp., 82 Fed. Res. Bull. 848 (1996)

82 Federal Reserve Bulletin 848

September, 1996

Orders Issued Under Section 4 of the Bank Holding Company Act

Banc One Corporation, Columbus, Ohio
CoreStates Financial Corp, Philadelphia, Pennsylvania
PNC Bank Corp., Pittsburgh, Pennsylvania
KeyCorp, Cleveland, Ohio
National City Corporation, Cleveland, Ohio

Order Approving a Proposal to Engage in Certain Data Processing Activities

Banc One Corporation, Columbus, Ohio; CoreStates Financial Corp, Philadelphia, Pennsylvania; PNC Bank Corp., Pittsburgh, Pennsylvania; KeyCorp, Cleveland, Ohio; and National City Corporation, Cleveland, Ohio (collectively, "Applicants"), bank holding companies within the meaning of the Bank Holding Company Act ("BHC Act"), have requested the Board's approval under section 4(c)(8) of the BHC Act (*12 U.S.C.* § *1843*(c)(8)) and section 225.23(a) of the Board's Regulation Y (12 C.F.R. 225.23(a)) for their joint subsidiary, Electronic Payment Services, Inc., Wilmington, Delaware ("EPS"), to engage in certain data processing activities pursuant to section 225.25(b)(7) of Regulation Y (12 C.F.R. 225.25(b)(7)).

Applicants, through EPS, would provide data processing and related services to banks and other automated teller machine ("ATM") owners ("ATM Deployers") in connection with the distribution through ATMs of tickets to concerts and other events, gift certificates, prepaid telephone cards, and other documents evidencing a prepayment for goods or services.[1]

Notice of the proposal, affording interested persons an opportunity to submit comments, has been published *(61 Federal Register 27,352 (1996))*. The time for filing comments has expired, and the Board has considered the proposal and all comments received in light of the factors set forth in section 4(c)(8) of the BHC Act.

Applicants are large commercial banking organizations headquartered in Ohio and Pennsylvania, and engage directly and through subsidiaries in a broad range of banking and permissible nonbanking activities in the United States.[2] EPS currently provides data processing and transmission services to banks and retail merchants that are members of its branded ATM and point-of-sale ("POS") networks. EPS also is engaged in developing and providing a variety of electronic payment, benefit transfer, and data interchange services.[3]

Proposed Activities

EPS proposes to provide data processing services to ATM Deployers in connection with the distribution through ATMs of tickets, gift certificates, prepaid telephone cards, and other documents evidencing a prepayment for goods or services.[4] EPS would provide the software and telecommunications channels necessary to transmit cardholder requests and card issuer authorizations, and related switching and account reconciliation services.[5]

EPS also would provide switching services and transaction processing to transmit account debiting, transaction authorization, and settlement between the ATM Deployer, or its bank, and the cardholder's bank. In certain cases, some

---

[1] For purposes of this order, ATM Deployers include depository financial institutions, retail merchants, and independent sales organizations that package and sell ATM services to merchants. In addition, a financial institution means a bank, bank holding company, thrift institution, thrift holding company, and subsidiaries of any of these companies.

[2] Asset and deposit information for each of the Applicants is contained in the Appendix.

[3] See Banc One Corporation et al., *79 Federal Reserve Bulletin 1158* (1993).

[4] The tickets contemplated by this proposal would include public transportation tickets and tickets to entertainment events. Gift certificates and prepaid telephone cards would be issued in fixed denominations for a specific merchant or group of merchants, and would evidence prepayment of the purchase price of merchandise or services to be selected by the bearer at some time in the future. ATM Deployers also would sell products that could be offered for sale directly by a financial institution such as mutual fund shares or insurance policies where permitted by applicable law.

[5] Specifically, EPS would provide "terminal driving services" which include:

> (1) Establishing and maintaining an electronic link between an ATM and a telecommunications switch to transmit cardholder requests and card issuer authorizations; and
> (2) Operating the feature and function displays on an ATM screen using computer software to permit an ATM to dispense various products in addition to currency.

of these services may be provided by third-parties, such as national ATM networks or third-party processors.

In a typical transaction, an ATM cardholder would select a particular product from a menu offered at an ATM. Electronic commands transmitted by EPS would verify that the deposit account or line of credit designated by the cardholder holds sufficient funds to make the purchase. After the authorization is received, the ATM then would dispense the product and a receipt in accordance with the Board's Regulation E (Electronic Fund Transfers).[6] Finally, the card-issuing bank would debit an amount equal to the cost of the purchase from the cardholder's designated account and transfer the funds to the account of the merchant or ATM Deployer, as appropriate, using settlement procedures established by the ATM network.

Closely Related to Banking Analysis

Section 4(c)(8) of the BHC Act provides that a bank holding company may, with Board approval, engage in any activity that the Board determines to be "so closely related to banking or managing or controlling banks as to be a proper incident thereto."[7] The Board previously has determined by regulation that processing and transmitting financial, banking, or economic data are activities that are closely related to banking and, therefore, permissible for bank holding companies under section 4(c)(8) of the BHC Act.[8] The Board also has specifically determined that a bank holding company may provide data processing and related services necessary to permit customers to use an ATM card to debit a deposit account or line of credit at an ATM terminal for cash and credit transactions, and for the purchase of travelers checks, money orders, and postage stamps.[9] In

---

[6] 12 C.F.R. 205.

[7] *12 U.S.C. § 1843*(c)(8). See *National Courier Association v. Board of Governors, 516 F.2d 1229, 1237 (D.C. Cir. 1975).* In addition, the Board may consider any other basis that may demonstrate that the proposed activity has a reasonable or close connection or relationship to banking or managing or controlling banks. See Board Statement Regarding Regulation Y, *49 Federal Register 806 (1984); Securities Industry Association v. Board of Governors, 468 U.S. 207, 210-11, n.5 (1984).*

[8] See 12 C.F.R. 225.25(b)(7). Regulation Y also requires that the data processing services be provided pursuant to a written agreement and places certain limitations on the facilities and hardware provided with the data processing services. Specifically, the facilities must be designed, marketed, and operated for the processing and transmission of financial, banking, or economic data; hardware must be provided only in conjunction with permissible software; and general purpose hardware must not constitute more than 30 percent of the cost of any packaged offering. EPS has committed that it will provide the proposed services pursuant to a written agreement and will provide facilities and hardware within the limitations established by Regulation Y.

[9] See The Bank of New York Company, et al., *80 Federal Reserve Bulletin 1107, 1109 (1994).* EPS currently conducts these activities. See Letters dated February 13, 1996, from the Federal Reserve Bank of Cleveland to Phyllis Dietz, Esq., and from the Federal Reserve Bank of Philadelphia to John F. Stefanowicz, CoreStates Financial Corp.

addition, the Board has determined that a bank holding company may provide data processing services that support the use of credit cards by consumers in the direct purchase of goods and services from merchants.[10]

The data processing activity proposed in this case involves providing the same type of data processing support as the Board previously has approved for credit card transactions and other more traditional types of ATM transactions. Based on all the facts of record, the Board has concluded that the activities proposed by EPS in this case are permissible data processing and transmission services encompassed within the Board's data processing regulation and, therefore, the activities are closely related to banking within the meaning of the BHC Act.

Proper Incident to Banking Analysis

In order to approve this proposal, the Board also must determine that the proposed activities are a proper incident to banking; that is, that the proposal "can reasonably be expected to produce benefits to the public, such as greater convenience, increased competition, or gains in efficiency, that outweigh possible adverse effects, such as undue concentration of resources, decreased or unfair competition, conflicts of interests, or unsound banking practices."[11]

As part of its review of these factors, the Board has considered the financial and managerial resources of Applicants and their respective subsidiaries and the effect the proposal would have on such resources.[12] Based on all the facts of record, the Board has concluded that financial and managerial considerations are consistent with approval of this proposal.

The Board expects that the proposed activities would result in benefits to consumers, merchants, and ATM Deployers. The proposed activities would allow consumers to purchase products at additional locations and during non-business hours, and would facilitate convenient payment for such products. The proposed activities also would enhance the ability of merchants to distribute products through new channels and would provide ATM Deployers with additional sources of transaction volume and resulting fee income. In addition, the proposed activities would increase the level of competition among existing providers of these services.

There is no evidence in the record that consummation of this proposal would result in any significantly adverse effects, such as undue concentration of resources, decreased or unfair competition, conflicts of interests, or unsound

---

[10] See Banc One Corporation, 81 Federal Reserve Bulletin 492 (1995); Citicorp, 76 Federal Reserve Bulletin 549 (1990); and Barclays Bank PLC, 71 Federal Reserve Bulletin 113 (1985).

[11] *12 U.S.C.* § *1843*(c)(8).

[12] See 12 C.F.R. 225.24. See also The Fuji Bank, Limited, *75 Federal Reserve Bulletin 94 (1989);* Bayerische Vereinsbank AG, *73 Federal Reserve Bulletin 155 (1987).*

banking practices, that are not outweighed by the public benefits of this proposal. Accordingly, and based on all the facts of record, the Board has concluded that the balance of the public interest factors it is required to consider under the proper incident to banking standard of section 4(c)(8) of the BHC Act is favorable and consistent with approval of this proposal.

Conclusion

Based on the foregoing and all the facts of record, the Board has determined to, and hereby does, approve this proposal subject to all the terms and conditions set forth in this order. The Board's determination also is subject to all the terms and conditions set forth in Regulation Y, including those in sections 225.7 and 225.23(g) (12 C.F.R. 225.7 and 225.23(g)), and to the Board's authority to require such modification or termination of the activities of a bank holding company or any of its subsidiaries as the Board finds necessary to assure compliance with, and to prevent evasion of, the provisions of the BHC Act and the Board's regulations and orders issued thereunder. The Board's decision is specifically conditioned on compliance with all the commitments made in connection with this proposal. These commitments and conditions shall both be deemed to be conditions imposed in writing by the Board in connection with its findings and decision, and, as such, may be enforced in proceedings under applicable law.

This transaction shall not be consummated later than three months after the effective date of this order, unless such period is extended for good cause by the Board or by the Federal Reserve Banks of Cleveland or Philadelphia, acting pursuant to delegated authority.

By order of the Board of Governors, effective July 1, 1996.

JENNIFER J. JOHNSON
Deputy Secretary of the Board

Appendix

Asset and Deposit Data as of December 31, 1995.

Banc One Corporation, with $90.2 billion in total consolidated assets, is the tenth largest commercial banking organization in the United States, controlling $67.4 billion in deposits. Banc One operates subsidiary banks in Ohio, Kentucky, Indiana, Michigan, Illinois, Wisconsin, Texas, Colorado, Arizona, California, Oklahoma, Utah, and West Virginia.

CoreStates Financial Corp, with $29.7 billion in total consolidated assets, is the 31st largest commercial banking organization in the United States, controlling $21.5 billion in deposits. CoreStates operates subsidiary banks in Pennsylvania, New Jersey, and Delaware.

PNC Bank Corp., with $73.5 billion in total consolidated assets, is the 12th largest commercial banking organization in the United States, controlling $21.5 billion in deposits. PNC operates subsidiary banks in Pennsylvania, Ohio, Kentucky, Indiana, New Jersey, Massachusetts, and Delaware.

KeyCorp, with $66.3 billion in total consolidated assets, is the 14th largest commercial banking organization in the United States, controlling $47.3 billion in deposits. KeyCorp operates subsidiary banks in Ohio, Indiana, Michigan, New York, Washington, Maine, Oregon, Idaho, Utah, Colorado, Wyoming, and Alaska.

National City, with $36.2 billion in total consolidated assets, is the 24th largest commercial banking organization in the United States, controlling $25.2 billion in deposits. National City operates subsidiary banks in Ohio, Indiana, and Kentucky.

VOTE:

Voting for this action: Chairman Greenspan, Vice Chair Rivlin, and Governors Kelley, Lindsey, Phillips, Yellen, and Meyer.

Appendix D9

Royal Bank of Canada, et al., 83 Fed. Res. Bull. 135 (1997)

83 Federal Reserve Bulletin 135

February, 1997

Orders Issued Under Section 4 of the Bank Holding Company Act

Royal Bank of Canada, Montreal, Canada
Norwest Corporation, Minneapolis, Minnesota
Stichting Prioriteit ABN AMRO Holding, Stichting Administratiekantoor ABN AMRO Holding, ABN AMRO Holding N.V., ABN AMRO Bank N.V., All of Amsterdam, The Netherlands
ABN AMRO North America, Inc., Chicago, Illinois

Order Approving Notices to Engage in Nonbanking Activities

Royal Bank of Canada, Montreal, Canada, a foreign banking organization that is subject to the Bank Holding Company ("BHC") Act; Norwest Corporation, Minneapolis, Minnesota; Stichting Prioriteit ABN AMRO Holding, Stichting Administratiekantoor ABN AMRO Holding, ABN AMRO Holding N.V., ABN AMRO Bank N.V., and ABN AMRO North America, Inc., bank holding companies within the meaning of the BHC Act, have requested the Board's approval under section 4(c)(8) of the BHC Act (*12 U.S.C.* § *1843*(c)(8)) and section 225.23 of the Board's Regulation Y (12 C.F.R. 225.23) each to acquire more than 5 percent of the voting interests in Integrion Financial Network, LLC, White Plains, New York ("Integrion"), and thereby engage in data processing and data transmission activities pursuant to section 225.25(b)(7) of the Board's Regulation Y (12 C.F.R. 225.25(b)(7)).[1]

[1] Royal Bank of Canada ("RBC"), Norwest Corporation ("Norwest") and Stichting Prioriteit ABN AMRO Holding ("ABN AMRO") and its subsidiaries listed above are hereafter collectively referred to as "Notificants".

Notice of the proposal, affording interested persons an opportunity to submit comments, has been published *(61 Federal Register 54,441 (1996))*. The time for filing comments has expired, and the Board has considered the notice and all comments received in light of the factors set forth in section 4(c)(8) of the BHC Act.

RBC, with total consolidated assets of approximately $131.6 billion,[2] is the largest commercial banking organization in Canada, and operates a branch in New York, New York; agencies in Los Angeles, California, and Miami, Florida; and a representative office in Chicago, Illinois.

Norwest, with total consolidated assets of $77.8 billion,[3] is the 12th largest commercial banking organization in the United States, and controls banks in Minnesota and 14 other states.

ABN AMRO, with total consolidated assets of $339.4 billion, is the largest commercial banking organization in the Netherlands, and controls seven depository institutions in Illinois and one commercial bank in New York. ABN AMRO Bank N.V. also operates branches in Boston, Massachusetts; Chicago, Illinois; New York, New York; Pittsburgh, Pennsylvania; and Seattle, Washington; and agencies in Atlanta, Georgia; Miami, Florida; Houston, Texas; and Los Angeles and San Francisco, California.

Each Notificant also engages in a number of nonbanking activities in the United States.

Proposed Activities

Integrion is a joint venture among Notificants, 12 national banks, one savings and loan holding company,[4] and Gemini Management Corporation, a subsidiary of International Business Machines Corporation ("IBM"). Integrion will design, develop, and operate a data processing and transmission system through which depository institutions and their affiliates would make available home banking and other financial services to their respective customers. Integrion will not itself provide home banking or other financial services. Instead, the data processing and data transmission system ("gateway") Integrion designs and

---

[2] Except as otherwise noted, asset and ranking data are as of December 31, 1995, and use exchange rates then in effect.

[3] Asset and ranking data for Norwest are as of June 30, 1996.

[4] The following national banks would become members of Integrion on consummation of the proposal: Bank of America NT & SA; NationsBank, N.A.; KeyBank, N.A.; Bank One, Columbus, N.A.; Mellon Bank, N.A.; Barnett Bank, N.A.; First Bank N.A.; PNC Bank, N.A.; Michigan National Bank; The First National Bank of Chicago; Comerica Bank-Ann Arbor, N.A.; and Fleet National Bank. Each of these national banks has applied to the Office of the Comptroller of the Currency to invest in Integrion through an operating subsidiary of the bank. Washington Mutual Inc., a savings and loan holding company, also would become a member of Integrion and has provided notice of its intent to invest in Integrion to the Office of Thrift Supervision.

operates will serve as a switch or interface, electronically connecting customers of member depository institutions with the member depository institutions themselves.[5]

Customers would connect to Integrion's gateway, and thus a member depository institution, using a variety of devices, including personal computers ("PCs"), touchtone telephones, or other electronic communication devices.[6] Once a customer is connected to the gateway, Integrion would electronically route and connect the customer to the appropriate member depository institution, using software developed by Integrion that would facilitate communications between the customer's PC (or other device) and the depository institution's hardware and software.[7] In this manner, the Integrion gateway will provide customers with access to the menu of electronic banking and financial services offered by their respective member depository institutions, including remote banking services;[8] bill-payment functions; and access to stock quotations.[9]

The proposed activities appear to be data processing and transmission activities that are permissible for bank holding companies under section 4(c)(8) of the BHC Act and section 225.25(b)(7) of the Board's Regulation Y. The Board previously has determined by regulation that certain data processing and transmission activities are closely related to banking and therefore permissible for bank holding companies under section 4(c)(8) of the BHC Act. Regulation Y permits bank holding companies to provide data processing and transmission

---

[5] Notificants do not currently anticipate that Integrion's facilities would be used by member depository institutions to store customer account data. Notificants do expect that Integrion would store limited amounts of data related to transactions conducted through the gateway, such as information relating to bill payment instructions transmitted to member depository institutions. Integrion is permitted to store and transmit data to the extent permissible under section 225.25(b)(7) of the Board's Regulation Y. 12 C.F.R. 225.25(b)(7).

[6] Customers using a PC may connect to the Integrion gateway through dedicated, private communications networks; through personal financial software programs; or through the Internet.

[7] Integrion has contracted with IBM to provide the telecommunications and data network infrastructure necessary for Integrion to electronically link member depository institutions with their customers. Under this contract, communications between Integrion and member depository institutions will be transmitted through an existing, proprietary IBM telecommunications and data network.

[8] It is expected that the remote banking services offered by a member depository institution would include the ability to gain access to account information, transfer funds between accounts, obtain information on available loan or deposit products, apply for a loan, establish additional accounts, order checks, or communicate electronically with a customer service representative.

[9] The individual banking and financial services that a customer would be able to gain access to through Integrion's gateway would depend on the products offered by the member depository institution. Such products and services would be offered by the member depository institution in its own name, and would be displayed to the customer using the graphics, logo, and service marks chosen and developed by the depository institution. Thus, it would appear to customers connecting to their depository institutions through the Integrion gateway that they are connected directly to the depository institution, and the data processing and transmission services provided by Integrion would be essentially transparent to consumers.

services, facilities, data bases, or access to such services, facilities, or data bases by any technological means, if the data to be processed or furnished are financial, banking, or economic in nature.[10] Regulation Y also provides that bank holding companies may engage in incidental activities that are necessary to carry on an activity that is closely related to banking.[11]

Internet Access

In addition to providing these services, Integrion's gateway will provide customers of member depository institutions with a means of connecting to the Internet, a nonproprietary computer network that contains significant amounts of data that are not financial, banking, or economic in nature.[12] As an accommodation to its member depository institutions and their customers, Integrion proposes to provide an electronic link to an Internet access provider.[13]

The Board previously has permitted bank holding companies providing permissible data processing and transmission services to financial institutions to process and transmit a limited amount of nonfinancial data for such institutions as an incidental activity.[14] Notificants contend that member depository institutions desire to offer Internet access to their customers in order to make their package of banking and financial services more marketable, and to permit the institutions to compete more effectively with nonbank financial service providers. Notificants have indicated that providing Internet access to customers of member depository institutions would constitute a small part of Integrion's overall data processing and transmission activities,[15] and would not require modification of the gateway's

---

[10] See 12 C.F.R. 225.25(b)(7); see also Cardinal Bancshares, Inc., *82 Federal Reserve Bulletin 674 (1996);* and The Royal Bank of Canada, *82 Federal Reserve Bulletin 363 (1996)* (bank holding companies may provide data processing and transmission services to financial institutions for purposes of allowing such institutions to offer electronic banking, bill payment, and stock quotation services). Notificants must provide these financial data processing and transmission services through Integrion in accordance with the limitations set forth in section 225.25(b)(7) of Regulation Y.

[11] See 12 C.F.R. 225.21(a)(2).

[12] Notificants must consult with the Federal Reserve System prior to providing, through Integrion, data processing or transmission services to any non-depository organization, or providing access to non-financial databases other than as described in this order, in order to permit the System to determine whether such activities are permissible under section 4 of the BHC Act and Regulation Y.

[13] Integrion could, for example, provide access to the Internet through an electronic link to IBM's proprietary network, which maintains connections to a wide variety of public and proprietary databases and computer networks, or to other Internet access providers.

[14] See BNCCORP, INC., *81 Federal Reserve Bulletin 295 (1995);* see also First National of Nebraska, Inc., *82 Federal Reserve Bulletin 82 (1996).*

[15] Notificants expect that less than 10 percent of Integrion's revenues would be derived from providing Internet access to customers of member depository institutions. Notificants have committed that Integrion will provide nonfinancial data processing and transmission services in accordance with the limitations in Regulation Y and relevant Board orders.

capabilities or systems. In addition, as noted above, Integrion would provide Internet access only as an accommodation to its member depository institutions, which in turn would offer Internet access to their customers only as part of a broader package of banking or financial services. In light of the foregoing, and based on all the facts of record, the Board has concluded that Integrion's provision of Internet access to customers of its member depository institutions is incidental to its permissible data processing and transmission activities.

Other Considerations

In order to approve this notice, the Board also must find that the performance of the proposed activities by Integrion "can reasonably be expected to produce benefits to the public, such as greater convenience, increased competition, or gains in efficiency, that outweigh possible adverse effects, such as undue concentration of resources, decreased or unfair competition, conflicts of interests, or unsound banking practices."[16] As part of the Board's evaluation of these factors, the Board considers the financial and managerial resources of the notificants and their subsidiaries and the effect the transaction would have on such resources.[17] The Board notes that the capital ratios of Norwest and ABN AMRO North America, Inc. meet applicable risk-based capital standards and that each of the foreign bank Notificants maintains capital equivalent to the capital levels that would be required of a U.S. banking organization. Based on all the facts of record, the Board has concluded that financial and managerial considerations are consistent with approval.

The Board believes that consummation of the proposal would enhance consumer convenience by expanding the availability of remote banking services and by making these services available in new ways. Consummation of the proposal would permit member depository institutions and their affiliates to deliver remote banking services to their customers more efficiently, and would establish a joint venture that pools the resources of a number of banking organizations for the purpose of developing data processing and transmission systems that would facilitate the creation and distribution of additional remote banking products that respond to consumer needs. In addition, the communications gateway operated by Integrion would allow member depository institutions and their affiliates to make existing remote banking services available to consumers through additional means, such as through personal financial software programs, screen phones, and the public Internet. There is no evidence in the record to indicate that consummation of the proposal would result in any significantly adverse effects, such as undue concentration of resources, decreased or unfair competi-

[16] *12 U.S.C.* § *1843*(c)(8).

[17] See 12 C.F.R. 225.24; see also The Fuji Bank, Limited, *75 Federal Reserve Bulletin 94 (1989)*; Bayerische Vereinsbank AG, *73 Federal Reserve Bulletin 155 (1987)*.

tion,[18] conflicts of interests, or unsound banking practices, that are not outweighed by the public benefits of this proposal.[19] On the basis of the foregoing and all the facts of record, the Board has concluded that the public benefits reasonably to be expected from Integrion's proposed activities outweigh any possible adverse effects from the proposal, and, therefore, that the activities are a proper incident to banking under section 4(c)(8) of the BHC Act.

Conclusion

Based on the foregoing and all the facts of record, including the commitments discussed in this order and all other commitments and representations made by Notificants in connection with the notices, and subject to the terms and conditions set forth in this order, the Board has determined that the notices should be; and hereby are, approved. The Board's determination is subject to all the conditions set forth in Regulation Y, including those in sections 225.7 and 225.23(g) of Regulation Y (12 C.F.R. 225.7 and 225.23(g)), and to the Board's authority to require such modification or termination of the activities of a bank holding company or any of its subsidiaries as the Board finds necessary to ensure compliance with, and to prevent evasion of, the provisions of the BHC Act and the Board's regulations and orders issued thereunder. The Board's decision is specifically conditioned on Notificants' compliance with the commitments made in connection with this notice and the conditions discussed in this order. The commitments and conditions relied on in reaching this decision shall be deemed to be conditions imposed in writing by the Board in connection with its findings and decision and, as such, may be enforced in proceedings under applicable law.

---

[18] The Board notes that, pursuant to the terms of Integrion's charter, Notificants and other members of Integrion will remain free to compete with each other and Integrion in the development and marketing of data processing and transmission networks similar to the Integrion gateway, as well as remote banking and other financial services.

[19] In considering the public interest factors in this case, the Board has carefully considered the measures that Integrion and member financial institutions will take to protect the account data and other financial information that will be transmitted through the gateway from electronic interception, interference, or fraud. The Board previously has noted that the nature of the risks associated with providing electronic banking services is not different from those associated with more traditional forms of banking. See Cardinal Bancshares, Inc., *82 Federal Reserve Bulletin 674, 676 (1996).* Among other security measures, Integrion and member depository institutions will use log-in passwords and encryption procedures to attempt to maintain the privacy and integrity of data transmitted. In addition, as part of its operations, Integrion will transmit data to member institutions through a private communications network.

By order of the Board of Governors, effective December 2, 1996.

JENNIFER J. JOHNSON
Deputy Secretary of the Board

VOTE:

Voting for this action: Chairman Greenspan, Vice Chair Rivlin, and Governors Kelley, Lindsey, Phillips, and Meyer. Absent and not voting: Governor Yellen.

Appendix E1
FDIC General Counsel's Opinion No. 8 (Stored Value Cards) (1996)

Federal Register: August 2, 1996 (Volume 61, Number 150)
Notices
Page 40489-40494

FEDERAL DEPOSIT INSURANCE CORPORATION

General Counsel's Opinion No. 8; Stored Value Cards and Other Electronic Payment Systems; Notices

AGENCY: Federal Deposit Insurance Corporation (FDIC or Corporation).

ACTION: Notice of FDIC General Counsel's Opinion No. 8.

SUMMARY: The FDIC has received inquiries on whether and under what circumstances funds underlying stored value cards may be considered deposits under the Federal Deposit Insurance Act. This General Counsel Opinion sets forth the Legal Division's conclusions on this issue.

FOR FURTHER INFORMATION CONTACT:
Marc J. Goldstrom, Counsel, Legal
Division, (202) 898-8807, Federal Deposit Insurance Corporation, 550
17th Street, NW., Washington, DC 20429.

Introduction

Insured depository institutions are increasingly utilizing new technology to offer novel and innovative products to customers. One such product is the stored-value card. A stored value card stores information electronically on a magnetic stripe or computer chip and can be used to purchase goods or services. The balance recorded on the card is debited at a merchant's point of sale terminal when the consumer makes a purchase. Generally, stored value cards contain all the information necessary to identify the card and its value. This has enabled point of sale terminals in most systems to be "offline".[1] In other words, it is unnecessary to contact a depository institution or database for transaction authorization.

Some stored value cards are designed to be used until their value is exhausted and then are disposed. Other more sophisticated stored value cards may be "reloadable". The cards may have multiple uses, such as credit and debit features, in addition to the stored value component. Also, a particular stored value card system may have multiple card issuers and multiple card-accepting merchants. Some cards (or the stored value component of some cards) may be utilized by whomever may be in possession of such card, while others require a personal identification number to use.

Consumers may typically load value[2] onto a card in a number of ways. A customer without a pre-existing depositor relationship with an insured institution may purchase a stored value card from that institution. A deposit account holder may load value onto the card by withdrawing from an account through a teller, via an ATM, or, potentially, via a specially equipped telephone or personal computer. At least one system would allow the consumer to transfer the stored value to another person's card.

Typically, stored value cards are touted as substitutes for cash. Technically, however, they are not cash, and they do not have the finality of cash. Although it may not be apparent to the consumer, a stored value card transaction must typically move through a complex payment system before a payment is completed. Moreover, what is actually stored on stored value cards is information that, through the use of programmed terminals, advises a prospective payee that rights to a sum of money can be transferred to the payee, who in turn can exercise such right and be paid.

In addition to the development of stored value cards, stored value systems are being developed for making payments over computer networks such as the Internet.

---

[1]While most stored value card systems are "offline," we understand that there are "online" stored value card systems (i.e., the primary record of the balance of funds available to the consumer is not maintained on the card itself, but at the depository institution or a central data facility). Such cards are similar to debit cards except that the cardholder specifically designates the amount of money that may be accessed through the card and once so designated, such funds may only be accessed through the card. So far as we are aware, the systems of this type are not currently being utilized by depository institutions. In its proposed amendment to Regulation E, 61 FR 19,696 (May 2, 1996), the Board of Governors of the Federal Reserve System has distinguished between "offline accountable," "offline unaccountable," and "online" stored value systems in determining whether the regulation applies to various types of stored value systems. This opinion does not use these distinctions. This is not intended as a criticism or rejection of the Board's classification system. Rather, it is indicative of the fact that these particular distinctions are not necessarily germane as to whether and under what circumstances the funds underlying a stored value card are "deposits" under the Federal Deposit **Insurance** Act (FDIA).

[2]The use of the phrase "load value onto a card," "electronic value," or any similar terms used in this opinion, is not meant to imply that the information loaded on stored value cards is legal tender or anything similar to legal tender. See 12 U.S.C. 5103. Rather, as discussed in the text below, such information is more in the nature of a right to be paid a sum of money.

In such systems funds may be accessed using a personal computer, and transferred to individuals, merchants, or companies. While this opinion addresses stored value cards, the Legal Division believes that in general the principles discussed herein would apply equally to stored value computer network payment products.

Types of Stored Value Systems[3]

In some systems the funds underlying the stored value card could remain in a customer's account until the value is transferred to a merchant or other third party, who in turn collects the funds from the customer's bank ("Bank Primary—Customer Account Systems").[4] In other systems, as value is downloaded onto a card, funds are withdrawn from a customer's account (or paid directly by the customer) and paid into a reserve or general liability account held at the institution to pay merchants and other payees as they make claims for payments ("Bank Primary—Reserve Systems").

In still other systems, the electronic value is created by a third party and the funds underlying the electronic value are ultimately held by such third party ("Bank Secondary Systems"). In such systems, depository institutions act as intermediaries in collecting funds from customers in exchange for electronic value. In some Bank Secondary Systems, the electronic value is provided to the institution to have available for its customers. As customers exchange funds for electronic value, the funds are held for a short period of time and then forwarded to the third party ("Bank Secondary—Advance Systems"). In other systems of this nature, the depository institution will exchange its own funds for electronic value from the third party and in turn exchange electronic value for funds with its customers ("Bank Secondary—Pre-Acquisition Systems").

In Bank Secondary Systems, the depository institution may have a contingent liability to redeem the electronic value from consumers and merchants. As such electronic value is redeemed, the institution may in turn exchange the electronic value for funds with the third party.

Primary Legal Issue

From the FDIC's perspective, the primary legal issue raised by the development of stored value card systems is whether and to what extent the funds or

---

[3]The classification of stored value systems described below is not intended to encompass all of the possible ways that stored value card systems may be structured. Rather, this classification system represents a mechanism to generalize the circumstances under which the funds underlying stored value cards may or may not be considered deposits within the meaning of the FDIA.

[4]Such a system would be similar to debit card systems, except that, unlike a debit card the information or value is on the card itself. The staff is not aware of any such system currently in development. It is our understanding, however, that such a system could be developed.

obligations underlying stored value cards constitute "deposits"[5] within the meaning of section 3(l) of the Federal Deposit Insurance Act (FDIA) and are therefore assessable and qualify for deposit insurance.[6] The FDIC General Counsel's legal opinion on this issue is contained herein. The opinion expressed herein is general in nature and based upon the information that the FDIC staff has gathered on stored value cards to date. No view is expressed on any specific stored value card system and the specific facts of any such system might cause the opinion expressed herein to change.

Applicable Statutes

An analysis of whether funds underlying the value on a stored value card are considered to be a part of the institution's assessment base and qualify for deposit **insurance** coverage begins with the definition of a deposit under section 3(l) of the FDIA. This section provides in pertinent part that:

The term "deposit" means—

1. The unpaid balance of money or its equivalent received or held by a bank or savings association in the usual course of business and for which it has given or is obligated to give credit, either conditionally or unconditionally, to a commercial, checking, savings, time, or thrift account, or which is evidenced by its certificate of deposit, thrift certificate, investment certificate, certificate of indebtedness, or other similar name, or a check or draft drawn against a deposit account and certified by the bank or savings association, or a letter of credit or a traveler's check on which the bank or savings association is primarily liable***
2. Trust funds as defined in this Act received or held by such bank or savings association, whether held in the trust department or held or deposited in any other department of such bank or savings association,

[5]Whether and to what extent the funds or obligations underlying stored value cards constitute "deposits" within the meaning of section 3(l) of the FDIA will in large part determine whether such funds are "insured deposits" under section 3(m) of the FDIA. An "insured deposit" is that portion of a "deposit" that is insured. It is the "net amount due to any depositor" for "deposits in an insured depository institution" (after deducting offsets) less any part thereof that is in excess of $100,000. 12 U.S.C. 1813(m), 1817(i), and 1821(a). Such net amount is also determined in accordance with regulations prescribed by the FDIC. See 12 C.F.R. Part 330.

[6]This opinion only addresses whether the funds underlying stored value cards constitute deposits under the FDIA. Such determinations are relevant for assessment and insurance purposes. There are other issues, not addressed by this opinion, which are of great importance to the FDIC and which the FDIC will continue to monitor as appropriate. Such issues include, but are not limited to, consumer disclosure matters, systemic risk, security, electronic funds transfer matters, reserve requirements, counterfeiting, monetary policy, and money laundering.

3. Money received or held by a bank or savings association, or the credit given for money or its equivalent received or held by a bank or savings association, in the usual course of business for a special or specific purpose, regardless of the legal relationship thereby established, including without being limited to, escrow funds, funds held as security for an obligation due to the bank or savings association or others (including funds held as dealers reserves) or for securities loaned by the bank or savings association, funds deposited by a debtor to meet maturing obligations, funds deposited as advance payment on subscriptions to United States Government securities, funds held for distribution or purchase of securities, funds held to meet its acceptances or letters of credit, and withheld taxes***
4. Outstanding draft (including advice or authorization to charge a bank's or a savings association's balance in another bank or savings association), cashier's check, money order, or other officer's check issued in the usual course of business for any purpose, including without being limited to those issued in payment for services, dividends, or purchases, and
5. Such other obligations of a bank or savings association as the Board of Directors, after consultation with the Comptroller of the Currency, Director of the Office of Thrift Supervision, and the Board of Governors of the Federal Reserve System, shall find and prescribe by regulation to be deposit liabilities by general usage***.

12 U.S.C. 1813(l).

Analysis

For purposes of this analysis, the most relevant provisions of section 3(l) of the FDIA are subsections (1) and (3). Synthesizing the requirements of these two subsections, in order for the funds underlying **stored value cards** to constitute deposits under section 3(l)(1) or (3) of the FDIA, 12 U.S.C. 1813(l)(1) & (3), the funds must represent: (1) An unpaid balance of money or its equivalent received or held by an institution; (2) in the usual course of business; and (3) either (a) the institution must have given or be obligated to give credit to a commercial, checking, savings, time, or thrift account; or (b) the funds must be held for a special or specific purpose.

An Unpaid Balance of Money or Its Equivalent Received or Held by an Institution

The first requirement is that there must be "an unpaid balance of money or its equivalent received or held by a bank or savings association." In each type of Bank Primary System described above, the institution will hold the funds to pay merchants and other payees. Consequently, this requirement of the statute would be satisfied.

In Bank Secondary—Advance Systems the funds may initially be received by the institution but later transferred to a third party. The issue then arises as to whether the fact that funds are received and held by an institution, albeit for a short time period, satisfies this requirement of the statute, thereby possibly creating a deposit liability during the period for which the institution holds the money.

In my opinion in Bank Secondary—Advance Systems funds held by an institution for a time period prior to transfer would meet the statutory requirement of "the unpaid balance of money or its equivalent received or held by a bank or savings association". In the analogous case of an institution selling travelers' checks issued by others, the FDIC staff has long held the opinion that the proceeds from such sale are deposits while held by the institution.[7] In my view, an institution holding funds prior to transfer to a third party in a Bank Secondary—Advance System is indistinguishable from the aforementioned travelers' check case. It is important to note, however, that the institution would owe the obligation to the third party, not the holder of the card. Thus, to the extent such funds may constitute a deposit, the "depositor" would be the third party. Moreover, any deposit liability for such funds would be extinguished upon transfer of the funds to the third party.

In Bank Secondary—Pre-Acquisition Systems the funds underlying the stored value are received or held by the third party. The institution in effect advances these funds on behalf of its customers and later collects funds from its customer in exchange for electronic value loaded onto stored value cards. Because the funds underlying the stored value are held by the third party, in my view, such funds are received or held by the third party, not the depository institution. Consequently, it appears that the requirement of "an unpaid balance of money or its equivalent received or held by [an institution]" would not be satisfied in Bank Secondary—Pre-Acquisition Systems.

Also in some Bank Secondary Systems the institution may by contract retain a contingent liability to redeem the electronic value from consumers and merchants. This raises the issue whether a contingent liability to redeem the electronic value represents an unpaid balance of money or its equivalent received or held by an institution. In interpreting 12 U.S.C. 1813(l)(1), the Supreme Court, in accordance with the purpose of the statute, imposed the requirement that a deposit of money or its equivalent be "hard earnings" that businesses and individuals have entrusted to banks. FDIC v. Philadelphia Gear Corp., 476 U.S. 426, 435 (1986). The Court held that a stand-by letter of credit does not fall within the

[7]See FDIC Staff Advisory Opinion 93-55 (August 6, 1993) (funds held for one business day by an agent bank selling travelers checks on behalf of a company issuing travelers' checks, are deposits of the bank under 3(l)(3) of the FDIA, until such funds are forwarded to the company).

meaning of section 3(l)(1) of the FDIA because this was only a contingent obligation and did not represent "hard earnings." Id. at 440.

Any contingent liability of an institution to redeem electronic value in a Bank Secondary System would in my view not constitute "hard earnings" and thus, in accordance with the Court's holding in Philadelphia Gear, would not satisfy the requirement of an unpaid balance of money or its equivalent received or held by a bank or savings association. In Bank Secondary Systems the "hard earnings" are ultimately held by the third party, not the institution

In the Usual Course of Business

Insured depository institutions are increasingly participating in stored value card systems. In light of this, the FDIC would likely view any funds received or held by institutions pursuant to participation in stored value card systems to be in the usual course of business.

The Institution Must Have Given or Be Obligated to Give Credit to an Account

To be a deposit under section 3(l)(1) of the FDIA, 12 U.S.C. 1813(l)(1), money or its equivalent must not only be held or received by an institution in the usual course of business, but must (unless another alternative condition is satisfied) be a payment for which the institution has given or is obligated to give credit to a commercial, checking, savings, time or thrift account. This requirement would not appear to be at issue in Bank Primary—Customer Account Systems because the funds remain credited to the customer's account until claims on such funds are made by payees. Assuming the other aforementioned requirements are met, the funds underlying Bank Primary—Customer Account Systems would appear to be deposits under section 3(l)(1) of the FDIA, 12 U.S.C. 1813(l)(1).

With respect to Bank Primary—Reserve Systems and both types of Bank Secondary Systems, stored value card products appear to be structured so that the institution does not credit and is not obligated to credit a commercial, checking, savings, time or thrift account. As described previously, when a customer purchases a stored value card in a Bank Primary—Reserve System funds are withdrawn from the customer's account (or paid directly by the customer) and paid into a reserve or general liability account maintained by the institution. Such accounts are routinely created and maintained by insured depository institutions. The FDIC does not consider such reserve or general liability accounts to be "deposits" within the meaning of section 3(l)(1) of the FDIA, 12 U.S.C. 1813(l)(1), because there does not appear to be an obligation to credit the funds to a commercial, checking, savings, time, or thrift account. In addition, the sample agreements which the FDIC staff has reviewed clearly indicate that the parties to a stored value card agreement, i.e., the insured depository institution and the purchaser of the card, do not intend that the funds be credited to one of the five enumerated accounts.

Similarly, in Bank Secondary Systems the funds which consumers pay to load value onto a stored value card are ultimately held by the third party originator of the stored value. In these cases also it would appear that no commercial, checking, savings, time or thrift account has been credited nor is the institution obligated to credit such an account.

The foregoing notwithstanding, at some point the institution may become obligated to credit a payee's deposit account maintained at that institution and thus create a deposit liability to the payee. For example, after a transaction wherein the value on the card is transferred from a consumer to a merchant, and the merchant requests that the funds underlying the electronic value be credited to the merchant's account, the institution would appear to be under an obligation to credit the merchant's account; thereby, possibly creating a deposit liability to the merchant.

If the Institution Has Not Given or Is Not Obligated to Give Credit to an Account; The Funds Must Be Held for a Special or Specific Purpose

If funds held by an institution underlying stored value cards are not deposits under section 3(l)(1) of the FDIA, 12 U.S.C. 1813(l)(1), because the institution is not obligated to credit an account, the analysis must turn to whether such funds may be considered deposits under section 3(l)(3) of the FDIA, 12 U.S.C. 1813(l)(3). In order to be considered a deposit under 3(l)(3) of the FDIA, the value underlying a stored value card must represent: (1) Money or its equivalent (or the credit given for money or its equivalent) received or held by an institution; (2) in the usual course of business; and (3) for a special or specific purpose.

The first two requirements are essentially the same as under section 3(l)(1) of the FDIA as discussed above. While section 3(l)(3) of the FDIA, 12 U.S.C. 1813(l)(3), does not require that the institution be obligated to credit the funds to an account, it does require that funds be held "for a special or specific purpose" in order to qualify as a deposit.

Congress included in the statute, without limitation, the following examples of a bank or savings association holding funds for a special or specific purpose: "escrow funds, funds held as security for an obligation due to the bank or savings association or others (including funds held as dealers reserves) or for securities loaned by the bank or savings association, funds deposited by a debtor to meet maturing obligations, funds deposited as advance payment on subscriptions to United States Government securities, funds held for distribution or purchase of securities, funds held to meet its acceptances or letters of credit, and withheld taxes***." 12 U.S.C. 1813(l)(3).

While Congress included in section 3(l)(3) a number of special or specific purposes for which money may be held to qualify as a deposit, the clause "without being limited to" means that the section does not state each and every such purpose. Courts have held that money covering a Clearing House Interpayment System ("CHIPS") release[8] and monies wired by a loan participant to the lead bank for the purpose of funding a participated loan,[9] each constitute funds held for a special or specific purpose within the meaning of this statute. The case law seems to suggest that to qualify as a deposit under 3(l)(3) the purpose for which the money is being held must at least be as specific as the purposes listed in the statute. See FDIC v. European American Bank & Trust Co., 576 F. Supp. 950, 957 (S.D.N.Y. 1983); Seattle-First Bank v. FDIC, 619 F. Supp. 1351, 1360 (D.C. Okl. 1985).

When an institution holds funds in exchange for electronic value embedded in a stored value card, the relevant questions are: (1) What is the purpose for which these funds are being held? and (2) Is that purpose at least as specific as the purposes enumerated in the statute? With respect to Bank Primary—Reserve Systems funds appear to be held by an institution to meet its obligations to payees as they make claims on such funds pursuant to general or miscellaneous and unrelated transactions undertaken within the stored value card system. It is my opinion that this purpose is fundamentally different from the examples listed in section 3(l)(3) of the FDIA, 12 U.S.C. 1813(l)(3). For example, an escrow account will typically have a very specific purpose associated with a particular transaction (or two or more related transactions). Similarly, funds underlying a letter of credit and funds held for purchasing securities are linked to a specific transaction or transactions.

The cases holding that certain funds are deposits within the meaning of section 3(l)(3) of the FDIA, 12 U.S.C. 1813(l)(3), also involve funds held with respect to a specific transaction. For example, in Seattle-First Bank the court held that monies wired by a loan participant to the lead bank at the lead bank's direction for the purpose of funding a participated loan were monies received for the special or specific purpose of funding the loan. 619 F Supp. at 1360. In that case, as in the examples contained within section 3(l)(3) of the FDIA, 12 U.S.C. 1813(l)(3), the funds held are for a purpose associated with a particular transaction or two or more related transactions.

---

[8]FDIC v. European American Bank & Trust Co., 576 F. Supp. 950, 957 (S.D.N.Y. 1983) (Money covering a CHIPS transfer has as specific a purpose as the money in the accounts listed by the statute. Just like money deposited to meet maturing obligations, money backing a CHIPS release is to insure payment to the recipient of the release.)

[9]Seattle-First Bank v. FDIC, 619 F. Supp. 1351, 1360 (D.C. Okl. 1985) (monies wired by a loan participant to the lead bank, at the lead's direction, for the purpose of funding a participated loan can become deposits within the meaning of 3(l)(3) when the wired funds are not drawn by the intended borrower. The funds were received for the special or specific purpose of funding the participated loan).

Conversely, a customer who transfers funds to an institution in exchange for electronic value may engage in any of a number of unrelated transactions. Indeed, when a customer has electronic value loaded onto a card he may have no idea as to what transactions he will use the card to engage in, nor whom the transferees may be. Thus, unlike the examples listed in the statute, funds held by an institution to redeem electronic value could be associated with general or miscellaneous unrelated transactions. Consequently, an institution holding funds to meet obligations to transferees in a Bank Primary—Reserve System does not appear to be as specific a purpose as the examples in the statute and in the cases finding deposit liabilities under section 3(l)(3) of the FDIA.[10] Therefore, in my view such funds would not be held for a special or specific purpose within the meaning of section 3(l)(3) of the FDIA, 12 U.S.C. 1813(l)(3).[11]

On the other hand, in the case of Bank Secondary—Advance Systems the funds are being held or received by the institution in order to pay the third party in consideration of the electronic value transferred by such third party to the institution and ultimately its customer. Thus, like the examples listed in the statute and the cases finding monies to be deposits under section 3(l)(3),[12] these funds are linked to a specific transaction. Moreover, these funds are analogous to funds held for one business day by an agent bank selling travelers checks on behalf of a company issuing travelers' checks. The FDIC staff considers such funds to be deposits of the bank under 3(l)(3) of the FDIA until such funds are forwarded to the company. See FDIC Staff Advisory Opinion 93-55, (August 6, 1993). Thus, in the case of Bank Secondary—Advance Systems, the funds being held or received in order to pay the third party may be considered held or received for a special or specific purpose within the meaning of section 3(l)(3) of the FDIA, 12 U.S.C. 1813(l)(3) and may therefore qualify as a deposit under such section. It is important to note, however, that such a deposit liability would be to the third party, not the institution's customer.

Other Subsections of the Statute Defining Deposit—Trust Funds

Trust funds are deposits under section 3(l)(2) of the FDIA, 12 U.S.C. 1813(l)(2). For purposes of the FDIA trust funds are funds held by an insured

---

[10]See Seattle-First Bank v. FDIC, 619 F. Supp. at 1360; FDIC v. European American Bank & Trust Co., 576 F. Supp. at 957.

[11]The funds underlying a stored value card in a Bank Primary—Reserve System could, in our view, be considered to be held for a special or specific purpose within the meaning of section 3(l)(3) of the FDIA, 12 U.S.C. 1813(l)(3), if the system is structured so that the ultimate payee can only be one pre-determined specific party. For example, if an institution were to issue a stored value card solely for the purchase of long-distance telephone services from a specific company, such funds could be considered to be held for a special or specific purpose.

[12]See Seattle-First Bank v. FDIC, 619 F. Supp. at 1360; FDIC v. European American Bank & Trust Co., 576 F. Supp. at 957.

depository institution in a fiduciary capacity, including funds held as trustee, executor, administrator, guardian, or agent. 12 U.S.C. 1813(p). The FDIC staff is not aware of stored value card systems in which funds are held by an institution in a fiduciary capacity.

Other Subsections of the Statute Defining Deposit—Certain Negotiable Instruments

Section 3(l)(4) of the FDIA, 12 U.S.C. 1813(l)(4), includes within the definition of deposit an "outstanding draft*** cashier's check, money order, or other officer's check***." Stored value obligations have been analogized to cashier's checks and money orders. Indeed, Bank Primary—Reserve System stored value cards operate in much the same way that these instruments do. Nonetheless, unlike the payment mechanisms listed in the statute, stored value cards are not negotiable instruments.[13] Moreover, unlike a cashier's check or money order, the institution is not drawing a check upon itself. Rather, the institution's customer transfers to a payee the rights to a sum of money being held at the institution and in making payment to the payee, the institution is recognizing that its customer has transferred that right. See FDIC v. European American Bank & Trust Co., 576 F. Supp. at 957.

Notwithstanding the fact that stored value card obligations operate in a manner similar to cashier's checks and money orders, I am of the view that there are differences between these instruments and stored value cards Moreover, for purposes of considering whether a payment mechanism is a deposit within the meaning of section 3(l)(4) of the FDIA, 12 U.S.C. 1813(l)(4) I believe that Congress did not intend to include payment mechanisms other than the negotiable instruments enumerated in the subsection. Id.[14]

Other Subsections of The Statute Defining Deposit—Authority of the FDIC to Promulgate a Regulation Finding That Funds Underlying Stored Value Cards are Deposits

In addition to the statutory definition of deposits under sections 3(l)(1)-(4) of the FDIA, 12 U.S.C. 1813(l)(1)-(4), section 3(l)(5) of the FDIA, 12 U.S.C. 1813(l)(5), gives the Board of Directors the authority, after consultation with the Comptroller of the Currency, Director of the Office of Thrift Supervision, and the Board of Governors of the Federal Reserve System, to find and prescribe by regulation other obligations of an insured depository institution to be deposit liabilities by general usage. The FDIC has not promulgated such a regulation.

---

[13]See U.C.C., Section 3-104(1).

[14]In my view the same conclusion would apply with respect to analogizing stored value cards to travelers' checks on which the institution is primarily liable, which are deposits under section 3(l)(1) of the FDIA, 12 U.S.C. 1813(l)(1).

Summary

In summary, in my opinion funds underlying Bank Primary—Customer Account Systems appear to be funds held by an institution, in the usual course of business, which remain credited to the customer's account until the payee makes a claim on the funds. Such funds would therefore appear to be deposits under section 3(l)(1) of the FDIA, 12 U.S.C. 1813(l)(1).

As a general matter, funds held by an institution to meet obligations under Bank Primary—Reserve Systems would appear not to be deposits under section 3(l)(1) of the FDIA, 12 U.S.C. 1813(l)(1), because the funds are not credited to or obligated to be credited to a commercial, checking, time, or thrift account.

It is my further opinion that the funds underlying Bank Primary—Reserve Systems are not deposits under section 3(l)(3) of the FDIA, 12 U.S.C. 1813(l)(3), because such funds are not held for a special or specific purpose. The examples of funds held for such purposes in the statute are all linked to one or more specific transactions. Conversely, the funds underlying stored value card transactions are not necessarily linked to a specific transaction.

In Bank Secondary—Pre-Acquisition Systems the funds underlying the stored value are, in my view, received or held by the third party, not the depository institution. Consequently, it appears that this requirement of section 3(l) (1) and (3) of the FDIA, 12 U.S.C. 1813(l)(1), (3), would not be satisfied in such systems.

The funds held by an institution in a Bank Secondary—Advance System would not create a deposit liability to the customer because the liability is owed to the third party for whom the institution is temporarily holding the funds. Such funds may create a deposit liability to the third party. The funds are held by the institution in the usual course of business prior to transferring such funds to the third party. The parties may or may not intend that the institution credit an account. Even if the institution is not obligated to credit such funds to an account, and thus such funds would not be a deposit under section 3(l)(1) of the FDIA, the funds may be deemed to be held for the specific purpose of transferring the funds to the third party and thus would be considered a deposit under section 3(l)(3) of the FDIA, 12 U.S.C. 1813(l)(3).

The fact that an institution may retain a contingent liability to redeem electronic value from consumers and merchants in Bank Secondary Systems does not meet the requirement of "money or its equivalent held by an institution" and therefore would not give rise to a deposit liability to the customer under either 3(l)(1) or (3) of the FDIA, 12 U.S.C. 1813(l)(1), (3).

With respect to the other provisions of section 3(l) of the FDIA, 12 U.S.C. 1813(l), the FDIC staff is not aware of stored value card systems in which funds will be held as trust funds. Thus, the funds underlying stored value cards would not be deposits under section 3(l)(2) of the FDIA, 12 U.S.C. 1813(l)(2). Similarly, while stored value cards have certain similarities to cashier's checks and money orders, they are not drafts drawn on the bank, nor are they negotiable instruments.

Consequently, they cannot be considered deposits under section 3(l)(4) of the FDIA, 12 U.S.C. 1813(l)(4).

Notwithstanding the question of whether and under what circumstances stored value card obligations are deposits within the meaning of section 3(l)(1)-(4) of the FDIA, 12 U.S.C. 1813(l)(1)-(4), section 3(l)(5) of the FDIA, 12 U.S.C. 1813(l)(5), gives the Board of Directors the authority to find and prescribe by regulation that other obligations of an insured depository institution are deposit liabilities by general usage. The FDIC has not promulgated such a regulation.

This General Counsel Opinion only addresses the extent to which funds underlying stored value cards may constitute a deposit under 12 U.S.C. 1813(l). It is not intended to address the way in which FDIC would act in its role as receiver. In the event of an institution's failure, to the extent that any funds underlying stored value cards are recognized as deposits, there may be recordkeeping issues and other issues as to who may be entitled to deposit insurance and in what amount. See 12 C.F.R. Part 330.

Finally, the FDIC would expect that institutions clearly and conspicuously disclose to their customers the insured or non-insured status of their stored value products, as appropriate.

By order of the Board of Directors, dated at Washington, D.C., this 16th day of July, 1996.

Federal Deposit Insurance Corporation
Jerry L. Langley,
Executive Secretary.
[FR Doc. 96-19697 Filed 8-1-96; 8:45 am]
BILLING CODE 6714-01-P

Table of Cases

LAW OF ELECTRONIC BANKING

Table of Cases

TABLE OF CASES

References are to sections.

Index

LAW OF ELECTRONIC BANKING

Index

INDEX

References are to sections or appendices.

C

D

E

G

J

N

O

T

$195.00